Fodor's®

Austria

EIGHTH EDITION

New

D0040622

The complete guide, thoroughly up-to-date

Packed with details that will make your trip

The must-see sights, off and on the beaten path

What to see, what to skip

Mix and match vacation itineraries

City strolls, countryside adventures

Smart lodging and dining options

Essential local dos and taboos

Transportation tips, distances, and directions

Key contacts, savvy travel tips

When to go, what to pack

Clear, accurate, easy-to-use maps

Books to read, videos to watch

Fodor's Travel Publications, Inc.
New York • Toronto • London • Sydney • Auckland
www.fodors.com

Fodor's Austria

EDITOR: Langdon Faust

Editorial Contributors: David Brown, Bonnie Dodson, Alan Levy, Willibald Picard, Marton Radkai, Helayne Schiff, M. T. Schwartzman (Gold Guide editor), Earl Steinbicker, George Sullivan, Lito Tejada-Flores, Charlotte van der Reyden, Angela Walker
Editorial Production: Stacey Kulig
Maps: David Lindroth, *cartographer*; Robert Blake, *map editor*
Design: Fabrizio La Rocca, *creative director*; Guido Caroti, *associate art director*; Jolie Novak, *photo editor*
Production/Manufacturing: Robert B. Shields
Cover Photograph: Uniphoto Picture Agency

Copyright

Eighth Edition

ISBN 0-679-00012-7

Special Sales

Fodor's Travel Publications are available at special discounts for bulk purchases for sales promotions or premiums. Special editions, including personalized covers, excerpts of existing guides, and corporate imprints, can be created in large quantities for special needs. For more information, contact your local bookseller or write to Special Markets, Fodor's Travel Publications, 201 East 50th Street, New York, NY 10022. Inquiries from Canada should be directed to your local Canadian bookseller or sent to Random House of Canada, Ltd., Marketing Department, 2775 Matheson Boulevard East, Mississauga, Ontario L4W 4P7. Inquiries from the United Kingdom should be sent to Fodor's Travel Publications, 20 Vauxhall Bridge Road, London SW1V 2SA, England.

PRINTED IN THE UNITED STATES OF AMERICA

10 9 8 7 6 5 4 3 2 1

CONTENTS

Maps

ON THE ROAD WITH FODOR'S

WHEN I PLAN A VACATION, the first thing I do is cast around among my friends and colleagues to find someone who's just been where I'm going. That's because there's no substitute for a recommendation from a good friend who knows your tastes, your budget, and your circumstances, someone who's just been there. Unfortunately, such friends are few and far between. So it's nice to know that there's *Fodor's Austria.*

In the first place, this book won't stay home when you hit the road. It will accompany you every step of the way, steering you away from wrong turns and wrong choices and never expecting a thing in return. Most important of all, it's written and assiduously updated by the kind of people you *would* hit up for travel tips if you knew them. They're as choosy as your pickiest friend, except they've probably seen a lot more of Austria. In these pages, they don't send you chasing down every town and sight in Austria but have instead selected the best ones, the ones that are worthy of your time and money. To make it easy for you to put it all together in the time you have, they've created short, medium, and long itineraries and, in cities, neighborhood walks that you can mix and match in a snap. Will this be the vacation of your dreams? We hope so.

About Our Writers

Our success in helping to make your trip the best of all possible vacations is a credit to the hard work of our extraordinary writers.

Even before **George W. Hamilton** first arrived in Vienna in 1960, his heart would beat in three-quarter time whenever he heard the intoxicating waltzes of Johann Strauss. Falling in love with the Austrian capital, George found a handy excuse to become a resident: He settled in as manager of the recording studio of the Vienna Symphony Orchestra. Along the way, our longtime area editor has helped found the orchestra's renowned Johann Strauss Ensemble and even discovered unrecorded waltzes. Among his favorite times in Austria are those brilliant spring days when the not-so-blue Danube manages to turn the proper Straussian shade. Music is not the only Austrian specialty George appreciates. His direct experience as hotelier and restaurateur served as the basis for the critical evaluations found in this guide's dining and lodging sections. "Whenever I pick up a cookbook on Austrian cuisine, I first check the recipe for goulash," he chuckles. "If it says anything other than equal parts onion and meat, the book is bogus." Today, as a reporter for the *Economist* and the *Financial Times* research units specializing in travel and economics, he loves to dine out with guests at the Vier Jahreszeiten or—for a more *gemütlich* evening—at the atmospheric Ofenloch.

Keith Besonen has written for the on-line magazines *Paper Daily, CuisineNet,* and *Salon.* He's fond of Austrian beer, and his favorite place to drink it is Brauhaus Nussdorf in Vienna.

Bonnie Dodson updated the Vienna, Side Trips from Vienna, the Danube Valley, Eastern Austria, Salzburg, Tirol, and Voralberg chapters. She is a native of Minneapolis and has a Master of Fine Arts in Professional Writing from the University of Southern California. During her five years living in Vienna, Bonnie has enjoyed traveling throughout Europe. Bonnie's husband, **Gary Dodson,** has lived in Tokyo, Bangkok, Buenos Aires, and Los Angeles, and is fluent in five languages. He now works for a pharmaceutical company in Vienna. Gary's passions are movies, travel, and wine, and he enjoys partaking of all three in Austria. He wrote the boxes on Austrian wine (with Bonnie) and Mozart.

Lito Tejada-Flores was born at 13,000 ft in the Bolivian Andes and has spent much of his life since in high places. He's shared his passion for mountain adventure in a series of books, films, and most recently his Breakthrough on Skis instructional videos. As a contributing editor to *Skiing* magazine, Lito has skied around the world. He is in love with the Alps, and visits Austria every chance he gets.

Marton Radkai is in many ways a typical Central European: his mother was Bavarian, his father Hungarian, but he was born in New York City. He was raised in France, England, and Switzerland, studied in Vermont and Massachusetts, and went on to become a radio announcer (WFCR in Amherst, Massachusetts) and then a travel writer and photographer, a translator, and an editor. He has spent the past 16 years in Central Europe, traveling the highways and byways of southern Germany, Austria, and Hungary. He is currently living in Munich.

Danke, vielen Danke (many thanks) to the directors of the Austrian National Tourist Offices in Vienna and in New York and the individual tourist offices for each of the provinces for their generous and considerable assistance in preparing this new edition. Ulrike Kinz of the Voralberg Tourist Office in Vienna and Thorsten Busch of the Lower Austria Tourist Office in Vienna were particularly helpful.

Connections

We're pleased that the American Society of Travel Agents continues to endorse Fodor's as its guidebook of choice. ASTA is the world's largest and most influential travel trade association, operating in more than 170 countries, with 27,000 members pledged to adhere to a strict code of ethics reflecting the Society's motto, "Integrity in Travel." ASTA shares Fodor's devotion to providing smart, honest travel information and advice to travelers, and we've long recommended that our readers—even those who have guidebooks and traveling friends—consult ASTA member agents for the experience and professionalism they bring to your vacation planning.

On Fodor's Web site (www.fodors.com), check out the new Resource Center, an online companion to the Gold Guide section of this book, complete with useful hot links to related sites. In our forums, you can also get lively advice from other travelers and more great tips from Fodor's experts worldwide.

How to Use This Book

Organization

Up front is the **Gold Guide,** an easy-to-use section arranged alphabetically by topic. Under each listing you'll find tips and information that will help you accomplish what you need to in Austria. You'll also find addresses and telephone numbers of organizations and companies that offer destination-related services and detailed information and publications.

The first chapter in the guide, **Destination: Austria,** helps get you in the mood for your trip. What's Where gets you oriented, Pleasures and Pastimes describes the activities and sights that make Austria unique, New and Noteworthy cues you in on trends and happenings, Fodor's Choice showcases our top picks, and Festivals and Seasonal Events alerts you to special events you'll want to seek out.

There are two city chapters in *Fodor's Austria* (Vienna and Salzburg) and several lengthy city sections in the eight regional chapters, which focus not simply on a particular province but often on regions to explore across several provinces. Each city chapter begins with Exploring information, which is divided into neighborhood sections; each recommends a walking or driving tour and lists sights in alphabetical order. Each regional chapter is divided by geographical area; within each area, towns are covered in logical geographical order, and attractive stretches of road and minor points of interest between them are indicated by the designation *En Route.* And within town sections, all restaurants and lodgings are grouped.

To help you decide what to visit in the time you have, all chapters begin with our recommended itineraries. The A to Z section that ends all chapters covers getting there and getting around. It also provides helpful contacts and resources.

At the end of the book you'll find **Portraits,** with a new essay on skiing in Austria, followed by suggestions for pretrip research, from recommended reading to movies on tape that use Austria as a backdrop, and a German vocabulary and menu guide.

Icons and Symbols

★	Our special recommendations
✕	Restaurant
🏠	Lodging establishment
✕🏠	Lodging establishment whose restaurant warrants a special trip
🦆	Good for kids (rubber duck)
☞	Sends you to another section of the guide for more information
✉	Address
☎	Telephone number

⊙ Opening and closing times

🎫 Admission prices (those we give apply to adults; substantially reduced fees are almost always available for children, students, and senior citizens)

Numbers in white and black circles ③ ❸ that appear on the maps, in the margins, and within the tours correspond to one another.

Dining and Lodging

The restaurants and lodgings we list are the cream of the crop in each price range. Price charts appear in the Pleasures and Pastimes section that follows each chapter introduction.

Hotel Facilities

We always list the facilities that are available—but we don't specify whether you'll be charged extra to use them: When pricing accommodations, always ask what's included. In addition, assume that all rooms have private baths unless noted otherwise. In addition, when you book a room, be sure to mention if you have a disability or are traveling with children, if you prefer a private bath or a certain type of bed, or if you have specific dietary needs or other concerns.

Assume that hotels operate on the **European Plan** (EP, with no meals) unless we note differently. Most hotels—except the most expensive options—include a free breakfast. In rural and resort areas, however, some hotels opt for half-board basis (breakfast and one meal a day must be taken), particularly in the Western Alps region—we note if this is the case in our reviews.

Restaurant Reservations and Dress Codes

Reservations are always a good idea; we mention them only when they're essential or are not accepted. Book as far ahead as you can, and reconfirm as soon as you arrive. Unless otherwise noted, the restaurants listed are open daily for lunch and dinner. We mention dress only when men are required to wear a jacket or a jacket and tie. Look for an overview of local dining-out habits in the Gold Guide and in the Pleasures and Pastimes section that follows each chapter introduction.

Credit Cards

The following abbreviations are used: **AE**, American Express; **DC**, Diners Club; **MC**, MasterCard; and **V**, Visa.

Don't Forget to Write

You can use this book in the confidence that all prices and opening times are based on information supplied to us at press time; Fodor's cannot accept responsibility for any errors. Time inevitably brings changes, so always confirm information when it matters—especially if you're making a detour to visit a specific place.

Were the restaurants we recommended as described? Did our hotel picks exceed your expectations? Did you find a museum we recommended a waste of time? Keeping a travel guide fresh and up-to-date is a big job, and we welcome your feedback, positive *and* negative. If you have complaints, we'll look into them and revise our entries when the facts warrant it. If you've discovered a special place that we haven't included, we'll pass the information along to our correspondents and have them check it out. So send us your thoughts via e-mail at editors@fodors.com (specifying the name of the book on the subject line) or on paper in care of the Austria editor at Fodor's, 201 East 50th Street, New York, NY 10022. In the meantime, have a wonderful trip!

Karen Cure

Karen Cure
Editorial Director

Austria

SMART TRAVEL TIPS A TO Z

Basic Information on Traveling in Austria, Savvy Tips to Make Your Trip a Breeze, and Companies and Organizations to Contact

AIR TRAVEL

BOOKING YOUR FLIGHT

Price is just one factor to consider when booking a flight: frequency of service and even a carrier's safety record are often just as important. Major airlines offer the greatest number of departures. Smaller airlines—including regional and no-frills airlines—usually have a limited number of flights daily. On the other hand, so-called low-cost airlines usually are cheaper, and their fares impose fewer restrictions, such as advance-purchase requirements. Safety-wise, low-cost carriers as a group have a good history—about equal to that of major carriers.

When you book, **look for nonstop flights** and **remember that "direct" flights stop at least once.** Try to **avoid connecting flights,** which require a change of plane. Two airlines may jointly operate a connecting flight, so ask if your airline operates every segment—you may find that your preferred carrier flies you only part of the way. International flights on a country's flag carrier are almost always nonstop; U.S. airlines often fly direct.

Ask your airline if it offers electronic ticketing, which eliminates all paperwork. There's no ticket to pick up or misplace. You go directly to the gate and give the agent your confirmation number—a real blessing if you've lost your ticket or made last-minute changes in travel plans. There's no worry about waiting on line at the airport while precious minutes tick by.

CARRIERS

When flying internationally, you must usually choose between a domestic carrier, the national flag carrier of the country you are visiting, and a foreign carrier from a third country. You may, for example, choose to fly

Austrian Airlines to Austria. National flag carriers have the greatest number of nonstops. Domestic carriers may have better connections to your home town and serve a greater number of gateway cities. Third-party carriers may have a price advantage.

➤ MAJOR AIRLINES: **Air Canada** (☎ 416/925–2311 or 800/268–7240). **Austrian Airlines** (☎ 800/843–0002). **Delta** (☎ 800/221–1212). Many major American air carriers—such as American, TWA, and United—do not service Vienna directly; they fly passengers to major European hubs, such as London or Zurich for transfers to flights with other airlines.

➤ FROM THE U.K.: **Austrian Airlines** (☎ 0171/434–7300). **British Airways** (☎ 0181/897–4000 or 0345/222–111 outside London). **Lauda Air** (☎ 0171/630–5924).

➤ WITHIN AUSTRIA: **Austrian Airlines** (☎ 01/7007-0; main Austrian office at Kärtner Ring 18, 1010 Vienna) and its subsidiary, Tyrolean, offer service from Vienna to Linz, Innsbruck, and points outside Austria. **Rheintalflug** (☎ 01/7007–6911 in Vienna, 05574/48800 in Vorarlberg, 071/435120) has service between Vienna and Altenrhein (Switzerland, near Bregenz), with bus connections for points in Vorarlberg. Winter schedules on all domestic lines depend on snow conditions.

CHARTERS

Charters usually have the lowest fares but are the least dependable. Departures are infrequent and seldom on time, flights can be delayed for up to 48 hours or can be canceled for any reason up to 10 days before you're scheduled to leave. Itineraries and prices can change after you've booked your flight.

In the U.S., the Department of Transportation's Aviation Consumer Protection Division has jurisdiction over charters and provides a certain degree of protection. The DOT requires that money paid to charter operators be held in escrow, so if you can't pay with a credit card, **always make your check payable to a charter carrier's escrow account.** The name of the bank should be in the charter contract. If you have any problems with a charter operator, contact the DOT (☞ Airline Complaints, *below*). If you buy a charter package that includes both air and land arrangements, remember that the escrow requirement applies only to the air component.

CONSOLIDATORS

Consolidators buy tickets for scheduled international flights at reduced rates from the airlines, then sell them at prices that beat the best fare available directly from the airlines, usually without restrictions. Sometimes you can even get your money back if you need to return the ticket. Carefully read the fine print detailing penalties for changes and cancellations, and **confirm your consolidator reservation with the airline.**

➤ CONSOLIDATORS: **Cheap Tickets** (☎ 800/377–1000). **Discount Travel Network** (☎ 800/576–1600). **Unitravel** (☎ 800/325–2222). **Up & Away Travel** (☎ 212/889–2345). **World Travel Network** (☎ 800/409–6753).

CUTTING COSTS

The least-expensive airfares to Austria are priced for round-trip travel and usually must be purchased in advance. It's smart to **call a number of airlines, and when you are quoted a good price, book it on the spot**—the same fare may not be available the next day. Airlines generally allow you to change your return date for a fee. If you don't use your ticket, you can apply the cost toward the purchase of a new ticket, again for a small charge. However, most low-fare tickets are nonrefundable. To get the lowest airfare, **check different routings.** Compare prices of flights to and from different airports if your destination or home city has more than one gateway. Also price off-peak flights, which may be significantly less expensive.

Travel agents, especially those who specialize in finding the lowest fares (☞ Discounts & Deals, *below*), can be especially helpful when booking a plane ticket. When you're quoted a price, **ask your agent if the price is likely to get any lower.** Good agents know the seasonal fluctuations of airfares and can usually anticipate a sale or fare war. However, waiting can be risky: The fare could go *up* as seats become scarce, and you may wait so long that your preferred flight sells out. A wait-and-see strategy works best if your plans are flexible. If you must arrive and depart on certain dates, don't delay.

If you plan to cover all of Austria, you may fly to Munich, Germany, and rent a car from there or take the train to Salzburg or Innsbruck. Since Germany is a little bit cheaper than Austria, this could prove a good deal, especially if you have a day to spare, and don't mind a very pretty 2-hour ride through Bavaria.

CHECK IN & BOARDING

Airlines routinely overbook planes, assuming that not everyone with a ticket will show up, but sometimes everyone does. When that happens, airlines ask for volunteers to give up their seats. In return these volunteers usually get a certificate for a free flight and are rebooked on the next flight out. If there are not enough volunteers, the airline must choose who will be denied boarding. The first to get bumped are passengers who checked in late and those flying on discounted tickets, so **get to the gate and check in as early as possible,** especially during peak periods.

Although the trend on international flights is to drop reconfirmation requirements, many airlines still ask you to reconfirm each leg of your international itinerary. Failure to do so may result in your reservation being canceled.

Always **bring a government-issued photo ID to the airport.** You may be asked to show it before you are allowed to check in.

FLYING TIMES

Flying time is 8 hours from New York, 11 hours from Chicago, and 13 hours from Los Angeles.

HOW TO COMPLAIN

If your baggage goes astray or your flight goes awry, complain right away. Most carriers require that you **file a claim immediately.**

➤ AIRLINE COMPLAINTS: **Federal Aviation Administration Consumer Hotline** (☎ 800/322–7873). **U.S. Department of Transportation Aviation Consumer Protection Division** (✉ C-75, Room 4107, Washington, DC 20590, ☎ 202/366–2220).

AIRPORTS & TRANSFERS

AIRPORTS

The major airport is Vienna's **Schwechat Airport**, about 12 mi southeast of the city.

➤ AIRPORT INFORMATION: **Schwechat airport** (☎ 43/1–71110).

TRANSFERS

If you are landing in Vienna, the cheapest way to get to the city is by bus, on the **Vienna Airport Lines** (☎ 01/5800–2300), which has two separate lines. One line goes to the City Air Terminal at the Hilton Hotel (near the city's First District) every 20 minutes between 6:30 AM and 11 PM, and less frequently after that; traveling time is 20 minutes. The other line goes to the Southern and Western train stations (Südbahnhof and Westbahnhof) in 20 and 35 minutes respectively. Departure times are every 30 minutes from 8:10 AM to 7:10 PM, hourly thereafter, and not at all 12:10–3:30 AM. Fare is AS70 one-way, AS130 for a round-trip. Another possibility is with a **Flughafentaxi**, a taxi with a special airport fare of AS350 one-way. Not all taxis accept credit cards, and don't forget, a tip is appreciated.

If you land in **Salzburg**, the bus line No. 77 shuttles every 15 minutes from the airport to the train station, otherwise take a taxi. If you land in **Munich**, the cheapest way of getting to town is with the S8 train that takes about 45 minutes to the main train station (Hauptbahnhof) with stops along the way and connecting rides.

BIKE TRAVEL

There are many cycling trails throughout Austria, along the Danube, around lakes, and in the Alps (☞ Outdoor Activities and Sports, *below*).

BIKES IN FLIGHT

Most airlines will accommodate bikes as luggage, provided they are dismantled and put into a box. Call to see if your airline sells bike boxes (about $5; bike bags are at least $100) although you can often pick them up free at bike shops. International travelers can sometimes substitute a bike for a piece of checked luggage for free; otherwise, it will cost about $100. Domestic and Canadian airlines charge a $25–$50 fee.

BOAT & FERRY TRAVEL

For leisurely travel between Vienna and Linz or eastward across the border into Slovakia or Hungary, consider taking a Danube boat. More than 300 km (187 mi) of Austria's most beautiful scenery awaits you, as you glide past castles and ruins, medieval monasteries and abbeys, and lush vineyards. One of the lovelier sections, particularly in spring, is the Wachau valley near Vienna.

Most of the immaculate white-painted craft carry about 1,000 passengers each on their three decks. As soon as you get on board, give the steward a good tip for a deck chair and ask him to place it where you will get the best views. Be sure to book cabins in advance. Day trips are also possible on the Danube. You can use boats to move from one riverside community to the next, and along some sections, notably the Wachau, the only way of crossing the river is using the little shuttles (in the Wachau, these are special motor-less boats that use the current to sail across).

Hydrofoils run daily from Vienna to Bratislava in Slovakia and to Budapest in Hungary. You can travel via the Danube to the Black Sea and back on river passenger ships.

➤ FARES & SCHEDULES: Contact your travel agent or, in Austria, the **Blue Danube Steamship Company/DDSG**

THE GOLD GUIDE / SMART TRAVEL TIPS

(✉ Friedrichstr. 7, A-1043 Vienna, ☎ 01/588–800.

BUS TRAVEL

BUS LINES

Austria features extensive national networks of buses run by post-office and railroads. Where Austrian trains don't go, buses do, and you'll find the railroad and post-office buses (bright yellow for easy recognition) in the remotest regions carrying passengers as well as mail. You can get tickets on the bus, and in the off-season there is no problem getting a seat, but on routes to favored ski areas during holiday periods reservations are essential. Bookings can be handled at the ticket office (there's one in most towns with bus service) or by travel agents. In most communities, bus routes begin and end at or near the railroad station, making transfers easy. Increasingly, coordination of bus service with railroads means that many of the discounts and special tickets available for trains apply to buses as well. There are private bus companies in Austria as well.

➤ PRIVATE BUS LINES: **Austrobus** (☎ 01/53411–0). **Blaguss Reisen** (☎ 022/ 50180–0).**Bundesbus** (☎ 01/71101). **Dr. Richard** (☎ 01/33100–0).

BUSINESS HOURS

BANKS

In most cities, banks are open weekdays 8–3, Thursday until 5:30 PM. Lunch hour is from 12:30 to 1:30. All banks are closed on Saturday, but you can change money at various locations (such as American Express offices on Saturday morning and major railroad stations around the clock), and changing machines are also found here and there in the larger cities.

MUSEUMS

Museum hours vary from city to city and museum to museum; if museums are closed one day, it is usually Monday. Few Austrian museums are open at night. In Summer, the Salzburg Zoo at Hellbrunn has nighttime opening for the diurnal animals.

SHOPS

In general, you'll find shops open weekdays from 8:30 or 9 until 6, with a lunchtime closing from noon to 1 or 1:30. In smaller villages, the midday break may run until 3. Many food stores, bakeries, and small grocery shops open at 7 or 7:30 and, aside from the noontime break, stay open until 6 or 6:30. Shops in large city centers take no noon break. On Saturday, shops stay open until noon or 1, except on the first Saturday of the month, when (except for food stores) they stay open until 5, a few until 6. Barbers and hairdressers traditionally take Monday off, but there are exceptions. Fashionable these days is for hairdressers to work evenings and nights on certain "good-for-haircutting" moon days! Also in the country, many shops close on Wednesday afternoon, and in parts of Burgenland close also on Thursday afternoon.

CAMERAS & COMPUTERS

EQUIPMENT PRECAUTIONS

Always **keep your film, tape, or computer disks out of the sun.** Carry an extra supply of batteries, and **be prepared to turn on your camera, camcorder, or laptop** to prove to security personnel that the device is real. Always **ask for hand inspection of film,** which becomes clouded after successive exposure to airport X-ray machines, and **keep videotapes and computer disks away from metal detectors.**

TRAVEL PHOTOGRAPHY

➤ PHOTO HELP: **Kodak Information Center** (☎ 800/242–2424). *Kodak Guide to Shooting Great Travel Pictures,* available in bookstores or from Fodor's Travel Publications (☎ 800/533–6478; $16.50 plus $4 shipping).

CAR RENTAL

Rates in Vienna begin at AS400 a day and AS600 a weekend for an economy car with a manual transmission, and unlimited mileage. This does not include tax on car rentals. Renting a car in Germany may be cheaper, but make sure the rental agency knows you are driving into Austria and that the car is equipped with an Autobahn sticker (☞ Car Travel, *below*) for Austria. When renting an RV be sure to compare prices and reserve early.

➤ MAJOR AGENCIES: **Alamo** (☎ 800/
522–9696, 0800/272–2000 in the
U.K.). **Avis** (☎ 800/331–1084, 800/
879–2847 in Canada, 008/225–533
in Australia). **Budget** (☎ 800/527–
0700, 0800/181181 in the U.K.).
Dollar (☎ 800/800–4000; 0990/
565656 in the U.K., where it is
known as Eurodollar). **Hertz** (☎
800/654–3001, 800/263–0600 in
Canada, 0345/555888 in the U.K.,
03/9222–2523 in Australia, 03/358–
6777 in New Zealand). **National
InterRent** (☎ 800/227–3876; 0345/
222525 in the U.K., where it is
known as Europcar InterRent).

➤ LOCAL AGENCIES: **Autoverleih
Buchbinder** (✉ Schlachthausgasse 38,
A–1030 Vienna, ☎ 01/717–50–0,
FAX 01/717–5022, with offices
throughout Austria).

➤ RVs: **Gebetsroither** (✉ Brunnerstr.
Industriegelände, A–2201 Hagen-
brunn, ☎ 02246/4150, FAX 02246/
4711). **Sun Cruiser** (✉ Hintere Ortstr.
65, A–2325 Himberg, ☎ 02235/
87550, FAX 02235/87550–83).

CUTTING COSTS

To get the best deal, **book through a
travel agent who is willing to shop
around.**

Also **ask your travel agent about a
company's customer-service record.**
How has the company responded to
late plane arrivals and vehicle
mishaps? Are there often lines at the
rental counter? If you're traveling
during a holiday period, does a
confirmed reservation guarantee
you a car?

Be sure to **look into wholesalers,**
companies that do not own fleets but
rent in bulk from those that do and
often offer better rates than traditional car-rental operations. Prices are
best during off-peak periods. Rentals
booked through wholesalers must be
paid for before you leave the United
States.

➤ RENTAL WHOLESALERS: **Auto Europe** (☎ 207/842–2000 or 800/223–
5555, FAX 800–235–6321). **Europe by
Car** (☎ 212/581–3040 or 800/223–
1516, FAX 212/246–1458). **DER
Travel Services** (✉ 9501 W. Devon
Ave., Rosemont, IL 60018, ☎ 800/
782–2424, FAX 800/282–7474 for

information or 800/860–9944 for
brochures). **Kemwel Holiday Autos**
(☎ 914/835–5555 or 800/678–
0678, FAX 914/835–5126).

INSURANCE

When driving a rented car you are
generally responsible for any damage
to or loss of the vehicle. Before you
rent, **see what coverage you already
have** under the terms of your personal auto-insurance policy and credit
cards.

Collision policies that car-rental
companies sell for European rentals
typically do not cover stolen vehicles.
Before you buy additional coverage
for theft, check with your credit-card
company and personal auto insurance—you may already be covered.

REQUIREMENTS

In Austria your own driver's license is
acceptable. An International Driver's
Permit is a good idea; it's available
from the American or Canadian
automobile association, and, in the
United Kingdom, from the Automobile Association or Royal Automobile Club. These international
permits are universally recognized,
and having one in your wallet may
save you a problem with the local
authorities.

SURCHARGES

Before you pick up a car in one city
and leave it in another, **ask about
drop-off charges or one-way service
fees,** which can be substantial. Note,
too, that some rental agencies charge
extra if you return the car before the
time specified in your contract. To
avoid a hefty refueling fee, **fill the
tank just before you turn in the car,**
but be aware that gas stations near
the rental outlet may overcharge.

CAR TRAVEL

Make absolutely sure your car is
equipped with the *Autobahnvignette,*
as it is called, a little trapezoidal
sticker with a highway icon and the
Austrian eagle, or with a calendar
marked with an M or a W. This
sticker allows use of the autobahn. It
costs AS550 for a year and is available at gas stations, tobacconists,
automobile-club outlets in neighboring countries or near the border. You

can also purchase a two-month Vignette for AS150, or a ten-day one for AS70. Prices are for vehicles up to 3.5 tons and RVs. For motorcycles it is AS220. Not having a Vignette (which is generally called the *Pickerl*) can lead to high fines. Get your Pickerl before driving to Austria!

Besides the Pickerl, if you are planning to drive around a lot, budget in a great deal of toll money: For example, the tunnels on the A10 autobahn cost AS 70 apiece, the Grossglockner Pass road will cost AS 350, and passing through the Arlberg tunnel costs AS130. Driving up some especially beautiful valleys, such as the Kaunertal in Tirol, or up to the Tauplitzalm in Styria, also costs money, around AS120.

The Austrian highway network is excellent, and roads are well maintained and well marked. Secondary roads may be narrow and winding. The main thorough routes (autobahns), especially the A10 down to Carinthia and Italy, are packed during both Austrian and German school holidays, as well as on weekends in summer. As a nod to the environment, less salt is being used on highways in winter, but few drivers seem to take heed of the greater hazard. Remember that in winter you will need snow tires and often chains, even on well-traveled roads. It's wise to check with the automobile clubs for weather conditions, since mountain roads are often blocked, and ice and fog are hazards.

AUTO CLUBS

Austria has two automobile clubs, ÖAMTC and ARBÖ, both of which operate motorist service patrols. You'll find emergency (orange-colored) phones along all the highways. If you break down along the Autobahn, the nearest phone will be pointed out by a small arrow on the guardrail. Otherwise, if you have problems, call **ARBÖ** (☎ 123) or **ÖAMTC** (☎ 120) from anywhere in the country. No area or other code is needed for either number. Both clubs charge nonmembers for emergency service. Remember to get proper coverage from your home club.

➤ IN AUSTRIA: **Austrian Automobile Club/ÖAMTC** (✉ Schubertring 1–3, A–1010 Vienna, ☎ 01/711–99–55).

➤ IN AUSTRALIA: **Australian Automobile Association** (☎ 06/247–7311).

➤ IN CANADA: **Canadian Automobile Association** (CAA, ☎ 613/247–0117).

➤ IN NEW ZEALAND: **New Zealand Automobile Association** (☎ 09/377–4660).

➤ IN THE U.K.: **Automobile Association** (AA, ☎ 0990/500–600), **Royal Automobile Club** (RAC, ☎ 0990/722–722 for membership, 0345/121–345 for insurance).

➤ IN THE U.S.: **American Automobile Association** (☎ 800/564–6222).

FROM THE U.K.

The best way to reach Austria by car from England is to take North Sea/Cross Channel ferries to Oostende or Zeebrugge in Belgium or Dunkirk in northern France. An alternative is the Channel Tunnel; motoring clubs can give you the best routing to tie into the continental motorway network. Then take the toll-free Belgian motorway (E5) to Aachen, and head via Stuttgart to Innsbruck and the Tirol (A61, A67, A5, E11, A7) or east by way of Nürnberg and Munich, crossing into Austria at Walserberg and then on to Salzburg and Vienna. Total distance to Innsbruck is about 1,100 km (650 mi); to Vienna, about 1,600 km (1,000 mi). The most direct way to Vienna is virtually all on the autobahn via Nürnberg, Regensburg, and Passau, entering Austria at Schärding. In summer, border delays are much shorter at Schärding than at Salzburg. The trip to Innsbruck via this route will take 2–3 days.

If this seems like too much driving, in summer you can **put the car on a train** in s'Hertogenbosch in central southern Netherlands on Thursday, or in Schaerbeek (Brussels) on Friday, for an overnight trip, arriving in Salzburg early the following morning and in Villach three hours later. **DER Travel Service** (✉ 18 Conduit St., London W1R 9TD, ☎ 0171/290–0111, FAX 0171/629–7442) has details of fares and schedules.

GASOLINE

Gasoline and diesel are readily available, but on Sunday stations in the more out-of-the-way areas may be closed. Stations carry only unleaded (*bleifrei*) gas, both regular and premium (super), and diesel. If you're in the mountains in winter with a diesel, and there is a cold snap (with temperatures threatening to drop below -4°F (-20°C), add a few liters of gasoline to your diesel, about 1:4 parts, to prevent it from freezing. Gasoline prices are the same throughout the country, slightly lower at discount and self-service stations. Expect to pay about AS11 per liter for regular, AS12.50 for premium. Oil in Austria is expensive, retailing at AS80 upward per liter. If need be, purchase oil, windshield-wipers, and other paraphernalia at big hardware stores.

ROAD MAPS

A set of eight excellent, detailed road maps is available from the Austrian Automobile Club/ÖAMTC (☞ *above*), at most service stations, and at many bookstores. The maps supplied without charge by the Austrian National Tourist Office are adequate for most needs, but if you will be covering much territory, the better ÖAMTC maps are a worthwhile investment.

RULES OF THE ROAD

Tourists from EU countries may bring their cars to Austria with no documentation other than the normal registration papers and their regular driver's license. A Green Card, the international certificate of insurance, is recommended for EU drivers and compulsory for others. All cars must carry a first-aid kit (including rubber gloves) and a red warning triangle to use in case of accident or breakdown. These are available at gas stations along the road, or at any automotive supply store or large hardware stores.

The minimum driving age in Austria is 18, and children under 12 years must ride in the back seat; smaller children require a restraining seat. Note that all passengers must use seat belts.

Drive on the right side of the street in Austria. Vehicles coming from the right have the right of way, except that at unregulated intersections streetcars coming from either direction have the right of way. No turns are allowed on red. In residential areas, the right of way can be switched around; The rule is, be careful at any intersection.

Drinking and driving: Since 1998, maximum blood-alcohol content allowed is 0.5 parts per thousand, which in real terms means very little to drink. Remember when driving in Europe, that the police can stop you anywhere at any time for no particular reason.

Unless otherwise marked, the speed limit on Autobahns is 130 kph (80 mph), although this is not always strictly enforced. On other highways and roads, the limit is 100 kph (62 mph), 80 kph (49 mph) for RVs or cars pulling a trailer weighing more than 750 kilos (about 1,650 lbs). In built-up areas, a 50 kph (31 mph) limit applies and is likely to be taken seriously. In some towns, special 30 kph (20 mph) limits apply. Remember that insurance doES not necessarily pay if it can be proved you were going above the limit when involved in an accident.

TRAFFIC

Traffic News: Austria has a fine English-language radio station called Blue Danube Radio broadcasting from 6 AM–7 PM, with regular traffic reports on the top of the hour and at the half mark, except in the case of an emergency. Set your radio to 103.8 Mhz.

CHILDREN & TRAVEL

CHILDREN IN AUSTRIA

Be sure to plan ahead and **involve your youngsters** as you outline your trip. When packing, include things to keep them busy en route. On sightseeing days try to schedule activities of special interest to your children. If you are renting a car don't forget to **arrange for a car seat** when you reserve.

➤ BABY-SITTING: In Vienna, **Austrian Academic Guest Service** (✉ Operngasse 24, A–1040, ☎ 01/587–3525).

FLYING

If your children are two or older, **ask about children's airfares.** As a general rule, infants under two not occupying a seat fly at greatly reduced fares or even for free.

In general the adult baggage allowance applies to children paying half or more of the adult fare. When booking, **ask about carry-on allowances for those traveling with infants.** In general, for babies charged 10% of the adult fare you are allowed one carry-on bag and a collapsible stroller, which may have to be checked; you may be limited to less if the flight is full.

Experts agree that it's a good idea to use safety seats aloft for children weighing less than 40 pounds. Airlines, however, can set their own policies: U.S. carriers allow FAA-approved models but usually require that you buy a ticket, even if your child would otherwise ride free, since the seats must be strapped into regular seats. Airline rules vary, so it's important to **check your airline's policy about using safety seats during takeoff and landing.** Safety seats cannot obstruct the movement of other passengers in the row, so get an appropriate seat assignment as early as possible.

When making your reservation, **request children's meals or a free-standing bassinet** if you need them; the latter are available only to those seated at the bulkhead, where there's enough legroom. Remember, however, that bulkhead seats may not have their own overhead bins, and there's no storage space in front of you—a major inconvenience.

GROUP TRAVEL

When planning to take your kids on a tour, look for companies that specialize in family travel.

➤ FAMILY-FRIENDLY TOUR OPERATORS: **Grandtravel** (✉ 6900 Wisconsin Ave., Suite 706, Chevy Chase, MD 20815, ☎ 301/986–0790 or 800/247–7651) for people traveling with grandchildren ages 7–17.

Families Welcome! (✉ 92 N. Main St., Ashland, OR 97520, ☎ 541/482–6121 or 800/326–0724, FAX 541/482–0660).

HOTELS

Most hotels in Austria allow children under a certain age to stay in their parents' room at no extra charge, but others charge them as extra adults; be sure to **ask about the cutoff age for children's discounts.**

In Trebesing, Carinthia, parents accompany the babies instead of the other way around; services for the babies are incredible. It began with Austria's **First Baby Hotel.**

➤ BEST CHOICES: **First Baby Hotel** (✉ Trebesing Bad 1, A–9852 Trebesing, ☎ 04732/2350–0, FAX 04732/2263).

CONSUMER PROTECTION

Whenever possible, **pay with a major credit card** so you can cancel payment or get reimbursed if there's a problem, provided that you can provide documentation. This is the best way to pay, whether you're buying travel arrangements before your trip or shopping at your destination.

If you're buying a package or tour, always **consider travel insurance** that includes default coverage (☞ Insurance, *below*).

➤ LOCAL BBBs: **Council of Better Business Bureaus** (✉ 4200 Wilson Blvd., Suite 800, Arlington, VA 22203, ☎ 703/276–0100, FAX 703/525–8277).

CUSTOMS & DUTIES

When shopping, **keep receipts** for all of your purchases. Upon reentering the country, **be ready to show customs officials what you've bought.** If you feel a duty is incorrect, appeal the assessment. If you object to the way your clearance was handled, get the inspector's badge number. In either case, first ask to see a supervisor, then write to the appropriate authorities, beginning with the port director at your point of entry.

IN AUSTRIA

Travelers over 17 who are residents of European countries—regardless of citizenship—may bring in duty-free 200 cigarettes or 50 cigars or 250 grams of tobacco, 2 liters of wine and 2 liters of 22% spirits or 1 liter of over 22% spirits, and 50 milliliters of perfume. These limits may be liberalized or eliminated under terms of the European Union agreement. Travelers from all other countries (such as those coming directly from the United States or Canada) may bring in twice these amounts. All visitors may bring gifts or other purchases valued at up to ECU175 or A$2,300 (about $190), although in practice you'll seldom be asked.

IN AUSTRALIA

Australia residents who are 18 or older may bring back $A400 worth of souvenirs and gifts (including jewelry), 250 cigarettes or 250 grams of tobacco, and 1,125 ml of alcohol (including wine, beer, and spirits). Residents under 18 may bring back $A200 worth of goods.

➤ INFORMATION: **Australian Customs Service** (Regional Director, ✉ Box 8, Sydney, NSW 2001, ☎ 02/9213–2000, FAX 02/9213–4000).

IN CANADA

Canadian residents who have been out of Canada for at least 7 days may bring in C$500 worth of goods duty-free. If you've been away less than 7 days but more than 48 hours, the duty-free allowance drops to C$200; if your trip lasts 24–48 hours, the allowance is C$50. You may not pool allowances with family members. Goods claimed under the C$500 exemption may follow you by mail; those claimed under the lesser exemptions must accompany you. Alcohol and tobacco products may be included in the 7-day and 48-hour exemptions but not in the 24-hour exemption. If you meet the age requirements of the province or territory through which you reenter Canada, you may bring in, duty-free, 1.14 liters (40 imperial ounces) of wine or liquor *or* 24 12-ounce cans or bottles of beer or ale. If you are 16 or older you may bring in, duty-free, 200 cigarettes and 50 cigars.

You may send an unlimited number of gifts worth up to C$60 each duty-free to Canada. Label the package UNSOLICITED GIFT—VALUE UNDER $60. Alcohol and tobacco are excluded.

➤ INFORMATION: **Revenue Canada** (✉ 2265 St. Laurent Blvd. S, Ottawa, Ontario K1G 4K3, ☎ 613/993–0534, 800/461–9999 in Canada).

IN NEW ZEALAND

Although greeted with a "Haere Mai" ("Welcome to New Zealand"), homeward-bound residents with goods to declare must present themselves for inspection. If you're 17 or older, you may bring back $700 worth of souvenirs and gifts. Your duty-free allowance also includes 4.5 liters of wine or beer; one 1,125-ml bottle of spirits; and either 200 cigarettes, 250 grams of tobacco, 50 cigars, or a combo of all three up to 250 grams.

➤ INFORMATION: **New Zealand Customs** (✉ Custom House, ✉ 50 Anzac Ave., Box 29, Auckland, New Zealand, ☎ 09/359–6655, ☎ 09/309–2978).

IN THE U.K.

If you are a U.K. resident and your journey was wholly within the European Union (EU), you won't have to pass through customs when you return to the United Kingdom. If you plan to bring back large quantities of alcohol or tobacco, check EU limits beforehand.

➤ INFORMATION: **HM Customs and Excise** (✉ Dorset House, ✉ Stamford St., London SE1 9NG, ☎ 0171/202–4227).

IN THE U.S.

U.S. residents may bring home $400 worth of foreign goods duty-free if they've been out of the country for at least 48 hours (and if they haven't used the $400 allowance or any part of it in the past 30 days).

U.S. residents 21 and older may bring back 1 liter of alcohol duty-free. In addition, regardless of your age, you are allowed 200 cigarettes and 100 non-Cuban cigars. Antiques, which the U.S. Customs Service defines as objects more than 100 years old, enter duty-free, as do original works of art done entirely by hand, including paintings, drawings, and sculptures.

You may also send packages home duty-free: up to $200 worth of goods for personal use, with a limit of one parcel per addressee per day (and no alcohol or tobacco products or perfume worth more than $5); label the package PERSONAL USE, and attach a list of its contents and their retail value. Do not label the package UNSOLICITED GIFT, or your duty-free exemption will drop to $100. Mailed items do not affect your duty-free allowance on your return.

➤ INFORMATION: **U.S. Customs Service** (Inquiries, ⊠ Box 7407, Washington, DC 20044, ☎ 202/927–6724; complaints, Office of Regulations and Rulings, ⊠ 1301 Constitution Ave. NW, Washington, DC 20229; registration of equipment, Resource Management, ⊠ 1301 Constitution Ave. NW, Washington DC 20229, ☎ 202/927–0540).

DINING

When dining out, you'll get the best value at simpler restaurants. Most post menus with prices outside. If you begin with the *Würstelstand* (sausage vendor) on the street, the next category would be the *Imbiss-Stube,* for simple, quick snacks. Many meat stores serve soups and a daily special at noon; a blackboard menu will be posted outside. A number of cafés also offer lunch, but watch the prices; some can turn out to be more expensive than restaurants. *Gasthäuser* are simple restaurants or country inns. Austrian hotels have some of the best restaurants in the country, often with outstanding chefs. In the past few years, the restaurants along the autobahns have developed into very fine places to eat, besides being architecturally interesting to look at.

MEALTIMES

Besides the normal three meals, Austrians sometimes throw in a few snacks in between, or forego one meal for a snack. The day begins with a very early Continental breakfast of rolls and coffee; *Gabelfrühstück,* a slightly more substantial breakfast with eggs or cold meat—possibly even a small goulash—at mid-morning; a main meal, usually served between noon and 2; afternoon *Jause* (coffee with cake) at teatime; and, unless dining out, a light supper to end the day, between 6 and 9, tending toward the later hour. Many restaurant kitchens close in the afternoon, but

some post a notice saying DURCHGE-HEND WARME KÜCHE, meaning that hot food is available even between regular mealtimes. In Vienna, some restaurants go on serving until 1 and 2 AM, a tiny number also through the night. The rest of Austria is more conservative.

DISABILITIES & ACCESSIBILITY

ACCESS IN AUSTRIA

The Austria National Tourist Office in New York has a guide to Vienna for people with disabilities and a special map of the city's accessible sights. The Hilton, InterContinental, and Marriott chain hotels plus a number of smaller ones are accessible.

➤ LOCAL RESOURCES: The **Austrian National Tourist Office** (☞ Visitor Information, *below*) can provide a guide to accessible Austrian hotels. Once in Austria, check with the **Österreichischer Zivilinvalidenverband** (⊠ Brigittenauer Lände 42, A–1200 Vienna, ☎ 01/330–6189) for more information. The **Sozialamt der Stadt Wien** (⊠ Gonzagagasse 23, A–1010, ☎ 01/531–14–0) and the **Vienna Tourist Office** (⊠ Obere Augartenstr. 40, A–1025, ☎ 01/211–14–0) also have a booklet on Vienna hotels and a city guide for travelers with disabilities.

MAKING RESERVATIONS

When discussing accessibility with an operator or reservations agent, **ask hard questions.** Are there any stairs, inside *or* out? Are there grab bars next to the toilet *and* in the shower/tub? How wide is the doorway to the room? To the bathroom? For the most extensive facilities meeting the latest legal specifications, **opt for newer accommodations,** which are more likely to have been designed with access in mind. Older buildings or ships may have more limited facilities. Be sure to **discuss your needs before booking.**

TRANSPORTATION

The railroads are both understanding and helpful. If prior arrangements have been made, taxis and private vehicles are allowed to drive right to the train platform; railway personnel will help with boarding and leaving trains; and with three days' notice, a special wheelchair can be provided for getting around train corridors. If you're traveling by plane, ask in advance for assistance or a wheelchair at your destination. A number of stations in the Vienna subway system have only stairs or escalators, but elevators are being added at major stations.

➤ COMPLAINTS: **Disability Rights Section** (✉ U.S. Department of Justice, Civil Rights Division, ✉ Box 66738, Washington, DC 20035–6738, ☎ 202/514–0301 or 800/514–0301, TTY 202/514–0383 or 800/514–0383, FAX 202/307–1198) for general complaints. **Aviation Consumer Protection Division** (☞ Air Travel, *above*) for airline-related problems. **Civil Rights Office** (✉ U.S. Department of Transportation, Departmental Office of Civil Rights, S-30, ✉ 400 7th St. SW, Room 10215, Washington, DC, 20590, ☎ 202/366–4648, FAX 202/366–9371) for problems with surface transportation.

TRAVEL AGENCIES & TOUR OPERATORS

As a whole, the travel industry has become more aware of the needs of travelers with disabilities. In the U.S., the Americans with Disabilities Act requires that travel firms serve the needs of all travelers. Note, though, that some agencies and operators specialize in making travel arrangements for individuals and groups with disabilities.

➤ TRAVELERS WITH MOBILITY PROBLEMS: **Access Adventures** (✉ 206 Chestnut Ridge Rd., Rochester, NY 14624, ☎ 716/889–9096), run by a former physical-rehabilitation counselor. **Accessible Journeys** (✉ 35 W. Sellers Ave., Ridley Park, PA 19078, ☎ 610/521–0339 or 800/846–4537, FAX 610/521–6959), for escorted tours exclusively for travelers with mobility impairments. **Flying Wheels Travel** (✉ 143 W. Bridge St., Box 382, Owatonna, MN 55060, ☎ 507/451–5005 or 800/535–6790, FAX 507/451–1685), a travel agency specializing in customized tours and itineraries worldwide. **Hinsdale Travel Service** (✉ 201 E. Ogden Ave., Suite 100, Hinsdale, IL 60521, ☎ 630/325–1335), a travel agency that benefits

from the advice of wheelchair traveler Janice Perkins.

DISCOUNTS & DEALS

Be a smart shopper and **compare all your options** before making any choice. A plane ticket bought with a promotional coupon may not be cheaper than the least expensive fare from a discount ticket agency. For high-price travel purchases, such as packages or tours, keep in mind that what you get is just as important as what you save. Just because something is cheap doesn't mean it's a bargain.

CLUBS & COUPONS

Many companies sell discounts in the form of travel clubs and coupon books, but these cost money. You must use participating advertisers to get a deal, and only after you recoup the initial membership cost or book price do you begin to save. If you plan to use the club or coupons frequently, you may save considerably. Before signing up, find out what discounts you get for free.

➤ DISCOUNT CLUBS: **Entertainment Travel Editions** (✉ 2125 Butterfield Rd., Troy, MI 48084, ☎ 800/445–4137; $20–$51, depending on destination). **Great American Traveler** (✉ Box 27965, Salt Lake City, UT 84127, ☎ 801/974 3033 or 800/548–2812, $49.95 per year). **Moment's Notice Discount Travel Club** (✉ 7301 New Utrecht Ave., Brooklyn, NY 11204, ☎ 718/234–6295; $25 per year, single or family). **Privilege Card International** (✉ 237 E. Front St., Youngstown, OH 44503, ☎ 330/746–5211 or 800/236–9732; $74.95 per year). **Sears's Mature Outlook** (✉ Box 9390, Des Moines, IA 50306, ☎ 800/336–6330; $19.95 per year). **Travelers Advantage** (✉ CUC Travel Service, ✉ 3033 S. Parker Rd., Suite 1000, Aurora, CO 80014, ☎ 800/548–1116 or 800/648–4037; $59.95 per year, single or family). **Worldwide Discount Travel Club** (✉ 1674 Meridian Ave., Miami Beach, FL 33139, ☎ 305/534–2082; $50 per year family, $40 single).

CREDIT-CARD BENEFITS

When you use your credit card to make travel purchases you may get free travel-accident insurance, collision-damage insurance, and medical or legal assistance, depending on the card and the bank that issued it. American Express, MasterCard, and Visa provide one or more of these services, so **get a copy of your credit card's travel-benefits policy.** If you are a member of an auto club, always **ask hotel and car-rental reservations agents about auto-club discounts.** Some clubs offer additional discounts on tours, cruises, and admission to attractions.

DISCOUNT RESERVATIONS

To save money, **look into discount-reservations services** with toll-free numbers, which use their buying power to get a better price on hotels, airline tickets, even car rentals. When booking a room, always **call the hotel's local toll-free number** (if one is available) rather than the central reservations number—you'll often get a better price. Always ask about special packages or corporate rates.

When shopping for the best deal on hotels and car rentals, **look for guaranteed exchange rates,** which protect you against a falling dollar. With your rate locked in, you won't pay more, even if the price goes up in the local currency.

➤ AIRLINE TICKETS: **800/FLY–4–LESS.**

➤ HOTEL ROOMS: **Hotels Plus** (☎ 800/235–0909). **International Marketing & Travel Concepts** (☎ 800/790–4682). **Steigenberger Reservation Service** (☎ 800/223–5652). **Travel Interlink** (☎ 800/888–5898).

PACKAGE DEALS

Packages and guided tours can save you money, but don't confuse the two. When you buy a package, your travel remains independent, just as though you had planned and booked the trip yourself. Fly/drive packages, which combine airfare and car rental, are often a good deal. If you **buy a rail/drive pass,** you'll save on train tickets and car rentals. All Eurail- and Europass holders get a discount on Eurostar fares through the Channel Tunnel.

ELECTRICITY

To use your U.S.-purchased electric-powered equipment, **bring a converter and adapter.** The electrical current in Austria is 220 volts, 50 cycles alternating current (AC); wall outlets take continental-type plugs, with two round prongs.

If your appliances are dual-voltage, you'll need only an adapter. Don't use 110-volt outlets, marked FOR SHAVERS ONLY, for high-wattage appliances such as blow-dryers. Most laptops operate equally well on 110 and 220 volts and so require only an adapter.

EMERGENCIES

➤ EMERGENCIES: **Police** (☎ 133). **Fire** (☎ 122). **Ambulance** (☎ 144).

GAY & LESBIAN TRAVEL

In Vienna, the twice-monthly magazine *Xtra!* runs a calendar of daily events and addresses.

➤ LOCAL RESOURCES: **Homosexuelle Initiative** (⊠ No-varagasse 40, A–1020 Vienna, ☎ 01/216–6604). **Rosa Lila Villa** (⊠ Linke Wienzeile 102, A–1060 Vienna, ☎ 01/586–8150).

➤ GAY- AND LESBIAN-FRIENDLY TRAVEL AGENCIES: **Corniche Travel** (⊠ 8721 Sunset Blvd., Suite 200, West Hollywood, CA 90069, ☎ 310/854–6000 or 800/429–8747, FAX 310/659–7441). **Islanders Kennedy Travel** (⊠ 183 W. 10th St., New York, NY 10014, ☎ 212/242–3222 or 800/988–1181, FAX 212/929–8530). **Now Voyager** (⊠ 4406 18th St., San Francisco, CA 94114, ☎ 415/626–1169 or 800/255–6951, FAX 415/626–8626). **Skylink Travel and Tour** (⊠ 3577 Moorland Ave., Santa Rosa, CA 95407, ☎ 707/585–8355 or 800/225–5759, FAX 707/584–5637), serving lesbian travelers. **Yellowbrick Road** (⊠ 1500 W. Balmoral Ave., Chicago, IL 60640, ☎ 773/561–1800 or 800/642–2488, FAX 773/561–4497).

HEALTH

MEDICAL PLANS

No one plans to get sick while traveling, but it happens, so **consider signing up with a medical-assistance company.** Members get doctor referrals, emergency evacuation or repatriation, 24-hour telephone hot lines for medical consultation, cash for emergencies, and other personal and legal assistance. Coverage varies by plan, so **review the benefits of each carefully.**

➤ MEDICAL-ASSISTANCE COMPANIES: **International SOS Assistance** (⊠ 8 Neshaminy Interplex, Suite 207, Trevose, PA 19053, ☎ 215/245–4707 or 800/523–6586, FAX 215/244–9617; ⊠ 12 Chemin Riant-bosson, 1217 Meyrin 1, Geneva, Switzerland, ☎ 4122/785–6464, FAX 4122/785–6424).

SHOTS & MEDICATIONS

No special shots are required before visiting Austria, but if you will be cycling or hiking through the eastern or southeastern parts of the country, get inoculated against encephalitis; it can be carried by ticks.

HOLIDAYS

All banks and shops are closed on national holidays: New Year's Day; Jan. 6, Epiphany; Easter Sunday and Monday; May 1, May Day; May 8, Ascension Day; Pentecost Sunday and Monday; May 29, Corpus Christi; Aug. 15, Assumption; Oct. 26, National Holiday; Nov. 1, All Saints' Day; Dec. 8, Immaculate Conception; Dec. 25–26, Christmas. Museums are open on most holidays and closed on Good Friday and Dec. 24. Banks and offices are closed on Dec. 8, but most shops are open.

INSURANCE

Travel insurance is the best way to **protect yourself against financial loss.** The most useful plan is a comprehensive policy that includes coverage for trip cancellation and interruption, default, trip delay, and medical expenses (with a waiver for preexisting conditions).

Without insurance, you will lose all or most of your money if you cancel your trip, regardless of the reason. Default insurance covers you if your tour operator, airline, or cruise line goes out of business. Trip-delay covers unforeseen expenses that you may incur due to bad weather or mechanical delays. It's important to compare the fine print regarding trip-delay coverage when comparing policies.

For overseas travel, one of the most important components of travel insurance is its medical coverage. Supplemental health insurance will pick up the cost of your medical bills should you get sick or injured while traveling. U.S. residents should note that Medicare generally does not cover health-care costs outside the United States, nor do many privately issued policies. Residents of the United Kingdom can buy an annual travel-insurance policy valid for most vacations taken during the year in which the coverage is purchased. If you are pregnant or have a pre-existing condition, make sure you're covered. British citizens should buy extra medical coverage when traveling overseas, according to the Association of British Insurers. Australian travelers should buy travel insurance, including extra medical coverage, whenever they go abroad, according to the Insurance Council of Australia.

Always **buy travel insurance directly from the insurance company**; if you buy it from a cruise line, airline, or tour operator that goes out of business you probably will not be covered for the agency or operator's default, a major risk. Before you make any purchase, **review your existing health and home-owner's policies** to find out whether they cover expenses incurred while traveling.

➤ TRAVEL INSURERS: In the U.S., **Access America** (⊠ 6600 W. Broad St., Richmond, VA 23230, ☎ 804/285–3300 or 800/284–8300). **Travel Guard International** (⊠ 1145 Clark St., Stevens Point, WI 54481, ☎ 715/345–0505 or 800/826–1300). In Canada, **Mutual of Omaha** (⊠ Travel Division, ⊠ 500 University Ave., Toronto, Ontario M5G 1V8, ☎ 416/598–4083, 800/268–8825 in Canada).

➤ INSURANCE INFORMATION: In the U.K., **Association of British Insurers** (⊠ 51 Gresham St., London EC2V 7HQ, ☎ 0171/600–3333). In Australia, the **Insurance Council of Australia** (☎ 613/9614–1077, FAX 613/9614–7924).

THE GOLD GUIDE / SMART TRAVEL TIPS

LANGUAGE

German is the official national language in Austria. In larger cities and in most resort areas, you will usually have no problem finding people who speak English; hotel staffs in particular speak it reasonably well, and many young Austrians speak it at least passably. However, travelers do report that they often find themselves in stores, restaurants, and railway and bus stations where it's hard to find someone who speaks English—so it's best to have some native phrases up your sleeve (☞ Chapter 12). Note that all public announcements on trams, subways and buses are in German. Train announcements usually are given in English as well, but if you have any questions, try to get answers before boarding.

LODGING

You can live like a king in a real castle in Austria or get by on a modest budget. Starting at the lower end, you can find a room in a private house or on a farm, or dormitory space in a youth hostel. Next up the line come the simpler pensions, many of them identified as *Frühstückspension,* (bed-and-breakfast). Then come the Gasthäuser, the simpler country inns. The fancier pensions in the cities can often cost as much as hotels; the difference lies in the services they offer. Most pensions, for example, do not staff the front desk around the clock. Among the hotels, you can find accommodations ranging from the most modest, with a shower and toilet down the hall, to the most elegant, with every possible amenity.

Austria has few very expensive ($$$$) hotels outside Vienna, Salzburg, and the major resorts, but has numerous expensive ($$$) ones, usually with swimming pools—sometimes indoor and outdoor—saunas, fitness rooms, and other amenities. The moderate ($$) accommodations in country areas or smaller cities and towns are generally more than adequate: Food, service, and cleanliness are of high standards. The newer inexpensive ($) seasonal hotels have private showers. *See* Lodging *in* Pleasures and Pastimes in individual chapters for prices, which vary widely among large cities,

resorts, and small country towns, as well as in peak season and in low. Outside of the largest cities, Austria remains a country of smaller innkeepers and family operations. This fact opens the way for a warm relationship with owners and staff, adding to the pleasures of a vacation.

The Austrian National Tourist offices (☞ Visitor Information, *below*) have detailed brochures (in German) on farm and village holidays, on family apartments, and on hotels specializing in families with small children.

APARTMENT & VILLA RENTALS

If you want a home base that's roomy enough for a family and comes with cooking facilities, **consider a furnished rental.** These can save you money, especially if you're traveling with a large group of people. Home-exchange directories list rentals (often second homes owned by prospective house swappers), and some services search for a house or apartment for you (even a castle if that's your fancy) and handle the paperwork. Some send an illustrated catalog; others send photographs only of specific properties, sometimes at a charge. Up-front registration fees may apply.

➤ RENTAL AGENTS: **Drawbridge to Europe** (⊠ 5456 Adams Rd., Talent, OR 97540, ☎ 541/512–8927 or 888/268–1148, ℻ 541/512–0978). **Europa-Let/Tropical Inn-Let** (⊠ 92 N. Main St., Ashland, OR 97520, ☎ 541/482–5806 or 800/462–4486, ℻ 541/482–0660). **Hometours International** (⊠ Box 11503, Knoxville, TN 37939, ☎ 423/690–8484 or 800/367–4668). **Interhome** (⊠ 124 Little Falls Rd., Fairfield, NJ 07004, ☎ 973/882–6864 or 800/882–6864, ℻ 973/808–1742). **Property Rentals International** (⊠ 1008 Mansfield Crossing Rd., Richmond, VA 23236, ☎ 804/378–6054 or 800/220–3332, ℻ 804/379–2073). **Rent-a-Home International** (⊠ 7200 34th Ave. NW, Seattle, WA 98117, ☎ 206/789–9377 or 800/488–7368, ℻ 206/789–9379). **Villas International** (⊠ 605 Market St., San Francisco, CA 94105, ☎ 415/281–0910 or 800/221–2260, ℻ 415/281–0919). **Hideaways International** (⊠ 767 Islington St., Portsmouth, NH 03801, ☎ 603/

430–4433 or 800/843–4433, FAX
603/430–4444; membership $99) is a
club for travelers who arrange rentals
among themselves.

CASTLES

➤ INFORMATION: **Schlosshotels und
Herrenhäuser in Österreich** (✉
Ferdinand-Hanusch-Pl. 1, A–5020
Salzburg, ☎ 0662/846825–0,
FAX 0662/846826).

FARM HOLIDAYS

➤ INFORMATION: **Farmhouse Holidays
in Austria** (✉ Hardtgasse 19, A–
1190 Vienna, ☎ 01/368–0111,
FAX 01/368–0111–3 provides information on basic as well as specialty
farms, such as organic farms or farms
for children, for the disabled, for
horseback riders.

HOSTELS

No matter what your age, you can
**save on lodging costs by staying at
hostels.** In some 5,000 locations in
more than 70 countries around the
world, Hostelling International (HI),
the umbrella group for a number of
national youth hostel associations,
offers single-sex, dorm-style beds and,
at many hostels, "couples" rooms and
family accommodations. Membership
in any HI national hostel association,
open to travelers of all ages, allows
you to stay in HI-affiliated hostels at
member rates (one-year membership
is about $25 for adults; hostels run
about $10–$25 per night). Members
also have priority if the hostel is full;
they're eligible for discounts around
the world, even on rail and bus travel
in some countries.

➤ HOSTEL ORGANIZATIONS: **Hostelling
International—American Youth Hos-
tels** (✉ 733 15th St. NW, Suite 840,
Washington, DC 20005, ☎ 202/783–
6161, FAX 202/783–6171). **Hostelling
International—Canada** (✉ 400-205
Catherine St., Ottawa, Ontario K2P
1C3, ☎ 613/237–7884, FAX 613/237–
7868). **Youth Hostel Association of
England and Wales** (✉ Trevelyan
House, ✉ 8 St. Stephen's Hill, St.
Albans, Hertfordshire AL1 2DY,
☎ 01727/855215 or 01727/845047,
FAX 01727/844126); membership in the
U.S. $25, in Canada C$26.75, in the
U.K. £9.30).

ROMANTIK HOTELS

For the coziest, most personal accommodations in elegant surroundings,
some say the best options are the
Romantik Hotels & Restaurants
found throughout Austria.

➤ RESERVATIONS: **DER Tours** (✉
11933 Wilshire Blvd., Los Angeles,
CA 90025, ☎ 310/479–4140 or 800/
421–4343). **Euro-Connection** (✉
Box 2397, 1819 207th Place SW,
Lynwood, WA 98036, ☎ 206/670–
1140 or 800/645–3876). **MLT Vacations** (✉ 5130 Highway 101,
Minnetonka, MN 55345, ☎ 612/
474–2540 or 800/362–3520). **Romantik Travel and Tours** (✉ 16932
Woodinville-Redmond Rd., Suite
A107, Box 1278, Woodinville, WA
98072, ☎ 206/486–9394 or 800/
826–0015).

MAIL

POSTAL RATES

Within Europe, all mail goes by air, so
there's no supplement on letters or
postcards. A letter of up to 20 grams
(about ¾ ounce) takes AS7, a post-
card AS6. To the United States or
Canada, a letter of up to 20 grams
takes AS13 for airmail. If in doubt,
mail your letters from a post office
and have the weight checked. The
Austrian post office also adheres
strictly to a size standard; if your
letter or card is outside the norm,
you'll have to pay a surcharge. Postcards via airmail to the United States
or Canada need AS8.50. Always place
an airmail sticker on your letters or
cards! Post offices have air-letter
(aerogram) forms for AS12 to any
overseas destination.

RECEIVING MAIL

When you don't know where you'll be
staying, **American Express** mail service
is a great convenience, with no charge
to anyone either holding an American
Express credit card or carrying American Express traveler's checks. Pick
up your mail at the local offices (✉
Kärntner Str. 21–23, A–1015 Vienna,
☎ 01/51540–0; ✉ Mozartpl. 5,
A–5020 Salzburg, ☎ 0662/8080–0;
✉ Brixner Str. 3, A–6020 Innsbruck,
☎ 0512/582491–0; and ✉ Bürgerstr.
14, A–4021 Linz, ☎ 0732/669013).
You can also have mail held at any

THE GOLD GUIDE / SMART TRAVEL TIPS

Austrian post office; letters should be marked *Poste Restante* or *Postlagernd*. You will be asked for identification when you collect mail. In Vienna, if not addressed to a specific district post office, this service is handled through the main post office (⊠ Fleischmarkt 19, A–1010 Vienna, ☏ 01/515–09–0).

MONEY

COSTS

A cup of coffee in a café will cost about AS28; a half-liter of draft beer, AS27–AS40; a glass of wine, AS38; a Coca-Cola, AS28; an open-face sandwich, AS28; a mid-range theater ticket AS200; a concert ticket AS250–AS500; an opera ticket AS600 upwards; a 1-mi taxi ride, AS35. Outside the hotels, laundering a shirt costs about AS30; dry cleaning a suit costs around AS130–AS140; a dress, AS100–AS120. A shampoo and set for a woman will cost around AS350–AS450, a manicure about AS150–AS180; a man's haircut (without shampoo) will cost about AS225–AS250.

CREDIT & DEBIT CARDS

Credit cards are coming into widespread use, but figure on using travelers checks and having cash available. Most Austrian travel agencies still take only Diner's Club cards, but Visa and MasterCard are quickly gaining broad acceptance. The multi-use Eurocheck card can be used to pay in many gas stations and restaurants. Some establishments have a minimum sum for use of credit cards; others may accept cards grudgingly.

Should you use a credit card or a debit card when traveling? Both have benefits. A credit card allows you to delay payment and gives you certain rights as a consumer (☞ Consumer Protection, *above*). A debit card, also known as a check card, deducts funds directly from your checking account and helps you stay within your budget. When you want to rent a car, though, you may still need an old-fashioned credit card. Although you can always *pay* for your car with a debit card, some agencies will not allow you to *reserve* a car with a debit card.

Otherwise, the two types of plastic are virtually the same. Both will get you cash advances at ATMs worldwide if your card is properly programmed with your personal identification number (PIN). Both offer excellent, wholesale exchange rates. And both protect you against unauthorized use if the card is lost or stolen. Your liability is limited to $50, as long as you report the card missing.

➤ ATM LOCATIONS: Cirrus (☏ 800/424–7787). Plus (☏ 800/843–7587) for locations in the U.S. and Canada, or visit your local bank.

CURRENCY

The Austrian unit of currency is the schilling (AS), subdivided into 100 groschen. At press time (summer 1998), the exchange rate was about AS12.58 to the dollar, AS20.66 to the pound sterling. These rates can and will vary. The schilling is pegged to the German mark at a constant 7-to-1 ratio. As of 1999 the Euro (ECU) will start being quoted. At presstime, 1 ECU = $1.10.

There are Austrian coins for 5, 10, and 50 groschen and for 1, 5, 10, and 20 schillings. The paper notes have AS20, AS50, AS100, AS500, AS1,000, and AS5,000 face value. There is little visible difference between the 100-and 500-schilling notes; be careful, since confusion could be expensive! Legally, foreign exchange is limited to licensed offices (banks and exchange offices); in practice, the rule is universally ignored. You can frequently pay with Deutschmarks, especially in regions near the border, in Salzburg, and in Tirol.

EXCHANGING MONEY

For the most favorable rates, **change money through banks.** Although fees charged for ATM transactions may be higher abroad than at home, Cirrus and Plus exchange rates are excellent, because they are based on wholesale rates offered only by major banks. You won't do as well at exchange booths in airports or rail and bus stations, in hotels, in restaurants, or in stores, although you may find their hours more convenient. To avoid lines at airport exchange booths, **get a bit of local currency before you leave home.**

➤ EXCHANGE SERVICES: **Chase Currency To Go** (☎ 800/935–9935; 935–9935 in NY, NJ, and CT). **International Currency Express** (☎ 888/842–0880 on the East Coast, 888/278–6628 on the West Coast). **Thomas Cook Currency Services** (☎ 800/287–7362 for telephone orders and retail locations).

TRAVELER'S CHECKS

Do you need traveler's checks? It depends on where you're headed. If you're going to rural areas and small towns, go with cash; traveler's checks are best used in cities. Lost or stolen checks can usually be replaced within 24 hours. To ensure a speedy refund, buy your own traveler's checks—don't let someone else pay for them: irregularities like this can cause delays. The person who bought the checks should make the call to request a refund.

OUTDOOR ACTIVITIES & SPORTS

The Austrians are great sports lovers and go in for a greater variety of sports than any other European nation (☞ Pleasures and Pastimes in Chapter 1).

BALLOONING

Filzmoos in the Salzburg province near the Styrian border is one of several ballooning centers.

➤ CONTACTS: **Austrian Aero-Club** (⊠ Prinz Eugen-Str. 12, A–1040 Vienna, ☎ 01/505–1028, FAX 01/505–7923). **Austrian Ballooning Club** (Endresstr. 79/4, A–1230 Vienna, ☎ 01/889–8222). **Balloon Sportclub Vienna** (⊠ Mariahilfer Str. 41–43, A–1060 Vienna, ☎ 01/587–8139–20).

BICYCLING

Cyclists couldn't ask for much more than the cycle track that runs the length of the Danube or the many cycling routes that crisscross the country, major cities included. Just about every lake is surrounded by bike paths, and there are other rivers, too, such as the Drau, that have trails. You can rent a city bike (21-gear) for AS150 per day (AS90, if you have a rail ticket in your hand) at any of about 130 railroad stations throughout the country and return it to another. With an all-day ticket (AS40), you can take your bike on the train with you anywhere in the country and leave it at another station with freight facilities for an AS45 return fee. If you have a *Vorteilscard* (☞ Discounts in Train Travel, *below*) it's all half price.

Tourist Offices have details (in German), including maps and hints for trip planning and mealtime and overnight stops that cater especially to cyclists. Ask for the booklet "Radtouren in Österreich." There's also a brochure in English: "Biking Austria—On the Trail of Mozart" that provides details in English on the cycle route through the High Tauern mountains in Salzburg Province.

➤ CONTACT: **Austria Radreisen** (⊠ Fritz–Holzingerstr. 546, A–4780 Schärding, ☎ 07712/5511–0, FAX 07712/4811).

BOATING AND SAILING

Small boats can be rented on all the lakes of the Salzkammergut region and on the large lakes in Carinthia. You can rent a rowboat on almost all of Austria's lakes and on the side arms of the Danube (Alte Donau and the Donauinsel) in Vienna.

Windsurfing (*Windsegeln*) is extremely popular, particularly on the Neusiedler See in Burgenland, on the Attersee in Upper Austria, and on the side arms of the Danube in Vienna. There are schools at all these locations with lessons and rentals.

➤ CONTACT: **Österreichischer Segel-Verband, the Austrian Yachting Club** (⊠ Grosse Neugasse 8, A–1040 Vienna, ☎ 01/587–8688, FAX 01/586–6171).

CAMPING

If your idea of a good holiday is the "great outdoors" and if your purse is a slender one, a camping holiday may be just the thing for you. Austrians love the idea and there are practically as many tourists under canvas as in the hotels and Gasthäuser. You'll find more than 450 campsites throughout the country, usually run by regional organizations, a few private. Most have full facilities, often including swimming pools and snack bars or grocery shops. Charges average about AS230 per day for a family of three, depending on the location and the range and quality of services offered. Many campsites have a fixed basic fee for three adults and one child, parking included. Camping is not restricted to the summer season; some sites are open year-round, with about 155 specifically set up for winter camping. For details, check with the tourist offices of the individual Austrian provinces.

➤ CONTACT: **Österreichischer Camping Club** (✉ Schubertring 1–3, A–1010 Vienna, ☎ 01/71199–1272, FAX 01/71199–1498).

FISHING

Among Austria's well-stocked lakes are the Traunsee, Attersee, Hallstätter See, and Mondsee in Upper Austria; the Danube, Steyr, Traun, Enns, Krems, and Alm rivers also provide good fishing. Tirol is another good region; try the Achensee, Traualpsee, Walchsee, Plansee, and nearby streams. Also try the Inn and Drau in East Tirol and the Ziller in the Zillertal. Styria provides some of the best trout fishing in Austria, as do the lakes in the Styrian Salzkammergut. Carinthian lakes and the streams in Lower Austria also abound in fish. Ask the Austrian National Tourist Office for the guidebook "Austrian Fishing Waters"; it includes licensing details. The separate provinces also have detailed brochures on waters and licensing. Unfortunately, the rights along many of the best streams have been given, meaning that no additional licenses will be issued, but ask at the local tourist office. Some hotels have fishing rights; we note these throughout the book.

GLIDING

From May to September you can glide solo or learn to glide at one of Austria's schools, at Zell am See (Salzburg province); Niederöblarn and Graz-Thalerhof (Styria); in Wiener Neustadt and Spitzberg bei Hainberg (Lower Austria). In Zell am See and at Wien-Donauwiese (Vienna) there are two-seater gliders, for instructor and passenger; at the other airfields you're on your own.

➤ CONTACT: **Austrian Aero Club** (✉ Prinz Eugen-Str. 12, A–1040 Vienna, ☎ 01/505–1028–74, FAX 01/505–7923).

GOLF

Austria now has more than 50 courses. Most are private, but for a greens fee you can arrange a temporary membership. Many courses are associated with hotels, so package arrangements can be made. Austrian National Tourist Offices have golfing brochures.

➤ CONTACTS: **Golf Green Austria** (✉ Bräuhausstr. 1a, A–5020 Salzburg, ☎ 0662/827852, FAX 0662/822098). **Österreichischer Golfverband** (✉ Prinz Eugen-Str. 12, A–1040 Vienna, ☎ 01/505–3245–0, FAX 01/505–4962).

HIKING AND CLIMBING

With more than 50,000 km (about 35,000 mi) of well-maintained mountain paths through Europe's largest reserve of unspoiled landscape, the country is a hiker's paradise. Three long-distance routes traverse Austria: E-4, the Pyrenees–Jura–Neusiedler See route, ending in Burgenland on the Hungarian border; E-5 from Lake Constance in Vorarlberg to the Adriatic; and E-6 from the Baltic, cutting across mid-Austria via the Wachau Valley region of the Danube and on to the Adriatic. Wherever you are in Austria, you will find shorter hiking trails requiring varying degrees of ability. Routes are well marked, and maps are readily available from bookstores, the Österreichische or Alpenverein/ÖAV, and the automobile clubs.

Of the more than 700 refuges in Austria, about a quarter are at altitudes of between 8,200 and 9,800 ft. Mountain guides typically charge AS2,250 a day for glacier tours and easy-to-moderate climbs, with the guides responsible for their own food. For more strenuous climbing and longer periods, you can arrange a fixed fee in advance. A tip is usual at the end of the climb.

If you're a newcomer to mountain climbing or want to improve your skill, schools in Tirol, Carinthia, Styria, and Salzburg province will take you on. Ask the ÖAV for addresses. All organize courses and guided tours for beginners and more advanced climbers.

Tourist offices have details on hiking holidays; serious climbers can write directly to **Österreichischer Alpenverein/ÖAV** (Austrian Alpine Club, ☞ *below*) for more information. Membership in the club (AS460, about $43) will give you a 50% reduction from the regular fees for overnights in the 275 mountain refuges it operates. Senior memberships have a reduced price.

➤ CONTACT: **Österreichischer Alpenverein/ÖAV** (✉ Wilhelm-Greil-Str. 15, A–6020 Innsbruck, ☎ 0512/595470, ℻ 0512/575528; in the U.K., ✉ 13 Longcroft House, Fretherne Rd., Welwyn Garden City, Hertfordshire AL8 6PQ, ☎ 01707/324835).

HORSEBACK RIDING

Whether you want to head off cross-country or just canter around a paddock, Austria offers many kinds of equestrian holidays, and some hotels have their own riding schools. Ask for the booklet "Riding Arena Austria" from the tourist office. The provinces of Styria, Burgenland, and Upper and Lower Austria are particularly popular with riders.

SKIING

Skiing is without doubt the emperor of winter sports, and Austria is one of the finest places—if not the finest—in which to learn or practice the far-from-gentle art of skiing (☞ Pleasures and Pastimes *in* Chapter 1 and Powder-Perfect Skiing *in* Chapter 12).

SNOWBOARDING

Snowboarders will find halfpipes and ample challenges in all major winter resorts. You can rent boards and take lessons in many Salzburg province, Tirol, Carinthia, and Vorarlberg ski areas.

SPECTATOR SPORTS

Soccer is a national favorite. Every town has at least one team, and rivalries are fierce; matches are held regularly in Vienna and Innsbruck. When Austrians aren't skiing, they like to watch the national sport; downhill and slalom races are held regularly in Innsbruck, Kitzbühel, Seefeld, and St. Anton. There's horse racing with pari-mutuel betting at the track in the Prater in Vienna. Tennis matches are held in Vienna, Linz, and Innsbruck.

WATERSPORTS AND SWIMMING

Waterskiing and sail skiing are popular on the Wörther See (where there's also spectacular night waterskiing with torches) and Millstätter See in Carinthia; on the Traunsee, Attersee, and Wolfgangsee in Salzkammergut; in Zell am See in Salzburg Province; and on the Bodensee (Lake Constance) in Vorarlberg. Waterskiing is not permitted on many of the smaller Austrian lakes, so check first. There are hundreds of places to swim throughout Austria, and with very few exceptions, the water is unpolluted. All the lakes in the Salzkammergut, Carinthia, and Tirol have excellent swimming, but are crowded in the peak season. In the Vienna area, the Alte Donau and Donauinsel arms of the Danube are accessible by public transportation and are suitable for families. It's best to go early to avoid the crowds on hot summer weekends. The Alte Donau beaches have changing rooms and checkrooms. Swimming in the Neusiedler See in Burgenland is an experience; you can touch bottom at virtually any place in this vast brackish lake. Swimming naked or at least partly so is fairly common.

PACKING

LUGGAGE

How many carry-on bags you can bring with you is up to the airline. Most allow two, but the limit is often reduced to one on certain flights. Gate agents will take excess baggage—including bags they deem oversize—from you as you board and add it to checked luggage. To avoid this situation, make sure that everything you carry aboard will fit under your seat. Also, get to the gate early, and request a seat at the back of the plane; you'll probably board first, while the overhead bins are still empty. Since big, bulky baggage attracts the attention of gate agents and flight attendants on a busy flight, make sure your carry-on is really a carry-on. Finally, a carry-on that's long and narrow is more likely to remain unnoticed than one that's wide and squarish.

If you are flying internationally, note that baggage allowances may be determined not by piece but by weight—generally 88 pounds (40 kilograms) in first class, 66 pounds (30 kilograms) in business class, and 44 pounds (20 kilograms) in economy.

Airline liability for baggage is limited to $1,250 per person on flights within the United States. On international flights it amounts to $9.07 per pound or $20 per kilogram for checked baggage (roughly $640 per 70-pound bag) and $400 per passenger for unchecked baggage. You can buy additional coverage at check-in for about $10 per $1,000 of coverage, but it excludes a rather extensive list of items, shown on your airline ticket.

Before departure, **itemize your bags' contents** and their worth, and label the bags with your name, address, and phone number. (If you use your home address, cover it so that potential thieves can't see it readily.) Inside each bag, **pack a copy of your itinerary.** At check-in, **make sure that each bag is correctly tagged** with the destination airport's three-letter code. If your bags arrive damaged or fail to arrive at all, file a written report with the airline before leaving the airport.

PACKING LIST

Dressing in Austria ranges from conservative to casual, and is somewhat dependent on age. Older people tend to dress solidly, slacks on women are as rare as loud sport shirts are on men. Young people tend to be very trendy, and the trend is basically U.S., with kids in baseball caps, baggy trousers, loud shirts with all kinds of things written on them in (sometimes poor) English. In the country or more rural areas of, say, Styria or Burgenland, things are a little less loud. Jeans are ubiquitous in Austria as everywhere, but are considered inappropriate at concerts (other than pop) or formal restaurants. For concerts and opera, women may want a skirt or dress, and men a jacket; even in

summer, gala performances at small festivals tend to be dressy. And since an evening outside at a Heuriger (wine garden) may be on your agenda, be sure to take a sweater or light wrap. Unless you're staying in an expensive hotel or will be in one place for more than a day or two, take hand-washables; laundry service gets complicated. Austria is a walking country, in cities and mountains alike. If intending to hike in the mountains, bring boots with sturdy soles and that rise above the ankle. For lots of city walking a good pair of sports shoes is needed.

Mountainous areas are bright, so bring sunscreen lotion, even in winter. Consider packing a small folding umbrella for the odd deluge, or a waterproof windbreaker of sorts. Sunglasses are a must as well, and if you intend to go high up in the mountains, make sure your sunglasses are good and prevent lateral rays. Mosquitoes can become quite a bother in summer around the lakes and along the rivers, especially the Danube and the swampy regions created by its old arms. Bring some good repellent.

In your carry-on luggage **bring an extra pair of eyeglasses or contact lenses** and **enough of any medication you take** to last the entire trip. You may also want your doctor to write a spare prescription using the drug's generic name, since brand names may vary from country to country. **Never put prescription drugs or valuables in luggage to be checked.** To avoid customs delays, carry medications in their original packaging. And don't forget to copy down and carry addresses of offices that handle refunds of lost traveler's checks.

PASSPORTS & VISAS

When traveling internationally, **carry a passport even if you don't need one** (it's always the best form of ID), and make **two photocopies of the data page** (one for someone at home and another for you, carried separately from your passport). If you lose your passport, promptly call the nearest embassy or consulate and the local police.

ENTERING AUSTRIA

U.S., Australian, Canadian, New Zealand, and U.K. citizens need only a valid passport to enter Austria for stays of up to three months.

PASSPORT OFFICES

The best time to apply for a passport or to renew is during the fall and winter. Before any trip, be sure to check your passport's expiration date and, if necessary, renew it as soon as possible. (Some countries won't allow you to enter on a passport that's due to expire in six months or less.)

➤ AUSTRALIAN CITIZENS: **Australian Passport Office** (☎ 13/1232).

➤ CANADIAN CITIZENS: **Passport Office** (☎ 819/994–3500 or 800/567–6868).

➤ NEW ZEALAND CITIZENS: **New Zealand Passport Office** (☎ 04/494–0700 for information on how to apply, 0800/727–776 for information on applications already submitted).

➤ U.K. CITIZENS: **London Passport Office** (☎ 0990/21010), for fees and documentation requirements and to request an emergency passport.

➤ U.S. CITIZENS: **National Passport Information Center** (☎ 900/225–5674; calls are charged at 35¢ per minute for automated service, $1.05 per minute for operator service).

SENIOR-CITIZEN TRAVEL

To qualify for age-related discounts, **mention your senior-citizen status up front** when booking hotel reservations (not when checking out) and before you're seated in restaurants (not when paying the bill). Note that discounts may be limited to certain menus, days, or hours. When renting a car, **ask about promotional car-rental discounts,** which can be cheaper than senior-citizen rates.

Austria has so many senior citizens that facilities almost everywhere cater to the needs of older travelers, with discounts for rail travel and museum entry. Check with the Austrian National Tourist Office to find what form of identification is required, but generally if you're 65 or over (women 62), once you're in Austria the railroads will issue you a *Seniorenpass*

(you'll need a passport photo and passport or other proof of age) entitling you to the senior citizen discounts regardless of nationality.

➤ EDUCATIONAL PROGRAMS: **Elderhostel** (⊠ 75 Federal St., 3rd floor, Boston, MA 02110, ☎ 617/426–8056). **Interhostel** (⊠ University of New Hampshire, ⊠ 6 Garrison Ave., Durham, NH 03824, ☎ 603/862–1147 or 800/733–9753, FAX 603/862–1113).

STUDENT TRAVEL

TRAVEL AGENCIES

To save money, **look into deals available through student-oriented travel agencies.** To qualify you'll need a bona fide student ID card. Members of international student groups are also eligible.

➤ LOCAL RESOURCES: Information on tickets, fares, and lodgings is available at the **Youth Information Center** in Vienna (⊠ Dr. Karl-Renner-Ring/Bellaria-Passage, ☎ 01/1799), open Monday–Saturday, noon–7 PM.

➤ STUDENT IDs & SERVICES: **Council on International Educational Exchange** (⊠ CIEE, ⊠ 205 E. 42nd St., 14th floor, New York, NY 10017, ☎ 212/822–2600 or 888/268–6245, FAX 212/822–2699), for mail orders only, in the United States. **Travel Cuts** (⊠ 187 College St., Toronto, Ontario M5T 1P7, ☎ 416/979–2406 or 800/667–2887) in Canada.

➤ STUDENT TOURS: **AESU Travel** (⊠ 2 Hamill Rd., Suite 248, Baltimore, MD 21210-1807, ☎ 410/323–4416 or 800/638–7640, FAX 410/323–4498),**Contiki Holidays** (⊠ 300 Plaza Alicante, Suite 900, Garden Grove, CA 92840, ☎ 714/740–0808 or 800/266–8454, FAX 714/740–2034).

TAXES

VALUE-ADDED TAX (VAT)

The Value Added Tax (VAT) in Austria is 20% generally but only 10% on food and clothing. If you are planning to take your purchases with you when you leave Austria (export them) you can get a refund. The shop will give you a form or a receipt, which must be presented at the border, where the wares are inspected. The Austrian government will send you your refund, minus a processing fee.

TELEPHONES

COUNTRY CODES

The country code for Austria for 43. When dialing an Austrian number from abroad, drop the initial 0 from the local area code.

Austria's telephone service is in a state of change as the country converts to a digital system. We make every effort to keep numbers up to date, but do recheck the number—particularly in Innsbruck, Linz, and Vienna—if you have problems getting the connection you want (a sharp tone indicates no connection or that the number has been changed). All numbers given in this guide include the city or town area code; if you are calling within that city or town, dial the local number only.

DIRECTORY & OPERATOR INFORMATION

For information on local calls, dial 1611; for assistance with long-distance service, dial 1616; and for information on direct dialing out of Austria, call 1613.

INTERNATIONAL CALLS

You can dial direct to almost any point on the globe from Austria. However, it costs more to telephone from Austria than it does to telephone to Austria. Calls from post offices are always the least expensive and you can get helpful assistance in placing a long-distance call; In large cities, these centers at main post offices are open around the clock.

To make a collect call—you can't do this from pay phones—dial the operator and ask for an R-Gespräch (pronounced air-ga-shprayk). Most operators speak English; if yours doesn't, you'll be passed to one who does.

The international access code for the United States and Canada is 001, followed by the area code and number. For Great Britain, first dial 0044, then the city code without the usual "0" (171 or 181 for London), and the number. Other country and many city codes are given in the front of tele-

phone books (in Vienna, in the A-H book).

AT&T, MCI, and Sprint international access codes make calling the United States relatively convenient, but you may find the local access number blocked in many hotel rooms. First ask the hotel operator to connect you. If the hotel operator balks, ask for an international operator, or dial the international operator yourself. One way to improve your odds of getting connected to your long-distance carrier is to travel with more than one company's calling card (a hotel may block Sprint, for example, but not MCI). If all else fails, call from a pay phone in the hotel lobby.

➤ ACCESS CODES: **AT&T Direct** (☎ 022–903–011; ☎ 800/435–0812 for other areas). **MCI WorldPhone** (☎ 022–903–012; ☎ 800/444–4141 for other areas). **Sprint International Access** (☎ 800/659–0043; ☎ 800/877–4646 for other areas).

LONG-DISTANCE CALLS

When placing a long-distance call to a destination within Austria, you'll need to know the local area codes, which can be found by consulting the telephone numbers that are listed in this guide's regional chapters. The following are area codes for Austria's major cities: Vienna, 01; Graz, 0316; Salzburg, 0662; Innsbruck, 0512; Linz, 0732. When dialing from outside Austria, the 0 should be left out. Note that calls within Austria are one-third cheaper between 6 and 8 AM on weekdays and from 1 PM on Saturday to 8 AM on Monday.

PUBLIC PHONES

Coin-operated pay telephones are dwindling in number. They take AS1, 5, 10, and 20 coins. A three-minute local call costs AS1. At the oldest coin-operated machines (they are huge and grey) drop in at least three one-schilling pieces, pick up the receiver and dial; when the party answers, push the indicated button and the connection will be made. If there is no response, your coin will be returned into the bin to the lower left. The smaller machines are more recent and don't have the button to connect. If your party has an answering machine you'll have to pay a little something. Most pay phones have instructions in English on them. Add AS1 when time is up to continue the connection.

If you plan to make many calls from pay phones, a *Wertkarte* is a convenience. You can buy this electronic phone card at any post office for AS190, AS95, or AS48, which allows AS200, AS100, or AS50 worth of calls from any *Wertkartentelephon*. You simply insert the card and dial; the cost of the call is automatically deducted from the card, and a digital window on the phone tells you how many units you have left (these are not minutes!). A few public phones in the cities also take American Express, Diners, Mastercard, and Visa credit cards.

Faxes can be sent from post offices and received as well, but neither service is very cheap.

TIPPING

Although virtually all hotels and restaurants include service charges in their rates, tipping is still customary, but at a level lower than in the United States. Tip the hotel doorman AS10–AS15 per bag, and the porter who brings your bags to the room another AS10 per bag. In very small country inns, such tips are not expected but are appreciated. In family-run establishments, tips are generally not given to immediate family members, only to employees. Tip the hotel concierge only for special services or in response to special requests. Room service gets AS10–AS20 for snacks or ice, AS20 for full meals. Maids normally get no tip unless your stay is a week or more or service has been special.

In restaurants, round up the bill by AS5 to AS50 or 5%–7%, depending on the size of the check and the class of the restaurant. Big tips are not usual in Austrian restaurants, since 10% has already been included in the prices. Hat-check attendants get AS7–AS15, depending on the locale. Washroom attendants get about AS2–AS5. Wandering musicians and the piano player get AS20, AS50 if they've filled a number of requests.

Round up taxi fares to the next AS5 or AS10; a minimum AS5 tip is customary. If the driver offers (or you ask for) special assistance, such as carrying your bags beyond the curb, an added tip of AS5–AS10 is in order.

TOUR OPERATORS

Buying a prepackaged tour or independent vacation can make your trip to Austria less expensive and more hassle-free. Because everything is prearranged, you'll spend less time planning.

Operators that handle several hundred thousand travelers per year can use their purchasing power to give you a good price. Their high volume may also indicate financial stability. But some small companies provide more personalized service; because they tend to specialize, they may also be more knowledgeable about a given area.

BOOKING WITH AN AGENT

Travel agents are excellent resources. In fact, large operators accept bookings made only through travel agents. But it's a good idea to **collect brochures from several agencies,** because some agents' suggestions may be influenced by relationships with tour and package firms that reward them for volume sales. If you have a special interest, **find an agent with expertise in that area**; ASTA (☞ Travel Agencies, *below*) has a database of specialists worldwide.

Make sure your travel agent knows the accommodations and other services. Ask about the hotel's location, room size, beds, and whether it has a pool, room service, or programs for children, if you care about these. Has your agent been there in person or sent others you can contact?

Do some homework on your own, too: Local tourism boards can provide information about lesser-known and small-niche operators, some of which may sell only direct.

BUYER BEWARE

Each year consumers are stranded or lose their money when tour operators—even very large ones with excellent reputations—go out of business. So **check out the operator.** Find out how long the company has been in business, and ask several travel agents about its reputation. If the package or tour you are considering is priced lower than in your wildest dreams, **be skeptical.** Try to **book with a company that has a consumer-protection program.** If the operator has such a program, you'll find information about it in the company's brochure. If the operator you are considering does not offer some kind of consumer protection, then ask for references from satisfied customers.

In the U.S., members of the National Tour Association and United States Tour Operators Association are required to set aside funds to cover your payments and travel arrangements in case the company defaults. It's also a good idea to choose a company that participates in the American Society of Travel Agent's Tour Operator Program (TOP). This gives you a forum if there are any disputes between you and your tour operator; ASTA will act as mediator.

➤ TOUR-OPERATOR RECOMMENDATIONS: **American Society of Travel Agents** (☞ Travel Agencies, *below*). **National Tour Association** (⊠ NTA, ⊠ 546 E. Main St., Lexington, KY 40508, ☎ 606/226–4444 or 800/755–8687). **United States Tour Operators Association** (⊠ USTOA, ⊠ 342 Madison Ave., Suite 1522, New York, NY 10173, ☎ 212/599–6599 or 800/468–7862, FAX 212/599–6744).

COSTS

The more your package or tour includes, the better you can predict the ultimate cost of your vacation. Make sure you know exactly what is covered, and **beware of hidden costs.** Are taxes, tips, and service charges included? Transfers and baggage handling? Entertainment and excursions? These can add up.

Prices for packages and tours are usually quoted per person, based on two sharing a room. If traveling solo, you may be required to pay the full double-occupancy rate. Some operators eliminate this surcharge if you agree to be matched with a roommate of the same sex, even if one is not found by departure time.

GROUP TOURS

Among companies that sell tours to Austria, the following are nationally known, have a proven reputation, and offer plenty of options. The classifications used below represent different price categories, and you'll probably encounter these terms when talking to a travel agent or tour operator. The key difference is usually in accommodations, which run from budget to better, and better-yet to best.

➤ SUPER-DELUXE: **Abercrombie & Kent** (⊠ 1520 Kensington Rd., Oak Brook, IL 60521-2141, ☎ 630/954–2944 or 800/323–7308, FAX 630/954–3324). **Travcoa** (⊠ Box 2630, 2350 S.E. Bristol St., Newport Beach, CA 92660, ☎ 714/476–2800 or 800/992–2003, FAX 714/476–2538).

➤ DELUXE: **Globus** (⊠ 5301 S. Federal Circle, Littleton, CO 80123-2980, ☎ 303/797–2800 or 800/221–0090, FAX 303/347–2080). **Maupintour** (⊠ 1515 St. Andrews Dr., Lawrence, KS 66047, ☎ 785/843–1211 or 800/255–4266, FAX 785/843–8351). **Tauck Tours** (⊠ Box 5027, 276 Post Rd. W, Westport, CT 06881-5027, ☎ 203/226–6911 or 800/468–2825, FAX 203/221–6866).

➤ FIRST-CLASS: **Brendan Tours** (⊠ 15137 Califa St., Van Nuys, CA 91411, ☎ 818/785–9696 or 800/421–8446, FAX 818/902–9876). **Caravan Tours** (⊠ 401 N. Michigan Ave., Chicago, IL 60611, ☎ 312/321–9800 or 800/227–2826, FAX 312/321–9845). **Collette Tours** (⊠ 162 Middle St., Pawtucket, RI 02860, ☎ 401/728–3805 or 800/340–5158, FAX 401/728–4745). **DER Tours** (⊠ 9501 W. Devon St., Rosemont, IL 60018, ☎ 800/937–1235, FAX 847/692–4141 or 800/282–7474, 800/860–9944 for brochures). **Gadabout Tours** (⊠ 700 E. Tahquitz Canyon Way, Palm Springs, CA 92262-6767, ☎ 619/325–5556 or 800/952–5068). **Trafalgar Tours** (⊠ 11 E. 26th St., New York, NY 10010, ☎ 212/689–8977 or 800/854–0103, FAX 800/457–6644).

➤ BUDGET: **Cosmos** (☞ Globus, *above*). **Trafalgar Tours** (☞ *above*).

PACKAGES

Like group tours, independent vacation packages are available from major tour operators and airlines. The companies listed below offer vacation packages in a broad price range.

➤ AIR/HOTEL: **Delta Vacations** (☎ 800/872–7786). **DER Tours** (☞ Group Tours, *above*). **TWA Getaway Vacations** (☎ 800/438–2929).

➤ FROM THE U.K.: **Eurobreak** (✉ 10–18 Putney Hill, London SW15 6AX, ☎ 0181/780–7700). **Kuoni Travel** (✉ Kuoni House, Dorking, Surrey RH5 4AZ, ☎ 01306/740-500). **Swiss Travel Service Ltd.** (✉ Bridge House, 55–59 High Rd., Broxbourne, Hertfordshire EN10 7DT, ☎ 01992/456–123). **Time Off Ltd.** (✉ Chester Close, Chester St., London SW1X 7BQ, ☎ 0171/235–8070). **Wallace Arnold Tours Ltd.** (✉ Gelderd Rd., Leeds LS12 6DH, ☎ 0113/231–0739; ✉ 62 George St., Croydon, CR9 1DN, ☎ 0181/686–9833).

THEME TRIPS

➤ ADVENTURE: **Himalayan Travel** (✉ 110 Prospect St., Stamford, CT 06901, ☎ 203/359–3711 or 800/225–2380, FAX 203/359–3669). **Wilderness Travel** (✉ 1102 Ninth St., Berkeley, CA 94710, ☎ 510/558–2488 or 800/368–2794).

Horizons—Adventures of a Lifetime (✉ Box 670565, Marietta, GA 30066, ☎ 800/246–3180, FAX 770/565–4233).

➤ BALLOONING: **Buddy Bombard European Balloon Adventures** (✉ 333 Pershing Way, West Palm Beach, FL 33401, ☎ 561/837–6610 or 800/862–8537, FAX 561/837–6623).

➤ BARGE/RIVER CRUISES: **Abercrombie & Kent** (☞ Group Tours, *above*). **KD River Cruises of Europe** (✉ 2500 Westchester Ave., Purchase, NY 10577, ☎ 914/696–3600 or 800/346–6525, FAX 914/696–0833).

➤ BICYCLING: **Backroads** (✉ 801 Cedar St., Berkeley, CA 94710-1800, ☎ 510/527–1555 or 800/462–2848, FAX 510-527–1444). **Butterfield & Robinson** (✉ 70 Bond St., Toronto, Ontario, Canada M5B 1X3, ☎ 416/864–1354 or 800/678–1147, FAX 416/

864–0541). **Classic Adventures** (✉ Box 153, Hamlin, NY 14464-0153, ☎ 716/964–8488 or 800/777–8090, FAX 716/964–7297). **Euro-Bike Tours** (✉ Box 990, De Kalb, IL 60115, ☎ 800/321–6060, FAX 815/758–8851). **Uniquely Europe** (✉ 1940 116th Ave. NE, Bellevue, WA 98004, ☎ 425/455–4445 or 800/927–3876, FAX 425/455–2111). **Vermont Bicycle Touring** (✉ Box 711, Bristol, VT, 05443-0711, ☎ 802/453–4811 or 800/245–3868, FAX 802/453–4806).

➤ CHRISTMAS/NEW YEAR'S: **Annemarie Victory Organization** (✉ 136 E. 64th St., New York, NY 10021, ☎ 212/486–0353, FAX 212/751–3149) is known for their spectacular "New Year's Eve Ball in Vienna" excursion. This highly respected organization has been selling out this tour—which includes deluxe rooms at the Bristol, the Imperial Palace Ball, and a Konzerthaus New Year's Day concert—for ten years running. In 1996, Annemarie Victory premiered a "Christmas in Salzburg" trip, with rooms at the Goldener Hirsch and a side trip to the Silent Night Chapel in Oberndorf. **Smolka Tours** (✉ 82 Riveredge Rd., Tinton Falls, NJ 07724, ☎ 732/576–8813 or 800/722–0057) also conducts festive holiday-season tours that include concerts and gala balls.

➤ FOOD AND WINE: **Herzerl Tours** (✉ 355 Lexington Ave., New York, NY 10017, ☎ 212/867–4830 or 800/684–8488, FAX 212/986–0717). **IST Cultural Tours** (✉ 225 W. 34th St., New York, NY 10122-0913, ☎ 212/563–1202 or 800/833–2111, FAX 212/594–6953).

➤ HIKING/WALKING: **Adventure Center** (✉ 1311 63rd St., #200, Emeryville, CA 94608, ☎ 510/654–1879 or 800/227–8747, FAX 510/654–4200). **Alpine Adventure Trails Tours** (✉ 322 Pio Nono Ave., Macon, GA 31204, ☎ 912/478–4007). **Mountain Travel-Sobek** (✉ 6420 Fairmount Ave., El Cerrito, CA 94530, ☎ 510/527–8100 or 800/227–2384, FAX 510/525–7710). **Uniquely Europe** (☞ Bicycling, *above*). **Wilderness Travel** (☞ Adventure, *above*).

➤ HISTORY & ART: **Five Star Touring** (✉ 60 E. 42nd St., #612, New York, NY 10165, ☎ 212/818–9140 or 800/

792–7827, FAX 212/818–9142). **IST Cultural Tours** (☞ Food and Wine, *above*). **Smolka Tours** (☞ Christmas/New Year's, *above*). **Herzerl Tours** (☞ Food and Wine, *above*). **Smithsonian Study Tours and Seminars** (✉ 1100 Jefferson Dr. SW, Room 3045, MRC 702, Washington, DC 20560, ☎ 202/357–4700, FAX 202/633–9250).

➤ MOTORCYCLING: **Beach's Motorcycle Adventures** (✉ 2763 W. River Pkwy., Grand Island, NY 14072-2053, ☎ 716/773–4960, FAX 716/773–5227). **Edelweiss Bike Travel** (✉ 129 Hillside Ave., Williston Park, NY 11596, ☎ 516/746–6761 or 800/877–2784, FAX 516/746–6690).

➤ MOUNTAIN CLIMBING: **Mountain Travel-Sobek** (☞ Hiking/Walking, *above*).

➤ MUSIC: **Dailey-Thorp Travel** (✉ 330 W. 58th St., #610, New York, NY 10019-1817, ☎ 212/307–1555 or 800/998–4677, FAX 212/974–1420). **IST Cultural Tours** (☞ Food and Wine, *above*). **Smolka Tours** (☞ Christmas/New Year's, *above*). **Herzerl Tours** (☞ Food and Wine, *above*).

➤ SKIING: **Value Holidays** (✉ 10224 N. Port Washington Rd., Mequon, WI 53092-5755, ☎ 414/241–6373 or 800/241–5329).

➤ SPAS: **Herzerl Tours** (☞ Food and Wine, *above*). **Spa-Finders** (✉ 91 5th Ave., #301, New York, NY 10003-3039, ☎ 212/924–6800 or 800/255–7727).

➤ TRAIN TOURS: **Abercrombie & Kent** (☞ Group Tours, *above*). For a special treat, hire your own private rail car once used by kings and heads of state. For details, contact **Le Majestic Nostalgie-Reisen** (✉ Franziskanerpl. 4, A-1010 Vienna, ☎ 01/512–1062).

TRAIN TRAVEL

Austrian train service is excellent: It's fast and, for Western Europe, relatively inexpensive, particularly if you take advantage of the discount fares. Trains on the mountainous routes are slow, but no slower than driving, and the scenery is gorgeous! Many of the remote rail routes will give you a look at traditional Austria, complete with Alpine cabins tacked onto mountainsides and a backdrop of snowcapped peaks.

For train schedules, ask at your hotel or stop in at the train station and look for large posters labeled AB-FAHRT (departures) and ANKUNFT (arrivals). In the Abfahrt listing you'll find the departure time in the main left-hand block of the listing and, under the train name, details of where it stops en route and the time of each arrival. There is also information about connecting trains and buses, with departure details. Workdays are symbolized by two crossed hammers, which means that the same might not be running on weekends or holidays. A little rocking horse means that a special playpen has been set up for children in the train. Women traveling alone may book special compartments on the night trains or long distance rides (ask for a *Damenabteilung*).

Austrian Federal Railways trains are identifiable by the letters that precede the train number on the timetables and posters. The IC (InterCity) or EC (EuroCity) trains are fastest, but a supplement of AS50 is included in the price of the ticket. EN trains have sleeping facilities. All tickets are valid without supplement on D (express), E (*Eilzug;* semi-fast), and local trains. The EC or IC supplement should be bought in the station with your ticket, in the train it will cost a few schillings more. Seat reservations are required on some trains; on most others you can reserve for AS30 up until a few hours before departure. Be sure to do this on the main line trains (Vienna–Innsbruck, Salzburg–Klagenfurt, Vienna–Graz, for example) at peak holiday times. The EC trains usually have a dining car with fairly good food. The trains originating in Budapest have good Hungarian cooking. Otherwise there is usually a fellow with a cart serving snacks and hot and cold drinks. Most trains are equipped with a card telephone in or near the restaurant car, or ask the conductor (who also sells the cards).

The difference between first and second class on Austrian trains is mainly a matter of space. First- and second-class sleepers, and couchettes (six to a compartment), are available on international runs, as well as on long trips within Austria. If you're driving and would rather watch the scenery than the traffic, you can put your car on a train in Vienna and take it to Salzburg, Innsbruck, Feldkirch, or Villach. You relax in a compartment or sleeper for the trip, and the car is unloaded when you arrive.

Railroad enthusiasts and those with plenty of time can treat themselves to rides on narrow-gauge lines found all over Austria that amble through Alpine meadows; some even make flower-picking stops in season. A few lines still run under steam power, and steam excursions are increasingly easy to find. Local stations have descriptive brochures with dates, points of origin, and fares.

DISCOUNT PASSES

To save money, **look into rail passes.** But be aware that if you don't plan to cover many miles, you may come out ahead by buying individual tickets.

Austria is one of 17 countries in which you can **use Eurailpasses,** which provide unlimited first-class rail travel, in all of the participating countries, for the duration of the pass. If you plan to rack up the miles, get a standard pass. These are available for 15 days ($538), 21 days ($698), one month ($864), two months ($1,224), and three months ($1,512).

In addition to standard Eurailpasses, **ask about special rail-pass plans.** Among these are the Eurail Youthpass (for those under age 26), the Eurail Saverpass (which gives a discount for two or more people traveling together), a Eurail Flexipass (which allows a certain number of travel days within a set period), the Euraildrive Pass and the Europass Drive (which combines travel by train and rental car). Whichever pass you choose, remember that you must **purchase your pass before you leave** for Europe.

Many travelers assume that rail passes guarantee them seats on the trains they wish to ride. Not so. You need to **book seats ahead even if you are using a rail pass**; seat reservations are required on some European trains, particularly high-speed trains, and are a good idea on trains that may be crowded—particularly in summer on popular routes. You will also need a reservation if you purchase sleeping accommodations.

Another option that gives you discount travel through various countries is the European East Pass, good for travel within Austria, the Czech Republic, Hungary, Poland, and Slovakia: cost is $199 for any 5 days unlimited travel within a one-month period.

The ÖBB, the Austrian rail service, offers a large number of discounts for various travel constellations. If you are traveling with a group of people, even small, there are percentages taken off for each member. Families can also get discounts. School children and students also get good deals. The Vorteilscard is valid for a year and costs AS1190, allowing 50% fare reduction on all rail travel. If you are planning lots of travel in Austria, it could be a good deal. Ask for other special deals, and check travel agencies. Children between 6 and 15 travel at half price, under 6 years of age for free.

A *Bundesnetzkarte* (full-network pass) gives you unlimited travel for a month (AS5,900 for first class, AS4,300 second class). The ticket is also good on the suburban rail system (S-Bahn) around Vienna, on all funiculars and cog railways and private lines, allows a 25% discount on ships on the Wolfgangsee and 50% for excursions on the Bodensee (Lake Constance). Apply at any large rail station. You will need a passport photo.

For AS350 and a passport photo, women over 60 and men over 65 can obtain a *Seniorenpass*, which carries discounts up to 50% on rail tickets. The pass also has a host of other benefits, including reduced-price entry into museums. Most rail stations can give you information.

Travelers under 26 should inquire about discount fares under the *Billet International Jeune* (BIJ). The special one-trip tickets are sold by Eurotrain

International, travel agents, and youth-travel specialists, and at rail stations.

➤ INFORMATION AND PASSES: **CIT Tours Corp.** (✉ 15 West 44th Street, 10th Floor, New York, NY 10036, ☎ 212/730–2400 or 800/248–7245 in the U.S., 800/387–0711 or 800/361–7799 in Canada). **DER Travel Services** (✉ 9501 W. Devon Ave., Rosemont, IL 60018, ☎ 800/782–2424, FAX 800/282–7474 for information or 800/860–9944 for brochures). **Rail Europe** (✉ 500 Mamaroneck Ave., Harrison, NY 10528, ☎ 914/682–5172 or 800/438–7245, FAX 800/432–1329; ✉ 2087 Dundas E, Suite 106, Mississauga, Ontario L4X 1M2, ☎ 800/361–7245, FAX 905/602–4198).

FROM THE U.K.

There's a choice of rail routes to Austria, but check services first; long-distance passenger service across the Continent is undergoing considerable reduction. There is daily service from London to Vienna via the *Austria Nachtexpress*. Check other services such as the *Orient Express*. If you don't mind changing trains, you can travel via Paris, where you change stations to board the overnight *Arlberg Express* via Innsbruck and Salzburg to Vienna. First- and second-class sleepers and second-class couchettes are available as far as Innsbruck.

When you have the time, a strikingly scenic route to Austria is via Cologne and Munich; after an overnight stop in Cologne, you take the *EuroCity Express Johann Strauss* to Vienna.

➤ INFORMATION AND RESERVATIONS: Contact **Eurotrain** (✉ 52 Grosvenor Gardens, London SW1W OAG, ☎ 0171/730–3402), which offers excellent deals for those under 26, or **British Rail Travel Centers** (☎ 0171/834–2345). For additional information, call **DER Travel Service** (☎ 0171/408–0111) or the **Austrian National Tourist Office** (☞ Visitor Information, *below*).

TRAVEL AGENCIES

A good travel agent puts your needs first. Look for an agency that has been in business at least five years, emphasizes customer service, and has someone on staff who specializes in your destination. In addition, **make sure the agency belongs to a professional trade organization,** such as ASTA in the United States. If your travel agency is also acting as your tour operator, *see* Buyer Beware in Tour Operators, *above*).

➤ LOCAL AGENT REFERRALS: **American Society of Travel Agents** (ASTA, ☎ 800/965–2782 24-hr hot line, FAX 703/684–8319). **Association of Canadian Travel Agents** (✉ Suite 201, 1729 Bank St., Ottawa, Ontario K1V 7Z5, ☎ 613/521–0474, FAX 613/521–0805). **Association of British Travel Agents** (✉ 55–57 Newman St., London W1P 4AH, ☎ 0171/637–2444, FAX 0171/637–0713). **Australian Federation of Travel Agents** (☎ 02/9264–3299). **Travel Agents' Association of New Zealand** (☎ 04/499–0104).

U.S. GOVERNMENT

Government agencies can be an excellent source of inexpensive travel information. When planning your trip, **find out what government materials are available.**

➤ ADVISORIES: **U.S. Department of State** (✉ Overseas Citizens Services Office, ✉ Room 4811 N.S., Washington, DC 20520; ☎ 202/647–5225 or FAX 202/647–3000 for interactive hot line; ☎ 301/946–4400 for computer bulletin board); enclose a self-addressed, stamped, business-size envelope.

➤ PAMPHLETS: **Consumer Information Center** (✉ Consumer Information Catalogue, Pueblo, CO 81009, ☎ 719/948–3334 or 888/878–3256) for a free catalog that includes travel titles.

VISITOR INFORMATION

➤ AUSTRIAN NATIONAL TOURIST OFFICE: **In the U.S.:** ✉ 500 5th Ave., 20th floor, New York, NY 10110, ☎ 212/944–6880, FAX 212/730–4568, or write to ✉ Box 1142, New York, NY 10108. **In Canada:** ✉ 2 Bloor St. E, Suite 3330, Toronto, Ontario M4W 1A8, ☎ 416/967–3381, FAX 416/967–4101; ✉ 1010 Sherbrooke St. W, Suite 1410, Montréal, Québec H3A 2R7, ☎ 514/849–3709, FAX 514/849–9577;

THE GOLD GUIDE / SMART TRAVEL TIPS

✉ 200 Granville St., Suite 1380, Granville Sq., Vancouver, British Columbia V6C 1S4, ☎ 604/683–5808 or 604/683–8695, 🖷 604/662–8528. **In the U.K.:** ✉ 30 St. George St., London W1R 0AL, ☎ 0171/629–0461. **Web site:** www.anto.com.

WHEN TO GO

Austria has two main tourist seasons. The weather usually turns glorious around Easter to mark the start of the summer season and holds until about mid-October, often later. Because much of the country remains "undiscovered," you will usually find crowds only in the major cities and resorts. May and early June, September, and October are the most pleasant months for travel; there is less demand for restaurant tables, and hotel prices tend to be lower.

A foreign invasion takes place between Christmas and New Year's Day, at which time many Viennese are already on the slopes of western Austria, and over the long Easter weekend, and hotel rooms in Vienna are at a premium. July and August and the main festivals (☞ Festivals and Seasonal Events *in* Chapter 1) are crowded times, but again, the Viennese head out for their vacations, so the city itself is relatively calm.

The winter-sports season starts in December, snow conditions permitting, and runs through April. You can ski as late as mid-June on the high glaciers, at altitudes of 8,000 feet or more. Although reservations are essential in the major ski resorts in season, travelers can frequently find rooms in private houses or small pensions if they're prepared to take a slight detour from the beaten path.

CLIMATE

Austria has four distinct seasons, all fairly mild. But because of altitudes and the Alpine divide, temperatures and dampness vary considerably from one part of the country to another; for example, northern Austria's winter is often overcast and dreary, while the southern half of the country basks in sunshine. The eastern part of the country, especially Vienna and the areas near the Czech border, can become bitterly cold in winter thanks to Continental influence.

The *Fön* (hair dryer) is a wind that makes the country as a whole go haywire. It comes from the south, is warm, and announces itself by very clear air, blue skies, and long wisps of cloud. Whatever the reason, the Alpine people (all the way to Vienna) begin acting up; some become obnoxiously aggressive, others depressive, many people have headaches, and (allegedly) accident rates rise. The Fön breaks with clouds and rain.

➤ FORECASTS: **Weather Channel Connection** (☎ 900/932–8437), 95¢ per minute from a Touch Tone phone.

The following are average monthly maximum and minimum temperatures for three cities in Austria:

Climate in Austria

VIENNA

Jan.	34F	1C	May	66F	19C	Sept.	68F	20C
	25	– 4		50	10		52	11
Feb.	37F	3C	June	73F	23C	Oct.	57F	14C
	27	– 3		57	14		45	7
Mar.	46F	8C	July	77F	25C	Nov.	45F	7C
	34	1		59	15		37	3
Apr.	59F	15C	Aug.	75F	24C	Dec.	37F	3C
	43	6		59	15		30	– 1

THE GOLD GUIDE / SMART TRAVEL TIPS

SALZBURG

Jan.	36F	2C	May	66F	19C	Sept.	68F	20C
	21	− 6		46	8		50	10
Feb.	39F	4C	June	72F	22C	Oct.	57F	14C
	23	− 5		52	11		41	5
Mar.	48F	9C	July	75F	24C	Nov.	46F	8C
	30	− 1		55	13		32	0
Apr.	57F	14C	Aug.	73F	23C	Dec.	37F	3C
	39	4		55	13		25	− 4

INNSBRUCK

Jan.	34F	1C	May	68F	20C	Sept.	70F	21C
	19	− 7		46	8		50	10
Feb.	39F	4C	June	75F	24C	Oct.	59F	15C
	23	− 5		52	11		41	5
Mar.	52F	11C	July	77F	25C	Nov.	46F	8C
	32	0		55	13		32	0
Apr.	61F	16C	Aug.	75F	24C	Dec.	36F	2C
	39	4		54	12		25	− 4

1 Destination: Austria

BEYOND THE SCHLAG

TODAY'S AUSTRIA—and in particular its capital, Vienna—reminds me of a formerly fat man who is now at least as gaunt as the rest of us but still allows himself a lot of room and expects doors to open wide when he goes through them. After losing two world wars and surviving amputation, annexation, and occupation, a nation that once ruled Europe now endures as a tourist mecca and a neutralized, somewhat balkanized republic.

Still, there are oases of perfection, such as those Sunday mornings from September to June when—if you've reserved months in advance—you can hear (but not see) those "voices from heaven," the Vienna Boys Choir, sing mass in the marble-and-velvet royal chapel of the Hofburg. Lads of 8 to 13 in sailor suits, they peal out angelic notes from the topmost gallery, and you might catch a glimpse of them after mass as you cut across the Renaissance courtyard for the 10:45 performance of the Lipizzaner stallions in the Spanish Riding School around the corner. Beneath crystal chandeliers in a lofty white hall, expert riders in brown uniforms with gold buttons and black hats with gold braid put these aristocrats of the equine world through their classic paces.

Just past noon, when the Spanish Riding School lets out, cross the Michaelerplatz and stroll up the Kohlmarkt to No. 14: Demel's, the renowned and lavish pastry shop founded shortly after 1848 by the court confectioner. It was an instant success with those privileged to dine with the emperor, for not only was Franz Josef a notoriously stodgy and paltry eater, but, when he stopped eating, protocol dictated that all others stop, too. Dessert at Demel's became a must for hungry higher-ups. Today's Demel's features a flawless midday buffet offering venison en croûte, chicken in pastry shells, beef Wellington, meat tarts, and frequent warnings to "leave room for the desserts."

Closer to the less costly level of everyday existence, my family and I would lay on a welcoming meal for visitors just off plane or train: a freshly baked slab of *Krusti Brot* to be spread with *Liptauer*, a piquant paprika cream cheese, and *Kräuter Gervais*, Austria's answer to cream cheese and chives, all washed down by a youngish white wine. Such simple pleasures as a jug of wine, a loaf of bread, and a spicy cheese or two are what we treasure as Austrian excellence in democratic days. And if our visitors really carried on about our wine, we would take them on the weekend to the farm it was from, for going to the source is one of the virtues of living in this small, unhomogenized land of 7.5 million people that is modern Austria.

"Is it safe to drink the water?" is still the question I'm asked most by visitors to Vienna. "It's not only safe," I reply, "it's recommended." Sometimes they call back to thank me for the tip. Piped cold and clean via Roman aqueducts from a couple of Alpine springs, the city's water has been rated the best in the world by connoisseurs as well as by authorities such as the Austrian Academy of Sciences and an international association of solid-waste-management engineers. Often on a summer evening, when our guests looked as though a cognac after dinner might be too heavy, I brought out a pitcher of iced tap water, and even our Viennese visitors smacked their lips upon tasting this refreshing novelty. But don't bother to try it in a tavern; except for a few radical thinkers and the converts I've made, virtually all Viennese drink bottled mineral water, and few waiters will condescend to serve you any other kind.

People say that after two decades in Vienna one must feel very Viennese, and maybe they're right, because here I am chatting about food and drink, which is the principal topic of Viennese conversation. So, before leaving the capital for the provinces, let me call your attention to three major culinary inventions that were all introduced to Western civilization in Vienna in the watershed year of 1683: coffee, the croissant, and the bagel.

That was the year the second Turkish siege of Vienna was at last repelled, when

King Jan Sobieski of Poland and Duke Charles of Lorraine rode to the rescue, thereby saving the West for Christianity. The Sultan's armies left behind their silken tents and banners, some 25,000 dead, and hundreds of huge sacks filled with a mysterious brownish bean. The victorious Viennese didn't know what to make of it—whether to bake, boil, or fry it. But one of their spies, Franz George Kolschitzky, a wheeler-dealer merchant who had traveled in Turkey and spoke the language, had sampled in Constantinople the thick black brew of roasted coffee beans that the Turks called *Kahve*. Though he could have had almost as many sacks of gold, he settled for beans—and opened history's first Viennese coffeehouse. Business was bad, however, until Kolschitzky tinkered with the recipe and experimented with milk, thus inventing the *Mélange*: taste sensation of the 1680s and still the most popular local coffee drink of the 1990s.

While Kolschitzky was roasting his reward, Viennese bakers were celebrating with two new creations that enabled their customers truly to taste victory over the Muslims: a bun curved like a crescent, the emblem of Islam (what Charles of Lorraine might have called *croissant* Austrians call *Kipferl*), and a roll shaped like Sobieski's stirrup, for which the German word was *Bügel*. The invention of the bagel, however, proved less significant, for it disappeared swiftly and totally, only to resurface in America centuries later, along with Sunday brunch.

One would be hard put to tell the sometimes smug and self-satisfied Viennese that Wien (the German name for the capital) is not the navel of the universe, let alone of Austria, but the person who could tell it to him best would be a Vorarlberger. The 305,600 citizens of Austria's westernmost province live as close to Paris as they do to Vienna, which tries to govern them; their capital, Bregenz, is barely an hour's drive from Zürich, but eight or more from Vienna, and the natives sometimes seem more Swiss than Austrian.

The Kleinwalsertal, a remote valley of Vorarlberg that juts into Bavaria, cannot be reached directly from Austria by car, bus, or train. A few summers ago, I joined some intrepid Austrians on a strenuous and sometimes treacherous two-day up- and downhill climb from Lech am Arlberg to the Kleinwalsertal. Along the way, we saw an eagle, vultures, and marmots, and I wouldn't have traded the trip for a sack of coffee beans—nor would I ever undertake such a venture again. When we tried to buy some coffee, the locals were reluctant to accept our schillings because the Deutschmark is their official currency. While the rest of Austria aspires to enter the European Union, the Kleinwalsertal, through monetary union, has been quietly living in it from its outset.

The northern reaches of Tirol and the western parts of Upper Austria also border on Germany and have a heartier, beerier character than the eastern and southern provinces. (There are nine provinces in all; Vienna, the capital, counts as a state, too, and its mayor is also a governor.) Although the glittering city of Salzburg, capital of rugged Salzburg province, perches right on the German border, 26 km (16 mi) from Berchtesgaden, Austrian traditions, folk customs and costumes, and the music of native son Mozart flourish there as nowhere else in the country—revered and cherished, revived and embroidered.

AUSTRIA BORDERS not just on Germany and Switzerland but also on Liechtenstein, Italy, Slovenia, the Czech Republic, Slovakia, and Hungary. In Austria's greenest province, Styria, one side of the road is sometimes in Slovenia, and you're never far from Hungary or Italy. Styria is so prickly about its independence, even from Austria, that it maintains its own embassies in Vienna and Washington. It is the source of Schilcher, Austria's best rosé wine, which you almost never see in Viennese restaurants. A few years ago, at a farmhouse near Graz, the Styrian capital, I was sipping some Schilcher that went with some wonderful lamb. "Where is this lamb from?" I asked my host.

"Right here," he replied. "Styrian lamb wins all kinds of prizes."

"Then why can't we find it in Vienna?" I wondered. "When we do get lamb, it comes all the way from New Zealand and costs a fortune."

"That's because we don't grow lambs or Schilcher for export," he replied, dead serious.

The influx and tastes of Balkan and Turkish workers have made lamb cheaper and plentiful all over Austria, and now, since the crumbling of the Iron Curtain, Austria is reluctantly becoming even more of a melting pot than it was in the days of the Habsburg empire. The province of Burgenland used to be part of Hungary, and it retains much of its Magyar character in villages where you open a door and find, instead of a courtyard, a whole street full of steep-roofed houses, people, and life. With the dissolution of the Austro-Hungarian Empire after World War I, Burgenland was ceded to Austria, pending a plebiscite in 1921. The population voted overwhelmingly to stay Austrian—except for the people of Ödenburg, which was then its capital and is now Sopron in Hungary. Later, but too late, it was discovered that Ödenburg's pro-Hungarians had registered the inhabitants of several cemeteries to achieve a majority. By enlisting their ancestors, they doomed their descendants to two generations behind the Iron Curtain and a difficult job of catching up.

Burgenland also boasts a culturally active Croatian minority, while Carinthia, Austria's southernmost province, has a proud Slovenian minority that is still fighting for the legal right not to Germanize the names of its villages.

The ultimate identity problem, however, belonged until recently to the province of Lower Austria, which is neither low nor south but takes its name from the part of the Danube it dominates on the map. Before 1986, Lower Austria had no capital city; its state offices were scattered around Vienna, the metropolis it envelops with forest. Upon its selection as the provincial seat, the small city of St. Pölten, with a core of lovely churches and cloisters that swirl around you like a Baroque ballet, danced onto the map of tourist destinations. Already coming to life as a sightseeing attraction, St. Pölten is starting to thrive as a center of government.

Any day of the year, you can take an express train at Vienna's Westbahnhof for an eight-hour, 770-km (480-mi) east–west crossing of most of the country, stopping at five of Austria's nine provincial capitals: St. Pölten; Linz, the Upper Austrian seat; Salzburg; Innsbruck, in Tirol; and Bregenz, in Vorarlberg. But you would be well rewarded, as the pages that follow will demonstrate, by disembarking at each one and giving it a day or two or more of your life.

— Alan Levy

WHAT'S WHERE

Poised in the heart of the continent, Austria is as topographically diverse as it is historically wealthy. Although it is one of Europe's smallest countries, Austria manages to pack within its border as many mountains, lakes, and picturesque cities as countries five times its size. Here is a quick overview to help you travel civilized roads, both back in time and forward.

Vienna

Think of Vienna and you think of operettas and psychoanalysis, Apfelstrudel and marble staircases, Strauss waltzes and Schubert melodies. Baroque and imperial, it goes without saying that the city has an Old World charm—a fact that the natives are both ready to acknowledge and yet hate being reminded of. Today, Vienna is a white-gloved yet modern metropolis, a place where Andrew Lloyd Webber's *Phantom of the Opera* plays in the same theater that premiered Mozart's *Magic Flute*. A walk through the city's neighborhoods—many dotted with masterpieces of Gothic, Baroque, and Secession architecture—offers a fascinating journey thick with history and peopled by the spirits of Empress Maria Theresa, Haydn, Beethoven, Metternich, Mozart, and Klimt.

Most visitors start along the Ring, the grand boulevard that surrounds the inner city; here, you'll find art treasures in the Fine Arts Museum; magnificent spectacles at the Vienna State Opera (one reason why Vienna remains for many the musical capital of the world); and the Hofburg, Vienna's gigantic Imperial Palace, whose chapel showcases the Vienna Boys Choir and whose stables shelter the Lipizzaner stallions (when they aren't prancing at the Spanish Riding School). The city comes alive during the "Merry Season"—the first two months of the year—when raised trumpets and opera capes adorn its great Fasching balls; then more than ever, Vienna moves in three-quarter time. Near the city are the legendary Vienna Woods, with the famous spa of **Baden,** the **Weinviertel** (Wine District), and poetic **Mayerling,** where Crown Prince Rudolf and his lover met a tragic end.

Eastern Austria

A great white stork glides to a landing on the chimney of the hooded roof of a house—a timeless image as far from the bustle of civilization as you can imagine and one common in Austria's easternmost province. For those familiar with other parts of Austria, this region's far-awayness offers the contrast of simple, homely, exceptionally charming pleasures: whitewashed Magyar-style houses, vast stretches of *puszta* (steppe), evenings filled with the haunting sounds of Gypsy music—legacies attesting to the fact that much of eastern Austria belonged to Hungary before World War I.

A region of castle-capped hills, fields of grain, and vineyards (some of the best Austrian wines, including the regal Trockenbeerenauslesen, are produced here), **Burgenland** has major sights, including **Lake Neusiedl**—so gigantic it's called the "Viennese Sea"—and the Old World town of **Eisenstadt**, site of the exquisite Esterházy Palace where famed composer Josef Haydn worked for many years (don't miss a concert in the palace's Haydn Hall). **Graz,** the capital of Styria—Austria's southeastern province—is the country's second-largest city and boasts a historic city center that is as strikingly preserved as any other.

The Danube Valley

The scenes along a trip down the Austrian Danube unfold like a picture book of history. In a parade of sights, Roman ruins, Baroque monasteries with "candle-snuffer" cupolas, and medieval castles-in-air beyond counting dot the length of the river, stoking the imagination with their legends and myths. Here is where Richard the Lion-Hearted spent years locked in a dungeon and where the Nibelungs—immortalized by Wagner—caroused at the top of their lungs in battlemented forts. Clearly, the Danube is liquid history, and you can enjoy drifting eight hours downriver in a steamer or—even better—traveling 18

hours upriver against the current.

Along the way you discover the **Wachau Valley** ("crown jewel of the Austrian landscape"), the Baroque abbey of **Melk,** and the robber castles of Studen and Werfenstein. A convenient base point is **Linz,** Austria's third-largest city (and its most underrated): its Old Town is filled with architectural treasures, glockenspiel chimes, and pastry shops that offer the best Linzer tortes around. The town is right on the Danube, which, if you catch it on a bright summer day, takes on the proper shade of Johann Strauss "blau."

Salzkammergut

Remember the first five minutes of *The Sound of Music,* the camera sweeping across mountains, forests, flower-strewn valleys, and lakes with romantic castles reflected in the water? It wasn't just Hollywood: Austria's own **Lake District** is really where Maria and the von Trapp children lived and sang, in movie and real life. The Salzkammergut, the country's "salt shaker" if you will, stretches across three states— from Salzburg through Styria to Upper Austria. The German word *Salz* is frequently encountered here; indeed, the entire economy has been based on salt mining for millennia. **Bad Ischl** is Austria's oldest brine spa and a charming turn-of-the-century resort where Emperor Franz Josef kept a villa (his birthday is still celebrated on August 18) and where Franz Lehár wrote *The Merry Widow.*

The clear blue Wolfgangsee was named after the town **St. Wolfgang** (whose *Weisses Rössl* inn inspired a famous operetta by Ralph Benatzky), where traffic in summer is fierce. Far quieter is **Hallstatt,** a picturesque village clamped between the dark waters of the Hallstättersee and the fierce-looking needles of the Dachstein range. It gave its name to a prehistoric era, thanks to an Iron Age burial ground excavated nearby. The setting of **Gosau lakes** is so superb it inspired some of Wagner's greatest music. Don't forget to go spelunking through the region's great salt caves (where Hitler once stored stolen art treasures).

Salzburg

Mozart, Mozart, Mozart! Birthplace of Wolfgang Amadeus, Salzburg is a world-class music mecca. If Mozart's native city did him little honor in his lifetime, it is making up for it now. His symphonies, masses, piano sonatas, and string quartets are heard in the city's churches, castles, palaces, and concert halls; his operas are enchantingly produced in the Marionette Theater; Mozartkugel candies delight countless chocolate lovers; and every summer, the Salzburg Music Festival draws a huge and very highbrow (and wealthy) crowd to the city and its myriad concert halls, especially to see the traditional annual production of *Jedermann,* or *Everyman,* the well-known tale of a man who sells his soul for eternal life.

Music is not all there is to offer in this stupendously Baroque city. There are churches and museums, the mighty Hohensalzburg fortress, old-fashioned cafés, narrow medieval streets, glorious fountains. The playful water gardens of Hellbrunn Castle remind us that not all archbishops were stern and unpleasant.

Carinthia

Carinthia—or Kärnten in German—is the country's sunniest (and southernmost) province. Here you'll find **the Austrian Riviera,** a happy blend of mountains, valleys, and placid blue-green lakes that rest serenely between the shoulders of low forested hills and reflect the golden-white light of the rocky faces of the Karawanken and Carnic Alps. Around the shores of the largest lake, the Wörther See, waterside gaiety emanates from the resorts at **Maria Wörth** and **Velden.**

Nature's glories are only part of Carinthia's allure, for many of its Alpine towns contain artistic treasures of the highest order. **Spittal** has Schloss Porcia, a renowned Renaissance palace (its arcaded courtyard is the sublime setting for summer concerts and plays); a great Romanesque basilica broods over tiny Gurk; **St. Veit an der Glan**'s town square is probably the most beautiful in the country, alive with sidewalk cafés in summer; and when you see the 9th-century Hochosterwitz Castle from afar, high atop a hill, you almost expect a dragon to appear in a puff of smoke or to hear troubadours warbling (the castle was the model for the one in Walt Disney's *Snow White*). **Klagenfurt** is the official capital of Carinthia, but **Villach** has emerged as the "secret" capital, no more so than when the town hosts the most riotous Carnival celebration in Austria.

Eastern Alps

If you want a region that conveniently packages the panoramic, the most gemütlich little towns in Austria, and an all-out array of sports, head for the Eastern Alps, magnificently sited within the regions of East Tirol, Salzburg Province, and West Styria. Most towns and villages in this region have not been scarred by bland, quick-fix architecture. No road in Europe matches the 48-km (30-mi) **Grossglockner High Alpine Highway,** which crosses this section of the Tauern mountains and affords a terrific view of **Heiligenblut,** a town cowering in an amphitheater of ragged peaks. On the winding way are spectacular views of the Grossglockner Group, most of which are well beyond the 10,000-ft mark. **Lienz,** a sunny town with a very Italianate flair, lies just south of this scenic mountainscape. There's excellent skiing in the Eastern Alps, but keep in mind the season for Alpine wildflowers is May to June.

Innsbruck and Tirol

Tirol has a great deal, if not everything: the Holy Roman Empire splendors of Innsbruck, Hansel-and-Gretel villages, majestic mountain peaks, masked Carnival revelers, and more—much more. The best base for exploration is **Innsbruck,** a modern and attractive town straddling the rushing Inn River that retains the late Gothic mansion the Goldenes Dachl (Golden Roof). It has beautiful works of architecture, including the "Golden Roof." The sports-minded will also find delightful skiing, snowboarding, hiking, mountain-biking, rafting, hang gliding—you name it, it's done, and if not in or around Innsbruck, then in Kitzbühel, one of the world's oldest ski resorts, or up the Ziller Valley, in the Ötz Valley.

Vorarlberg

"What God has put asunder by a mountain, let no man join by a tunnel"—so said the Vorarlbergers of old. Once the Arlberg Tunnel linked Austria's westernmost province to the rest of the country, the secret was out. Vorarlberg—nicknamed the *Ländle,* the "Little Province"—was really Austria's Switzerland: cheaper in some ways, perhaps less efficient in others.

Tops on all visitors' lists are the fresh air and aria-making of the **Bregenz Music Festival** on Lake Constance; the **Bregen-**

zerwald—forests of Wagnerian romanticism; the **Schubert Festival in Hohenems**; and the endless, powdery snows of its skiing regions. **Lech** is for the wealthy, but try the Brandner Valley east of Bludenz for remoteness or the **Lüner Lake** for its icy waters, or spend a night in the Hotel Traube in Schruns, where Ernest Hemingway played cards in the winter of 1926.

PLEASURES AND PASTIMES

Mozart Mania

Had you been in Innsbruck on August 13, 1993, you would have had a most graphic illustration of what music is to Austria. Suddenly all 23 church spires of the city started pealing away. It was a "city concert" for all the town's bells by the Spanish composer Llorenc Barber. It can happen in Austria: You're walking along thinking of nothing special, and you are suddenly hearing a concert, a recital, an orchestra rehearsing, a soprano going through her scales. You can sit in the Mirabellgarten in Salzburg enjoying coffee and cake, and listen to the opera singers rehearsing. You can be swimming in the Wörthersee in Carinthia and 20 minutes later attending a Brahms recital in Pörtschach, where the great romantic composer spent time (and wrote his Fourth Symphony). That's musical Austria.

It's not only Mozart whose music pours from churches and concert halls, even from the instruments of street musicians— it's music in general that seems to be the spiritual fuel of the country. Wherever you go in Austria, you'll be confronted with classical, jazz, pop, folk, techno, punk, you name it. In summer, if you can't afford the prices of Salzburg and have not packed your best threads, then go to the more congenial Bregenz music festival, or explore the innumerable offerings of the Carinthian Summer in Ossiach.

As for Vienna itself, no city can boast such a roster of fine composers and performers. From the huge Empire and beyond, they poured in in droves (assuming they were not born there)—the better-known being Mozart (naturally), Beethoven, Schubert, Haydn, Johannes Brahms, Mahler, Richard Strauss, Johann Strauss the Younger (no relation), and Arnold Schönberg.

Schnitzels, Strudels, and Sachertortes

Food in Austria is extremely varied. All the gastronomic traditions of the old Empire have left their mark here, so be prepared for genuine Hungarian *pörkölt* (what we call goulash) and *lecsó* (red pepper and tomato stew), and for heavenly Bohemian desserts. The *Palatschinken* are originally Hungarian as well, thin pancakes that can be stuffed around chocolate, marmalade, or a farmer's-cheese stuffing (*Topfen*). Serb *cevapcici* (kebabs) and *rasnici* also appear on menus with fair frequency, even in Austrian establishments, as does *Serbische Bohnensuppe,* a mighty Serb bean soup.

The national gastronomy itself includes lean spareribs and heavy-caliber bread or potato dumplings (also a Bohemian legacy) mixed with bacon or liver or stuffed with anything from cracklings (*Grammel*) to apricots (*Marillen*). In Carinthia (and to an extent in Burgenland), you should try *Sterz* (also called polenta), filling and healthy cornmeal dishes that have roots in Italy and Slovenia as well. From western Austria comes *Kaiserschmarrn,* the "emperor's nonsense" eaten with cranberry jam. The Styrians have their salads, goat's and sheep's cheeses, their various soups, garlic soup, pumpkin soup (*Kürbiskremsuppe*), and a basic soup of meat and root vegetables (*Wurzelfleisch*). In some friendly country *Heuriger* in Lower Austria, you can try blood sausage; *Blunz'n,* with mashed potatoes; or the standard *Schweinsbraten,* pork roast. And there is more: the famous *Wiener schnitzel* (veal scallop, breaded, deep-fried in fresh oil); *Schinkenfleckerl* (broad flat noodles with ham— a Bohemian recipe), and the cheap but delicious *Beuschl* (lung and heart of beef in a thick sauce always served with a giant Knödel). *Tafelspitz mit Kren* is boiled beef fillet with horseradish.

Venison (*Wild*) is a specialty that crosses restaurant class boundaries. A nice *Rehrücken mit Serviettenknödel* (saddle of deer with a bread dumpling cooked wrapped in cloth) at a four-star establishment is something to write home about. By the same token, you may find a robust *Gamsgulasch* (chamois goulash) in a rustic little hut near the summit of a Styrian mountain, or excellent smoked sausages and hams being offered by a Carinthian *Almbauer* at a few tables outside his summer farm in the mountains.

You need not go thirsty either on your travels. Austria has excellent water, which can be drunk from the tap or straight from the spring at times, and that, good brewers will tell you, makes for excellent beer. Murau in Styria has a top brewery, with a fine restaurant attached. Some swear by Vienna's own Ottakringer. All the orchards in the country also make for terrific fruit juices. The new kid on the block for the past few years is elderberry (*Hollunder*), which comes in dry reds or whites and which—like wine—can be *gespritzt*, mixed with either tap water (*stilles Wasser*) or mineral water (*Mineral*). The *Sommergespritzter* is one-third wine, two-thirds water.

Austria's wines range from good to outstanding. Don't hesitate to ask waiters for advice, even in the simpler restaurants, and as with the food, go for the local wine, if possible. For a light, dry white wine, try the Grüner Veltliner. The Welschriesling is a slightly heavier, fruitier wine. In some areas, the wines have their own special names, for example, Styrians are particularly proud of their Schilcher, a generally dry rosé. The reds, too, are well represented, especially in Burgenland. Blauer Portugieser, Traminer, and Zweigelt tend to be on the lighter side. For a slightly heavier red, select a Blaufränkisch or Blauer Burgunder. A novelty, if you happen to be traveling around Heiligenbrunn in Burgenland, is the powerful Uhudler, made of ungrafted vines that originally came from the United States to make European vines resistant to devastating phylloxera. The Austrian government prohibited making it because of its high alcohol content, but after Austria joined the EU in 1995, the prohibition was lifted for fear other European nations would catch on and turn a good penny making this quintessential Austrian wine.

Souvenirs, Austrian-Style

Not so long ago, almost any store on Vienna's Kärntnerstrasse could boast that it once created its exquisite jewelry, fine leather goods, or petit-point handbags (as Viennese as St. Stephen's Cathedral)

for the imperial Habsburgs. The court has vanished, but the *Hoflieferanten* (court suppliers) still maintain their name and at times the old-fashioned grace, slightly fawning touch, and lots of *Gnä Frau* and *der Herr* thrown in for good measure.

There are various types of souvenirs to take home and enjoy, of course: fine glassware from Riedel's in Kufstein (founded 1756); Swarovski crystal; ceramics from a variety of manufacturers, including Gmunder (from Traun near Salzburg); and Augarten porcelain, Europe's oldest china after Meissen. These wares are distributed throughout the country in large and loud shops in the pedestrian zones of Vienna, Salzburg, Graz, Innsbruck, Klagenfurt, and so on. The same applies to traditional clothing: *Trachten, Lederhosen, Dirndls,* and the like can be purchased at such places as Lanz (Vienna and Salzburg), Geiger (in Salzburg), Giesswein (in Vienna) or by keeping a sharp eye out for the magic word *Trachten* while driving about. You may accidentally stumble over some treasures in small towns such as Tamsweg or Feldkirchen in Carinthia, or run across a farmer's market where honest-to-goodness handmade traditional clothing and ornamentations are being sold alongside sheep, boar, or deer skins, leatherware of all sorts, the best plum schnapps, and elderberry and wild raspberry syrups. As for pottery and crockery, you may prefer to take home some of the cottage-industry ware from Stoob in Burgenland or a set of wooden plates that simply get better by the year.

Sipping a cooled Schilcher on a warm summer evening on your porch at home may be the best way of remembering a terrific trip to Austria (don't forget customs restrictions, ☞ The Gold Guide).

Powder-Perfect Skiing

Skiing is without doubt the queen of winter sports, and Austria is one of the finest places—if not the finest—in which to learn or practice the far-from-gentle art of skiing. For information on planning skiing vacations in Austria, *see* Chapter 12.

The Great Outdoors

Austria is one of the most participant-sport-minded countries in the world. Babies barely out of diapers practically learn to walk on skis. At a snowflake's notice,

AUSTRIAN WINE REGIONS

AUSTRIAN VINTNERS ARE beginning to be taken seriously in the world market after successfully rebounding from the scandal of the mid-1980s, when a few unscrupulous merchants added antifreeze to their wines. And they've gone a long way toward changing the outdated image of the simple, undemanding white of the *Heurigen* (wine taverns), usually served gespritzt (mixed with seltzer water) and drunk at a picnic table on a hot summer day.

The majority of grapes grown in Austria are still traditional varieties, with 80% of these used for white wines like Grüner Veltliner and Welschriesling. Of the reds, Zweigelt is the most widely grown; Blaufränkisch is capable of greater complexity; and Blauer Portieser produces pleasant, softer wines. But winegrowers are becoming more venturesome and are experimenting with chardonnay, Riesling, pinot noir, and cabernet sauvignon.

There are five major wine-growing regions: the Wachau, which encompasses the lush Danube Valley west of Vienna; the Weinviertel (Wine Quarter), extending from the area north of Vienna to the Czech border; Burgenland, the province east of Vienna that was formerly part of Hungary; and southern Styria, bordering on Slovenia and reminiscent of Tuscany with its gently rolling hills. Within the city limits of Vienna itself are a number of family-owned vineyards that maintain their own Heurigen.

Each wine region has its own character. Burgenland and southern Styria have warmer climates, which make for full-bodied red wines, while the Wachau's cool climate is tempered by the Danube River valley and produces more Germanic, Rhine-style whites. The Weinviertel boasts of having the least rainfall and most sunny days of all the wine-growing regions in Austria, and it has been producing wine since the Middle Ages.

Burgenland consists of two different territories: the hilly, wooded southern area and the flatlands around the vast Neusiedlersee (Lake Neusiedl), including Carnuntum, where vineyards were established as early as Celtic and Roman times. This is red wine country, famous for its Zweigelt and Blaufränkisch, and it also produces some very good dessert wines.

Though southern Styria is also blessed with a warm climate, it produces a great number of white wines as well as red. Chardonnay is rich and full-bodied here, and you will also find the spicy, fragrant Traminer and Welchriesling, the most common varietal in Styria. But Styrians swear by their Schilcher, a tart, peach-colored rosé that is unique to the region.

The Wachau produces light, fruity white wines, most notably Grüner Veltliner and Riesling, as well as some of the country's best Sekt (sparkling wine); the Kamptal, set back from the river, makes the area's best reds. The Weinviertel is also known principally for light, fresh whites, but interesting things are being done with chardonnay and Weiss Grau Burgunder (Pinot Gris).

Austrian wines have been steadily improving for the last decade, and the long, hot summer of 1997 produced one of the best vintages of the century. It's a perfect time to start sampling their charms.

half the population takes to the slopes; in summer they all head for the lakes and rivers—even to the Danube at Vienna—or to go canoeing, rafting, canyoning, rock-climbing, mountain biking, or spelunking. Tennis is a standard fixture in the Austrian sports world, and golf is on the rise. But one of the great sports, again thanks to the mountains, is hiking, known as *das Wandern.* This can mean anything from a leisurely stroll along the shores of Lake Fuschl to a major hike through the Karawanken in Carinthia lasting several days. Tourist offices inevitably have a *Wanderkarte,* a walking map, to help guide you on your way up, across, around, and down mountains. In fact, there are walking paths that crisscross the Alps, and if you are really a hot hiker, you can stay at refuges on the way and hardly ever come in contact with the "civilized" world of the valleys. Even Vienna is surrounded and traversed by hiking paths: You can bring a special pad along distributed by the tourist office, and a specific sights you'll find a stamp. Bring enough stamps back to the tourist office, and you will receive a pin.

Do not underestimate the mountains. Either have someone along who knows them or have your Wanderkarte and keep your eyes pealed for the telltale markings on the trees and rocks indicating where the road is going. Getting caught in the dark somewhere in the Rax mountains of Lower Austria or around Kühtai in Tirol will suddenly make little Austria feel like the wilds of Washington State. Bring good hiking boots that go over your ankles, thick socks, water-resistant clothing, good sunglasses, headgear, and sunblock. A compass can also be of assistance.

A final note on hiking: There are very stringent rules for hikers. First, try to avoid disturbing wildlife (that's why mountain biking is often forbidden). Further, leave no garbage behind, including cigarette butts. Do not set fires. If you have a dog along, keep it on a leash or walking close to you—foresters have the right to shoot any roaming dogs, and they are sometimes very trigger-happy and rude. Finally, large posters usually near ski lifts or at rest stations in the mountains indicate what plants are protected (the Edelweiss, for example, and several types of gentian as well), and the law is enforced.

NEW AND NOTEWORTHY

The year opens with the annual **New Year's Day concert** by the Vienna Philharmonic, conducted by Lorin Maazel, with the musical selection for the gala event a secret until 10 days before the performance. On New Year's Eve, the Vienna State Opera, the Volksoper, and opera houses in other cities mount Strauss' comic opera *Die Fledermaus.* Other cities have followed Vienna's lead and also offer New Year's concerts.

The main musical event of 1999 is the 100th anniversary of the death of the king of the waltz, **Johann Strauss the Younger,** and the 150th anniversary of the death of his father. Austria plans to mark the year with a celebration of Strauss operettas and waltzes, and both the Vienna State Opera and the Volksoper will host performances of several of both composers' works. The highlight of the festival on the lake at Mörbisch in Burgenland will be a Strauss operetta.

Getting tickets to the glamorous **Opernball** in Vienna depends on luck and speed. Earmark February 11, 1999, or alternatively March 2, 2000, to take part in this quintessentially Viennese event. Vienna will be **Waltzing in 2000** as it hosts an international dance tournament with Viennese Waltz competition November 17–19, 2000. It's bound to be as exciting as one of the classic balls.

New in the **Vienna art world** is the renovation of the rambling Messepalast building, located on the Ring near the Kunsthistorisches Museum. Plans are under way to turn it into a museum for post-1918 art, with works by Egon Schiele forming the nucleus of the collection. The Messepalast was previously used as a convention center and concert venue.

Near the United Nations center in the 22nd District, a massive new complex called **Donau City,** or Danube City, is under construction. When it's completed, it will house restaurants, shops, and movie theaters. As of press time, the new four-star Forum Hotel, part of the Inter-Continental Hotel Group, is scheduled to open there in late 1998.

A new addition to Stephansplatz is the **Jewish Welcome Center,** located at No. 10. Vienna's Jewish population shrank from more than 200,000 before World War II to just 12,000 today. Along with trying to keep in touch with emigrants all over the world, the Welcome Center provides information on where to visit important Jewish landmarks and former Jewish neighborhoods in the city.

A new monetary currency will make its debut on January 1, 1999, when the conversion to the **euro** begins for all members of the European Union, Austria included. Some payment systems (mainly in trade) will begin using the euro immediately. The rates of conversion between the euro and local currencies will be irrevocably fixed, which should eliminate commission charges when exchanging currency. Consumers will continue chiefly to use their own national currency because euro banknotes and coins will not yet be available, but the gradual introduction of dual pricing of goods and services will enable people slowly to get used to the new money. Eventually, the euro will become a currency in its own right and participating national currencies will no longer be listed on foreign exchange markets. By January 1, 2002, at the latest, new euro banknotes and coins will be put into circulation and the old national currencies will be withdrawn. In Austria this will be done over a period of three months, after which euro banknotes and coins alone will have legal tender status.

Once every six years, Thiersee in Tirol holds its traditional **passion play** from May to October. Just about the entire village participates in the event, which is next scheduled for 1999.

FODOR'S CHOICE

No two people agree on what makes a perfect vacation, but it's fun and helpful to known what others think. Here's a compendium from the must-see lists of hundreds of Austrian travelers. For detailed information about these memories-in-themaking, refer to the appropriate chapters in this book.

Quintessential Austria

★ **New Year's Day concert in Vienna's Musikverein.** You've seen it on television, but now you're *here* in the Golden Hall—its gilt bare-breasted ladies supporting the balconies, the walls festooned with floral displays—sharing in the excitement of a Vienna Philharmonic concert seen and heard by millions around the world.

★ **Waltzing around the clock at a Fasching ball.** Whether you go to the Opera Ball or the Zuckerbäckerball (sponsored by pastry cooks), remember that gala etiquette states a gentleman can kiss only a lady's hand.

★ **Taking a boat through the Wachau on the Danube.** The vineyards are glowing in all fall colors or the apricot and cherry trees are in bloom. Spring or fall or warm breezy summer, this is heaven on earth. The setting sun always makes the villages radiate, and the great Baroque monastery of Melk seems like poured gold.

★ **A summer evening in Styria.** The hills of the Southern Wine Road (südliche Weinstrasse) are dotted with little familyrun Heurigen, where the wine is excellent, the food simple and good, the people hospitable. Often, the house's garden serves as a guest garden (*Gastgarten*); you can stay as long as the place stays open, meet other people, and make friends.

★ **The Lipizzaner stallions at the Spanish Riding School.** Where else can you see horses dance a minuet to Mozart? For sheer elegance, the combination of the chestnut-colored riding habits of the trainers and the pure white of the horses' coats can't be beat.

★ **A hike up a mountain.** Pack a bag with water, bread, cheese, cold cuts, and fresh fruit, and spend a day roaming the mountains, crossing icy streams, traversing cool forests, meeting cows and sheep—maybe the odd deer or fox, or kindred walker, or farmer. What's good for the body is good for the soul!

Sights to Remember

★ **Gosau am Dachstein.** In a vista that many consider one of the most beautiful in Austria, the Dachstein massif seems to pose for the tourist's camera. The mountain's ermine mantle of snow is mirrored in the Gosau lakes below—a vision so breathtaking it inspired some of Wagner's greatest music.

★ **Vienna from the Leopoldsberg.** The metropolis sprawls on a plain embraced on the one side by hills, traversed on the other by the flows and canals of the Danube, its barges like toys. Every detail of the city is visible on a clear day, the great Ferris wheel of the Prater, St. Stephen's Cathedral, the refinery of Schwechat. You can see way into the distance almost all the way to Bratislava.

★ **Salzburg from the Kapuzinerberg after the first snow.** A blanket of white softens the somber gray of the city and brings buildings and squares to life; you'll see features you've overlooked before, with the solid Festung watching patiently over the Christmas-card scene.

★ **Hallstatt on a misty morning.** At the "world's prettiest lakeside village," the surrounding mountains often disappear into the mist, leaving the unforgettable shadowy outline of the church and town buildings hugging the lakeshore.

Unforgettable Drives

★ **The Wachau when its apricot trees are in blossom.** In spring, the narrow Danube Valley becomes a riot of fruit trees in delicate pastel blossom sweeping up hillsides from the very riverbanks.

★ **Grossglockner Highway between East Tirol and Salzburg Province.** This engineering masterpiece challenges the driver but brings, one after another, glorious panoramas of snow-swept Alpine horizons and lush meadows. Take the side route up to the vast glacier whose runoff feeds the many mountain streams.

Taste Treats

★ **Sampling wine at a romantic *Heuriger* in Rust.** The Burgenland red wines taste their best when enjoyed outdoors at wooden tables accompanied by chunks of country bread and spicy *Liptauer* cheese spread, fresh radishes, and slivers of bell peppers; the vintner will set you up with a memorable picnic.

★ ***Käsekrainer* (sausage stuffed with cheese) in the arcaded side passageway at the Naschmarkt, at the Karlsplatz end across from Theater an der Wien.** One bite of this crunchy, grilled sausage oozing with melted cheese will spoil you forever

for an Oscar Mayer cheesedog. The best way to eat a Käsekrainer is with a soft, fresh Semmel roll and a dollop of mild, sweet mustard on the side.

★ ***Stollen* (cake) with coffee at the Café Zauner in Bad Ischl.** A favorite of Emperor Franz Josef—both the café and its pastries—is still very popular today, enhanced by outdoor tables directly overlooking the river; this is a pilgrimage regularly made by Austrians as well as tourists.

Great Hotels

★ **Österreichischer Hof, Salzburg.** From its vantage point along the banks of the Salzach with a staggering view opposite of the Old City and looming fortress, this grande dame of Salzburg hotels has gone out of its way to provide beauty and comfort in each of the exquisitely decorated rooms. The danger is that you won't want to leave the hotel to explore the sights. $$$$

★ **Palais Schwarzenberg, Vienna.** It's hard to believe you're in the heart of the city at this secluded hotel, set in its own vast, formal park. Built in the early 1700s, the palace is still privately owned and retains a sense of history while offering luxuriously appointed rooms. Guests are made to feel at home, whether strolling through the gardens or sipping a drink in front of a roaring fire in the drawing room on cold winter nights. $$$$

★ **Schloss Obermayerhofen, Bad Waltersdorf.** The elegance of the castle and the beauty of the surrounding countryside make this a perfect place to get away from it all. The ancient rooms are decorated with museum-worthy tapestries and antiques. After returning from an invigorating hike, nothing could be more magical than changing for dinner and walking down a pathway lined with blazing torches to the gourmet restaurant. $$$$

Memorable Restaurants

★ **Artner, Vienna.** Spectacular wines and goat cheese from the Artner Winery in the Carnuntum region east of Vienna are highlighted in this upscale eatery. The food is superb, offering traditional Austrian fare as well as exotic dishes, and it's fun to sample a different wine with each course. $$

★ **Tiroler Stuben, Innsbruck.** Friedrich Wolf concentrates on ingredients in this comfortable, relaxed restaurant, bringing in fresh fish and lamb from France several times weekly. Treatments vary, but dishes are imaginative without being superficial, adding up to very fine dining indeed. $$$

★ **Zum Eulenspiegel, Salzburg.** This little cottage looks as if it's straight out of a fairy tale, and happily the food matches the unique setting. The house is hundreds of years old and full of wonderful nooks and crannies reached by odd staircases. Mullioned windows, gleaming dark-wood-paneled walls, white linen, and candlelight make for an unforgettable evening. This isn't kitsch; it's genuine Old World authentic. $$$

★ **Zum Roten Wolf, Langelebarn.** Just a few miles west of Vienna, this rustic country inn with wooden booths and beamed ceilings is one of the best-kept secrets around. Don't go if you're in a hurry, but settle in for a leisurely, spectacular meal, complete with a choice of good wines at reasonable prices. $$$

Historic Towns/ Picturesque Squares

★ **Hauptplatz, Linz.** The spacious main square of the Upper Austrian capital has been handsomely restored; church spires rather than skyscrapers shape the skyline. The square is the site for local markets just as it was centuries ago, with many of the same buildings gracing the scene.

★ **Old City, Graz.** Narrow winding streets tucked below the city's "mountain" invite exploration. The old quarter exudes charm and has attracted a host of boutiques and tiny restaurants, all wedged willy-nilly into odd corners. This is one of Austria's better-kept secrets.

★ **Steyr, Upper Austria.** Wonderfully colorful decorative facades address the main square, brooded over by the castle above. Tiny, half-concealed stairways lead upward to the castle area, while other stone steps take you down the opposite side to the riverbank. The setting is an ensemble worthy of Hollywood; in this case, it's all charmingly real.

Classic Cafés

★ **Café Central, Vienna.** Nothing embodies the spirit of Old World Viennese café society than this grand, plush coffeehouse not far from the Hofburg Palace. Trotsky supposedly plotted the Russian Revolution here, using the alias Bronstein. In the late afternoon an all-woman orchestra plays Viennese waltzes.

★ **Tomaselli, Salzburg.** An almost reverent atmosphere pervades this enduring temple to café culture, but you'll find the usual accoutrements, such as a stack of newspapers to accompany your coffee and dessert.

Churches and Abbeys

★ **Melk, Lower Austria.** Probably the most impressive of Europe's abbeys, Melk perches like a magnificent yellow-frosted wedding cake overlooking the Danube, its ornate library holding rows of priceless treasures. If you can visit only one abbey in all of Europe, Melk should be among the top contenders.

★ **St. Florian, Upper Austria.** This abbey, where composer Anton Bruckner was organist, is impressive for its sheer size alone. Add to the symmetrical structure the glorious church and the representational rooms, and you have one of Austria's religious highlights.

★ **St. Stephen's Cathedral, Vienna.** The country's Catholic life centers on St. Stephen's, rebuilt after burning during the last days of World War II. It is one of Europe's finest Gothic structures, with two different towers, one of which can be climbed on foot; the other has an elevator and holds the *Pummerin,* Austria's largest bell. Like the exterior, the interior of the cathedral is a masterpiece, especially of the stone-carving art.

Parks and Gardens

★ **Mirabell Gardens, Salzburg.** For an idyllic view, look up through the formal garden to the castle (Festung) dominating the city, but don't miss the droll Baroque side garden with its amusing stone dwarfs.

★ **Schönbrunn, Vienna.** Was the palace an excuse for the gardens, or vice versa? The manicured trees, the symmetrical walkways, the discoveries at various intersections—all add to the pleasure of exploration here. Climb to the Gloriette, which is now a moderately good café, for a sweeping perspective of the gardens and the city beyond.

FESTIVALS AND SEASONAL EVENTS

JAN. 1➤ The New Year opens in Vienna with the world-famous concert by the **Vienna Philharmonic Orchestra**; write a year—or more—in advance (✉ Vienna Philharmonic, Musikverein, Bösendorferstr. 12, A–1010 Vienna, ☎ 01/505–6525). Those who can't get into the Philharmonic concert can try for one of the performances of the Johann Strauss operetta *Die Fledermaus* or another light delight in the **Volksoper** (✉ Währinger Strasse 78, A–1090 Vienna, ☎ 01/513–1513 credit-card orders) or at the intimate **Kammeroper** (✉ Fleischmarkt 24, A–1010 Vienna, ☎ 01/513–1513 credit-card orders). Those who want to dance their way into the new year can do so at the **Kaiserball** in the elegant rooms of the Hofburg (✉ WKV, Hofburg, Heldenplatz, A–1014 Vienna, ☎ 01/587–3666–14).

JAN. 6➤ Children disguised as the Magi walk the streets, especially out in the country, knock at doors, sing a song and recite poems about coming from afar, and ask for a small donation. They then chalk a "C+M+B" and the year on entrance door frames to bless the house for a year. Also special at this time is the ancient pre-Christian custom of the *Perchtenlauf*, masked figures that go on a rampage, mostly found in Salzburg Province, in Bad Gastein, for example.

WEEK OF JAN. 27➤ **Mozart's Birthday** is celebrated in Salzburg with a little festival featuring operas, recitals, and theme concerts (✉ Mozarteum, Schwarzstr. 26, A–5020 Salzburg, ☎ 0622/872996).

FEB.➤ **Fasching** (or Fasnacht, as its called in the western part of the country), the carnival period before Lent, can become very wild with huge processions of disguised figures, occasional unwilling participation by spectators, who may even suffer (light) blows. In Tirol, things are organized so that each town has a specific year to perform its festivities. The entire country starts going to dances—and the ball season begins. In Vienna, which is comparatively quiet at this time, the ball season opens on the Thursday before Fasching.

FEB. 11, 1999, AND MARCH 2, 2000➤ The Opera House in Vienna is transformed into the world's most elegant ballroom for the annual **Opernball**. Order tickets early (✉ Staatsoper, Ringstrasse 2, A–1010 Vienna, ☎ 01/514–44–2606, FAX 01/514–44–2624).

LATE-MAR.–EARLY APR.➤ **Easter Festival,** Salzburg's "other" major music festival, offers opera and concerts of the highest quality, with ticket prices to match (✉ Hofstallgasse 1, A–5020 Salzburg, ☎ 0662/8045–361).

MID-MAY–MID-JUNE➤ The **Wiener Festwochen** takes place in Vienna—a festival of theater, music, films, and exhibitions (✉ Lehargasse 11, A–1060 Vienna, ☎ 0222/582–2222).

JUNE 2➤ The religious holiday **Corpus Christi** is celebrated throughout Austria with colorful processions and parades. In the Lungau region of Land Salzburg, villagers dress up in local costumes. Equally colorful are the processions of gaily decorated boats and barges on the Traun and Hallstätter lakes.

MID-JUNE➤ A **Schubert Festival** with top international artists is held in Feldkirch in Vorarlberg.

JUNE 21➤ **Midsummer Night** is ablaze with bonfires throughout the country, with the liveliest celebrations taking place in the mountains of Tirol and in the Wachau region along the Danube in Lower Austria.

JULY–AUG.➤ **Carinthian Summer** combines concerts, opera, and literature in the modern Congress House in Villach and the exquisite monastery and Baroque chapel in Ossiach (✉ Carinthischer Sommer, Gumpendorferstr. 76, A–

1060 Vienna, ☎ 01/596–8198 through May; ✉ Stift Ossiach, A–9570 Ossiach, ☎ 04243/2510 June–Aug.).

Musical Summer/Klang-Bogen in Vienna has nightly recitals in one of the city's many palaces or orchestral concerts in the courtyard of the city hall (✉ KlangBogen Wien, Stadiongasse 29, A–1010 Vienna, ☎ 01/4000–8410, ℻ 01/4000–99–8410).

The **Bregenz Festival** increases in prestige from year to year and has become one of Europe's outstanding music festivals, noted particularly for its opera performances on the lake (✉ Bregenzer Festspiele, Box 311, A–6901 Bregenz, ☎ 05574/4920–223).

The **Salzburg Festival** brings together the world's greatest musical artists for a citywide celebration. Write several months in advance (✉ Salzburger Festspiele, Postfach 140, A–5010 Salzburg, ☎ 0662/8045–322).

AUTUMN

SEPT. 1➤ This date marks the start of the **theater and music season** in Vienna.

EARLY SEPT.➤ A series of **trade fairs** packs Vienna during the first weeks of the month; the most interesting is the Hit consumer electronics show, where new products are showcased.

The **Haydn Festival** takes place in Eisenstadt in Burgenland (✉ Burgenländische Haydn Festspiele, Schloss Esterházy, A–7000 Eisenstadt, ☎ 02682/618660).

The **International Bruckner Festival** makes Linz come alive: Theater, concerts, fireworks, and art exhibits extend to the St. Florian monastery, where the composer Anton Bruckner worked and is buried (✉ Untere Donaulände 7, A–4010 Linz, ☎ 0732/775230).

MID-OCT.➤ **Viennale** in Vienna shows films ranging from the avant-garde to retrospectives (✉ Wiener Filmfestwochen Viennale, Stiftsgasse 6, A–1070 Vienna, ☎ 0222/526–5947).

NOV. 11➤ **St. Martin's Day** (*Martinigansl* or *Ganslessen,* "Martin's goose" or "goose eating") is as good as a holiday; restaurants throughout the country serve traditional roast goose and red cabbage in honor of the patron saint of publicans and innkeepers. The most enthusiastic

celebrations, including village parades, take place in Burgenland, of which Martin is the patron saint.

DEC. 5 AND 6➤ On **St. Nicholas' Day** (Dec. 6) the original Father Christmas, who fills stockings of good children, is honored in family surroundings. Sometimes in Lower Austria and Vienna, and more often in Tirol, on December 5, you catch a few rowdies dressed up in wild clothes with horns and huge red tongues hanging out of their mouths: You've met the *Krampus,* the darker side of St. Nick! *Christkindl* (Christ Child) festivals, in December throughout the country, are open-air markets selling toys, favors, decorations, and food. The town of Christkindl in Styria comes into its glory each year at this time.

DEC. 24➤ The **Christmas Eve** service in the tiny memorial chapel at Oberndorf, north of Salzburg, features the singing of *Silent Night,* which Franz Gruber wrote when he was an organist here in the early 19th century. **Christmas Eve midnight mass** at St. Stephen's Cathedral in Vienna is an impressive, if crowded, event; get an entrance pass at the cathedral in advance.

2 Vienna

Magnificent, magnetic, and magical, Vienna beguiles one and all with Old World charm and courtly grace. It is a place where head waiters still bow as if saluting a Habsburg prince, where Lipizzaner stallions dance minuets to Mozart—a city that waltzes and works in three-quarter time. Like a well-bred grande dame, Vienna doesn't hurry, and neither should you. Saunter through its stately streets—peopled by the spirits of Beethoven and Strauss, Metternich, and Freud—marvel at its Baroque palaces, and dream an afternoon away at a cozy Kaffeehaus.

THE CITIZENS OF VIENNA, it has been said, properly waltz only from the waist down, whirling around the crowded dance floor while holding their upper bodies motionless and ramrod straight. The sight can be breathtaking in its sweep and splendor, and its elegant coupling of freewheeling exuberance and rigid formality—of license and constraint—is quintessentially Viennese. Viennese town palaces, Baroque mansions built mostly during the 18th century that can be found all over the inner city, present in stone and stucco a similar artful synthesis of license and constraint as the dance that was so often performed inside them. They make Vienna a Baroque city that is, at its best, an architectural waltz.

Updated by Bonnie Dodson

Today, visitors who tour Vienna can easily feel they're doing so in three-quarter time. As they explore its churches filled with statues of golden saints and pink-cheeked cherubs, wander through its treasure-packed museums, or while away the afternoon in those multitudinous meccas of mocha (the inevitable cafés), they can begin to feel lapped in lashings of rich, delicious, whipped cream—the beloved *Schlagobers* that garnishes most Viennese pastries. The ambience of the city is predominantly ornate and fluffy: white horses dancing to elegant music; snow frosting the opulent draperies of Empress Maria Theresa's monument, set in the formal patterns of "her" lovely square; a gilded Johann Strauss, playing gracefully among a grove of green trees; rich decorations, secretly filling the interior courtyards of town houses that present a severe face to the outside world; the transformation of grim Greek legends by the voluptuous music of Richard Strauss; the tangible, geometric impasto of Klimt's paintings; the stately pavane of a mechanical clock. All these will create in the visitor the sensation of a metropolis that likes to be visited and admired—and which indeed is well worth admiring and visiting.

For many centuries, this has been the case. One of the great capitals of Europe, Vienna was for centuries home to the Habsburg rulers of the Austro-Hungarian Empire. Today the empire is long gone, but many reminders of the city's imperial heyday remain, carefully preserved by the tradition-loving Viennese. When it comes to the arts, the glories of the past are particularly evergreen, thanks to the cultural legacy created by the many artistic geniuses nourished here.

From the late 18th century on, Vienna's culture—particularly its musical forte—was famous throughout Europe. Haydn, Mozart, Beethoven, Schubert, Brahms, Strauss, Mahler, and Bruckner all lived in the city, producing music that is still played in concert halls all over the world. And at the tail end of the 19th century the city's artists and architects—Gustav Klimt, Egon Schiele, Oskar Kokoschka, Josef Hoffmann, Otto Wagner, and Adolf Loos among them—brought about an unprecedented artistic revolution, a revolution that swept away the past and set the stage for the radically experimental art of the 20th century.

At the close of World War I the Austro-Hungarian Empire was dismembered, and Vienna lost its cherished status as the seat of imperial power. Its influence was much reduced, and its population began to decline (unlike what happened in Europe's other great cities), from around 2 million to the current 1.7 million. Today, however, the city's future looks brighter, for with the collapse of the Iron Curtain, Vienna may at long last regain its traditional status as the hub of Central Europe.

For many first-time visitors, the city's one major disappointment concerns the Danube River. The inner city, it turns out, lies not on the river's main stream but on one of its narrow offshoots, known as the Danube

Canal. As a result, the sweeping river views expected by most newcomers fail to materialize.

The Romans are to blame, for when Vienna was founded as a Roman military encampment around AD 100, the walled garrison was built not on the Danube's main stream but rather on the largest of the river's eastern branches, where it could be bordered by water on three sides. The wide, present-day Danube did not take shape until the late 19th century, when its various branches were rerouted and merged to prevent flooding.

The Romans maintained their camp for some 300 years (the emperor Marcus Aurelius is thought to have died in Vindobona, as it was called, in 180) and finally abandoned the site around 400. The settlement survived the Roman withdrawal, however, and by the 13th century growth was sufficient to require new city walls to the south. According to legend, the walls were financed by the English: In 1192 the local duke kidnapped King Richard I (the Lion-Hearted), en route from the Third Crusade, and held him prisoner in Dürnstein, upriver, for two years until he was expensively ransomed.

Vienna's third set of walls dates from 1544, when the existing walls were improved and extended. The new fortifications were built by the Habsburg dynasty, which ruled the Austro-Hungarian Empire for an astonishing 640 years, beginning with Rudolf I in 1273 and ending with Karl I in 1918. The walls stood until 1857, when Emperor Franz Josef finally decreed that they be demolished and replaced by the famous tree-lined Ringstrasse (Ring Street).

During medieval times the city's growth was relatively slow, and its heyday as a European capital did not begin until 1683, after a huge force of invading Turks laid siege to the city for two months, to be finally routed by an army of Habsburg allies. Among the supplies that the fleeing Turks left behind were sacks filled with coffee beans. It was these beans, so the story goes, that gave a local entrepreneur the idea of opening the first public coffeehouse; they remain a Viennese institution to this day.

The passing of the Turkish threat produced a Viennese building boom, and the Baroque style was the architectural order of the day. Flamboyant, triumphant, joyous, and extravagantly ostentatious, the new art form—imported from Italy—transformed the city into a vast theater in the 17th and 18th centuries. Life became a dream—the gorgeous dream of the Baroque, with its gilded madonnas and cherubs; its soaring, twisted columns; its painted heavens on the ceilings, its sumptuous domes. In the 19th century, a reaction set in—the Biedermeier epoch, when middle-class industriousness and sober family values set a new style. Then came the Strauss era—that lighthearted period that conjures up imperial balls, "Wine, Women, and Song," heel-clicking, and hand-kissing. Today, visitors will find that all these eras have left their mark on Vienna, making it a city possessed of a special grace. It is this grace that gives Vienna the distinctive architectural character that sets the city so memorably apart from its great rivals—London, Paris, and Rome.

Pleasures and Pastimes

Café Society

They used to say that there were more cafés and coffeehouses in Vienna than there were banks in Switzerland. Whether or not this can still be claimed, you can't savor the true flavor of Vienna without visiting some of its Meccas of Mocha. Every afternoon at 4, the coffee-and-pastry ritual of *Kaffeejause* takes place from one end of the city to the other. Regulars take their *Stammtisch* (usual table) and sit until they go home for dinner. They come to gossip, read the papers, negotiate business, play cards, meet a spouse (or someone else's), or—who knows?—just have a cup of coffee. Whatever the reason, Viennese use cafés and coffeehouses as club, pub, bistro, and even a home away from home. (Old-timers recall the old joke: "Pardon me, would you mind watching my seat for a while so I can go out for a cup of coffee?")

In fact, to savor the atmosphere of the coffeehouse, you must allow time. There is no need to worry about outstaying one's welcome, even over a single small cup of coffee—so set aside a morning or afternoon, and take along this book. For historical overtones, head for the Café Central—where Stalin and Trotsky hatched the Russian Revolution; for Old World charm, check out the opulent Café Landtmann (even its plush velvet interior is chocolate-colored) or the elegant Café Sacher (famous for its cake); for the smoky art scene, go to the Café Hawelka. Wherever you go, never ask for just a cup of coffee; request, at the very least, a mocha *mit Obers* (with whipped cream) from the *Herr Ober,* or any of many other delightful variations (☞ Cafés *in* Dining, *below*).

The Heurigen

It is a memorable experience to sit at the edge of a vineyard on the Kahlenberg with a tankard of young white wine and listen to the *Schrammel* quartet playing sentimental Viennese songs. The wine taverns, called *Heurigen* (the single appellation is *Heuriger*) for the new wine that they serve, are very much a part of and typical of the city (although not unique to Vienna). Heurigen sprang up in 1784 when Joseph II decreed that owners of vineyards could open their own private wine taverns. The Viennese discovered that it was cheaper to go out to the wine than to bring it inside the city walls where taxes were levied. The Heuriger owner is supposed to be licensed to served only the produce of his own vineyard, a rule long more honored in the breach than in the observance (it would take a sensitive palate indeed to differentiate among the various vineyards).

These taverns (☞ Heurigen *in* Dining, *below*) in the wine-growing districts on the outskirts of the city (in such villages as Neustift am Walde, Sievering, Nussdorf, and Grinzing) vary from the simple front room of a vintner's house to ornate establishments. The true Heuriger is open for only a few weeks a year to allow the vintner to sell a certain quantity of his production tax-free for consumption on his own premises. The commercial establishments keep to a somewhat more regular season but still sell wine only from their own vines.

The choice is usually between a "new" and an "old" white wine and a red, but you can also ask for a milder or sharper wine according to your taste. Most Heurigen are happy to let you sample the wines before order. You can also order a *Gespritzter,* half wine and half soda water. The waitress will bring you the wine, usually in a ¼-liter mug or liter carafe, but you get your own food from the buffet. The wine tastes as mild as lemonade, but it packs a punch. If it isn't of good quality, you will know by a raging headache the next day.

Jugendstil Jewels

From 1897 to 1907, the Vienna Secession movement gave rise to one of the most spectacular manifestations of the pan-European style known as Art Nouveau. Viennese took to calling the look *Jugenstil,* or the "young style." In such dazzling edifices as Otto Wagner's Wienzeile majolica-adorned mansion and Adolf Loos's Looshaus, Jugendstil architects rebelled against the prevailing 19th-century historicism that had created so many imitation Renaissance town houses and faux

Grecian temples. Josef Maria Olbrich, Josef Hoffman, and Otto Schön-
thal took William Morris's Movement, added dashes of Charles Ren-
nie Mackintosh and flat-surface Germanic geometry, and came up
with a luxurious style that shocked turn-of-the-century Viennese (and
infuriated Emperor Franz Josef). Many artists united to form the Vienna Secession—whose most famous member was painter Gustav
Klimt—and the Wiener Werkstätte, which transformed the objects of
daily life with a sleek modern look. Today, Jugendstil buildings are among
the most fascinating structures in Vienna. The shrine of the movement
is the world-famous Secession Building—the work of Josef Maria Olbrich—the cynosure of all eyes on the Friedrichstrasse.

Museums and Marvels

You could spend months just perusing Vienna's 90 museums. Subjects
range alphabetically from art to wine, and in between are found such
oddities as bricks and burials, such marvels as carriages and clocks,
and such memorials as Mozart and martyrs. If your time is short, the
one museum not to be overlooked is the Kunsthistorisches Museum,
Vienna's famous art museum. This is one of the great museums of the
world, with masterworks by Titian, Rembrandt, Vermeer, Velasquez,
and an outstanding collection of Brueghels.

Given a little more time, the Schatzkammer, or Imperial Treasury, is
well worth a visit, for its opulent bounty of crown jewels, regal attire,
and other trappings of court. The sparkling new Silberkammer, a museum of court silver and tableware, is fascinating for its "behind-the-
scenes" views of state banquets and other elegant representational
affairs. The best-known museums tend to crowd up in late morning
and mid-afternoon hours; you can beat the mobs by going earlier or
around the noon hour, at least to the larger museums that are open
without a noontime break.

The Sound—and Sights—of Music

What closer association to Vienna is there but music? Boasting one of
the world's greatest concert venues (Musikverein), two of the world's
greatest symphony orchestras (Vienna Philharmonic and Vienna Symphony), and one of the top opera houses (Staatsoper), it's no wonder
that music and the related politics are subjects of daily conversation.
During July and August—just in time for tourists—the city hosts the
Vienna Summer of Music, with numerous special events and concerts.

For the musical tourist who is excited at the prospect of treading in
the footprints of the mighty, seeing where masterpieces were committed to paper, or standing where a long-loved work was either praised
or damned at its first appearance, Vienna is tops: The city is saturated
with musical history. There is the apartment where Mozart wrote his
last three symphonies, the house where Schubert was born, and, just
a tram ride away, the path that inspired Beethoven's Pastoral Symphony.
Just below, you'll find a handy list of these musical landmarks.

Of course, there is also music to delight as well as inspire. The statue
of Johann Strauss II in the Stadtpark tells all. To see him, violin tucked
under his chin, is to imagine those infectious waltzes, "Wine, Women,
and Song," "Voices of Spring," and best of all, the "Emperor." But quite
possibly you will not need to imagine them. Chances are, somewhere
in the distance, an orchestra will be playing them. Head for the The-
atre an der Wien to hear great operetta (*Die Fledermaus* and *The
Merry Widow* both premiered here) or to the Volksoper. While the traditional classics are the main fare for the conservative, traditional Viennese, acceptance of modern music is growing, as are the audiences
for pop and jazz.

Musicians' residences abound, and many are open as museums. The most famous are Mozart's Figarohaus and Beethoven's Pasqualatihaus, which are discussed in the city sections below. Vienna has many other music landmarks scattered over the city—here's a sample: **Schubert**—a native of the city, unlike most of Vienna's other famous composers—was born at Nussdorferstrasse 54 (☎ 01/317–3601, U-Bahn U2/Schottenring, then Streetcar 37 or 38 to Canisiusgasse), in the Ninth District, and died in the Fourth District at Kettenbrückengasse 6 (☎ 01/581–6730, U-Bahn U4/Kettenbrückengasse). **Joseph Haydn's house,** which includes a Brahms memorial room, is at Haydngasse 19 (☎ 01/596–1307, U-Bahn U4/Pilgramgasse or U3/Zieglergasse) in the Sixth District. **Beethoven's Heiligenstadt residence,** where at age 32 he wrote the "Heiligenstadt Testament," an anguished cry of pain and protest against his ever-increasing deafness, is at Probusgasse 6 in the 19th District (☎ 01/375408, U-Bahn U4/Heiligenstadt, then Bus 38A to Wählamt). The home of the most popular composer of all, waltz king **Johann Strauss the Younger,** can be visited at Praterstrasse 54 (☎ 01/214–0121, U-Bahn U4/Nestroypl.), in the Second District; he lived here when he composed "The Blue Danube Waltz" in 1867. All the above houses contain commemorative museums. Admission is AS25; a block of 10 AS25 tickets for city museums costs AS160. All are open Tuesday–Sunday 9–12:15 and 1–4:30.

Stepping Out in Three-Quarter Time

Ever since the 19th-century Congress of Vienna—when pundits laughed "*Elle danse, mais elle ne marche pas*" (the city "dances, but it never gets anything done")—Viennese extravagance and gaiety have been world famous. Fasching, the season of Prince Carnival, was given over to court balls, opera balls, masked balls, Chambermaids' and Bakers' balls, and a hundred other gatherings, many held within the glittering interiors of Baroque theaters and palaces. Presiding over the dazzling evening gowns and gilt-splashed uniforms, towering headdresses, flirtatious fans, *chambres séparées*, "Wine, Women, and Song," *Die Fledermaus,* "Blue Danube," hand-kissing, and gay abandon was the baton of the waltz emperor, Johann Strauss. White-gloved women and men in white tie would glide over marble floors to his heavenly melodies. They still do. Now, as in the days of Franz Josef, Vienna's old three-quarter-time rhythm strikes up anew each year during Carnival, from New Year's Eve until Mardi Gras.

During January and February, as many as 40 balls may be held in a single evening, the most famous—some say too famous—being the Opernball. This event transforms the Vienna Opera House into the world's most beautiful ballroom (and transfixes all of Austria when shown live on national television). For a price, anyone can attend, but corporate interests often buy up most of the tickets. The invitation to the Opernball reads, "*Frack mit Dekorationen,*" which means that it's time to dust off your Legion of Honor medal and women mustn't wear white (reserved for debutantes). Remember that you must dance the *Linkswalzer*—the counterclockwise, left-turning waltz that is the only way to dance in Vienna. After your gala evening, finish off the morning with a *Kater Frühstuck*—a hangover breakfast—of goulash soup. For a rundown on the major balls that the public can attend during the winter season, *see* Nightlife *in* Nightlife and the Arts, *below.*

EXPLORING VIENNA

To the Viennese, the most prestigious address of Vienna's 23 *Bezirke,* or districts, is the First District (the inner city, bounded by the Ringstrasse and the Danube Canal). The Second through Ninth districts surround the inner city (starting with the Second District across the Danube Canal and running clockwise); the 10th through 23rd districts form a second concentric ring of suburbs. The vast majority of sightseeing attractions are to be found in the First District. For hard-core sightseers who wish to supplement the key attractions that follow, the tourist office (☞ Contacts and Resources *in* Vienna A to Z, *below*) has a booklet, "Vienna from A–Z" (AS60), that gives short descriptions of some 250 sights around the city, all numbered and keyed to a fold-out map at the back, as well as to numbered wall plaques on the buildings themselves. Note that the nearest U-Bahn (subway) stop to most city attractions described below is included at the end of the service information (☞ Subway system map *in* Getting Around *in* Vienna A to Z, *below*). The more important churches have coin-operated (AS10) tape machines that give an excellent commentary in English on the history and architecture of the church.

Vienna is a city to explore and discover on foot. The description of the city on the following pages is divided into eight areas: seven that explore the architectural riches of central Vienna and an eighth that describes Schönbrunn Palace and its gardens. Above all, *look up* as you tour Vienna: Some of the most fascinating architectural and ornamental bits are on upper stories or atop the city's buildings.

Numbers in the text correspond to numbers in the margin and on the Vienna, Hofsburg, and Schönbrunn Palace maps.

Great Itineraries

IF YOU HAVE 1 DAY

Touring Vienna in a single day is a proposition as strenuous as it is unlikely, but those with more ambition than time should first get a quick view of the lay of the city by taking a streetcar ride around the Ringstrasse, the wide boulevard that encloses the heart of the city. Then spend the time until early afternoon exploring the city center, starting at Vienna's cathedral, the **Stephansdom** ①, followed by a stroll along the Graben and Kärntnerstrasse, the two main pedestrian shopping streets in the center. About 1 PM, head for **Schönbrunn Palace** ㊺ to spend the afternoon touring the magnificent royal residence, or visit the **Kunsthistoriches Museum** ㊼, one of the great art museums of the world. After the museum closes at 6 PM, relax over coffee at a café; then spend a musical evening at a concert, opera, or operetta or a convivial evening at a Heuriger, one of the wine restaurants for which Vienna is also famous.

IF YOU HAVE 3 DAYS

Given more time, day one can be a little less hectic, and in any case, you'll want more time for the city center. Rather than going on the do-it-yourself streetcar ride around the Ringstrasse, take an organized sightseeing tour, which will describe the highlights. Plan to spend a full afternoon at **Schönbrunn Palace** ㊺. Reserve the second day for art, tackling the exciting **Kunsthistoriches Museum** ㊼ before lunch and the magnificent collection of Old Master drawings of the **Albertina Museum** ㊱ and the impressive **Belvedere Palace** ㊽. For a contrasting step into modern art in the afternoon—don't miss Klimt's legendary *The Kiss* at the Belvedere. Do as the Viennese do, and fill in any gaps with stops at cafés, reserving evenings for relaxing over music or wine. On the third day, head for the world-famous **Spanische Reitschule** ㉖ and watch the Lipizzaners prance through morning training. While you're in the neighborhood, view the sparkling court jewels in the Imperial Treasury, the **Schatzkammer** ㊱, and the glitzy **Silberkammer** ㉜, the museum of court silver and tableware, and take in one of Vienna's most spectacular Baroque settings, the glorious Grand Hall of the **Hofbibliothek Prunksaal** ㉙. For a total contrast, head out to the Prater amusement park (☞ The Inner City, *below*) in late afternoon for a ride on the giant Ferris wheel and end the day in a wine restaurant on the out-skirts, such as Sievering or Nussdorf.

IF YOU HAVE 7 DAYS

Spend your first three days as outlined in the itinerary above. Then begin your fourth day getting better acquainted with the Fourth District—the heart of the city. Treasures here range from Roman ruins to the resi-dences of Mozart and Beethoven, the **Figarohaus** ㉝ and the **Pasqualati-haus** ⑲; then, slightly afield, the **Freud Apartment** ㉚ (in the Ninth District) or the oddball **Hundertwasserhaus** (in the Third, ☞ The Inner City, *below*). Put it all in contemporary perspective with a backstage tour of the magnificent **Staatsoper** ㉗, the opera house. For a country break on the fifth day, take a tour of the **Vienna Woods** (☞ Chapter 3) or the Danube Valley, particularly the glorious **Wachau district** (☞ Chapter 5), where vineyards sweep down to the river's edge. On the sixth day, fill in some of the blanks with a stroll around the **Naschmarkt** (☞ Pomp and Circumstance, *below*) food-market district, taking in the nearby **Secession Building** ㊟ with Gustav Klimt's famous Beethoven Frieze. Don't overlook the superb Jugendstil buildings on the north side of the market. If you're still game for museums, head for any one of the less usual offerings, such as the Jewish Museum, the Musical In-struments Museum, or the Ephesus Museum, in the **Hofburg** (☞ An Imperial City, *below*), or visit the city's historical museum, **Historisches Museum der Stadt Wien** ㉜; by now, you'll have acquired a good con-cept of the city and its background, so the exhibits will make more sense. Cap the day by visiting the **Kaisergruft** ㉟ in the Kapuzinerkirche to view the serried ranks of Habsburgs responsible for so much of Vienna.

The Inner City: Historic Heart of Vienna

A good way to break the ice on your introduction to Vienna is to get a general picture of its layout as presented to the cruising bird or airplane pilot. There are several beautiful vantage points from which you can look down and over the city—including the terrace of the Upper Belvedere Palace—but the city's preeminent lookout point, offering fine views in all directions, is gained from Stephansdom by toiling up the 345 steps of Alt Steffl (Old Stephen, its south tower) to the observation platform. The young and agile will make it up in 8 to 10 minutes; the slower-paced will make it in closer to 20. An elevator, and no exertion, will present you with much the same view from the terrace. From atop, you can see that St. Stephen's is the veritable hub of the city's wheel.

Most of Vienna lies roughly within an arc of a circle, with the straight line of the Danube as its chord. Its heart, the Innere Stadt (Inner City) or First District—in medieval times, the entire city of Vienna—is bounded by the Ringstrasse (Ring), which forms almost a circle, with a narrow arc cut off by the Danube Canal, diverted from the main river just above Vienna and flowing through the city to rejoin the parent stream just below it. The city spreads out from the Stephansdom, ac-cented by the series of magnificent buildings erected—beginning in the 1870s, when Vienna reached the zenith of its imperial prosperity—around the Ringstrasse: the Opera House, the National Art Gallery and the National Museum of Natural History, the "New Wing" of the Hof-burg, the House of Parliament, the Rathaus, the University, and the Votivkirche. For more than eight centuries, the enormous bulk of the cathedral has remained the nucleus around which the city has grown. The bird's-eye view can be left until the last day of your visit when the city's landmarks will be more familiar. First day or last, the vistas are memorable, especially if you catch them as the cathedral's famous *Pum-merin* (Boomer) bell is tolling.

A Good Walk

Stephansplatz, in the heart of the city, is the logical starting point from which to track down Vienna's past and present, as well as any acquaintance (natives believe that if you wait long enough at this intersection of eight streets you'll run into anyone you're searching for). Although it's now in what is mainly a pedestrian zone, **Stephansdom** ①, the mighty cathedral, marks the point from which distances to and from Vienna are measured. Visit the cathedral (it's quite impossible to view all its treasures, so just soak up its reflective Gothic spirit) and consider climbing its 345-step Alt Steffl tower or descending into its Habsburg crypt. Vienna of the Middle Ages is encapsulated in the streets in back of St. Stephen's Cathedral. You could easily spend half a day or more just prowling the narrow streets and passageways—Wollzeile, Bäckerstrasse, Blutgasse—typical remnants of an early era.

Wander up the Wollzeile, cutting through the narrow Essiggasse and right into the Bäckerstrasse, to the **Universitätskirche** ② or Jesuitenkirche, a lovely Jesuit church (the pink and green interior is topped by a trompe-l'oeil ceiling painted by Andrea Pozzo in 1705) where masses are sung in Latin on many Sunday mornings. Note the contrasting Academy of Science diagonally opposite (Beethoven premiered his Battle Symphony in its Ceremonial Hall). Follow the Sonnenfelsgasse, ducking through one of the tiny alleys on the right to reach the Bäckerstrasse; turn right at Gutenbergplatz into the Köllnerhofgasse, right again into tiny Grashofgasse, and go through the gate into the surprising **Heiligenkreuzerhof** ③, a peaceful oasis (unless a a handicrafts market is taking place). Through the square, enter the Schönlaterngasse (Beautiful Lantern Street) to admire the house fronts—film companies at times block this street to make shots in the picturesque atmosphere—on your way to the **Dominikanerkirche** ④, the Dominican church with its marvelous Baroque interior. As you follow Predigergasse and Falkestrasse, in back of the church is the architectural contrast of the **Postsparkasse** ⑤ and former War Ministry, facing each other. Retrace your steps, following Postgasse into **Fleischmarkt** ⑥. Nearby Hoher Markt, reached by taking Rotenturmstrasse west to Lichtensteg or Bauernmarkt, was part of the early Roman encampment, witness the **Roman ruins** under **Hoher Markt** ⑦. The extension of Fleischmarkt ends in a set of stairs leading up past the eccentric Kornhäusal Tower. Up the stairs to the right on Ruprechtsplatz is **Ruprechtskirche** ⑧, St. Rupert's Church, allegedly the city's oldest. Take Sterngasse down the steps, turn left into Marc Aurel-Strasse and right into Salvatorgasse to discover the lacework **Maria am Gestade** ⑨, Maria on the Banks, which once sat above a small river, now underground.

TIMING

If you're pressed for time and happy with facades rather than what's behind them, this route could take half a day, but if you love to look inside and stop to ponder and explore the myriad narrow alleys, figure at least a day for this walk. During services, wandering around the churches will be limited, but otherwise, you can tackle this walk about any time at your convenience.

Sights to See

❹ **Dominikanerkirche** (Dominican Church). The Postgasse, to the east of Schönlaterngasse, introduces an unexpected visitor from Rome: the Dominikanerkirche. Built in the 1630s, some 50 years before the Viennese Baroque building boom, its facade is modeled after any number of Roman churches of the 16th century. The interior illustrates why the Baroque style came to be considered the height of bad taste during the 19th century and still has many detractors today. "Sculpt till you drop" seems to have been the motto here, and the viewer's eye is given no respite. This sort of Roman architectural orgy never really gained a foothold in Vienna, and when the great Viennese architects did pull out all the decorative stops—Hildebrandt's interior at the Belvedere Palace, for instance—they did it in a very different style and with far greater success. ⊠ *Postg. 4,* ☎ *01/512–7460. U-Bahn: U3 Stubentor/Dr.- Karl-Lueger-Pl.*

❻ Fleischmarkt. Fleischmarkt and the picturesque tiny Griechengasse just beyond the glittering 19th-century Greek Orthodox church are part of the city's oldest core. This corner of the inner city has a medieval feel that is quite genuine; there has been a tavern at Fleischmarkt 11 for some 500 years. The wooden carving on the facade of the current Griechenbeisl restaurant commemorates Max Augustin—best known today from the song "Ach du lieber Augustin"—an itinerant musician who sang here during the plague of 1679.

NEED A BREAK?   Take a pause for coffee at the corner of Fleischmarkt and Wolfengasse, at the **Café Vienne** (⊠ Fleischmarkt 20), famous for baking what may be the biggest and most enticing cakes in the city.

❸ Heiligenkreuzerhof. Tiny side streets and alleys run off of Sonnenfelsgasse, parallel to Bäckerstrasse. Amid the narrow streets is Heiligenkreuzerhof (Holy Cross Court), one of the city's most peaceful backwaters. This complex of buildings dates from the 17th century but got an 18th-century face-lift. Appropriately, the restraint of the architecture—with only here and there a small outburst of Baroque spirit—gives the courtyard a distinct feeling of retreat. The square is a favorite site for seasonal markets at Easter and Christmas, and for occasional outdoor art shows.

❼ Hoher Markt. This square was badly damaged during World War II, but the famous Anker Clock at the east end survived the artillery fire. The huge mechanical timepiece took six years (1911–17) to build and still attracts crowds at noon when the full panoply of mechanical figures representing Austrian historical personages parades by. The figures are identified on a plaque to the bottom left of the clock. The graceless buildings erected around the square since 1945 are not aging well and do little to show off the square's lovely Baroque centerpiece, the St. Joseph Fountain (portraying the marriage of Joseph and Mary), designed in 1729 by Joseph Emanuel Fischer von Erlach, son of the great Johann Bernhard Fischer von Erlach. The Hoher Markt does harbor one wholly unexpected attraction, however: underground ☞ **Roman ruins.**

OFF THE BEATEN PATH   **HUNDERTWASSERHAUS** – To see one of Vienna's most amazing buildings, travel eastward from Schwendenplatz or Julius-Raab Platz along Radetzkystrasse to the junction of Kegelgasse and Löwengasse. Here, you'll find the Hundertwasserhaus, a 50-apartment public-housing complex designed by Friedensreich Hundertwasser, Austria's best-known living painter. The structure looks as though it was decorated by a crew of mischievous circus clowns wielding giant crayons. The building caused a sensation when it was erected in 1985 and still draws crowds of sightseers. ⊠ *Löweng. and Kegelg. U-Bahn: U1 or U4/Schwedenpl., then Streetcar N to Hetzgasse.*

KRIMINAL MUSEUM (CRIMINAL MUSEUM) – This might be the strangest museum in the city, and it is certainly the most macabre. The vast collection is entirely devoted to murder in Vienna of the most gruesome kind, with the most grisly displays contained appropriately in the cellar. Murderers and their victims are depicted in photos and newspaper clippings,

Vienna

TO PRATER

Schottenring
Gonzagag.
Zelinkag.
Esslingg.
Werdertorg.
Neutorg.
Heinrichsg.
Franz Josefs Kai
Obere Donaustrasse
Danube Canal
Hollandstrasse
Taborstr.
Praterstrasse

Rudolfs-pl.
Golsdorfg.
Salztorg.
Salztorbr.
Concordia-pl.
Salzgries
Fürberg.-Schwett.
Salvatorgasse
Sterng.
Marc-Aurel-Str.
Morzin-pl.

9

Wipplingerstr.
Judenpl.
Hoher
Judengasse
Raben Steig
Fleischmarkt
Marienbr.
Schwedenbr.

8

Schweden-pl.
Laurenzer-berg
Danube Canal
Franz Josefs Kai
Aspernbr.
Untere Donaustr.
Radetzkystr.
Julius-Raab-Pl.

10

11
Seitzerg.
Tuchlauben
Landskrong.
Bauernmkt.
Markt
Rotg.
Lugeck
Köllnerhof.
Sonnenfelsg.
Bäckerstr.
Schön laterng.
Postg.
Wiesingerstr.
Dominikanerbastei
Rosenbursenstr.
Biberstr.

7

6

3

2

5
Georg-Coch-Pl.

Brandstätte
Jasomirg.
Goldschm.g.
Graben
Rotenturmstr.
Stephanspl.
Wollzeile
Postg.

22

4

Hübs-burgerg.
Bräunerstr.
Stock-im-Eisen-Platz
Schulerstr.
Zedlitzg.
Dr. Karl Luegerpl.
Stubenring
Weiskch.

21

1

53
Domg.
Grünangerg.
Kumpfg.
Stubenbastei
Weiskch.str.
Vord. Zollamtsstr.
Landstrasser
Hint. Zollamtsstr.

52
Blutg.
Singerstr.
Riemerg.
Liebenbgg.

Bahnhof Wien-Mitte

Dorotheerg.
Spiegelg.
Plankeng.
Liftengg.
Rauhensteing.
Ballg.
Franziskaner-pl.

20

Neuer Markt
M. d' Avianog.
Himmelpfortg.
Seilerstätte
Weihburgg.

55

AE **54**

Central Air Terminal

Führ.-Teppichhof-richg.
Tegetthof-str.
Johannesg.
Scheffg.
Parkring
Landstrasser Hauptstrasse
Inzeildenstr.

Albertina-pl.
Ahnag.
Fichteg.
Krugerstr.
Hegelg.

i

57
Kärntnerstrasse
Walfischg.
Schwarzenbergstr.
Johannesg.
Stadtpark

Mahlerstr.
Opern Passage
Kärntner Ring
Schubertring
Lothringerstr.
Beatrixgasse
Rechte Bahngasse

Bösendorfer-str.
Akademie-str.

Musikverein

Karlsplatz

Schwarzenberg-pl.

Konzerthaus
Am Heumkt.
Salesianerg.

61

60
Argentinierstr.
Prinz Eugen-Str.
Rennweg

62

and many of the actual instruments used in the killings are displayed, with axes seeming to be the most popular. There are even skeletons and mummified heads, as well as several photo enlargements of victims at the scene of the murder. A visit here certainly gives a different perspective on life in this cultured, elegant city. Though the accompanying text is in German, you get the picture. The Criminal Museum is across the Danube Canal from Schwedenplatz, about a 15-minute walk from Ruprecht- skirche, the Hoher Markt, or the Heilegenkreuzerhof. ⊠ *Grosse Sperlg. 24,* ☎ *01/214–4678.* ☎ *AS60.* ☉ *Open Tues.–Sun. 10–5. Streetcar N from Schwedenplatz along Taborstrasse to Obere Augartenstrasse.*

KUNSTHAUS WIEN – Near the Hundertwasserhaus (☞ *above*) you'll find another Hundertwasser project, an art museum, which mounts outstand- ing international exhibits in addition to showings of the colorful Hundert- wasser works. Like the apartment complex nearby, the building itself is pure Hundertwasser, with irregular floors, windows with trees growing out of them, and sudden architectural surprises, a wholly appropriate setting for modern art. ⊠ *Untere Weissgerberstr. 13,* ☎ *01/712– 0491–0,* ☎ *AS60.* ☉ *Daily 10–7. U-Bahn: U1 or U4/Schwedenpl., then Streetcar N to Radetzkypl.*

❾ Maria am Gestade (St. Mary on the Banks). The middle-Gothic, seven-sided tower of Maria am Gestade, crowned by a delicate cupola, is a sheer joy to the eye and dispels the idea that Gothic must necessarily be austere. Built around 1400 (but much restored in the 17th and 19th centuries), the church incorporated part of the Roman city walls into its foundation; the north wall, as a result, takes a slight but noticeable dogleg to the right halfway down the nave. Like St. Stephen's, Maria am Gestade is rough-hewn Gothic, with a simple but forceful facade. The church is especially beloved, however, because of its unusual de-tails—the pinnacled and saint-bedecked gable that tops the front fa-cade, the stone canopy that hovers protectively over the front door, and (most appealing of all) the intricate openwork lantern atop the south-side bell tower. Appropriately enough in a city famous for its pastry, the lantern lends its tower an engaging suggestion of a sugar caster, while some see an allusion to hands intertwined in prayer. ⊠ *Passauer Pl./Salvatorg. U-Bahn: U1, U3 Stephansplatz.*

❺ Postsparkasse (Post Office Savings Bank). The Post Office Savings Bank is one of modern architecture's greatest curiosities. It was designed in 1904 by Otto Wagner, whom many consider the father of 20th-cen-tury architecture. In his famous manifesto, *Modern Architecture,* Wag-ner condemned 19th-century revivalist architecture and pleaded for a modern style that honestly expressed modern building methods. Ac-cordingly, the exterior walls of the Post Office Savings Bank are mostly flat and undecorated; visual interest is supplied merely by varying the pattern of the bolts that were used to hold the marble slabs in place on the wall surface during construction. Later architects were to em-brace Wagner's beliefs wholeheartedly, although they used different, truly modern building materials: glass and concrete rather than mar-ble. The Post Office Savings Bank was indeed a bold leap into the fu-ture, but unfortunately the future took a different path and today the whole appears a bit dated. Go inside for a look at the restored and func-tioning Kassa-Saal, or central cashier's hall, to see how Wagner car-ried his concepts over to interior design. ⊠ *Georg-Coch-Pl. 2,* ☎ *01/ 51400.* ☉ *Lobby weekdays 8–3.*

OFF THE   **PRATER** – Vienna's most famous park and most beloved attraction for
BEATEN PATH   children can be found by heading out northeast from the historic city
               center, across the Danube Canal along Praterstrasse: the famous Prater,

the city's foremost amusement park. In 1766, to the dismay of the aristocracy, Emperor Joseph II decreed that the vast expanse of imperial parklands known as the Prater would henceforth be open to the public. East of the inner city between the Danube Canal and the Danube proper, the Prater is a public park to this day, notable for its long promenade (the Hauptallee, more than 4½ km/3 mi in length); its sports facilities (a golf course, a stadium, a racetrack, and a swimming pool, for starters); the landmark giant Ferris wheel (Riesenrad); the traditional, modern amusement-park rides; a number of less-innocent indoor, sex-oriented attractions; a planetarium; and a small but interesting museum devoted to the Prater's long history. If you look carefully, you can discover a handful of children's rides dating to the 1920s and '30s that survived the fire that consumed most of the Volksprater in 1945. The best-known attraction is the 200-ft Ferris wheel that figured so prominently in the 1949 film *The Third Man*. One of three built in Europe at the end of the last century (the others were in England and France but have long since been dismantled), the wheel was badly damaged during World War II and restored shortly thereafter. Its progress is slow and stately (a revolution takes 10 minutes), the views from its cars magnificent, particularly toward dusk. Try to eat at the famous Schweizerhaus (☒ Strasse des 1 Mai, 116, ☎ 01/728–0152), which has been serving frosty mugs of beer, roast chicken and *Stelze* (a huge hunk of crispy roast pork on the bone) for more than 100 years. Its informal setting with wooden plank tables indoors or in the garden in summer adds to the fun. Credit cards are not accepted. ☒ *Park free, Riesenrad AS45.* ☉ *Apr., daily 10 AM– 11 PM; May–Sept., daily 9 AM–midnight; Oct., daily 10–10; Nov., daily 10–8; Dec., weekends 10–6. U-Bahn: U1/Praterstern.*

Roman ruins. The ruins are under the ☞ Hoher Markt, on what was once the main east–west axis of the Roman encampment of Vindobona, and the foundations of several officers' houses built in the 2nd century have been uncovered. The officers lived well: Their houses even had central heating, and you can see the pipes that carried the hot water. The excavations are entered through the sushi snack bar in the passageway at No. 3; a short, descriptive pamphlet in English is available at the ticket table. ☒ *Hoher Markt/Fischhof 3,* ☎ *01/535–5606.* ☒ *AS25.* ☉ *Tues.–Sun. 9–12:15 and 1–4:30. U-Bahn: U1, U3 Stephansplatz.*

❽ Ruprechtskirche (St. Ruprecht's Church). Ruprechtsplatz, another of Vienna's time-warp backwaters, lies to the north of the Kornhäusel Tower. The church in the middle, Ruprechtskirche, is the city's oldest. According to legend it was founded in 740; the oldest part of the present structure (the lower half of the tower) dates from the 11th century. Set on the ancient ramparts overlooking the Danube Canal, it is serene and unpretentious. Try the one door, though it's usually locked. You can look in through the grill, but the lack of windows generally obscures what can be seen of the arcaded, unadorned interior. ☒ *Ruprechtspl. U-Bahn: U1, U4 Schwedenpl.*

Schönlaterngasse (Beautiful Lantern Street). Once part of Vienna's medieval Latin Quarter, Schönlaterngasse is rapidly becoming so again. Among the street's Baroque houses (note the colorfully painted facades) and chic shops you'll find the house known as the **Basiliskenhaus** (House of the Basilik, ☒ Schönlaterng. 7). According to legend, it was first built for a baker; on June 26, 1212, a foul-smelling basilisk (half-rooster, half-toad, with a glance that could kill) took up residence in the courtyard well, poisoning the water. An enterprising apprentice dealt with the problem by climbing down the well armed with a mirror; when the basilisk saw its own reflection, it turned to stone. The petrified creature can still be seen in a niche on the building's facade. Today, modern science accounts for the contamination with a more prosaic explanation: natural-gas seepage. Be sure to take a look in the house's miniature courtyard for a trip back to medieval Vienna (the house itself is private). The picturesque street is named for the ornate wrought-iron wall lantern at Schönlaterngasse 6. Just a few steps from the Basilikenhaus, take a look into the Baroque courtyard at Schönlaterngasse 8—one of the city's prettiest. A blacksmith workshop, **Alte Schmiede** (Old Smithy, ✉ Schönlaterng. 9), is now a museum.

❶ Stephansdom (St. Stephen's Cathedral). This soaring structure enshrines the heart of Vienna, although it is curious to note that in its earliest days, as the parish church which was built in the years 1144–47, it stood outside the walls of the city. Vienna can thank a period of hard times for the Mother Church for the distinctive silhouette of the cathedral. Originally the structure was to have had matching 445-ft-high spires, a standard design of the era, but funds ran out, and the north tower to this day remains a happy reminder of what gloriously is not. The lack of symmetry creates an imbalance that makes the cathedral instantly identifiable from its profile alone. The cathedral, as well as the Staastoper and some other major buildings, were very heavily damaged in World War II. Since then, it has risen from the fires of destruction like a phoenix, and like the phoenix, it is a symbol of regeneration.

It is difficult now, sitting quietly in the shadowed peace, to tell what was original and what parts of the walls and vaults were reconstructed. No matter: Its history-rich atmosphere is dear to all Viennese. That noted, St. Stephen's possesses a fierce presence that is blatantly un-Viennese. It is a stylistic jumble ranging from 13th-century Romanesque to 15th-century Gothic. Like the exterior, St. Stephen's interior lacks the soaring unity of Europe's greatest Gothic cathedrals, with much of its decoration dating from the later Baroque era.

The wealth of decorative sculpture in St. Stephen's can be demoralizing to the nonspecialist, so if you wish to explore the cathedral in detail, you may want to buy the admirably complete English-language description sold in the small room marked Schriften und Opferkerzen (Pamphlets and Votive Candles). One particularly masterly work, however, should be seen by everyone: the stone pulpit attached to the second freestanding pier on the left of the central nave, carved by Anton Pilgram around 1510. The delicacy of its decoration would in itself set the pulpit apart, but even more intriguing are its five sculpted figures. Carved around the outside of the pulpit proper are the four Latin Fathers of the Church (from left to right: St. Augustine, St. Gregory, St. Jerome, and St. Ambrose), and each is given an individual personality so sharply carved as to suggest satire, perhaps of living models. There is no satire suggested by the fifth figure, however; below the pulpit's stairs Pilgram sculpted a fine self-portrait, showing himself peering out a half-open window. Note the toads, lizards, and other creatures climbing the spiral rail alongside the steps up to the pulpit. As you walk among the statues and aisles, remember that many notable events occurred here, including the marriage of Mozart in 1782 and his funeral in December 1791.

St. Stephen's was devastated by fire in the last days of World War II, and the extent of the damage may be seen by leaving the cathedral through the south portal, where a set of preconstruction photographs commemorates the disaster. Restoration was protracted and difficult, but today the cathedral once again dominates the center of the city. Note the "05" carved into the stone to the right of the outer massive front door. The "0" stands for Österreich, or Austria, and the "5" is for the fifth letter of the alphabet. This translates into OE, the abbre-

MOZART

WOLFGANG AMADEUS Mozart (1756–91) bequeathed the world incomparable musical riches, and no devotee would want to pass up a trip to his native Austria. Certainly, it's easy to find the places he lived in or visited, all carefully restored or marked by memorial plaques. But a knowledge of his troubled relations with his homeland makes the experience a poignant one.

From the beginning of Wolfgang's precocious career, his father, frustrated in his own musical ambitions at the Archbishopric in Salzburg, looked beyond the boundaries of the Austro-Hungarian Empire to promote the boy's fame. At the age of six, he was presented to the royal courts of Europe and caused a sensation with his skills as an instrumentalist and impromptu composer.

As he grew up, however, his virtuosity lost its power to amaze and he was forced to make his way as an "ordinary" musician, which then meant finding a position at court. In this he was not much more successful than his father had been, in spite of what would seem to be the decisive advantage of genius. In Salzburg he was never able to rise beyond the level of organist (allowing him, as he noted with sarcastic pride, to sit above the cooks at table), and his attempts to have his compositions performed were rebuffed.

In disgust, he severed his ties with the Archbishop and tried his luck in Vienna, where despite the popularity of his operas and the admiration of his peers (Joseph Haydn early recognized him as the greatest composer of the time) he was able to obtain only an unpaid appointment as assistant Kapellmeister at St. Stephen's months before his death.

By then he had been invited by friends to come to London (where Haydn later made a fortune), and subscriptions had been taken up in Hungary and the Netherlands that would have paid him handsomely. But it was too late. Whatever the truth of the theories still swirling around his untimely death, the fact remains that not only was he not given the state funeral he deserved, but he was buried in an unmarked grave after a hasty, sparsely attended funeral.

If one is inclined to accuse Mozart's fellow countrymen of neglect, they would seem to have made up for it with a vengeance. The visitor to Vienna and Salzburg can hardly ignore the barrage of Mozart candies, wine, beer, coffee mugs, T-shirts, baseball caps—not to mention the gilded statues that make do for a nonexistent monumental tomb. Indeed, he has become a thriving brand-name industry and one of the centerpieces of Austrian tourism.

And Mozart, always one to appreciate a joke, even at his own expense, would surely see the irony in the belated veneration.

— Gary Dodson

viation for Österreich, and was a covert sign of resistance to the Nazi annexation of Austria. The bird's-eye views from the cathedral's beloved **Alte Steffl** tower will be a highlight for some. The tower is 450 ft high and was built between 1359 and 1433. The climb or elevator ride up is rewarded with vistas that extend to the rising slopes of the Wienerwald. ⊠ *Stephanspl.,* ☎ *01/515–52–526.* ⌦ *Each tour AS40, elevator AS40.* ⊙ *Daily 6 AM–10 PM. Tour Mon.–Sat. at 10:30 and 3, Sun. at 3; evening tour July–Aug., daily at 7; catacombs tour Mon.–Sat. at 10, 11, 11:30, 2, 2:30, 3:30, 4, and 4:30, Sun. at 2, 2:30, 3:30, 4, and 4:30; North Tower elevator to Pummerin bell Apr.–Sept., daily 9–6, and Oct.–Mar., daily 8–5. U-Bahn: U1, U3 Stephanspl.*

<table>
<tr><td>NEED A
BREAK?</td><td>If you're in the mood for ice cream, head for Zanoni & Zanoni (⊠ Am Lugeck 7, ☎ 01/7979) near St. Stephen's between Rotenturmstrasse and Bäckerstrasse and open 365 days a year. Here you'll have trouble choosing from among 25 or more flavors of smooth, Italian-style gelato, including mango, caramel, and chocolate chip. There are also tables for those who want to rest their feet and enjoy a sundae.</td></tr>
</table>

② **Universitätskirche** (Jesuit Church). The east end of Bäckerstrasse is punctuated by Dr.-Ignaz-Seipel-Platz, named for the theology professor who was chancellor of Austria during the 1920s. On the north side is the Universitätskirche, or Jesuitenkirche, built around 1630. Its flamboyant Baroque interior contains a fine trompe-l'oeil ceiling fresco by that master of visual trickery Andrea Pozzo, who was imported from Rome in 1702 for the job. You may hear a Mozart or Haydn mass sung here in Latin on many Sundays. ⊠ *Dr.-Ignaz-Seipl-Pl.,* ☎ *01/512–1335–0. U-Bahn: U3 Stubentor/Dr.-Karl-Lueger-Pl.*

Bittersweet Vienna: Baroque Gems and Cozy Cafés

As the city developed and expanded, the core quickly outgrew its early confines. New urban centers sprang up, to be ornamented by government buildings and elegant town residences. Since Vienna was the beating heart of a vast empire, nothing was spared to make the edifices as exuberant as possible, with utility often a secondary consideration. The best architects of the day were commissioned to create impressions as well as buildings, and they did their job well. That so much has survived is a testimony to the solidness both of the designs and of the structures on which the ornamentation has been overlayed.

Those not fortunate enough to afford town palaces were relegated to housing that was often confining and far less than elegant. Rather than suffer the discomfitures of a disruptive household environment, the city's literati and its philosophers and artists took refuge in cafés, which in effect became their combined salons and offices. To this day, cafés remain an important element of Viennese life. Many residents still have their *Stammtisch,* or regular table, at which they appear daily. Talk still prevails—but increasingly so do handy radio telephones and even laptops.

A Good Walk

Start in the Wipplingerstrasse at the upper (west) end of Hoher Markt to find touches of both the imperial and the municipal Vienna. On the east side is the **Altes Rathaus,** which served as the City Hall until 1885; on the west, the **Bohemian Court Chancery** ⑩, once diplomatic headquarters for Bohemia's representation to the Habsburg court. Turn south into the short Fütterergasse to reach **Judenplatz,** in the Middle Ages the center of Judaism in Vienna. A clockwatcher's delight is down at the end of Kurrentgasse in the form of the **Uhrenmuseum** (Clock Museum); around the corner through the Parisgasse to Schulhof, a children's delight is the **Puppen- und Spielzeug-Museum** (Doll and Toy Museum). Follow Schulhof into the huge **Am Hof** square, boasting the **Kirche am Hof** ⑪ and what must be the world's most elegant fire station. The square hosts an antiques and collectibles market most of the year on Thursdays and Friday, plus other ad hoc events. Take the miniscule Irisgasse from Am Hof into the Naglergasse, noting the mosaic Jugendstil facade on the pharmacy in the Bognergasse, to your left. Around a bend in the narrow Naglergasse is the **Freyung,** an irregular square bounded on the south side by two wonderfully stylish palaces, including **Palais Ferstel** ⑫, now a shopping arcade, and the elegantly restored **Palais Harrach** next door, now an outpost of the Kunsthistoriches Museum. Opposite, the privately run **Kunstforum** art museum mounts varied and outstanding exhibitions. The famous **Kinsky Palace** ⑬ at the beginning of Herrengasse is still partly a private residence. The north side of the Freyung is watched over by the **Schottenkirche** ⑭, a Scottish church that was, in fact, established by Irish monks. The complex also houses a small but worthwhile museum of the order's treasures. Follow Teinfaltstrasse from opposite the Schottenkirche, turning right into Schreyvogelgasse. Climb the ramp on your right past the so-called Dreimäderlhaus at Schreyvogelgasse 10—note the ornate facade of this pre-Biedermeier patrician house—to reach Molker Bastei, where Beethoven lived in the **Pasqualatihaus** ⑮, now housing a museum memorializing the composer. Follow the ring south to Löwelstrasse, turning left into Bankgasse; then turn right into Abraham-a-Santa Clara-Gasse (the tiny street that runs off the Bankgasse) to Minoritenplatz and the **Minoritenkirche** ⑯, the Minorite Church, with its odd, hat-less tower. Inside is a kitschy mosaic *Last Supper*. Landhausgasse will bring you to Herrengasse, and diagonally across the street, in the back corner of the Palais Ferstel, is the **Café Central** ⑰, one of Vienna's hangouts for the famous. As you go south up the Herrengasse, on the left is the odd Hochhaus, a 20th-century building once noted as Vienna's skyscraper. Opposite are elegant Baroque former town palaces, now used as museum and administration buildings by the province of Lower Austria.

TIMING

The actual distances in this walk are relatively short, and you could cover the route in 1½ hours or so. But if you take time to linger in the museums and sample a coffee with whipped cream in the Café Central, you'll develop a much better understanding of the contrasts between old and newer in the city. You could easily spend a day following this walk, if you were to take in all of the museums; note that these, like many other Viennese museums, are closed on Mondays.

Sights to See

Altes Rathaus (Old City Hall). Opposite the Bohemian Chancery (☞ *below*) stands the Altes Rathaus, dating from the 14th century but sporting 18th-century Baroque motifs on its facade. The interior passageways and courtyards, which are open during the day, house a Gothic chapel (open at odd hours); a much-loved, Baroque wall-fountain (Georg Raphael Donner's **Andromeda Fountain** of 1741); and display cases exhibiting maps and photos illustrating the city's history.

Am Hof. Am Hof is one of the city's oldest squares. In the Middle Ages the ruling Babenberg family built their castle on the site of No. 2; hence the name of the square, which means simply "at court" The grand residence hosted such luminaries as Barbarossa and Walter vonder Vogelweide, the famous Minnesinger who features in Wagner's *Tannhauser.* The Baroque **Column of Our Lady** in the center dates from 1667, marking the Catholic victory over the Swedish Protestants in the Thirty Years' War (1618–48). The onetime **Civic Armory** at the northwest corner

has been used as a fire station since 1685 (the high-spirited facade, with
its Habsburg eagle, was "Baroqued" in 1731) and today houses the
headquarters of Vienna's fire department. The complex includes a
firefighting museum (open only on Sunday mornings). Presiding over
the east side of the square is the noted Kirche Am Hof (☞ *below*). In
Bognergasse to the right of the Kirche Am Hof, around the corner from
the imposing Bank Austria headquarters building, at No. 9, is the
Engel Pharmacy, with a Jugendstil mosaic depicting winged women col-
lecting the elixir of life in outstretched chalices. At the turn of the century the inner city was dotted with storefronts decorated in a similar
manner; today this is the sole survivor. Around the bend from the Naglergasse is the picturesque Freyung square (☞ *below*).

⑩ Bohemian Court Chancery. One of the architectural jewels of the Inner
City can be found at Wipplingerstrasse 7, the former Bohemian Court
Chancery, built between 1708 and 1714 by Johann Bernhard Fischer von
Erlach. Fischer von Erlach and his contemporary Johann Lukas von Hildebrandt were the reigning architectural geniuses of Baroque Vienna; they
designed their churches and palaces during the building boom that followed the defeat of the Turks in 1683. Both had studied architecture in
Rome, and both were deeply impressed by the work of the great Italian
architect Francesco Borromini, who had brought to his designs a wealth
and freedom of invention that were looked upon with horror by most
contemporary Romans. But for Fischer von Erlach and Hildebrandt, Borromini's ideas were a source of triumphant architectural inspiration, and
when they returned to Vienna they produced between them many of the
city's most beautiful buildings. Alas, narrow Wipplingerstrasse allows
little more than a oblique view of this florid facade. The back side of the
building, on Judenplatz, is less elaborate but gives a better idea of the
design concept. The building first served as diplomatic and representational offices of Bohemia (now a part of the Czech Republic) to the Vi-
enna-based monarchy and, today, still houses government offices.

⑰ Café Central. Part of the ☞ **Palais Ferstel** complex, the Café Central
is one of Vienna's more famous cafés, its full authenticity blemished
only by complete restoration in recent years. In its prime (before World
War I), the café was "home" to some of the most famous literary figures of the day, who ate, socialized, worked, and even received mail
here. The denizens of the Central favored political argument; indeed,
their heated discussions became so well known that in October 1917,
when Austria's foreign secretary was informed of the outbreak of the
Russian Revolution, he dismissed the report with a facetious reference
to a well-known local Marxist, the chess-loving (and presumably
harmless) "Herr Bronstein from the Café Central." The remark was
to become famous all over Austria, for Herr Bronstein had disappeared and was about to resurface in Russia bearing a new name: Leon
Trotsky. No matter how crowded the café may become, you can linger
as long as you like over a single cup of coffee and a newspaper from
the huge international selection provided. Across the street at Herrengasse
17 is the **Café Central Konditorei,** an excellent pastry and confectionery
shop associated with the café. ⊠ *Herreng. 14,* ☎ *01/533–3763. AE,
DC, MC, V. Closed Sun. U-Bahn: U3 Herrengasse.*

The Freyung. Naglergasse, at its curved end, flows into Heidenschuss,
which in turn leads down a slight incline from Am Hof to one of Vienna's most prominent squares, the Freyung, meaning "freeing." The
square was so named because for many centuries the monks at the adjacent Schottenhof (☞ *below*) possessed the privilege of offering sanctuary for three days. In the center of the square stands the allegorical
Austria Fountain (1845), notable because its Bavarian designer, one

Ludwig Schwanthaler, had the statues cast in Munich and then supposedly filled them with cigars to be smuggled into Vienna for black-market sale. Around the sides of the square are some of Vienna's greatest patrician residences, including the Ferstel, Harrach, and Kinsky palaces (☞ *below*).

Judenplatz. From the 13th to the 15th century, Judenplatz—off Wipplingerstrasse—was the center of Vienna's Jewish ghetto. Today the square's centerpiece is a rectangular block intended as a Holocaust memorial; the architect's concept was a stylized stack of books to recall Jewish strivings toward learning. Nearby is a statue of the 18th-century Jewish playwright Gotthold Ephraim Lessing, erected after World War II.

⓭ **Kinsky Palace.** Just one of the architectural treasures that comprise the urban set piece of the Freyung (☞ *above*), the Palais Kinsky is the square's best-known palace, one of the most sophisticated pieces of Baroque architecture in the city. Located at Freyung 4, it was built between 1713 and 1716 by Hildebrandt. Its only real competition comes a few yards farther on: the Greek temple facade of the Schottenhof (☞ *below*), which is at right angles to the Schottenkirche, up the street from the Kinsky Palace.

⓫ **Kirche Am Hof.** On the east side of the Am Hof square, the Kirche Am Hof, or the Church of the Nine Choirs of Angels, is identified by its sprawling Baroque facade, designed by Carlo Carlone in 1662. The somber interior lacks appeal, but the checkerboard marble floor may remind you of Dutch churches. ⊠ *Am Hof 1. U-Bahn: U3 Herrengasse.*

Kunstforum. The huge gold ball atop the doorway on the Freyung at the corner of Renngasse marks the entrance to the Kunstforum, an extensive art gallery run by Bank Austria featuring outstanding temporary exhibitions. ⊠ *Freyung 8,* ☎ *01/711–91–5742.* ☜ *AS90.* ☻ *Thurs.–Tues. 10–6, Wed. 10–9. U-Bahn: U3 Herrengasse.*

⓰ **Minoritenkirche** (Church of the Minorite Order). The Minoritenplatz is named after its centerpiece, the Minoritenkirche, a Gothic affair with a strange stump of a tower, built mostly in the 14th century. The front is brutally ugly, but the back is a wonderful, if predominantly 19th-century, surprise. The interior contains the city's most imposing piece of kitsch: a large mosaic reproduction of Leonardo da Vinci's *Last Supper,* commissioned by Napoléon in 1806 and later purchased by Emperor Francis I. ⊠ *Minoritenpl. 2A,* ☎ *01/533–4162. U-Bahn: U3 Herrengasse.*

⓬ **Palais Ferstel.** At Freyung 2 stands the recently restored Palais Ferstel, which is not a palace at all but a commercial shop-and-office complex designed in 1856 and named for its architect, Heinrich Ferstel. The facade is Italianate in style, harking back, in its 19th-century way, to the Florentine palazzi of the early Renaissance. The interior is unashamedly eclectic: vaguely Romanesque in feel and Gothic in decoration, with here and there a bit of Renaissance or Baroque sculpted detail thrown in for good measure. Such eclecticism is sometimes dismissed as mindlessly derivative, but here the architectural details are so respectfully and inventively combined that the interior becomes a pleasure to explore. The 19th-century stock-exchange rooms upstairs are now gloriously restored and used for conferences and concerts. ⊠ *Freyung 2.*

Palais Harrach. Next door to the Palais Ferstel (☞ *above*) is the newly renovated Palais Harrach, part of which now houses a small but worthwhile gallery of paintings and art objects from the main Kunsthistorisches Museum (which has far more treasures than space in which to display them) as well as special exhibits. ⊠ *Freyung 3,* ☎ *01/533–7811.* ☜ *AS90.* ☻ *Wed.–Mon. 10–6.*

⑮ Pasqualatihaus. Beethoven lived in the Pasqualatihaus while he was composing his only opera, *Fidelio,* as well as his Seventh Symphony and Fourth Piano Concerto. Today his apartment houses a small commemorative museum (in distressingly modern style). After navigating the narrow and twisting stairway, you might well ask how he maintained the jubilant spirit of the works he wrote there. This house is around the corner from the *Third Man* Portal (☞ *below*). ⊠ *8 Mölker Bastei,* ☎ *01/535–8905.* ⊡ *AS25.* ۞ *Tues.–Sun. 9–12:15 and 1–4:30. U-Bahn: U2 Schottentor.*

🐾 **Puppen und Spielzeugmuseum** (Doll and Toy Museum). As appealing as the clockworks of the Uhrenmuseum located just next door is this doll and toy museum, with its collections of dolls, dollhouses, teddies, and trains. ⊠ *Schulhof 4,* ☎ *01/535–6860.* ⊡ *AS60.* ۞ *Tues.–Sun. 10–6. U-Bahn: U1, U3 Stephansplatz.*

Schottenhof. Found on the Freyung square (☞ *above*) and designed by Joseph Kornhäusel in a very different style from his Fleischmarkt tower, the Schottenhof is a shaded courtyard. The facade typifies the change that came over Viennese architecture during the Biedermeier era (1815–48). The Viennese, according to the traditional view, were at the time so relieved to be rid of the upheavals of the Napoléonic Wars that they accepted without protest the ironhanded repression of Prince Metternich, chancellor of Austria, and retreated into a cozy and complacent domesticity. Restraint also ruled in architecture, with Baroque license rejected in favor of a new and historically "correct" style that was far more controlled and reserved. Kornhäusel led the way in Vienna; his Schottenhof facade is all sober organization and frank repetition. But in its marriage of strong and delicate forces it still pulls off the great Viennese-waltz trick of successfully merging seemingly antithetical characteristics. *U-Bahn: U2 Schottentor.*

NEED A BREAK?   In summer, **Wienerwald** restaurant, in the tree-shaded courtyard of the Schottenhof (☞ *above*), is ideal for relaxing over lunch, coffee, or a glass of wine.

⑭ Schottenkirche. In 1758–61 the famous Italian painter Canaletto did paintings of the Freyung square (☞ *above*) looking north toward the Schottenkirche; the pictures hang in the Kunsthistorisches Museum, and the similarity to the view you see about 240 years later is arresting. In fact, a church has stood on the site of the Schottenkirche since 1177; the present edifice dates to the mid-1600s, when it replaced its predecessor, which had collapsed after the architects of the time had built on weakened foundations. The interior, with its ornate ceiling and a decided surplus of cherubs and angels' faces, is in stark contrast to the plain exterior. The adjacent small **Museum im Schottenstift** includes the best of the monastery's artworks, including the celebrated late-Gothic high altar, dating to about 1470. The winged altar is fascinating for its portrayal of the Holy Family in flight into Egypt—with Vienna clearly identifiable in the background. ⊠ *Freyung 6,* ☎ *01/534980.* ⊡ *Church free, museum AS40, special exhibits AS50.* ۞ *Church Thurs.–Sat. 10–5, Sun. noon–5; museum Tues.–Sun. 10–6. U-Bahn: U2 Schottentor.*

Third Man Portal. The doorway at Schreyvogelgasse 8 (up the incline) was made famous in 1949 by the classic film *The Third Man* (☞ Close-up box, *below*); it was here that Orson Welles, as the malevolently knowing Harry Lime, stood hiding in the dark, only to have his smiling face illuminated by a sudden light from the upper-story windows of the house across the alley. The film enjoys a renaissance each summer in the Burg Kino and is fascinating for its portrayal of a post-

THE THIRD MAN

PROBABLY NOTHING HAS done more to create the myth of postwar Vienna than Carol Reed's classic 1949 film, *The Third Man*. The bombed-out ruins of this proud, imperial city created an indelible image of devastation and corruption in the war's aftermath. Vienna was then divided into four sectors, each commanded by one of the victorious American, Russian, French, and British armies. But their attempts at rigid control could not prevent a thriving black market.

In the film, Joseph Cotten plays Holly Martins, a pulp-fiction writer who comes to Vienna in search of his friend, Harry Lime (Orson Welles). He makes the mistake of delving too deeply in Lime's affairs, even falling in love with his girlfriend, Anna Schmidt (Alida Valli), with fatal consequences.

Many of the sites where the film was shot still remain and are easily visited. Harry Lime appears for the first time nearly one hour into the film in the doorway of Anna's apartment building at No. 8 Schreyvogelgasse, around the corner from the Mölker-Bastei (a remnant of the old city wall). He then runs to Am Hof, a lovely square lined with Baroque town houses and churches, which appears much closer to Anna's neighborhood than it actually is.

The famous scene between Lime and Martins on the Ferris wheel was filmed on the Riesenrad at the Prater, the huge amusement park across the Danube canal. While the two friends talk in the enclosed compartment, the wheel slowly makes a revolution, with all Vienna spread out below them.

In the memorable chase at the end of the movie, Lime is seen running through the damp, sinister sewers of Vienna, hotly pursued by the authorities. In reality, he would not have been able to use the sewer system as an escape route because the tunnels were too low and didn't connect between the different centers of the city. But a movie creates its own reality. In fact, a more feasible, if less cinematic, possibility of escape was offered by the labyrinth of cellars that still connected many buildings in the city.

Lime's funeral is held at the Zentralfriedhof (Central Cemetery), reachable by the 71 streetcar. This is the final scene of the movie, where Anna Schmidt walks down the stark, wide avenue (dividing sections 69 and 70), refusing to acknowledge the wistful presence of Holly Martins.

After touring sewers and cemeteries, a pick-me-up might be in order. You couldn't do better than to treat yourself to a stop at the Hotel Sacher, used for a scene in the beginning of the movie when Holly Martins is using the telephone in the lobby. The bar in the Sacher was a favorite hangout of director Carol Reed, and when filming finally wrapped, he left a signed note to the bartender, saying: "To the creator of the best Bloody Marys in the whole world."

— Bonnie Dodson

war Vienna still in ruins. To get here from the nearby and noted Schot-tenkirche (☞ *above*), follow Teinfaltstrasse one block west to Schreyvo-gelgasse on the right.

Uhrenmuseum (Clock Museum). Kurrentgasse leads south from the east end of Judenplatz; the beautifully restored 18th-century houses on its east side make this one of the most unpretentiously appealing streets in the city. And at the far end of the street is one of Vienna's most ap-pealing museums: the Uhrenmuseum, or Clock Museum (enter to the right on the Schulhof side of the building). The museum's three floors display a splendid array of clocks and watches—more than 3,000 timepieces—dating from the 15th century to the present. The ruckus of bells and chimes on any hour is impressive, but try to be here at noon for the full cacophony. Right next door is the Puppen und Spielzeug-museum (☞ *above*). ⊠ *Schulhof 2,* ☎ *01/533–2265.* ☜ *AS50.* ☉ *Tues.– Sun. 9–4:30. U-Bahn: U1, U3 Stephansplatz.*

Vienna's Shop Window: From Michaelerplatz to the Graben

The compact area bounded roughly by the back side of the Hofburg palace complex, the Kohlmarkt, the Graben, and Kärntnerstrasse be-longs to the oldest core of the city. Remains of the Roman city are just below the present-day surface. This was and still is the commercial heart of the city, with shops and markets for various commodities; today, the Kohlmarkt and Graben in particular offer the choicest luxury shops, overflowing into the Graben end of Kärnter Strasse. The area is marvelous for its visual treats, ranging from the squares and varied architecture to shop windows. The evening view down Kohlmarkt from the Graben is an inspiring classic, with the night-lit gilded dome of Michael's Gate to the palace complex as the glittering backdrop.

A Good Walk

Start your walk through this fascinating quarter at **Michaelerplatz** ⑱, one of Vienna's most evocative squares, where the feel of the imperial city remains very strong; the buildings around the perimeter present a synopsis of the city's entire architectural history: medieval church spire, Renaissance church facade, Baroque palace facade, 19th-century apartment house, and 20th-century bank. Look in on Michaelerkirche (St. Michael's Church). Opposite the church is the once-controversial **Looshaus** ⑲, considered a breakthrough in modern architecture (visi-tors are welcome to view the restored lobby). From Michaelerplatz, take the small passageway to the right of the church; in it on your right is a relief dating to 1480 of Christ on the Mount of Olives. Follow the Stallburggasse through to Dorotheergasse, and turn right to discover the **Dorotheum,** the government-run auction house and the Vienna equiv-alent of Christie's or Sotheby's. On your right in the Dorotheergasse (toward the Graben) is the enlarged **Jewish Museum** ⑳, which in-cludes a bookstore and café. On the left is the famous Café Hawelka, home to the contemporary art and literature crowd. Turn right in the Graben to come to **Stock-im-Eisen** ㉑; the famous nail-studded tree trunk is encased in the corner of the building with the Bank Austria offices. Opposite and impossible to overlook is the aggressive **Neues Haas-Haus,** an upmarket restaurant and shopping complex. Wander back through the **Graben** for the full effect of this harmonious street and look up to see the ornamentation on the buildings. Pass the **Pest-säule** (Plague Column), which shoots up from the middle of the Graben like a geyser of whipped cream. Just off to the north side is **Peterskirche** ㉒, St. Peter's Church, a Baroque gem almost hidden by its surroundings. At the end of the Graben, turn left into the **Kohlmarkt** ㉓ for the classic view of the domed arch leading to the Hofburg, the imperial palace complex. Even if your feet aren't calling a sit-down strike, finish up at **Demel** ㉔, at Kohlmarkt 14, with some of the best *patisseries* in the world.

TIMING

Inveterate shoppers, window or otherwise, will want to take time to pause before or in many of the elegant shops during this walk, which then could easily take most of a day or even longer. If you're content with facades and general impressions, the exercise could be done in a bit over an hour, but it would be a shame to bypass the narrow side streets. In any case, look into St. Michael's and consider the fascinating Dorotheum, itself easily worth an hour or more.

Sights to See

㉔ **Demel** (⌧ Kohlmarkt 14, ☏ 01/535–1717–0), Vienna's best-known pastry shop, offers a dizzying selection, and if you possess a sweet tooth, a visit will be worth every groschen. Chocolate lovers will want to participate in the famous Viennese Sachertorte debate by sampling Demel's version and then comparing it with its rival at the **Sacher Café,** which is in Hotel Sacher (☞ Lodging, *below*). For considerably less elegance with a touch of the Formica-cool '50s, but excellent coffee and good pastries as well as value, go instead to the **Arabia** café (⌧ Kohlmarkt 5, ☏ 01/503–0929).

Dorotheum. The narrow passageway just to the right of St. Michael's, with its large 15th-century relief depicting Christ on the Mount of Olives, leads into the Stallburggasse. The area is dotted with antiques stores, attracted by the presence of the Dorotheum, the famous Viennese auction house that began as a state-controlled pawnshop in 1707 (affectionately known as "Aunt Dorothy" to its patrons). Merchandise coming up for auction is on display at Dorotheergasse 17. The showrooms—packed with everything from carpets and pianos to cameras and jewelry and postage stamps—are well worth a visit. Some wares are not for auction but for immediate sale. ⌧ *Dorotheerg. 17,* ☏ *01/515–60–0.* ☉ *Weekdays 8–6, Sat. 8–noon. U-Bahn: U1, U3 Stephanspl.*

The Graben. One of Vienna's major crossroads, the Graben, leading west from Stock-im-Eisen-Platz, is a street whose unusual width gives it the presence and weight of a city square. Its shape is due to the Romans, who dug the city's southwestern moat here, adjacent to the original city walls. The Graben's centerpiece is the effulgently Baroque ☞ **Pestsäule.**

㉕ **Jewish Museum.** The former Eskeles Palace, once an elegant private residence, is now home to the city's Jüdisches Museum der Stadt Wien. Permanent exhibitions tell of the momentous role that Viennese-born Jews played in realms from music to medicine, art to philosophy, both in Vienna—until abruptly halted in 1938—and in the world at large. Changing exhibits add contemporary touches. The museum complex includes a café and bookstore. ⌧ *Dorotheerg. 11,* ☏ *01/535–0431.* ☞ *AS70.* ☉ *Sun.–Fri. 10–6, Thurs. 10–9. U-Bahn: U1, U3 Stephansplatz.*

㉓ **Kohlmarkt.** The Kohlmarkt, aside from its classic view of the domed entryway to the imperial palace complex of the Hofburg, is best known as Vienna's most elegant shopping street. The shops, not the buildings, are remarkable, although there is an entertaining odd-couple pairing: No. 11 (early 18th century) and No. 9 (early 20th century). The mixture of architectural styles is similar to that of the Graben, but the general atmosphere is low-key, as if the street were consciously deferring to the showstopper dome at the west end. The composers Haydn and Chopin lived in houses on the street, and indeed, the Kohlmarkt lingers in the memory when flashier streets have faded.

⑲ Looshaus. In 1911, Adolf Loos, one of the founding fathers of 20th-century modern architecture, built the Looshaus on august Michaelerplatz, facing the Imperial Palace entrance. It was considered nothing less than an architectural declaration of war. After two hundred years of Baroque and neo-Baroque exuberance, the first generation of 20th-century architects had had enough. Loos led the revolt against architectural tradition; *Ornament and Crime* was the title of his famous manifesto, in which he inveighed against the conventional architectural wisdom of the 19th century. Instead, he advocated buildings that were plain, honest, and functional. When he built the Looshaus for Goldman and Salatsch (men's clothiers) in 1911, the city was scandalized. Archduke Franz Ferdinand, heir to the throne, was so offended that he vowed never again to use the Michaelerplatz entrance to the Imperial Palace. Today the Looshaus has lost its power to shock, and the facade seems quite innocuous; argument now focuses on the postmodern Neues Haas-Haus (☞ *below*) opposite St. Stephen's Cathedral. The recently restored interior of the Looshaus remains a breathtaking surprise; the building now houses a bank, and you can go inside to see the stylish chambers and staircase. ⊠ *Michaelpl. 3. U-Bahn: U3 Herrengasse.*

⑱ Michaelerplatz. One of Vienna's most historic squares, this small plaza is now the site of an excavation revealing Roman plus 18th- and 19th-century layers of the past. The excavations are a latter-day distraction from the Michaelerplatz's most noted claim to fame—the eloquent entryway to the palace complex of the Hofburg.

In 1945 American soldiers forced open the doors of the crypt in the **Michaelerkirche** for the first time in 150 years and made a singular discovery. Lying undisturbed over the centuries were the mummified remains of former wealthy parishioners of the church—even the finery and buckled shoes worn at their burial was preserved by the perfect temperatures contained within the crypt. Fascinatingly ghoulish tours are offered hourly, for AS40, given first in German and then in English. Visitors are led down into the shadowy gloom and through a labyrinth of passageways, pausing at several tombs (many of which are open in order to view the remains) with a little explanation of the cause of death given at each site. *U-Bahn: U3 Herrengasse.*

Neues Haas-Haus. Stock-im-Eisen-Platz is home to central Vienna's most controversial (for the moment, at least) piece of architecture: the Neues Haas-Haus designed by Hans Hollein, one of Austria's best-known living architects. Detractors consider its aggressively contemporary style out of place opposite St. Stephen's, seeing the cathedral's style parodied by being stood on its head; advocates consider the contrast enlivening. Whatever the ultimate verdict, the new restaurant and shopping complex has not been the expected commercial success; its restaurants may be thriving, but its boutiques are not. ⊠ *Stephanspl. 12.* ☉ *Shops weekdays 9–6, Sat. 9–noon.*

Pestsäule (Plague Column). Erected by Emperor Leopold I between 1687 and 1693 in thanks to God for delivering the city from a particularly virulent plague, today the representation looks more like a host of cherubs doing their best to cope with the icing of a wedding cake wilting in the hot sunshine. Staunch Protestants may be shocked to learn that the foul figure of the Pest stands also for the heretic plunging away from the "True Faith" into the depth of hell. But they will have to get used to the fact that the Catholic Church has triumphed over Protestantism in Austria and frequently recalls the fact on stone and on canvas. ⊠ *Graben.*

㉒ Peterskirche (St. Peter's Church). Considered the best example of church Baroque in Vienna—certainly the most theatrical—the Peterskirche was constructed between 1702 and 1708 by Lucas von Hildebrandt. According to legend, the original church on this site was founded in 792 by Charlemagne, a tale immortalized by the relief plaque on the right side of the church. The facade possesses angled towers, graceful tower tops (said to have been inspired by the tents of the Turks during the siege of 1683), and an unusually fine entrance portal. Inside the church, the Baroque decoration is elaborate, with some fine touches (particularly the glass-crowned galleries high on the walls to either side of the altar and the amazing tableau of the martyrdom of St. John Nepomuk), but the lack of light and the years of accumulated dirt create a prevailing gloom, and the much-praised ceiling frescoes by J. M. Rottmayr are impossible to make out. Just before Christmastime each year, the basement crypt is filled with a display of nativity scenes. The church is shoehorned into tiny Petersplatz, just off the Graben. ⊠ *Peterspl. U-Bahn: U1, U3 Stephanspl.*

㉑ **Stock-im-Eisen.** In the southwest corner of Stock-im-Eisen-Platz, set into the building on the west side of Kärntnerstrasse, is one of the city's odder relics: the Stock-im-Eisen, or the "nail-studded stump." Chronicles first mention the Stock-im-Eisen in 1533, but it is probably far older, and for hundreds of years any apprentice metalsmith who came to Vienna to learn his trade hammered a nail into the tree trunk for good luck. During World War II, when there was talk of moving the relic to a museum in Munich, it mysteriously disappeared; it reappeared, perfectly preserved, after the threat of removal had passed.

An Imperial City: The Hofburg

A walk through the Imperial Palace, known as the **Hofburg,** brings you back to the days when Vienna was the capital of a mighty empire. You can still find in Vienna shops vintage postcards and prints that show the revered and bewhiskered Emperor Franz Josef starting out on a morning drive from his Hofburg palace in his carriage. Today, at the palace—which faces Kohlmarkt on the opposite side of Michaelerplatz—you can walk in his very footsteps, gaze at the old tin bath the emperor kept under his simple iron bedstead, marvel at his bejeweled christening robe, and feast your eyes on great works of art, impressive armor, and some of the finest Baroque interiors in Europe along the way.

Until 1918 the Hofburg was the home of the Habsburgs, rulers of the Austro-Hungarian Empire. As a current tourist mecca, it has become a vast smorgasbord of sightseeing attractions: The Imperial Apartments, two Imperial treasuries, *six* museums, the National Library, and the famous Winter Riding School all vie for attention. The entire complex takes a minimum of a full day to explore in detail; if your time is limited (or if you want to save most of the interior sightseeing for a rainy day), you should omit the Imperial Apartments and all the museums mentioned below except the Kunsthistorisches Museum, the new museum of court silver and tableware, the Silberkammer, and probably the Schatzkammer. An excellent multilingual, full-color booklet describing the palace in detail is for sale at most ticket counters within the complex; it gives a complete list of attractions and maps out the palace's complicated ground plan and building history wing by wing.

Vienna took its imperial role seriously, as evidenced by the sprawling Hofburg complex, today, as then, the seat of government. But this is generally understated power; while the buildings cover considerable area, the treasures lie inside, not to be flamboyantly flaunted. Certainly under Franz Josef II, the reign was beneficent—witness the broad Ringstrasse he ordained and the array of museums and public buildings it hosts. With few exceptions (Vienna City Hall and the Votive Church), rooflines are kept to an even level, creating an ensemble effect that helps integrate the palace complex and its parks into the urban landscape without making a domineering statement. Diplomats still bustle in and out of high-level international meetings in the elegant halls. Horse-drawn carriages still traverse the Ring and the roadway that cuts through the complex. Ignore the cars and tour buses and you can easily imagine yourself in a Vienna of a hundred or more years ago.

Architecturally, the Hofburg—like St. Stephen's—is far from refined. It grew up over a period of 700 years (its earliest mention in court documents is 1279, at the very beginning of Habsburg rule), and its spasmodic, haphazard growth kept it from attaining any sort of unified identity. But many of the bits and pieces are fine, and one interior (the National Library) is a tour de force.

A Good Walk

When you begin to explore the Hofburg you realize that the palace complex is like a nest of boxes, courtyards opening off courtyards and wings (*trakts*) spreading far and wide. First tackle **Josefsplatz** ㉕, the remarkable square that interrupts Augustinerstrasse, ornamented by the equestrian statue of Josef II—many consider this Vienna's loveliest square. Indeed, the beautifully restored imperial decor adorning the roof of the buildings forming Josefsplatz is one of the few visual demonstrations of Austria's onetime widespread power and influence. On your right to the north is the **Spanische Reitschule** ㉖, the Spanish Riding School—one part of Vienna known throughout the world—where the famous white horses reign. Across Reitschulgasse under the arches are the **Lipizzaner Museum** ㉗ and the Imperial Stables. To the south stands the **Augustinerkirche** ㉘, St. Augustine's Church, where the Habsburg rulers' hearts are preserved in urns. The grand main hall of the **Hofbibliothek Prunksaal** ㉙, the National Library, is one of the great Baroque treasures of Europe, a sight not to be missed (enter from the southwest corner of Josefsplatz).

Under the Michaelerplatz dome is the entrance to the **Kaiserappartements** ㉚, hardly the elegance you would normally associate with royalty, but Franz Josef II, the residing emperor from 1848 to 1916, was anything but ostentatious in his personal life. For the representational side, however, go through into the **In der Burg** ㉛ courtyard and look in at the elegant **Silberkammer** ㉜ museum of court silver and tableware. Go through the **Schweizertor** ㉝, the Swiss gate, to the south off of In der Burg, to reach the small **Schweizer Hof** ㉞ courtyard with stairs leading to the **Hofburgkapelle** ㉟, the Imperial Chapel where the Vienna Boys Choir makes its regular Sunday appearances. In a back corner of the courtyard is the entrance to the **Schatzkammer** ㊱, the Imperial Treasury, overflowing with jewels, robes, and royal trappings. From In der Burg, the roadway leads under the **Leopold Wing** ㊲ of the complex into the vast park known as **Heldenplatz** ㊳, or Hero's Square. The immediately obvious heroes are the equestrian statues of Archduke Karl and Prince Eugene of Savoy. The Hofburg wing to the south with its concave facade is the **Neue Burg** ㊴, the "new" section of the complex, now housing four specialized museums. Depending on your interests, consider the **Ephesus Museum** ㊵, with Roman antiquities; the **Collection of Musical Instruments** ㊶, where you also hear what you see; the impressive **Collection of Weapons** ㊷, with tons of steel armor, or the **Ethnological Museum** ㊸, including Montezuma's headdress. Ahead, the **Burgtor** ㊹ gate separates the Hofburg complex from the Ringstrasse. The quiet oasis in back of the Neue Burg is the **Burggarten** ㊺. Catch your breath and marvel that you've seen only a small part of the Hofburg—a large part of it still houses the offices of the Austrian government and cannot be visited by the public.

TIMING
You could spend a day in the Hofburg complex. For most of the smaller museums, figure on anything from an hour upward.

Sights to See

28 Augustinerkirche (Church of the Augustinian Order). Across Josefsplatz from the Riding School is the entrance to the Augustinerkirche, built during the 14th century and possessing the most unified Gothic interior in the city. But the church is something of a fraud; the interior, it turns out, dates from the late 18th century, not the early 14th. A historical fraud the church may be, but a spiritual fraud it is not. The view from the entrance doorway is stunning: a soaring harmony of vertical piers, ribbed vaults, and hanging chandeliers that makes Vienna's other Gothic interiors look earthbound by comparison. The imposing Baroque organ sounds as fine as it looks, and the Sunday morning High Mass—frequently by Mozart or Haydn—sung here can be the highlight of a trip. To the right of the main altar in the small Loreto Chapel stand silver urns in serried ranks; they contain the hearts of Habsburg rulers. This rather morbid sight is viewable after early mass on Sunday, Monday, or by appointment. ✉ *Josefspl.,* ☎ *01/533–7099–0. U-Bahn: U3 Herrengasse.*

45 Burggarten. The intimate Burggarten in back of the Neue Burg is a quiet oasis that includes a statue of a contemplative Kaiser Franz Josef and an elegant statue of Mozart, moved here from the Albertinaplatz after the war, when the city's charred ruins were rebuilt. The former greenhouses under the wall of the Augustine church are being restored into a café complex replete with palms and winter garden setting. ✉ *Access from Opernring and Hanuschg./Goetheg. U-Bahn: U2 Babenbergerstr.*

44 Burgtor. The failure to complete the ☞ **Hofburg** building program left the old main palace gate stranded in the middle of the Heldenplatz(☞ *below*).

41 Collection of Musical Instruments. This Neue Burg (☞ *below*) museum houses pianos that belonged to Brahms, Schumann, and Mahler. An acoustic guided tour allows you actually to hear the various instruments on headphones as you move from room to room. 🎟 *Combined ticket with Ephesus Museum (☞ below) and Collection of Weapons (☞ below) museums AS30 (AS80 for special exhibits).* ☉ *Tues.–Sun. 10–6. U-Bahn: U2 Babenbergerstrasse.*

42 Collection of Weapons. Rivaling the armory in Graz as one of the most extensive arms-and-armor collections in the world is this Neue Burg (☞ *below*) museum. Enter at the triumphal arch set into the middle of the curved portion of the facade. 🎟 *Combined ticket with Ephesus Museum(☞ below) and Collection of Musical Instruments (☞ above) AS30 (AS80 for special exhibits).* ☉ *Tues.–Sun. 10–6. U-Bahn: U2 Babenbergerstrasse.*

40 Ephesus Museum. One of the museums in the Neue Burg (☞ *below*), the Ephesus Museum contains exceptional Roman antiquities unearthed by Austrian archaeologists in Turkey at the turn of the century. 🎟 *Combined ticket with Collection of Musical Instruments (☞ above) and Collection of Weapons (☞ above) museums AS30 (AS80 for special exhibits).* ☉ *Tues.–Sun. 10–6. U-Bahn: U2 Babenbergerstrasse.*

43 Ethnological Museum (Museum für Völkerkunde). This anthropological museum is entered at the west end pavilion in the Neue Burg (☞ *below*). Montezuma's feathered headdress is a highlight of its collection. 🎟 *AS30.* ☉ *Wed.–Mon. 10–4.*

The Hofburg (Imperial Palace)

Augustinerkirche, **28**
Burggarten, **45**
Burgtor, **44**
Collection of Musical Instruments, **41**
Collection of Weapons, **42**
Ephesus Museum, **40**

Ethnological Museum, **43**
Heldenplatz, **38**
Hofbibliothek Prunksaal, **29**
Hofburgkapelle, **35**
In der Burg, **31**
Josefsplatz, **25**

Kaiserappartements, **30**
Leopold Wing, **37**
Lipizzaner Museum, **27**
Neue Burg, **39**
Schatzkammer, **36**
Schweizer Hof, **34**

Schweizertor, **33**
Silberkammer, **32**
Spanische Reitschule, **26**

38 **Heldenplatz.** The long wing with the concave bay on the south side of the square is the youngest section of the palace, called the Neue Burg (☞ *below*). Although the Neue Burg building plans were not completed and the Heldenplatz was left without a discernible shape, the space nevertheless is punctuated by two superb equestrian statues of Archduke Karl and Prince Eugene of Savoy. The older section on the north includes the offices of the federal president.

29 **Hofbibliothek Prunksaal** (National Library). This is one of the grandest Baroque libraries in the world, in every sense a cathedral of books. Its centerpiece is the spectacular Prunksaal—the Grand Hall of the National Library—which probably contains more book treasures than any comparable collection outside the Vatican. The main entrance to the ornate reading room is in the left corner of Josefsplatz. Designed by Fischer von Erlach the Elder just before his death in 1723 and completed by his son, the Grand Hall is full-blown High Baroque, with trompe-l'oeil ceiling frescoes by Daniel Gran. The library may not be to everyone's taste, but in the end it is the books themselves that come to the rescue. They are as lovingly displayed as the gilding and the frescoes, and they give the hall a warmth that the rest of the palace decidedly lacks. On the third floor is an intriguing museum of globes that should not be overlooked. ⊠ *Josefspl. 1, at top of stairs inside,* ☎ *01/543–100 library or 01/534–10–297 museum.* 🎫 *Library AS40, museum AS20.* ☉ *Library Nov.–May, Mon.–Sat. 10–noon; June–Oct., Mon.–Sat. 10–4 (hrs vary depending on exhibitions); museum Mon.–Wed. and Fri. 11–noon, Thurs. 2–3. U-Bahn: U3 Herrengasse.*

35 **Hofburgkapelle** (Chapel of the Imperial Palace). The Vienna Boys Choir (Wiener Sängerknaben) sings mass at 9:15 on Sunday, Monday, and holidays from September to June. Alas, the arrangement is such that you *hear* the choirboys but don't see them; their soprano and alto voices peal forth from a gallery behind the seating area. ⊠ *Hofburg, Schweizer Hof,* ☎ *01/533–9927.*

31 **In der Burg.** This prominent courtyard of the Hofburg complex features a statue of Francis II and the noted ☞ **Schweizertor** gateway. Note the clock on the far upper wall at the north end of the courtyard: It tells time by the sundial, also gives the time mechanically, and even, above the clock face, indicates the phase of the moon.

25 **Josefsplatz.** Josefsplatz is the most imposing of the Hofburg courtyards, with an equestrian **statue of Emperor Joseph II** (1807) in the center.

30 **Kaiserappartements** (Imperial Apartments). The long, repetitive suite of conventionally luxurious rooms has a sad and poignant feel. The decoration (19th-century imitation of 18th-century rococo) tries to look regal, but much like the empire itself in its latter days, it is only going through the motions and ends up looking merely official. Among the few signs of genuine life are Emperor Franz Josef's spartan, iron field bed, on which he slept every night, and Empress Elizabeth's wooden gymnastics equipment, on which she exercised every morning. Amid all the tired splendor they look decidedly forlorn. ⊠ *Hofburg, Schweizer Hof,* ☎ *01/587–5554–515.* 🎫 *AS70, combined ticket with Silberkammer (☞ below) AS90, tour AS20 per museum.* ☉ *Daily 9–5. U-Bahn: U2 Herrengasse.*

37 **Leopold Wing.** A long tract of offices known as the Leopold Wing separates the In der Burg courtyard from the vast Heldenplatz (☞ *above*).

27 **Lipizzaner Museum.** If you're interested in learning more about the Lipizzaners, visit this museum, located in what used to be the old imperial pharmacy. Exhibitions document the history of the Lipizzans, including paintings, photographs, and videos giving an overview from the 16th century to the present. A highlight is a visit to the stables, where you can see the horses up-close through a glass window. ⊠ *Reitschulg. 2,* ☎ *01/526–4184–30,* FAX *01/526–4186.* ☑ *AS50; combined ticket with morning training session AS130.* ⊘ *Daily 9–6.*

㊴ Neue Burg. The Neue Burg stands today as a symbol of architectural overconfidence. Designed for Emperor Franz Josef in 1869, this "new chateau" was part of a much larger scheme that was meant to make the Hofburg rival the Louvre, if not Versailles. The German architect Gottfried Semper planned a twin of the present Neue Burg on the opposite side of the Heldenplatz, with arches connecting the Neue Burg and its twin with the other pair of twins on the Ringstrasse, the Kunsthistorisches Museum (Museum of Art History), and the Naturhistorisches Museum (Museum of Natural History). But World War I intervened, and with the empire's collapse the Neue Burg became merely the last in a long series of failed attempts to bring architectural order to the Hofburg. (From its main balcony, in April 1938, Adolf Hitler, telling a huge cheering crowd below of his plan for the new German empire, declared that Vienna "is a pearl! I am going to put it into a setting of which it is worthy!") Today, visitors flock to the Neue Burg because it houses no fewer than four specialty museums: the ☞ **Ephesus Museum, Collection of Musical Instruments, Ethnological Museum,** and **Collection of Weapons.** ⊠ *Heldenpl.,* ☎ *01/525240.*

㊱ Schatzkammer (Imperial Treasury). The entrance to the Schatzkammer, or Imperial Treasury, with its 1,000 years of treasures, is tucked away at ground level behind the staircase to the Hofburgkapelle. The elegant display is a welcome antidote to the monotony of the Imperial Apartments, for the entire Treasury was completely renovated in 1983–87, and the crowns and relics and vestments fairly glow in their new surroundings. Here you'll find such marvels as the Holy Lance—reputedly the lance that pierced Jesus' side—the Imperial Crown (a sacred symbol of sovereignty once stolen on Hitler's orders), and the Saber of Charlemagne. Don't miss the Burgundian Treasure, connected with that most romantic of medieval orders of chivalry, the Order of the Golden Fleece. ⊠ *Schweizer Hof,* ☎ *01/533–7931.* ☑ *AS60.* ⊘ *Wed. and Fri.–Mon. 10–6, Thurs. 10–9. U-Bahn: U2 Herrengasse.*

�34 Schweizer Hof. This courtyard was named after the Swiss Guards who were once stationed here. In the southeast corner (at the top of the steps) is the entrance to the Hofburgkapelle (☞ *above*).

�33 Schweizertor (Swiss Gate). Dating from 1552 and decorated with some of the earliest classical motifs in the city, the Schweizertor leads from In der Burg through to the oldest section of the palace, a small courtyard known as the Schweizer Hof (☞ *above*). The gateway is painted maroon, black, and gold; it gives a fine Renaissance flourish to its building facade.

㊲ Silberkammer (Museum of Court Silver and Tableware). The large courtyard on the far side of the Michaelertor rotunda is known as In der Burg; here on the west side is the entrance to the sparkling new Silberkammer. There's far more than forks and fingerbowls here; stunning decorative pieces vie with glittering silver and gold for attention. Highlights include Franz Josef's vermeil banqueting service, the Jardinière given to Empress Elizabeth by Queen Victoria, and gifts from Marie-Antoinette to her brother, Josef II. The presentation of full table settings gives an idea of court life both as a daily routine and on festive occasions. ⊠ *Hofburg, Michalertrakt,* ☎ *01/533–1044.* ☑ *AS70, combined ticket with Kaiserappartements (☞ above) AS90.* ⊘ *Daily 9–5.*

★ ㉖ **Spanische Reitschule** (Spanish Riding School). Located between Augustinerstrasse and the Josefsplatz is the world-famous Spanish Riding School, a favorite for centuries, and no wonder: Who can resist the sight of the stark white Lipizzaners going through their masterful paces? For the last 300 years they have been perfecting their *haute école* riding demonstrations to the sound of Baroque music in a ballroom that seems to be a crystal-chandeliered stable. The breed was started in 1580, and the horses proved themselves in battle as well as in the complicated "dances" for which they are famous. The interior of the riding school, the 1735 work of Fischer von Erlach the Younger, is itself an attraction—surely Europe's most elegant sports arena—and if the prancing horses begin to pall, move up to the top balcony and examine the ceiling. The school's popularity is hardly surprising, and tickets to some performances must be ordered in writing many weeks in advance. Information offices have a brochure with the detailed schedule (performances are usually March–December, with the school on vacation in July and August). Generally the full, 80-minute shows take place Sunday at 10:45 AM plus selected Wednesdays at 7 PM. Check for hour-long morning performances on Saturday at 10; tickets for Saturday shows are available only from ticket and travel agencies (a list of these agencies is included in a free leaflet about the Spanish Riding School available from the Austrian National Tourist Office; the leaflet also includes the full-year schedule of performances).

Morning training sessions (without music), held Tuesday–Saturday, with a few in February and August on Mondays as well, are usually open to the public. Tickets can be bought *only* at the door for these morning training sessions (the relocated entrance is currently next to the Schweizertor, in the In der Burg courtyard, but might be moved back to Josefsplatz, so check), and the line starts forming between 9 and 9:30 for the opening at 10. Note, however, there are special training sessions on Saturday mornings that are accompanied by music—these tickets are available only by reservation through ticket agencies. Note that ticket agencies (legally) add a commission of 22%–25% to the face price of the ticket. For Sunday and Wednesday performance ticket orders, write to Spanische Reitschule (✉ Hofburg, A 1010 Vienna). Pick up reserved tickets at the office under the Michaelerplatz rotunda dome. ✉ *Michaelerpl. 1, Hofburg,* ☎ *01/533–9031–0,* 𝔽𝔸𝕏 *01/535–0186.* 🎫 *Seats AS250–AS900, standing room AS200, Sat. morning training session with music AS250, other morning training session AS100.* ☉ *Mar.–June and Sept.–mid-Dec. Closed tour wks.*

The Ringstrasse and Its Environs

Along with the Hofburg, the Ringstrasse is Vienna's major urban set piece. This grand series of thoroughfares bounds the heart of Vienna, the Innere Stadt (Inner City), or First District. It follows the lines of what were, until an imperial decree ordered their leveling in 1857, the defenses of the city. By the 1870s, Vienna had reached the zenith of her imperial prosperity, and this found ultimate expression in the series of magnificent buildings erected around the Ringstrasse—the Opera House, the Kunsthistoriches Museum, the Natural History Museum, and the Rathaus, University, and Votivkirche.

A Good Walk

Is there a best way to explore the Ring? You can walk it from one end to the other—from where it begins at the Danube Canal to where it returns to the canal after its curving flight. Or, you can explore it whenever you happen to cross it on other missions. While it is a pleasant sequence of boulevards, seeing its succession of rather pompous buildings all in one walk can be overpowering. Or, you can obtain the best of both options by following this suggested itinerary, which leavens the bombast of the Ring with some of Vienna's most fascinating sights.

Immediately across the Ringstrasse from the Hofburg are twin buildings, both museums. To the west is the **Naturhistorisches Museum** ㊻; to the east, the **Kunsthistorisches Museum** ㊼, the art museum packed with world-famous treasures. Allow ample time for exploration here. Farther to the west of the museum square is the compact **Spittelberg Quarter** ㊽ of tiny streets between Burggasse and Sibensterngasse, often site of handicraft and seasonal fairs. The **Volksgarten** ㊾ on the inside of the Ringstrasse to the north of the museum square numbers a café and rose garden among its attractions; look also for the small memorial to Franz Josef's wife, Empress Elizabeth, in the back corner. Tackle the Ringstrasse buildings by starting with the Justizpalast (Ministry of Justice), moving along to Parliament, the Rathaus (City Hall), the Burgtheater opposite on the inside of the Ring, then the Universität (the main building of Vienna's university) beyond, again on the outside of the Ring. Next to the university stands the neo-Gothic Votivkirche. If you still have time and energy, walk farther along the Ring to discover the Börse (Stock Exchange) at the corner of the Ring and Wipplingerstrasse. The outside end of Hohenstaufengasse leads into Liechtensteinstrasse, which will bring you to Berggasse. Turn right to reach No. 19, the **Freud Apartment** ㊿, now a museum and research facility. By continuing along Liechtensteinstrasse four blocks or taking the D streetcar two stops from the Bösre, you will arrive at Fürstengasse, where the **Museum Moderner Kunst** �51 is incongruously housed in the legendary Palais Liechtenstein.

TIMING

If you can, plan for Vienna's Louvre—the Kunsthistorisches Museum—early in the day before the crowds arrive, although the size of crowds depends greatly on whatever special shows the museum may be exhibiting. As for the main sights off the Ringstrasse, you could easily lump visits to the Freud Apartment and the Museum of Modern Art together, figuring on about a half day for the two combined.

Sights to See

㊿ **Freud Apartment.** Not far from the historic Hofburg district, beyond the Votivkirche at the Schotterning along the Ringstrasse, you can skip over several centuries and visit that outstanding symbol of 20th-century Vienna: Sigmund Freud's apartment at Berggasse 19 (Apartment 6, one flight up; ring the bell and push the door simultaneously); this was his residence from 1891 to 1938. The five-room collection of memorabilia is mostly a photographic record of Freud's life, with some documents, publications, and a portion of his collection of antiquities also on display. The waiting-room furniture is authentic, but the consulting room and study furniture (including the famous couch) can be seen only in photographs. ⊠ *Bergg. 19*, ☎ *01/319–1596.* ⌑ *AS60.* ☉ *July– Sept., daily 9–6; Oct.–June, daily 9–4. U-Bahn: U2 Schottentor.*

㊼ **Kunsthistorisches Museum** (Museum of Fine Art). One of the finest art collections in the world, housed in palatial splendor, the Kunsthistorisches Museum is the jewel of Vienna's museums. Its glories are the Italian and Flemish collections, assembled by the Habsburgs over many centuries. Even a cursory description would run on for pages, but a brief selection of the museum's most important works will give you an idea of the riches to be enjoyed. The large-scale works concentrated in the main galleries shouldn't distract you from the equal share of masterworks in the more intimate side wings. The Flemish wing ranges from Rogier van der Weyden's *Triptych Crucifixion* and Holbein's *Portrait* *of Jane Seymour, Queen of England,* to a fine series of Rembrandt portraits and Vermeer's peerless *Allegory of the Art of Painting* (currently being restored). The group of paintings by Pieter Brueghel the Elder is the largest in existence and contains the world-renowned *Peasant Wedding* and *Hunters in the Snow.* The grand style of the 17th-century is represented by Rubens's towering altarpieces and his *Nude of Hélène Fourment.* In the Italian wing are works by Titian, including his *Portrait of Isabella d'Este,* whose fiercely intelligent eyes make you realize why she was the first lady of the Renaissance, and Giorgione's *The Three Philosophers,* an enigmatic composition in uniquely radiant Venetian coloring. A short list of other highlights includes Raphael's *Madonna in the Meadow,* Correggio's *Jupiter Embracing Io,* Parmigianino's *Cupid Cutting a Bow,* Guercino's *Return of the Prodigal Son,* and Caravaggio's *Madonna of the Rosary.* One level down is the remarkable, less-visited *Kunstkammer,* displaying priceless objects created for the Habsburg emperors. These include curiosities made of gold, silver, and crystal (including Cellini's famous salt cellar), and more exotic materials, such as ivory, horn, and gemstones, as well as a lovely Della Robbia Madonna and a female portrait bust by Laurana. ⌖ *Maria-Theresien-Pl.,* ☎ *01/525240.* ⌖ *AS45 (more for special exhibits).* ⊙ *Tues.–Sun. 10–6, picture gallery Thurs. 6–9 PM.*

Museum für angewandte Kunst (MAK) (Museum of Applied Arts). This fascinating museum contains a large collection of Austrian furniture, porcelain, art objects, and priceless Oriental carpets; the Jugendstil display devoted to Josef Hoffman and his followers at the Wiener Werkstätte is particularly fine. The museum also features a number of changing exhibitions of contemporary, with artists ranging from Chris Burden to Nam June Paik. The museum also houses the popular MAK Cafe (☞ Dining, *below*). ⌖ *Stubenring 5,* ☎ *01/711–36–0.* ⌖ *Standing exhibits AS30, special exhibits AS90.* ⊙ *Tues.–Wed. and Fri.–Sun. 10–6, Thurs. 10–9. U-Bahn: U3 Stubentor.*

�51 **Museum Moderner Kunst** (Museum of Modern Art). The official address of the Museum Moderner Kunst, housed in the celebrated **Palais Liechtenstein**, may be at Fürstengasse 1, but Liechtensteinstrasse is the address by which most Viennese know it. The large 18th-century mansion was originally the Liechtenstein Summer Palace; today it houses the national collection of 20th-century art and the outstanding private Ludwig collection, mainly of Austrian artists. Artists from Gustav Klimt to Robert Rauschenberg and Nam June Paik are represented, and a more inappropriate environment for modern art would be hard to imagine. Twentieth-century art and 18th-century architecture here declare war on each other and fight to an uneasy draw. Still, if you can shut out the architecture (or the art, depending on your taste), the museum is well worth a visit. ⌖ *Fürsteng. 1,* ☎ *01/317–6900.* ⌖ *AS45.* ⊙ *Tues.–Sun. 10–6. U-Bahn: U2 Schottentor, then Streetcar D to Fürstengasse.*

㊻ **Naturhistorisches Museum** (Natural History Museum). The formal museum complex just outside the Ring has two elements—to the east is the celebrated Kunsthistorisches Museum, to the west is the Naturhistorisches Museum, or Natural History Museum. This is home of, among other artifacts, the famous Venus of Willendorf, a tiny statuette thought to be some 20,000 years old and symbol of the Iron Age Hallstatt civilization. The reconstructed dinosaur skeletons understandably draw the greatest attraction. ⌖ *Maria-Theresien-Pl.,* ☎ *01/521–77–0.* ⌖ *AS45.* ⊙ *Wed.–Mon. 9–6. U-Bahn: U2, U3 Volkstheater.*

Ringstrasse. Late in 1857, Emperor Franz Josef issued a decree announcing the most ambitious piece of urban redevelopment Vienna had ever seen. The inner city's centuries-old walls were to be torn down, and the *glacis*—the wide expanse of open field that acted as a protective buffer between inner city and outer suburbs—was to be filled in. In their place was to rise a wide, tree-lined boulevard, upon which would stand an imposing collection of new buildings that would reflect Vienna's special status as the political, economic, and cultural heart of the Austro-Hungarian Empire. During the 50 years of building that followed, many factors combined to produce the Ringstrasse as it now stands, but the most important was the gradual rise of liberalism after the failed Revolution of 1848. By the latter half of the Ringstrasse era, support for constitutional government, democracy, and equality—all the concepts that liberalism traditionally equates with progress—was steadily increasing. As the Ringstrasse went up, it became the definitive symbol of this liberal progress; as Carl E. Schorske put it in his *Fin-de-Siècle Vienna,* it celebrated "the triumph of constitutional *Recht* (right) over imperial *Macht* (might), of secular culture over religious faith. Not palaces, garrisons, and churches, but centers of constitutional government and higher culture dominated the Ring."

The highest concentration of public building occurred in the area around the Volksgarten, where are clustered (moving from south to north, from Burgring to Schottenring) the ☞ **Kunsthistorisches Museum,** the ☞ **Naturhistorisches Museum,** the **Justizpalast** (Palace of Justice), the **Parliament** (Parliament), the **Rathaus** (City Hall), the **Burgtheater** (National Theater), the **Universität** (University of Vienna), the **Votivkirche** (Votive Church), and slightly farther along, the **Börse** (Stock Exchange) on Schottenring. As an ensemble, the collection is astonishing in its architectural presumption: It is nothing less than an attempt to assimilate and summarize the entire architectural history of Europe. As critics were quick to notice, however, the complex suffers from a serious organizational flaw: Most of the buildings lack effective context. Rather than being the focal points of an organized overall plan, they are plunked haphazardly down on an avenue that is itself too wide to possess a unified, visually comprehensible character.

To some, the monumentality of it all is overbearing; others, however, find the architectural panorama exhilarating, and growth of the trees over 100 years has served to put the buildings into different perspective. There is no question but that the tree-lined boulevard with its broad sidewalks gives the city a unique ribbon of green and certainly the distinction that the emperor sought. *U-Bahn for Volksgarten: U2 Lerchenfelder Strasse.*

㊽ Spittelberg Quarter. The Spittelberg quarter, one block northwest of Maria-Theresien-Platz off the Burggasse, offers a fair visual idea of Vienna outside of the city walls a century ago. Most buildings have been replaced, but the engaging 18th-century survivors at Burggasse 11 and 13 are adorned with religious and secular decorative sculpture, the latter with a niche statue of St. Joseph, the former with cherubic work-and-play bas-reliefs. For several blocks around—walk down Gutenberggasse and back up Spittelberggasse—the 18th-century houses have been beautifully restored. The sequence from Spittelberggasse 5 to 19 is an especially fine array of Viennese plain and fancy. Around holiday times, particularly Easter and Christmas, the Spittelberg quarter, known for arts and handicrafts, hosts seasonal markets offering unusual and interesting items.

㊾ Volksgarten. Just opposite the Hofburg is a green oasis with a beautifully planted rose garden, a 19th-century Greek temple, and a rather wistful white marble monument to Empress Elizabeth—Franz Josef's Bavarian wife, who died of a dagger wound inflicted by an Italian anarchist in Geneva in 1898. If not overrun with latter-day hippies, these can offer appropriate spots to sit for a few minutes and consider Vienna's most ambitious piece of 19th-century city planning: the famous Ringstrasse.

Monarchs and Mozart: From St. Stephen's to the Opera House

The cramped, ancient quarter behind St. Stephen's Cathedral offers a fascinating contrast to the luxurious expanses of the Ringstrasse and more recent parts of Vienna. This was—and still is—concentrated residential territory in the heart of the city. Mozart lived here; later, Prince Eugene and others built elegant town palaces as the smaller buildings were replaced. Streets—now mostly reserved for pedestrians—are narrow, and tiny alleyways abound. Facades open into courtyards that once housed the carriages and horses. The magnificent State Opera House shares with St. Stephen's the honor of being one of the city's most familiar and beloved landmarks.

A Good Walk

To pass through these streets is to take a short journey through history and art. In the process—as you visit haunts of Mozart, kings, and emperors—you can be easily impressed with a sense of exactly how Vienna's glittering Habsburg centuries unfolded. Start from St. Stephen's Cathedral by walking down Singerstrasse to Blutgasse and turn left into the **Blutgasse District** ⑤—a neighborhood redolent of the 19th century. At the north end in Domgasse is the so-called **Figarohaus** ㊿, now a memorial museum, the house in which Wolfgang Amadeus Mozart lived when he wrote the opera *The Marriage of Figaro*. Follow Domgasse east to Grünangergasse, which will bring you to Franziskanerplatz and the Gothic-Renaissance Franziskanerkirche (St. Francis Church). Follow the ancient Ballgasse to Rauhensteingasse, turning left onto **Himmelpfortgasse**—"The Gates of Heaven Street." Prince Eugene of Savoy had his town palace here at No. 8, now the **Finanzministerium** ㊽, living here when he wasn't enjoying his other residence, the Belvedere Palace. Continue down Himmelpfortgasse to Seilerstätte and turn right into Annagasse with its beautiful houses, which brings you back to the main shopping street, **Kärnter Strasse,** where you can find everything from Austrian jade to the latest Jill Sander turnouts. Turn left, walking north two blocks, and take the short Donnergasse to reach **Neuer Markt** square and the Providence Fountain. At the southwest corner of the square is the **Kaisergruft** ㊺ in the Kapuzinerkirche, the burial vault for rows of once-ruling Habsburgs. Tegetthofstrasse south will bring you to Albertinaplatz, the square noted for the obvious war memorial and even more for the **Albertina Museum** ㊾, one of the world's great collections of Old Master drawings and prints. The southeast side of the square is bounded by the famous **Staatsoper** ㊼, the State Opera House; check for tour possibilities or, better, book tickets for a great *Der Rosenkavalier.*

TIMING

A simple walk of this route could take you a full half day, assuming you stop occasionally to survey the scene and take it all in. The restyled Figarohaus is worth a visit, but note the odd closing hours and schedule accordingly. The Kaisergruft in the Kapuziner church is impressive for its shadows of past glories, but there are crowds, and you may have to wait to get in; the best times are early morning and around lunchtime. Tours of the State Opera House take place in the afternoons; check the schedule posted outside one of the doors on the arcaded Kärntnerstrasse side. Figure about an hour each for the various visits and tours.

Sights to See

56 **Albertina Museum.** Some of the greatest Old Master drawings—including Dürer's legendary *Praying Hands*—are housed in this unassuming building, home to the world's largest collection of drawings, sketches, engravings, and etchings. Dürer leads the list, but there are many other highlights, including works by Rembrandt, Michelangelo, and Correggio. In fact, the holdings are so vast that only a limited number can be shown at one time, and some drawings are so delicate that they can be shown only in facsimile. The building is undergoing restoration, and at press time (spring 1998)—possibly for the next two years—the collection is being housed in the Akademiehof. The Akademiehof is across from the Secession (the building with the gold cabbage-shape ball on top). The closest U-Bahn stop is Karlsplatz. Entrance to the collection is at Makartplatz 3. ⊠ *Augustinerstr. 1,* ☎ *01/534–83–0.* ☉ *Call for hrs during renovation.*

52 **Blutgasse District.** The small block bounded by Singerstrasse, Grünangergasse, and Blutgasse is known as the Blutgasse District. Nobody knows for certain how the gruesome name—*Blut* is German for "blood"—originated, although one legend has it that Knights Templar were slaughtered here when their order was abolished in 1312, although in later years the narrow street was known in those unpaved days as Mud Lane. Today the block is a splendid example of city renovation and restoration, with cafés, small shops, and galleries tucked into the corners. You can look inside the courtyards to see the open galleries that connect various apartments on the upper floors, the finest example being at Blutgasse 3. At the corner of Singerstrasse sits the 18th-century **Neupauer-Breuner Palace,** with its monumental entranceway and inventively delicate windows. Opposite at Singerstrasse 17 is the **Rottal Palace,** attributed to Hildebrandt, with its wealth of classical wall motifs. For a contrast, turn up the narrow Blutgasse, with its simple 18th-century facades.

53 **Figarohaus.** One of Mozart's 11 rented Viennese residences, the Figarohaus has its entrance at Domgasse 5, on the tiny alley behind St. Stephen's (although the facade on Schulerstrasse is far more imposing). It was in this house that Mozart wrote *The Marriage of Figaro* and the six quartets dedicated to Joseph Haydn (who once called on Mozart here, saying to Leopold, Mozart's father, ". . . your son is the greatest composer that I know in person or by name"). The apartment he occupied now contains a small commemorative museum—"created," alas, by an architect more interested in graphic blandishment than a sense of history; you'll have to use your imagination to picture how Mozart lived and worked here. ⊠ *Domg. 5,* ☎ *01/513–6294.* ☒ *AS25.* ☉ *Tues.–Sun. 10–12:15 and 1–4:30. U-Bahn: U1, U3 Stephansplatz.*

54 **Finanzministerium** (Ministry of Finance). The architectural jewel of Himmelpfortgasse, this imposing abode—designed by Fischer von Erlach in 1697 and later expanded by Hildebrandt—was originally the town palace of Prince Eugene of Savoy. As you study the Finanzministerium, you'll realize its Baroque details are among the most inventively conceived and beautifully executed in the city; all the decorative motifs are so softly carved that they appear to have been freshly squeezed from a pastry tube. The Viennese are lovers of the Baroque in both their architecture and their pastry, and here the two passions seem visibly merged. Such Baroque elegance may seem inappropriate for a finance ministry, but the contrast between place and purpose could hardly be more Viennese. ⊠ *8 Himmelpfortg. 8.*

Take a break at a landmark café in one of the most charming squares in Vienna, between Himmelpfortgasse and Singerstrasse. The **Kleines Cafe** (⌖ Franziskanerpl. 3), open daily, is more for coffee, cocktails, and light snacks than pastries, and few places are more delightful to sit and relax on a warm afternoon and evening. In summer tables are set outside on the intimate cobblestone square where the only sound is the tinkling fountain and occasional chiming of bells from the ancient Franciscan monastery next door. Before heading on, be sure to take a short stroll up Ballgasse, the tiny 18th-century street opposite the café.

Himmelpfortgasse. The maze of tiny streets including Ballgasse, Rauhensteingasse, and Himmelpfortgasse (literally, "Gates of Heaven Street") masterfully conjures up the Vienna of the 19th century. The most impressive house on the street is the Ministry of Finance (☞ *above*). The back side of the Steffl department store on Rauhensteingasse now marks the site of the house in which Mozart died in 1791. There's a commemorative plaque that once identified the streetside site together with a small memorial corner to Mozart on the fifth floor of the store.

⑤ Kaisergruft (Imperial Burial Vault). In the basement of the Kapuzinerkirche, or Capucin Church (on the southwest corner of the Neuer Markt), is one of the more intriguing sights in Vienna: the Kaisergruft, or Imperial Burial Vault. The crypts contain the partial remains of some 140 Habsburgs (the hearts are in the Augustinerkirche and the entrails in St. Stephen's) plus one non-Habsburg governess ("She was always with us in life," said Maria Theresa, "why not in death?"). Perhaps this is the wrong way to approach the Habsburgs in Vienna, starting with their tombs, but it does give you a chance to get their names in sequence as they lie in their serried ranks, their coffers ranging from the simplest, though positive, explosions of funerary conceit with decorations of skulls and other morbid symbols to the lovely and distinguished tomb of Maria Theresa and her husband. Designed while the couple still lived, their monument shows the empress in bed with her husband—awaking to the Last Judgment as if it were just another weekday morning, while the remains of her son (the ascetic Josef II) lie in a simple casket at the foot of the bed as if he were the family dog. ⌖ *Neuer Markt/Tegetthoffstr. 2,* ☎ *01/512–6853–0.* ▣ *AS40.* ◷ *Daily 9:30–4. U-Bahn: U1, U3 Stephansplatz.*

Kärntnerstrasse. The Kärntnerstrasse remains Vienna's leading central shopping street. These days Kärntnerstrasse is much maligned. Too commercial, too crowded, too many tasteless signs, too much gaudy neon—the complaints go on and on. Nevertheless, when the daytime tourist crowds dissolve, the Viennese arrive regularly for their evening promenade, and it is easy to see why. Vulgar the street may be, but it is also alive and vital, possessing an energy that the more tasteful Graben and the impeccable Kohlmarkt lack. For the sightseer beginning to suffer from an excess of art history, classic buildings, and museums, a Kärntnerstrasse window-shopping pause will be welcome.

Neuer Markt. The centerpiece in the Neuer Markt square, Georg Raphael Donner's **Providence Fountain,** has not had a happy life. Put up in 1739, it was at the time the very latest word in civic improvement, with elegantly mannered nude statuary meant to personify the Danube and four of its tributaries. The Empress Maria Theresa, however, was offended; she disapproved of nudity in art. The figures were removed and put away and later nearly melted down for munitions. They were finally restored in 1801 but were once again taken away (to be replaced by the present copies) in 1873. The original figures can be studied in quiet at the Lower Belvedere Palace (☞ Pomp and Circumstance: South of the Ring to the Belvedere, *below*).

57 **Staatsoper** (State Opera House). The famous Vienna Staatsoper on the Ring vies with the cathedral for the honor of marking the emotional heart of the city—it is a focus for Viennese life and one of the chief symbols of resurgence after the cataclysm of World War II. Its directorship is one of the top jobs in Austria, almost as important as that of president, and one that comes in for even more public attention. Everyone thinks they could do it just as well, and since the huge salary comes out of the taxes, they feel they have every right to criticize, often and loudly. The first of the Ringstrasse projects to be completed (in 1869), the opera house suffered disastrous bomb damage in the last days of World War II (only the outer walls, the front facade, and the main staircase area behind it survived). The auditorium is plain when compared to the red and gold eruptions of London's Covent Garden or some of the Italian opera houses, but it has an elegant individuality that shows to best advantage when the stage and auditorium are turned into a ballroom for the great Opera Ball.

The construction of the Opera House is the stuff of legend. When the foundation was laid, the plans for the Opernring were not yet complete, and in the end the avenue turned out to be several feet higher than originally planned. As a result, the Opera House lacked the commanding prospect that its architects, Eduard van der Nüll and August Sicard von Sicardsburg, had intended, and even Emperor Franz Josef pronounced the building a bit low to the ground. For the sensitive van der Nüll (and here the story becomes a bit suspect), failing his beloved emperor was the last straw. In disgrace and despair, he committed suicide. Sicardsburg died of grief shortly thereafter. And the emperor, horrified at the deaths his innocuous remark had caused, limited all his future artistic pronouncements to a single immutable formula: *Es war sehr schön, es hat mich sehr gefreut* ("It was very nice, it pleased me very much").

Renovation could not avoid a postwar look, for the cost of fully restoring the 19th-century interior decor was prohibitive. The original basic design was followed in the 1945–55 reconstruction, meaning that sight lines from some of the front boxes are poor at best. These disappointments hardly detract from the fact that this is one of the world's half dozen greatest opera houses, and experiencing a performance here can be the highlight of a trip to Vienna. Tours of the Opera House are given regularly, but starting times vary according to opera rehearsals; the current schedule is posted at the east-side entrance under the arcade on the Kärntnerstrasse marked GUIDED TOURS, where the tours begin. Alongside under the arcade is an information office that also sells tickets to the main opera and the Volksoper. ⊠ *Opernring 2,* ☎ *01/514–440.* 🎫 *Tour AS60.* ☉ *Summer, weekdays 11–3; other times call for information. U-Bahn: U1, U2, U4 Karlsplatz.*

Pomp and Circumstance: South of the Ring to the Belvedere

City planning in the late 1800s and early 1900s clearly was essential to manage the growth of the burgeoning imperial capital. The elegant Ringstrasse alone was not a sufficient showcase, and anyway, it focused on public rather than private buildings. The city fathers as well as private individuals commissioned the architect Otto Wagner to plan and undertake a series of projects. The area around Karlsplatz and the fascinating open food market remains a classic example of unity of design. Not all of Wagner's concept for Karlsplatz was realized, but enough remains to be convincing and to convey the impression of what might have been. The unity concept predates Wagner's time in the former garden setting of Belvedere Palace, one of Europe's greatest architectural triumphs.

A Good Walk

The often overlooked **Academy of Fine Arts** ⑧ is an appropriate starting point for this walk, as it puts into perspective the artistic arguments taking place around the turn of the century. While the Academy represented the conservative viewpoint, a group of modernist revolutionaries broke away and founded the Secessionist movement, with its culmination in the gold-crowned **Secession Building** ⑨. Now housing changing exhibits and Gustav Klimt's provocative *Beethoven Frieze*, the museum stands appropriately close by the Academy; from the Academy, take Makartgasse south one block. The famous **Naschmarkt** open food market starts diagonally south from the Secession; follow the rows of stalls southwest. Pay attention to the northwest side of the Linke Wienzeile, to the Theater an der Wien at the intersection with Millöckergasse (Mozart and Beethoven personally premiered some of their finest works at this opera house–theater) and to the **Otto Wagner Houses.** Head back north through the Naschmarkt; at the top end, cross Wiedner Hauptstrasse to your right into the park complex that forms Karlsplatz, creating a setting for the classic **Karlskirche** ⑥. Around **Karlsplatz,** note the Technical University on the south side, the Otto Wagner subway station buildings on the north. Across Lothringer Strasse on the north side are the Künstlerhaus art exhibit hall and the Musikverein. The out-of-place and rather undistinguished modern building to the left of Karlskirche houses the worthwhile **Historisches Museum der Stadt Wien** ⑥. Cut through Symphonikerstrasse (a passageway through the modern complex) and take Brucknerstrasse to **Schwarzenbergplatz.** The Jugendstil edifice on your left is the French Embassy; ahead is the Russian War Memorial. On a rise behind the memorial sits Palais Schwarzenberg, a jewel of a onetime summer palace and now a luxury hotel. Follow Prinz Eugen-Strasse up to the entrance of the **Belvedere Palace** ⑥ complex on your left. Besides the palace itself are other structures and, off to the east side, a remarkable botanical garden. After viewing the palace and the grounds, you can exit the complex from the lower building, Untere Belvedere, into Rennweg, which will steer you back to Schwarzenbergplatz.

TIMING

The first part of this walk, taking in the Academy of Fine Arts and the Secession, plus the Naschmarkt and Karlsplatz, can be accomplished in an easy half day. The Museum of the City of Vienna is good for a couple of hours, more if you understand some German. Give the Belvedere Palace and grounds as much time as you can. Organized tours breeze in and out—without so much as a glance at the outstanding modern art museum—in a half hour or so, not even scratching the surface of this fascinating complex. If you can, budget up to a half day here, but plan to arrive fairly early in the morning or afternoon before the busloads descend. Bus tourists aren't taken to the Lower Belvedere, so you'll have that and the formal gardens to yourself.

Sights to See

⑧ **Academy of Fine Arts.** An outsize statue of the German author Schiller announces the Academy of Fine Arts on Schillerplatz. (Turn around and note his more famous contemporary Goethe, pompously seated in an overstuffed chair, facing him from across the Ring.) The Academy was founded in 1692, but the present Renaissance Revival building dates to the late 19th century. The idea was conservatism and traditional values, even in the face of a growing Movement that scorned formal rules. It was here in the 1920s that an aspiring Adolf Hitler was refused acceptance on grounds of insufficient talent. The academy includes a museum focusing on Old Masters. The collection is mainly of interest to specialists, but Hieronymus Bosch's famous *Last Judgment* tryptich hangs here, an imaginative, if gruesome, speculation of the hereafter. ✉ *Schillerpl. 3,* ☎ *01/588–16–225.* 💷 *AS50.* ☉ *Tues. and Thurs.–Fri. 10–2; Wed. 10–1 and 3–6; weekends 9–1. U-Bahn: U1, U2, U4 Karlsplatz.*

OFF THE
BEATEN PATH

AM STEINHOF CHURCH – Otto Wagner's most exalted piece of Jugendstil architecture is not in the inner city but in the suburbs to the west: the Am Steinhof Church, designed in 1904 during his Secessionist phase. Head out to the church by taking the U4 subway line, which is adjacent to the Otto Wagner Houses (☞ *below*). On the grounds of the Vienna City Psychiatric Hospital, Wagner's design unites mundane functional details (rounded edges on the pews to prevent injury to the patients and a slightly sloped tile floor to facilitate cleaning) with a soaring, airy dome and glittering Jugendstil decoration (stained glass by Koloman Moser). The church is open once a week for guided tours (in German). ✉ *Baumgartner Höhe 1,* ☎ *01/910–60–2391.* 💷 *Free.* ☉ *Sat. 3–4. U-Bahn: U4/Unter-St.-Veit, then Bus 47A to Psychiatrisches Krankenhaus; or U2/ Volkstheater, then Bus 48A.*

★ ⑥ **Belvedere Palace.** Baroque architect Lucas von Hildebrandt's most important Viennese work is wedged between Rennweg (entry at No. 6A) and Prinz Eugen-Strasse (entry at No. 27): the Belvedere Palace. In fact the Belvedere is two palaces with extensive gardens between. Built outside the city fortifications between 1714 and 1722, the complex originally served as the summer palace of Prince Eugene of Savoy; much later it became the home of Archduke Franz Ferdinand, whose assassination in 1914 precipitated World War I. Though the lower palace is impressive in its own right, it is the much larger upper palace, used for state receptions, banquets, and balls, that is Hildebrandt's acknowledged masterpiece. The usual tourist entrance for the Upper Belvedere is the gate on Prinz-Eugen-Strasse, for the Lower Belvedere, the Rennweg gate—but for the most impressive view of the upper palace, approach it from the south garden closest to the South Rail Station. The upper palace displays a remarkable wealth of architectural invention in its facade, avoiding the main design problem common to all palaces because of their excessive size: monotony on the one hand and pomposity on the other. Hildebrandt's decoration here approaches the rococo, that final style of the Baroque era when traditional classical motifs all but disappeared in a whirlwind of seductive asymmetric fancy. The main interiors of the palace go even further: Columns are transformed into muscle-bound giants, pilasters grow torsos, capitals sprout great piles of symbolic imperial paraphernalia, and the ceilings are set aswirl with ornately molded stucco. The result is the finest rococo interior in the city.

Today both the upper and lower palaces of the Belvedere are noted museums devoted to Austrian painting. The **Österreichisches Barockmuseum** (Austrian Museum of Baroque Art) in the lower palace at Rennweg 6a displays Austrian art of the 18th century (including the original figures from Georg Raphael Donner's Providence Fountain in the Neuer Markt)—and what better building to house it. Next to the Baroque Museum (outside the west end) is the converted Orangerie, devoted to works of the medieval period.

The main attraction in the upper palace's **Österreichische Galerie** (Austrian Gallery) is the legendary collection of 19th- and 20th-century Austrian paintings, centering on the work of Vienna's three preeminent early 20th-century artists: Gustav Klimt, Egon Schiele, and Oskar Kokoschka. Klimt was the oldest, and by the time he helped found the Secession movement, he had forged a highly idiosyncratic painting style that combined realistic and decorative elements in a way that was completely revolutionary. *The Kiss*—his greatest painting and one of the icons of modern art—is here on display. Schiele and Kokoschka went even further, rejecting the decorative appeal of Klimt's glittering abstract designs and producing works that completely ignored conventional ideas of beauty. Today they are considered the fathers of modern art in Vienna. Modern music, too, has roots in the Belvedere complex: the composer Anton Bruckner lived and died here in 1896 in a small garden house now marked by a commemorative plaque. ⊠ *Prinz-Eugen-Str. 27,* ☎ *01/798–0700 or 01/795–570.* ⊡ *AS60 to all Belvedere museums.* ☉ *Tues.–Sun. 10–5. U-Bahn: U1, U2, U4 Karlsplatz, then Streetcar D to Belvederegasse.*

⑥¹ Historisches Museum der Stadt Wien (Museum of Viennese History). Housed in an incongruously modern building at the east end of the regal Karlsplatz, this museum possesses a dazzling array of Viennese historical artifacts and treasures: models, maps, documents, photographs, antiquities, stained glass, paintings, sculpture, crafts, and reconstructed rooms. Paintings include Klimts and Schieles, and there's a life-size portrait of the composer Alban Berg painted by his contemporary Arnold Schönberg. Alas, display information and designations in the museum are only in German, and there's no guidebook in English. ⊠ *Karlspl.,* ☎ *01/505–8747–0.* ⊡ *AS50.* ☉ *Tues.–Sun. 9–4:30. U-Bahn: U1, U2, U4 Karlsplatz.*

★ ⑥⁰ Karlskirche. Dominating the Karlsplatz is one of Vienna's greatest buildings, the Karlskirche, dedicated to St. Charles Borromeo. At first glance, the church seems like a fantastic vision—one blink and you half expect the building to vanish. For before you is a giant Baroque church framed by enormous freestanding columns, mates to the famous Trajan's Column of Rome's ancient Forum. These columns may be out of keeping with the building as a whole but were conceived with at least two functions in mind: One was to portray scenes from the life of the patron saint, carved in imitation of Trajan's triumphs, and thus help to emphasize the Imperial nature of the building; and the other was to symbolize the Pillars of Hercules, suggesting the right of the Habsburgs to their Spanish dominions, which the emperor had been forced to renounce. Whatever the reason, the end result is an architectural tour de force.

The Karlskirche was built in the early 18th century on what was then the bank of the River Wien and is now the southeast corner of the park complex. The church had its beginnings in a disaster. In 1713 Vienna was hit by a brutal plague outbreak, and Emperor Charles VI made a vow: If the plague abated, he would build a church dedicated to his namesake, St. Charles Borromeo, the 16th-century Italian bishop who was famous for his ministrations to Milanese plague victims. In 1715 construction began, using an ambitious design by Johann Bernhard Fischer von Erlach that combined architectural elements from ancient Greece (the columned entrance porch), ancient Rome (the Trajaneseque columns), contemporary Rome (the Baroque dome), and contemporary Vienna (the Baroque towers at either end). When it was finished, the church received a decidedly mixed press. History, incidentally, delivered a negative verdict: In its day the Karlskirche spawned no imitations, and it went on to become one of European architecture's most famous curiosities. Notwithstanding, seen lit at night, the building is magical in its setting.

The main interior of the church utilizes only the area under the dome and is surprisingly conventional given the unorthodox facade. The space and architectural detailing are typical High Baroque; the fine vault frescoes, by J. M. Rottmayr, depict St. Charles Borromeo imploring the Holy Trinity to end the plague. ⊠ *Karlspl.,* ☎ *01/504–61–87.* ☉ *Weekdays 7:30–7, Sat. 8–7, Sun. 9–7. U-Bahn: U1, U2, U4 Karlspl.*

Karlsplatz. Like the space now occupied by the Naschmarkt, Karlsplatz was formed when the River Wien was covered over at the turn of the century. At the time Wagner expressed his frustration with the result—too large a space for a formal square and too small a space for an informal park—and the awkwardness persists to this day. The buildings surrounding the Karlsplatz, however, are quite sure of themselves: The area is dominated by the classic **Karlskirche** (☞ *above*), made less dramatic by the unfortunate reflecting pool with its Henry Moore sculpture, wholly out of place, in front. On the south side of the Resselpark, that part of Karlsplatz named for the inventor of the ship's screw propeller, stands the **Technical University** (1816–18). In a house that occupied the space closest to the church, Italian composer Antonio Vivaldi died in 1741; a plaque marks the spot. On the north side across the heavily traveled roadway are the **Künstlerhaus** (the exhibition hall in which the Secessionists refused to exhibit, built in 1881 and still in use) and the **Musikverein** (☞ Music *in* Nightlife and the Arts, *below*). The latter, finished in 1869, is now home to the Vienna Philharmonic. The downstairs lobby and the two halls upstairs have been gloriously restored and glow with fresh gilding. The main hall has what may be the world's finest acoustics; this is the site of the annual, globally televised New Year's Day concert.

Some of Otto Wagner's finest Secessionist work can be seen two blocks east on the northern edge of Karlsplatz. In 1893 Wagner was appointed architectural supervisor of the new Vienna City Railway, and the matched pair of small pavilions he designed for the Karlsplatz **train station** in 1898 are among the city's most ingratiating buildings. Their structural framework is frankly exposed (in keeping with Wagner's belief in architectural honesty), but they are also lovingly decorated (in keeping with the Viennese fondness for architectural finery). The result is Jugendstil at its very best, melding plain and fancy with grace and insouciance. The pavilion to the southwest is utilized as a small, specialized museum. In the course of redesigning Karlsplatz, it was Wagner, incidentally, who proposed moving the fruit and vegetable market to what is now the Naschmarkt (☞ *below*).

Naschmarkt. The area between Linke and Rechte Wienzeile has for 80 years been home to the Naschmarkt, Vienna's main outdoor produce market, certainly one of Europe's—if not the world's—great open-air markets, where packed rows of polished and stacked fruits and vegetables compete for visual appeal with braces of fresh pheasant in season; the nostrils, meanwhile, are accosted by spice fragrances redolent of Asia or the Middle East. *U-Bahn: U1, U2, U4 Karlsplatz.*

NEED A BREAK? | Who can resist exploring the Naschmarkt without picking up a snack as you go along. The stands marked *Imbiss* (snack) will sell you a *Hühnerschnitzel-Semmel* (chicken schnitzel inside a Viennese roll); **Heindl & Co. Palatschinkenkuch'l** (pancake kitchen) sells a wide variety of meat and dessert crepes; and the **Naschmarkt Bäckerei** has pastries. You can find a *Stehkaffee* (literally, "stand-up coffee")—limited seats but high tables on which to lean—at the **Anker** pastry and bakery shops.

Otto Wagner Houses. The Ringstrasse-style apartment houses that line the Wienzeile are an attractive, if generally somewhat standard, lot, but two stand out: **Linke Wienzeile 38 and 40**—the latter better known as the "Majolica House"—designed (1898–99) by the grand old man of Viennese fin-de-siècle architecture, Otto Wagner, during his Secessionist phase. A good example of what Wagner was rebelling against can be seen next door, at **Linke Wienzeile 42,** where decorative enthusiasm has blossomed into Baroque Revival hysteria. Wagner had come to believe that this sort of display was nothing but empty pretense and sham; modern apartment houses, he wrote in his pioneering text *Modern Architecture,* are entirely different from 18th-century town palaces, and architects should not pretend otherwise. Accordingly, he banished classical decoration and introduced a new architectural simplicity, with flat exterior walls and plain, regular window treatments meant to reflect the orderly layout of the apartments behind them. There the simplicity ended. For exterior decoration, he turned to his younger Secessionist cohorts Joseph Olbrich and Koloman Moser, who designed the ornate Jugendstil patterns of red majolica-tile roses (No. 40) and gold stucco medallions (No. 38) that gloriously brighten the facades of the adjacent houses—so much so that their Baroque-period neighbor is ignored. The houses are private.

Schwarzenbergplatz. A remarkable urban ensemble, the Schwarzenbergplatz comprises some notable sights. The center of the lower square off the Ring is marked by an oversize equestrian Prince Schwarzenberg—he was a 19th-century field marshal for the imperial forces. Admire the overall effect of the square and see if you can guess which building is the newest; it's the one on the northeast corner (No. 3) at Lothringer Strasse, an exacting reproduction of a building destroyed by war damage in 1945 and dating only to the 1980s. The military monument occupying the south end of the square behind the fountain is the **Russian War Memorial,** set up at the end of World War II by the Soviets; the Viennese, remembering the Soviet occupation, call its unknown soldier the "unknown plunderer." South of the memorial is the stately **Schwarzenberg Palace,** designed as a summer residence by Johann Lukas von Hildebrandt in 1697, completed by Fischer von Erlach father and son, and now (in part) a luxury hotel (☞ Dining and Lodging, *below*). The delightful formal gardens wedged between Prinz Eugen-Strasse and the Belvedere gardens can be enjoyed from the hotel restaurant's veranda.

★ ⑤ **Secession Building.** If the Academy of Fine Arts represents the conservative attitude toward the arts in the late 1800s, then its antithesis can be found immediately behind it to the southeast: the Secession Pavilion. Restored in the mid-1980s after years of neglect, the Secession building is one of Vienna's preeminent symbols of artistic rebellion. Rather than looking to the architecture of the past, like the revivalist Ringstrasse, it looked to a new antihistoricist future. It was, in its day, a riveting trumpet blast of a building and is today considered by many to be Europe's first example of full-blown 20th-century architecture.

The Secession began in 1897 when 20 dissatisfied Viennese artists, headed by Gustav Klimt, "seceded" from the Künstlerhausgenossenschaft, the conservative artists' society associated with the Academy of Fine Arts. The movement promoted the radically new kind of art known as Jugendstil, which found its inspiration in both the organic, fluid designs of Art Nouveau and the related but more geometric designs of the English Arts and Crafts Movement. (The Secessionists founded an Arts and Crafts workshop of their own, the famous Wiener Werkstätte, in an effort to embrace the applied arts.) The Secession building was the movement's exhibition hall, designed by the architect Joseph Olbrich and completed in 1898. The lower story, crowned by the entrance motto *Der Zeit Ihre Kunst, Der Kunst Ihre Freiheit* ("To Every Age Its Art,

To Art Its Freedom"), is classic Jugendstil: The restrained but assured decoration (by Koloman Moser) beautifully complements the facade's pristine flat expanses of cream-color wall. Above the entrance motto sits the building's most famous feature, the gilded openwork dome that the Viennese were quick to christen "the golden cabbage" (Olbrich wanted it to be seen as a dome of laurel, a subtle classical reference meant to celebrate the triumph of art). The plain white interior— "shining and chaste," in Olbrich's words—was also revolutionary; its most unusual feature was movable walls, allowing the galleries to be reshaped and redesigned for every show. One early show, in 1902, was an exhibition devoted to art celebrating the genius of Beethoven; Gustav Klimt's *Beethoven Frieze*, painted for the occasion, has now been restored and is permanently installed in the building's basement. ⊠ *Friedrichstr. 12,* ☎ *01/587–5307–0.* 🖃 *AS90.* ☉ *Tues.–Fri. 10–6, weekends 10–4. U-Bahn: U1, U2, U4 Karlsplatz.*

OFF THE
BEATEN PATH

ZENTRALFRIEDHOF – Taking a streetcar out of Schwarzenbergplatz, music lovers will want to make a pilgrimage to the **Zentralfriedhof** (Central Cemetery, ⊠ 11th District on Simmeringer Hauptstr.), which contains the graves of most of Vienna's great composers: Ludwig van Beethoven, Franz Schubert, Johannes Brahms, the Johann Strausses (father and son), and Arnold Schönberg, among others. The monument to Wolfgang Amadeus Mozart is a memorial only; the approximate location of his unmarked grave can be seen at the now deconsecrated St. Marx-Friedhof at Leberstrasse 6–8. *Streetcar 71 to St. Marxer Friedhof, or on to Zentralfriedhof Haupttor/2*

Splendors of the Habsburgs: A Visit to Schönbrunn Palace

The glories of imperial Austria are nowhere brought together more convincingly than in the Schönbrunn Palace (Schloss Schönbrunn) complex. Brilliant "Maria Theresa Yellow"—she, in fact, caused Schöbrunn to be built—is everywhere in evidence. Imperial elegance flows unbroken throughout the grounds and the setting, and the impression even today is interrupted only by tourists. This is one of Austria's primary tourist sites, although sadly, few stay long enough to discover the real Schönbrunn (including the little maiden with the water jar, after whom the complex is named). While the assorted outbuildings might seem eclectic, they served as centers of entertainment when the court moved to Schönbrunn in the summer, accounting for the zoo, the priceless theater, the fake Roman ruins, the greenhouses, and the walkways. In Schönbrunn, you step back three hundred years into the heart of a powerful and growing empire and follow it through to defeat and demise in 1917.

A Good Walk

The usual start for exploring the Schönbrunn complex is the main palace. There's nothing wrong with that approach, but as a variation, consider first climbing to the **Gloriette** ⓖ on the hill overlooking the site, for a bird's-eye view to put the rest in perspective (take the stairs to the Gloriette roof for the ultimate experience). While at the Gloriette, take a few steps west to discover the **Tiroler House** ⓖ and follow the zigzag path downhill to the palace; note the picture-book views of the main building through the woods. Try to take the full tour of the **Schönbrunn Palace** ⓖ rather than the shorter, truncated version. Check whether the ground-floor back rooms (*Berglzimmer*) are open to viewing. After the palace guided tour, take your own walk around the grounds. The Schöner Brunner, the namesake fountain, is hidden in the woods to the southeast; continue along to discover the convincing (but fake) Roman Ruins. At the other side of the complex to the west are the excellent

Tiergarten ⑥⑥ (zoo), the **Palmenhaus** ⑥⑦ (tropical greenhouse), and the attached **Schmetterlinghaus** (butterfly house). Closer to the main entrance, both the **Wagenburg** ⑥⑧ (carriage museum) and Schlosstheater (palace theater) are frequently overlooked treasures. Before heading back to the city center, visit the **Hofpavillion** ⑥⑨, the private subway station built for Emperor Franz Josef, located to the west across Schönbrunner Schlossstrasse.

TIMING

If you're really pressed for time, the shorter guided tour will give you a fleeting impression of the palace itself, but try to budget at least half a day to take the full tour and include the extra rooms and grounds as well. The 20-minute hike up to the Gloriette is a bit strenuous but worthwhile, and there's now a café as reward at the top. The zoo is worth as much time as you can spend, and figure on at least a half hour to an hour each for the other museums. Tour buses begin to unload for the main building about mid-morning; start early or utilize the noon lull to avoid the worst crowds. The other museums and buildings in the complex are far less crowded.

Sights to See

⑥③ **Gloriette.** At the crest of the hill, topping off the Schönbrunn Palace, sits a Baroque masterstroke: Johann Ferdinand von Hohenberg's incomparable Gloriette, now restored to its original splendor. Perfectly scaled for its setting, the Gloriette—a palatial pavilion that once offered royal guests a place to rest and relax on their tours of the palace grounds and that now houses an equally welcome café—holds the whole vast garden composition together and at the same time crowns the ensemble with a brilliant architectural tiara. This was a favorite spot of Maria Theresa's, though in later years she grew so fat it took six men to carry her in her palanquin to the summit.

⑥⑨ **Hofpavillon.** The most unusual interior of the palace complex, the restored imperial subway station known as the Hofpavillon is just outside the palace grounds (at the northwest corner, a few yards east of the Hietzing subway station). Designed by Otto Wagner in conjunction with Joseph Olbrich and Leopold Bauer, the Hofpavillon was built in 1899 for the exclusive use of Emperor Franz Josef and his entourage. Exclusive it was: The emperor used the station only once. The exterior, with its proud architectural crown, is Wagner at his best, and the lustrous interior is one of the finest examples of Jugendstil decoration in the city. ⊠ *Schönbrunner Schloss-Str., next to Hietzing subway station,* ☎ *01/877–1571.* ⊡ *AS25.* ⊙ *Tues.–Sun. 9–12:15 and 1–4:30. U-Bahn: U4 Hietzing.*

⑥⑦ **Palmenhaus.** On the grounds to the west of Schönbrunn Palace is a huge greenhouse filled with exotic trees and plants. ⊠ *Nearest entrance Hietzing,* ☎ *01/877–5087–406.* ⊡ *AS40, combined ticket with Schmetterlinghaus (☞ below) AS65.* ⊙ *May–Sept., daily 9:30–6 (last admission at 5:30); Oct.–Apr., daily 9:30–5 (last admission at 4:30).*

Schmetterlinghaus. Close by the Palmenhaus (☞ *above*) is another Schönbrunn Palace favorite, given over to hordes of live butterflies, orchids, and other floral displays. ⊠ *Nearest entrance Hietzing,* ☎ *01/877–5087–421.* ⊡ *AS40, combined ticket with Palmenhaus (☞ above) AS65.* ⊙ *May–Sept., daily 10–5 (last admission at 4:30); Oct.–Apr., daily 10–3:30 (last admission at 3).*

★ ⑥⑤ **Schönbrunn Palace.** Designed by Johann Bernhard Fischer von Erlach in 1696, Schönbrunn Palace, the huge Habsburg summer residence, lies well within the city limits, just a few subway stops west of Karlsplatz on line U4. The vast and elegantly planted gardens are open daily

Schönbrunn Palace and Park

from dawn till dusk, and multilingual guided tours of the palace interior are offered daily. A visit inside the palace is not included in most general city sightseeing tours, which offer either a mercilessly tempting drive past or else an impossibly short half hour or so to explore. The four-hour commercial sightseeing bus tours of Schönbrunn offered by tour operators cost several times what you'd pay if you tackled the easy excursion yourself; their advantage is that they get you there and back with less effort. Go on your own if you want time to wander the magnificent grounds.

The most impressive approach to the palace and its gardens is through the front gate, located on Schönbrunner Schloss-Strasse halfway between the Schönbrunn and Hietzing subway stations. The vast main courtyard is ruled by a formal design of impeccable order and rigorous symmetry: Wing nods at wing, facade mirrors facade, and every part stylistically complements every other. The courtyard, however, turns out to be a mere appetizer; the feast lies beyond. The breathtaking view that unfolds on the other side of the palace is one of the finest set pieces in all Europe and one of the supreme achievements of Baroque planning. Formal *allées* (garden promenades) shoot off diagonally, the one on the right toward the zoo, the one on the left toward a rock-mounted obelisk and a fine false Roman ruin. But these, and the woods beyond, are merely a frame for the astonishing composition in the center: the sculpted fountain; the carefully planted screen of trees behind; the sudden, almost vertical rise of the grass-covered hill beyond, with the ☞ **Gloriette** on top.

Within the palace, the magisterial state salons are quite up to the splendor of the gardens, but note the contrast between these chambers and the far more modest rooms in which the rulers—particularly Franz Josef—lived and spent most of their time. Of the 1,400 rooms, 40 are open to the public on the regular tour, and 2 are of special note: the Hall of Mirrors, where the six-year-old Mozart performed for Empress Maria Theresa in 1762 (and where he met six-year-old Marie Antoinette for the first time, developing a little crush on her), and the Grand Gallery, where the Congress of Vienna (1815) danced at night after carving up Napoléon's collapsed empire during the day. Ask about viewing the ground-floor living quarters (*Berglzimmer*), where the walls are fascinatingly painted with palm trees, exotic animals, and tropical views. As you go through the palace, take an occasional glance out the windows; you'll be rewarded by a better impression of the beautiful patterns of the formal gardens, punctuated by hedgerows and fountains. These window vistas were enjoyed by rulers from Maria Theresa and Napoléon to Franz Josef. ⊠ *Schönbrunner Schloss-Str.,* ☎ *01/81113.* ☜ *Grand tour of palace interior (40 rooms) AS140, self-guided grand tour (40 rooms) AS110, self-guided imperial tour (20 rooms) AS80.* ⊙ *Apr.–Oct., daily 8:30–5; Nov.–Mar., daily 8:30–4:30. U-Bahn: U4 Schönbrunn.*

Schönbrunn Palace Park. The palace grounds boast a bevy of splendid divertissements, including a grand zoo (☞ Tiergarten, *below*) and carriage museum (☞ Wagenburg, *below*). Climb to the Gloriette for a panoramic view out over the city as well as the palace complex. If you're exploring on your own, seek out the intriguing Roman ruin, now used as a backdrop for outdoor summer opera. The marble *schöner Brunnen* ("beautiful fountain"), with the young girl pouring water from an urn, is nearby. The fountain gave the name to the palace complex. ⊙ *May–Oct., daily 9–5. U-Bahn: U4 Schönbrunn.*

Ⓒ ⑥⑥ **Tiergarten.** Claimed to be the world's oldest, the zoo has retained its original Baroque decor and, today, has acquired world-class recognition under director Helmut Pechlaner. New settings have been created for both animals and public; in one case, the public looks out into a new, natural display area from one of the Baroque former animal houses. The zoo is constantly adding new attractions and undergoing renovations, so there's plenty to see. ☎ *01/877–1236–0.* ☜ *AS90.* ⊙ *Nov.–Jan., daily 9–4:30; Oct. and Feb., daily 9–5; Mar., daily 9–5:30; Apr., daily 9–6; May–Sept., daily 9–6:30. U-Bahn. U1.*

⑥④ **Tiroler House.** This charming building to the west of the Gloriette was a favorite retreat of Empress Elizabeth; it now includes a small restaurant (open according to season and weather).

Ⓒ ⑥⑧ **Wagenburg** (Carriage Museum). Most of the carriages are still roadworthy and, indeed, Schönbrunn dusted off the gilt-and-black royal funeral carriage that you see here for the burial ceremony of Empress Zita in 1989. ⊠ *Wagenburg,* ☎ *01/877–3244.* ☜ *AS30.* ⊙ *Nov.–Mar., Tues.–Sun. 10–4; Apr.–Oct., daily 9–6. U-Bahn: U4 Schönbrunn.*

DINING

Ever since joining the European Union a few years ago, Austria has undergone a culinary revolution, and nowhere is this more evident than in Vienna. It has emerged from its provincial stagnation with flying colors and now offers its share of world-class restaurants, and they're not only limited to the luxury establishments.

In a first-class restaurant you will pay as much as in most other major Western European capitals. But you can still find good food at refreshingly low prices in the simpler restaurants, particularly at neighborhood *Gasthäuser* in the suburbs. If you eat your main meal at noon (as the Viennese do), you can take advantage of the luncheon specials.

Vienna's restaurant fare ranges from Arabic to Yugoslav, with strong doses of Chinese, Italian, and Japanese, but assuming you've come for what makes Vienna unique, our listings focus not on exotic spots but on places where you'll meet the Viennese and experience Vienna.

Many restaurants are closed one or two days a week (often weekends), and most serve meals only 11:30–2 and 6–10. An increasing number now serve after-theater dinners, but reserve in advance. The pocket-size paperback book *Wien wie es isst* (in German; from almost any bookstore) gives up-to-date information on the restaurant, café, and bar scene. For an overview on the pleasures of Austrian cuisine, *see* "Schnitzels, Strudels, and Sachertortes" *in* Pleasures and Pastimes *in* Chapter 1.

CATEGORY	COST*
$$$$	over AS500
$$$	AS300–AS500
$$	AS150–AS300
$	under AS150

per person, including a small glass of open house wine or beer, service (usually 10%), sales tax (10%), and additional small tip (3%–5%)

Restaurants

$$$$ ✕ **Altwienerhof.** Inauspiciously tucked away in one of Vienna's drabber neighborhoods lies a culinary treasure, opened in 1928, in the same family ever since, and well known throughout the country. Guests dine in elegant rooms decorated with French tapestries, or in the beautiful, glass-enclosed winter garden, which overlooks a quiet courtyard. The chef-owner is renowned for his French-based cuisine and light, delicate sauces. The menu changes seasonally and fresh seafood is flown in daily. Look for *loup de mer,* a mild white fish in saffron sauce, and a side dish of potato mousseline with black truffles and fried parsley. *Wine Spectator* has proclaimed Altwienerhof's 25,000-bottle wine collection as one of the great wine cellars of the world, the only restaurant in Austria to be so honored. ⊠ *Herklotzg. 6,* ☎ *01/892–6000,* FAX *01/892–6000–8. Reservations essential. Jacket and tie. AE, DC, MC, V. Closed Sun. and last 3 wks of Jan.*

$$$$ ✕ **Imperial.** This exquisite restaurant in the Imperial hotel (☞ Lodging, *below*) now ranks with the top eateries in the city, and as soon as you're seated in the intimate, wood-paneled room you know you're in for a treat. Chef Stefan Hierzer is from Styria, and you'll find many Styrian specialties on the menu. The cream of potato soup with white truffle oil is especially delicious, and other good choices include Styrian beef with *Krautfleckerl*—little pasta squares with slivers of cabbage in a *Kübiskernöl* (pumpkin seed oil) sauce—or turbot with caviar, artichokes, yellow peppers, and snow peas. Service is friendly and attentive without being intrusive. ⊠ *Kärntner Ring 16,* ☎ *01/50110–0,* FAX *01/50110–410. AE, DC, MC, V. No lunch.*

$$$$ ✕ **Korso.** For many, this is Vienna's top restaurant, and chef Reinhard
★   Gerer is known throughout Austria for his creative touch. The setting for such gastronomic excellence is appropriate, with gleaming wood-paneled walls, beveled glass, and tables set with fine linen, sparkling Riedel crystal, and fresh flowers. Specialties include *Felchen,* a delicate white fish served with glass noodles, or lobster with white beans, arugula, and black polenta. If money is no object, have the chef prepare a special tasting menu, with a different wine to accompany each course. Some readers have complained of snooty service. ⊠ *Mahlerstr. 2,* ☎ *01/515–16–546,* FAX *01/515–16–550. Reservations essential. Jacket and tie. AE, DC, MC, V. Closed Aug. No lunch Sat.*

$$$$ ✕ **Le Siècle.** Guests at the Radisson/SAS Palais Hotel and others come here to dine in pampered elegance on a variety of seafood, flown in fresh daily. Tempting items on the ever-changing menu might include marinated salmon with a dill mustard sauce to start, followed by lightly fried turbot fillet with white asparagus and artichoke-and-truffle mousse. Desserts, like the delicate citrus fruit terrine, are inspired and steer away from traditional heavy cakes and strudels. ⊠ *Parkring 16,* ☎ *01/515–17–3440. Reservations essential. Jacket and tie. AE, DC, MC, V. Closed weekends and July and Aug.*

$$$$ ✕ **Palais Schwarzenberg.** This restaurant, in a former private 18th-century palace, has one of the most impressive settings in Vienna, but be sure to book a table on the glassed-in terrace; you'll be surrounded inside by greenery, with a view out over the formal gardens. Try not to fill up on the variety of freshly baked breads and olives that are first brought to the table, because you'll want to order some of the tempting appetizers, such as risotto with spinach, black truffles and fontina cheese, or ribbon pasta with breast of quail in a mushroom sauce, before going on to the main course. Fish is nicely done here, and a good choice is grilled turbot with potato ravioli. ⊠ *Schwarzenbergpl. 9,* ☎ *01/798–4515–600,* 🖷 *01/798–4714. Reservations essential. Jacket and tie. AE, DC, MC, V.*

$$$$ ✕ **Steirereck.** This is generally conceded to be the most famous restau-
★ rant in Austria, and it consistently ranks high on critics' lists. The setting is elegant, and extra touches include a bread trolley overflowing with freshly baked breads and, at the end of the meal, an outstanding selection of cheeses from Steirereck's own cheese cellar. Fish choices are plentiful and may include delicate smoked catfish, turbot in an avocado crust, or char with mashed potatoes on a bed of white garlic sauce. Also good is the quail in red wine sauce with zucchini cannelloni or lamb with crepes and spinach cooked simply with garlic and olive oil. ⊠ *Rasumofskyg. 2,* ☎ *01/713–3168,* 🖷 *01/713–5168–2. Reservations essential. Jacket and tie. AE, DC, MC, V. Closed weekends.*

$$$$ ✕ **Zu den Drei Husaren.** One of Vienna's oldest restaurants, the "Three
★ Hussars" has triumphantly regained its reputation as a gourmet temple over the last few years, and the friendly staff will put you at ease while you settle in for a relaxing, luxurious evening. The friendly staff will put you at ease while you settle in for a relaxing, luxurious evening, although the enticing but unpriced evening hors d'oeuvre trolley can send your bill soaring. The menu offers traditional Viennese cuisine as well as a superb veal cutlet with pesto fettuccine or guinea fowl with stuffed morel mushrooms. Even if dessert is not your thing, you shouldn't pass up such exquisite delights as *Husarenpfannkuchen,* the house crepes. The only caveat is that the enticing but unpriced evening hors d'oeuvre trolley can send your bill soaring. ⊠ *Weihburgg. 4,* ☎ *01/ 512–1092,* 🖷 *01/512–1092–18. Reservations essential. Jacket and tie. AE, DC, MC, V. Closed mid-July–mid-Aug.*

$$$ ✕ **Do & Co.** The spectacular setting at the top of the modern Neues
★ Haas-Haus building smack in the middle of Stephansplatz would make this worthwhile for the view alone, but the food is also excellent and varied, with a nouvelle Asian touch featuring fragrant, tangy wok creations. For heartier appetites there are numerous meat choices, such as the popular combination King crab and Uruguayan steak. There is also a fantastic, though pricey, sushi bar at lunchtime. In the evenings, make sure to book a table by the window so you can see the sunset over the spires of St. Stephen's and the rooftops of the city; in warm weather, ask for a table outside on the balcony. ⊠ *Stephanspl. 12,* ☎ *01/535–3969. Reservations essential. AE, DC, MC, V.*

66

Vienna Dining

KEY

AE American Express Office

i Tourist Information

0 _____ 1/4 mile

0 _____ 1/4 km

$$$ ✕ **Fadinger.** Some of the best nouvelle Austrian cuisine in the city can be found at this small, plainly decorated restaurant near the Börse (the Vienna Stock Exchange). The widely varied menu includes light-as-a-feather fish dishes, such as salmon in a crispy potato crust, as well as hearty but never heavy meat courses. The *Zwiebelrostbraten*, skirt steak topped with crispy fried onions, is outstanding. ✉ *Wipplingerstr. 29*, ☎ *01/533–4341. Reservations essential. No credit cards. Closed weekends.*

$$$ ✕ **Griechenbeisl.** An inn has been on this site since 1457, next to the glittering gold Greek Orthodox church, in one of the prettiest areas in the city. Now housed within the half-timbered walls is a old-fashioned kitchen that serves traditional, delicious Viennese dishes, such as thick and hearty goulash soup, Wiener schnitzel, and *Apfelstrudel*. In summer tables are set up in the charming small square in front of the restaurant. ✉ *Fleischmarkt 11*, ☎ *01/533–1941. AE, DC, MC, V.*

$$$ ✕ **Neu Wien.** As the name says, this is a taste of the new Vienna. The
★   vaulted interior is enlivened by cheeky modern art, and service is friendly and efficient. The eclectic menu changes frequently, but look for the herbed goat cheese salad with basil oil dressing; *Zanderfilet*, a crispy pike perch with a cream beet sauce; or veal with tagliatelle in a truffle sauce. Top it all off with a bottle of smooth Vranac from Montenegro. ✉ *Bäckerstr. 5*, ☎ *01/512–0999. Reservations essential. MC, V. Closed weekends in summer. No lunch.*

$$$ ✕ **Schnattl.** If you're not outdoors in the idyllic courtyard, the setting could be described as cool postmodern: The main room has now acquired a warmer patina but is relatively unadorned, letting you concentrate instead on the attractively set tables and excellent cuisine (which offers occasional surprises such as medallions of mountain ram). Traditional dishes like roast pork are transformed with such touches as a light mustard sauce, lamb with a trace of rosemary, with offerings dependent on season and availability of fresh ingredients. The real bargain here is the daily AS75 lunch special. ✉ *Lange G. 40*, ☎ *01/405–3400. AE, DC. Closed Sun., 2 wks around Easter, and late Aug.–mid-Sept. No lunch Sat.*

$$$ ✕ **Zu ebener Erde und erster Stock.** This gem of a historic house near
★   the Volkstheater was named after a play by Nestroy and means "the ground level and first floor." Upstairs is the cozy Biedermeier room with crocheted pillows and old family photos on the walls, and downstairs is an informal room that appeals to diners who want a light, pretheater meal. *Kürbis* (pumpkin) figures prominently on the menu, from the salted, roasted pumpkin seeds that are brought for you to nibble on while deciding what to order to the pumpkin cream soup to the delicious pumpkin risotto and branzino in rosemary broth. The thyme gnocchi and beef roulade stuffed with mozzarella and eggplant is also wonderful. For dessert try the light *Topfenknödel* with plums. ✉ *Burgg. 13*, ☎ *01/523–6254. Reservations essential. AE, V. Closed Sat. lunch, Sun.–Mon., and 1st 3 wks of Aug.*

$$$ ✕ **Zum Kuckuck.** Once you step inside this intimate, vaulted-ceiling restaurant, you enter Old Vienna and leave the modern world behind. Tables are set with pink linen, pewter candlesticks, and fresh flowers, and old prints from Emperor Franz Josef's time adorn the walls. Sip a glass of *Sekt* (Austria sparkling wine) with blood orange juice while perusing the extensive menu. The kitchen offers good, honest cooking, from beef rouladen marinated in red wine to duck in a honey–green peppercorn sauce. ✉ *Himmelpfortg. 15*, ☎ *01/512–8470*, ℻ *01/774–1855. AE, DC, MC, V. Closed Sun.*

$$ ✕ **A Tavola.** Ever since this casual, trendy Italian restaurant opened,
★   it's been hard to get a table. As soon as you're seated, a variety of delicious breads and deep green olive oil are placed in front of you, but it's still hard to resist ordering a bowl of thick, chunky tomato soup

or an arugula salad for a starter. Pasta dishes are a specialty, including the unusual and tasty spaghetti with curry, black olives and chicken breast, but there's also a plentiful choice of beef, chicken, and fish dishes, and pheasant in season. ⊠ *Weihburgg. 3–5,* ☎ *01/512–7955. Reservations essential. AE, DC, MC, V. Closed Mon.*

$$ ✕ **Artner.** This modern, nicely lit restaurant has one of the most in-
★ novative menus in the city, plus it has the unique feature of showcasing fantastic wines and goat cheese from its own 350-year-old winery in the Carnuntum region east of Vienna. Start with a salad of field greens and grilled goat cheese, then go on to mahimahi wrapped in a palm leaf and served with red rice in a mango-coconut sauce, or sesame-crusted pike perch with Oriental noodles and cilantro pesto. Lamb and veal dishes are also temptingly offered. This is one of the few kitchens in Vienna that stay open all afternoon. It's located just around the corner from Taubstummengasse, one subway stop from St. Stephen's on the U1. ⊠ *Florag. 6 (entrance on Neumanng.),* ☎ *01/503–5033,* 𝔽𝔸𝕏 *01/503–5034. AE, DC, MC, V. No lunch weekends.*

$$ ✕ **Bei Max.** The decor is somewhat bland, but the tasty Carinthian specialties—the cheese-and-meat-filled ravioli known as *Käsnudeln* and *Fleischnudeln* in particular—pack this friendly restaurant. You'll also find such classic standards as *Tafelspitz* (boiled beef), as well as outstanding desserts. The *Kletzennudeln,* a form of bread pudding with dried fruit and cinnamon, is a house feature. ⊠ *Landhausg. 2/Herreng.,* ☎ *01/533–7359. No credit cards. Closed weekends, last wk of July, and 1st 3 wks of Aug.*

$$ ✕ **Boheme.** This charming restaurant in the Spittelberg area is a favorite hangout of opera singers, and autographed pictures of some of the opera-loving owner's more famous patrons line the walls. Opera arias play in the background, and the ambience is casual and relaxed. Start with a tasty salad of field greens and fried zucchini in a yogurt dressing or the simple sliced tomatoes with olives and fresh mozzarella; then go on to pork medallions with potato cakes in a mushroom cream sauce or the more traditional roast duck with dumplings and *Rotkraut* (red cabbage). ⊠ *Spittelbergg. 19,* ☎ *01/523–3173. AE, DC, MC, V. Closed Sun. No lunch.*

$$ ✕ **Figlmüller.** Known for its gargantuan Wiener schnitzel, which is so large it overflows the plate, Figlmüller is always packed. Guests share the benches, the long tables, and the experience. Food choices are limited, and everything is à la carte. There are two entrances; one is off the passageway from Stephansdom. The small enclosed "greenhouse" in the passageway entry is more popular than the inside rooms. ⊠ *Wollzeile 5,* ☎ *01/512–6177. No credit cards. Closed Aug.*

$$ ✕ **Gösser Bierklinik.** The rooms go on and on in this upstairs (more formal) and downstairs (preferred) complex, which dates back four centuries. The fare is as solid as the house; the Wiener schnitzel here is first class. The salad bar is new. And there's a menu in English. The beer, of course, is Austrian, from the Gösser brewery in Styria. ⊠ *Steindlg. 4,* ☎ *01/535–6897. AE, DC, MC, V. Closed Sun.*

$$ ✕ **Lale.** Vienna has a substantial Turkish population, and this modern, inviting restaurant in the heart of the Schwedenplatz area serves some of the best Turkish cuisine in the city. Specialties include *Huhnerspiess,* chunks of tender grilled chicken breast on a skewer, served with yogurt and tomato sauce, and a wide variety of lamb dishes. The vegetarian *Döner* sandwich is a mouthwatering combination of grilled eggplant, feta, spinach, and hummus in a soft, freshly baked bun—perfect for a takeout lunch. ⊠ *Franz-Josef-Kai 29,* ☎ *01/535–2736. No credit cards.*

$$ ✕ **Lebenbauer.** Located in the shadow of the Freyung, this long-standing vegetarian restaurant even has a nonsmoking room, rare in this part of Europe. The menu offers both vegetarian and whole-grain items, and there's a lot to choose from. Specialties include *Hirsegröstl*, a millet hash with pumpkin seeds in an oyster mushroom sauce, and gluten-free pasta with smoked salmon and shrimp in a dill cream sauce. There are also several free-range chicken and fish entrées, all lightly prepared. ✉ *Teinfaltstr. 3,* ☎ *01/533–5556–0. AE, DC, MC, V. Closed 1st 2 wks of Aug. No lunch Sun., no dinner weekends.*

$$ ✕ **Livingstone.** If you're homesick for a hamburger and fries, this is the place to go. Buns are homemade, and the Austrian beef is of the finest quality. But if the tropical-colonial setting straight out of a 1940s Bogart movie makes you want to try something more adventurous, you won't be disappointed. The open kitchen allows you to glimpse some of the exotic food being prepared, such as pasta with smoked tofu, tiger shrimp, squash, and green chili peppers in a garlic-ginger sesame oil sauce. ✉ *Zelinkag. 4,* ☎ *01/533–3393. AE, DC, MC, V. No lunch.*

$$ ✕ **MAK Cafe.** In the Museum für angewandte Kunst, also known as MAK, this is one of the "scene" places in Vienna. The menu changes frequently and includes lots of vegetarian and pasta items. One staple is the delicious pierogi stuffed with either potatoes or minced beef. In summer sit outside in the shaded inner courtyard. ✉ *Stubenring 3–5,* ☎ *01/714–0121. No credit cards. Closed Mon.*

$$ ✕ **Schlossgasse 21.** There are three different settings in this popular restaurant, in the old Margareten area. The cavernous main room is for casual diners; the Hofstöckl offers a more elegant, intimate ambience; and the lovely garden courtyard entices everyone in fine weather. The food here is varied and delicious. You can make a meal of the *Baurensalat*—farmer's salad with field greens, Styrian sheep's cheese, and white beans in a Kürbiskernöl (pumpkin seed oil) dressing—and main courses offer everything from a real Argentine steak sandwich to *Käseschnitzel* (fried cheese) to exotic Asian dishes. The Hofstöckl has a schnapps bar with more than 50 varieties to choose from. ✉ *Schlossg. 21,* ☎ *01/544–0767. No credit cards. No lunch Oct.–Apr., no lunch weekends May–Sept. U-Bahn: U4/Pilgrimg.*

$$ ✕ **Strandcafé.** If you want to have a good meal directly on the banks of the Danube though away from the city center in the 22nd District, this is the place to go. The specialty of the house is the meaty, garlicky spareribs, served on a wooden plank, but you can also choose from a variety of Viennese dishes, including the delicious *Huhnerschnitzel* (fried, breaded fillet of chicken breast) and crispy french fries. ✉ *Florian-Berndl-G. 20,* ☎ *01/203–6747. No credit cards. U-Bahn: U1/Alte Donau.*

$$ ✕ **Wrenkh.** The menu here is eclectic, and everything is vegetarian and made from the freshest ingredients. Start with the miso soup and then go on to wild rice risotto with mushrooms or Greek fried rice with vegetables, sheep's cheese, and olives. The minimalist-style café section offers lunch specials at a great value, while the more elegant adjacent room is perfect for a nice, relaxed lunch or dinner. On Sundays there is a brunch buffet. There is also a nonsmoking room. ✉ *Bauernmarkt 10,* ☎ *01/533–1526. AE, DC, MC, V. Closed Sun., except 1st Sun. of month, open for brunch.*

$ ✕ **Brezl Gwölb.** Housed in a medieval pretzel factory between Am Hof and Judenplatz, this snug restaurant fills up fast at night. Try the scrumptious *Tyroler G'röstl*, a kind of hash served in a blackened skillet, or the *Kasnockerl*, spaëtzle in a pungent cheese sauce. Try to get a table downstairs in the real medieval cellar, which looks like a set from *Phantom of the Opera*. ✉ *Ledererhof 9,* ☎ *01/533–8811. AE, DC, MC, V.*

$ ✕ **Fischer Braü.** This is known as Vienna's number one brewery restau-
★ rant, and though it's located in the 19th District, it's worth the effort
to get here. Several varieties of their own fresh beer are featured, and
the menu is extensive, but nothing fancy. You can choose from stuffed
baked potatoes, salads, or Wiener schnitzel, huge and served with a
side order of potato salad. Especially scrumptious is the golden-fried
Hühnerschnitzel (chicken breast). The beer garden with its twinkling
lights strung through the trees is packed on summer evenings, so come
early to get a table. Every Sunday there is a popular jazz brunch, with
live music. ⊠ *Billrothstr. 17,* ☎ *01/319–6264. No credit cards. No
lunch, except Sun. brunch.*

$ ✕ **Plutzer Bräu.** At the top of the quaint, cobblestone Spittelberg dis-
trict, this sleek, modern brew pub always seems to draw a crowd. The
beer, microbrewed on the premises, is excellent, and there are many kinds
to try. To go along with a glass or two, have a rack of tender spareribs,
a *Putenschnitzel* (fried, breaded turkey breast), or just a nice big salad
with strips of grilled chicken. In summer tables are set outside on the
pedestrian street. ⊠ *Schrankg. 2,* ☎ *01/526–1215. No credit cards.*

$ ✕ **Rosenberger Marktrestaurant.** Downstairs under a huge (artificial)
tree you'll find a cluster of cafeteria islands offering soups, excellent
grilled specialties, vegetables, pastas, salads, desserts, and fresh juices
and other beverages, all prepared to order and attractively (if somewhat confusingly) presented. You can leave your valuables in one of
the free lockers while you make and enjoy your selection. Look for seasonal specialties such as asparagus and fresh chilled melon. Take your
choice to any of the side rooms, some decorated with musical instruments, some with antique kitchenware and dishes. ⊠ *Maysederg. 2/
Fürichg. 3,* ☎ *01/512–3458. No credit cards.*

$ ✕ **Spatzennest.** This is simple, hearty Viennese cooking at its best, lo-
cated on a quaint, cobblestone pedestrian street straight out of a 1930s
Hollywood movie set in Old Vienna. Tasty dishes include Wiener
schnitzel, roast chicken, and pillowy fried spaëtzle with slivers of ham
and melted cheese. It's especially delightful in summer, when tables are
set outside. It can be smoky indoors. ⊠ *Ulrichspl. 1,* ☎ *01/520–
1659. No credit cards. Closed Fri.–Sat.*

$ ✕ **Trzesniewski.** "Unpronounceably good" is the (correct) motto of this
tiny sandwich shop, a Viennese tradition for decades. If a quick snack
will suffice, three or four of the open sandwiches and a *Pfiff* (⅛ liter,
or ¹⁄₁₀ quart) of beer, or a vodka, may be just the needed pickup. Share
one of the few tables, or stand up at one of the counters. You'll be surprised at the elegance of many of the customers. ⊠ *Dorotheerg. 1,* ☎
01/512–3291. No credit cards. Closed Sun. No dinner Sat.

Wine Taverns

In-town wine restaurants cannot properly be called *Heurigen,* since they
are not run by the vintner, so the term is *Weinkeller* (wine restaurant, or
cellar). Many of them extend a number of levels underground, particularly in the older part of the city. Mainly open in the evening, they are
intended primarily for drinking, though you can always get something
to eat from a buffet, and increasingly, full dinners are available. As at
their country cousins, wine is served by the mug. Some of the better wine
restaurants follow; no credit cards are accepted except where noted.

$$ ✕ **Augustinerkeller.** This ground-floor Keller is open at noontime as
★ well as in the evening. The spit-roasted chicken is excellent, as is the
filling *Stelze* (roast knuckle of pork). For dessert, try the *Apfelstrudel,*
moist and warm from the oven. There's kitschy live music at night. ⊠
Augustinerstr. 1/Albertinerpl., ☎ *01/533–1026. MC, V.*

$$ ✕ **Esterházykeller.** This maze of rooms offers some of the best Keller wines in town plus a typical Vienna menu noontime and evenings, as well as a hot and cold buffet, but the atmosphere may be too smoky for some. ⊠ *Haarhof 1,* ☎ *01/533–3482. Closed weekends.*

$$ ✕ **Melker Stiftskeller.** Down and down you go, into one of the friendli-
★ est Kellers in town, where Stelze is a popular feature, along with out-standing wines by the glass or, rather, mug. ⊠ *Schotteng. 3,* ☎ *01/ 533–5530. MC. Closed Sun. No lunch.*

$ ✕ **Zwölf Apostel-Keller.** You pass a huge wood statue of St. Peter on the way downstairs to the two underground floors in this deep-down cellar in the oldest part of Vienna. The young crowd comes for the good wines and the atmosphere, and there's buffet food as well. ⊠ *Sonnenfelsg. 3,* ☎ *01/512–6777. No lunch.*

Heurigen

Few cities the size of Vienna boast wine produced within city limits, and even fewer offer wines ranging from good to outstanding. But in various suburban villages—once well outside the center but now parts of the urban complex—the fringes of the city have spawned charac-teristic wine taverns and restaurants, sometimes in the vineyards them-selves. Summer and fall are the seasons for visiting the Heurigen, though often the more elegant and expensive establishments, called *Noble-Heurige,* stay open year-round. Heurigen are concentrated in several outskirts of Vienna: Stammersdorf, Grinzing, Sievering, Nuss-dorf, Neustift, and a corner of Ottakring. Perchtoldsdorf, just outside Vienna, is also well known for its wine taverns.

Our favorite district is Stammersdorf, across the Danube. Try **Robert Helm** for good wines, a small but complete buffet including desserts from the house kitchen, and a wonderfully inviting tree-shaded gar-den. Call to confirm that this is open; it sometimes closed for irregu-lar periods. ⊠ *Stammersdorfer Str. 121,* ☎ *01/292–1244. No credit cards. Closed Sun. and Mon.*

Wine and food are both outstanding at **Wieninger,** with its spacious gar-den and series of typical vintner's rooms. Wieningers's bottled wines are ranked among the country's best. ⊠ *Stammersdorfer Str. 78,* ☎ *01/ 292–4106. No credit cards. Closed Mon. and mid-Dec.–Jan. 2.*

The Grinzing district today suffers from mass tourism, with very few exceptions; one is **Zum Martin Sepp,** where the wine, food, service, and ambience are all good. ⊠ *Cobenzlg. 32,* ☎ *01/324–4875. DC, V.*

East of the Grinzing village center, **Zimmermann** has excellent wines and buffet foods, an enchanting tree-shaded garden, and an endless collec-tion of small paneled rooms and vaulted cellars. ⊠ *Armbrusterg. 5/ Grinzinger Str.,* ☎ *01/318–8975. AE, DC, MC, V. Closed Sun. No lunch.*

In Sievering, vintner **Haslinger** offers both good wines and a small but tasty buffet. The atmosphere is plain but honest both indoors and in the small, typical vine-covered garden outside in summer. ⊠ *Agnesg. 3,* ☎ *01/440–1347. No credit cards. Closed Mon.*

In Neustift am Walde, **Shreiberhaus** has one of the prettiest terraced gardens in the city, with picnic tables stretching straight up into the vineyards. The buffet offers a delicious array of dishes, such as spit-roasted chicken, salmon pasta, and a huge selection of tempting grilled vegetables and salads. The golden Traminer wine is excellent. ⊠ *Rath-str. 54,* ☎ *01/440–3844. No credit cards.*

In Nussdorf seek out **Schübel-Auer** for its series of atmospheric rooms and good wines. ⊠ *Kahlenberger Str. 22,* ☎ *01/372222. No credit cards. Closed Sun., Jan., and July.*

Heiligenstadt is home to **Mayer am Pfarrplatz**—the legendary Heuriger in Beethoven's former abode—where the atmosphere in the collection of rooms is genuine, the à la carte offerings and buffet more than abundant, and the house wines excellent. You'll even find some Viennese among the tourists. ⊠ *Heiligenstädter Pfarrpl. 2,* ☎ *01/371287. AE, DC, MC, V. No lunch weekdays or Sat.*

Cafés

One of the quintessential Viennese institutions, the coffeehouse, or café, is club, pub, and bistro all rolled into one. For decades, a substantial part of Austrian social life has revolved around them (though now less than in the past) as Austrians by and large are rather reluctant to invite strangers to their homes and prefer to meet them in the friendly, but noncommittal, atmosphere of the café.

To savor the atmosphere of the coffeehouses you must take your time; set aside an afternoon, a morning, or at least a couple of hours, and settle down in one of your choice. Read or catch up on your letter writing: There is no need to worry about outstaying one's welcome, even over a single small cup of coffee, better identified as a *kleiner Schwarzer* (black) or *kleiner Brauner* (with milk). (Of course, in some of the more opulent coffeehouses, this cup of coffee can cost as much as a meal.)

Coffee is not just coffee in Austria. It comes in many forms and under many names. Morning coffee is generally *Melange* (half coffee, half milk) or, with little milk, a *Brauner.* The usual after-dinner drink is *Mokka,* very black, and most Austrians like it heavily sweetened. Restaurants that serve Balkan food offer *Türkischer,* or Turkish coffee, a strong, thick brew. Most delightful are the coffee-and-whipped-cream concoctions, universally cherished as *Kaffee mit Schlag,* a taste that is easily acquired and a menace to all but the very thin. The coffee may be either hot or cold. A customer who wants more whipped cream than coffee asks for a *Doppelschlag.* Hot black coffee in a glass with one knob of whipped cream is an *Einspänner* (literally, "one-horse coach"). Then you can go to town on a *Mazagran,* black coffee with ice and a tot of rum, or *Eiskaffee,* cold coffee with ice cream, whipped cream, and biscuits. Or you can simply order a *Portion Kaffee* and have an honest pot of coffee and jug of hot milk.

The typical Viennese café, with polished brass or marble-topped tables, bentwood chairs, supplies of newspapers, and tables outside in good weather, is a fixed institution, of which there are literally hundreds. All cafés serve pastries and light snacks in addition to beverages. Many offer a menu or fixed lunch at noon, but be aware that some can get rather expensive. No credit cards are accepted unless noted.

Of course, when tourists think of Viennese cafés, Demel (☞ Exploring Vienna, *above*) and Café Sacher (☞ Lodging, *below*) leap to mind, but they are hardly typical. When you want a quick (but excellent) coffee and dessert, look for an **Aida** café; they are scattered throughout the city. If all you want is just a fast but delicious cup of coffee, head for **Café de l'Europe** at Graben 31, where if you stand at one of the tall tables you pay only AS20. A seat will double the price. **Eduscho** is a coffee chain located throughout the city, offering a cup of regular coffee for just AS8, though no place to sit.

Here's a sampling of the best of the traditional cafés: **Alte Backstube** (⌧ Lange G. 34, ☎ 01/406–1101), in a gorgeous Baroque house—with a café in front and restaurant in back—was once a bakery and is now a museum as well. **Bräunerhof** (⌧ Stallburggasse 2, ☎ 01/512–3893) has music on some afternoons. **Café Central** (⌧ Herrengasse 14, ☎ 01/ 535–4176–0) is where Stalin and Trotsky played chess. **Frauenhuber** (⌧ Himmelpfortgasse 6, ☎ 01/512–4323) has its original turn-of-the-century interior and a good choice of desserts. **Landtmann** (⌧ Dr.-Karl-Lueger-Ring 4, ☎ 01/532–0621) is an elegant turn-of-the-century café, reputed to have been a favorite of Freud's. In fine weather you can sit outside on the front terrace, offering glorious views of the city. **Museum** (⌧ Friedrichstr. 6, ☎ 01/586–5202), original interior by the architect Adolf Loos, draws a mixed crowd and has lots of newspapers. **Schwarzenberg** (⌧ Kärntner Ring 17, ☎ 01/512–7393), with piano music in late afternoons, is highly popular, particularly its sidewalk tables in summer. **Tirolerhof** (⌧ Tegetthoffstr. 8/Albertinapl., ☎ 01/512–7833), with ample papers and excellent desserts, is popular with students.

Café Hawelka (⌧ Dorotheergasse 12, ☎ 01/512–8230) deserves special mention; whole books have been written at and about this shabby gathering place—its international clientele ranges from artists to politicians. Hawelka is jammed any time of day, so you share a table (and the very smoky atmosphere). In a city noted for fine coffee, Hawelka's is superb, even more so when accompanied by a freshly baked *Buchterln* (sweet roll, evenings only).

Pastry Shops

Viennese pastries are said to be the best in the world. In all shops you can buy them to enjoy on the premises, usually with coffee, as well as to take out. A 200-year-old institution is **Demel** (☞ Exploring Vienna, *above*). **Gerstner** (⌧ Kärntnerstr. 15, ☎ 01/496377) is in the heart of the bustling Kärntnerstrasse and is one of the more modern Viennese cafés. Popular here is the Bruegel torte, a marzipan pastry especially concocted for their branch in the Kunsthistorisches Museum. **Heiner** (⌧ Kärntnerstr. 21-23, ☎ 01/512–6863–0; ⌧ Wollzeile 9, ☎ 01/512–4838–0) is dazzling for its crystal chandeliers as well as for its pastries. **Oberlaa** (⌧ Neuer Markt 16, ☎ 01/513–2936) has irresistible confections, cakes, and bonbons, as well as light lunches and salad plates, served outdoors in summer. **Sluka** (⌧ Rathauspl. 8, ☎ 01/406–8896–0) has special dietetic desserts, snacks, and an appetizer buffet and serves outdoors in summer.

LODGING

In Vienna's best hotels the staff seems to anticipate your wishes almost before you express them. Such service, of course, has its price, and if you wish, you can stay in Vienna in profound luxury. For those with more modest requirements, ample rooms are available in less expensive but entirely adequate hotels. Pensions, mainly bed-and-breakfast establishments often managed by the owner, generally represent good value. A number of student dormitories are run as hotels in summer, offering about the most reasonable quarters of all. And several apartment-hotels accommodate those who want to stay longer.

When you have only a short time to spend in Vienna, you will probably want to stay in the inner city (the First District, or 1010 postal code) or fairly close to it, within walking distance of the most important sights, restaurants, and shops. Although most of the hotels there are in the more expensive categories, excellent and reasonable accommodations can be found in the Sixth, Seventh, and Eighth districts and put you close to the major museums. You'll also find a group of moderate ($$) and inexpensive ($) hotels in the Mariahilfer Strasse–Westbahnhof area, within easy reach of the city center by subway.

For the high season, Easter–September, and around the Christmas–New Year holidays, make reservations a month or more in advance. Vienna is continually the site of some international convention or other, and the city fills up quickly.

Our hotel categories correspond more or less to the official Austrian rating system, with five stars the equivalent of our very expensive ($$$$) category. Color television is usual in the top two categories; breakfast is included with all *except* the highest category. Air-conditioning is rare except in the larger, newer chain hotels. These seem constantly to be hosting convention or seminar groups, making service somewhat less personal, but there are exceptions, as noted.

CATEGORY	COST*
$$$$	over AS2,700
$$$	AS1,200–AS2,700
$$	AS950–AS1,200
$	under AS950

All prices are for two persons in a standard double room, including local taxes (usually 10%), service (15%), and breakfast (except in most $$$$ hotels).

$$$$ ⊞ **Bristol.** This hotel has one of the finest locations in Europe, on the Ring next to the Opera House. The accent here is on tradition, from the brocaded walls to the Biedermeier period furnishings in the public rooms and some of the bedrooms. The house dates from 1892, and during the 1945–55 occupation it was the U.S. military headquarters. The view is better from rooms on the Kärntnerstrasse or the Ring, and some rooms have balconies facing the Opera. The Bristol also houses the acclaimed Korso restaurant (☞ Dining, *above*). ⊠ *Kärntner Ring 1, A–1010,* ☎ *01/515–16–0,* FAX *01/515–16–550. 141 rooms with bath. 2 restaurants, bar, health club. AE, DC, MC, V.*

$$$$ ⊞ **Das Triest.** This is a little off the beaten track but still within easy
★   walking distance of the city center. Recently totally redone by Sir Terence Conran, it's now Vienna's most chic hotel, giving guests the feeling that they are onboard an ultrasleek new ocean liner, which is surprising, considering it was once the stables of the old Vienna-Trieste posthouse. The extra little touches in the rooms here are plentiful; even the doorknobs feel nice to the touch. The hotel also features an excellent Italian restaurant, and breakfast is included in the room rate (unusual for a Vienna hotel in its class). ⊠ *Wiedner Hauptstr. 12, A–1010,* ☎ *01/589–180,* FAX *01/589–1818. 73 rooms with bath. Restaurant, bar, café, health club. AE, DC, MC, V.*

$$$$ ⊞ **Hilton.** The public areas have been restyled for a more contemporary look, and the bedrooms are a cut above the usual Hilton standard in size and individuality of decor. The suites are particularly spacious; who could resist breakfast on a suite balcony with a 180-degree view of the city? The upper rooms are quietest; the no-smoking floor is so popular that you need to book at least two to three weeks in advance. Special winter rates are available. The airport bus terminal is part of the complex; the U3 and U4 subway lines, trains, and buses stop at the terminal across the street; yet you're within an easy walk of the city center. ⊠ *Am Stadtpark, A–1030,* ☎ *01/717–00–0,* FAX *01/713–0691. 600 rooms with bath. 2 restaurants, bar, café, no-smoking floor, sauna, health club, parking (fee). AE, DC, MC, V.*

$$$$ ⊞ **Imperial.** The hotel is as much a palace today as when it was formally opened in 1873 by Emperor Franz Josef. The emphasis is on Old

76

Vienna Lodging

Vienna elegance and privacy, which accounts for the heads of state and celebrities staying here. Michael Jackson checks in regularly, and other guests have included Bruce Springsteen and Elizabeth Taylor. The beautiful rooms are furnished in antique style, though only the first three floors are part of the original house and have high ceilings; subsequent floors were added in the late 1930s. Don't overlook the grand marble staircase and ornate reception rooms. The hotel also houses the Imperial restaurant (☞ Dining, *above*), and the Imperial Cafe, which features the famed Imperial torte. ✉ *Kärntner Ring 16, A–1010,* ☎ *01/501–10–0,* FAX *01/501–10–410. 128 rooms with bath. Restaurant, café, piano bar, no-smoking rooms. AE, DC, MC, V.*

$$$$ 🏨 **Palais Schwarzenberg.** Set against a vast formal park, the palace, built in the early 1700s, seems like a country estate, so it's hard to believe you're in the heart of the city. Each room is individual and luxuriously appointed, with the family's original artwork adorning the walls. Bathrooms are sleekly done, with heated towel racks and long, deep bathtubs. A newly renovated wing with ultramodern suites by Italian designer Paolo Piva has recently opened at the far end of the park. You don't have to be a guest here to come for a drink, coffee, or light lunch, served outside on the terrace in summer or beside a roaring fireplace in the main sitting room in winter. ✉ *Schwarzenbergpl. 9, A–1030,* ☎ *01/798–4515–0,* FAX *01/798–4714. 44 rooms with bath. Restaurant, bar, pool, free parking. AE, DC, MC, V.*

$$$$ 🏨 **Radisson/SAS Palais.** Two former fin-de-siècle palaces have come together to form this recently renovated hotel, which boasts a superb location on the Ring and also Le Siècle (☞ Dining, *above*), one of Vienna's top seafood restaurants. The staff is ready to help with anything. Ask for a room facing the Stadtpark. ✉ *Parkring 16, A–1010,* ☎ *01/515–170,* FAX *01/51–22–216. 246 rooms with bath. 2 restaurants, bar, café, health club. AE, DC, MC, V.*

$$$$ 🏨 **Sacher.** One of the grand old hotels, the Sacher dates from 1876, and it has retained its sense of history over the years while providing luxurious, modern-day comfort. The corridors are a veritable art gallery, and the exquisitely furnished bedrooms also contain original artwork. The location directly behind the Opera House could hardly be more central. The ratio of staff to guests is more than two to one, and among the traditional luxury hotels, the Sacher probably offers the best value. Meals in the Red Room or Anna Sacher Room are first-rate, with both a Continental and Viennese menu. The Café Sacher, of course, is legendary (☞ Exploring Vienna, *above*). British director Carol Reed filmed some of his classic 1949 film *The Third Man* in the reception area. ✉ *Philharmonikerstr. 4, A–1010,* ☎ *01/514–56–0,* FAX *01/514–57–810. 108 rooms with bath. 2 restaurants, bar, café, no-smoking rooms. AE, DC, MC, V.*

$$$ 🏨 **Altstadt.** This small hotel was once a patrician home, and it's a real gem. Rooms are large with all the modern comforts, though they retain an antique feel. The English-style lounge has a fireplace and plump floral sofas. Upper rooms have views out over the city roofline. The management is personable and helpful. You're one streetcar stop or a pleasant walk from the main museums. ✉ *Kirchengasse 41, A–1070,* ☎ *01/526–3399,* FAX *01/523–4901. 25 rooms with bath. Bar. AE, DC, MC, V.*

$$$ 🏨 **Austria.** This older house, tucked away on a tiny cul-de-sac, offers the ultimate in quiet and is only five minutes' walk from the heart of the city. The high-ceiling rooms are pleasing in their combination of dark wood and lighter walls; the decor is mixed, with Oriental carpets on many floors. Rooms without full bath are in the $$ category. There is a nice courtyard terrace that is perfect for sipping coffee after a day of sightseeing. You'll feel at home here, and the staff will help you find your way around town or get opera or concert tickets. ✉ *Wolfengasse*

3 (Fleischmarkt), A–1010, ☎ *01/515–23–0,* ☎ *01/515–23–505. 46 rooms, 42 with bath. AE, DC, MC, V.*

$$$ ⚏ **Biedermeier im Sünnhof.** This jewel of a hotel is tucked into a renovated 1820s house that even with all modern facilities still conveys a feeling of old Vienna. The rooms are compact but efficient, the public areas tastefully done in the Biedermeier style, and the service is friendly. The courtyard passageway around which the hotel is built has attracted a number of interesting boutiques and handicrafts shops, but at times there is an excess of coming and going as tour groups are accommodated. It's about a 20-minute walk or a 6-minute subway ride to the center of the city. ✉ *Landstrasser Hauptstr. 28, A–1030,* ☎ *01/716–71–0,* ☎ *01/716–71–503. 204 rooms with bath. Restaurant, bar, parking (fee). AE, DC, MC, V.*

$$$ ⚏ **Europa.** Newly renovated from top to bottom, this 1957-vintage hotel offers modern, functional rooms. The selling point here is the great location. Rooms on the Neuer Markt side are quieter than those on Kärntnerstrasse. ✉ *Neuer Markt 3, A–1010,* ☎ *01/515–94–0,* ☎ *01/513–8138. 113 rooms with bath. Restaurant, bar, café. AE, DC, MC, V.*

$$$ ⚏ **Fürstenhof.** This turn-of-the-century building, directly across from the Westbahnhof, describes its large rooms as "old-fashioned comfortable" and you reach them via a marvelous hydraulic elevator. Furnishings are a mixed bag. The side rooms are quieter than those in front. Rooms without bath are in the $$ category. A very nice breakfast is included in the price. ✉ *Neubaugürtel 4, A–1070,* ☎ *01/523–3267,* ☎ *01/523–3267–26. 58 rooms, 39 with bath. AE, DC, MC, V.*

$$$ ⚏ **König von Ungarn.** In a 16th-century house in the shadow of St. Stephen's Cathedral, this hotel began catering to court nobility in 1815. (Mozart lived in the house next door when he wrote *The Marriage of Figaro*.) A superb redesign turned it into a modern hotel, and you could hardly hope for a happier result. The hotel radiates charm, from the greenery in the wood-paneled atrium lobby to the antiques of various periods and the pine country furnishings in the bedrooms. The rooms are not overly large, but each is individually and appealingly decorated. Those in back are somewhat quieter. Insist on written confirmation of bookings. ✉ *Schulerstr. 10, A–1010,* ☎ ☎ *01/515–84–0. 32 rooms with bath. Restaurant, bar. DC, MC, V.*

$$$ ⚏ **Kummer.** In the heart of the shopping district, the imposing, Georgian-style exterior of this old hotel has an equally noble lobby with a grand, sweeping staircase. Each comfortably furnished room is different, and the ones facing the busy Mariahilferstrasse have soundproofed windows. Some rooms have an alcoved sitting area. The hotel is also close to the Westbahnhof and major museums. ✉ *Mariahilferstr. 71a, A–1060,* ☎ *01/58895,* ☎ *01/587–8133. 100 rooms with bath. Restaurant, bar. AE, DC, MC, V.*

$$$ ⚏ **Royal.** Just around the corner from St. Stephen's and Kärntnerstrasse, this modern hotel is on the site of a former pilgrim hostel from the early 16th century. It was destroyed in World War II and rebuilt in 1960. Rooms are pleasantly decorated, though despite the prime location, none have a view. The hotel's Italian restaurant, Firenze Enoteca, is favored by opera singers, including Pavarotti. In summer the restaurant also operates on the rooftop terrace with a spectacular view of the Graben and St. Stephen's. ✉ *Singerstr. 3, A–1010,* ☎ *01/51568–0,* ☎ *01/513–9698. 77 rooms with bath. 2 restaurants. AE, DC, MC, V.*

$$$ ⚏ **Wandl.** The restored facade identifies a 300-year-old house that has been in family hands as a hotel since 1854. You couldn't find a better location, tucked behind St. Peter's Church, just off the Graben. The hallways are punctuated by cheerful, bright openings along the glassed-in inner court. The rooms are modern, but some are a bit plain and charmless, despite parquet flooring and red accents. Ask for one of the rooms done in period furniture, with decorated ceilings and gilt mirrors; they're palatial, if slightly overdone. ⊠ *Peterspl. 9, A–1010,* ☎ *01/534–55–0,* FAX *01/534–55–77. 138 rooms with bath. Bar. AE, DC, MC, V.*

$$–$$$ ⛨ **Altwienerhof.** Don't be put off by the rather unappealing neighborhood this small hotel is located in, just one subway stop away from the Westbahnhof. The selling point here are the spacious, comfortable rooms, most with modern, ultraluxurious bathrooms and some with a view over the lovely inner courtyard. Owner Frau Kellner is very helpful and friendly and can arrange tickets to any concert in the city. Guests also have an opportunity to partake of the reasonably priced half board at the hotel's restaurant (☞ Dining, *above*), one of the top-ranked eateries in Austria. A rich buffet breakfast (included in the room price) is served in the Winter Garden or in the flower-filled courtyard in summer. ⊠ *Herklotzg. 6, A–1150,* ☎ *01/892–6000,* FAX *01/892–6000–8. 23 rooms with bath. AE, DC, MC, V.*

$$–$$$ ⛨ **Kärntnerhof.** Behind the "Schönbrunn yellow" facade of this ele-
★   gant 100-year-old house on a quiet cul-de-sac lies one of the friendliest small hotels in the center of the city. Don't let the dated and uninteresting lobby put you off; take the gorgeously restored Biedermeier elevator to the rooms upstairs. They contain either brown or white reproduction furniture, and the baths are modern. The staff is adept at getting theater and concert tickets for "sold-out" performances and happily puts together special outing programs for guests. Pets are welcome here. ⊠ *Grashofg. 4, A–1010,* ☎ *01/512–1923–0,* FAX *01/513–2228–33. 43 rooms with bath. Parking (fee). AE, DC, MC, V.*

$$–$$$ ⛨ **Neuer Markt.** You're in the heart of the city at this attractive pastel-yellow pension, situated in a lofty position at the head of the pretty square bearing the same name. Rooms are modern and comfortable, and the staff is very friendly and helpful, making you feel right at home. ⊠ *Seilerg. 9, A–1010,* ☎ *01/512–2316,* FAX *01/513–9105. 37 rooms with bath. AE, DC, MC, V.*

$$–$$$ ⛨ **Pension Aclon.** On the upper floors of a gray but gracious older building just off the Graben (with the famous Café Hawelka downstairs; ☞ Cafés, *above*), this family-run hostelry is attractively done up in Old Vienna style, with lots of plants, dark woods, and nice faux-marble baths. Rooms on the inner court are quieter, though the street in front carries no through traffic. The smaller rooms have modern decor, while the larger rooms are decorated in Biedermeier style. ⊠ *Dorotheerg. 6–8, A–1010,* ☎ *01/512–7940–0,* FAX *01/513–8751. 22 rooms, 14 with bath. No credit cards.*

$$–$$$ ⛨ **Pension Aviano.** Tucked away in a corner of the Neuer Markt, this small pension is close to the Opera House. Rooms are cheerful and quiet, and the two junior suites have a charming turret where you can sit and gaze out over the rooftops of Vienna. In summer breakfast tables are set outside on the balcony overlooking the inner courtyard. ⊠ *Marco d'Avianog. 1, A–1010,* ☎ *01/512–8330,* FAX *01/512–8330–6. 17 rooms with bath. DC, MC, V.*

$$–$$$ ⛨ **Pension Nossek.** This family-run establishment on the upper floors
★   of a 19th-century office and apartment building lies at the heart of the pedestrian and shopping area. The rooms have high ceilings and are eclectically but comfortably furnished; those on the front have a magnificent view of the Graben. Do as the many regular guests do and book early. ⊠ *Graben 17, A–1010,* ☎ *01/533–7041–0,* FAX *01/535–3646. 27 rooms, 22 with bath. No credit cards.*

$$–$$$ ⛨ **Pension Pertschy.** Housed in a former town palace just off the Graben, this pension is as central as you can get. A massive arched portal leads to a yellow courtyard, around which the house is built. A few rooms contain lovely old ceramic stoves (just for show). Most rooms are spacious, and each one is comfortable, though overall the furniture

is a bit kitschy. Baths are satisfactory. Use the elevator, but don't overlook the palatial grand staircase. ⊠ *Habsburgergasse 5, A–1010,* ☎ *01/534–49–0,* ℻ *01/534–49–49. 43 rooms with bath. DC, MC, V.*

$$–$$$ 🛏 **Pension Riedl.** Located on the upper floors of a lovely 19th-century building overlooking the Postsparkassenamt, this Secession-style building was designed by Otto Wagner. Rooms are nicely furnished and comfortable. A full breakfast is included. ⊠ *Georg–Coch–Platz 3/4/10, A–1010,* ☎ *01/512–7919,* ℻ *01/512–79198. 8 rooms with bath. DC, MC, V. Closed first 2 wks of Feb.*

$$ 🛏 **Pension Baroness.** One flight up, behind the drab facade of this turn-of-the-century apartment house, are comfortable rooms with contemporary furnishings, many quite spacious and many completely renovated in 1990. The front rooms are noisy, but the nearby streetcar stop is a convenience. ⊠ *Lange G. 61, A–1080,* ☎ *01/405–1061,* ℻ *01/405–1061–61. 38 rooms with bath. Bar. MC, V.*

$$ 🛏 **Pension Christina.** This quiet pension, just steps from Schwedenplatz and the Danube Canal, offers mainly smallish modern rooms, warmly decorated with attractive dark-wood furniture set off against beige walls. ⊠ *Hafnersteig 7, A–1010,* ☎ *01/533–2961–0,* ℻ *01/533–2961–11. 33 rooms with bath. MC, V.*

$$ 🛏 **Pension City.** You'll be on historic ground here: In 1791 the playwright Franz Grillparzer was born in the house that then stood here; a bust and plaques in the entryway commemorate him. On the second floor of the present 100-year-old house, located about three minutes away from St. Stephen's Cathedral, the rooms are newly outfitted in a successful mix of modern and 19th-century antique furniture against white walls. The baths are small but complete. ⊠ *Bauernmarkt 10, A–1010,* ☎ *01/533–9521,* ℻ *01/535–5216. 19 rooms with bath. AE, DC, MC, V.*

$$ 🛏 **Pension Grun.** A minimum stay of three nights is required here, but if you're staying that long you can't beat the five-minute walk to the city center. It's around the corner from the happening Schwedenplatz area and the Bermuda Triangle, where a lot of the most fun bars and nightclubs are located. Rooms are spacious and there's a comfortable sitting room. ⊠ *Gonzagag. 1, 3rd floor, Suite 19, A–1010,* ☎ *01/533–2506. 3 rooms with bath. AE, DC, MC, V.*

$$ 🛏 **Zur Wiener Staatsoper.** The hotel's florid facade, with oversize torsos supporting its upper bays, is pure 19th-century Ringstrasse style. The rooms are less well defined in style, small yet comfortable. The baths are adequate. And you'll find yourself within steps of the Opera House and Kärntnerstrasse. ⊠ *Krugerstr. 11, A–1010,* ☎ *01/513–1274–0,* ℻ *01/513–1274–15. 22 rooms with bath. AE, MC, V.*

$ 🛏 **Pension Reimer.** Friendly and comfortable, this hotel is in a prime location just off the Mariahilferstrasse. Rooms have high ceilings and large windows, and the atmosphere throughout is nice and cheerful. Breakfast is included. ⊠ *Kircheng. 18, A–1070,* ☎ *01/523–6162,* ℻ *01/524–3782. 14 rooms with bath. MC, V.*

$ 🛏 **Pension Wild.** This friendly, family-run pension on several floors of
★ an older apartment house draws a liberal, relaxed younger crowd to one of the best values in town. Rooms are simple but modern, with light-wood furniture and pine-paneled ceilings. Each wing has a kitchenette. The breakfast room–TV lounge is bright and attractive, and you're close to the major museums. ⊠ *Lange G. 1, A–1080,* ☎ *01/406–5174,* ℻ *01/402–2168. 14 rooms without bath. Sauna, exercise room. AE, DC, MC, V.*

Seasonal Hotels

Student residences, which operate as hotels July–September, can provide excellent bargains in the inexpensive ($) category. They have single or double rooms, all (unless noted) with bath. You can book by calling any of the **Rosenhotels** (☎ 01/911–4910, FAX 01/910–0269) or central booking for the student residence hotels of the **Albertina group** (☎ 01/521–74930, FAX 01/521–1968). Unless otherwise noted, credit cards are accepted.

🏠 **Academia.** Among this group, this is a fairly luxurious choice. ✉ *Pfeilg. 3a, A–1080,* ☎ *01/401–760. 368 rooms. Restaurant, bar.*

🏠 **Accordia.** Belonging to the Albertina group, this is the newest of the seasonal hotels and is fairly close to the center. ✉ *Grosse Schiffg. 12, A–1020,* ☎ *01/521–7493. 95 rooms.*

🏠 **Ambiente.** This accommodation is an Albertina member near the U.S. embassy, a quiet location. ✉ *Boltzmanng. 10, A–1090,* ☎ *01/ 521–7493. 50 rooms.*

🏠 **Auge Gottes.** For bargain hunters, this choice is among the very cheapest. ✉ *Nussdorfer Str. 75, A–1090,* ☎ *01/317–6344. 79 rooms without bath.*

🏠 **Avis.** This option even features its own restaurant and bar. ✉ *Pfeilg. 4, A–1080,* ☎ *01/401–740. 72 rooms. Restaurant, bar. AE, MC, V.*

🏠 **Haus Technik.** An Albertina member, this place is fairly close to the center. ✉ *Schäfferg. 2, A–1040,* ☎ *01/521–7493. 104 rooms. Restaurant.*

🏠 **Rosenhotel Burgenland 3.** For weary travelers, the restaurant is a boon but tips the house into the $$ category. ✉ *Bürgerspitalg. 19, A–1060,* ☎ *01/597–9347,* FAX *01/597–9475–9. 140 rooms. Restaurant, bar. AE, MC, V.*

🏠 **Studentenheim der Musikhochschule.** This choice offers the most central location of any of the seasonal hotels, in the heart of the city. ✉ *Johannesg. 8, A–1010,* ☎ *01/514–84–0,* FAX *01/514–84–49. 85 rooms, some with bath.*

NIGHTLIFE AND THE ARTS

The Arts

Dance

Under new directors, the **ballet evenings** that are on the Stadtsoper and Volksoper schedule (☎ 01/514–44–0) are now much improved and finally up to international standards. Vienna also has theaters offering contemporary dance, representing Austria's up-and-coming choreographers and theater artists. Check out **Szene Wien** (✉ Hauffg. 26, A–1110, ☎ 01/749–3341, FAX 01/749–2206) and **dietheater Wien** (✉ Karlspl. 5, A–1010, ☎ 01/587–8774, FAX 01/587–8774) for their seasonal programs.

Film

Film has enjoyed a recent renaissance, with viewers seeking original rather than German-dubbed versions. Look for films in English at **Burgkino** (✉ Opernring 19, ☎ 01/587–8406)—in summer, Carol Reed's classic *The Third Man* with Orson Welles is a regular feature; also try **de France** (✉ Schottenring 5/Hessg. 7, ☎ 01/317–5236); **Flotten** (✉ Mariahilferstr. 85, ☎ 01/586–5152); **Haydn** (✉ Mariahilferstr. 57, ☎ 01/587–2262); and **Votiv-Kino** (✉ Währinger Str. 12, ☎ 01/ 317–3571). Art and experimental films are shown at the **Stadtkino** (✉ Schwarzenbergpl. 7, ☎ 01/712–6276).

The film schedule in the daily newspaper *Der Standard* lists foreign-language films (*Fremdsprachige Filme*) separately. In film listings, *OmU* means original language with German subtitles.

The **Filmmuseum** in the Albertina shows original-version classics with a heavy focus on English-language films and organizes retrospectives of the works of artists, directors, and producers. The monthly program is posted outside, and guest memberships (AS40 per day) are available. It is closed July, August, and September. ⊠ *Augustinerstr. 1,* ☎ *01/533–7054.* ⚞ *AS110, AS50 with AS200 yearly membership.*

Galleries

A host of smaller galleries centers on the Singerstrasse and Grünangergasse, although there are many more scattered about the city.

Music

Vienna is one of the main music centers of the world. Contemporary music gets its hearing, but it's the hometown standards—the works of Beethoven, Brahms, Haydn, Mozart, and Schubert—that draw the Viennese public. A monthly program, put out by the city tourist board and available at any travel agency or hotel, gives a general overview of what's going on in opera, concerts, jazz, theater, and galleries, and similar information is posted on billboards and fat advertising columns around the city.

Vienna is home to four full symphony orchestras: the great Vienna Philharmonic, the outstanding Vienna Symphony, the broadcasting service's ORF Symphony Orchestra, and the Niederösterreichische Tonkünstler. There are also hundreds of smaller groups, from world-famous trios to chamber orchestras.

The most important concert halls are in the buildings of the Gesellschaft der Musikfreunde, called the **Musikverein** (⊠ Dumbastr. 3; ticket office at Karlspl. 6, ℻ 01/505–86–819401), which contains the Grosser Musikvereinssaal and the Brahmssaal and the **Konzerthaus** (⊠ Lothringerstr. 20, ☎ 01/712–4686, 01/712–1211 ticket window, ℻ 01/712–2872), which houses the Grosser Konzerthaussaal, Mozart-saal, and Schubertsaal halls.

Concerts are also given in the small **Figarosaal** of Palais Palffy (⊠ Josefspl. 6, ☎ 01/512–5681–0), the **concert studio of the broadcasting station** (⊠ Argentinierstr. 30A, ☎ 01/501–01–8881), and the **Bösendorfersaal** (⊠ Graf Starhemberg-G. 14, ☎ 01/504–6651). Students of the **music school** regularly give class recitals in the school's concert halls during the academic year; look for announcements posted outside for dates and times (⊠ Seilerstätte 26 and Johannesg. 8, ☎ 01/588–06–0).

Although the **Vienna Festival** (☎ 01/589–22–0), held early May to mid-June, wraps up the primary season, the summer musical scene is bright, with something scheduled every day. Outdoor symphony concerts are performed weekly in the vast arcaded courtyard of the Rathaus (entrance on Friedrich Schmidt-Pl.). You can catch musical events in the Volksgarten and in the St. Augustine, St. Michael's, Minorite, and University churches; at Schönbrunn Palace they're outside in the courtyard as well as part of an evening guided tour.

Mozart concerts are performed in 18th-century costume and powdered wigs in the large hall, or Mozartsaal, of the Konzerthaus (☞ *above*); operetta concerts are held in the Musikverein (☞ *above*), and the Hofburg and Palais Ferstel. There are no set dates, so inquire through hotels and travel and ticket agencies for availabilities. Note, however, that some of these concerts, including intermission lasting possibly an hour, are rather expensive affairs put on for tourists and are occasionally of disappointing quality.

Church music, the mass sung in Latin, can be heard Sunday mornings during the main season at St. Stephen's; in the Franciscan church, St. Michael's; the Universitätskirche; and, above all, in the Augustinerkirche. The Friday and Saturday newspapers carry details. St. Stephen's also has organ concerts most Wednesday evenings from early May to late November.

The **Vienna Boys Choir** (Wiener Sängerknaben) sings mass at 9:15 AM in the Hofburgkapelle (⊠ Hofburg, Schweizer Hof, ☎ 01/533–9927, FAX 01/533–9927–75) from mid-September to late June. Written requests for seats should be made at least eight weeks in advance (⊠ Hofmusikkapelle Hofburg, A–1010 Vienna). You will be sent a reservation card, which you exchange at the box office (in the Hofburg courtyard) for your tickets. Tickets are also sold at ticket agencies and at the box office (open daily 11:30–1 and 3–5). Each person is allowed a maximum of two tickets. General seating costs AS60, prime seats in the front of the church AS340. It's important to note that only the 10 side balcony seats allow a view of the choir. Those who purchase floor seats, standing room, or center balcony will not be able to see the boys. On Sunday at 8:45 AM all unclaimed pre-ordered tickets are sold. If you've missed the Vienna Boys Choir at the Sunday mass, you may be able to hear them in a more popular program in the Konzerthaus.

TICKETS

Most theaters now reserve tickets by telephone against a credit card; you pick up your ticket at the box office with no surcharge. The same applies to concert tickets. Ticket agencies (☞ Contacts and Resources *in* Vienna A to Z, *below*) charge a minimum 22% markup and generally deal in the more expensive seats. Expect to pay (or tip) a hotel porter or concierge at least as much as a ticket-agency markup for hard-to-get tickets. Tickets to musicals and some events including the Vienna Festival are available at the **"Salettl" gazebo** kiosk alongside the Opera House on the Kärntnerstrasse. Tickets to that night's musicals are reduced by half after 2 PM (☎ 01/588–85).

Opera and Operetta

The **Staatsoper** (State Opera House, ⊠ Opernring 2, ☎ 01/514–4429–69 or 01/514–440), one of the world's great opera houses, has been the scene of countless musical triumphs and a center of unending controversies over how it should be run and by whom. (When Lorin Maazel was unceremoniously dumped as head of the Opera not many years ago, he pointed out that the house had done the same thing to Gustav Mahler a few decades earlier.) A performance takes place virtually every night September–June, drawing on the vast repertoire of the house, with emphasis on Mozart and Verdi. (Opera here is nearly always performed in the original language, even Russian.) Guided tours of the Opera House are held year-round. The opera in Vienna is a dressy event, and even designer jeans are not socially acceptable. Evening dress and black tie, though not compulsory, are recommended for first-night performances and in the better seats.

Light opera and operetta are performed at the **Volksoper** (⊠ Währingerstr. 78, ☎ 01/514–440) outside the city center at Währingerstrasse and Währinger Gürtel (third stop on Streetcar 41, 42, or 43, from "downstairs" at Schottentor, U2, on the Ring). Prices here are significantly lower than in the main opera, and performances can be every bit as rewarding. Mozart is sung here, too, but in German, the language of the house.

You'll find musicals and operetta also at the **Raimundtheater** (⊠ Wallg. 18, ☎ 01/599–77–0), **Ronacher** (⊠ Seilerstätte/Himmelpfortg., ☎ 01/514–110), and the **Theater an der Wien** (⊠ Linke Wienzeile 6, ☎ 01/588–30–0). Opera and operetta are performed on an irregular schedule at the **Kammeroper** (⊠ Fleischmarkt 24, ☎ 01/512–01–000).

In summer, look for outdoor opera performances on the grounds of **Schönbrunn Palace** (☞ Exploring Vienna, *above*); Mozart's *Don Giovanni* here is a memorable experience. Book early, since the Schönbrunn performances are regular sellouts. There's standing room available. Also in summer, light opera or operetta performances by the Kammeroper ensemble are given in the exquisite **Schlosstheater** at Schönbrunn. Ticket agencies will have details.

TICKETS

Tickets to the **state theaters** (Opera, Volksoper, Burgtheater, and Akademietheater) can be charged against your credit card. You can order them by phoning up to a month before the performance (☎ 01/513–1513) or buy them in person up to a month in advance at the Theaterkassen, the central box office. ⊠ *Theaterkassen, back of Opera, Hanuschg. 3, in courtyard,* ☎ *01/514–44–2959 or 01/514–44–2960.* ☉ *Weekdays 8–6, Sat. 9–2, Sun. and holidays 9–noon.*

You can get information and tickets for **Opera and Volksoper** at the ticket office for those theaters. ⊠ *Kärntnerstr. 40, Staatsoper arcade,* ☎ *01/514–44–2958.* ☉ *Weekdays 10–1 hr before performance, Sat. 10–noon.*

You can write ahead for tickets as well. The nearest **Austrian National Tourist Office** can give you a schedule of performances and a ticket order form. Send the form (no payment is required) to the ticket office (⊠ Kartenvorverkauf Bundestheaterverband, Goetheg. 1, A–1010 Vienna), which will mail you a reservation card; when you get to Vienna, take the card to the main box office to pick up and pay for your tickets.

Theater

Vienna's **Burgtheater** (⊠ Dr.-Karl-Lueger-Ring 2, A–1010 Vienna; ☞ State Theaters, *above*, for ticket details) is one of the leading German-language theaters of the world. Its current director has replaced the German classics with more modern and controversial pieces. The Burg's smaller house, the **Akademietheater** (⊠ Lisztstr. 1), draws on much the same group of actors for classical and modern plays. Both houses are closed during July and August.

The **Kammerspiele** (⊠ Rotenturmstr. 20, ☎ 01/533–2833) does modern plays. The **Theater in der Josefstadt** (⊠ Josefstädterstr. 26, ☎ 01/402–7631–0) stages classical and modern works year-round in the house once run by the great producer and teacher Max Reinhardt. The **Volkstheater** (⊠ Neustiftg. 1, ☎ 01/523–3501–0) presents dramas, comedies, and folk plays.

For theater in English (mainly standard plays), head for **Vienna's English Theater** (⊠ Josefsg. 12, ☎ 01/402–1260). Another option is the equally good **International Theater** (⊠ Porzellang. 8, ☎ 01/319–6272).

Nightlife

Balls

The gala Vienna evening you've always dreamed about can become a reality: Among the many balls given during the Carnival season, several welcome the public—at a wide range of prices, from about AS700 to AS3,000 per person. Dates change every year, but most balls are held in January and February. Some of the more popular balls are the Blumen Ball (Florists' Ball), Kaffeesieder Ball (Coffee Brewers' Ball), Bon-

bon Ball (Confection Ball), and the most famous and expensive of them all, the Opernball (Opera Ball). You can book tickets with a Eurocheck or through hotel concierges (for more information call ☎ 01/211140, ᖴᴀX 01/216–8492).

For a background on these festive events, *see* Stepping Out in Three-Quarter Time *in* Pleasures and Pastimes, *above.*

Bars and Lounges

Vienna has blossomed in recent years with delightful and sophisticated bars. Head for the "Bermuda Triangle," an area in the First District roughly defined by Judengasse, Seitenstättengasse, Rabensteig, and Franz-Josefs-Kai. Here you will find dozens of bars, both intimate and large, like First Floor, Krah-Krah, and Ma Pitom. Near the Börse on Zelinkagasse is the classy Planter's Club. Back toward Stephansplatz, on Bäckerstrasse, check out Weinorgel, Oswald & Kalb; on Blutgasse, Chamäleon; on Singerstrasse, the Galerie Bar. The American Bar on Kärntner Durchgang has an original Adolf Loos turn-of-the-century interior.

Cabaret

Cabaret has a long tradition in Vienna. To get much from any of it, you'll need good German with some Viennese vernacular as well, plus knowledge of local affairs. **Simpl** (✉ Wollzeile 36, ☎ 01/512–4742) continues earning its reputation for barbed political wit but has had to give way to some newcomers at **Kabarett Niedermair** (✉ Lenaug. 1A, ☎ 01/408–4492).

Casinos

Try your luck at the casino **Cercle Wien** (✉ Kärntnerstr. 41, ☎ 01/512–4836) in a former town palace redone in dark wood paneling and millions of twinkling lights. Games include roulette and blackjack. You'll need your passport for entry identification.

Discos

The disco scene is big in Vienna, and the crowd seems to follow the leader from one "in" spot to the next. A few continually draw full houses.

Try **Atrium** (✉ Schwarzenbergpl. 10, ☎ 01/505–3594); **Queen Anne,** still very much "in" (✉ Johannesg. 12, ☎ 01/512–0203); and **U–4,** popular with a mixed group, early thirties and younger (✉ Schönbrunnerstr. 222, ☎ 01/815–8307).

Irish Pubs

After Austria joined the European Union several years ago, Irish pubs started popping up all over the place. Along with British and Irish ex-patriots you can find a substantial Viennese crowd, and most are open all day long. Offering light dishes to go along with Guinness on tap is **Flanagan's** (✉ Schwarzenbergstr. 1–3, ☎ 01/513–7378). Live Irish music is offered some nights at the **Irish Pub** (✉ Naglerg. 7 [entrance on Körblerg], ☎ 01/532–9438). The place to go for Murphy's Red Irish beer, Harp's on tap, and Irish stew is **Little Stage Irish Pub** (✉ Ramperstorfferg. 66, A–1050). You can eat fish-and-chips in a book-lined room at the popular **Molly Darcy's** (✉ Teinfaltstr. 6, ☎ 01/533–2311).

Jazz Clubs

Vienna is increasingly good for jazz, though places where it can be heard tend to come and go. Nothing gets going before 9 PM. Live groups appear almost nightly at **Jazzland** (✉ Franz-Josefs-Kai 29, ☎ 01/533–2575); **Papa's Tapas** (✉ Schwarzenbergpl. 10, ☎ 01/505–0311); and **Roter Engel** (✉ Rabensteig 5, ☎ 01/535–4105). **Porgy & Bess** (✉ Spiegelg. 2, ☎ 01/512–8438–0) has gained a reputation for good jazz, although the future of the club is uncertain.

Nightclubs

Vienna has no real nightclub tradition, although there are a number of clubs in town. Most of the ones with floor shows are horribly expensive and not very good; some are outright tourist traps. The two where you run the least risk are **Casanova,** where singles can sit reasonably peacefully at the upstairs bar (⊠ Dorotheerg. 6, ☎ 01/512–9845), and the upscale **Moulin Rouge** (⊠ Walfischg. 11, ☎ 01/512–2130). The leading spots for dancing are the **Eden Bar,** which always has a live band and is for the well-heeled, mature crowd (⊠ Lilieng. 2, ☎ 01/512–7450); **Chattanooga,** which often has a live band and draws a younger crowd (⊠ Graben 29a, ☎ 01/533–5000); and **Volksgarten** (⊠ Volksgarten, Burgring 1, ☎ 01/533–0518–0), where a mixed younger set comes, particularly in summer for outdoor dancing.

OUTDOOR ACTIVITIES AND SPORTS

Participant Sports

Bicycling

Look for the special pathways either in red brick or marked with a stylized cyclist in yellow. Note and observe the special traffic signals at some intersections. You can take a bike on the subway (except during rush hours) for half fare, but only in cars with a blue shield on the door, and only on stairs or elevators with the "bike" shield, not the escalators. The city tourist office has a brochure in German with useful cycling maps, plus a leaflet "See Vienna by Bike" with tips in English. At most bookstores you can purchase a cycling map of Vienna put out by a local cycling organization known as ARGUS (⊠ Frankenberggasse 11, ☎ 01/505–8435). You can rent a bike starting at about AS40 per hour, leaving your passport or other identification as a deposit.

Rent a bike year-round at the Westbahnhof, Wien Nord (Praterstern), or Floridsdorf rail station. Or, pick up a bike at one of the following: **Radverleih Hochschaubahn** (☎ 12/729–5888), mid-March–October, in the Prater amusement park, by Hochschaubahn, slightly right after the Ferris wheel; **Radverleih Praterstern,** April–October, at street level under Praterstern North rail station; or at **Hammermayer/Radsport Nussdorf** (⊠ Donaupromenade, ☎ 01/374598), next to the Nussdorf DDSG dock.

Pedal Power (⊠ Ausstellungsstr. 3, A–1020, ☎ 01/729–7234, ℻ 01/729–7235) offers guided bike tours of Vienna and the surrounding vicinity, from April to October, including the main sights of the city, or tours to the outlying vineyards for a glass of wine. It's also possible to rent a bike and do your own exploring. Three-hour guided tours cost AS280 (AS230 for students); a five-hour bike rental on your own is AS300; for a full day, AS395.

Other rental locations are available from tourist offices.

Boating

Both the Alte Donau (Old Danube), a series of lakes to the north of the main stream, and the Neue Donau, on the north side of the Donauinsel (the artificial island in the river), offer good waters for paddleboats, rowboats, kayaks, sailboats, and Windsurfers. The Danube itself is somewhat fast-moving for anything but kayaks. Rent boats from **Auzinger Boote** (⊠ Laberlweg 22, ☎ 01/235788), **Eppel** (⊠ Wagramer Str. 48, ☎ 01/235168), **Irzl** (⊠ Florian Berndl-G. 33–34, ☎ 01/203–6743), **Karl Hofbauer** (⊠ Neue Donau at Reichsbrücke; ⊠ Obere Alte Donau 185; ☎ 01/204–3435–0), and **Newrkla** (⊠ Obere Alte Donau, ☎ 01/386105). For details about sailing and sailing events, check with **Haus des Sports** (⊠ Prinz-Eugen-Str. 12, ☎ 01/505–3742–0).

Golf

The top in-town golf course is at **Freudenau** in the Prater (☎ 01/728–9564–0, ℻ 01/728–5379). But this 18-hole, par-70 course is so popular from April to November, even with the weekday AS800 fee, that you'll probably need to be invited or have an introduction from a member to play; on weekends, membership or an invitation is required.

There are alternatives, but these, too, are generally overbooked. Weekdays, of course, will be best for any of the courses, particularly those farther from Vienna. Try one of the following: **Brunn am Gebirge,** an 18-hole, par-72 course about 10 km (6 mi) to the southwest (⊠ Rennweg 50, ☎ 02236/33711, ℻ 02236/33863); **Colony Club Gutenhof,** 10 km (6 mi) to the southeast, with two courses of 18 holes, par-73 each, at Himberg (⊠ Gutenhof, ☎ 02235/87055–0); **Ebreichsdorf,** 27 km (17 mi) south of Vienna, an 18-hole, par-72 course (⊠ Schlossallee 1, ☎ 02254/73888); **Golfclub Am Wienerberg,** a 9-hole, par-35 course on the south side of Vienna, open March–November (⊠ Gutheil Schoder-G. 9, ☎ 01/66123–0); or **Hainburg,** 50 km (31 mi) east of Vienna, with 18 holes, par-72 (⊠ Auf der Heide, ☎ 02165/62628, ℻ 02165/65331).

Health and Fitness Clubs

Try **Fitness Center Harris** (⊠ Niebelungeng. 7, ☎ 01/587–3710), **Fitness Center Stadtpark** (⊠ Kursalon, Johannesg. 33, ☎ 01/714–7775), or **Zimmermann Fitness** (⊠ Kaiserstr. 43, ☎ 01/526–2000; ⊠ Kreuzg. 18, ☎ 01/406–4625), which is for women only.

Ice-Skating

The **Wiener Eislaufverein** (⊠ Lothringer Str. 22, behind InterContinental Hotel, ☎ 01/713–6353–0) has outdoor skating with skate rentals, October–March. Weekends are crowded. For indoor skating, check the **Wiener Stadthalle** (⊠ Vogelweidpl. 14, ☎ 01/981–00–0).

Jogging

Jogging paths run alongside the Danube Canal, and runners also frequent the Stadtpark and the tree-lined route along the Ring, particularly the Parkring stretch. Farther afield, in the Second District, the Prater Hauptallee, 4 km (2½ mi) from Praterstern to the Lusthaus, is a favorite.

Riding

Splendid bridle paths crisscross the Prater park. To hire a mount, contact the **Reitclub Donauhof** (⊠ Hafenzufahrtstr. 63, ☎ 01/728–3646 or 01/728–9716) or **Reitclub Prater/Reitschule Sylvia Kühnert** (⊠ Dammhaufen 62, ☎ 01/728–1335).

Skiing

A nearby slope, **Hohe Wand,** west of the city in the 14th District, offers limited skiing, with a ski lift and man-made snow when the heavens refuse. Take Bus 49B from the Hütteldorf stop of the U4 subway. Serious Viennese skiers (that includes nearly everybody) will take a train or bus out to nearby Niederösterreich (Lower Austria), with the area around the **Semmering** (☞ Chapter 4), about an hour from the city, one of the favorite locations for a quick outing.

Swimming

Vienna has at least one pool for each of its 23 districts; most are indoor pools, but some locations have an outdoor pool as well. An indoor favorite is **Rogner's** (⊠ Strohbachg. 7–9, ☎ 01/587–0844–0), complete with water slide.

For a less formal environment, head for the swimming areas of the Alte Donau or the Donauinsel (☞ Boating, *above*). The pools and the Alte Donau (paid admission) will be filled on hot summer weekends, so the Donauinsel can be a surer bet. Some beach areas are shallow and suitable for children, but the Donauinsel has no lifeguards, though there are rescue stations for emergencies. Changing areas are few, lockers nonexistent, so don't take valuables. And don't be tempted to jump into the Danube Canal; the water is definitely not for swimming, nor is the Danube itself, because of heavy undertows and a powerful current.

The city has information on all places to swim; contact the **Magistratesabteilung 44** (✉ ☎ 01/601120). Ask for directions to reach the following:

Donauinsel Nord is a huge free recreation area with a children's section and nude bathing. **Donauinsel Süd** is free and offers good swimming and boating and a nude bathing area. It's harder to get to and less crowded than other areas, and food facilities are limited. **Gänsehäufel** is a bathing island in the Alte Donau with paid admission, lockers, changing rooms, children's wading pools, topless and nude areas, and restaurants; on sunny weekends, it's likely to be full by 11 AM or earlier. **Krapfenwaldbad** is an outdoor park-pool tucked among the trees on the edge of the Vienna Woods, full of Vienna's beautiful people and singles. Get there early on a sunny Sunday or you won't get in. **Stadionbad** is an enormous sports complex popular with the younger crowd; go early. For the fun of it, ride the miniature railway (*Liliputbahn*) from behind the Ferris wheel in the Prater amusement park to the Stadion station and walk the rest of the way.

Tennis

Though Vienna has plenty of courts, they'll be booked solid. Try anyway; your hotel may have good connections. **Sportservice Wien-Sport** (✉ Bacherpl. 14, ☎ 01/545–1201–0) operates a central court-booking service (100 courts in summer, three halls in winter). Top businesspeople and political leaders head to **Tennis Point Vienna** (✉ Nottendorferg./Baumg., ☎ 01/799–9997) for the 10 indoor courts, squash, sauna, and an outstanding fitness studio; there is a bar and an excellent and remarkably reasonable restaurant as well. **Vereinigte Tennisanlagen** (✉ Prater Hauptallee 5, ☎ 01/728–1811) has courts in other locations as well. Or you can try **Tennisplätze Arsenal** (✉ Arsenalstr. 1, by Südbahnhof, ☎ 01/798–2132; ✉ Faradayg. 4, ☎ 01/798–7265; ✉ Gudrunstr. 31, ☎ 01/602–1521), which has 57 sand courts; **Tennisplätze Stadionbad** (✉ Prater Hauptallee, ☎ 01/720–2070); or **Wiener Eislaufverein** (✉ Lothringer Str. 22, behind Inter-Continental Hotel, ☎ 01/713–6353–0).

Spectator Sports

Football (Soccer)

Matches are played mainly in the **Ernst–Happel–Stadion** (stadium) in the Prater (✉ Meiereistr. 7, ☎ 01/728–0854) and the **Hanappi Stadium** (✉ Keisslerg. 6, ☎ 01/914–3490–0). Indoor soccer takes place in the **Stadthalle** (✉ Vogelweidpl. 14, ☎ 01/981–00–01). Tickets can usually be bought at the gate, but the better seats are available through ticket agencies (☞ Contacts and Resources *in* Vienna A to Z, *below*).

Horse Racing

The racetrack (flat and sulky racing) is in the Prater (✉ Galopprennpl. Freudenau, ☎ 01/728–9535–0), and the season runs April–November. The highlight is the Derby, which takes place the third Sunday in June.

Tennis

Professional matches are played in the Prater or in the Stadthalle (☞ Football [Soccer], *above*). Ticket agencies will have details.

SHOPPING

Shopping Districts

The Kärntnerstrasse, Graben, and Kohlmarkt pedestrian areas in the **Inner City** claim to have the best shops in Vienna, and for some items, such as jewelry, some of the best anywhere, although you must expect high prices. The side streets within this area have developed their own character, with shops offering antiques, art, clocks, jewelry, and period furniture. **Ringstrassen Galerie,** the new shopping plaza at Kärntner Ring 5–7, brings a number of shops together in a modern complex, although most of these stores have other, larger outlets elsewhere in the city. Outside the center, concentrations of stores are on **Mariahilfer Strasse** straddling the Sixth and Seventh districts; **Landstrasser Hauptstrasse** in the Third District; and, still farther out, **Favoritenstrasse** in the 10th District.

A collection of attractive small boutiques can be found in the **Palais Ferstel** passage at Freyung 2 in the First District. A modest group of smaller shops has sprung up in the **Sonnhof** passage between Landstrasser Hauptstrasse 28 and Ungargasse 13 in the Third District. The **Spittelberg** market, on the Spittelberggasse between Burggasse and Siebensterngasse in the Seventh District, has drawn small galleries and handicrafts shops and is particularly popular in the weeks before Christmas and Easter. Christmas is the time also for the tinselly **Christkindlmarkt** on Rathausplatz in front of City Hall; in protest over its commercialization, smaller markets specializing in handicrafts have sprung up on such traditional spots as Am Hof and the Freyung (First District), also the venue for other seasonal markets.

Vienna's **Naschmarkt** (between Linke and Rechte Wienzeile, starting at Getreidemarkt) is one of Europe's great and most colorful food and produce markets. Stalls open at 5 or 6 AM, and the pace is lively until 1 or 2 PM. Saturday is the big day, when farmers come into the city to sell at the back end of the market. It's closed Sunday.

ANTIQUES

You will find the best antiques shops located in the First District, many clustered close to the Dorotheum auction house, in the Dorotheergasse, Stallburggasse, Plankengasse, and Spiegelgasse. You'll also find interesting shops in the Josefstadt (Eighth) district, with prices considerably lower than those in the center of town. Wander up Florianigasse and back down Josefstädter Strasse, being sure not to overlook the narrow side streets.

D&S (⊠ Dorotheerg. 12, ☎ 01/512–1011) specializes in old Viennese clocks. For Art Deco, look to **Galerie bei der Albertina** (⊠ Lobkowitzpl. 1, ☎ 01/513–1416). Look in at **Glasgalerie Kovacek** (⊠ Spiegelg. 12, ☎ 01/512–9954) to see a remarkable collection of glass paperweights and other glass objects. Another Art Deco option is **Kunsthandel Junker** (⊠ Dortheerg. 12, ☎ 01/513–2208). You'll find paintings and furniture in many shops in this area, including **Kunst Salon Kovacek** (⊠ Stallburggasse 2, ☎ 01/512–8358). **Peter Feldbacher** (⊠ Annag. 6, ☎ 01/512–2408) has items ranging from glass to ceramics to furniture.

Auctions

The **Dorotheum** (⊠ Dorotheerg. 17, ☎ 01/515–60–0) is a state institution dating to 1707, when Emperor Josef I determined that he didn't want his people being exploited by pawnbrokers. The place is intriguing, with goods ranging from furs to furniture auctioned almost daily. Information on how to bid is available in English. Some items are for immediate cash sale.

Flea Markets

Every Saturday (except holidays), rain or shine, from about 7:30 AM to 4 or 5, the **Flohmarkt** in back of the Naschmarkt, stretching along the Linke Wienzeile from the Kettenbrücken U4 subway station, offers a staggering collection of stuff ranging from serious antiques to plain junk. Haggle over prices. On Thursdays and Fridays from late spring to mid-fall, an outdoor combination arts-and-crafts, collectibles, and flea market takes place on **Am Hof.** On Saturday and Sunday in summer from about 10 to 6 an outdoor **art and antiques market** springs up along the Danube Canal, stretching from the Schwedenbrücke to beyond the Salztorbrücke. Lots of books are sold, some in English, plus generally better goods and collectibles than at the Saturday flea market. Bargain over prices all the same.

Department Stores

The **Steffl** department store (⊠ Kärntnerstr. 19) is moderately upscale without being overly expensive. The larger department stores are concentrated in Mariahilfer Strasse. By far the best is **Peek & Cloppenburg** (⊠ Mariahilfer Str. 26–30), definitely upscale; outstanding gourmet shops and restaurants are in the basement. Farther up the street you will find slightly cheaper goods at **Gerngross** (⊠ Mariahilfer Str. and Kircheng.) and cheaper still at **Stafa** (⊠ Mariahilfer Str. 120).

Specialty Stores

BOOKS

Several good stores whose stock includes books in English are on the Graben and Kärntnerstrasse in the First District. For bookstores specializing in English-language books, *see* Contacts and Resources *in* Vienna A to Z, *below.*

CERAMICS AND PORCELAIN

Ceramics can be found at **Berger** (⊠ Weihburgg. 17, ☎ 01/512–1434). Gmunden primitive country ceramics are at **Pawlata** (⊠ Kärntnerstr. 14, ☎ 01/512–1764). More country ceramics can be found at **Plessgott** (⊠ Kärntner Durchgang, ☎ 01/512–5824). Check out Viennese porcelain patterns at **Augarten** (⊠ Graben/Stock-im-Eisen-Pl 3, ☎ 01/512–1494), **Albin Denk** (⊠ Graben 13, ☎ 01/512–4439), **Rosenthal** (⊠ Kärntnerstr. 16, ☎ 01/512–3994), and **Wahliss** (⊠ Kärntnerstr. 17, ☎ 01/512–1729–0).

CRYSTAL AND GLASS

Select famous Vienna glassware at **Bakalowits** (⊠ Spiegelg. 3, ☎ 01/512–6351–0). **Lobmeyr** (⊠ Kärntnerstr. 26, ☎ 01/512–0508–0), another glassware vendor, also has a small museum of its creations upstairs; the firm supplied the crystal chandeliers for the Metropolitan Opera in New York City, a gift from Austria.

Exquisite Riedl crystal is available from **Albin Denk** (⊠ Graben 13, ☎ 01/512–4439), **Berndorf** (⊠ Wollzeile 12, ☎ 01/512–2944), and **Rasper & Söhne** (⊠ Graben 15, ☎ 01/534–33–0).

GIFT ITEMS

Niederösterreichisches Heimatwerk (☞ Women's Clothing, *below*) has handmade folk objects and textiles.

Österreichische Werkstätten (⊠ Kärntnerstr. 6) offers outstanding and unusual handmade handicrafts, gifts, and quality souvenirs ranging from jewelry to textiles.

Souvenir in der Hofburg (⊠ Hofburgpassage 1 and 7) is another source of more traditional gift items.

92

Vienna Shopping

93

Wiener Geschenke (⊠ Reitschulg. 4/Michaelerpl.) has a nice selection of quality gift and traditional souvenir items and is open Sunday during part of the year.

JADE

Discover interesting pieces of Austrian jade at **Burgenland** (⊠ Opernpassage, ☏ 01/587−6266).

JEWELRY

Carius & Binder (⊠ Kärntnerstr. 17, ☏ 01/512−6750) is good for watches.

Haban (⊠ Kärntnerstr. 2, ☏ 01/512−6730−0; ⊠ Graben 12, ☏ 01/512−1220) has a fine selection of watches and jewelry.

A. Heldwein (⊠ Graben 13, ☏ 01/512−5781) sells elegant jewelry, silverware, and watches.

A. E. Köchert (⊠ Neuer Markt 15, ☏ 01/512−5828−0) has outstanding original creations.

Eleonora Kunz (⊠ Neuer Markt 13, ☏ 01/512−7112) sells stunning modern pieces for men and women.

Schullin (⊠ Kohlmarkt 7, ☏ 01/533−9007−0) has some of the most original work found anywhere.

MEN'S CLOTHING

Clothing in Vienna is far from cheap but is of good quality. The best shops are in the First District:

Sir Anthony (⊠ Kärntnerstr. 21−23, ☏ 01/512−6835), **E. Braun** (⊠ Graben 8, ☏ 01/512−5505−0), **House of Gentlemen** (⊠ Kohlmarkt 12, ☏ 01/533−3258), **Ita** (⊠ Graben 18, ☏ 01/533−6004−0), **Malowan** (⊠ Opernring 23, ☏ 01/587−6296), **Silbernagel** (⊠ Kärntnerstr. 15, ☏ 01/512−5312), **Teller** in the Third District (⊠ Landstrasser Hauptstr. 88−90, ☏ 01/712−6397) for particularly good value, **Venturini** (⊠ Spiegelg. 9, ☏ 01/512−8845) for custom-made shirts.

For men's *Trachten,* or typical Austrian clothing, including lederhosen, try **Loden-Plankl** (⊠ Michaelerpl. 6, ☏ 01/533−8032), and go to **Collins Hüte** (⊠ Opernpassage, ☏ 01/587−1305) to get the appropriate hat.

MUSIC

Look for CDs at the **Virgin Megastore** (⊠ Mariahilferstr. 37−39, ☏ 01/588370), if you haven't got the same thing at home. **Carola** is best for pop LPs and CDs (⊠ Albertinapassage by Opera House, ☏ 01/586−4114). **EMI** (⊠ Kärntnerstr. 30, ☏ 01/512−3675) has a wide selection of pops, plus classics upstairs.

Havlicek (⊠ Herreng. 5, ☏ 01/533−1964) features classics and is particularly knowledgeable and helpful. **da Caruso** (⊠ Operng. 4, ☏ 01/513−1326) specializes in classics, with an emphasis on opera.

NEEDLEWORK

For Vienna's famous petit point, head for **Petit Point Kovacec** (⊠ Kärntnerstr. 16, ☏ 01/512−4886) or **Stransky** (⊠ Hofburgpassage 2, ☏ 01/533−6098).

SHOES AND LEATHER GOODS

Try **Humanic** (⊠ Kärntnerstr. 51, ☏ 01/512−5892; ⊠ Singerstr. 2, ☏ 01/512−9101), **Nigst** (⊠ Neuer Markt 4, ☏ 01/512−4303), **Popp & Kretschmer** (⊠ Kärntnerstr. 51, ☏ 01/512−6421−0), and **Zak** (⊠ Kärntnerstr. 36, ☏ 01/512−7257).

The couturier to Vienna is **Adlmüller** (⊠ Kärntnerstr. 41, ☎ 01/512–6650–0). Check also **Flamm** (⊠ Neuer Markt 12, ☎ 01/512–2889), E. Braun, Ita, or Malowan (☞ Men's Clothing, *above*). You'll find modern young styling at **Maldone** (⊠ Kärntnerstr. 4, ☎ 01/512–2761; ⊠ Kärntnerstr. 12, ☎ 01/512–2234; ⊠ Graben 29, ☎ 01/533–6091; ⊠ Hoher Markt 8, ☎ 01/533–2555).

Check out the selection of dirndls and women's *Trachten,* the typical Austrian costume with white blouse, print skirt, and apron, at **Lanz** (⊠ Kärntnerstr. 10, ☎ 01/512–2456), **Loden-Plankl** (☞ Men's Clothing, *above*), **Niederösterreichisches Heimatwerk** (⊠ Herreng. 6, ☎ 01/533–3495), **Resi Hammerer** (⊠ Kärntnerstr. 29–31, ☎ 01/512–6952), and **Tostmann** (⊠ Schotteng. 3a, ☎ 01/533–5331, ℻ 01/533–6864).

VIENNA A TO Z

Arriving and Departing

By Boat

If you arrive in Vienna via the Danube, the DDSG/Blue Danube ship will leave you at **Praterlände** near Mexikoplatz (⊠ Friedrichstr. 7, ☎ 01/588–800). The Praterlände stop is a two-block taxi ride or hike from the Vorgartenstrasse U1/subway station, or you can take a taxi directly into town.

By Bus

International long-distance bus service (Bratislava, Brno) and most postal and railroad buses arrive at the **Wien Mitte** central bus station (⊠ Landstrasser Hauptstr. 1b, ☎ 01/711–07–3850 or 01/711–01), across from the Hilton Hotel.

By Car

Vienna is 300 km (187 mi) east of Salzburg, 200 km (125 mi) north of Graz. Main routes leading into the city are the A1 Westautobahn from Germany, Salzburg, and Linz and the A2 Südautobahn from Graz and points south.

On highways from points south or west or from the airport, ZENTRUM signs clearly mark the route to the center of Vienna. From there, however, finding your way to your hotel can be no mean trick, for traffic planners have installed a devious scheme prohibiting through traffic in the city core (the First District) and scooting cars out again via a network of exasperating one-way streets. In the city itself a car is a burden, though very useful for trips outside town.

By Plane

Vienna's airport (☎ 01/7007–0 for flight information) is at Schwechat, about 19 km (12 mi) southeast of the city. **Austrian Airlines** (☎ 01/1789), **Air Canada** (☎ 0664/432–2197 for mobil phone), **Delta** (☎ 01/512–6646–0), and **Lauda Air** (☎ 01/514770) fly into Schwechat from North America. The North American services of Austrian, Delta, and Swissair are shared under joint flight numbers and may be flown in and out of Vienna by any of the three lines.

Buses leave the airport frequently for the **city air terminal** (⊠ Am Stadtpark, ☎ 01/5800–33369), by the Hilton. The cheapest way into town is the S7 **train** (called the *Schnellbahn*), which shuttles every half hour between the airport and the Landstrasse/Wien–Mitte (city center) and Wien–Nord (north Vienna) stations; the fare is AS34 and it takes about 35 minutes. Follow the picture signs of a train to the basement of the airport. Your ticket is also good for an immediate transfer to your destination within the city on the streetcar, bus, or U-Bahn. **Buses** also run every hour (every half hour on weekends and holidays Apr.–Sept.) from the airport to the Westbahnhof (West Train Station) and the Südbahnhof (South Train Station). Be sure you get on the right bus! The one-way fare for all buses is AS70. A **taxi** from the airport to downtown Vienna costs about AS350–AS500; agree on a price in advance. Cabs (legally) do not meter this drive, as airport fares are more or less fixed (legally again) at about double the meter fare. The cheapest cab service to the airport is C+K Airport Service (☎ 01/1731, FAX 01/689–6969), charging a set price of AS270. C+K will also meet your plane at no extra charge if you let them know your flight information in advance.

By Train

Trains from Germany, Switzerland, and western Austria arrive at the **Westbahnhof** (West Station), on Europaplatz, where the Mariahilfer Strasse crosses the Gürtel. If you're coming from Italy or Hungary, you'll generally arrive at the **Südbahnhof** (South Station, ⊠ Wiedner Gürtel 1). The current stations for trains to and from Prague and Warsaw are **Wien Nord** (North Station, ⊠ Praterstern) and **Franz-Josef Bahnhof** (⊠ Julius-Tandler-Pl.). **Central train information** (☎ 01/1717) will have details and taped schedule information (in German) for trains to and from the west (☎ 01/1552) or for trains to and from the south (☎ 01/1553).

Getting Around

Vienna is divided into 23 numbered districts. Taxi drivers may need to know which district you seek, as well as the street address. The district number is coded into the postal code with the second and third digits; thus A–1010 (the "01") is the First District, A–1030 is the Third, A–1110 is the 11th, and so on. Some sources and maps still give the district numbers, either in Roman or Arabic numerals, as Vienna X or Vienna 10.

Vienna is a city to tackle on foot. With the exception of the Schönbrunn and Belvedere palaces and the Prater amusement park, most sights are concentrated in the center, the First District (A–1010), much of which is a pedestrian zone anyway.

By Bus and Streetcar

Vienna's public transportation system is fast, clean, safe, and easy to use. Get public transport maps at a tourist office or at the transport-information offices (*Wiener Verkehrsbetriebe*), underground at Karlsplatz, Stephansplatz, and Praterstern. You can transfer on the same ticket between subway, streetcar, bus, and long stretches of the fast suburban railway, *Schnellbahn* (*S-Bahn*). Buy single tickets for AS20 from dispensers on the streetcar or bus; you'll need exact change. The ticket machines at subway stations (*VOR-Fahrkarten*) give change and dispense 24-hour, 72-hour, and eight-day tickets, as well as single tickets separately and in blocks of two and five. At *Tabak-Trafik* (cigarette shops/newsstands) or the underground *Wiener Verkehrsbetriebe* offices you can get a block of five tickets for AS85, each ticket good for one uninterrupted trip in more or less the same general direction with unlimited transfers. Or you can get a three-day ticket for AS130, good on all lines for 72 hours from the time you validate the ticket; there's also a 24-hour ticket for AS50. If you're staying longer, get an eight-day ticket (AS265), which can be used on eight separate days or by any number of persons (up to eight) at any one time. **Tabak-Trafik Almassy** (⊠ Stephanspl. 4, to the right behind cathedral, ☎ 01/512–

5909) is open every day from 8 AM to 7 PM and has tickets as well as film and other items.

Ask at tourist offices or your hotel about a *Vienna-Card;* costing AS180, the card combines 72 hours' use of public transportation and discounts at certain museums and shops.

The first streetcars run from about 5:15 AM. From then on, service (barring gridlock on the streets) is regular and reliable, and most lines operate until about midnight. Where streetcars don't run, buses do; route maps and schedules are posted at each bus or subway stop.

Should you miss the last streetcar or bus, special night buses with an N designation operate at half-hour intervals over several key routes; the starting (and transfer) points are the Opera House and Schwedenplatz. The night-owl buses take a special fare of AS25, tickets available on the bus; normal tickets, your 72-hour, and *Vienna-Card* are not valid.

Within the heart of the city, bus lines 1A, 2A, and 3A are useful crosstown routes. These carry a reduced fare of AS8.50 per trip if you have bought the *Kurzstrecke* ticket (AS34), good for four trips or up to four people on one trip (with no transfer). The *Kurzstrecke* tickets are also valid for two stops on the subway or shorter distances on the streetcar lines.

By Car

Traffic congestion within Vienna has gotten out of hand, and driving to in-town destinations generally takes longer than public transportation. City planners' solutions have been to make driving as difficult as possible, with one-way streets and other tricks, and a car in town is far more of a burden than a pleasure. Drivers not familiar with the city literally need a navigator. The entire First and Sixth through Ninth districts are limited-parking zones and require that a *Parkschein,* a paid-parking chit available at most newsstands and tobacconists, be displayed on the dash during the day. Overnight street parking in the First and Sixth through Ninth districts is restricted to residents with special permits; all other cars are subject to expensive ticketing or even towing, so in these districts be sure you have off-street garage parking.

By Horse Cab

A *Fiaker,* or horse cab, will trot you around to whatever destination you specify, but this is an expensive way to see the city. A short tour of the inner city takes about 20 minutes and costs AS500; a longer one including the Ringstrasse takes about 40 minutes and costs AS800, for the whole Fiaker. The carriages accommodate four (five if someone sits next to the coachman). Starting points are Heldenplatz in front of the Hofburg, Stephansplatz beside the cathedral, and across from the Albertina, all in the First District. For longer trips, or any variation of the regular route, agree on the price first.

By Subway

Five subway lines (*U-Bahn*), whose stations are prominently marked with blue *U* signs, crisscross the city. Karlsplatz and Stephansplatz are the main transfer points between lines. The last subway (U4) runs at about 12:30 AM.

By Taxi

Taxis in Vienna are relatively inexpensive. The initial charge is AS26 for as many as four people daytime, AS27 nighttime, weekends, and holidays. AS16 is added for radio cabs ordered by phone and for each piece of luggage that must go into the trunk, and a charge is added for waiting beyond a reasonable limit. It's customary to round up the fare

98

Vienna Subways

to cover the tip. Taxis can be flagged on the street (when the roof light is on), taken from regular stands, or ordered by phone (☎ 01/313–00, 01/401–00, or 01/601–60–0). Service is usually prompt, but when you hit rush hour, the weather is bad, or you need to keep to an exact schedule, call ahead and order a taxi for a specific time. If your destination is the airport, ask for a reduced-rate taxi. For the cheapest taxi to the airport, *see* Between the Airport and City Center, *above*.

For a chauffeured limousine call **Göth** (☎ 01/713–7196), **Mazur** (☎ 01/604–2233), **Tibor Adler** (☎ 01/216–0990), or **Peter Urban** (☎ 01/713–5255 or 713–3781).

Contacts and Resources
Car Rentals
Rental cars can be arranged at the airport or in town. Major firms include:

Avis (✉ Airport, ☎ 01/7007–2700; ✉ Opernring 3–5, ☎ 01/587–6241), **Budget** (✉ Airport, ☎ 01/7007–2711; ✉ Hilton Hotel, Am Stadtpark, ☎ 01/714–6565–0), **Europcar** (✉ Airport, ☎ 01/7007–3316; ✉ Erdberg Park & Ride, ☎ 01/799–6176), **Hertz** (✉ Airport, ☎ 01/7007–2661; ✉ Kärntner Ring 17, ☎ 01/512–8677; 01/713–1596 for international reservations), **National** (✉ Europcar/InterRent at airport, ☎ 01/7007–3316; ✉ Denzel Autovermietung, Kärntner Ring 14, ☎ 01/505–4200; ☎ 01/505–4166 for international reservations).

Buchbinder (✉ Schlachthausg. 38, ☎ 01/717–50–0) is a local firm with particularly favorable rates and clean cars.

Doctors and Dentists
If you need a doctor and speak no German, ask your hotel, or in an emergency, phone your consulate.

Embassies

Canadian Embassy (✉ Laurenzerberg 2, on the 3rd floor of Haupt-post building complex, ☎ 01/531–38–01). **U.K. Embassy and Consulate** (✉ Jauresg. 10, ☎ 01/71613–5151). **U.S. Embassy** (✉ Boltzmanng. 16, ☎ 01/313–39). **U.S. Consulate** (✉ Gartenbauprom-enade, Parkring 12A, Marriott building, ☎ 01/313–39).

Emergencies

The emergency numbers are ☎ 133 for the **police,** ☎ 144 for an **ambulance,** and ☎ 122 for the **fire department.**

English-Language Bookstores

The leading sources of books in English are **Big Ben Bookstore** (✉ Serviteng. 4a, ☎ 01/319–6412), **British Bookstore** (✉ Weihburgg. 24–26, ☎ 01/512–1945–0), and **Shakespeare & Co.** (✉ Sterng. 2, ☎ 01/535–5053). **Alphaville** (✉ Schleifmühlg. 5, ☎ 01/585–1966) mainly rents videotapes.

English-Language Radio

"Blue Danube Radio" on FM at 103.8 and 91.0 MHz carries news, music, and information in English (and some in French) throughout the day and early evening, with major newscasts at noon and 6 PM.

Guided Tours

EXCURSIONS

All three bus tour operators (☞ Orientation Tours, *below*) offer short trips outside of the city. Check their offerings and compare packages and prices to be sure you get what you want. Your hotel will have brochures.

ORIENTATION TOURS

When you're pressed for time, a good way to see the highlights of Vienna is via a sightseeing bus tour, which gives you a once-over-lightly of the heart of the city and allows a closer look at Schönbrunn and Belvedere palaces. You can cover almost the same territory on your own by taking either Streetcar 1 or 2 around the Ring and then walking through the heart of the city (☞ Self-Guided Tours, *below*). For tours, contact one of the following: **Cityrama/Gray Line** (✉ Börseg. 1, ☎ 01/534–1312, FAX 01/534–1328), **CityTouring Vienna** (✉ Penzingerstr. 46, ☎ 01/894–1417–0, FAX 01/894–3239),or **Vienna Sightseeing Tours** (✉ Stelzhammerg. 4/11, ☎ 01/712–4683–0, FAX 01/712–714–1141).

Vienna Sightseeing Tours and CityTouring Vienna run 1¼-hour "get acquainted" tours daily. All three have tours of about three hours (AS350), including brief visits to Schönbrunn and Belvedere palace grounds. If you want to see the Schönbrunn interior, you'll have to pay a separate entrance fee, with some operators offering a 30-minute or one-hour stop, or in some cases leaving you to find your way back to the center of town yourself. All three firms offer a number of other tours as well (your hotel will have detailed programs) and provide hotel pickup for most tours.

For a wide range of interesting guided tours, including informative walks through the old Jewish Quarter and a *Third Man* tour from the classic film starring Orson Welles, contact **Vienna Walks and Talks** (✉ Wiethestr. 69/1, A–1220, ☎ 01/774–8901 or 01/602–3367, FAX 01/774–8933).

STREETCAR TOURS

From early May through September, a 1929 vintage streetcar leaves each Saturday at 11:30 AM and 1:30 PM and Sunday, Monday, and holidays at 9:30 and 11:30 AM and 1:30 PM from the Otto Wagner Pavilion at Karlsplatz for a guided tour. For AS200 (AS180 if you have the *Vienna-Card*), you'll go around the Ring, out past the big Ferris wheel in the Prater and past Schönbrunn and Belvedere palaces in the course of the two-hour trip. The old-timer trips are popular, so get tickets in advance at the **transport-information office** underground at Karlsplatz, weekdays 7 AM–6 PM, weekends and holidays 8:30–4 (☎ 01/7909–44026).

PERSONAL GUIDES

Guided walking tours (in English) are a great way to see the city highlights. Tour topics range from "Unknown Underground Vienna" to "1,000 Years of Jewish Tradition" and "Vienna Around Sigmund Freud." Tours take about 1½ hours, are held in any weather provided at least three people turn up, and cost AS108 plus any entry fees. No reservations are needed. Get a list of the guided-tour possibilities at the city information office (✉ Kärntnerstr. 38). Ask for the monthly brochure "Walks in Vienna," which details the tours, days, times, and starting points. You can also arrange to have your own privately guided tour for AS1,116 for a half day.

SELF-GUIDED TOURS

Get a copy of "Vienna Downtown Walking Tours" by Henriette Mandl from any bookshop. The six tours take you through the highlights of central Vienna with excellent commentary and some entertaining anecdotes, which most of your Viennese acquaintances won't know. The booklet "Vienna from A–Z" (in English, AS70; available at bookshops and city information offices) explains the numbered plaques attached to all major buildings.

Late-Night Pharmacies

In each area of the city one pharmacy stays open 24 hours; if a pharmacy is closed, a sign on the door will tell you the address of the nearest one that is open. Call 01/1550 for names and addresses (in German) of the pharmacies open that night.

Lost and Found

If you've lost something valuable, check with the police at the **Fundamt** (✉ Wasag. 22, ☎ 01/313–44–0 or 01/313–44–9211). If your loss occurred on a train, check the **Bundesbahn Fundamt** (✉ Railway lost property office, ☎ 01/5800). If you were coming in from Salzburg, call the office at the **Westbahnhof** (☎ 01/5800–32996) 8–noon; from Villach or the south, call the **Südbahnhof** (☎ 01/5800–35656). Losses on the subway system or streetcars can be checked by calling the **Zentrale Fundstelle** (☎ 01/7909–43500).

Ticket Agencies

American Express (✉ Kärntnerstr. 21–23, A–1015, ☎ 01/515–40–0, FAX 01/515–40–70), **Carta Austria** (✉ Goldschmiedg. 10, ☎ 01/536–01), **Cosmos** (✉ Kärntner Ring 17, A–1010, ☎ 01/515–33–0, FAX 01/513–4147), or **Vienna Ticket Service** (✉ Postfach 160, A–1043, ☎ 01/534170, FAX 01/534–1726).

Travel Agencies

American Express (✉ Kärntnerstr. 21–23, ☎ 01/515–40–0, FAX 01/515–40–70), **Carlson/Wagon-Lits** (✉ Kärntner Ring 2, ☎ 01/501–60–0, FAX 01/501–60–65), **Cosmos** (✉ Kärntner Ring 15, ☎ 01/515–33–0, FAX 01/513–4147), **Ruefa Reisen** (✉ Fleischmarkt 1, ☎ 01/534–04–0, FAX 01/534–04–394), and **Österreichisches Verkehrsbüro** (✉ Friedrichstr. 7, opposite the Secession Building, ☎ 01/588–00–0, FAX 01/986–8533).

Visitor Information

The main point for information (walk-ins only) is the **Vienna City Tourist Office** (Fremdenverkehrsstelle der Stadt Wien, ⊠ Kärntnerstr. 38), in back of the Opera House and around the corner from the Hotel Sacher, open daily 9–7. For phone inquiries call the Central Tourist Office (☎ 01/211140).

If you need a room, go to **Information-Zimmernachweis,** operated by the Verkehrsbüro in the Westbahnhof (☎ 01/892–3392) and in the Südbahnhof (☎ 01/505–3132). At the airport, the **information and room-reservation office** in the arrivals hall (☎ 01/7007–2828) is open daily 8:30 AM–9 PM. None of these offices can arrange room bookings by telephone; you must deal in person.

If you're driving into Vienna, get information or book rooms at **Information-Zimmernachweis** at the end of the Westautobahn at Wientalstrasse/Auhof (☎ 01/979–1271) or at the end of the Südautobahn at Triesterstrasse 149 (☎ 01/616–0071 or 01/616–0070).

3 Side Trips from Vienna

*From the Vienna Woods
to the Weinviertel*

*Is it the sun or the soil? The dreamy
castle-capped peaks? Whatever the
reason, the idyllic regions outside
Vienna have always offered perfectly
pastoral escapes for Viennese. Rich in
scenic splendor, this countryside is
also saturated with musical history.
Here, Beethoven was inspired to write
his* Pastoral Symphony, *Johann
Strauss set the Vienna Woods to
music, and a glass of intoxicating
Retzer Wein urged Richard Strauss to
compose the "Rosenkavalier Waltz."
From the elegant spa of Baden to
mysterious Mayerling, this region
is a day-tripper's delight.*

THE VIENNESE ARE UNDENIABLY LUCKY. Few populaces enjoy such glorious—and easily accessible—options for day-tripping. For many the first destination is, of course, the Wienerwald, the fabled Vienna Woods. The Vienna Woods is a large range of rolling, densely wooded hills, extending from Vienna's doorstep to the outposts of the Alps in the south. This region is crisscrossed by country roads and hiking paths, dotted with forest lodges and inns, and solidifies every now and then into quaint little villages and market towns. In addition to such natural pleasures, the regions outside of Vienna offer something for everyone. Turning south to Mayerling leads you to the site where in 1889 the successor to the Austrian throne presumably took his own life after shooting his secret love—a mystery still unresolved. You can opt to head northeast, into wonderfully encompassing woods and gently rolling hills sprinkled with elegant summer palaces, and, to the north, to take one long, liquid adventure by exploring the Weinstrasse (Wine Road), along which vast expanses of vineyard produce excellent, mainly white wines. Another choice is to follow the trail of the defensive castles that protected the land from invaders from the north, or you can even trace the early days of Masonry in Austria—both Haydn and Mozart were members of what was then a secret and forbidden brotherhood.

Updated by
Bonnie Dodson

Pleasures and Pastimes

Bicycling
The Carnuntum region and the southeast corner of the Weinviertel, a region known as the Marchfeld, offer outstanding cycling, with a number of marked routes. Cycle paths follow the southern bank of the Danube past Carnuntum (Petronell) through Bad Deutsch–Altenburg to Hainburg, and other parts of the region are flat enough to offer fine cycling without exertion. In the Marchfeld, another marked route close to the March river includes the Baroque castles at Marchegg, Schlosshof, and Niederweiden.

Castles
To take advantage of the fact that the Danube forms a natural line of defense, barons and bailiffs decided centuries ago to fortify bluffs along the river. Castles were the best answer, and a wonderful string of these more or less follows the course of the Thaya river, starting in Weitra and Heidenreichstein close to the Czech border, then eastward to Raabs, Riegersburg, and Hardegg. The 17th- and 18th-century structures vary from turreted hilltop fortresses to more elegant moated bastions, but all were part of a chain against invaders. Several are basically intact, the others restored, and all are impressive relics well worth visiting. Castle concerts have become popular during summer months, when the buildings are open for tours as well.

Dining
With very few exceptions, food in this region, while influenced by Vienna cuisine, is simple. The basics are available in abundance: roast meats, customary schnitzel variations, game in season, fresh vegetables, and standard desserts such as *Palatschinken* (crepes filled with jam or with nuts topped with chocolate sauce). Imaginative cooking is rare; this is not tourist country, and the local population demands little beyond reasonable quality and quantity.

Wines are equally taken for granted, although four of the areas included here are designated as separate wine regions—the Weinviertel, or wine quarter to the north of Vienna; the Kamptal, which divides the Weinviertel from the Waldviertel to the west; the Carnuntum–Petronell region, just below the Danube to the southeast of Vienna; and the Thermen region, south and southwest of the capital. The specialties are mainly white wines, with the standard types, Grüner Veltliner and Rieslings and increasingly Weissburgunder, predominating. Reds are coming more into favor, with lighter reds such as Zweigelt and even rosés to be found in the northern areas, the heavier reds such as Blaufränkisch and St. Laurent and the spicier Gewürztraminer and Müller–Thurgau whites in the south. Most of the vintners work small holdings, so output is limited. The wine market in Poysdorf, center of Austria's largest wine region, offers an opportunity to sample a wide choice of area wares.

Restaurant prices include taxes and a service charge, but it is customary to give the waiter an additional tip of 3%–5%, usually rounding up the bill to the nearest AS5 or AS10.

CATEGORY	COST*
$$$$	over AS350
$$$	AS200–AS350
$$	AS150–AS200
$	under AS150

per person for a typical two-course meal, including a small glass of wine or beer but excluding a tip.

Hiking and Walking

The celebrated Vienna Woods to the west and southwest of Vienna are crisscrossed by hundreds of easy hiking paths, numbered, color-coded, and marked for destinations. Excellent hiking maps available from most bookstores will give ideas and routes. Paths will take you through woods, past meadows and vineyards, alongside streams and rivers, with an occasional tavern hidden away deep in the woods where you can stop for refreshment or a cold snack. Deer, wild boar, and a host of small animals inhabit these preserves. The area is protected, and development is highly restricted, making it ideal for pleasurable hiking.

Lodging

Accommodations in the countryside around Vienna are pretty basic. This is underdeveloped tourist territory, prime turf for the more adventuresome, with rooms frequently to be found as an adjunct to the local *Gasthaus.* Nearly all are family-run; the younger members will speak at least some school English. You'll probably have to carry your own bags, and elevators to upper floors are scarce. Booking ahead is a good idea, as most places have relatively few rooms, particularly rooms with full bath. Window screens are almost unknown in Austria, as bugs are few, but in farming areas, both flies and occasionally mosquitoes can be a nuisance in the warmer seasons. Since you'll want windows open at night, take along a can of bug spray and you'll sleep more peacefully. The standard country bed covering is a down-filled feather bed, so if you're allergic to feathers or want more warmth, ask for blankets. Even the simpler hotels will be spotless, and almost without exception, you'll be offered a tasty breakfast, which can range from fresh rolls with cold cuts and cheese and tea or coffee to an ample buffet spread with cereals and fruit as well, included in the room price. Hotel room rates usually include breakfast—although check to be sure.

CATEGORY	COST*
$$$$	over AS 1,300
$$$	AS1,000–AS1,300
$$	AS600–AS1,000
$	under AS600

All prices are for a standard double room for two, including taxes and service charge.

Exploring Vienna's Environs

The region surrounding Vienna divides itself logically into four areas. The Vienna Woods, that huge, unspoiled belt of forest green stretching westward south of the Danube, was celebrated by composers Beethoven, Schubert, and Strauss and remains a favorite of the Viennese today. The towns to the south—Mödling, Baden, and Bad Vöslau—mark the east end of the rolling, wooded hills. There the fertile Vienna Basin begins, sweeping east to the low, wooded Leitha Mountains, which shelter the Putzta Plain extending on into Hungary. The northern part of the basin widens into the Danube Valley, forming the Carnuntum agricultural and wine region, with Slovakia to the east.

North of the Danube, two great regions are divided by the Kamp River, with the wooded Waldviertel (or Forest District) to the northwest adjoining the Czech Republic, and the rolling hills of the agricultural Weinviertel (or Wine District) to the northeast, bordering on the Czech Republic and on Slovakia, where the March River flows into the Danube.

Great Itineraries

The four districts surrounding Vienna are compact, and each can be explored in a day or two. To pursue the lives of the famous composers Schubert and Beethoven, take the route to the south, to Mödling and Baden; for Haydn's birthplace, go to the east to Rohrau, then possibly on to Eisenstadt (☞ Chapter 4). To tour a chain of defensive castles, head for the forested Waldviertel. To enjoy rolling hills and vast expanses of vineyards and to sample their output, seek out the Weinviertel to the north.

Numbers in the text correspond to numbers in the margin and on the Baden and Environs and the Waldviertel and Weinviertel maps.

South of the Danube

IF YOU HAVE 1 DAY

To get a taste of the fringes of the Vienna Woods to the capital's south and west, head for **Mödling** ② and **Baden** ⑦. Both are smaller communities with unspoiled 17th-century town centers on a scale easy to assimilate. The route to Baden runs through the band of rolling wooded hills that mark the eastern edge of the Vienna Woods. The hills are skirted by vineyards forming a "wine belt," which also follows the valleys south of Vienna.

IF YOU HAVE 3 DAYS

With more time, you might spend two days in the Vienna Woods area, starting off with two particularly picturesque towns, **Perchtoldsdorf** ① and **Mödling** ②—with perhaps a look at the grand garden of **Schloss Laxenburg** ③—then following the scenic *Weinstrasse* (wine road) through the lush vineyard country to the noted wine-producing village of **Gumpoldskirchen** ⑥. Overnight in 🖬 **Baden** ⑦; then spend your second day taking in the sights of the fashionable spa town, including its grand Kurpark and Casino. Set out in the afternoon for mysterious 🖬 **Mayerling** ⑧. After an evocative dawn and morning there, head for the great abbey at **Heiligenkreuz** ⑨, continuing on to Vienna.

North of the Danube

IF YOU HAVE 1 DAY

The decision will have to be woods or wine, if you're tight on time. If woods, then head for **Waidhofen an der Thaya** ⑳, returning via picturesque **Raabs an der Thaya** ㉑, **Geras** ㉔, and **Horn** ⑪. If wine, start at the bustling shipbuilding city of Korneuburg, and then head northward to the border town of **Laa an der Thaya** ㉘ and return via **Poysdorf** ㉙, famous as a wine center.

Baden and Environs

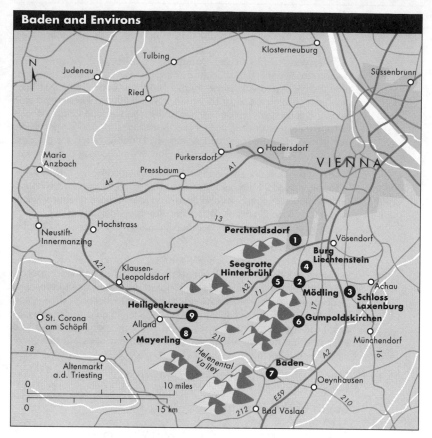

IF YOU HAVE 3 DAYS

Spend a leisurely two days tracking the castles of the Waldviertel, starting at **Ottenstein** ⑬; moving on to **Zwettl** ⑭, with its magnificent abbey; overnighting at the noted castle–hotel–Masonic museum in 🏰 **Rosenau** ⑮; and continuing on to **Weitra** ⑯, with its painted facades, for the start of the defensive castles route. The next mighty castle is at **Heidenreichstein** ⑲; follow the castle route with an overnight in 🏰 **Raabs an der Thaya** ㉑ and proceed onward to **Schloss Riegersburg** ㉒ and **Burg Hardegg** ㉓, overlooking the river forming the border with the Czech Republic. A stop in the ancient city of **Retz** ㉗ will give you a taste of the wine country; to end your excursion, head on to **Laa an der Thaya** ㉘ and **Poysdorf** ㉙.

When to Tour Vienna's Environs

Most of the regions around Vienna are best seen in the temperate seasons between mid-March and mid-November. The Waldviertel, however, with its vast stands of great forest, offers picture-book scenery throughout the year. The combination of oaks and evergreens offers a color spectrum ranging from intense early spring green, through the deep green of summer, and into traces of autumn foliage, particularly in the Kamp River valley; in winter, occasional spectacular displays of hoarfrost and snowswept vistas turn the region into a glittering three-dimensional Christmas card.

ON THE ROAD TO BADEN AND MAYERLING

This short, though history-rich, tour takes you to Baden through the legendary band of rolling wooded hills of the Vienna Woods that border Vienna on the west. The hills are skirted by vineyards forming a "wine belt," which also follows the valleys south of Vienna. You can visit this area easily in a day's outing, either by car or by public transportation, or you can spend the night in Baden, Mödling, or Alland for a more leisurely tour, visiting Mayerling, Heiligenkreuz, and a few other sights in the area.

Perchtoldsdorf

❶ *12 km (7½ mi) southwest of Vienna center.*

Just over the Vienna city line to the southwest lies Perchtoldsdorf, a charmingly picturesque market town with many wine taverns, a 13th-century Gothic parish church, and the symbol of the town—an imposing stone tower completed in 1511, once forming a piece of the town's defense wall. Familiarly known as Pedersdorf, the town is a favorite excursion spot for the Viennese, who come mainly for the good local wines. Wander around the compact town square to admire the Renaissance houses, some with arcaded courtyards. The Pestsäule (Plague Column) in the center of the square, which gives thanks for rescue from the dread 16th-century plague, was created by the famous Baroque architect Fischer von Erlach and is similar to the Plague Column that adorns the Graben in Vienna (☞ Vienna's Shop Window: From Michaelerplatz to the Graben *in* Chapter 2). The most recent version of *The Three Musketeers*, starring Chris O'Donnell and Charlie Sheen, was partly filmed here within the old defense walls. Without a car, you can reach Perchtoldsdorf from Vienna by taking the S-Bahn, or train, from the Westbahnbof, to Liesing, and then a short cab ride to the town.

Dining

$$$$ ✕ **Jahreszeiten.** This elegant, formal yet relaxed restaurant is in the capable hands of Günter Winter, whose reputation as a top chef continues to grow. The menu reflects international cuisine with an Austrian flair. You might be offered game and spring lamb in season, or try any of the fish offerings, perhaps sweet-sour shrimp on saffron rice. Finish with *Topfensouffle*, a delicately light cheesecake concoction. Beyond the kitchen, the atmosphere, like the tables, is set to perfection, and the menu is supplemented by wines from an outstanding cellar, international as well as local. ✉ *Hochstr. 17*, ☎ *01/865–3129. Reservations essential. AE, DC, MC, V. Closed Mon., Easter wk, and late July–early Aug. No lunch Sat. or dinner Sun.*

Mödling

20 km (12½ mi) southwest of Vienna.

❷ Founded in the 10th century, **Mödling** has a delightful town center, now a pedestrian zone. Here you can admire centuries-old buildings, most one- or two-story, which give the town an intimate feeling. Composers Beethoven and Schubert appreciated this in the early 1800s; Mödling was one of Beethoven's favored residences outside of Vienna. Note the domineering **St. Othmar Gothic parish church** on a hill overlooking the town proper, a Romanesque 12th-century charnel house (where the bones of the dead were kept), and the town hall, which has a Renaissance loggia. Later eras added art nouveau, which mixes happily with the several 16th- and 17th-century buildings.

❸ A couple of miles east of Mödling is **Schloss Laxenburg,** a complex consisting of a large Baroque Neues Schloss (New Castle), a small 14th-century Altes Schloss (Old Castle), and an early 19th-century neo-Gothic castle set into the sizable lake. The large park is full of birds and small game, such as roe deer and hare, and is decorated with statues, cascades, imitation temples, and other follies. The park and grounds are a favorite with the Viennese for Sunday outings. The Altes Schloss was built in 1381 by Duke Albrecht III as his summer residence, and several Habsburg emperors spent summers in the Neues Schloss, which now houses the International Institute of Applied Systems Analysis. Opposite is the large Baroque Convent of the Charitable Sisters. The castle is currently occupied by a research institute and is generally not open to the public, but the gardens are open daily. ⊠ *Schlosspl. 1,* ☎ *02236/ 712–26–0.* ⌸ *Garden AS15, boat to castle AS5, tour AS45.* ⊙ *Gardens daily 10–5; tours 11, 2, and 3.*

☕ ❹ A couple of miles east of Mödling is **Burg Liechtenstein,** an imposing medieval castle perched formidably on a crag overlooking the Vienna Woods. The pale stone walls and turrets have withstood marauding armies and the elements for more than 800 years, but the interior has been largely restored and includes a squires' hall, kitchen, bedchambers, a chapel, and even a medieval toilet. Not to be missed is the Tower Room, with its 13th-century red Italian marble fireplace and carved wooden spiral staircase. The Tower Room was the last refuge in case of an attack, and you can see where boiling water and refuse were poured onto the invaders. In summer concerts are held in the courtyard. ⊠ *Maria Enzersdorf,* ☎ *02236/44294.* ⌸ *AS50.* ⊙ *Apr.–Oct., Tues.– Sun. 9:30–5.*

☕ ❺ West of Mödling on Route 11 is the **Seegrotte Hinterbrühl,** a fascinating but now somewhat commercialized underground sea, created years ago when a mine filled up with water. You can take a 45-minute motorboat trip and look at the reflections through the arched caverns of the mine. Some of the recent film *The Three Musketeers,* starring Charlie Sheen and Chris O'Donnell, was filmed here. ⊠ *Grutschgasse 2, Hinterbrühl,* ☎ *02236/26364.* ⌸ *AS50.* ⊙ *Apr.–Oct., daily 9–5; Nov.– Mar., daily 9–3:30.*

Dining

$$$ ✕ **Hotel-Restaurant Höldrichsmühle.** Höldrichsmühle, where a mill has turned since the 12th century, is now the spot for a famed 200-year-old country inn. Legend holds that the linden tree and the well found here inspired composer Franz Schubert to one of his better-known songs. Stop at this traditional restaurant for fish, game, or various wild mushroom dishes in season. ⊠ *Gaadnerstr. 34,* ☎ *02236/26274–0. No credit cards.*

Gumpoldskirchen

❻ *4 km (2½ mi) west of Mölding.*

From Mödling, follow the scenic Weinstrasse (an unnumbered road to the west of the rail line) through the lush vineyard country to the famous wine-producing village of Gumpoldskirchen, home of one of Europe's most pleasant white wines. This tiny village on the eastern slopes of the last Alpine rocks has lived for wine for two thousand years, and its white wines enjoy a fame that is widespread. At one stage, there was more Gumpoldskirchner on the world markets than the village could ever have produced—a situation reminiscent of the medieval glut of pieces of the True Cross. **Vintners' houses** line the main street, many of them with the typical large wooden gates that lead to the vine-covered courtyards where the Heuriger (wine of the latest vintage) is served by the owner and his family at simple wooden tables with benches. Gumpoldskirchen also has an arcaded Renaissance town hall, a market fountain made from a Roman sarcophagus, and the (private) castle of the Teutonic knights, whose descendants still own some of the best vineyard sites in the area.

Dining

$$ ✕ **Altes Zechhaus.** Perched at the the top of the Old Town, this centuries-old drinking tavern is still going strong. Choose from the tempting array of salads downstairs and then order a hearty schnitzel, spit-roasted chicken, or duck, which will be brought to your table piping hot. Try to get a table upstairs in the wood-beamed Gothic Room, where plank tables are set against ancient stone walls and mullioned windows. Be sure to check out their house wine with its bawdy label, on display in the foyer. ⊠ *Kirchenpl. 1,* ☎ *02252/62247,* FAX *02252/ 63541. AE, DC, MC, V.*

Baden

★ ❼ *7 km (4½ mi) south of Gumpoldskirchen, 32 km (20 mi) southwest of Vienna.*

The Weinstrasse brings you to the serenely elegant spa town of Baden. Since antiquity, Baden's sulfuric thermal baths have attracted the ailing and the fashionable from all over the world. When the Romans came across the springs, they dubbed the town Aquae; the Babenbergs revived it in the 10th century; and when the Russian czar Peter the Great visited in 1698, Baden's golden age began. Austrian emperor Franz II spent 31 successive summers here: Every year for 12 years before his death in 1835, the royal entourage moved from Vienna for the season. Later in the century, Emperor Franz Josef II was a regular visitor, becoming the inspiration for much of the regal trappings the city still sports. In Baden, Mozart composed his "Ave Verum"; Beethoven spent 15 summers here and wrote large sections of his Ninth Symphony and *Missa Solemnis* when he lived at Frauengasse 10; here Franz Grillparzer wrote his historical dramas; and Josef Lanner, both Johann Strauss (father and son), Carl Michael Ziehrer, and Karl Millöcker composed and directed many of their waltzes, marches, and operettas.

For many people the primary reason for a visit to Baden is the lovely, sloping **Kurpark** in the center of town, where occasional outdoor public concerts still take place. Operetta is performed under the skies in the Summer Arena (the roof closes if it rains); in winter, it is performed in the Stadttheater. People sit quietly under the old trees or walk through the upper sections of the Kurpark for a view of the town from above. The old Kurhaus, now enlarged and renovated, incorporates a convention hall. ⊠ *Kaiser Franz Ring.*

The ornate **casino**—with a bar, restaurant, and gambling rooms—still includes traces of its original 19th-century decor but has been enlarged and overlaid with glitz that rivals that of Las Vegas. ⊠ *Kaiser Franz Ring 1–3, Kurpark,* ☎ *02252/44496–0.* ☉ *Casino daily from 1* PM, *gambling daily from 3* PM.

Music lovers will want to visit the **Beethoven House** (⊠ Rathausgasse 10, ☎ 02252/86800–231). Admission is AS20, and hours are Tuesday–Friday 4–6, weekends 9–11 and 4–6. Children of all ages will enjoy the enchanting **Doll and Toy Museum** (⊠ Erzherzog Rainer-Ring 23, ☎ 02252/41020). Admission is AS20, and the museum is open Tuesday–Friday 4–6, weekends 9–11 and 4–6.

One of the pleasures associated with Baden is getting there. You can reach the city directly from Vienna by bus or, far more fun, interurban streetcar, in about 50 minutes—the bus departs from the Ring directly opposite the Opera House; the blue streetcar departs from the Ring across from the Bristol Hotel. Both drop you in the center of Baden. By car from Vienna, travel south on Route A2, turning west at the junction of Route 305. It is possible, with advance planning, to go on to Mayerling and Heiligenstadt on post office buses (☎ 01/711–01).

Dining and Lodging

$$$$ ╳📧 **Grand Hotel Sauerhof.** "Schönbrunn yellow" marks this appeal-
★   ing country house, which has been elegantly renovated, with rooms in old-Vienna style. The hotel caters heavily to seminars and group activities, but individual guests are not ignored, and accommodations are very comfortable. It is also possible to go for a day's outing to their Beauty Farm and pamper yourself with the full body treatment. The hotel's Rauhenstein restaurant is excellent (try the veal with a red-wine mushroom sauce, or for dessert, the famous house crepes). ✉ *Weilburgstr. 11–13, A–2500,* ☎ *02252/41251–0,* ⨳ *02252/48047. 88 rooms. Restaurant, bar, indoor pool, sauna, tennis court, exercise room. AE, DC, MC, V.*

$$$$ ╳📧 **Schloss Weikersdorf.** You're in a restored Renaissance castle but just minutes away from the center of Baden. The setting on the edge of a vast public park offers bonuses of a rose garden and boating on the lake. Rooms and baths are luxuriously outfitted. ✉ *Schlossgasse 9–1, A–2500,* ☎ *02252/48301,* ⨳ *02252/48301–150. 104 rooms. Restaurant, bar, indoor pool, sauna, tennis courts, bowling. AE, DC, MC, V.*

$$$–$$$$ ╳📧 **Krainerhütte.** This friendly house, in typical Alpine style, with balconies and lots of natural wood, has been family-run since 1876. The location on the outskirts of town is ideal for relaxing or exploring the surrounding woods. Facilities are up-to-date, and the restaurant offers a choice of cozy rooms or an outdoor terrace along with international and Austrian cuisine, with fish and game from the hotel's own reserves. ✉ *Helenental, A–2500,* ☎ *02252/44511–0,* ⨳ *02252/44514. 60 rooms. Restaurant, indoor pool, sauna, tennis court. AE, MC, V. Closed mid-Jan.–early Feb.*

Mayerling

❽   *11 km (7 mi) northwest of Baden, 29 km (18 mi) west of Vienna.*

Scenic Route 210 takes you through the quiet Helenental Valley west of Baden to Mayerling, scene of a tragedy that is still impetuously discussed and disputed by the Austrian public, press, and historians at the slightest provocation and still provides a torrid subject for moviemakers and novelists in many other parts of the world. On the snowy evening of January 28, 1889, the 30-year-old Habsburg heir, Crown Prince Rudolf, Emperor Franz Josef's only son, and his 17-year-old mistress, Baroness Marie Vetsera, met a violent and untimely end at the emperor's hunting lodge at Mayerling. Most historians believe it was a suicide pact between two desperate lovers (the Pope had refused an annulment to Rudolf's own unhappy marriage to Princess Stephanie of Belgium). There are those, however, who feel Rudolf's pro-Hungarian political leanings might be a key to the tragedy. Given information gleaned from private letters that have recently come to light, it is also possible Rudolf was hopelessly in love with a married woman and killed himself in despair, taking Marie Vetsera with him. In an attempt to suppress the scandal—the full details are not known to this day—the baroness's body, propped up between two uncles, was smuggled back into the city by carriage (she was buried hastily in nearby Heiligenkreuz). The bereaved emperor had the hunting lodge where the suicide took place torn down and replaced with a rather nondescript Carmelite convent. Mayerling remains beautiful, haunted—and remote: The village is infrequently signposted.

Heiligenkreuz

❾ *4 km (2½ mi) west of Mayerling, 14 km (8¾ mi) west of Mödling.*

Heiligenkreuz, in the heart of the southern section of the Vienna Woods, is a magnificent Cistercian abbey with a famous Romanesque and Gothic church, founded in 1135 by Leopold III. The church itself is lofty and serene, with beautifully carved choir stalls (the Cistercians are a singing order) surmounted by busts of Cistercian saints. The great treasure here is the relic of the cross that Leopold V is said to have brought back from his crusade in 1188. The cloisters are interesting for the Chapel of the Dead, where the brothers lie in state guarded by four gesticulating skeletons holding a candelabra. The chapter house contains the tombs of Babenberg rulers. On a corner of the abbey grounds, you can follow the Baroque stations of the cross along paths lined with chestnut and linden trees. ⊠ *Heiligenkreuz 1,* ☎ *02258/8703.* ⚑ *Abbey free, tour AS60.* ⊙ *Tours Mon.–Sat. 10, 11, 2, 3, and 4; Sun., 11, 2, 3, and 4 (additional tour at 5 daily in summer).*

From Vienna, reach Heiligenkreuz by taking Route A21 southwest or via bus from Südtirolerplatz.

Dining and Lodging

$$$ ✕▥ **Gasthof Zur Linde.** In the heart of the Vienna Woods, some 24 km (15 mi) northwest of Mayerling, lies the small town of Laaben bei Neulengbach—equally distant (about 22½ km/14 mi northwest of Mayerling) from Mayerling and Heiligenkreuz, in the shadow of the 2,900-ft Schöpfl Mountain. This charming, family-run country inn offers an excellent base from which to explore the countryside. Rooms are modest but complete and comfortable, with rustic decor. The popular restaurant, with its several wood-beamed rooms, sets the right atmosphere for international and regional cuisine, with seasonal specialties such as lamb, asparagus, and game featured. You might find roast pork marinated in apple cider or fresh local trout. ⊠ *Hauptpl. 28, A–3053 Laaben bei Neulengbach,* ☎ *02774/8378–0,* ⍐ *02774/8378–20. 10 rooms. Restaurant. No credit cards. Closed Tues., Wed., mid-Feb.– Mar., and 2 wks in Nov.*

THE WALDVIERTEL

The "Forest District" north of the Danube and to the northwest of Vienna was long dormant, out of the mainstream and cut off from neighboring Czechoslovakia by a sealed border until 1990. Today, with the reopening of many crossing points, the Waldviertel has reawakened. Here, gentle hills bearing stands of tall pine and oak are interspersed with small farms and friendly country villages. The region can be seen in a couple of days, longer when you pause to explore the museums, castles, and other attractions. Zwettl and Raabs an der Thaya, where facilities are more modest and much less expensive than those of the major tourism routes, make good bases for discovering this area.

The main rail line from Vienna to Prague passes through the Waldviertel, making the region accessible by train. In addition, post office buses cover the area fairly well and with reasonable frequency. Bus hubs are Horn, Waidhofen, and Zwettl. An express bus service runs between Vienna and Heidenreichstein via Waidhofen an der Thaya.

Kleinwetzdorf

⑩ *52 km (32½ mi) northwest of Vienna.*

The celebrated Austrian field marshal Joseph Wenzel Graf von Radetsky (1766–1858) is buried at **Heldenberg,** near the tiny village of Kleinwetzdorf, in elegant but lugubrious surroundings. The great field marshal was instrumental in defeating Napoléon in 1814, thus saving the Habsburg crown for the young Francis Joseph II. Radetzky's tomb, arranged for by a wealthy uniform supplier, is marked by an obelisk set in a park studded with dozens of larger-than-life busts of Austrian royalty and nobility. Follow the marked path to the west back of the park past the memorial to young emperor Franz Josef II to reach the lion-guarded memorial to Radetzky's military campaigns in Italy and Hungary. The whole complex is a slightly eerie phantasmagoria—but historically fascinating. ⊠ *Heldenberg 46,* ☎ *02956/2372.* 🎟 *Free.* ☾ *Daily dawn–dusk.*

The small, 17th-century **Schloss Wetzdorf** has a **Radetzky museum,** although of all the memorials to the field marshal, probably Johann Strauss father's "Radetzky March" is the best known. Half-hidden to the south of the castle is a freestanding arched gate surmounted with wonderful reclining lions. The castle's **Schlosstaverne** (only open on weekends and holidays) offers light snacks and basics such as Wiener schnitzel, coffee, and cooling drinks. The courtyard makes a delightful setting in good weather. ⊠ *Kleinwetzdorf 1,* ☎ *02956/2372.* 🎟 *Tour AS40, parking free.* ☾ *Tour May–Oct., weekends holidays 10–6.*

Dining and Lodging

$$–$$$ ✕🏨 **Restaurant Naderer.** A fine "food-with-a-view" spot, the Naderer is at the top of the hill above Maissau, 14 km (9 mi) northwest of Kleinwetzdorf on Route 4. The cuisine is of a standard that draws guests from as far away as Vienna. You can expect the standards such as roast pork and chicken, but you'll also find excellent goose, duck, lamb, and game in season. The cakes from the house kitchens are particularly good. Most of the excellent wines come from the surrounding vineyards. In summer, lunching on the terrace overlooking the valley can be a particularly pleasurable experience. Twelve hotel rooms are available for overnights. ⊠ *Am Berg 44, A–3712 Maissau,* ☎ *02958/82334. 12 rooms with bath. AE, DC, MC, V.*

Horn

32 km (20 mi) northwest of Kleinwetzdorf, 81 km (50½ mi) northwest of Vienna.

⑪ **Horn** lies at the eastern edge of the Waldviertel. Remnants of the impressive fortification walls, with its watchtowers built in 1532 to defend against invading Turks, are still obvious. Wander through the core of the old city, which dates from the 15th century. Note the painted Renaissance facade on the house (1583) at Kirchenplatz 3. **St. Stephen's parish church** on the edge of the cemetery out of the center boasts a Gothic choir and late-Gothic stone chancel. The Baroque **Piaristen church,** built in 1660, features a 1777 altar painting by the renowned regional artist Kremser Schmidt. The castle, started in the 1500s and completely rebuilt in the 18th century, sits at the edge of the large, attractive Schlosspark. Horn is host to an international chamber-music festival in summer.

⑫ About 5 km (3 mi) west of Horn, at Altenburg on Route 38, **Stift Altenburg** was built in 1144 and rebuilt in 1645–1740 after its destruction by the Swedes. The library and the frescoed translucent

The Waldviertel and the Weinviertel

SLOVAKIA

CZECH REPUBLIC

Morava

March

WEINVIERTEL

WALDVIERTEL

Vienna

Danube

Litschau
Kautzen
Brand
Heidenreichstein
Dobersberg
Thaya
Drosendorf
Znojmo
Raabs an der Thaya ㉑
Waidhofen an der Thaya ⑳
Gross Siegharts
Gross Siegharts
Sigmundsherberg
Geras ㉔
Schloss Riegersburg ㉓
㉒
Burg Hardegg ㉓
Retz ㉗
Haugsdorf
Guntersdorf
Hollabrunn
Eggenburg
Maissau
Rosenburg ㉕
Horn ⑪ ㉕
Stift Altenburg ⑫
Ottenstein ⑬
Rastenfeld
Neupölla
Kamp
Museum of Medicine and Meteorology ⑭
Truppenübungsplatz
Neu-Nagelberg ⑲
Schrems
Vitis
Waldegg
Kirchberg am Walde
Göpfritz
Schwarzenau
Großglobnitz
Gmünd ⑰
Weitra ⑯
Großschönau
Schweiggers
Rosenau ⑮
Zwettl ⑭
Großgerungs
Langschlag
Rappottenstein
Ottenschlag
Würnsdorf
Spitz
Krems
Oberrohrendorf
Grafenegg
Langenlois
Kirchberg am Wagram
Großweikersdorf
Kleinwetzdorf ⑩
Heldenberg
Maissau
Göllersdorf ㉖
Stockerau
Tulln
Traisen
Herzogenberg
St Pölten
Melk
Danube
A1
Laa an der Thaya ㉘
Staatz
Mistelbach
Wilfersdorf
Poysdorf ㉙
Bernhardsthal
Schrattenberg
Drasenhofen
Břeclav
Hohenau
Dürnkrut
Angern
Wolkersdorf
Gaweinstal
Ernstbrunn
Leobendorf
Korneuburg
Deutsch-Wagram
Strasshof ㉛ ㉚
Marchegg Safari Park ㉛
Gänserndorf ㉚
Schloss Niederweiden ㉜
Schlosshof ㉝ ㉞
Engelhartstetten
Carnuntum ㉟
Orth
Rohrau ㊱
Purkersdorf

N

0   20 miles
0   30 km

ceilings by the master artist Paul Troger are glorious. ✉ *Altenburg 1,* ☎ *02982/3451 or 02982/2725,* 𝟤𝟤𝟤 *02982/345113.* 🎫 *Free, tours AS50.* ☉ *Daily; tours Easter–Nov. 1, daily at 10, 11, and 4, and Nov. 2–Easter by appointment.*

⑬ Almost 35 km (21 mi) west of Altenburg, on Route 38 in Rastenfeld, the castle (✉ Ottenstein 1, ☎ 02826/254) at **Ottenstein,** now a hotel-restaurant, has a number of impressive reception rooms and parts dating to 1178. Ottenstein defied the invading Swedes in 1645 only to be devastated by the Russians in 1945. Sports enthusiasts will find boating and swimming in the reservoir and golf at Niedergrünbach. The ruined Lichtenfels castle nearby can be explored.

Zwettl

⑭ *49 km (31 mi) west of Horn, 125 km (78 mi) northwest of Vienna.*

Zwettl lies in the heartland of the Forest District. The town center, squeezed between a river bend, is attractive for its gabled houses and colorful pastel facades. The city wall, dating from the Middle Ages, still includes eight defensive towers. But Zwettl is best known for the vast **Stift Zwettl,** a Cistercian abbey, dating from 1138, about 2¼ km (1½ mi) west of the town. The Zwettl abbey, perched above the Kamp River, was established as an outpost of the abbey at Heiligenkreuz in the Vienna Woods (☞ Heiligenkreuz, *above*). The imposing south gate in the cloisters remains from the original edifice; the church, with its massive Gothic choir, was completed in 1348. Later renovations added the glorious Baroque touches, with the west wall crowned by a 292-ft tower. An international organ festival is held here annually from the end of June to the end of July. ☎ *02822/550–17 or 02822/550–57.* 🎫 *AS50.* ☉ *Tour Apr.–June and Oct., Mon.–Sat. at 10, 11, 2, and 3, Sun. at 11, 2, and 3; July–Sept., additional tour daily at 4. Closed Nov.–Easter.*

About 2 km (1 mi) north of Zwettl on Route 36, at Dürnhof, a fascinating **Museum of Medicine and Meteorology** is housed in a cloister chapel built in 1294. Exhibits follow the development of medicine from earliest times to the present, and the courtyard garden of medicinal herbs adds another dimension to the history. ☎ *02822/53180.* 🎫 *AS40.* ☉ *May–Oct., Tues.–Sun. 10–6.*

Dining and Lodging

$$ ✕ **Stiftstaverne-Restaurant.** Set within the Zwettl abbey, this spacious tavern complex serves good Austrian country fare such as grilled chicken and roast pork with bread dumplings and occasional regional specialties such as Waldviertel potato dumplings. The outstanding beer, fresh from the nearby brewery, alone is alone worth a stop, as are the wines, which come from the abbey's own cellars. ✉ *Stift Zwettl,* ☎ *02822/550–36. No credit cards. Closed 1st 2 wks of Feb. and Tues. Nov.–Easter.*

$$ 🏨 **Gasthof Hamerlingsaal.** The cream-color plain facade gives way to a relatively simple but modernized family-run hotel set somewhat to the east of the town center. Rooms are comfortable enough, and the buffet breakfast is ample. ✉ *Galgenbergstr. 3, A–3910,* ☎ *02822/52344–0,* 𝟤𝟤𝟤 *02822/52344–85. 24 rooms with bath. No credit cards.*

Rosenau

⑮ *8 km (5 mi) west of Zwettl.*

Schloss Rosenau, with its prominent central tower, is an impressive Renaissance structure built in 1590 with later Baroque additions. The castle was ravaged by the Soviets in 1945, then rebuilt as a hotel and museum complex housing the unique **Freimaurer-Museum** (Freemasonry Museum). A secret room once used for lodge ceremonies was discovered during the renovations and is now part of the museum. Displays show the ties of Haydn and Mozart to freemasonry, and many exhibits are in English, reflecting the origins of the brotherhood. ☎ 02822/58221. ☞ AS50, with tour AS70. ⊙ Mid-Apr.–Oct., daily 9–5; call for tour times.

Dining and Lodging

$$$–$$$$ ✕🏨 **Schloss Rosenau.** Set in an elegant castle, this small hotel offers
★ country quiet and modern rooms furnished in period style. The theme of the hotel is the rose, and roses are everywhere, even strewn throughout the rooms, making it a very romantic retreat. The wood-paneled restaurant is one of the best in the area, featuring garlic soup, bread soup, and lamb or game in season. In summer, food seems to taste even better on the sunny outdoor terrace, which overlooks great expanses of grain fields set about a jewel of a tiny castle. ⊠ ☎ 02822/58221, ℻ 02822/58222–8. 18 rooms. Restaurant, indoor pool, sauna, fishing. AE, DC, MC, V. Closed mid-Jan.–Feb.

Weitra

★ ⑯ 16 km (11 mi) northwest of Rosenau.

The small town of Weitra, set along the main road of LH71, is renowned for its stunning, ornate painted house facades (sgraffiti) dating from the 17th and 18th centuries. A charming small brewery has been in business here since 1321. And the tradition is well founded: In 1645, 33 Weitra citizens held the right to operate a brewery. The 15th-century fortress **Schloss Weitra,** with its Renaissance features, is privately owned, but following extensive renovations in 1993 parts are now open to the public; the rococo theater, ceremonial hall, the tower, and the extensive Schlosskeller (with an exhibition on beer brewing) are particularly worthwhile. This is the most westerly of the line of castles built to defend against possible invaders from the north. ☎ 02856/3311. ☞ AS60. ⊙ Mid-May–late Oct., Wed.–Sun. 10–5.

Dining and Lodging

$$ ✕🏨 **Gasthof Waschka.** This is a typical Austrian gasthaus with plain wooden banquets and a smoky haze in the air. But Hadmar Bräu is fresh on tap, named after Hadmar II, the founder of Weitra, and the specialty of the house is the tasty Waldviertler Knödelgröstl, a hefty portion of fried potato dumplings mixed with crispy onions and fried egg. There are rooms upstairs for overnighters. ⊠ Rathauspl. 8, A–3970, ☎ 02856/2296. 12 rooms. Restaurant, bar, sauna. No credit cards. Closed Wed.

Gmünd

16 km (10 mi) north of Weitra, 55 km (34½ mi) northwest of Horn.

⑰ The town of **Gmünd** was curiously divided in 1918 when the border with Czechoslovakia was established. The actual line passes through a few houses and backyards, but with the barbed-wire defenses removed, the border is now a harmless affair. The core of the old town remains in Austria and is worth viewing for the painted facades (sgraffiti) around the main square. Adjacent to the square is the once-moated (private) castle, which dates from the 16th century.

Railroad fans have a field day in Gmünd; the Czechs still use some steam locomotives for switching, and on the Austrian side Gmünd is one of
↺ the main points on the delightful narrow-gauge **Waldviertler Bahn** (☎

02852/52588), which runs occasional steam excursions plus some regular services. The excursion runs generally include a club car with refreshments.

Ⓒ The **Naturpark Blockheide Gmünd-Eibenstein** wildlife preserve to the northeast of the town center, open free to the public all year, includes a geological open-air museum and a stone marking the 15th meridian east of Greenwich. No one knows the source of the huge granite boulders that adorn the park. ✉ *Schremserstr. 6,* ☎ *02852/53817.*

Northwest of Schrems, a detour west from Route 30, on Route 303, leads to **Neu–Nagelberg,** pressed against the Czech border and a center of glass making since 1740. Among the operating glassworks that you can visit in order to see how glass is made and blown is **Glasstudio Zalto** (✉ Neu–Nagelberg 58, ☎ 02859/7237–0). Another, **Stölzle Kristall** (✉ Hauptstr. 45, Alt–Nagelberg, ☎ 02859/7531–0), has a showroom and factory outlet.

Heidenreichstein

⑲ *9 km (5½ mi) southwest of Gmünd, 51 km (32 mi) northwest of Horn.*

★ Ⓒ The scenic route north from Schrems parallels the narrow-gauge railway to Heidenreichstein, noted for the massive moated **Burg Heidenreichstein** with its corner towers, which has never been captured by enemy forces since it was built in the 15th century; some of the walls, 10 ft thick, went up in the 13th century. This is one of the most remarkable "water" castles in Austria. Water—or moated—castles were surrounded by a body of water (natural or artificial) for defense purposes, whereas the "hill" castles used steep, often rocky and inaccessible slopes for protection. The building is in remarkable condition, the best preserved of all moated castles in Austria, and some of the rooms are furnished with pieces dating from the 15th and 16th centuries. It is open for tours only. ✉ *Schremserstr. 1,* ☎ *02862/523725.* 🎟 *Tour AS60.* ☉ *Tours mid-Apr.–mid-Oct., Tues.–Sun. at 9, 10, 11, 2, 3, and 4.*

Waidhofen an der Thaya

⑳ *14 km (9 mi) east of Heidenreichstein, 32 km (20 mi) north of Zwettl, 37 km (23 mi) northwest of Horn.*

Route 5 between Heidenreichstein and Waidhofen an der Thaya is particularly scenic. Waidhofen itself is a three-sided, walled defense city typical of those of the 13th century. Fires destroyed much of the early character of the town, but the town square, rebuilt at the end of the 19th century, has a pleasing unity. The town is dominated by its Baroque **parish church,** locally known as the Cathedral of the Thaya Valley; the rococo chapel to Mary includes a Madonna of 1440 and distinguished portraits marking the stations of the cross. Outside the city walls, the **Bürgerspitalkapelle** has a side altar with a Gothic carved-wood relief of Madonna and child and 13 assistants, dating from about 1500.

Raabs an der Thaya

㉑ *21 km (13 mi) northeast of Waidhofen an der Thaya, 42 km (26 mi) northwest of Horn.*

The Thaya River wanders leisurely thorough Raabs an der Thaya, an unusually attractive village watched over by an 11th-century **Burg Raabs** perched dramatically on a rock outcropping and reflected in the river below. This was one of the chain of defensive castles through the Waldviertel region. The river is popular for fishing and swimming. ☎ *02846/8365.* 🎟 *AS50.* ☉ *June–Sept., weekends 10–5; call to confirm.*

Dining and Lodging

$$ ✕⌨ **Hotel Thaya.** A friendly, family-run hotel directly on the river, the
★ Thaya offers comfortable, modern, if slightly spartan rooms in the new
annex. Rooms directly overlooking the river are the favorites. The restaurant prepares such solid local specialties as roast pork and veal. ✉ *Hauptstr. 14, A–3820,* ☎ *02846/8202–0,* ℻ *02846/8202–20. 25 rooms. Restaurant, bar, beer garden, sauna, exercise room, dance club, parking. No credit cards.*

OFF THE
BEATEN PATH
DROSENDORF – Northeast of Raabs along Route 30 is the border town of Drosendorf, with a castle built in 1100 and a historic center typical of a small walled community. The encircling wall is virtually intact and complete with watchtowers.

En Route The intriguing ruins of the Kollmitz castle to the southeast of Raabs
on the way to Riegersburg can be explored, and a bit farther along are
the ruins of Eibenstein castle, another link in the 16th- and 17th-century defense chain along the border with Bohemia.

Riegersburg

28 km (17½ mi) east of Raabs an der Thaya, 33 km (20½ mi) north of Horn, 18½ km (11½ mi) northwest of Retz.

㉒ The impressive **Schloss Riegersburg** was originally moated before the
substantial edifice was given a Baroque makeover in 1731 and again
virtually rebuilt after the Russians inflicted heavy damage in 1945. Note
the window variations and the classic figures that ornament the roofline.
The whole castle was renovated in 1992–93, highlighting the elegance
of the public rooms and its period furnishings, now back in place. ☎
02916/332 or 02916/425. ⛩ *Tour AS85, combination ticket with the Hardegg castle AS130.* ☉ *Apr.–June and Sept.–mid-Nov., daily 9–5; July–Aug., daily 9–7.*

 ㉓ Hardegg, about 6 km (4 mi) east of Riegersburg on an unnumbered road,
is the smallest village in Austria. It features a wonderfully eclectic **Burg
Hardegg,** which stands mightily on a rock promontory high above the
Thaya River, watching over the Czech Republic. (The river midstream
marks the boundary; as recently as 1990, the pedestrian bridge was impassable, the border sealed, and Czech border defenses concealed in the
woods opposite.) The earliest parts of the castle date from 1140. The
armory and armament collection, chapel, and the museum's exhibits on
the emperor Maximilian in Mexico alone are worth a visit. In addition,
the kitchen and other working rooms of the castle give a real feeling of
the daily life of an earlier era. An English-speaking guide is available for
small-group tours. ✉ *Hardegg,* ☎ *02949/8225.* ⛩ *Castle AS65, tour
AS25, combination ticket with the Riegersburg castle AS130.* ☉ *Apr.–
June and Sept.–mid-Nov., daily 9–5; July–Aug., daily 9–6.*

Geras

㉔ *14 km (8½ mi) southwest of Riegersburg, 22 km (14 mi) north of Horn,
23 km (14½ mi) southeast of Raabs an der Thaya.*

Another of the Waldviertel's great abbeys, the **Stift Geras,** is situated
at Geras. Established in 1120, the impressive complex has had from
its beginnings close ties to its agricultural surroundings. The abbey was
given a glorious full-blown Baroque treatment in the course of rebuilding
following a fire in 1730, including a translucent fresco by the noted
Paul Troger in the 18th-century Marble Hall, now often used for concerts. While the abbey still functions as a religious center, the complex

is also a noted school for arts and crafts. ✉ *Hauptstr. 1,* ☎ *02912/ 7345–289.* ☞ *AS50.* ⊙ *Tour May–Oct., Tues.–Sat. at 10, 11, 2, 3, and 4, Sun. at 11, 2, 3, and 4.*

Dining and Lodging

$$$ ✕⌂ **Stiftsrestaurant und Hotel "Alter Schüttkasten."** A former granary outbuilding of the abbey has been turned into a modern hotel with all the amenities. Rooms are comfortable; those on the front look out over the fields toward the abbey. The restaurant offers seasonal specialties such as fish and game in addition to pork, beef, and other regional standards. ✉ *Vorstadt 11, A–2093,* ☎ *02912/7332,* ☒ *02912/7332–33. 26 rooms. Restaurant, bar, sauna, parking. DC.*

Kamptal

Rosenburg is 23 km (14½ mi) south of Geras, 80 km (50 mi) northwest of Vienna.

㉕ The gloriously scenic Kamp River valley (Kamptal), running from **Rosenburg** in the north some 30 km (19 mi) south roughly to Hadersdorf am Kamp, technically belongs to the Waldviertel, though for the amount of wine produced here, it might as well be a part of the Weinviertel, the Wine District to the east. The river, road, and railroad share the frequently narrow and twisting route that meanders some 25 km (15½ mi) through the valley from Rosenburg south to Langenlois. The villages along the route—Gars am Kamp, Schönberg am Kamp, Zöbing, Strass, and Langenlois—are all known for excellent wines, mainly varietal whites. Strass in particular has become an active center of viticulture, and many vintners offer wine tastings. Castle ruins dot the hilltops above the woods and vineyards; the area has been populated since well before 900 BC. Scattered through the valley are some noted eateries and hotels; the best are reviewed below. Route 34 takes you through more vineyards to Kollersdorf, where Route 3 east will return you to Vienna.

♻ The massive fortress **Burg Ferwaltung Hoys** dates from 1200 and dominates the north entrance to the Kamptal Valley. Its features include the original jousting field as a forecourt and impressive reception rooms inside, where armor and other relics of the period are on display. Curious Renaissance balconies and small courtyards are incorporated into the design, although the variety in the 13 towers added in the 15th century is the touch that immediately catches the eye. The first Sunday of the month falconry demonstrations are performed in medieval costumes. ✉ *Rosenburg am Kamp,* ☎ *02982/2911.* ☞ *AS65 (includes tour); demonstration AS65; combination ticket AS100.* ⊙ *Apr.– mid-Nov., daily 9–5; falconry demonstration Apr.–Nov., daily at 11 and 3; tour begins 1 hr before demonstration.*

Dining and Lodging

$$$$ ✕ **Gut Oberstockstall.** A former cloister in Oberstockstall, just north
★ of Kirchberg am Wagram, houses this country inn, where the rustic setting indoors is charming and the courtyard garden idyllic in summer. Nearly all ingredients come from the farm itself, guaranteeing top freshness; preparation is individual and imaginative. The specialties of the house include beef, lamb, duck, game in season, and delicious desserts—all to the accompaniment of the house's own outstanding wines. ✉ *Kirchberg am Wagram,* ☎ *02279/2335. No credit cards. Closed Sun.–Tues., mid-Dec.–Feb., and last 2 wks of Aug.*

$$–$$$ ✕ **Pfiffig.** The ruins of the ancient castle above Gars am Kamp provide the dramatic setting for this excellent family-run restaurant serving regional specialties and other choices such as tender *Tafelspitz* (boiled beef). The rooms are elegant and offer a showcase for local artists.

The excellent wines understandably come from the neighborhood. ⊠ *Gars am Kamp,* ☎ *02985/30500. No credit cards. Closed Mon.– Tues. and Jan.*

$–$$ ✕ **Brundlmayer.** This country Heuriger in the center of Langenlois offers outstanding wines from one of Austria's top vintners, as well as a tasty hot-and-cold buffet, all in an indoor rustic setting or outdoors in the Renaissance courtyard. The simple but delicious fare might include variations on Schinkenfleckerl, the popular dish of baked ham and noodles, goat cheese, or dried, lightly-smoked ham. ⊠ *Walterstr. 14, Langenlois,* ☎ *02734/2883. No credit cards. Closed Mon.–Wed. and mid-Dec.–early Mar.*

$$–$$$ ✕▥ **Schlosstaverne Mörwald.** Beyond the golden facade of this elegant
★ tavern across from Schloss Grafeneg you'll find a friendly and welcoming atmosphere. Rooms are comfortably furnished in beiges and reds. The restaurant offers game in season and local cuisine with international touches. The strawberries in early summer taste even better outdoors on the sunny dining terrace. ⊠ *A–3485 Haitzendorf,* ☎ *02735/2616,* ℻ *02735/2298–6. 6 rooms. Restaurant. MC, V. Closed Jan.–Feb.*

THE WEINVIERTEL

The Wine District takes its name from rustic and delightful rolling countryside north of Vienna. The Weinviertel is bounded by the Danube on the south, the Thaya River and the reopened Czech border on the north, the March River and Slovakia to the east. No well-defined line separates the Weinviertel from the Waldviertel to the west; the Kamp River valley, officially part of the Waldviertel, is an important wine region. Whether wine, crops, or dairies, this is farming country, its broad expanses of vineyards and farmlands broken by patches of forest and neat villages. A tour by car, just for the scenery, can be made in a day; you may want two or three days to savor the region and its wines— these are generally on the medium-dry side. Don't expect to find here the elegant facilities found elsewhere in Austria; prices are low by any standard, and village restaurants and accommodations are mainly Gasthäuser that meet local needs. This means that you'll rub shoulders over a glass of wine or a beer with country folk.

Göllersdorf

㉖ *10 km (6 mi) north of Stockerau West interchange on Rte. 303/E59.*

The rolling hills and agricultural lands of the southwest Weinviertel around Hollabrunn offer little excitement other than panoramas and scenic pleasures, but one exception is the **Schloss Schönborn,** about 2 km (1 mi) south of Göllersdorf on Route 303. The castle was laid out in 1712 by that master of Baroque architecture, Johann Lukas von Hildebrandt. Today the castle is in private hands, but the harmony of design can be appreciated from the outside. The parish church in Göllersdorf is also a Baroque Hildebrandt design of 1740 overlaid on a Gothic structure dating to the mid-1400s.

Retz

★ ㉗ *43 km (27 mi) north of Göllersdorf, 70 km (44 mi) north of Vienna.*

Retz, at the northwest corner of the Weinviertel, is a charming town with an impressive rectangular central square formed by buildings dating mainly to the 15th century. Take time to explore Retz's tiny streets leading from the town square; the oldest buildings and the wall and gate-tower defenses survived destruction by the Swedish armies in 1645 during the Thirty Years' War. The Dominican church (1295) at the southwest corner of the square also survived, and it is interesting for its long, narrow design. The pastel Biedermeier facades along with the sgraffiti add appeal to the square, which is further marked by the impressive city hall with its massive Gothic tower in the center. The landmark of the town is the pretty **Windmühle,** a Dutch windmill set incongruously in the middle of the vineyards on the edge of town. Follow the markers leading up to the summit, where you can sit and rest on benches offering a stunning view of the surrounding countryside.

Retz is best known for its red wines. Here you can tour **Austria's largest wine cellar,** tunneled 65 ft under the town, and at the same time taste wines of the area. Some of the tunnels go back to the 13th century, and at the end of the 15th century each citizen was permitted to deal in wines and was entitled to storage space in the town cellars. Efforts to use the cellars for armaments production during World War II failed because of the 88% humidity. The temperature remains constant at 8°C–10°C (47°F–50°F). Entrance to the cellars is at the Rathauskeller, in the center of town. ⊠ *Hauptpl.,* ☎ *02942/2700.* ⊡ *Tour AS80.* ⊙ *Tour Mon.–Sat. at 10:30 and 2, Sun. at 10:30, 2, and 4; call to confirm tour times.*

Dining and Lodging

$$$$ ✕⊡ **Althof Retz/Hotel Burghof.** A new hotel has been tucked into an ancient estate building just off the town square. Take your choice of the upscale Hotel Burghof or the slightly less expensive Althof, which also serves as a training hotel. Both are done in whites and light wood. Rooms are modern, comfortable, and with all facilities. The restaurant has been less successful, but the standards and regional specialties are fine. The excellent wines naturally come mainly from the area. ⊠ *Althofgasse 14, A–2070,* ☎ *02942/3711–0,* ℻ *02942/3711–55. 65 rooms. Restaurant, parking. No credit cards.*

Laa an der Thaya

㉘ *39 km (24 mi) east of Retz, 65 km (41 mi) north of Vienna.*

From 1948 until about 1990, Laa an der Thaya was a town isolated by the Cold War, directly bordering what was then Czechoslovakia. Laa is considerably livelier now that the border is open. (As long as you have your passport with you, you can cross into the Czech Republic and return without complication.) The town's huge central square is adorned with a massive neo-Gothic city hall, in stark contrast to the low, colorful buildings that form the square. A good time to visit is mid-September during the Onion Festival, when all varieties of onions are prepared in every imaginable way in food stalls set up throughout the village. If you're traveling from Retz to Laa an der Thaya, retrace your way south on Route 30 to Route 45.

Laa boasts a **Bier Museum,** located in the town fortress, that traces the history of beer (the nearby Hubertus brewery has been in business since 1454) and maintains an imposing collection of beer bottles. ☎ *02522/ 2501.* ⊡ *AS20.* ⊙ *May–Sept., weekends 2–4.*

Dining

$$ ✕ **Restaurant Weiler.** Light woods and country accessories set the tone
★   in this family-run restaurant; in summer dinner is served in the outdoor garden. Try the delicate cream of garlic soup or the house specialty, game in season. For dessert, the delicious cakes of the house are temptingly displayed in a showcase. ⊠ *Staatsbahnstr. 60,* ☎ *02522/2379. No credit cards. Closed Mon., 2 wks in Feb., and July. No dinner Sun.*

Poysdorf

㉙ *22 km (13 mi) southeast of Laa an der Thaya, 61 km (38 mi) north of Vienna.*

Poysdorf is considered by many the capital of the Weinviertel. Wine making here goes back to the 14th century. Poysdorf vintages, mainly whites, rank with the best Austria has to offer. Narrow paths known as *Kellergassen* (cellar streets) on the northern outskirts are lined with wine cellars set into and under the hills. A festival in early September marks the annual harvest. At the **wine market** (⊠ Singerstr. 2) in the center of town, you can taste as well as buy; the market is open Monday–Thursday 8–5, Friday 8–6, and weekends 10–noon and 2–6.

The town **museum** includes a section on viticulture and wine making. ⊠ *Brunner Str. 9,* ☎ *02552/3209.* ⊡ *AS40.* ☉ *Easter–Oct., Mon.– Wed. 9–noon and 1–5; call to confirm.*

Dining

$$-$$$ ✕ **Zur Linde.** This friendly family-run restaurant with rustic decor 16
★ km (10 mi south of Poysdorf is setting higher standards for such traditional fare as roast pork, stuffed breast of veal, flank steak, and fresh game in season. Desserts are excellent; try the extraordinary *Apfelstrudel* (apple strudel). A major attraction here is the remarkable range of wines from the neighborhood at altogether reasonable prices. ⊠ *Bahnhofstr. 49, Mistelbach,* ☎ *02572/2409. AE, DC, MC, V. Closed Mon., late Jan.–mid-Feb., and late July–mid-Aug. No dinner Sun.*

$$ ✕ **Gasthaus Schreiber.** Choose the shaded garden under huge trees or the country-rustic decor indoors. The typical Austrian fare—roast pork, stuffed breast of veal, boiled beef, filet steak with garlic—is commendable, as is the house-made ice cream. The wine card lists more than 60 area labels. ⊠ *Bahnstr. 2,* ☎ *02552/2348. No credit cards. Closed Tues. and late Jan.–mid-Feb. No dinner Mon.*

Gänserndorf

㉚ *41 km (26 mi) south of Poysdorf, 30 km (19 mi) northeast of Vienna.*

☉ Three kilometers (2 miles) south of Gänserndorf, the **Safari-Park und Abenteuerpark** (Safari Park and Adventure Park) allows visitors to drive through re-created natural habitats of live wild animals, many of which (lions and tigers) are hardly indigenous to Austria. The adventure takes five to six hours, allowing time for the petting zoo and the extra animal shows, which start every half hour. For those without a car, a safari bus leaves for the circuit every hour. ⊠ *Siebenbrunner Str.,* ☎ *02282/70261–0,* ⱻ *02282/70261–27.* ⊡ *AS185.* ☉ *Palm Sunday– Oct., weekdays 9:30–4, weekends 9–4:30.*

Strasshof

㉛ *3 km (2 mi) southwest of Gänserndorf.*

The area to the north of Gänserndorf includes one of Austria's few gas and oil fields, where operating pumps patiently pull up crude to be piped to the refinery about 20 km (12½ mi) south. Underground, exhausted gas wells serve as natural storage tanks for gas coming to Western Europe from Russia.

☉ The **Heizhaus,** north of Strasshof, is a fascinating private collection of dozens of steam locomotives and railroad cars stored in a vast engine house. Enthusiasts have painstakingly rebuilt and restored many of the engines; steam locomotives are up and running on the first Sunday of each month. The complex includes transfer table, water towers, and coaling station, and visitors can climb around among many of the locomotives awaiting restoration. The collection includes—at least for the time being—many of the operative locomotives from the Technical Museum in Vienna, now closed for extensive renovations. ⊠ *Sillerstr. 123,* ☏ *02287/3027.* ⊠ *AS60, steam days AS70, including parking and tour.* ☉ *Mid-Apr.–Oct., Sun. 10–4.*

Dining

$$$$ ✕ **Marchfelderhof.** In nearby Deutsch Wagram, this sprawling complex, with its eclectic series of rooms bounteously decorated with everything from antiques to hunting trophies, has a reputation for excess in the food department as well. The menu's standards—Wiener schnitzel, roast pork, lamb—are more successful than the more expensive efforts at innovation. Deutsch Wagram is 9 km (5½ mi) southwest of Strasshof on Route 8, 17 km (11 mi) northeast of Vienna on Route 8. ⊠ *Bockfliesser Str. 31, Deutsch Wagram,* ☏ *02247/2243–0,* ℻ *02247/ 2236–13. AE, DC, MC, V. Closed Mon. and late Dec.–early Feb.*

Marchegg

16 km (10 mi) southeast of Gänserndorf, 43 km (27 mi) east of Vienna.

The tiny corner of the lower Weinviertel to the southeast of Gänserndorf is known as the Marchfeld, for the fields stretching east to the March River, forming the border with Slovakia. In this region—known as the granary of Austria—three elegant Baroque castles in the area are worth a visit; all have been totally renovated in recent years and given over to changing annual exhibits, concerts, and other public activities. These country estates have lost none of their gracious charm over the centuries.

32 The northernmost of the group is the castle at **Marchegg,** the oldest parts dating to 1268. What you see today is the Baroque overlay added in 1733 to the basic building of the Middle Ages. The castle now houses a hunting museum. To reach Marchegg from Gänserndorf, take Route 8a 6 km (4 mi) east to Route 49, then Route 49 10 km (6 mi) south. ☏ *02285/224.* ⊠ *AS40.* ☉ *Mid-Mar.–Nov., Tues.–Sun. 9– noon and 1–5.*

33 The castle at **Schlosshof** is a true Baroque gem, a product of that master designer and architect Johann Lukas von Hildebrandt, who in 1732 reconstructed the four-sided castle into an elegant U-shape building, opening up the eastern side to a marvelous Baroque formal garden that gives way toward the river. The famed Italian painter Canaletto captured the view before the reconstruction. The castle—once owned by Empress Maria Theresa—is now used for changing annual exhibits, but you can walk the grounds without paying admission. The castle is about 8 km (5 mi) south of Marchegg. ⊠ *Schlosshof,* ☏ *02285/6580.* ⊠ *AS70, combination ticket with Schloss Niederweiden AS100.* ☉ *Apr.– Oct., daily 10–5.*

34 **Schloss Niederweiden,** about 4 km (2½ mi) southwest of Schlosshof and north of Engelhartstetten, was designed as a hunting lodge and built in 1694 by that other master of the Baroque, Fischer von Erlach. This jewel was subsequently owned by Prince Eugene and Empress Maria Theresa, who added a second floor and the mansard roofs. Annual exhibits now take place here in summer, and in a Vinothek (wine shop) you can sample the wines of the surrounding area. ☏ *02214/2803.* ⊠ *AS70, combination ticket with Schlosshof AS100.* ☉ *Apr.–Oct., daily 10–5; Vinotek weekends 10–6.*

Carnuntum

32 km (20 mi) east of Vienna.

㉟ The remains of the important legionary Roman fortress **Carnuntum,** which once numbered 55,000 inhabitants, is in the tiny village of Petronell, reachable by the S7, a local train that departs from Wien Mitte/Landstrasse or Wien-Nord. Though by no means as impressive as Roman ruins in Italy and Spain, Carnuntum still merits a visit, with three amphitheaters (the first one seating 8,000) and the foundations of former residences, baths, and trading centers, some with mosaic floors. The ruins are quite spread out, with the impressive remains of a Roman arch, the **Heidentor** (Pagan's Gate), a good 15 minutes' walk from the main excavations. A pleasant path along the north end of the ruins leads past a dilapidated 17th-century palace once belonging to the Counts of Traun, to the remains of a Roman bath. In summer Greek plays are sometimes performed in English at the main amphitheater (☎ 02163/ 3400). ⊠ *Petronell,* ☎ *02163/33770.* 🎟 *AS45.* ⊘ *Apr.–Oct., weekdays 9–5, weekends 9–6.*

Many of the findings from the excavations at Carnuntum are located 4 km (2½ mi) northeast of Petronell in the village of Bad Deutsch-Altenburg, in the **Museum Carnuntum.** The pride of the collection is a carving of Mithras killing a bull. ⊠ *Badgasse 40–46, Petronell,* ☎ *02163/33770.* 🎟 *AS60, combination ticket with Carnuntum AS85.* ⊘ *Tues.–Sun. 10–5; closed Dec. 15–Jan. 15.*

㊱ Just 5 km (3 mi) south of Petronell, in the tiny village of **Rohrau,** is the **birthplace of Joseph Haydn.** The quaint reed-thatched cottage where in 1732 Haydn, son of the local blacksmith, was born is now a small museum, with a pianoforte he is supposed to have played, as well as letters and other memorabilia. After Haydn had gained worldwide renown, he is said to have returned to his native Rohrau and knelt to kiss the steps of his humble home. ⊠ *Hauptstr. 60, Rohrau,* ☎ *02164/ 2268.* 🎟 *AS20.* ⊘ *Tues.–Sun. 10–5.*

Also in Rohrau is the cream-and-beige palace, **Schloss Harrach,** where Haydn's mother worked as a cook. The palace has one of the best private art collections in Austria, with emphasis on 17th- and 18th-century Spanish and Italian paintings. ⊠ ☎ *02164/2252.* 🎟 *AS70.* ⊘ *Open Apr.–Oct., Tues.–Sun. 10–5.*

OFF THE
BEATEN PATH

ARTNER WEINBAU – Some of the best wines and freshly made *Ziegenkäse* (goat cheese) in the region can be found in the tiny village of Höflein, 12 km (7½ mi) southwest of Petronell. Artner has been a family business since 1650, and owner Hannes Artner is proud to offer tastings of his wines, including Chardonnay Barrique, cabernet sauvignon, and Blauer Zweigelt Kirchtal. Check for the opening times of the new outdoor *Heurigen* during selected weeks from May to August, when the new wine is available for tasting. ⊠ *Höflein Hauptstr. 58, Höflein,* ☎ *02162/63142.*

BRATISLAVA

60 km (37½ mi) east of Vienna.

Despite its close proximity to Vienna (just over the Slovakian border and one hour by train), Bratislava is unfortunately ignored by most travelers. Bratislava (or Pressburg, as the Austrians call it) was once a flourishing city of the Austro-Hungarian empire. It fell into decline under communism, but in the last few years a lot of work has gone into restoring the Staré Mesto (Old Town), and at long last its former glory is well on the way to being recaptured. There is a palpable air of vitality and industriousness to the city, and new restaurants and businesses are springing up all the time. Winding cobblestone streets are lined with freshly painted Baroque town houses and little shops, the squares are shaded and full of cafés with outdoor tables in summer, and a charming medieval archway leads to a pretty bridge decorated with wrought-iron and statues, now a haven for street artists and vendors. Watching over the whole city is the hulkingly impressive Hrad (castle), which had to be totally rebuilt in 1811 after being destroyed by fire.

Though you can spend an entire afternoon just enjoying lunch and shopping for inexpensive, exquisite Slovakian crystal, you shouldn't miss a visit to the **Primaciálny palác** (Primate's Palace), a classically elegant, pale pink former bishop's residence. The strikingly beautiful Hall of Mirrors was the scene for the signing of the Bratislava Peace Treaty of 1805 by Napoléon and Habsburg emperor Franz I, following Napoléon's victory at the Battle of Austerlitz. ⊠ *Namestie 1,* ☎ *no phone.* 🔳 *20 crowns.* ⊘ *Tues.–Sun. 10–5.*

Also worth a visit is the art museum, located in the **Mirbachov palác** (Mirbach Palace), where a commendable collection of 18th- and 19th-century European art is displayed. Concerts are sometimes performed here on Sunday mornings. ⊠ *Frantiskánske namestie, 11,* ☎ *07/5331– 556.* 🔳 *20 crowns.* ⊘ *Tues.–Sun. 10–5.*

As hotels are overpriced, with no apparent mid-range level, it's best to make Bratislava a day outing. Driving is not recommended, since the street layout is confusing and parking is difficult. Trains leave twice a day from the Sudbahnhof. Don't be deterred by the decaying communist city that engulfs you upon arrival as you emerge from the train station; just head straight for the Old Town, though be aware that Bratislava taxi drivers tend to overcharge foreigners (you can't always trust the meters), so it's best to agree on a price beforehand. For more information on Bratislava contact the **Slovakian Travel Office** in Vienna (☞ Contacts and Resources *in* Side Trip from Vienna A to Z, *below*).

Dining

$ ✕ **Cervený rak.** In the historic center near the 14th-century Michael's Gate, this restaurant at the sign of the red lobster offers typical Slovakian meals, such as breaded pork and dumplings or goulash. In summer there are tables set outside in the courtyard with a medieval wall as a backdrop. ⊠ *Michalská ul. 26,* ☎ *07/331375. No credit cards.*

$ ✕ **Modrá Hviezoa.** This popular restaurant is tucked right against the lower walls of the castle, and the climb up the narrow, winding street lets you work up an appetite for the hearty Slovakian meat and chicken dishes (most with dumplings) served here. Try to get a table in the dramatic, cavelike dining room, with its low ceilings and candlelight. ⊠ *Beblavého 14,* ☎ *07/332747. No credit cards.*

SIDE TRIPS FROM VIENNA A TO Z

Arriving and Departing

By Car

The autobahn A1 traverses the Vienna Woods in the west; the A2 autobahn runs through the edge of the Vienna Woods to the south. The A4 autobahn is a quick way to reach the Carnuntum region. The Waldviertel and Weinviertel are accessed by major highways but not autobahns.

By Train

The main east–west train line cuts through the Vienna Woods; the main north–south line out of Vienna traverses the eastern edge of the Vienna Woods. The main line to Prague and onward runs through the Waldviertel. Train service in the Weinviertel is regular to Mistelbach, irregular after that. The rail line east out of Vienna to the border town of Wolfstal cuts through the Carnuntum region. The line to the north of the Danube to Bratislava runs through the middle of the Marchfeld.

Getting Around

By Bus

Buses are a good possibility for getting around, although if you're not driving, a combination of bus and train is probably a better answer in many cases. Frequent scheduled bus service runs between Vienna and Baden, departing from across from the Opera House in Vienna to the center of Baden. Connections are available to other towns in the area. Bus service runs between Vienna and Carnuntum–Petronell, and on to Hainburg. Service to the Waldviertel is less frequent but is available between Vienna and Horn, Zwettl, Waidhofen, and Raabs an der Thaya. From these points, you can get buses to other parts of the Waldviertel. An express bus service runs between Vienna and Heidenreichstein via Waidhofen an der Thaya. In the Weinviertel, bus service is fairly good between Vienna and Laa an der Thaya and Poysdorf.

By Car

Driving through these regions is by far the best way to see them, since you can wander the byways and stop whenever and wherever you like.

By Train

Take the interurban train between Vienna and Baden for a delightful variation on the car or bus routine. Local trains on the Westbahn (main east–west line) will drop you off at stations in the Vienna Woods, but connections can be tricky unless you plan on an "out-and-back" excursion.

The main rail line from Vienna to Prague passes through the **Waldviertel,** making the region accessible by train, but you'll need a bus connection to reach the smaller towns.

Train service into the **Weinviertel** is fairly good but selective in the destinations you can reach on a direct trip. The suburban express line (*Schnellbahn*) runs between Vienna and Mistelbach, and to Gänserndorf and beyond to Bernhardsthal on the Czech border.

The suburban trains running from Wien-Mitte (Landstrasser Hauptstrasse) stop at Petronell, with service about once an hour. **Carnuntum** is about a 10-minute walk from the Petronell station. Trains go on to Hainburg, stopping at Bad Deutsch-Altenburg.

Contacts and Resources

Car Rentals

Cars can be rented from all leading companies at the Vienna airport (☞ Vienna A to Z *in* Chapter 2) or, in Baden, from **Autoverleih Buchbinder** (☏ 02252/48693) or **Autoverleih Schmidt** (☏ 0663/803289 mobil phone).

Emergencies

Police: ☏ 133, **fire:** ☏ 122. For **ambulance** or medical emergency, ☏ 144.

Guided Tours

The Vienna Woods is one of the standard routes offered by the sight-seeing-bus tour operators in Vienna, and it usually includes a boat ride through the "underground sea" grotto near Mödling. These short tours give only a quick taste of the region; if you have more time, you'll want to investigate further. For details, check with your hotel or with **Cityrama** (☎ 01/534–13–12), **CityTouring Vienna** (☎ 01/894–1417–0), or **Vienna Sightseeing Tours** (☎ 01/712–4683–0).

Visitor Information

Get information in Vienna before you start out, at the **tourist office of Lower Austria** (✉ Walfischg. 6, A–1010 Vienna, ☎ 01/513–8022, FAX 01/513–8022–30). There are several helpful regional tourist offices: **March–Donauland** (✉ Hauptpl. 296, A–2405 Bad Deutsch–Altenburg, ☎ 02163/3555, FAX 02163/3556), **Waldviertel** (✉ Hamerlingstr. 2, A–3910 Zwettl, ☎ 02822/54109–0, FAX 02822/54109–36), **Weinviertel** (✉ Liechtensteinstr. 1, A–2170 Poysdorf, ☎ 02552/3515, FAX 02552/3715), **Wienerwald** (✉ Hauptpl. 11, A–3002 Purkersdorf, ☎ 02231/62176, FAX 02231/65510).

Local tourist offices are generally open weekdays. The offices for the Vienna Woods region are as follows: **Baden** (✉ Brusattipl. 3, ☎ 02252/44531–57, FAX 02252/80733), **Gumpoldskirchen** (✉ Schrannenpl. 1, ☎ 02252/62421), **Mödling** (✉ Elisabethstr. 2, ☎ 02236/26727, FAX 02236/41632), **Perchtoldsdorf** (✉ Hauptpl., ☎ 01/86683–34).

The Waldviertel district has numerous tourist offices: **Gars am Kamp** (✉ Hauptpl. 82, ☎ 02985/2680), **Gmünd** (✉ Stadtpl. 19, ☎ 02852/50526–38, FAX 02852/54514), **Horn** (✉ Wiener Str. 4, ☎ 02985/2371), **Raabs an der Thaya** (✉ Hauptstr. 25, ☎ 02846/8365–0, FAX 02846/8365–21), **Waidhofen an der Thaya** (✉ Hauptpl. 1, ☎ 02842/51500), **Zwettl** (✉ Dreifaltigkeitspl. 1, ☎ 02822/52233).

The Weinviertel region has several tourist centers: **Gänserndorf** (✉ Rathauspl. 1, ☎ 022822651–0), **Laa an der Thaya** (✉ Rathaus, ☎ 02522/2501–29), **Poysdorf** (✉ Singerg. 2, ☎ 02552/2200), **Retz** (✉ Hauptpl. 30, ☎ 02942/2700).

For information on Bratislava, contact the **Slovakian Travel Office** (✉ Parkring 12, A–1010 Vienna, ☎ 01/512–0199, FAX 01/512–5916–85).

4 Eastern Austria

*Burgenland, Graz,
and the Styrian Wine Country*

*Despite its proximity to vibrant
Vienna, Eastern Austria offers rustic
pleasures and simple treasures: the
sight of a stork alighting on the
chimney atop a Mother Goose house;
an evening filled with the haunting
sounds of Gypsy music; vistas of lush
vineyards; and the city of Graz, whose
preserved Old City is a time-warped
marvel. In Burgenland, discover vast
Lake Neusiedl, so shallow you can
wade across it, and Eisenstadt, alive
with the sound of Joseph Haydn's
celebrated music.*

By Earl
Steinbicker

Updated by
Bonnie Dodson

NO PART OF THE NATION offers a greater range of scenery than the area loosely defined as Eastern Austria, yet, despite its proximity to Vienna, it is largely overlooked by foreign tourists. Not that the region lacks for visitors—long a favorite of Austrians, it is now becoming increasingly popular with Hungarians and other Eastern Europeans. Accordingly, most of the visitors are cost-conscious and demand strict value for their money, ensuring that prices will remain lower here than in other parts of the country for some time.

There are no singularly great sights in the region—no Schönbrunn Palace, no Salzburg, no not-to-be-missed five-star attractions; still, the aggregate of worthwhile sights is most impressive. You'll find a largely unspoiled land of lakes, farms, castles, villages, and vineyards. It's also a sports lover's paradise and is rich in history, with a distinguished musical past and—yes—one genuine city, Graz, whose sophistication and beauty may surprise you. In short, this is an ideal destination for experienced travelers who have already explored Vienna, Salzburg, the Tirol, and other better-known parts of Austria.

Eastern Austria, as it is defined here, consists of Burgenland, most of Styria (Steiermark), and a small section of Lower Austria (Niederösterreich)—three distinct provinces with little in common. The geography varies from haunting steppes and the mysterious Lake Neusiedl (Neusiedler See) in the east to the low, forested mountains of the south; the industrial valleys of the center and west; and the more rugged mountains of the north, where Austrian skiing began. Culturally, Eastern Austria is strongly influenced by neighboring Hungary and Slovenia, especially in its earthy and flavorful cuisines. Along with hearty food, the region is noted for its wines, many of which never travel beyond the borders.

We begin with Burgenland, intriguing both for its flatness and for the shallow Lake Neusiedl, with its reed-lined shore forming a natural nature preserve. Storks come in the thousands to feed in the lake, and stork families, in turn, obligingly nest atop nearby chimneys—allegedly bringing luck to the household below (and assuring travelers of some great photos). Off to the east, the lake gives way to the vast Hungarian plain, interrupted by occasional thatched-roof farmhouses and picturesque pole-and-pail wells. Music lovers will want to make the pilgrimage to Eisenstadt, where the great composer Joseph Haydn (1732–1809) was in the employ of Prince Esterházy. The impressive Esterházy castle stands as it did in Haydn's time, with its spacious theater-auditorium in which Haydn conducted his own operas and orchestral works almost nightly for the prince's entertainment.

The route from Burgenland southwest to Graz achieves an end-around run, circling the eastern tail of the Alps through a territory marked by monumental defensive castles built to ward off invaders from the east. Graz, Austria's second-largest city, boasts one of Europe's best-preserved Renaissance town centers, dating to an era when Graz, not Vienna, was the capital. The compact pedestrian zone that forms the city core sets imaginations on fire, with eye-catching discoveries around every corner. History notwithstanding, the city today is a pulsating metropolis, a surprise even to many Austrians. Styria offers the chance to visit one of Europe's oldest and still-revered religious pilgrimage sites at Mariazell. The dramatic onward route northward can be accomplished by rail or road; the latter climbs to above 3,000 ft at Annaberg in a series of more than a dozen hairpin turns. The easier route to Vienna via the

Semmering Pass achieves the same elevation and also offers some magnificent panoramas, including views of the snowcapped Schneeberg.

Pleasures and Pastimes

Dining

When choosing a restaurant, keep in mind that each province has its own cooking style. In Burgenland, the local Pannonian cooking, strongly influenced by neighboring Hungary, features such spicy dishes as *gulyas* (goulash) flavored with paprika. You'll also find fish from Lake Neusiedl, goose, game, and an abundance of fresh, local vegetables. Styria, bordering on Slovenia (formerly northern Yugoslavia), has a hearty cuisine with Serbian overtones; a typical dish is *Steirisches Brathuhn* (roast chicken turned on a spit). The intensely nutty *Kürbiskernöl* (pumpkin-seed oil) is used in many soup and rice dishes, as well as in salad dressings. Such Balkan specialties as *cevapcici* (spicy panfried sausages) are also often found on Styrian menus. You are most likely to encounter the more urbane Viennese cooking in Lower Austria, where you can get Wiener schnitzel nearly everywhere.

Many of the restaurants listed in the chapter are actually country inns that provide overnight accommodations as well as meals, as noted in the reviews. Restaurant prices include taxes and a service charge, but it is customary to give the waiter an additional tip of 3%–5%.

CATEGORY	COST*
$$$$	over AS500
$$$	AS300–AS500
$$	AS200–AS300
$	under AS200

per person for a typical three-course meal, excluding drinks and additional tip

The Great Outdoors

Eastern Austria is prime **hiking country,** and most tourist regions have marked trails. You'll need a local hiking map (*Wanderkarte*), usually for sale at a town's tourist office—whose staff can also suggest short rambles in the vicinity. Some particularly good places for walks are around Lake Neusiedl and Güssing in Burgenland; in the Mur Valley of Styria, especially the Bärenschützklamm at Mixnitz; around Mariazell; and atop the Schneeberg, Rax, and Semmering in Lower Austria.

For the truly ambitious, several long-distance trails cut through this region, among them the Nordalpen-Weitwanderweg past the Raxalpe to Rust and the Oststeiermärkischer-Hauptwanderweg from western Austria to Riegersburg. There's no need to carry either food or a tent, because you stay overnight in staffed huts. Camping is strongly discouraged for both safety and environmental reasons.

The *puszta* (steppe) to the east of Lake Neusiedl is known as the Seewinkel, a perfect place for **horseback riding** (*reiten*), and horses (*pferde*) can be hired in several villages. Ask at the local tourist office. Weekends are particularly popular, so book your steed well in advance.

Lodging

Accommodations in Eastern Austria range from luxury city hotels to mountain and lakeside resorts to castles and romantic country inns, and all are substantially lower in price than those in Vienna or Salzburg. Every town and village also has simpler *Gasthäuser,* which give good value as long as you don't expect a private bath. Accommodations in private homes are cheaper still. These bargains are usually identified by signs reading ZIMMER FREI (room available) or FRÜHSTÜCKSPENSION (bed-and-breakfast).

The tourist information office (*Fremdenverkehrsverein, Fremden-verkehrsamt,* or *Gästeinformation*) in virtually every town can usually find you a decent place to sleep if you haven't made a reservation (☞ Visitor Information *in* Eastern Austria A to Z, *below*). Hotel room rates include taxes and service, and usually breakfast—although you should always ask about the latter.

CATEGORY	COST*
$$$$	over AS2,000
$$$	AS1,000–AS2,000
$$	AS700–AS1,000
$	under AS700

All prices are for a standard double room for two, including taxes and ser-vice charge.

Wines

Eastern Austria vies with Lower Austria as source of the country's best wines. In both Burgenland and Styria, you can travel among villages and sample local vintages on "wine routes." Outstanding white wines predominate, although there are increasingly excellent reds and rosés as well. Burgenland's vineyards, mostly around Lake Neusiedl, pro-duce wines that tend to be slightly less dry, with perhaps the best ex-amples coming from the village of Rust and the areas around Donnerskirchen, Purbach, and Jois. Some of the sweet dessert wines (*Spätlese,* late harvest, and *Eiswein,* pressed from frozen grapes) are extraordinary, and all Burgenland wines are gaining a reputation for high quality. Many vintners happily share samples of their wares and will provide bread and cheese as accompaniment. In Styria, the wines from south of Graz along the Slovenian border and near Leibnitz are superb, especially the tangy Schilcher rosé.

Exploring Eastern Austria

The Eastern Austrian countryside has been fought over many times, which in part explains the host of defensive hilltop castles overlook-ing the flatter outlands to the east. Both conqueror and conquered have left their marks. The topography here, which ranges from the flat puszta of the north to the rolling hills of the south, demonstrates that there's more to Austria than the Alps. Graz is the only real city here; other centers are little more than villages in comparison.

Great Itineraries

Travelers who tackle Eastern Austria usually design their trip around three different destinations—Burgenland, the city of Graz, and the moun-tain route to Vienna—and the following suggested itineraries highlight these destinations.

Numbers in the text correspond to numbers in the margin and on the Burgenland, Eastern Styria and Lower Austria, and Graz maps.

IF YOU HAVE 1 DAY

Travelers with only a day at their disposal could head for **Eisenstadt** ⑧ and along the west shore of **Lake Neusiedl** to **Rust** ⑥, then return to Vienna via **Wiener Neustadt** ㊶. Another good (but full) one-day ex-cursion is to **Mariazell** ㊲, or to **Puchberg am Schneeberg** ㊵, both reachable from Vienna by car or train.

IF YOU HAVE 3 DAYS

Pick **Eisenstadt** ⑧ as a first stop, spending a half day here, and then move onward to the west shore of **Lake Neusiedl** to **Rust** ⑥ for brief stops before continuing southward to 🏰 **Graz** ⑬ for two overnights, with a day spent exploring the city. From Graz, head northward via

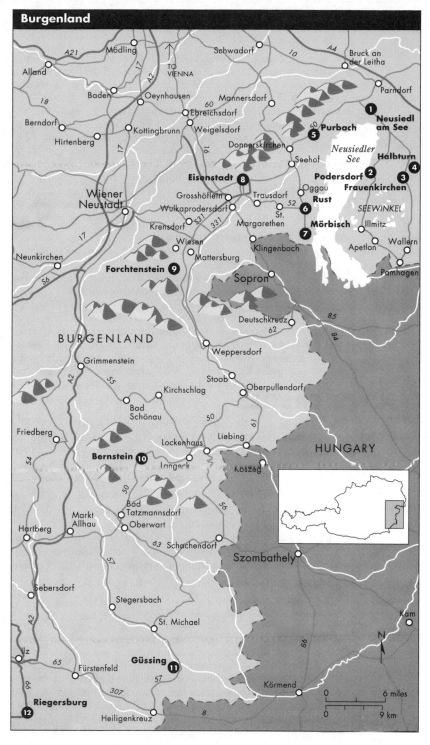

Burgenland

Bruck an der Mur ㉙, over the pass at **Semmering** ㊴, and **Wiener Neustadt** ㊶ to Vienna.

IF YOU HAVE 5–7 DAYS

A leisurely pursuit of Eastern Austria is highly rewarding. Get better acquainted with the curiously flat puszta on the eastern side of **Lake Neusiedl**; then head back over to the western side and spend your first overnight in 🔲 **Rust** ⑥. The next day head to the historic town of 🔲 **Eisenstadt** ⑧ and follow in the footsteps of famed Baroque-era composer Joseph Hayden and the Esterházy princes. Follow the Burgenland wine route south, and for contrast, spend two nights and a day discovering the delightful Altstadt and bustling metropolis that is 🔲 **Graz** ⑬. Take in the magnificent abbey at **Seckau** ㉛ and the vast **Eisenerz** ㉞ open-pit iron ore mines, with an overnight in nearby 🔲 **Leoben/Niklasdorf** ㉚ before continuing north for the attractions of Lower Austria. You might consider an overnight at 🔲 **Semmering** ㊴ on the way back to Vienna.

When to Tour Eastern Austria

Spring, summer, and fall are the seasons for Eastern Austria, unless you're a winter sports enthusiast, when downhill skiers head for Lower Austria and the less crowded slopes of Styria. Other than coming across festival goers and, in summer, visitors to the shores of Lake Neusiedl, you'll find relatively few tourists in this region. Graz functions year-round, but its treasures are less touted and crowds are unknown; Christmas in Graz is a visual spectacle, with whole sections of the city turned into a Christmas market. Winter in the area is an enigma: The Semmering mountains mark the eastern tail end of the Alps—north of the divide can be overcast and dreary while the area to the south basks in sunshine.

LAND OF CASTLES

This tour demonstrates that there's more to Austria than the Alps; it travels the length of Burgenland from the flat puszta of the north to the rolling castle-capped hills of the south before turning west to Styria, ending at Austria's second city, Graz. Although it is possible to cover the entire route of about 300 km (185 mi) in a single day, a leisurely pace is preferable.

Burgenland, a region of castles, fields of grain, and vineyards, is a narrow, fertile belt of agricultural land stretching some 170 km (106 mi) from the Slovak (former Czechoslovak) border, along the Hungarian frontier, and south to Slovenia (formerly northern Yugoslavia). Only 65 km (40 mi) across at its widest point, the region narrows to a mere 4 km (2½ mi).

The name Burgenland, meaning land of castles, dates only from 1921; prior to World War I this area was a part of Hungary. Throughout its long history it has been a battleground between east and west. It was part of the ancient Roman province of Pannonia, occupied by Celts, Roman settlers, Ostrogoths, and Slavs. After them came the Bavarians, Hungarians, and Austrians, followed by invading Turks. This legacy of conflict has continued into the late 20th century, with the tensions of the Iron Curtain a stark fact of life until 1989. The opening of the Hungarian border has again brought change and increased Burgenland's appeal to tourists.

Lake Neusiedl

Located in the north part of Burgenland, one of the region's chief attractions, Lake Neusiedl occupies a strange world. One of the largest lakes in Europe, it is the Continent's only true steppe lake—a bizarre body of warm brackish water. Its sole tributary is far too small to replenish the water lost through evaporation, and there is no outflow at all. Underground springs feed it, but when they fail it dries up, which last happened in the 1860s. At present the water is nowhere more than about 7 ft deep; its many shallower sections make it possible (but dangerous) to wade across the lake. Its depth has varied dramatically, however, at times nearly engulfing the villages on its banks. Most of its 124-square-mi surface area is in Austria, but the southern reaches extend into Hungary.

What really sets Lake Neusiedl apart is the thick belt of tall reeds—in some places more than a mile wide—that almost completely encircles it. This is the habitat of a large variety of birds (more than 250 species) that nest near the water's edge. The lake is also a paradise for anglers, boaters, and windsurfers; other activities include swimming and, along its banks, bicycling.

The flat plains around Lake Neusiedl, with their tiny hamlets and unspoiled scenery, are perfect for leisurely bicycling. Practically every village has a bike-rental shop (*Fahrradverleih* or *Radverleih*), but demand is so great that it's a good idea to reserve in advance. A bike route encircles the lake, passing through Hungary on the southern end (you can shorten the route by taking the ferry between Illmitz beach and Mörbisch). This and many other routes are described in a German-language map-brochure called "Radeln in Burgenland," available free at tourist offices.

Neusiedl am See

❶ *51 km (32 mi) southeast of Vienna.*

Neusiedl am See, at the north end of the lake for which it is named, is a pleasant resort town with good facilities. Direct hourly commuter trains from Vienna have made it very popular, so you won't be alone here. To reach the lake itself, follow the main street for three blocks east of the Hauptplatz and turn right on Seestrasse, a mile-long causeway that leads through the reeds to the lake, where you can rent small boats, swim, or just laze on the beach.

Near the water's edge is the **Seemuseum,** which has a well-rounded exhibit of local flora and fauna. ⊠ *Seebad,* ☎ *02167/2229.* ⌦ *AS20.* ⊗ *May–Oct., daily 9–noon and 1–5.*

In Neusiedel am See itself, visit the ruins of the 13th-century hill fortress Ruine Tabor, a 15th-century parish church near the town hall, and the **Pannonisches Heimatmuseum** (Museum of Local Pannonian Life). ⊠ *Kalvarienbergstr. 40,* ☎ *02167/8173.* ⌦ *Donation suggested.* ⊗ *May–Oct., Tues.–Sat. 2:30–6:30, Sun. 10–noon and 2:30–6:30.*

Lodging

$$$ ⊞ **Hotel Wende.** This sprawling three-story hotel complex is close to the lake and has many standard amenities, but don't expect the charm of a country inn. The comfortable rooms with balconies are of adequate size, and the restaurant is well regarded. ⊠ *Seestr. 40, A–7100,* ☎ *02167/8111–0,* ⨎ *02167/8111–649. 105 rooms with bath. Restaurant, bar, indoor pool, sauna, exercise room, bicycles. No credit cards. Closed late Jan.–mid-Feb.*

Podersdorf

❷ *14 km (8½ mi) south of Neusiedl am See.*

The region east of Lake Neusiedl is the beginning of the unusual Hungarian puszta, the great flat steppe marked with occasional windmills and characteristic wells with long wooden poles for drawing up water—a circular tour of about 70 km (44 mi) by car (or bicycle) would cover nearly everything of interest before returning you to Neusiedl am See. Some of the picturesque houses in Podersdorf have typical thatched roofs, and their chimneys are often adorned in summer with storks nesting after wintering in Egypt. Podersdorf has excellent swimming.

The **Natur und Tierlehrpfad**—a nature trail with cement casts of native bird and animal groupings—and a windmill (open for limited times only) educate tourists. ⊠ *Mühlstr. 26,* ☎ *02177/2227.* ▨ *AS25.* ⊙ *Mid-May–mid-Sept., daily 6 AM–7 PM.*

Dining and Lodging

$$ ✕ **Gasthof zur Dankbarkeit.** The kitchen offers fine local fare as well
★ as creative dishes with occasional Hungarian touches, served in comfortable *Stuben.* The menu changes daily, but you might find chicken-liver pâté, lamb sausages, rabbit, or rack of venison. The courtyard garden makes a delightful setting in summer. The excellent wines come from neighboring vineyards. ⊠ *Hauptstr. 39,* ☎ *02177/2223. DC, V. Closed Mon.–Thurs.*

$$–$$$ ☷ **Haus Attila.** In this small, simple, family-run lakefront hotel, the balconied rooms overlooking the lake are especially appealing. The Karner family also runs the nearby smaller (and slightly cheaper) **Seewirt** (⊠ Strandpl. 1, ☎ 02177/2415). ⊠ *Strandpl. 8, A–7141,* ☎ *02177/2415,* ℻ *02177/2465–30. 34 rooms with bath. Restaurant, sauna. No credit cards. Closed Jan.–Feb.*

En Route Podersdorf marks the beginning of the **Seewinkel,** a flat, marshy area dotted with small lakes and ponds, much of which is a wildlife sanctuary. The national park in **Illmitz** has a noted biological station and a nature trail (☎ 02175/2328–0). Beyond Illmitz, the road goes through Apetlon to **Pamhagen,** a border hamlet with a small zoo exhibiting animals and birds native to the Hungarian steppes.

Frauenkirchen

❸ *7½ km (4½ mi) east of Podersdorf, 16½ km (10¼ mi) southeast of Neusiedl am See.*

Frauenkirchen is known mainly for its **pilgrimage church,** rebuilt in 1702 after its 14th-century predecessor was destroyed by invading Turks and again restored following World War II. The Baroque interior has a much-venerated wooden statue of the Virgin, from the 13th century. Note the miniature Mount Calvary depiction alongside the church.

Dining

$$ ✕ **Altes Brauhaus.** No signs of the old brewery, other than the hearty regional fare, remain at this attractive country inn directly opposite the Pilgrimage Church. The dining rooms have varying rustic decor (the large back one caters to groups), and in summer there's also garden dining under the huge chestnut tree. Try the smooth garlic soup and follow with lamb, goose, or venison during the specialty weeks. Keep an eye out for regional and Hungarian specialties, such as meat-filled pancakes. ⊠ *Kirchenpl. 27,* ☎ *02172/2201. AE, DC, MC, V. Closed mid-Jan.–Feb. and Mon.–Tues. mid-Sept.–mid-July.*

Halbturn

❹ *5 km (3 mi) northwest of Frauenkirchen, 14 km (8½ mi) southeast of Neusiedl am See.*

Halbturn contains the exquisite Baroque **Schloss Halbturn,** an imperial hunting lodge built in 1710 by Lukas von Hildebrandt, the great architect of the period. This restored jewel was once used by Empress Maria Theresa as a summer residence and is noted for its ceiling frescoes. Devastated by Russian troops in the occupation following World War II, then rebuilt in the 1970s, the castle in summer now houses special annual exhibitions. You can stroll through the large, wooded surrounding park anytime, but in late spring when the red and pink chestnut trees are in bloom, the spectacle easily rivals a Monet landscape. In the courtyard, a shop sells excellent wines from the Halbturn vineyards, and a small art museum displays a copy of Gustav Klimt's impressive *Beethoven Frieze,* with the decided advantage over the Vienna original that here you can see the details up close. ⊠ *Schloss Halbturn,* ☏ *02172/8577.* 💷 *AS60.* ◷ *May–Oct., daily 9–6.*

Purbach

❺ *13 km (8½ mi) southwest of Neusiedl am See.*

Purbach, like the nearby wine villages of Breitenbrunn and Donnerskirchen, retains traces of its medieval fortifications. Look for the bust of a Turk atop a chimney in the town center; legend has it that when the invaders withdrew in 1532, one hungover, sleepy Turk missed the retreat and, fearing retribution, climbed down a chimney for safety. He was discovered, became an honored citizen, and lived in Purbach happily ever after. The wines of this area, the reds in particular, are outstanding and merit stopping for samples. In late fall and early winter you'll still see bunches of shriveled grapes on the leafless vines; these will be turned into rare Spätlese and still-rarer Eiswein dessert wines.

Dining and Lodging

\$\$\$–\$\$\$\$ ✕ **Nikolauszeche.** This is one of Burgenland's best restaurants, noted
★ for its elegant country decor in a 15th-century Renaissance house (it is a member of the Romantik Hotels & Restaurants group) as well as for its excellent regional cuisine. Specialties vary with the season, but you might find local goat cheese with olive oil, roast leg of lamb with rosemary and scalloped potatoes, or a pink fillet of young goat with mushroom cream sauce. There is an excellent selection of local wines, including some from the house's own winery. ⊠ *Bodenzeile 3,* ☏ *02683/5514,* 🖷 *02683/5077. AE, DC, MC, V. Closed mid-Dec.– mid-Mar.*

\$\$–\$\$\$ ✕🛏 **Am Spitz.** This country inn, at the end of an attractive row of wine cellars, is known for its local Burgenland and Pannonian cooking. The restaurant is in a former cloister, and the outside garden enjoys an exquisite floral setting, looking down over the lake. The menu changes daily but always features fresh fish, possibly including a spicy Hungarian fish soup, a cassoulet of lake fish in basil cream, and roast veal steak. The somewhat plain and modern associated *Gasthof* (\$\$) is pleasant but less gemütlich. ⊠ *Waldsiedlg. 2, A–7083,* ☏ *02683/5519. 14 rooms with bath. Restaurant. No credit cards. Closed Mon.–Tues. and late Dec.–Mar.*

Rust

6 *14 km (9 mi) south of Purbach, 28 km (17½ mi) southwest of Neusiedl am See.*

Picturesque Rust is easily the most popular village on the lake for its colorful pastel facades and for lake sports. Tourists flock here in summer to see for themselves the famed sights of storks nesting atop the Renaissance and Baroque houses in the town's well-preserved historic center. Be sure to look for *Steckerl,* a delicious local fish caught from the Neusiedlersee and grilled barbecue-style with spices. It's available in most restaurants, but only in the hot months of summer. If you're heading from Purbach, leave Route 50 at Seehof and follow the local road past Oggau to arrive in Rust.

Visit the restored Gothic **Fischerkirche** (Fishermen's Church) off the west end of the Rathausplatz. Built between the 12th and 16th centuries, it is surrounded by a defensive wall and is noted for its 15th-century frescoes and an organ from 1705. ⊠ *Conradpl. 1,* ☎ *02685/502.* ▦ *AS10.* ⊘ *May–Sept., Mon.–Sat. 10–noon and 2:30–6, Sun. 11–noon and 2–6.*

A causeway leads through nearly a mile of reeds to the **Seebad** beach and boat landing, where you can take a sightseeing boat round-trip or to another point on the lake, rent boats, swim, or enjoy a waterside drink or snack at an outdoor table of the Seerestaurant Rust.

Rust is also renowned for its outstanding wines. There are wine-tasting opportunities at the **Weinakademie** (⊠ Hauptstr. 31, ☎ 02685/6451, FAX 02685/6431). Two of the better family-owned wineries that offer tastings are **Weingut Feiler-Artinger** (⊠ Hauptstr. 3, ☎ 02685/237, FAX 02685/6552) and **Ernst Triebaumer** (⊠ Raiffeisenstr. 9, ☎ 02685/528).

You can sample the excellent local vintages, along with a light lunch, in a number of friendly cafés, cellars, and the typical *Heurige,* where young wines are served by their makers. A favorite spot is the **Rathauskeller** (⊠ Rathauspl. 1) open daily except Wednesday from 11:30 AM. The Ruster Blaufränkisch red wine is particularly good, resembling a well-rounded Burgundy.

Dining and Lodging

$ ✕ **Schandl.** For good, simple food to go along with the excellent wine from the family's winery, join the locals at this popular *Buschenschank* (inn). The buffet offers a selection of sausages, salads, cheese, and pickles as well as a few hot dishes that change daily. There is a pleasant courtyard for outdoor dining in summer. ⊠ *Hauptstr. 20,* ☎ *02685/ 265. No credit cards. Closed Tues. and Nov.–Mar.*

$$$ ✕▦ **Rusterhof.** A lovingly renovated *Burgher* house—the town's oldest—at the top of the main square is home to an excellent and imaginative restaurant. Light natural woods and vaulted ceilings set the atmosphere in the series of smaller rooms; in summer there's an outside garden. The menu depends on what's fresh and might include grilled fish or saddle of hare in *Eiswein* sauce. Finish with a rhubarb compote. The complex also includes four very nice apartments for guests. ⊠ *Rathauspl. 18, A–7071,* ☎ *02685/6416. 4 rooms. Restaurant. V. Closed Jan.–Apr.*

$$$ ▦ **Seehotel.** Set on the very edge of Lake Neusiedl, this rambling, modern complex contrasts strikingly with the bordering historic village. The comfortable guest rooms are contemporary Scandinavian in style; ask for one facing the lake. The kitchen is excellent. Golfers get reduced greens fees at the nearby Donnerskirchen course. ⊠ *Am Seekanal 2– 4, A–7071,* ☎ *02685/381–0,* FAX *02685/381–419. 110 rooms with*

bath. 2 restaurants, bar, indoor pool, sauna, tennis courts, exercise room, squash, beach, boating. AE, DC, MC, V.

Mörbisch

❼ *5½ km (3½ mi) south of Rust.*

Mörbisch is the last lakeside village before the Hungarian border. Considered by many to be the most attractive settlement on the lake, the town is famous for its low, whitewashed, Magyar-style houses, whose open galleries are colorfully decorated with flowers and bunches of grain. The local vineyards produce some superb white wines, especially the fresh-tasting Welschriesling and the full-bodied Muscat-Ottonel. Here, too, a causeway leads to a beach on the lake, where an international operetta festival is held each summer (☞ Nightlife and the Arts, *below*). A leisurely activity is to tour the countryside in a typical open **horse-drawn wagon.** Operators in several lakeside villages will arrange this, including Johann Mad (✉ Ruster Str. 14, ☎ 02685/8250) and Evi Wenzl (✉ Weinbergg. 12, ☎ 02685/8401).

Lodging

$$–$$$ 🏨 **Hotel Steiner.** Though in the center of the village, the family-run Steiner is also close to the vineyards and Lake Neusiedl. The somewhat plain modern exterior conceals rustic-style accommodations with all of the conveniences. ✉ *Hauerstr. 1, A–7072,* ☎ *02685/8444–0. 52 rooms with bath. Restaurant, indoor pool, sauna, bicycles. No credit cards. Closed Dec.–Mar.*

Nightlife and the Arts

At the **Mörbisch Lake Festival,** held on Fridays, Saturdays, and Sundays mid-July–August on Burgenland's Lake Neusiedl, operettas are performed outdoors on a floating stage. For information, contact the Mörbisch tourist office or the festival office (Seefestspiele Mörbisch) in Schloss Esterházy in Eisenstadt (☎ 02682/63384) or, during July and August, in Mörbisch itself (☎ 02685/8181–0, ℻ 02685/8334).

Eisenstadt

❽ *22 km (14 mi) northwest of Mörbisch, 48 km (30 mi) south of Vienna, 26 km (16¼ mi) west of Wiener Neustadt.*

Burgenland's provincial capital, Eisenstadt, scarcely more than a village, nevertheless has an illustrious history and enough sights to keep you busy for a half, if not a full, day. It is connected to Neusiedl am See by train and to Vienna and places throughout Burgenland by bus. From Rust, take Route 52 west past St. Margarethen and Trausdorf to the capital.

Although the town has existed since at least the 12th century, it was not of any importance until the 17th, when it became the seat of the Esterházys, a princely Hungarian family that traces its roots to Attila the Hun. The original Esterházy made his fortune by marrying a succession of wealthy landowning widows. Esterházy support was largely responsible for the Habsburg reign in Hungary under the Dual Monarchy. At one time, the family controlled a far-flung agro-industrial empire, and it still owns vast forest resources. The composer Joseph Haydn lived in Eisenstadt for some 30 years while in the service of the Esterházys. When Burgenland was ceded to Austria after World War I, its major city, Sopron, elected to remain a part of Hungary, and so in 1925 tiny Eisenstadt was made the capital of the new Austrian province.

In addition to what's listed below, Eisenstadt has a few other attractions that its tourist office can tell you about, including the Museum of Austrian Culture, the Diocesan Museum, the Fire Fighters Museum, Haydn's little garden house, and an assortment of churches.

★ **Schloss Esterházy,** the yellow-facaded former palace of the ruling princes, reigns over the town. Built in the Baroque style between 1663 and 1672 on the foundations of a medieval castle, it was later modified and is still owned by the Esterházy family, who lease it to the provincial government for use mostly as offices. Part of the recently mounted exhibition on the Esterházy family is still open; the rooms alone are worth viewing. The lavishly decorated **Haydn Room,** an impressive concert hall where the composer conducted his own works from 1761 until 1790, is still used for presentations of Haydn's works, with musicians often dressed in period garb. It can be seen on guided tours (in English on request) lasting about 30 minutes. The **park** behind the schloss is pleasant for a stroll or a picnic; in late August it is the site of the Burgenland wine week. The **Schloss-Café Zachs,** opposite the west end of the Schloss Esterházy at Glorietteallee 1, is open daily until 1 AM for snacks and refreshments. ⊠ *Esterházy Pl.,* ☎ *02682/63384.* ⌑ *AS60.* ⊙ *Easter–May and Oct., daily 8:30–5; June–Sept., daily 8:30–6; Nov.– Easter, weekdays 8:30–5; guided tour hourly.*

At the crest of the Esterházystrasse perches the **Bergkirche,** an ornate Baroque church that includes the strange *Kalvarienberg,* an indoor Calvary Hill representing the Way of the Cross with life-size figures placed in cavelike rooms along an elaborate path. At its highest point, the trail reaches the platform of the belfry, offering a view over the town and this section of Burgenland. The magnificent wooden figures were carved and painted by Franciscan monks more than 250 years ago. The main part of the church contains the tomb of Joseph Haydn, who died in 1809 in Vienna. When the body was returned to Eisenstadt for burial 11 years later at the request of Prince Esterházy, it was unaccountably headless. A search for the head ensued, but it was not discovered until 1932. It had been under glass in the possession of the Gesellschaft der Musikfreunde, the main Viennese musical society. Finally, in 1954 Haydn's head was returned to Eisenstadt, to be buried with his body in a crypt inside the church. ⊠ *Josef Haydn Pl. 1,* ☎ *02682/62638.* ⌑ *AS25.* ⊙ *Apr.–Oct., daily 9–noon and 2–5.*

Wertheimergasse and Unterbergstrasse were boundaries of the Jewish ghetto from 1671 until 1938. During that time, Eisenstadt had a considerable Jewish population; today the **Austrian Jewish Museum** (Österreichisches Jüdisches Museum) recalls the experience of all Austrian Jews throughout history. A fascinating private synagogue in the complex survived the 1938 terror and is incorporated into the museum. ⊠ *Unterbergstr. 6,* ☎ *02682/65145.* ⌑ *AS25.* ⊙ *Late May–late Oct., Tues.–Sun. 10–5.*

The **Landesmuseum** (Burgenland Provincial Museum) brings the history of the region to life with displays on such diverse subjects as Roman culture and the area's wildlife. There's a memorial room to the composer Franz Liszt, along with more relics of the town's former Jewish community. ⊠ *Museumg. 5,* ☎ *02682/62652-0.* ⌑ *AS80.* ⊙ *Tues.– Sun. 9–noon and 1–5.*

Joseph Haydn lived in the simple house on Haydn Gasse from 1766 until 1778. Now the **Haydn Museum,** it contains several of the composer's original manuscripts and other memorabilia. The house itself, and especially its flower-filled courtyard with the small back rooms, is unpretentious but quite delightful. ⊠ *Haydn Gasse 21,* ☎ *02682/ 62652-29.* ⌑ *AS20.* ⊙ *Easter–late Oct., daily 9–noon and 1–5.*

Dining and Lodging

$$ ✗ **Zum Eder.** This sunny atrium restaurant in the center of town offers friendly service and a wide variety of selections. The emphasis here is on light, healthy dishes, including white pork fillet with fresh spinach and a large salad with grilled strips of chicken, and there are several vegetarian items to choose from as well, such as tasty carrot and celery lasagne. ⊠ *Hauptstr. 25,* ☎ *02682/62645. No credit cards.*

$ ✗ **Haydnbräu.** A red-tiled floor against white stucco walls and lots of natural wood provide the right setting for the "First Burgenland Restaurant-Brewery." Indeed, the excellent beer comes directly from polished copper vats behind the bar. The food, too, is good, for either snacks or a main meal; try the beef in spicy beer pepperoni sauce or fried calamari in beer batter. ⊠ *Pfarrg. 22,* ☎ *02682/61561. No credit cards.*

$$ ✗⌂ **Gasthof Ohr.** This personal, family-run hotel and restaurant is about a 10-minute easy walk from the town center. The immaculate rooms are comfortably attractive, done in natural woods and white with color accents; those in the back are quieter. The rustic wood-paneled restaurant offers specialty weeks—goose, game, new asparagus—in addition to Austrian and regional standards such as schnitzel and Hungarian fish soup. In summer, the canopied outdoor dining terrace is a green oasis. Wine comes from the family vineyards. ⊠ *Ruster Str. 51, A–7000,* ☎ *02682/62460,* ℻ *02682/64481. 24 rooms with bath. Restaurant. MC, V.*

$$$ ⌂ **Hotel Burgenland.** Considered the province's best, this strikingly contemporary hotel has everything you'd expect in a first-class establishment. It's near the town center, and the large rooms are bright and airy. The restaurants, alas, have been inconsistent, although the glassed-in winter-garden café offers a pleasant pastel setting for a coffee or snack. ⊠ *Schubertpl. 1, A–7000,* ☎ *02682/696,* ℻ *02682/65531. 88 rooms with bath. 2 restaurants, bar, indoor pool, sauna. AE, DC, MC, V.*

Nightlife and the Arts

Eisenstadt devotes much cultural energy to one of its favorite sons. In the first half of September, it plays host to the annual **Haydn Festival** in the Esterházy Palace. Many of the concerts are by world-famous performers, and admission prices vary with the event. Other concerts featuring the works of Joseph Haydn run from mid-May to early October. Contact the Haydnfestspiele office (☎ 02682/61866–0, ℻ 02682/61805) in Schloss Esterházy (☞ *above*) or the local tourist office. Eisenstadt's **Haydn Quartet,** in 18th-century costumes, plays short matinee concerts of the master's works at 11 AM Tuesday and Friday, from mid-May to late October, at the Esterházy Palace (☎ 02682/63384, ℻ 02682/63384–20); tickets are AS80.

En Route   Heading southwest from Eisenstadt brings you to the narrow waist of Burgenland, squeezed between Lower Austria and Hungary. The leading attraction here is Forchtenstein; take Route S31 for 20 km (12½ mi) to Mattersburg, then a local road 3 km (2 mi) west.

Forchtenstein

❾ *23 km (14½ mi) southwest of Eisenstadt.*

In the summer, people throng to the small village of Forchtenstein for its strawberries, but its enduring dominant feature is the medieval hilltop castle, **Burg Forchtenstein.** This formidable fortress was built in the early 14th century, enlarged by the Esterházys around 1635, and twice defended Austria against invading Turks. Captured enemy soldiers were put to work digging the castle's 466-ft-deep well, famous for its echo. As befits a military stronghold, there is a fine collection of weapons in the armory and booty taken from the Turks; there's also

THE CASTLE ROAD

IF YOU ARE HEADING SOUTH from Vienna to Graz on the A2 autobahn, the flat plains give way suddenly to steeply wooded hills and rocky gorges, with tantalizing glimpses of proud and seemingly inaccessible castles perched atop craggy promontories. More than a dozen castles along the Schlösserstrasse (Castle Road) have withstood the invading armies of the Huns and Turks to repose today in all their splendor as museums or hotels.

You can begin the tour by dipping into the eastern edge of Styria, leaving the autobahn at the Hartberg exit to visit **Schloss Hartberg,** a castle dating from the 13th century and now a museum, with occasional summer concerts. From Hartberg take Highway 54 south to Kaibing, where there will be signs for St. Johann bei Herberstein and **Schloss Herberstein,** famous for its Florentine-style courtyard and animal and nature park. You can also inspect the castle's weaponry collection and stroll in the Baroque garden. **Schloss Stubenberg,** north along the lakeside drive Stubenbergsee, is a fortresslike structure with an impressive ceramics display and summer concerts. The Allhau exit off the A2 autobahn a short distance north of Hartberg takes you to Highway 50 and Bernstein (☞ *below*). This is home to **Burg Bernstein,** now a hotel but once the castle owned by Count Almásy, the character played by Ralph Fiennes in *The English Patient.*

East of Bernstein on Highway 50 is **Lockenhaus** (☎ 02616/2394, FAX 02616/2766), the castle with the most grisly history in Austria. In the 16th century, Countess Elisabeth Bathory was infamous for luring virgin peasant girls to her employ with promises of a dowry after two years' servitude; most girls never made it out alive. Obsessed with retaining her beauty, the depraved countess tortured and killed more than 500 girls, believing that bathing in their blood would keep her young. As a member of the nobility, the countess was never tried for her crimes. The castle is now a very nice hotel, with a medieval restaurant serving simple food like roast chicken and sausages.

Highway 50 south of Bernstein takes you to Stadtschlaining, the home of **Burg Schlaining,** famous for its weaponry collection, chapel, and palatial rooms (closed Monday). Highway 57 south of Highway 50 leads to **Burg Güssing** (☞ *below*), not far from the Slovenian and Hungarian borders. After this the Castle Road continues on into Styria, southeast of Graz, with several more noteworthy castles to visit or stay in.

A drive along the Castle Road can take anywhere from four or five hours to a couple of days, depending on how many of the castles you stop to visit—either to tour or to spend the night in. Even if you're in a hurry, it's relatively easy to get off and on the A2 autobahn to visit a castle. The best time to visit this area is between April and October, because most of the castles are closed during the winter months. For more information about the Castle Road, contact the Büro Die Schlösserstrasse (✉ Schloss Kornberg, A–8330 Feldbach, ☎ 03152/7419, FAX 003152/5824).

– Bonnie Dodson

an exhibition of stately carriages. ⌂ *Burgpl. 1,* ☎ *02626/81212.* ⌑ *AS60.* ☉ *Apr.–Oct., daily 8–11:30 and 1–4.*

Dining and Lodging

$$$ ✕ **Reisner.** The delicately prepared traditional food served at this popular restaurant attracts people from all over the region. You can eat in the somewhat formal dining room or in a rustic tavern favored by the locals, with the offerings matching the setting. Some typical dishes are trout with a ragout of fresh vegetables; excellent steaks; and, for dessert, rhubarb tart and poppy seed parfait. ⌂ *Hauptstr. 141,* ☎ *02626/ 63139. AE. Closed Wed.–Thurs. and early Mar.*

$ ⌸ **Gasthof Sauerzapf.** This simple country inn on the main road just five minutes west of the castle has recently modernized its rooms. ⌂ *Rosalienstr. 9, A–7212,* ☎ *02626/81217. 14 rooms with bath. Restaurant. No credit cards.*

En Route You can get to Bernstein from Forchtenstein by returning to the highway from Burg Forchtenstein and taking S31 and Route 50 south past Weppersdorf and Stoob, the latter famous for its pottery. The road then goes through Oberpullendorf and close to Lockenhaus, where a renowned music festival is held each summer in the 13th-century castle (☞ Nightlife and the Arts *in* Bernstein, *below*).

Bernstein

⑩ *73 km (45 mi) south of Forchenstein.*

The small village of Bernstein is one of few sources of *Edelserpentin,* a dark green serpentine stone also known as Bernstein jade. Jewelry and objets d'art made locally from the town's stone are on display in the **Felsenmuseum** (Stone Museum), located partly within a former mine. ⌂ *Potsch, Hauptpl. 5,* ☎ *03354/6620–0.* ⌑ *AS50.* ☉ *Mar.–Oct., daily 9–noon and 1:30–6; Nov.–Dec., daily 9–noon and 1:30–5.*

Shops in town explain cutting and exhibit stones. A visit to the **Piringer** shop and museum includes a look into the caves from which the Edelserpentin is hewn. ⌂ *Hauptpl. 3 and 7,* ☎ *03354/6504 or 03354/6506.* ⌑ *AS15.* ☉ *Mid-Mar.–mid-Dec., daily 9–noon and 1:30–5:30.*

Overlooking the village is **Burg Bernstein,** a 12th-century fortress that was rebuilt in the 17th century. Part of it is now a romantic castle-hotel, but the rest may be visited. ☎ *03354/6382.* ⌑ *AS50.* ☉ *May–Oct., daily 9–noon and 1–5; Nov.–Apr., by appointment.*

OFF THE BEATEN PATH

SOUTH BURGENLAND OPEN-AIR MUSEUM – South of Bernstein in Bad Tatzmannsdorf is the Freilichtmuseum (South Burgenland Open-Air Museum), which displays wonderfully restored old barns, farmhouses, and stables from the region, giving a feeling of life as experienced a century or more ago. ⌂ *Josef-Hölzel-Allee 1,* ☎ *03353/8284 or 03353/ 8717.* ⌑ *AS10.* ☉ *Oct.–May, daily 8–4; June–Aug., daily 8–6.*

Dining and Lodging

$ ✕ **Gasthof Heanznhof-Frühwirth.** In this typical Gasthof in the center of town you'll find unusually good regional cooking with strong Hungarian overtones: thick spicy soups, goose, duck, and other game in season. ⌂ *Hauptstr. 59,* ☎ *03354/6503. No credit cards. Closed Jan. and Thurs. Nov.–Mar.*

$$$–$$$$ ⌸ **Burg Bernstein.** This medieval castle, built in the 12th century, became a hotel in 1953, with indoor plumbing being the only concession to modern life. It has gained a certain fame of late because it once belonged to Count Almásy, the character portrayed by Ralph Fiennes in *The English Patient.* It's now owned by an offshoot of the family,

and you can still find Count Almásy's books on the shelves in the corridors, and his room is preserved the way he left it. The hilltop location gives it a bird's-eye view of the peaceful Tauchen Valley, just west of the village of Bernstein. The rooms, which tend to be large, look much as they must have in the mid-1800s. Meals, prepared by Countess Berger-Almásy herself, are served with regional wines in the Rittersaal, a baronial hall. ⊠ *Schlossweg 1, A–7434,* ☎ *03354/6382,* FAX *03354/6520. 14 rooms with bath. Pool, sauna, fishing, hunting. AE, DC, MC, V. Closed mid-Oct.–Apr.*

Nightlife and the Arts

The **International Chamber Music Festival** (Kammermusikfest) of Lockenhaus, 15 km (9½ mi) east of Bernstein, takes place during the first half of July in a 13th-century castle. World-famous musicians are invited to this intimate festival, and the audience may attend morning rehearsals. Violinist Gidon Kremer is the musical sparkplug behind the festival. Call the local church office (*Pfarramt*) for information, reservations, and accommodations (☎ 02616/2224, FAX 02616/2023).

Güssing

⓫ *54 km (34 mi) south of Bernstein, 13 km (8½ mi) north of Heiligenkreuz, Hungary.*

Güssing is yet another of Burgenland's castle-dominated villages. From Bernstein many travelers arrive via Route 50 past Bad Tatzmannsdorf, then follow Route 57.

The classic 12th-century fortress **Burg Güssing,** perched high on a solitary volcanic outcrop, has wonderful views of the surrounding countryside. It also has a fine collection of Old Master paintings (including portraits by Lucas Cranach), weapons, and armor, and a Gothic chapel with a rare 17th-century cabinet organ. In recent years, an exhibition celebrating fairy tales has been on view, with rooms devoted to Hansel and Gretel and Snow White. ☎ *03322/43400 or 03322/42491.* ✍ *Castle museum and fairy-tale exhibition AS75.* ☉ *May–Oct., daily 10–6 (last admission at 5).*

If you stop in Güssing to explore its castle, consider also visiting the **Naturpark Güssing** (Güssing Game Park), where a variety of wild animals indigenous to Eastern Austria reside in more than a square mile of open space. Observation posts are scattered throughout, and you should take your time at them—the animals have to come to you. ⊠ *1 km (½ mi) northeast of Güssing,* ☎ *03322/42419–0.* ✍ *AS15.* ☉ *Daily dawn–dusk.*

Dining and Lodging

$$ ✕▥ **Gasthof Gibiser.** Its proximity to Hungary has inspired the cre-
★ ative dishes served at this classic, white, villa-style country inn. The Pannonian cuisine combines the best of Austrian and Hungarian culinary traditions to produce such specialties as cabbage soup and steak stuffed with goose liver. For overnight guests there are several quiet rooms plus a few rustic thatched-roof cottages in the garden. ⊠ *Heiligenkreuz 81, A–7561,* ☎ *03325/4216–0,* FAX *03325/4246–44. 12 rooms with bath, 3 cottages. AE, DC, MC, V. Closed 1st 2 wks of Feb., late Dec., and Mon. in winter.*

Riegersburg

⓬ *57 km (35 mi) southwest of Güssing, 56 km (34¾ mi) east of Graz.*

To arrive at Riegersburg from Güssing, stay on Route 57 to the frontier village of Heiligenkreuz-im-Laftnitztal; then take Route 65 west to

Fürstenfeld, leaving Burgenland and crossing into Styria. Continue on to Ilz, and then turn south on Route 66 to Riegersburg. Riegersburg is a quiet agricultural community overshadowed by the massive fortress that perches atop an extraordinary volcanic outcropping. The rock has had its attraction over the centuries; archaeological finds have established that there were settlements here more than 6,000 years ago.

Rising some 600 ft above the valley below is the mighty and well-restored **Riegersburg Castle,** one of Austria's great defensive bastions. Originally built in the 11th century on the site of Celtic and Roman strongholds, it has never been humbled in battle, not even in 1945, when its German occupants held out against the Russians. The present structure dates from the 17th century and is entered by way of a heavily defended, winding path, so be prepared to climb for 20 to 30 minutes. (Taxis will take travelers with disabilities up; check with the Zehethofer BP filling station in town, or call them at ☎ 03153/8281.) The castle has weapons displays, rooms with period furnishings, and a separate museum of witchcraft and magic. Needless to say, the views are magnificent. ☎ *03153/8213–0.* ◪ *Each museum AS60, both museums AS95.* ۞ *Apr.–Oct., daily 9–5.*

Adjacent to the Riegersburg Castle you can observe free flight of birds of prey at **Greifvogelwarte Riegersburg** (Birds-of-Prey Keep). At various hours, falcons and eagles are set loose from a stand within the aviary preserve (returning to the keepers' care—and tempting meals, of course). ☎ *03153/7390.* ◪ *AS50.* ۞ *Mon.–Sat. at 11 and 3; Sun. at 11, 2, and 4, weather permitting.*

Dining and Lodging

$$ **×🕾 Gasthof Fink Zur Riegersburg.** This venerable, family-run coun-
★ try inn near the foot of the castle is prettily adorned with flower boxes and shutters. Its large, paneled dining room—complete with ceiling beams—is bright and airy, and there's also garden dining in season. The Austrian cuisine is hearty, with such dishes as bratwurst with sauerkraut and dumplings, and roast beef with cornmeal. A fine selection of Styrian wines is offered. ⊠ *Riegersburg 29, A–8333* ☎ *03153/ 0216,* 🖾 *03153/7357. 33 rooms with bath. Restaurant. AE, DC, MC, V. Closed Feb.*

GRAZ AND ITS ENVIRONS

200 km (125 mi) southwest of Vienna, 285 km (178 mi) southeast of Salzburg.

Native son Arnold Schwarzenegger hasn't managed to give Graz quite the cultural cachet that Mozart bestowed on Vienna and Salzburg. So this second-largest Austrian city (and capital of the province of Styria) has had to work harder to grab the spotlight. The Styriarte summer music festival has become one of the most prestigious cultural events in the country, and the opera now attracts top companies like the Bolshoi. With its skyline dominated by the squat 16th-century clock tower, the city has a well-preserved medieval center whose Italian Renaissance look gives it a Mediterranean feel in contrast to other Austrian cities.

Lying in a somewhat remote corner of the country and often overlooked by tourists, Graz is easily reached from Vienna or Salzburg and provides the urban highlight of an itinerary through southeastern Austria. The name Graz derives from the Slavic *gradec,* meaning "small castle"; there was probably a fortress atop the Schlossberg hill as early as the 9th century. This strategic spot guarded the southern end of the narrow Mur Valley—an important approach to Vienna—from invasion by the Turks. By the 12th century, a town had developed at the foot of the hill, which in time became an imperial city of the ruling Habsburgs. Graz's glory faded in the 17th century when the court moved to Vienna, but the city continued to prosper as a provincial capital, especially under the enlightened 19th-century rule of Archduke Johann.

If you're staying in the city for more than a day, you might want to make a short excursion or two into the countryside. Ask at the information office for the detailed folder in English, "Excursions around Graz," with suggestions as well as travel directions. Three favorite trips—to Stübing bei Graz, Piber, and Bärnbach—can each be done in a few hours.

A Good Walk

On the left bank of the River Mur at the center of the Old City is the **Hauptplatz** ⑬, which was converted from a swampy pastureland to a town square by traveling merchants in 1164. It wasn't until 1550 that the Rathaus (City Hall) was built, but little remains now of the original structure. Modernized over the centuries until it began to look out of place in the Renaissance-style square, its facade was restored to the initial design in 1966. Facing the Rathaus is the impressive Erzherzog Johann Brunnen (Prince Johann Fountain). Before leaving the Hauptplatz, go to the corner of Sporgasse for a look at the Baroque Luegg Haus, which gets its name from the German phrase *ums Eck lugen,* or "peering around the corner."

Backtrack to your left to the narrow, medievallike Franziskanergasse just off the Hauptplatz, and walk its short length to the Franziskanerplatz and the Franziskanerkirche, a church and Franciscan monastery dating from 1240, with a 14th-century choir, a 16th-century nave, and a 17th-century tower. The area is known as the Kälbernes Viertel, or Butcher's Quarter, because in the Middle Ages it was where the butchers had their stalls offering meat and sausages for sale. Return to the Hauptplatz and turn right along Schmiedgasse, or Blacksmith's Lane, which is lined with old burgher houses. If you're up for visiting a series of museums, make a detour by going right on Landhausgasse, then an almost immediate left onto Raubergasse to the entrance to the natural history section of the **Landesmuseum Joanneum** ⑭. The entrance to the applied arts department, displaying works by Lucas Cranach and Pieter Brueghel the Younger, is on Neutorgasse, parallel to but west of Raubergasse.

Take Landhausgasse northeast to Herrengasse. The Gemaltes Haus at No. 3 is a centuries-old ducal residence. At the corner of Herrengasse and Stempfergasse, note the Bären Apotheke (the Chemist at the Sign of the Bear) for its rococo exterior. On Herrengasse, but facing south, is the **Landhaus** ⑮, the home of the Styrian Parliament. Take a moment to enter the arcaded courtyard, which was designed by Italian architect Domenico dell'Allio in Renaissance Lombardy style. Adjoining the Landhaus is the **Landeszeughaus** ⑯, once the most important armory of southern Austria. Today it houses more than 30,000 exhibition pieces, mainly from the 16th and 17th centuries. Across the street at Herrengasse 13 is a house where Napoléon Bonaparte supposedly once spent the night.

Continue south on Herrengasse to the **Stadtpfarrkirche** ⑰, a splendid church dating from the early 16th century, worth a visit, and on to Hans-Sachs-Gasse. Turn left, then left again onto Engegasse, passing Bischofsplatz and going on to **Glockenspielplatz** ⑱, famous for the wood-carved, life-size Styrian couple who dance to the sound of the Glockenspiel (chimes). Just past the square is the Mehlplatz, which is lined with his-

Graz

toric houses and has a number of pubs and bars. In summer it's perfect for sipping a beer in one of the many beer gardens. Go back through Glockenspielplatz and go left on Abraham-St. Clara-Gasse, then left again onto Bürgergasse. Almost immediately to your right some steps lead to the late-Gothic **Domkirche** ⑲ and the Mausoleum of Emperor Ferdinand II. Leave the cathedral and go left onto Burggasse (not Bürgergasse), through the castle gateway (*Burgtor*) to the **Burg** ⑳ and the Stadtpark, the vast city park, with its fountains, pathways, and park benches offering relaxation.

After a respite at the Stadtpark, go back through the castle grounds and through the Burgtor, turn right onto Hofgasse, or Court Lane, and follow it to Sporgasse. Sporgasse (Spur Lane) was where spur makers and weaponry makers of the 14th and 15 centuries lived and worked. Go left on Sporgasse, and if you're still game after passing Luegg Haus from the beginning of the tour, go right onto Sackstrasse to **Herberstein Palace** ㉑, home to a collection of modern Styrian art, and the **Palais Khuenburg** ㉒, which now houses the city museum. Emerging from the Stadtmuseum, go right to Schlossbergplatz.

Schlossbergplatz is the base of the **Schlossberg** ㉓, known as Palace Mountain. This is where the fortress guarding Graz was located and where you'll mount the steep steps leading to the famous **Uhrturm** ㉔. This clock tower is the most famous landmark in Graz. Continue following the path upward to the Glockenturm, the bell tower that is part of the original fortress on the Schlossberg. This winds up the end of the walking tour, and if you're too tired to go back on foot to the center of the city, consider taking the Schlossbergbahn, the funicular that carries the weary down to Kaiser-Franz-Josef-Kai at 15-minute intervals.

TIMING

Nearly all tourist attractions in Graz are conveniently located in the compact Altstadt, or Old City quarter, which can easily be explored on foot in an hour or so, not including any stops. With several stops, a walk through the Old City of Graz can take all day. If you're pressed for time, choose which part of the old city you'd rather see: the lower section, with its churches, historical houses, and museums, or the upper town, with its winding wooded paths, famous clock tower, and the Schlossberg, the lookout point of the city. The best time to visit is between April and October when the weather is at its most inviting, but tourist attractions are open year-round.

Sights to See

⑳ **Burg.** The scanty remains of this former imperial palace now house government offices. Most of this uninspired structure is from the 19th and 20th centuries, but two noteworthy vestiges of the original 15th-century stronghold remain: the **Burgtor** (palace gate), which opens into the sprawling **Stadtpark** (municipal park); and the unusual 49-step, 26-ft carved stone double-spiral **Gothic staircase** of 1499, in the hexagonal tower at the far end of the grand courtyard.

⑲ **Domkirche.** On the south exterior wall is a rather faded 15th-century fresco called the *Landplagenbild,* which graphically depicts contemporary local torments—the plague, the locusts, and the Turks. Step inside to see the outstanding high altar made of colored marble, the choir stalls, Raphael Donner's 1741 tomb of Count Cobenzl, and Konrad Laib's *Crucifixion* of 1457. The 15th-century reliquaries on either side of the triumphal arch leading to the choir were originally the hope chests of Paola Gonzaga, daughter of Ludwig II of Mantua. The Baroque **Mausoleum** of Emperor Ferdinand II, who died in 1637, adjoins the cathedral. Its sumptuous interior is partly an early design by

native son Fischer von Erlach and his only work to be seen in Graz.
⊠ *Burgg. 3.* 🎫 *Free.* 🕙 *May–Sept., Mon.–Sat. 11–noon and 2–3;
tour Oct.–Apr., Mon.–Sat. at 11.*

⑱ Glockenspielplatz. Every day at 11 AM and 3 and 6 PM two mullioned
windows open in the mechanical clock high above the square, revealing a wooden man adorned in lederhosen, a tankard of beer in his up-
raised fist, and a dirndl-clad Austrian maiden. An old folk tune plays
and they dance on the window ledges before returning to their hidden
perch. The musical box was erected in 1903 by the owner of the house.
Look into the courtyard at No. 5, which has an impressive 17th-cen-
tury open staircase. The house at No. 7 has an arcaded Renaissance
courtyard.

NEED A
BREAK?

You can wait for the musical show right under the glockenspiel at the
trendy **Glockenspiel Café** (⊠ Glockenspielpl. 4). The coffee, sandwiches,
and pastries are all excellent, and there are plenty of outdoor tables
from which to enjoy the passing parade. The café is closed Sunday.

★ ⑬ Hauptplatz (Main Square). This triangular area was first laid out in
1164 and is used today as a lively open-air produce market. In its center stands the **Erzherzog Johann Brunnen** (Archduke Johann Fountain),
dedicated to the popular 19th-century patron whose enlightened policies did much to develop Graz as a cultural and scientific center. The
four female figures represent what were Styria's four main rivers;
today only the Mur and the Enns are within the province. The **Luegg
House**, at the corner of Sporgasse, is noted for its Baroque stucco facade. On the west side of the square are Gothic and Renaissance
houses. The late-19th-century **Rathaus** (City Hall) totally dominates
the south side of the main square. From the Neue-Welt-Gasse and
Schmiedgasse you get a superb view of the Hauptplatz.

㉑ Herberstein Palace. This 17th-century former city residence of the ruling princes now houses the **Neue Galerie** (New Hallery). Its collection
of paintings and sculpture from the 19th century to the present includes
works by such Austrian artists as Egon Schiele, along with the newest
in Styrian art. ⊠ *Sackstr. 16,* ☎ *0316/829155.* 🎫 *AS40.* 🕙 *Tues.–
Sat. 10–5.*

⑭ Landesmuseum Joanneum. This is the oldest public museum in Austria,
founded by Archduke Johann in 1811. Actually, this is part of a large
complex of museums devoted to different subjects, several of which are
in other parts of town. The **Alte Galerie** (Old Gallery) is a world-famous
collection of art from the Middle Ages through the Baroque period. Among
its treasures are works by Pieter Brueghel the Younger and both Hans
and Lucas Cranach, the noted *Admont Madonna* wood carving from
1400, and a medieval altarpiece depicting the murder of Thomas à
Becket. ⊠ *Natural history: Rauberg. 10, 0316/8017–4700; applied
arts: Neutorg. 45,* ☎ *0316/8017–4700.* 🎫 *AS60.* 🕙 *Natural history section Tues.–Sun. 9–4, applied arts section Tues.–Sun. 10–4.*

🐣 ⑯ Landeszeughaus. This provincial arsenal is possibly the most noted attraction in Graz. Virtually unchanged since it was built in 1643, this
four-story armory still contains the 16th- and 17th-century weapons
intended for use by Styrian mercenaries in fighting off the Turks.
Nearly 30,000 items are on display, including more than 3,000 suits
of armor (some of which are beautifully engraved), thousands of hal-
berds, swords, firearms, cannons, and mortars. (Pieces from this collection were shown in the United States and Canada in 1992.) Probably
the most important collection of its type in the world, it is now being
rearranged for better presentation—to turn the displays into a "living

exhibition" highlighting unusual items in contrast to the sheer quantity on hand. Call for possible new winter and evening hours. ⊠ *Herreng. 16,* ☎ *0316/8017–4810.* ⊠ *AS80.* ☉ *Apr.–Oct., Tues.–Sun. 9–5, Nov.–Mar., Tues.–Sun. 10–3.*

⑮ Landhaus. The Styrian provincial parliament house was built between 1557 and 1565 by Domenico dell' Allio in the Italian Renaissance style. Its arcaded courtyard is magnificently proportioned and features a 16th-century fountain that is an unusually fine example of old Styrian wrought-iron work. ⊠ *Herreng. 16.*

㉒ Palais Khuenburg. This was the birthplace in 1863 of Archduke Franz Ferdinand, heir to the throne of the Austro-Hungarian Empire. His assassination at Sarajevo in 1914 led directly to the outbreak of World War I. The palace is now home to the **Stadtmuseum** (City Museum), whose exhibits trace the history of Graz and include an old-time pharmacy. ⊠ *Sackstr. 18,* ☎ *0316/822580–0.* ⊠ *AS50.* ☉ *Tues. 10–9, Wed.–Sat. 10–6, Sun. 10–1.*

㉓ Schlossberg (Palace Mountain). The view from the summit of Graz's midtown mountain takes in all of the city and much of central Styria. A stone staircase beginning at Schlossbergplatz leads to the top, but since it is a 395-ft climb, you may prefer to use the **Schlossbergbahn** funicular railway (Kaiser-Franz-Josef-Kai 38) for AS20. The defensive fortress, whose ramparts were built to prevent the invading Turks from marching up the Mur Valley toward Vienna, remained in place until 1809, when a victorious Napoléon had them dismantled after defeating the Austrians. The town paid a large ransom to preserve two of the castle's towers, but the rest was torn down and is today a well-manicured and very popular park. Atop the Schlossberg and a few steps east of the funicular station is the **Glockenturm** (bell tower), an octagonal structure from 1588 containing Styria's largest bell, the famous 4-ton Liesl. This is also the departure point for guided walking tours of the Schlossberg, conducted daily, every hour from 9 to 5, except in winter. The **Open-Air Theater,** just yards to the north, is built into the old casemates of the castle and has a sliding roof in case of rain. Both opera and theater performances are held here in summer.

NEED A
BREAK?   The **Schlossberg Café** (☎ 0316/823050) at the top of the funicular railway, has garden tables with a sweeping view across Graz. Among its specialties are *Germknödel* (a sweet dumpling in poppyseed sauce) and *Most* (a light nonalcoholic wine).

Schloss Eggenberg. This 17th-century palace is located on the very edge of the city and is surrounded by a large deer park. Built around an arcaded courtyard lined with antlers, this fine example of the high-Baroque style contains the gorgeous **Prunkräume** (State Apartments) noted for their elaborate stucco decorations and frescoes, as well as three branch museums of the Joanneum. During the summer, candlelit chamber concerts are held here. The **Jagdmuseum** (Hunting Museum), on the first floor, displays antique weapons, paintings, and realistic dioramas. The **Abteilung für Vor- und Frühgeschichte** (Pre- and Early History Museum) has a remarkable collection of Styrian archaeological finds, including the small and rather strange Strettweg Ritual Chariot dating from the 7th century BC. The **Münzensammlung** (Numismatic Museum) is tucked away in a corner on the ground floor. The attractive outdoor café in the park surrounding the castle is the perfect place to fortify yourself before or after visiting the museums. ⊠ *Eggenberger Allée 90,* ☎ *0316/583– 264–0.* ⊠ *AS80.* ☉ *Apr.–Oct., Tues.–Sun. 9–5, tours at 10, 11, noon, 2, 3, and 4.*

⑰ Stadtpfarrkirche. The city parish church was built early in the 16th century and later received its Baroque facade and 18th-century spire. Tintoretto's *Assumption of the Virgin* decorates the altar. Badly damaged in World War II, the stained-glass windows were replaced in 1953 by a Salzburg artist, Albert Birkle, who portrayed Hitler and Mussolini as malicious spectators at the scourging of Christ (left window behind the high altar, fourth panel from the bottom on the right). Across the street begins a narrow lane named after Johann Bernhard Fischer von Erlach, the great architect of the Austrian Baroque, who was born in one of the houses here in 1666. ⊠ *Herreng. 23,* ☎ *0316/829624–0.* ☉ *7–7.*

㉔ Uhrturm (Clock Tower). This most famous landmark of Graz dates to the 16th century, though the clock mechanism is two centuries younger. The clock has four giant faces that might at first confuse you—until you realize that the *big* hands tell the hour and the *small* hands the minutes. At the time the clock was designed, this was thought to be easier to read at a distance. The 16th-century wooden parapet above the clock was once a post for firefighters, who kept a lookout on the city and sounded the alarm in case of fire.

Dining and Lodging

$$$–$$$$ ✕ **Casino-Restaurant.** It's no gamble when you dine in Graz's best restaurant, even if you have to pass the roulette wheels to reach the dining salons. The atmosphere is appropriately elegant and glitzy, if a bit dimly lit. Try the changing multicourse fixed menu or select from regional and international specialties such as Styrian chicken with rosemary potatoes and sautéed peppers, roast lamb in cheese crust, and duck breast in a honey herb sauce. Desserts are excellent, berry compote with marzipan crust or elderberry sherbet being recommended examples. The wine list includes regional and international choices; wines by the glass are somewhat limited. ⊠ *Landhausg. 10,* ☎ *0316/821380. Jacket and tie. AE, DC, MC, V. No lunch.*

$$$ ✕ **Hofkeller.** With its dark, wood-paneled walls, this popular place looks more like a old burgher cellar than an Italian restaurant. The blackboard menu changes daily, but there's usually a good choice of simple salads to start with, such as arugula with shaved Parmesan, as well as several pasta dishes, including a few vegetarian choices, such as manicotti stuffed with ricotta and spinach. Fish is always featured and is lightly prepared. ⊠ *Hofg. 8,* ☎ *0316/832439. No credit cards. Closed Sun.*

$$$ ✕ **Landhauskeller.** The Landhaus complex (☞ Sights to See, *above*), which includes the provincial parliament and the armory, also includes a favorite traditional restaurant, with its comfortably rustic dining rooms and courtyard, set within the ancient arcaded Landhaus itself. Among the variety of hearty Styrian dishes that may be served are *Tafelspitz* (boiled beef) and ragout of veal. The menu is extensive and there are excellent Styrian wines, too. ⊠ *Schmiedg. 9,* ☎ *0316/830276. AE, DC, MC, V. Closed Sun. and late Dec.–mid-Jan.*

$$$ ✕ **Quergasse.** This upstairs restaurant on a tiny, cobblestone alleyway
★ has beautifully frescoed rooms serving as a backdrop to the excellent, innovative cuisine. The menu is always changing but may offer smoked duck breast in a *Zweigelt* peanut sauce or monkfish in an olive pine-nut crust with basil gnocchi. ⊠ *Bürgerg. 4,* ☎ *0316/813830. AE, DC, MC, V. Closed Sun. No lunch.*

$$ ✕ **Keplerkeller.** The astronomer Johannes Kepler is supposed to have lived here at the end of the 16th century, but, alas, there's no proof. It is, nevertheless, an atmospheric wine cellar with heavy paneling and rustic decor, set between the Landeszeughaus and the Glockenspielplatz in the pedestrian zone of the Old City. There is a lovely Renaissance courtyard for alfresco dining and live music after 9 PM. The menu features local specialties like Styrian beef salad, Styrian pan-roasted beef, and *Tafelspitz* (boiled beef), and locally made strudel, along with the usual schnitzels. The Keplerkeller is especially popular for its selection of local wines in open carafes. ⊠ *Stempferg. 6,* ☎ *0316/822449. AE, DC, MC, V. Closed Sun. No lunch.*

$$ ✕ **Stainzerbauer.** Local residents return again and again to this cozy
★ restaurant, one block south of the cathedral, to eat at their regular tables or, in summer, in the cool courtyard. The popular Styrian specialties may include such hearty dishes as pork ribs on a wooden plank with garlic bread, or *Perlhuhn,* guinea fowl stuffed with spinach and cheese and served with pumpkin pasta. Be sure to try the crispy salad tossed with *Kürbiskernöl* (pumpkin-seed oil) and yogurt dressing. ⊠ *Bürgerg. 4,* ☎ *0316/821106. AE, DC, MC, V. Closed Sun. and holidays.*

$ ✕ **Mangold's Vollwertrestaurant.** Located near Südtirolerplatz, this popular vegetarian restaurant offers a variety of tasty dishes, served cafeteria-style. ⊠ *Griesg. 10,* ☎ *0316/918002. No credit cards. No dinner Sat. Closed Sun.*

$$$$ ✕🏨 **Schloss Obermayerhofen.** The queen of all the castle hotels is 60 km (37 mi) north of Graz, and would make a fine stop if you take the Castle Drive from Vienna to Graz (☞ Close-up box, *above*). No expense was spared in providing luxurious modern-day comfort while retaining the ancient feel of the castle, and no two rooms (furnished with antiques and tapestries) are alike. This is a perfect spot to stay while exploring the countryside, or making a day trip to Graz, 40 minutes away. The gourmet restaurant serves such tempting items as salmon tartare on a bed of crispy potato strips or panfried pike perch with white truffle mashed potatoes. The menu changes frequently. ⊠ *A–8272 Sebersdorf/Bad Waltersdorf,* ☎ *03333/2503,* 𝔽𝔸𝕏 *03333/ 2503–50, 20 rooms. Restaurant. Jan. 6–Feb.*

$$$$ 🏨 **Schlossberghotel.** This lovely old town house, tucked up against the
★ foot of the Schlossberg, is owned by a former race car driver who turned it into a hotel in 1982. The owner's wife is an avid art collector, and the tastefully furnished rooms display provincial antiques as well as 18th-century portraits, while the corridors are filled with modern artworks and an interesting variety of old Styrian lamps. The outdoor pool, on a rocky terrace, offers a spectacular view of the city. ⊠ *Kaiser-Franz-Josef-Kai 30, A–8010,* ☎ *0316/8070–0,* 𝔽𝔸𝕏 *0316/8070–160. 55 rooms with bath. Bar, pool, sauna, exercise room, meeting rooms, parking. AE, DC, MC, V.*

$$$–$$$$ 🏨 **Hotel Erzherzog Johann.** Travelers who prefer a traditionally elegant city hotel will be happy with this Old World establishment in a
★ 16th-century building. Its location, just steps from the Hauptplatz in the Old City, is perfect for tourists. Rooms are furnished charmingly in Biedermeier style and open onto a sunny atrium. ⊠ *Sackstr. 3–5, A–8010,* ☎ *0316/811616,* 𝔽𝔸𝕏 *0316/811515. 62 rooms with bath. Restaurant, bar, café, sauna. AE, DC, MC, V.*

$$$ 🏨 **Hotel Europa.** Opened in 1986, this modern hotel is directly across from the main train station, 1½ km (1 mi) west of the Old City. Its thoroughly contemporary design and interiors and ease of access make it popular with both businesspeople and tourists. An underground shopping mall connects it directly with the rail station and air terminal. ⊠ *Bahnhofgürtel 89, A–8020,* ☎ *0316/7076–0,* 𝔽𝔸𝕏 *0316/7076–606. 114 rooms with bath, 4 suites. Restaurant, bar, café, sauna. AE, DC, MC, V.*

$$$ 🏨 **Hotel Weitzer.** This impressive, pale-yellow turn-of-the-century building sits across the Mur River from the Old City, yet it's within easy walking distance of all major attractions. Rooms are modern yet comfortably cozy. ⊠ *Grieskai 12–14, A–8020,* ☎ *0316/703–0,* 𝔽𝔸𝕏

0316/703–88. 150 rooms with bath. Restaurant, bar, sauna, conference rooms. AE, DC, MC, V.

$$–$$$ ⛫ **Hotel Gollner.** A friendly, atmospheric, older hotel near the Opera House on the edge of the Old City, the Gollner has long been a favorite of the theatrical and operatic crowd. Its soundproof rooms are comfortably large and have been recently renovated; those still without a private bath are less expensive. ✉ *Schlögelg. 14, A–8010,* ☎ *0316/ 822521–0,* ℻ *0316/822527–7. 50 rooms, 46 with bath. Bar, sauna, exercise room. AE, DC, MC, V.*

$–$$$ ⛫ **Hotel Mariahilf.** A comfortable old hotel in the center of things, the Mariahilf is just across the river from the Old City. Although the location is fairly busy, the rooms are quiet thanks to soundproofing. Those without private bath rate in the $ category. ✉ *Mariahilferstr. 9, A– 8020,* ☎ *0316/713163–0,* ℻ *0361/717652. 44 rooms, 33 with bath. Restaurant. AE, DC, MC, V.*

$$ ⛫ **Rosenhotel Steiermark.** An exceptional value, this recent and very modern student accommodation, two blocks northeast of the university, functions as a hotel from early July until late September. Naturally, it attracts a young crowd and has an institutional feel, but if you want a clean room with a private bath at a low price, this is a good choice. ✉ *Liebigg. 4, A–8010,* ☎ *0316/381–503–0,* ℻ *0316/381– 503–62. 121 rooms with bath. Restaurant, bar, parking. AE, DC, MC, V. Closed Oct.–June.*

$ ⛫ **Hotel Strasser.** This friendly budget hotel, just two blocks south of the main train station, offers acceptable accommodations at rock-bottom prices. There is no elevator, the toilets are down the hall, and it is a bit noisy, but the rooms are large, comfortable, and clean, and the cozy restaurant is a good value. ✉ *Eggenberger Gürtel 11, A–8020,* ☎ *0316/713977,* ℻ *0316/916856. 40 rooms with bath. Restaurant, parking. No credit cards.*

Nightlife and the Arts

Graz is noted for its avant-garde theater and its opera, concerts, and jazz. The Graz tourist office distributes the quarterly "Graz Guide," with information in English, and the "Graz Stadtanzeiger" (City Informer), a free monthly guide in German.

The **Styriarte** festival (late June to mid-July), under the direction of Nikolaus Harnoncourt, gathers outstanding musicians from around the world. Performances take place at Schloss Eggenburg and various halls in Graz. For program details contact the tourist office (☞ Visitor Information *in* Eastern Austria A to Z, *below*) or Styriarte (✉ Palais Attems, Sackstr. 17, A–8010 Graz, ☎ 0316/825–000, ℻ 0316/877–3836).

The annual **Styrian Autumn Festival** (Steirische Herbst), a sometimes shocking celebration of the avant-garde in experimental theater, music, opera, dance, jazz, film, video, and other performing arts, is held in Graz in October. Contact Styriarte (☞ *above*) or the tourist office for details.

The 19th-century **Graz Opera House** (✉ Kaiser-Josef-Pl. 10, ☎ 0316/ 8000, ℻ 0316/8008–565), with its resplendent rococo interior, was completely renovated in 1984. Famed as a showcase for young talent and experimental productions as well as more conventional works, it stages three to five performances a week late September–June. Tickets are generally available until shortly before the performances; call for information.

Graz, a major university town, has a lively theater scene known especially for its experimental productions. Its **Schauspielhaus,** built in 1825, is the leading playhouse, and there are smaller theaters scattered around town. Contact the tourist office for current offerings.

Popular **candlelight concerts** are held in the Eggenberg Palace on Monday evenings from mid-July to mid-September at 8 PM. Ask the Graz tourist office for details. During July and August, students and, occasionally, faculty of the **American Institute of Musical Studies** (AIMS) (☎ 0316/327066, FAX 0316/325574) offer concerts. For information, check with the tourist office or the institute.

Graz's **after-hours scene** is centered on the area around Prokopigasse, Bürgergasse, and Glockenspielplatz. Here you'll find activity until the early morning hours. The crowd moves around, so check with the tourist office for the current "in" spots. The **Casino Graz** (✉ Landhausg. 10, ☎ 0316/832578) at the corner of Landhausgasse and Schmiedgasse in the Old City, is open daily from 3 PM. It offers French and American roulette, blackjack, baccarat, and punto banco. The entrance fee of AS260 gets you AS300 worth of chips. A passport is required, you must be at least 21, and men are expected to wear a jacket and tie.

Shopping

Be on the lookout for traditional skirts, trousers, jackets, and coats of gray and dark green woolen loden cloth; dirndls; modern sportswear and ski equipment; handwoven garments; and objects of wrought iron. The **Heimatwerk** shop at Paulustorgasse 4 is associated with the local folklore museum and stocks a good variety of regional crafts and products. For a wide selection of conventional goods, try the leading department store, **Kastner & Öhler,** at Sackstrasse 7, just off the Hauptplatz.

The many smart **boutiques** in the streets surrounding Sackstrasse carry typical cosmopolitan wares.

Stübing bei Graz

🖐 ㉕   *15 km (9 mi) northwest of Graz.*

The attraction in Stübing bei Graz is the **Austrian Open-Air Museum** (Österreichisches Freilichtmuseum), which covers some 100 acres of hilly woodland. Here is a fascinating collection of about 80 authentic farmhouses, barns, Alpine huts, working water mills, forges, and other rural structures dating from the 16th century through the early 20th century, moved to this site from every province of Austria. Buildings that otherwise would have been lost in the rush to "progress" have been preserved complete with their original furnishings. Most of the buildings are open to visitors, and in several artisans can be seen at work, sometimes in period costume. There is a restaurant and outdoor café by the entrance. You can reach Stübing bei Graz from Graz via Route 67 to Gratkorn, by train (15 minutes) to Stübing and a 2-km (1-mi) walk from there, or by municipal bus (40 minutes) from Lendplatz. ✉ *Stübing bei Graz,* ☎ *03124/53700.* ⚑ *AS75.* ☉ *Apr.–Oct., Tues.–Sun. 9–5 (last admission at 4).*

Piber

★ 🖐 ㉖   *44 km (27 mi) west of Graz.*

The hamlet of Piber on the northeast outskirts of Köflach (take Route 70 to and beyond Köflach) is devoted to raising horses, and from the **Lipizzaner Stud Farm** come the world-famous stallions that perform at the Spanish Riding School in Vienna (☞ The Hofburg *in* Chapter 2). These snow-white horses trace their lineage back to 1580, when Archduke Karl of Styria established a stud farm at Lipiza near Trieste, using stallions from Arabia and mares from Spain. After World War I, when Austria lost Lipiza, the farm was transferred to Piber. Born black, the steeds gradually turn white between the ages of two and seven. To get to Piber from Graz you can drive (take Route 70) or take a bus (75 minutes) or a train (about an hour), with departures every hour or two. Some trains split en route; be sure to board the correct car. Walk or take a taxi the 3 km (2 mi) between Köflach and Piber. ✉ *Bundesgestüt Piber,* ☎ *03144/3323.* ▣ *Tour AS100.* ◷ *Apr.–Oct.; 1-hr tour 9, 10:15, 1:30, and 3:15.*

Bärnbach

33 km (21 mi) west of Graz, 3 km (2 mi) north of Voitsburg.

Bärnbach offers the amazing visual sight of the **Church of St. Barbara.** Completely redone in 1988 by the contemporary Austrian painter Friedensreich Hundertwasser, its exterior is a fantasy of abstract religious symbols in brilliant colors and shapes.

At the interesting **Stölzle Glass Center,** you can watch glass blowing and purchase original glass articles. ✉ *Hochregisterstr. 1,* ☎ *03142/ 62950.* ▣ *AS55.* ◷ *Nov.–Mar., weekdays 9–1; Apr.–Oct., weekdays and Sun. 9–1.*

THROUGH STYRIA TO VIENNA

The mountainous green heartland of Styria embraces a region where ancient Romans once worked the surrounding mines of what are accurately called the Iron Alps. Here in West Styria, the atmosphere can change abruptly from industrial to tourist and can often combine the two—as at the Erzberg, literally a mountain of iron. The prime destination, however, remains Mariazell. In the past, royalty—not only the Habsburgs but princes of foreign countries as well—went there, not for social pleasures but for religious reasons, for Mariazell has a double personality. It is a summer and winter pleasure resort and a renowned place of pilgrimage. The evening candlelit processions through the village to its famed basilica are beautiful and inspiring.

To tour this region, you can head southwest—after a scenic ride north through the Mur Valley to the historic crossroads of Bruck an der Mur— to Judenburg and possibly Murau and even continue into Salzburg province. Another option is to start toward Judenburg but turn northwest beyond Leoben to the abbey at Admont and then either return to Bruck via Eisenerz or continue north through Upper Austria to Amstetten or via Steyr to Linz on the Danube. Back at Bruck an der Mur, where several highways and rail lines converge, you can head north to Mariazell and then continue on one of the country's most scenic mountain drives (or rail trips) back to the Danube Valley.

Peggau

㉗ *20 km (12 mi) north of Graz.*

Just north of the industrial town of Peggau (rail stop: Peggau-Deutschfeistritz) is the famous **Lurgrotte,** the largest stalactite and stalagmite cave in Austria. Conducted tours lasting an hour follow a subterranean stream past illuminated sights, and there is a small restaurant at the entrance. To get to Peggau from Graz, head north on Route 67, driving through the heavily forested, narrow Mur Valley toward Bruck an der Mur. (A rail line parallels the road, with trains every hour or two making local stops near the points of interest.) ☎ *03127/2580.* ▣ *Tours AS50.* ◷ *Apr.–Oct., daily 9–4.*

Mixnitz

20 km (12 mi) north of Peggau.

㉘ Mixnitz is the starting point for a rugged 4½-hour hike through the wild **Bärenschützklamm,** a savage gorge that can be negotiated only on steps and ladders but is nevertheless worth visiting for its spectacular foaming waterfalls. Beyond it are peaceful mountain meadows and finally the 5,650-ft **Hochlantsch** mountain.

Bruck an der Mur

㉙ *55 km (34 mi) north of Graz.*

Bruck an der Mur is known primarily as Styria's major traffic junction, a point where four valleys and two rivers converge and where several highways and main rail lines come together. Although most of the busy town is devoted to industry, its compact historic center, dating partially from the 13th century, is well worth a short visit.

The architecturally distinguished main square, **Koloman-Wallisch-Platz,** is four blocks west of the train station. On the square's northeast corner stands the late-15th-century **Kornmesserhaus,** a magnificent example of secular architecture in the late-Gothic style, noted especially for its elaborate loggia and arcades. The filigreed **Eiserner Brunnen** is across the square. This ornamental wrought-iron well housing dating from 1620 is considered to be the best piece of ironwork in Styria, a province noted for its metalwork. The **Rathaus** (Town Hall) facing it is also attractive and houses a small museum of local life (⊠ Heimatmuseum, ☎ 03862/51521–0). On the hill behind the square is the **Pfarrkirche** (Parish Church), built between the 13th and 15th centuries, which has an interesting late-Gothic sacristy door of wrought iron.

Overlooking the town, just two blocks northeast of its center, are the remains of **Burg Landskron,** a 13th-century fortress that once defended the confluence of the Mur and Mürz rivers. Today only its clock tower remains intact, but the view is worth the short climb. The small park surrounding the Landskron ruins, on the Schlossberg hill, makes a wonderful spot for a picnic. Buy your supplies at one of the shops in the streets below.

Dining

$$$ ✕ **Schnepf'n Wirt.** This comfortably elegant country inn is well regarded
★ locally for its imaginative variations on Austrian cuisine. It is on the western edge of town, in the hamlet of Unteraich along the Mur River. Among the dishes you might find are a parfait of goose liver with leafy salad, fillet of sole with asparagus, beef tournedos broiled with horseradish crust, and chocolate mousse with fresh berries. Ask about the excellent regional wines, although others are also available. ⊠ *Unteraich 23,* ☎ *03862/51474. AE, DC, MC, V. Closed Mon.–Tues. and 2 wks in Aug. No dinner Sun.*

Leoben

㉚ *16 km (10 mi) southwest of Bruck an der Mur.*

Interesting side trips fan out in several directions from the main junction of Bruck an der Mur. One takes you southwest by car (Route S6), train, or bus to Leoben, the largest town in central Styria and the center of an important mining and heavy-industry region. Most of the attractions are in the charming **Altstadt** (Old City), near the Hauptplatz. Here, six blocks south of the train station, you will find some historic sights, including the **Altes Rathaus** (Old City Hall) of 1568, the **Pest-**

säule (Plague Column) of 1717, and the handsome 17th-century **Hackl-haus** with its densely decorated Baroque facade. Walking one block west brings you to the **Museum der Stadt Leoben** (⊠ Kirchg. 6, ☎ 03842/4062–227), a municipal museum of local history, industry, art, and nature. Next door is the **Stadtpfarrkirche** (City Parish Church) of 1660; a block to the south is the **Mautturm** (Customs Tower) of 1615, locally called the *Schwammerl,* because it resembles a mushroom.

Across the Mur River from the Mautturm is the **Maria-am-Wasser Kirche,** a Gothic church with outstanding 15th-century stained-glass windows.

The suburb of Göss, 2 km (1 mi) south, is home of the famous Gösser beer, made in a former monastery founded in 1020. The small beer museum is open Friday–Monday, noon–8 PM; the **brewery** itself may be toured by prior arrangement (⊠ Brauhausstr., ☎ 03842/2090–0).

Lodging

$$ 🏨 **Brücklwirt.** This low-slung, modern hotel-restaurant on the main highway through Niklasdorf, 5 km (3 mi) northeast of Leoben, is quieter since the advent of the autobahn, but passing trains are still noisy. The rooms are smallish but comfortable, and the tiled baths are immaculate and bright; rooms in the back are quieter and have a magnificent view across green fields to the hills beyond. The restaurant serves a worthy selection of regional and Austrian specialties. In summer, dining on the candlelit terrace is a delight. ⊠ *Leobener Str. 90, A–8712 Leoben/Niklasdorf,* ☎ *03842/81727,* FAX *03842/81727–5. 21 rooms with bath. Restaurant, indoor pool, sauna, tennis, parking. AE, DC, MC, V.*

Seckau

③ *33 km (20½ mi) southwest of Leoben.*

For 550 years Seckau was the episcopal center of Styria, and its abbey is well worth a detour. The famed **Seckau Abbey** was founded in 1140 and over the years has been a significant religious center. The original Romanesque style of its church is visible despite later additions, and the complex contains several outstanding features of various periods, from the late-Renaissance mausoleum of Archduke Karl II to the strikingly modern apocalyptic frescoes in the Angels' Chapel by the 20th-century painter Herbert Boeckl. The whole complex of buildings bears rich testimony to the wealth that was lavished upon it—from stained-glass windows to wrought-iron fittings, paintings, and sculptures. The abbey is north of the small industrial town of Knittelfeld, which is southwest of Leoben on Route S6/E7. ☎ *03514/234–300.* 💰 *Donation requested.* ☉ *Tour Sun. at 11:45 and 2:45, other days and times by appointment.*

Judenburg

③ *15 km (9 mi) southwest of Knittelfeld.*

The ancient and attractive hill town of Judenburg overlooks the steelworks along the Upper Mur River valley. Its origins date to prehistoric times—the famous Strettweg Ritual Chariot (now on display at Schloss Eggenberg in Graz) was found here—but the town's name derives from a medieval colony of Jewish merchants.

From its Hauptplatz rises the lofty **Stadtturm,** a 240-ft-high watchtower built between 1449 and 1520, which you can ascend. The tower is open May and June, Friday–Sunday 10–6; July–September, daily 10–6; and October, Friday–Sunday 10–5. The early 16th-century **Pfarrkirche** next to the Stadtturm has some excellent sculptures, especially of the Virgin Mary.

The small **Stadtmuseum** around the corner offers dioramas depicting local history and a display of minerals from nearby mines. ⊠ *Kaserng. 27*, ☎ *03572/85053*. ⊠ *Donation requested*. ⊙ *Weekdays 9–noon*.

Just across the river from the Stadtmuseum, on Feldgasse, stands the 12th-century **Magdalenenkirche,** a Romanesque church with 14th-century frescoes and medieval stained-glass windows.

Murau

★ ㉝   *47 km (29½ mi) west of Judenburg.*

Murau is a stunningly picturesque, well-preserved medieval town where you can see stretches of the ancient town wall; the Pfarrkirche from 1296 with its ancient frescoes and late-Gothic "lantern of the dead" in the churchyard; the dominating Schloss Obermurau, a 13th-century castle that was rebuilt in the 17th century; and the Altes Rathaus, the Old Town Hall that was once a part of the fortifications. Stroll along the river, looking up at the timbered houses atop the wall, to get the full effect of the town's medieval defensive character.

The **Murau brewery** (⊠ Raffaltpl. 17), with more than 500 years' brewing tradition, has a small museum and a souvenir shop, but stop in the ground-floor Brauhaus restaurant to sample the brews and possibly have a filling meal of Styrian specialties as well.

If you ever dreamed of becoming a steam-locomotive engineer (*Lokführer*), Murau is your place. The narrow-gauge **Murtalbahn** (Mur Valley Railroad), which is more than 100 years old and is operated by the Steiermärkische Landesbahnen (Styrian Provincial Railways), gives engine-driving lessons on Thursday from early July until early September, ranging from 15 minutes on just a locomotive to longer periods with passenger cars attached; bring your friends, stock the bar car, and hire the local brass band to provide inspiration while you shovel the coal! The steam line also provides regular passenger service on the 37-km (23-mi) stretch between Murau and Tamsweg several days a week from late June to mid-September. ☎ *03532/2233 or 0316/2231–20.*

Eisenerz

★ ㉞   *30 km (18¾ mi) northwest of Leoben.*

The old mining town of Eisenerz is fascinating not only for its own attractions but also for the huge mountain of remarkably pure iron ore next to it. The community huddles around the Gothic parish church of **St. Oswald,** first built in 1282 and fortified as a bastion against the invading Turks in 1532. Its fantastically embellished interior is well worth seeing. West of the parish church stands the famous **Schichtturm,** an old tower whose bell once signaled the change of shifts at the mines.

The 17th-century building now housing the **Eisenerz Stadtmuseum** was converted to an elegant hunting lodge by Emperor Francis Joseph; the museum today is devoted to mining and ironworking, as well as to local life and culture. ⊠ *Im Kammerhof,* ☎ *03848/3615.* ⊠ *AS36.* ⊙ *May–Oct., daily 9–5; Nov.–Apr., Tues.–Fri. 9–noon.*

Just south of the town is its reason for being: the rust-colored, towering **Erzberg.** This mountain of iron ore has been worked since ancient times and still yields an ore that is 34% pure iron. Its present height is about 4,800 ft, although it was once much higher. Strip mining has given it a steplike appearance, similar to that of a ziggurat. Guided *Schaubergwerke* tours lasting about 1½ hours are conducted through the underground workings. It's cool inside no matter what the outside temperature, so take warm clothing. You can also tour the great stepped workings; transportation is via a crawler-truck fitted with seats. The trip takes about an hour. ✉ *Lower station of cableway, near road from Präbichl,* ☎ *03848/4531–470 or 03848/3700.* ⛺ *Schaubergwerke AS120, Tagebau (open mines) AS140, both tours AS230.* ⊙ *Schaubergwerke tour May–Oct., daily at 10, 12:30, and 3; Tagebau tour May–Oct., daily by appointment with ticket office.*

Near Erzberg, southeast on Route 115, is the 6,250-ft **Polster** mountain, which can be ascended by chairlift, offering great panoramic views to the west across the iron mountain.

En Route
★ Route 115 between Trofaiach and Hieflau to the northwest takes you through the scenic **Erzbach Valley,** with sensational vistas of snowcapped peaks to the southwest. The highway passes through the ancient mining town of **Vordernberg,** where Romans once worked with iron. Northeast of Eisenerz is a hidden mountain lake of great beauty, the **Leopoldsteiner See,** worth the slight detour. Between Hieflau to Admont, Route 112 parallels the spectacular **Gesäuse Ravine,** where the Enns River with its plunging waterfalls surges through limestone formations. The magnificent 7,770-ft Hochtor peak can be seen to the south. This is among the wildest scenery in the Alps, and it's a favorite challenge for rock climbers.

Admont

★ ㉟ *40 km (25 mi) west of Eisenerz.*

The small market town of Admont is dominated by its famous Benedictine abbey, **Stift Admont,** founded in the 11th century but almost entirely rebuilt after a disastrous fire in 1865. Of the earlier structures, only the glorious Baroque **library** survived intact. Fortunately, its treasures were also saved and are on view, including a Bible belonging to Martin Luther and a New Testament edited by Erasmus. The main building, 236 ft long, contains some 150,000 volumes and is noted for its 18th-century ceiling frescoes by Bartholomeo Altomonte as well as for its statues called *The Four Last Things* (Death, Judgment, Hell, and Heaven). There is also an extensive natural-history museum with lots of insects, an art museum, and a museum of local life. Many travelers visit this abbey from Bruck an der Mur, crossing mountainous country through western Styria, via Routes S6, 113, and A9 almost to Liezen, then east Route 117 east. The total distance is 100 km (62 mi); both trains and a limited bus service operate over the entire route, with changes required. ☎ *03613/2312–47.* ⛺ *AS40.* ⊙ *May–Sept., daily 10–1 and 2–5; Apr. and Oct., daily 10–noon and 2–4; Nov.–Mar. by appointment.*

Thörl

㊱ *15 km (9 mi) north of Bruck an der Mur.*

A popular excursion from Bruck an der Mur takes you north to Mariazell, a historic pilgrimage center. Along the way on Route 20, you'll discover the village of Thörl, dominated by the ruined 15th-century stronghold of **Schloss Schachenstein** (privately owned). Nearby stands a curious roadside chapel with an unusually carved Calvary dating from 1530. Just north is the popular mountain health resort of **Aflenz Kurort,** from which a chairlift ascends the 5,110-ft Bürgeralm. It operates daily during the ski season, but only Friday–Monday and on holidays the rest of the year. The village church, dating partially from the 12th century, is noted for its rustic stonework.

♻ The delightful narrow-gauge **Thörler Bahn** railroad (☎ 03862/221–2910), which marked its 100th anniversary in 1993, runs with its steam locomotives from Kapfenberg to Thörl-Aflenz on selected Tuesdays, Saturdays, and Sundays late June–mid-September. The rambling trip takes 1½ hours.

En Route Headed north on Route 20, you'll climb to over 4,000 ft as the road crosses the **Seeberg Pass,** from which you can see the surrounding mountain ranges of Hochschwab and Veitschalpe. A descent to the valley is followed by another rise to Mariazell.

Mariazell

37 *42 km (26¼ mi) north of Thörl.*

An excursion to Mariazell—famed for its pilgrimage church and gingerbread—is an adventure, thanks to the winding road that brings you there. The town has been a place of pilgrimage since 1157, when the Benedictines established a priory here. After Louis I, King of Hungary, attributed his victory over the Turks in 1377 to the intervention of its Virgin, Mariazell's reputation for miracles began to spread. As a year-round resort, Mariazell offers a wide range of sports and recreation; in winter there's a good ski school for beginners and young people.

The impressive **Mariazeller Basilica** stands resolutely over the town square. The present structure replaced the original church during the 14th century and was itself enlarged in the late 17th century by the Italian architect Domenico Sciassia. Its exterior is unusual, with the original Gothic spire and porch flanked by squat, bulbous Baroque towers. Step inside to see the incredibly elaborate plasterwork and paintings. In the **Gnadenkapelle** (Chapel of Miracles), the nave holds the main object of pilgrimage: the 12th-century statue of the Virgin of Mariazell. It stands under a silver baldachin designed in 1727 by the younger Fischer von Erlach and behind a silver grille donated by Empress Maria Theresa, who took her first communion here. Following her example, thousands of youngsters neatly turned out in white are brought annually from all over Austria to Mariazell for their first communion, usually on or around Whitsun. The **high altar** of 1704, by the elder Fischer von Erlach—the leading architect of the Austrian Baroque—is in the east end of the nave. Don't miss seeing the **Schatzkammer** (treasury) for its collection of votive offerings from medieval times to the present. Walls are covered with plaques, many of them illustrated, given in thanks for assorted blessings, including rescues ranging from runaway horses to shipwrecks. ▨ *Basilica free, Schatzkammer 20AS.* ☉ *Schatzkammer May–Oct. 30, weekdays 10:30–noon and 2–3, weekends 10–3.*

Pay a visit to the **Heimatmuseum** (Regional Museum of Local Life), at Wienerstrasse 35. Bruno Habertheuer's **mechanical Nativity figurines** are at the **stations of the cross** on Calvary Hill (⊠ Kalvarienberg 1, ☎ 03382/2366). The nativity scene with its 130 moving figures took 18 years to build. Admission to the museum is AS10.

♻ The **Museumtramway,** the world's oldest steam tramway, dating to 1884, operates between Mariazell and the Erlaufsee, for a 20-minute ride of about 3½ km (2 mi) to a lovely lake. For AS150 extra charge, you can accompany the engineer in the cab. ⊠ *Bahnhof Mariazell,* ☎ *03882/3014,* ℻ *03882/3393.* ▨ *Round-trip AS50.* ☉ *July–Sept., weekends, hourly 9:30–late afternoon.*

The famous narrow-gauge **Mariazellerbahn** rail line ambles over an 84-km (52½ mi) route between Mariazell and St. Pölten, coursing magnificent valleys and surmounting mountain passes in the process. This remarkable engineering achievement—the line incorporates 21 tunnels and 75 bridges and viaducts—was built in 1907 and electrified in 1911. The cars are modern but the sensation is one of ages long past. About five trains a day traverse the route in each direction. In St. Pölten, the narrow-gauge line connects with the main east–west rail route. For schedules, contact the Austrian Federal Railways system (☎ 03882/2366).

Dining and Lodging

$$ ✕ **Jägerwirt.** In what is basically a tourist town, this restaurant, directly across from the basilica, offers traditional country atmosphere and solid Austrian cuisine at fair prices. Besides the usual steaks and Wiener schnitzels, the menu may include such items as boiled pork with grated horseradish and breast of veal with dumplings. ✉ *Hauptpl. 2,* ☎ *03882/2362. No credit cards. Closed Mon., most of Dec., and 2 wks around Easter.*

$$$ 🏨 **Hotel Feichtegger.** Although this is a five-story modern hotel near the basilica and the cable car, its ambience is one of quiet, understated luxury. The well-equipped guest rooms have balconies. ✉ *Wiener Str. 6, A–8630,* ☎ *03882/2416–0,* 🅵🅰🆇 *03882/2416–80. 48 rooms with bath. Restaurant, bar, indoor pool, sauna, exercise room. AE, DC, MC, V. Closed 2 wks in mid-Dec.*

$$$ 🏨 **Mariazellerhof.** This small, cheerfully modern chalet-style hotel one block west of the basilica is known for its gingerbread snacks; the spicy aroma fills the house. Its comfortable rooms have balconies. ✉ *Grazer Str. 10, A–8630,* ☎ *03882/2179–0,* 🅵🅰🆇 *03882/2179–51. 10 rooms with bath, 4 with shower. Café. DC, MC. Closed last 3 wks of Jan.*

Outdoor Activities and Sports

The skiing on 4,150-ft **Bürgeralpe** is quickly reached by the Bürgeralpebahn cable car from a lower station just two blocks north of the basilica. Paths from the upper station fan out in several directions for country walks in summer. ✉ *Wienerstr. 28,* ☎ *03882/2555.* 🎫 *Roundtrip AS85.* ☉ *Late Apr.–June, early–mid-Oct., and mid- to late Nov., daily 9–5; July–Aug., daily 8:30–5:30; Sept., daily 8:30–5; Dec., daily 8–4; Jan.–Mar., daily 8–5.*

Shopping

Parts of town are permeated by the spicy aroma of baking **gingerbread** for which Mariazell is famous, and you'll see the decorated cookies everywhere.

THE MOUNTAIN ROUTE TO VIENNA

The most direct route from Bruck an der Mur northward to Vienna is also in some ways the most interesting. It takes you through the cradle of Austrian skiing, past several popular resorts, and over the scenic Semmering Pass and offers an opportunity to ride a 19th-century steam cogwheel train to the top of the highest mountain in this part of the country, a peak that often remains snowcapped into the summer. It also takes you to Wiener Neustadt, a small, historic city. This area's proximity to Vienna makes day trips or weekend excursions from the capital practical.

Mürzzuschlag

❸❽ *37 km (23 mi) northeast of Bruck an der Mur, 92 km (57 mi) north of Graz.*

The resort town of Mürzzuschlag is popular for both winter and summer sports. From Bruck an der Mur, head northeast on S6, past the industrial town of Kapfenberg, and take the exit marked for the resort. It is regarded as the birthplace of Austrian skiing and, in a sense, of the Winter Olympics, since the first Nordic Games were held here in 1904, but the main focus of ski activity has long since moved west to the Tirol.

Mürzzuschlag is popular with the Viennese and preserves its past glories in the excellent **Winter-Sports-Museum,** which displays equipment past and present from around the world. ⊠ *Wiener Str. 79,* ☎ *03852/ 3504.* ⊑ *AS30.* ⊙ *Tues.–Sun. 9–noon and 2–5.*

The **Brahms Museum,** Austria's only museum dedicated to composer Johannes Brahms, a German who adopted Austria as his home, is in Mürzzuschlag, where he spent many summers. The museum also hosts a number of chamber music concerts and recitals. ⊠ *Wienerstr. 4.* ⊑ *AS40.* ⊙ *May–Sept., daily 10–noon and 2–6; Oct.–Apr., daily 2–6.*

Semmering

39 *14 km (8½ mi) northeast of Mürzzuschlag, 90 km (56¼ mi) southwest of Vienna.*

Climbing along Route 306, high atop the Semmering Pass, at a height of 3,230 ft, lies the boundary between the provinces of Styria and Lower Austria. A bridle path has existed on this mountainous route since at least the 12th century, but the first road was not built until 1728. Today's highway is an engineering wonder, particularly on the Lower Austrian side, where the new road high on concrete stilts leaps over deep valleys; the old road snakes up in a series of switchback curves. The Styrian side is less dramatic, but offers distant alpine vistas. Given the technologies of the era, the railway—completed in 1854—that crosses the divide is a technical marvel, with its great viaducts and tunnels, and is still the main north–south rail route. At the top is Semmering, the first town in Lower Austria, a resort on a south-facing slope overlooking the pass. Sheltered by pine forests and built on terraces reaching as high as 4,250 ft, Semmering is considered to have a healthy atmosphere and has several spa-type hotels and pensions. The Semmering area plus the nearby Rax and Schneeberg regions are immensely popular in winter with the Viennese skiers. This is the area in which most Viennese first learn to ski, meaning that there are slopes ranging from gentle to the more challenging, although they are no match for the rugged Alpine stretches of Tirol and Salzburg province.

OFF THE
BEATEN PATH

HÖLLENTAL – A delightful side trip can be made from Semmering into the Höllental (Valley of Hell), an extremely narrow and romantic gorge cut by the Schwarza stream between two high mountains, the Raxalpe and the Schneeberg (snow mountain). From Hirschwang, at the beginning of the valley you can ride the **Raxbahn cable car** to a plateau on the Raxalpe at 5,075 ft. ☎ *02666/52497.* ⊑ *Round-trip AS185.* ⊙ *High season, daily 8–5:30 at ½-hr intervals; other months, daily 9–4:30 at ½-hr intervals.*

Dining and Lodging

$$$ ✕⌂ **Panoramahotel Wagner.** The view over the surrounding mountains provides the setting for this renovated hotel, which delights in the personal touch. The kitchen has established itself as the best in the area; try the lamb or fish. The excellent beer comes from a tiny brewery in the valley below. ⊠ *Hochstr. 267, A–2680,* ☎ *02664/2512–0,* FAX *02664/2512–61. 26 rooms with bath. Restaurant, sauna. DC, MC. Closed Wed.–Thurs. and Oct.–mid-Dec.*

$$–$$$ ✗🍽 **Belvedere.** Recently renovated, this old Alpine-style mountain inn is well known for its hearty Austrian food. Though located in town, it has an outdoor garden for dining in fine weather. Expect to find such offerings as fresh cream of asparagus soup, pork chops, and roast chicken. ✉ *Hochstr. 60, A–2680,* ☎ *02664/2270. 19 rooms with bath. Restaurant, indoor pool, sauna. AE, DC, MC, V. Closed mid- to late Apr.*

$$$–$$$$ 🍽 **Hotel Panhans.** This classic and popular mountain lodge resort is set near the center of town; it is frequently booked for conventions. Built in 1888, the main lodge has retained its characteristic Art Nouveau ambience despite a 1982 modernization. In 1993 a luxurious annex connected by an enclosed walkway was added behind the main building; it offers imaginative minisuites for honeymooners, stargazers (telescopes provided), and those who want their own open hearth. The elegant *Kaiser Karl* restaurant is ambitious but inconsistent and occasionally disappointing; the more relaxed *Wintergarten* restaurant is a better choice. Wines are excellent, and the hotel has its own Vinotek for tastings. ✉ *Hochstr. 32, A–2680,* ☎ *02664/8181–0,* ℻ *02664/8181–513. 112 rooms with bath. Restaurant, bar, café, indoor pool, sauna, exercise room, dance club. AE, DC, V.*

Puchberg am Schneeberg

④⓪ *33 km (21 mi) north of Semmering.*

People flock to the quiet mountain resort of Puchberg am Schneeberg largely to ride to the top of the Schneeberg mountain, Lower Austria's highest peak. You get to Puchberg via regular trains from Vienna, Wiener Neustadt, or points south. From Vienna, the railroads have a package ticket that includes the regular rail connection, the cog railway, and a chit for lunch at one of the mountaintop restaurants. From Höllental, continue north into the alley for 18 km (11 mi), passing through the wildest section, to Schwarzau im Gebirge. Then circle the north slope of the Schneeberg via the Klostertal to the resort.

☺ The marvelous, old narrow-gauge **Puchberg cog-wheel steam train** ascends to a plateau near Schneeberg's summit. Although many use the rail line as a starting point for mountain hiking, the journey itself is an exciting outing. Allow the better part of a day for this trip, since the ride takes 1⅓ hours each way and the trains are none too frequent, some running on a schedule and others according to demand. This excursion is very popular; make reservations well in advance—particularly for weekends and holidays—at any rail station in Europe. If you don't already have them, make reservations at Puchberg for the return down trip before you board for the trip up. Bring along a light sweater or jacket even in summer; it can be both windy and cool at the top. Ordinary walking shoes are sufficient unless you wander off the main trails, in which case you'll need hiking boots, along with some mountain experience.

The steam engines, dating from the 1890s, are built at a peculiar angle to the ground to keep their fireboxes level while climbing. The wooden cars they haul are of equal vintage, with hard seats. A rest stop is made at the **Baumgartner Haus,** where you can get refreshments before continuing up past the timberline and through two tunnels (close the windows or suffocate!). Near the upper station hut at altitude 5,892 ft is the small **Elizabeth Chapel** and the **Berghaus Hochschneeberg,** a simple lodge with a restaurant and overnight guest facilities. From here, you can walk to the **Kaiserstein** for a panoramic view and to the **Klosterwappen** peak, at 6,811 ft above sea level. Real stick-to-your-ribs mountain food, draft beer, and plenty of gemütlichkeit are served up at the inexpensive **Damböck Haus,** a rustic hut operated by the Austrian Touring Club (*ÖTK*). It's only a 15-minute walk from the upper station of the Puchberg line.

Allow about two to three hours total for these walks. Maps are available at the lodge. The last train down usually leaves about 4:30 or 5:30 PM; later runs are made if traffic warrants. Eurailpass and Euro Domino card holders may use their passes but must make seat reservations. ⊠ *Schneeberg Bahn, Bahnhof Puchberg,* ☎ *02636/2225–0.* ☒ *Round-trip AS250.* ☽ *Late Apr.–early Nov.*

Lodging

$ 🏠 **Berghaus Hochschneeberg.** The only way to reach this simple mountaintop lodge, other than by climbing, is by the famous old steam cog railway from Puchberg. You arrive to find panoramic views and a sturdy stone hotel, as old as the railway (1898), set in peaceful surroundings. Although there are few modern conveniences (one bathroom per floor, running water in rooms, TV only in the reception room), staying here is an invigorating experience. There are wonderful paths to hike. ⊠ *Hochschneeberg, A–2734,* ☎ *02636/2257. 25 rooms without bath. Restaurant, sauna. No credit cards. Closed Nov.–Apr.*

Wiener Neustadt

41   *19 km (12 mi) southeast of Puchberg am Schneeberg, 45 km (28¼ mi) south of Vienna, 38 km (23¾ mi) northeast of Semmering, 27 km (16¾ mi) west of Eisenstadt.*

Although today's Wiener Neustadt is a busy industrial center built on the ashes of its prewar self, enough of its past glories survived World War II's bombings to make a visit worthwhile. The small city was established in 1194 as a fortress to protect Vienna from the Hungarians. During the mid-15th century it was an imperial residence, and in 1752 it became, and still is, the seat of the Austrian Military Academy.

Begin your exploration of the Old City at the **Hauptplatz,** the largely traffic-free main square, which contains several rebuilt medieval houses with Gothic arcades standing opposite the 16th-century **Rathaus** (City Hall).

The mighty **Stadtpfarrkirche** (Town Parish Church), also known as the Liebfrauenkirche, rises imposingly out of the center of Domplatz, or cathedral square. Begun in the 13th century, the church had cathedral status from 1468 until 1784, and a number of choirs and chapels were added during that period. Note the ornate entryway on the south side, dating to about 1230. Styles are mixed between Roman and Gothic, but the interior is impressive for its unity of columned walls and ribbed ceiling. Look for the painted wooden figures of the Apostles dating to about 1500, a mural of the Last Judgment from about 1300, and the splendid tomb of Cardinal Khlesl with a bust carved in 1630 attributed to the school of Giovanni Bernini, the master of the Italian Baroque.

A narrow lane called the Puchheimgasse leads to the 12th-century **Reckturm,** a defensive tower said to have been built with part of the ransom money paid to free Richard the Lion-Hearted. Down Baumkirchnerring at the corner of Wiener Strasse is the 14th-century **Church of St. Peter-an-der-Sperr,** once a defense cloister, now an exhibition gallery. The greatest treasure in the **Stadtmuseum,** which is in a one-time Jesuit residence on Wiener Strasse, is the *Corvinusbecher,* an elegant 32-inch-high goblet from 1487 that was a gift from the Hungarian king who conquered the town.

To the east of the Hauptplatz, on Neuklostergasse, is the **Neukloster Church,** part of a Cistercian convent founded in 1250. Behind the high altar in the richly Baroque interior is the tomb of Eleanor of Portugal (died 1467), wife of the emperor Frederick III.

The massive **Burg** on Grazer Strasse, a castle begun in the 13th century and rebuilt as an imperial residence in the 15th century, was designated the Austrian Military Academy by order of Empress Maria Theresa in 1752. The Nazis took it over in 1938, and its first German commandant was General Erwin Rommel, the Desert Fox. The complex was battered by bombing in 1943 and 1945 but subsequently rebuilt. Enter its grounds to visit the famous 15th-century **Church of St. George,** whose gable is decorated with, among others, 14 Habsburg coats of arms. Beneath the gable is a statue of Friedrich III curiously inscribed "A.E.I.O.U.," which some believe stand for the Latin words that mean "Austria will rule the world." Inside the church, under the steps of the high altar, the remains of Emperor Maximilian I are buried.

Dining and Lodging

$$$–$$$$ ✕ **Gelbes Haus.** The 1906 Art Deco "Yellow House" slightly north of the center offers limited but outstandingly prepared dishes served in tasteful surroundings. Look for consommé with meat-filled strudel, Tafelspitz and breast of duck with goose liver, and, for dessert, figs with apple-cinnamon parfait. The homemade sherbets are also outstanding. The wine selection is broad, by the glass as well as the bottle. ⊠ *Kaiserbrunng. 11,* ☎ *02622/26400. DC, MC, V. Closed Sun.*

$$$ ✕🏨 **Hotel Corvinus.** A low, modern, and exceptionally pleasant hotel next to the city park, the recently built Corvinus is two blocks east of the train station and only a few minutes' stroll from the main square. It caters primarily to business travelers. The restaurant is recommended. ⊠ *Bahng. 29–33, A–2700,* ☎ *02622/24134,* 𝖥𝖠𝖷 *02622/ 24139. 68 rooms with bath. Restaurant, bar, sauna, meeting rooms. AE, DC, MC, V.*

Nightlife and the Arts

The **Wiesen Jazz Festival** attracts top-name performers from America and around the world for a couple of days in early July in Wiesen, Burgenland (12 km/7½ mi, southeast of Wiener Neustadt). For information, contact Landesverband Burgenland Tourismus (☞ Visitor Information *in* Eastern Austria A to Z, *below*).

EASTERN AUSTRIA A TO Z

Arriving and Departing

By Bus

There is good service to Neusiedl am See, Eisenstadt, and Güssing in Burgenland; Mariazell in Styria; and Wiener Neustadt in Lower Austria. Direct express service to Graz is infrequent. Most buses leave Vienna from the Wien Mitte Bus Station on Landstrasser Hauptstrasse, opposite the air terminal and Hilton Hotel, but be sure to check first, since some services to the south may depart from the bus terminal area at Südtirolerplatz, to the west of the Südbahnhof rail station. The major bus services connecting Vienna to towns in Eastern Austria are **Blaguss Reisen** (☎ 01/501–80–0, 𝖥𝖠𝖷 01/501–80–125) and **Bundesbus** (☎ 01/71101).

By Car

Two main autobahns traverse this region: the incomplete A3 between Vienna and Eisenstadt and the heavily traveled A2 between Vienna and past Wiener Neustadt to Graz and farther south. Northern Burgenland can be reached via the A4 autobahn east out of Vienna.

By Plane
The northern part of Eastern Austria is served by Vienna's international airport at Schwechat, 19 km (12 mi) southeast of the city center (☞ Vienna A to Z *in* Chapter 2).

Graz has its own international airport at Thalerhof, just south of the city, with flights to and from Vienna, Innsbruck, Linz, Paris, Munich, Frankfurt, Düsseldorf, and Zürich. Austrian Airlines and its subsidiary Tyrolean Airways, as well as Lufthansa, are the major carriers. Call for information (☎ 0316/2902–0).

By Train
Vienna and Graz are the logical rail arrival or departing points for this part of Austria. The main international north–south route connecting Vienna and northeastern Italy runs through this region and is traversed by EuroCity trains from Munich, Salzburg, Linz, Klagenfurt, and Venice, as well as other cities in neighboring countries. Nearly all long-distance trains going through this region meet at Bruck an der Mur, where connections can be made.

Getting Around

By Bus
Post office and railroad buses cover the area thoroughly, although services are less frequent in less populated areas further distant from city centers. Take trains for the main routes.

By Car
Driving is the best way to explore Eastern Austria, especially if you're visiting the smaller towns and villages or if your time is limited. Route 10 from Vienna to Lake Neusiedl in Burgenland is the preferred scenic alternative to the new A4 autobahn. Graz is connected to Vienna by both A2 and a more scenic mountain road, Route S6 over the Semmering Pass to Bruck an der Mur, then south through the Mur Valley. Driving in the Graz city center is not advisable, because there are many narrow, one-way, and pedestrian streets and few places to park.

By Streetcar
In Graz, streetcars and buses (☎ 0316/887411 information) are an excellent way of traveling within the city. Single tickets (AS20) can be bought from the driver, and one-day and multiple-ride tickets are also available. All six streetcar routes converge at Jakominiplatz near the south end of the Old City. One fare may combine streetcars and buses as long as you take a direct route to your destination.

By Taxi
In Graz, taxis can be ordered by phone (☎ 0316/878, 0316/899, 0316/222, or 0316/444).

By Train
If you're not driving, take trains on the main routes; services are fast and frequent. Trains depart from Vienna's Südbahnhof (South Station) hourly for the one-hour ride to Neusiedl am See. Connections can be made there for Eisenstadt and Pamhagen. There is also express service every two hours from the same station in Vienna to Graz, 2½ hours away, with intermediate stops at Wiener Neustadt, Mürzzuschlag, and Bruck an der Mur, and connections to Puchberg am Schneeberg, Semmering, and points west. Trains for Mariazell depart from Vienna's Westbahnhof (West Station), with a change at St. Pölten. Call for information (☎ 01/1717 departures from Vienna; 0316/1717 Graz's main station).

Contacts and Resources

Bicycling

Bicycling is enormously popular in the flatlands around Lake Neusiedl. Try the following for rentals: in **Illmitz,** Polay (⊠ Florianig. 5, ☎ 02175/3161); in **Mörbisch,** Posch (⊠ Blumentalg. 9, ☎ 02685/8242); in **Neusiedl am See,** Bahnhof (⊠ train station, ☎ 02167/8284) and Hotel Wende (⊠ Seestr. 40, ☎ 02167/8111−0); in **Podersdorf,** Fahrradverleih Tauber (⊠ Strandpl. 1, ☎ 02177/2204) and Rad-Sport Waldherr (⊠ Hauptstr. 42, ☎ 02177/2297); in **Rust,** Schneeberger (⊠ Rathauspl. 15, ☎ 02685/6442).

Boating

You can hire boats (*Bootsvermietung* or *Bootsverleih*) around Lake Neusiedl. Expect to pay about AS50 per hour for a rowboat, AS80 for a pedal boat, and AS120 for an electric boat; sailboat prices vary widely. Rent from: **Baumgartner** (⊠ Neusiedl am See, ☎ 02167/2782), **Friedrich Lang** (⊠ Mörbisch, ☎ 02685/8381), **Knoll** (⊠ Podersdorf, ☎ 02177/2431), **Ruster Freizeitcenter** (⊠ Rust, ☎ 02685/595), or **Stefan Gangl** (⊠ Illmitz, ☎ 02175/2158).

Car Rentals

Cars can be rented at all airports and in Graz from **Avis** (⊠ Schlögelg. 10, ☎ 0316/812920, FAX 0316/841178; or at the airport), **Buchbinder** (⊠ Keplerstr. 93−95, ☎ 0316/717330, FAX 0316/718843), **Budget** (⊠ airport, ☎ 0316/2902−342), **Europcar** (⊠ airport, ☎ 0316/296757), and **Hertz** (⊠ Andreas-Hofer-Pl. 1, ☎ 0316/825007, FAX 0316/810288).

Emergencies

Police, ☎ 133. **Fire,** ☎ 122. **Ambulance,** ☎ 144. In Graz, **Medical Service,** ☎ 141.

Guided Tours

ORIENTATION TOURS

Relatively few guided tours visit Eastern Austria, and those that do are in German, although English may be available on request. Inquire when booking. General orientation tours depart from Vienna and last one to four days. The one-day tours are usually to Lake Neusiedl and include a boat ride or to the Semmering mountain region with a cable-car ride. Reputable operators include the following: **Cityrama Sightseeing** (⊠ Börseg. 1, A−1010 Vienna, ☎ 01/534−1312, FAX 01/534−13−28); **CityTouring Vienna** (⊠ Penzingerstr. 46, A−1140 Vienna, ☎ 01/894−1417−0, FAX 01/894−3239); **Vienna Sightseeing Tours** (⊠ Stelzhammerg. 4/11, A−1031 Vienna, ☎ 01/712−4683−0, FAX 01/712−714−1141).

TOURS OF GRAZ

Minibus sightseeing tours of Graz are conducted on weekdays May−October. Guided walking tours of the Old City, in English and German, are held April−October, daily at 2, and November−March, Saturday at 2. Guided tours of the Schlossberg are conducted daily April−mid-October, departing hourly 9−5 from the Glockenturm near the upper station of the Schlossberg funicular. For prices, bookings, and current schedules of all tours, contact the city tourist office (☞ Visitor Information, *below*).

Horseback Riding

The area around Lake Neusiedl is ideal for riding. Livery stables on the east side of the lake include two at **Podersdorf,** Frankl (☎ 02177/2251) and Lang (☎ 02177/2764). A different adventure is riding Icelandic ponies, possible at the Schwarz stables (☎ 02610/42020) in **Neckenmarkt** in south Burgenland.

Late-Night Pharmacies

To find a pharmacy open late in Graz, call ☎ 18.

Travel Agencies

Check in Graz with **Reisebüro Kuoni** (✉ Sackstr. 6, ☎ 0316/824571–0, FAX 0316/824571–6) or **Ruefa** (✉ Opernring 9, ☎ 0316/829775–0, FAX 0316/829775–23).

Visitor Information

The regional tourist information office for Burgenland province is the **Landesverband Burgenland Tourismus** (✉ Schloss Esterházy, A–7000 Eisenstadt, ☎ 02682/63384, FAX 02682/63384–20). Lower Austria has a tourist office in Vienna: the **Niederösterreichisches Landesreisebüro** (✉ Walfischg. 6, A–1010 Vienna, ☎ 01/513–8022, FAX 01/513–8022–30). For Styria, the provincial tourist office is **Steirische Tourismus** (✉ St. Peter Hauptstr. 243, A–8042 Graz, ☎ 0316/403033–0, FAX 0316/403033–10).

For **Graz,** the quarterly *Graz-Guide* brochure, available from the tourist office (✉ Herrengasse 16, ☎ 0316/835241–11), includes a city map and provides information on current events.

There are several helpful local *Fremdenverkehrsamt* (tourist offices). **Bruck an der Mur:** Tourismusverband (✉ An der Postwiese 4, A–8600 Bruck an der Mur, ☎ 03862/54722, FAX 03862/54910). **Eisenstadt:** Eisenstadt Tourismus (✉ Schloss Esterházy, A–7000 Eisenstadt, ☎ 02682/63384, FAX 02682/633–8420). **Graz:** Grazer Tourismus (✉ Herrreng. 16, A–8010 Graz, ☎ 0316/835241–11, FAX 0316/837987; ✉ Platform 1 of main train station, ☎ 0316/916837). **Mariazell:** Tourismusverband (✉ Hauptpl. 13, A–8630 Mariazell, ☎ 03882/2366, FAX 03882/3945). **Neusiedl am See:** Tourismusbüro (✉ Hauptpl. 1, A–7100 Neusiedl am See, ☎ 02167/2229, FAX 02167/2637). **Rust:** Gästeinformation (✉ Rathaus, A–7071 Rust, ☎ 02685/202–18, FAX 02685/502). **Wiener Neustadt:** Fremdenverkehrsverein (✉ Hauptpl. 1–3, A–2700 Wiener Neustadt, ☎ 02622/23531–468, FAX 02622/23531–498).

5 The Danube Valley

A tonic in any season, a trip up the Austrian Danube unveils a parade of storybook-worthy sights: fairy-tale castles-in-air, medieval villages, and Baroque abbeys crowned with "candle-snuffer" cupolas. The Danube itself is a marvel—on a summer day it even takes on the proper shade of Johann Strauss blue. Along its banks, you'll discover the beautiful Wachau Valley and cheery Linz, whose pastry shops produce the best Linzer tortes around.

Updated by
Bonnie Dodson

TO THE SIGHTSEER, a trip along the Austrian Danube unfolds rather like a treasured picture book of history. Roman ruins (some built by Emperor Claudius), remains of medieval castles-in-air, and Baroque monasteries crowned with "candle-snuffer" cupolas perch precariously above the river, compelling the imagination with their legends and myths. This is where Isa—cousin of the Lorelei—lured sailors to the shoals, where Richard the Lion-Hearted was locked in a dungeon for years, and where the Nibelungs—immortalized by Wagner—caroused operatically in battlemented forts. Once, Roman sailors used to throw coins into the perilous whirlpools around Grein to placate Danubius, the river's tutelary god. Today, thanks to the technology of modern dams, travelers have the luxury of seeing this part of Austria from the tame deck of a comfortable river steamer. In clement weather, the nine-hour trip upriver to Linz is highly rewarding. If you have more time to spare, the voyage onward to Passau may be less dramatic but gives more time to take in the picturesque vineyards and the castles perched like so many eagles' aeries on crags above bends in the river.

Even more of the region's attractions can be discovered traveling by car or bus. You can explore plunging Gothic streets, climb Romanesque towers, and linger over a glass of wine at vaulted Weinkellers. River and countryside form an inspired unity here, with fortress-topped outcroppings giving way to broad pastures that swoop down to the very riverbanks. Many visitors classify this tour as one of Europe's great trips: Here you feel you can almost reach out and touch the riverside towns and soak up the intimacy unique to this stretch of the valley. In this chapter, we follow the course of the Danube upstream from Vienna as it winds through Lower Austria (Niederösterreich) and a bit of Upper Austria (Oberösterreich) to Linz, past monasteries and industrial towns, the riverside vineyards of the lower Weinviertel, and the fragrant expanses of apricot and apple orchards.

Linz, Austria's third-largest city (and its most underrated), is a key industrial center. It's also a fine town for shopping; the stores are numerous and carry quality merchandise, often at more reasonable prices than in Vienna or the larger resorts. Concerts and operas performed at Linz's modern Brucknerhaus make every bit as good listening as those in Vienna or Salzburg.

It is, however, the Danube, originating in Germany's Black Forest and emptying into the Black Sea, that is our focal point: The route that brought the Romans to the area and contributed to its development remains one of Europe's important waterways, with four national capitals on its banks—Vienna, Bratislava, Budapest, and Belgrade. It was not only the Romans who posited "Whoever controls the Danube controls all Europe." The Kuenringer (the robber knights who built many of the hilltop castles) thrived by sacking the baggage caravans of the early Crusaders; later, castles were financed through slightly more legitimate means—Frederick Barbarossa, leading his army downstream, had to pay a crossing toll at Mauthausen. Subsequently, cities sprang up to serve as ports for the salt, wood, ores, and other cargo transported on the river. Today, modern railroads and highways parallel most of the blue Danube's course.

This is a wonderful trip to take in early spring or in the fall after the grape harvest, when the vineyards turn reddish blue and a bracing chill settles over the Danube; the Empress Maria Theresa would arrive in Linz in May, just as the fruit trees were about to bloom. No matter when you come, be sure to try some of those fruits in a Linzer torte (a filling of brandy-flavored apricots, raspberries, or plums under a latticed pastry crust), a treat as satisfyingly rich and copious as the Danube Valley itself.

Pleasures and Pastimes

Abbeys

While castles galore dot the area—ranging from crumbling mountaintop ruins to wonderfully restored edifices replete with gargoyles—the real gems in these environs are the abbeys, majestic relics of an era when bishops were as influential as kings. The greatest are Melk, Klosterneuburg, Kremsmünster, St. Florian, and Göttweig, all of which have breathlessly imposing scope and elegance.

Bicycling

The trail along the Danube must be one of the great bicycle routes of the world. For much of the way (the exception being the Korneuburg–Krems stretch) you can bike on either side of the river. Some small hotels will even arrange to pick up you and your bike from the cycle path. You'll find bicycle rentals at most riverside towns and at rail stations. The terrain around Linz is relatively level, and within the city there are 89 km (55 mi) of marked cycle routes. In the areas of Eferding, St. Florian, through the Enns River valley, and around Steyr, the territory is generally good for cycling, with gentle hills and special routes.

Dining

Wherever possible, restaurants capitalize on the river view, and alfresco dining overlooking the Danube is one of the region's unsurpassed delights. Simple *Gasthäuser* are everywhere, but better dining is more often found in the country inns. The cuisine is basically Austrian, although desserts are often brilliant local inventions, including the celebrated Linzer torte and Linzer Augen, jam-filled cookies with three "eyes" in the top cookie.

Wine is very much the thing in the lower part of the Weinviertel, particularly in the Wachau region on the north bank of the Danube. Here you'll find many of Austria's best white wines, slightly dry and with a touch of fruity taste. In some of the smaller villages, you can sample the vintner's successes directly in his cellars. Restaurants, from sophisticated and stylish to plain and homey, are often rated by their wine offerings as much as by their chef's creations.

CATEGORY	COST*
$$$$	over AS500
$$$	AS300–AS500
$$	AS200–AS300
$	under AS200

per person for a typical three-course meal with a glass of house wine

Hiking

You could hardly ask for better hiking country: From the level ground of the Danube Valley, hills rise on both sides, giving great views when you reach the upper levels. There are *Wanderwege* (marked hiking paths) virtually everywhere; local tourist offices have maps and route details. Around Linz you might retrace the route of the Linz–Budweis horse-drawn tramway, Continental Europe's first railway, or trek from one castle to another. You can hike in the Mühlviertel from Freistadt to Grein and even get your pack transferred from hotel to hotel.

Lodging

Accommodation options range from castle hotels where you'll be treated like a king to quieter but elegant, usually family-run country inns to standard city hotels in Linz. The region is compact, so you can easily stay in one place and drive to a nearby locale to try a different restaurant. Rates understandably reflect the quality of service and amenities and usually include breakfast, which may range from a fast to a feast.

CATEGORY	COST*
$$$$	over AS1,500
$$$	AS1,000–AS1,500
$$	AS700–AS1,000
$	under AS700

All prices are for a standard double room, including tax and service.

Exploring the Danube Valley

Although much of the river is tightly wedged between steep hills rising from a narrow valley, the north and south banks of the Danube present differing vistas. The hills to the north are terraced so that the vineyards can catch the sun; the orchards, occasional meadows, and shadowed hills on the south are as visually appealing if less dramatic. Upstream from the Wachau region the valley broadens, giving way to farmlands and the industrial city of Linz straddling the river.

Great Itineraries

The Wachau section of the Danube Valley is a favorite outing for Viennese seeking a pleasant Sunday drive and a glass or two of good wine, but for foreign visitors to treat the region this casually would cause them to miss some of Austria's greatest treasures. Once there, castles and abbeys beckon, picturesque villages beg to be explored, and the vine-covered wine gardens prove nearly irresistible.

Numbers in the text correspond to numbers in the margin and on the Lower Danube Valley, Upper Danube Valley, and Linz maps.

IF YOU HAVE 3 DAYS

Start out early from Vienna, planning for a stop to explore the medieval center of **Krems** ③. The Vinotek Und's eponymous Kloster will give you a good idea of the regions's best wines. From Krems, you can scoot across the river to visit Stift Göttweig at **Göttweig** ㊷ or you can leave it until the return trip. Spend a night in a former cloister, now an elegant hotel, in ⊡ **Dürnstein** ⑤ in the shadow of the ruined castle where Richard the Lion-Hearted was imprisoned. An early morning climb up to the ruin or a jog along the Danube shoreline will reward you with great views. Take time to explore the town before heading along the Danube, crossing to ⊡ **Melk** ㊴, rated one of the greatest abbeys in Europe. This is high Baroque at its most glorious. Follow the river road on to ⊡ **Göttweig** ㊷ and have lunch on the terrace at the abbey. The abbey's Baroque chapel is breathtaking. Continuing eastward, follow the river as closely as possible (signs indicate Zwentendorf and Tulln) to **Klosterneuburg** ㊻, an imposing abbey that was once seat of the powerful Babenburger kings, and onward to Vienna.

IF YOU HAVE 5 DAYS

A more leisurely schedule would follow the same basic route but permit a visit at either **Burg Kreuzenstein,** near **Korneuburg** ① or **Schloss Grafenegg** near **Haitzendorf** ② before stopping in **Krems** ③ and **Weinkolleg Kloster Und** (☞ Krems, *below*), and overnighting in ⊡ **Dürnstein** ⑤. Spend the morning exploring the town, including the colorfully restored Baroque Stiftskirche. In the afternoon, discover the wine villages of **Weissenkirchen** ⑥ and **Spitz** ⑦. Plan on two overnights in ⊞ **Linz** ⑪–㉕, to discover the city itself and to fit in a side trip across the river north to the walled city of **Freistadt** ㉖ and then on to **Kefermarkt** ㉗, to view the 42-ft-high intricately carved, wood winged altar dating to 1497. On day four, take in **Kremsmünster** ㉜ and **St. Florian** ㉛; then proceed to ⊞ **Melk** ㊱. The fifth day will be full, but start with the Melk abbey, then the abbey at **Göttweig** ㊷, and move onward to **Klosterneuburg** ㊻.

IF YOU HAVE 7 DAYS

Additional time would allow far better acquaintance with this region. Located to the northwest of the Wachau, the Mühlviertel—the mill region north of Linz—turned out thousands of yards of linen from flax grown in the neighboring fields in the last century. You might follow the "textile trail," which takes you to museums tracing this bit of history. On your way along the northern Danube bank, visit the fascinating theater in **Grein** ⑨ and view the curious chancel in the church at **Baumgartenberg** ⑩. From ⊞ **Linz** ⑪–㉕, take trips upriver to **Eferding** ㉘, **Hartkirchen** ㉙, and **Aschach** ㉚, and south to ⊞ **Steyr** ㉞; you might also consider an overnight in this charming medieval city with its vast center square framed in pastel facades. From Steyr, attractive back roads will bring you to the walled town of **Waidhofen an der Ybbs** ㊲, parts of which date to the Turkish invasion of the 1600s. Rather than trying to pack three abbeys into one day, spread out the pleasures, dining in **Mautern** ㊶ and overnighting in ⊞ **Tulln** ㊹ before heading on to **Klosterneuburg** ㊻ and, finally, returning to Vienna.

When to Tour the Danube Valley

The Wachau—both north and south Danube banks—is packed wall-to-wall with visitors in late April to early May, but of course there's a reason: The apricot and apple trees are in glorious blossom, and bright orange poppies blanket the fields. Others prefer the chilly early to mid-autumn days, when a blue haze cradles the vineyards. Throughout the region, winter is drab. Seasons hardly withstanding, crowds jam the abbey at Melk; you're best off going first thing in the morning, before the tour buses arrive, or at midday when the throngs have receded.

THE WACHAU, NORTH BANK OF THE DANUBE

Unquestionably the most lovely stretches of the Danube's Austrian course run from the outskirts of Vienna, through the narrow defiles of the Wachau to the Nibelungengau—the region where the mystical race of dwarfs, the Nibelungs, are supposed to have settled, at least for a while. If you're taking the tour by train, take Streetcar D to Vienna's Franz Josefs Bahnhof, where you'll depart. If you're driving, the trickiest part may be getting out of Vienna. Follow signs to Prague to get across the Danube. Once across, avoid the right-hand exit marked Prague, which leads to the autobahn, and continue ahead, following signs for Prager Strasse and turning left at the traffic light. Prager Strasse (Route 3) heads toward Langenzersdorf and Korneuburg.

Korneuburg

❶ *18 km (11¼ mi) northwest of Vienna.*

Until recently, Korneuburg was the center of Austrian shipbuilding, where river passenger ships, barges, and transfer cranes were built for Russia, among other customers. Stop for a look at the imposing neo-

Lower Danube Valley

NORTH BANK
TOUR CONTINUES
ON MAP BELOW

Vienna

Korneuburg **1**

Haitzendorf **2**

Krems **3**

Mautern

Göttweig **42**

41

Stein Und **4**

Dürnstein **6**

5

Weissenkirchen

Spitz **7**

Maria
Taferl

Melk **39**

40

Schallaburg

Ybbs an
der Donau **38**

WACHAU

NIBELUNGENAU

St. Pölten

43

44 Tulln

45 Greifenstein

46 Klosterneuburg

6 miles

9 km

N

Gothic city hall (1864), which dominates the central square and towers over the town.

★ Atop a hillside 3 km (2 mi) beyond Korneuburg along Route 3 sits **Burg Kreuzenstein,** a castle with fairy-tale turrets and towers. Using old elements and Gothic and Romanesque bits and pieces brought to this site of a previously destroyed castle, Count Wilczek built Kreuzenstein from 1879 to 1908 to house his late-Gothic collection of art objects. You would never suspect the building wasn't absolutely authentic if the tour guides weren't so forthcoming. You'll see rooms full of armaments, the festival and banquet halls, library, chapel, even the kitchens. It is possible to reach Kreuzenstein via the suburban train (S-Bahn) to Leobendorf and a ¾-hour hike up to the castle. ⊠ *Leobendorf bei Korneuburg,* ☎ *02262/66102.* ▣ *AS80.* ⊙ *Mid-Mar.–mid-Nov., Tues.–Sun. 9–5; last tour at 4.*

Haitzendorf

❷ *51 km (38½ mi) west of Korneuburg.*

The tiny farming community of Haitzendorf (to reach it from Korneuburg, take Route 3, 33 km/21 mi past Stockerau; then turn right at Graftenwörth) features a church dating to the 14th century. In early summer, the vast strawberry fields surrounding the town yield a delicious harvest, which you can pick yourself.

A lush meadow and woodland area also surrounds the best-known site,
★ the turreted **Schloss Grafenegg.** The moated Renaissance castle dating to 1533 was stormed by the Swedes in 1645 and rebuilt from 1840 to 1873 in the English Gothic Revival style. Greatly damaged during the 1945–55 occupation, it was extensively restored in the 1980s. Look for such fascinating details as the gargoyle waterspouts, and don't miss the chapel. ☎ *02735/2205–14.* ▣ *AS60.* ⊙ *Mid-Apr.–Oct., Tues.– Sun. daily 10–5.*

Krems

★ ❸ *12 km (7 mi) west of Haitzendorf, 80 km (50 mi) northwest of Vienna, 26 km (16¼ mi) north of St. Pölten.*

Krems marks the beginning (when traveling upstream) of the Wachau section of the Danube. This delightful old town along Route 3 celebrated its 1,000th birthday in 1995 and is closely tied to Austrian history; here the ruling Babenbergs set up a dukedom in 1120, and the earliest Austrian coin was struck in 1130. In the Middle Ages, Krems looked after the iron trade while neighboring Stein traded in salt and wine, and over the years Krems became a center of culture and art. Today the area is the heart of a thriving wine production, and narrow streets, a Renaissance Rathaus, a parish church that is one of the oldest in Lower Austria, and a pedestrian zone make Krems an attractive city to wander through.

A 14th-century former Dominican cloister, farther along the street, now serves as the **Historisches Museum der Stadt Krems** (Krems Historical Museum), with a wine museum that holds occasional tastings. ⊠ *Körnermarkt 13,* ☎ *02732/801–338.* ▣ *AS30.* ⊙ *Easter–late Oct., Tues.–Sat. 9–noon and 2–5, Sun. 9–noon.*

Dining and Lodging

$$$ ✕ **Zum Kaiser von Österreich.** At this landmark located in the Old City district, you'll find excellent regional cuisine along with an outstanding wine selection (some of these vintages come from the backyard). The inside rooms are bright and pleasant, but the outside tables in sum-

mer are even more inviting. Owner-chef Haidinger learned his skills at Bacher, across the Danube in Mautern, so look for fish dishes along with specialties such as potato soup and roast shoulder of lamb with scalloped potatoes. ⊠ *Körnermarkt 9,* ☎ *02732/86001,* FAX *02732/ 86001–4. DC, MC, V. Closed Mon.*

$$$ ✕⊞ **Am Förthof.** An inn has existed on the riverside site of this mod-
★   ern hotel for hundreds of years. The rooms are comfortable and bal-
conied; those in front have a view of the Danube and Göttweig abbey across the river—and the sounds of the traffic. The dining room and in summer the inviting courtyard garden offer good regional cuisine; the chef's ambitions occasionally surpass his achievements, but the sump-
tuous breakfasts are an assured culinary experience. ⊠ *Förthofer Donaulände 8, A–3500,* ☎ *02732/83345 or 02732/81348,* FAX *02732/ 83345–40. 20 rooms. Restaurant, pool, sauna. DC, MC, V.*

$–$$ ✕⊞ **Alte Post.** You're allowed to drive into the pedestrian zone to this romantic house in the heart of the old town, next to the Steinener Tor (Stone Gate). The rooms are in comfortable country style (full baths are scarce), but the real feature here is dining on regional specialties or sipping a glass of the local wine in the arcaded Renaissance courtyard. The staff is particularly friendly, and cyclists are welcome. ⊠ *Obere Land-
str. 32, A–3500,* ☎ *02732/82276–0,* FAX *02732/84396. 26 rooms, 7 with bath. Restaurant, bicycles. No credit cards. Closed Jan.–mid-Mar.*

En Route Between Krems and Stein, in a beautifully restored Capuchin cloister
★   in the tiny town of Und, is the **Weinkolleg Kloster Und.** The building also houses the tourist office and a small wine museum, where you can taste (and buy) more than 100 Austrian wines. ⊠ *Undstr. 6, Krems–
Stein,* ☎ *02732/73073–0,* FAX *02732/73074–85.* ☞ *AS130 (includes tasting).* ⊙ *Mid-Jan.–Dec. 24, daily 11–7.*

Stein

❹ *5 km (3 mi) east of Krems.*

A frozen-in-time hamlet that has, over time, become virtually a suburb of the adjacent city of Krems, Stein is dotted with lovely 16th-cen-
tury houses, many on the hamlet's main street, Steinlanderstrasse. The former 14th-century **Minoritenkirche,** just off the main street in the pedestrian zone, now serves as a museum with changing exhibits. A few steps beyond the Minoritenkirche, an imposing square Gothic tower iden-
tifies the 15th-century **St. Nicholas parish church,** whose altar paint-
ing and ceiling frescoes were done by Kremser Schmidt. The upper part of the Gothic charnel house (1462), squeezed between the church and the hillside, has been converted to housing. Notice, too, the many architecturally interesting houses, among them the former tollhouse, with rich Renaissance frescoes. Stein was the birthplace of Ludwig Köchel, the cataloger of Mozart's works, which are referred to by their Köchel numbers.

Dürnstein

❺ *4 km (2½ mi) west of Stein, 90 km (56 mi) northwest of Vienna, 34 km (21¼ mi) northeast of Melk.*

If a beauty contest was held among the towns along the Wachau Danube, chances are Dürnstein would be the winner, hands down—
as you'll see when you arrive along with droves of tourists. The town is small; leave the car at one end and walk the narrow streets.

Set among terraced vineyards, the town is landmarked by its gloriously Baroque **Stiftskirche,** dating from the early 1700s, which sits on a cliff overlooking the river—this cloister church's combination of luminous blue facade and stylish Baroque tower is considered the most beautiful of its kind in Austria. After taking in the Stiftskirche, most visitors head up the hill, climbing 500 ft over the town, to the famous **Richard the Lion-Hearted Castle** where Leopold V held Richard the Lion-Hearted of England, caught on his way back home from the Crusades. In the tower of this castle, Richard was imprisoned (1192–93) until he was rescued by Blondel, the faithful minnesinger. It's said that Blondel was able to locate his imprisoned king when he heard his master's voice completing the verse of a song he was singing. The rather steep 30-minute climb to the ruins will earn you a breathtaking view up and down the Danube Valley and over the hills to the south.

Dining and Lodging

$$$ ✕ **Loibnerhof.** Here, in an idyllic setting on the banks of the Danube,
★ you'll dine on inventive variations on regional themes: Wachauer fish soup, crispy roast duck, and various grilled fish or lamb specialties. The house is famous for its *Butterschnitzel,* an exquisite variation on the theme of ground meat (this one's panfried veal with a touch of pork). The garden is enchanting in summer, but on weekends it's packed, and service tends to suffer. ✉ *Unterloiben 7,* ☎ *02732/82890–0,* FAX *02732/82890–3. No credit cards. Closed Mon.–Tues. and mid-Jan.–mid-Feb.*

$$$$ ✕⌂ **Richard Löwenherz.** The impressive vaulted reception and dining
★ rooms of this former convent are beautifully furnished with antiques, reflecting the personal warmth and care of the family management. The inviting open fire, stone floors, and friendly touches make this one of the most romantic of the Romantik Hotels group. Though all rooms are spacious and comfortable, the balconied guest rooms in the newer part of the house are more modern in decor and furnishings. Wander through the grounds and gardens, admiring the crumbling ruined walls from earlier centuries. A terrace overlooking the Danube offers stunning views. The outstanding restaurant is known for its regional specialties and local wines. ✉ *A–3601,* ☎ *02711/222,* FAX *02711/222–18. 40 rooms. Restaurant, bar, pool. AE, DC, MC, V. Closed Nov.–mid-Mar.*

$$$$ ✕⌂ **Schlosshotel Dürnstein.** This 17th-century early Baroque castle,
★ on a rocky terrace with exquisite views over the Danube, offers genuine elegance and comfort. The best rooms look onto the river, but all are unusually bright and attractive; of moderate size, they have comfortable seating and country antiques throughout. Half-board is standard. The kitchen matches the quality of the excellent wines from the area, and the tables set outside on the large stone balcony overlooking the river makes dining here a memorable experience. Even if you don't stay at the hotel, it's worth a stop for a delicious lunch or a leisurely afternoon pastry and coffee. ✉ *A–3601,* ☎ *02711/212,* FAX *02711/351. 37 rooms. Restaurant, bar, indoor and outdoor pools, sauna, exercise room. AE, DC, MC, V. Closed Nov.–Mar.*

$$$ ⌂ **Sänger Blondel.** Behind the yellow facade is a very friendly, traditional family hotel with elegant country rooms of medium size that have attractive paneling and antique decorations. The staff is particularly helpful and can suggest excursions in the area. The hotel is known for its restaurant, which features local specialties and a wide range of salads and lighter dishes. ✉ *No. 64, A–3601,* ☎ *02711/253–0,* FAX *02711/253–7. 16 rooms. Restaurant. No credit cards. Closed mid-Nov.–mid-Mar. and 1 wk in early July.*

Weissenkirchen

❻ *5 km (3 mi) west of Dürnstein, 22 km (14 mi) northeast of Melk.*

Tucked among vineyards, just around a bend in the Danube, is Weissenkirchen, a picturesque town that was fortified against the Turks in

1531. A fire in 1793 laid waste to much of the town, but the 15th-century parish church of **Maria Himmelfahrt,** built on earlier foundations, largely survived. The south nave dates to 1300, the middle nave to 1439, the chapel to 1460. The Madonna on the triumphal arch goes back to the Danube school of about 1520; the Baroque touches date to 1736; and to complete the picture, the rococo organ was installed in 1777.

On the Marktplatz, check out the 15th-century **Teisenhoferhof,** which has a charming Renaissance arcaded courtyard. The building now houses the Wachau museum and contains many paintings by Kremser Schmidt. ⊠ *Marktpl.,* ☎ *02715/2268.* 🎫 *AS20.* ⊙ *Apr.–Oct., Tues.– Sun. 10–5.*

Dining and Lodging

$$$ ✕ **Jamek.** Josef Jamek is known for his outstanding wines; his wife, ★ Edeltraud, for what she and her chefs turn out in the kitchen of this fine restaurant, which is also their home. You dine in one of several rooms tastefully decorated with 18th-century touches. Creative variations on typical Austrian specialties are emphasized; lamb and game in season are highlights. Wines are from the nearby family vineyards. ⊠ *Joching 45,* ☎ *02715/2235,* 𝔽𝔸𝕏 *02715/2483. Reservations essential. No credit cards. Closed Sun.–Mon., mid-Dec.–mid-Feb., and 1st 2 wks of July; but call to confirm days open. No dinner Thurs.*

$$ ✕ **Gasthaus Erwin Schwarz.** Here's an insider's tip: This is the best restaurant in the area, offering delicious regional cooking in a former farmhouse and butcher's shop. There is virtually nothing in the village of Nöhagen, which is 7 km (4½ mi) north of Weissenkirchen, yet people come from miles around to dine here. The restaurant raises its own animals, and all produce is grown on the premises. ⊠ *Nöhagen 13, Nöhagen,* ☎ *02717/8209. No credit cards. Closed Mon.–Tues., and Mon.–Thurs. Nov.–mid-Apr.*

$$$ 🏨 **Raffelsbergerhof.** This stunning Renaissance building (1574), once ★ a shipmaster's house, has been tastefully converted into a hotel with every comfort. The rooms are attractively decorated without being overdone. The family management is particularly friendly, and there's a quiet garden to complement the gemütlich public lounge. ⊠ *A–3610,* ☎ *02715/2201,* 𝔽𝔸𝕏 *02715/2201–27. 12 rooms. MC. Closed Nov.–Apr.*

Spitz

❼ *5 km (3 mi) southwest of Weissenkirchen, 17 km (10½ mi) northeast of Melk.*

Picturesque Spitz is set off the main road and back from the Danube, sitting like a jewel in the surrounding vineyards and hills. One vineyard, the "Thousand Bucket Hill," is said to produce that much wine in a good year. A number of interesting houses in Spitz go back to the 16th and 17th centuries. The late-Gothic 15th-century **parish church** contains Kremser Schmidt's altar painting of the martyrdom of St. Mauritius. Note the carved wood statues of Christ and the 12 apostles, dating to 1380, on the organ loft. Just beyond Spitz and above the road is the ruin of the **castle Hinterhaus,** to which you can climb.

A side road here marked to Ottenschlag (Route 217) leads up the hill, and about 7 km (4½ mi) beyond Mühldorf, to **Burg Oberranna,** a well-preserved castle surrounded by a double wall and dry moat. The original structure dates to 1114–25, the St. George chapel possibly even earlier. Part of the castle has been renovated into a hotel (☞ Lodging, below). ⊠ *Ober-Ranna 1, Mühldorf,* ☎ *02713/8221.* 🎫 *AS20.* ⊙ *May– Oct., Sat. 3–5, Sun. 2–6.*

Lodging

$$$ ⊞ **Burg Oberranna.** This 12th-century castle—a noted historic sight in itself (☞ *above*)—has been successfully turned into a charming and comfortable hotel, great as a base for hiking and also perfect for those who just want to get away. Some rooms include a kitchenette and sitting room. ⊠ *Ober-Ranna 1, A–3622 Mühldorf,* ☎ *02713/8221,* ℻ *02713/8366. 11 rooms, 4 suites. Café, kitchenettes. AE, V. Closed Nov.–Apr.*

En Route   The vistas are mainly of the other side of the Danube, looking across at Schönbühel and Melk, as you follow a back road via Jauerling and Maria Laach to Route 3 at Aggsbach. Shortly after Weitenegg the Wachau ends, and you come into the part of the Danube Valley known as the **Nibelungenau,** where the Nibelungs—who inspired the great saga *Nibelungenlied,* source of Wagner's *Ring*—are supposed to have settled for a spell. If you have always thought of the Nibelungs as a mythical race of dwarfs known only to old German legends and Wagner, dismiss that idea here. The Nibelungs existed, though not as Wagner describes them, and this area was one of their stomping grounds.

Maria Taferl

❽   *49 km (31 mi) southwest of Spitz, 13 km (8 mi) west of Melk, 7½ km (4¼ mi) northeast of Persenbeug/Ybbs an der Donau.*

Crowning a hill on the north bank is the two-towered **Maria Taferl Basilica,** a pilgrimage church with a spectacular outlook. It's a bit touristy, but the church and the view are worth the side trip.

About 5 km (3 mi) up a back road is **Schloss Artstetten,** a massive square castle with four round defense towers at its corners. This is the burial place of Archduke Franz Ferdinand and his wife, Sophie, whose double assassination in 1914 in Sarajevo was one of the immediate causes of World War I. ⊠ *Artstelten,* ☎ *07413/8302.* ☜ *AS70.* ⊙ *Apr.–Oct., daily 9–5:30.*

Lodging

$$$ ⊞ **Krone–Kaiserhof.** Two hotels under the same family management share each other's luxurious facilities. The Krone looks out over the Danube Valley, while the Kaiserhof has views of the nearby Baroque pilgrimage church. Both have rooms done a bit slickly in country style, and the restaurants are popular. An associated guest house ($) is less elegant but also shares facilities. Cyclists staying overnight will be picked up free at Marbach or Klein Pöchlarn landing stations on the Danube. ⊠ *A–3672,* ☎ *07413/6355–0,* ℻ *07413/6355–83. 72 rooms. 2 restaurants, bar, café, indoor and outdoor pools, sauna, miniature golf, exercise room. V. Closed Jan.–Feb.*

Grein

❾   *32 km (20 mi) west of Maria Teferl, 20 km (12 mi) west of Persenbeug/Ybbs an der Donau.*

Set above the Danube, Grein is a picture-book town complete with castle. The river bend below, known for years as the "place where death resides," was one of the most hazardous stretches of river until the reefs were blasted away in the late 1700s. Take time to see the intimate rococo **Stadttheater** in the town hall, built in 1790 by the populace and still occasionally used for concerts or plays. ⊠ *Rathaus,* ☎ *07268/6680.* ☜ *AS30.* ⊙ *Tour Apr.–late Oct., daily at 9, 10:30, and 2:30.*

Baumgartenberg

❿   *11 km (7 mi) west of Grein, 17½ km (11 mi) east of Mauthausen.*

The small village of Baumgartenberg is worth a visit for its ornate Baroque **parish church.** Note the lavish stucco-work and exquisitely carved 17th-century pews—and the unusual chancel supported by a tree trunk. The church is the only reminder of a once-famed Cisterican abbey, founded in 1141 by Otto von Machland, that used to thrive here. Outside the town is the picturesque **castle of Klam,** which used to belong to playwright August Strindberg; it now contains a small museum.

LINZ

130 km (81¼ mi) east of Salzburg, 185 km (115½ mi) west of Vienna.

The capital of Upper Austria, set where the Traun River flows into the Danube, Linz has a fascinating old-city core and an active cultural life. In 1832 it had a horse-drawn train to Czechoslovakia that was the first rail line on the Continent. Once known as the "Rich Town of the River Markets" because of its importance as a medieval trading post, it is today the center of Austrian steel and chemical production, both started by the Germans in 1938. A city of contrasts, Linz has Austria's largest medieval square and is home to one of the country's most modern multipurpose halls, the Brucknerhaus, which is used for concerts and conventions.

With the city's modern economic success, Linz's attractions for tourists have been generally overlooked. Nevertheless, Linz boasts beautiful old houses on the Hauptplatz; a Baroque cathedral with twin towers and a fine organ over which composer Anton Bruckner once presided; and its "city mountain," the Pöstlingberg, with a unique railway line to the top. Extensive redevelopment, restoration, and the creation of traffic-free zones continue to transform Linz. The heart of the city—the Altstadt (Old City)—has been turned into a pedestrian zone; either leave the car at your hotel or use the huge new parking garage under the main square in the center of town. Distances are not great, and you can take in the highlights in the course of a two-hour walking tour.

A Good Walk

The center of the Old City is the Hauptplatz, with its pretty pastel town houses. Dominating the square is the **Pillar to the Holy Trinity** ⑪, which was erected in 1723 in gratitude for the survival of Linz from the threat of war, fire, and the dreaded plague. Head down Klostergasse to the **Minoritenkirche** ⑫, which is worth a stop to inspect the church's rococo interior before visiting the adjacent **Landhaus** ⑬, a rambling Renaissance building with three inner courtyards. In the arcaded courtyard is the late-15th-century Fountain of the Planets, with Jupiter as the crowning glory.

Turn right on Altstadtgasse, and at Number 17 is the **Mozart Haus** ⑭, where Mozart stayed as a guest of the Count of Thun and composed the Linz Symphony in his spare time. At Number 10 is the **Kremsmünstererhaus** ⑮, with its turrets and onion domes, where Emperor Friedrich III supposedly died in August 1493. Turn left from Altstadtgasse onto Hofgasse (one of the prettiest corners in the city), and climb the quaint narrow street that leads up to the Rudolfstor, one of the entrances to **Linz Castle** ⑯. Since its earlier days as a prime fortress on the Danube, it has served as a hospital, army barracks, and even a prison before becoming a provincial museum. The view from the castle promontory is one of the most impressive spots in Linz. Walk through the castle grounds to Martinskirche, one of the oldest churches in Austria, with its nave dating from 799.

Linz

URFAHR

TO NEUE GALERIE

Danube

Obere Donaustr.

PÖSTLINGBERG

Hauptstrasse

Nibelungen-Brücke

Obere Donaulände

Untere Donaulände

Fabrikstrasse

Kaisergasse

Kaisergasse

Zollamtstrasse

Altes Rathaus

Lederergasse

Rathausgasse

Museumstrasse

Elisabethstrasse

Hofgasse

Pfarrgasse

Graben

Fadingerstrasse

Domgasse

Graben

Pochestrasse

Bethlehemstrasse

Tummelplatz

Alstadt

Theatergasse

Klosterstrasse

Marienstrasse

Dametzstrasse

Promenade

Promenade

Herrenstrasse

Landstrasse

Klammstrasse

Harrachstrasse

Walterstrasse

Spittelwiese

Bischofstrasse

Mozartstrasse

Kapuzinerstrasse

Steingasse

Baumbachstrasse

Rudigierstrasse

J.K.-Vogel-Strasse

N

Hopfengasse

Stifterstrasse

Hafnerstrasse

Herrenstrasse

Sailerstätte

Landstrasse

Bismarckstrasse

Humboldtstrasse

TO RAILROAD STATION

Langgasse

Bürgerstrasse

Wurmstrasse

Alter Dom, **23**
Bischofshof, **17**
Carmelitenkloster, **19**
Deutschordens-
kirche, **21**
Kepler Haus, **25**
Kremsmünsterer-
haus, **15**
Landhaus, **13**
Linz Castle, **16**

Minoritenkirche, **12**
Mozart Haus, **14**
Neuer Dom, **18**
Nordico, **22**
Pillar to the Holy
Trinity, **11**
Stadtpfarrkirche, **24**
Ursulinenkirche, **20**

Follow Römerstrasse along the castle walls down to the Promenade, veering right when you get to Herrenstrasse. Where Bichofstrasse meets Herrenstrasse is the **Bischofshof** ⑰, which was built between 1721 and 1726 for the Kremsmünster monastery and is still the seat of the bishop of Linz. The west end of Bishofstrasse angles onto Baumbachstrasse, which is the setting for the **Neuer Dom** ⑱, the massive 19th-century cathedral, which can hold up to 20,000 penitents. Note the Linz Window depicting the history of Linz before heading back to Herrenstrasse.

Turn right and shortly afterward left onto Rudigierstrasse. Follow this to Landstrasse, where you'll make another left. Two Baroque churches are located here, the **Carmelitenkloster** ⑲, modeled after St. Joseph's in Prague, and across the street, the **Ursulinenkirche** ⑳. Between these two churches is Harrachstrasse, which holds another Baroque gem, the **Deutschordenskirche** ㉑, or seminary church, located shortly after you cross Dametzgasse. After you're finished inspecting the high altar by Hildebrandt, backtrack along Harrachstrasse to Dametzstrasse, where you'll turn right. At the corner of Dametzstrasse and Bethlehemstrasse is the **Nordico** ㉒, the city museum, which was originally an early 17th-century town house used by the Kremsmünster monastery for nearly 200 years as a Jesuit training center for young Scandinavian men. Now it houses a collection that ranges from archaeological finds to the Biedermeier era.

Keep going along Dametzstrasse until you reach the Graben, where you turn left and walk for a short while before turning right on Domgasse. Here is the **Alter Dom** ㉓, the old city cathedral where Anton Bruckner played the organ for 12 years, beginning in 1856. From here follow Domgasse around to the **Stadtpfarrkirche** ㉔, near the intersection to Kollegiumgasse. This was originally a Romanesque basilica before being rebuilt in the Baroque style in the mid-17th century. In the entrance hall and entrance to the tower staircase you can see Gothic cross-ribbing on the vaulted ceiling.

Go left from the church onto Kollegiumgasse, then left into the Pfarrplatz. From the northwest edge of the square, head down Rathausgasse to Number 5, the last stop on the walking tour, the **Kepler Haus** ㉕, the home of astronomer Johannes Kepler. He lived here with his family for 10 years, beginning in 1612. More than a hundred years later Linz's first printing shop was established here. Rathausgasse leads into the Hauptplatz, which brings you back to the starting point of the tour.

TIMING

Of course the best time to visit Linz is from May to September, but fortunately the main tourist attractions are open year-round. Touring the Old City takes two to three hours, depending on how many of the sights you stop to visit. If you're pressed for time, head straight for Linz Castle. You'll pass through the loveliest parts of the city, and from the heights of the castle grounds you'll be able to enjoy stupendous views of the Danube.

Numbers in the text correspond to numbers in the margin and on the Linz map.

Sights to See

㉓ **Alter Dom** (Old Cathedral). Hidden away off the Graben, a narrow side street off of the Taubenmarkt above the Hauptplatz, is this Baroque gem (1669–78), whose striking feature is the single nave together with the side altars. Anton Bruckner was organist here from 1856 to 1868. ☉ *Daily 7–noon and 3–7.*

Altes Rathaus (Old City Hall). Located at the lower end of the main square, the original 1513 building was mainly destroyed by fire and replaced in 1658–59. Its octagonal corner turret and lunar clock, as well as some vaulted rooms, remain, and you can detect traces of the original Renaissance structure on the Rathausgasse facade. The present exterior dates from 1824. The approach from Rathausgasse 5, opposite the Kepler Haus, leads through a fine arcaded courtyard. On the facade here you'll spot portraits of Emperor Friedrich III, the mayors Hoffmandl and Prunner, the astronomer Johannes Kepler, and the composer Anton Bruckner. ⊠ *Hauptpl.*

⑰ Bischofshof (Bishop's Residence). At the intersection of Herrenstrasse and Bischofstrasse is this impressive mansion, which dates from 1721. Graced by a fine wrought-iron gateway, this remains the city's most important Baroque secular building. The design is by Jakob Prandtauer, the architectural genius responsible for the glorious Melk and St. Florian abbeys.

⑲ Carmelitenkloster. This magnificent Baroque church on Landstrasse was modeled on St. Joseph's in Prague. ⊠ *Langg. 17,* ☎ *0732/663410.* ⊙ *Daily 7–11:30 and 3–6.*

㉑ Deutschordenskirche. This former seminary church from 1723 is a beautiful yellow-and-white Baroque treasure with an elliptical dome, designed by Johann Lukas von Hildebrandt, who also designed its high altar. ⊠ *Harrachstr.,* ☎ *no phone.* ⊙ *Daily 8–6.*

Elisabethinenkloster. This church dates to the mid-18th century. Note the unusually dynamic colors in the dome fresco by Altomonte. ⊠ *Bethlehemstr. 23,* ☎ *0732/76760.*

Ⓒ Märchengrotte (Fairy-tale Grotto) Railroad. Trains run through a colorful imaginary world at the top of the ☞ **Pöstlinberg**. It's entertaining for the rest of the family as well as the kids. ⊠ , ☎ *0732/7801–7506.* 🎟 *AS40.* ⊙ *Sat. before Palm Sunday–Apr. and Oct., daily 9–4:45; May–Sept., daily 9–5:45.*

㉕ Kepler Haus. The astronomer Johannes Kepler lived here from 1612 to 1622; Linz's first printing shop was established in this house in 1745. ⊠ *Rathausgasse 5.*

⑮ Kremsmünstererhaus. Emperor Friedrich III is said to have died here in 1493. The building was done over in Renaissance style in 1578–80, and a story was added in 1616, with two turrets and onion domes. There's a memorial room to the emperor here; his heart is entombed in the Linz parish church, but the rest of him is in St. Stephen's cathedral in Vienna (☞ Chapter 2). The traditional rooms are now home to one of Linz' best restaurants, the Kremsmünsterer Stuben (☞ Dining and Lodging, *below*). ⊠ *Altstadt 10.*

⑬ Landhaus. The early Renaissance monastery adjoining the ☞ **Minoritenkirche** is now the Landhaus, with its distinctive tower, seat of the provincial government. Look inside to see the arcaded courtyard with the 1852 Planet Fountain and the Hall of Stone on the first floor, above the barrel-vaulted hall on the ground floor; for a more extensive look at the interior, inquire at the local tourist office for their scheduled guided tours. The beautiful Renaissance doorway (1570) is of red marble. ⊠ *Klosterstr. 7.*

⑯ Linz Castle. The massive four-story building in Tummelplatz was rebuilt by Friedrich III around 1477, literally on top of a castle that dated from 799. Note the **Friedrichstor** (the Friedrich Gate), with the same *A.E.I.O.U.* monogram also found in Krems, and the two interior courtyards. The castle houses the Upper Austrian provincial museum—weapons, musical instruments, nativity scenes, Upper Austrian art, and prehistoric and Roman relics. ✉ *Tummelpl. 10,* ☎ *0732/774419.* 🎫 *AS40.* ☉ *Tues.–Fri. 9–5, weekends 10–4.*

⑫ Minoritenkirche. Situated at the end of the Klosterstrasse, this church was once part of a monastery. The present building dates from 1752 to 1758 and has a delightful rococo interior with side altar paintings by Kremser Schmidt and the main altar by Bartolomeo Altomonte. ✉ *Klosterstr. 7,* ☎ *0732/77200.* 🎫 *Free.* ☉ *July–Sept., daily 7:30–4; Oct.–June, Mon.–Sat. 7:30–11 AM, Sun. 7:30–noon.*

⑭ Mozart Haus. This three-story Renaissance town house, actually the Thun Palace, has a later Baroque facade and portal. Mozart arrived here in 1783 with his wife to meet an especially impatient patron (Mozart was late by 14 days). As the composer forgot to bring any symphonies along with him, he set about writing one in the space of four days. The result: the sublime Linz Symphony in 1783. The palace now houses the local tourist office and private apartments, but the courtyard can be viewed. ✉ *Altstadt 17.*

Neue Galerie. Across the river in the Urfahr district is one of Austria's best modern art museums. The fine collection is well balanced, featuring mainly contemporary international and Austrian artists. ✉ *Blütenstr. 15, Urfahr,* ☎ *0732/7070–3600.* 🎫 *AS40.* ☉ *May–Oct., Mon.–Wed. and Fri. 10–6, Thurs. 10–10, Sat. 10–1; Nov.–Apr., Fri.–Wed. 10–6, Thurs. 10–10.*

⑱ Neuer Dom (New Cathedral). In 1862 the bishop of Linz engaged one of the architects of the Cologne cathedral to develop a design for a cathedral in neo-Gothic French-cathedral style and modestly ordered that its tower not be higher than that of St. Stephen's in Vienna. The result was the massive 400-ft tower, shorter than St. Stephen's by a scant 6½ ft. ✉ *Baumbachstr.,* ☎ *0732/777885.* 🎫 *Free.* ☉ *Daily 7:30–7.*

㉒ Nordico. At the corner of Dametzstrasse and Bethlehemstrasse, you'll find the city museum, dating from 1610. Its collection follows local history from pre-Roman times to the mid-1880s. ✉ *Bethlehemstr. 7,* ☎ *0732/7070–1912.* 🎫 *Free, except for special exhibits.* ☉ *Weekdays 9–6, weekends 2–5.*

⑪ Pillar to the Holy Trinity. One of the symbols of Linz is the 65-ft Baroque column in the center of the Hauptplatz square. Completed in 1723 of white Salzburg marble, the memorial offers thanks by an earthly trinity—the provincial estates, city council, and local citizenry—for deliverance from the threats of war (1704), fire (1712), and plague (1713). From March through October, there's a flea market here each Saturday (except holidays), from 7 AM to 2 PM.

★ **Pöstlingberg.** With a glass of chilled white wine, drink in the grand vista over Linz and the Danube from one of the flower-hung restaurants located at the top of Linz's "city mountain." At the summit is the **Church of Sieben Schmerzen Mariens,** an immense and splendidly opulent twin-towered Baroque pilgrimage church (1748), visible for leagues as a landmark of Linz. Also on the mountain is the ☞ **Märchengrotte (Fairy-tale Grotto) Railroad.** An electric railway, the **Pöstlingbergbahn,** gives a scenic ride up the mountain. To reach the base station for the railway, take Streetcar 3 across the river to Urfahr, Linz's left bank. Note the railway's unusual switches, necessary because the car wheel flanges ride the outside of the rails rather than the (usual) inside. When the line was built in 1898, it boasted the steepest incline of any noncog railway in Europe. In summer, the old open-bench cars are used. On a clear day the view at the top takes in a good deal of Upper Austria south of the Danube, with a long chain of the Austrian Alps on the horizon. ☎ *0732/7801–7002.* 🎫 *Round-trip AS35, combined ticket with Streetcar Line 3 AS48 (tickets available at Tourist Information).* ⊙ *Daily, every 20 min, 5:30 AM–8:20 PM.*

㉔ Stadtpfarrkirche. This city parish church dates from 1286 and was rebuilt in Baroque style in 1648. The tomb in the right wall of the chancel contains Friedrich III's heart. The ceiling frescoes are by Altomonte, and the figure of Johann Nepomuk (a local saint) in the chancel is by Georg Raphael Donner, in a setting by Hildebrandt. ⊠ *Domg.* ⊙ *Mon.–Sat. 8–7, Sun. 9–7.*

⑳ Ursulinenkirche. The towers at this Baroque church are one of the identifying symbols of Linz. Inside is a blaze of gold and crystal ornament. Note the Madonna figure wearing a hooded Carmelite cloak with huge pockets used to collect alms for the poor. ☎ *0732/771644.* ⊙ *Church daily 1–6, towers daily 8–6.*

Dining and Lodging

$$$$ ✕ **Kremsmünsterer Stuben.** In a beautifully restored historic house in
★ the heart of the Old City, you'll find an attractive wood-paneled restaurant offering everything from regional specialties to a six-course dinner. You might choose from saddle of hare or fillet of venison as a main course as you relax in the comfortable, traditional ambience of the city's best restaurant. ⊠ *Altstadt 10,* ☎ *0732/782111,* FAX *0732/784130. Reservations essential. Jacket and tie. AE, DC, MC, V. Closed Sun., 2 wks in Jan., and 2 wks in Aug. No lunch Sat. and Mon.*

$$$$ ✕ **Verdi.** Linz's favored dinner restaurant is in Lichtenberg, about 3 km (2 mi) north of the center, off Leonfelder Strasse. The cuisine is regional Austrian, with Italian and French overtones; the name refers to the opulent green-hued decor. Some complain of overemphasis on presentation, but this hardly deters the many regulars. Choose game in season or tender lamb. ⊠ *Pachmayrstr. 137,* ☎ *0732/733005. No credit cards. Closed Sun., Mon., and 3 wks in Jan.*

$$ ✕ **Ursulinenhof.** The decor is modern and unremarkable in this restaurant adjacent to the 18th-century Ursulinen Abbey, but the quality of the food makes up for what it might be lacking in atmosphere. Specialties include saltimbocca with corn-fed chicken and saffron wild rice or seafood lasagne. ⊠ *Landstr. 31,* ☎ *0732/774686. No credit cards. Closed Sun.*

$ ✕ **Glockenspiel.** This atmospheric coffeehouse is in the oldest patrician town house on the Hauptplatz. It is warm and inviting, with a vaulted ceiling, polished wood decor, and intimate tables that beckon you to sit and enjoy a mélange and fresh pastry. ⊠ *Hauptpl. 18,* ☎ *0732/795399. No credit cards.*

$ ✕ **K & K Hofbäckerei** (Fritz Roth). The tantalizing aroma of freshly baked bread will beckon you to this Old World bakery just off the Hauptplatz. Choose from a variety of tempting breads and pastries, order a cup of coffee, and then take a seat in the cozy adjoining candlelit room. The friendly owner speaks English. ⊠ *Pfarrg. 17,* ☎ *0732/784110. No credit cards. Closed Sun. No dinner.*

$ ✕ **Traxlmayr.** Proud with the patina of age, this is one of Austria's great
★ old-tradition coffeehouses. You can linger all day over one cup of coffee, reading the papers (*Herald Tribune* included) in their bentwood holders, and then have a light meal. In winter it's extremely smoky, but in summer you can sit outside on the charming terrace and watch passersby. Ask for the specialty, Linzer Torte, with your coffee. ⊠ *Promenade 16,* ☎ *0732/773353. No credit cards. Closed Sun.*

In case you want to see the world.

At American Express, we're here to make your journey a smooth one. So we have over 1,700 travel service locations in over 120 countries ready to help. What else would you expect from the world's largest travel agency?

do more

AMERICAN EXPRESS

http://www.americanexpress.com/travel

Travel

In case you want to
be welcomed there.

We're here to see that you're always welcomed at establishments everywhere. That's why millions of people carry the American Express® Card – for peace of mind, confidence, and security, around the world or just around the corner.

do more

And just in case.

We're here with American Express® Travelers Cheques
and Cheques *for Two*® They're the safest way to carry
money on your vacation and the surest way to get a
refund, practically anywhere, anytime.

Another way we help you...

do more

AMERICAN
EXPRESS

Travelers
Cheques

$$$$ ⊞ **Schillerpark.** You're close to the south end of the pedestrian zone but still reasonably near the center and the sights in this very modern glass complex. The rooms have clean lines, with contemporary furnishings, and some have waterbeds. The buffet breakfast is outstanding and included in the room price. The casino is in the same building. ✉ *Rainerstr. 2–4, A–4020,* ☎ *0732/6950–0,* FAX *0732/6950–9. 111 rooms. 2 restaurants, 2 bars, café, no-smoking floor, sauna. AE, DC, MC, V.*

$$$ ⊞ **Drei Mohren.** Directly across from the Landhaus Park and in the very heart of the city center, this modest hotel offers simple, yet comfortable and quiet rooms and a nice buffet breakfast. The staff is friendly and helpful. ✉ *Promenade 17, A–4020,* ☎ *0732/772626–0,* FAX *0732/772626–6. 25 rooms. AE, DC, MC, V.*

$$–$$$ ⊞ **Wolfinger.** This charming, traditional hotel in an old building is a
★ favorite of regular guests, in part because of the friendly staff, and its location couldn't be more central. The medium-size rooms have been recently modernized, with comfortable new furniture and bright fabrics. Those in the front are less quiet but give a view of city activities. ✉ *Hauptpl. 19, A–4020,* ☎ *0732/773291–0,* FAX *0732/773291–55. 45 rooms. AE, DC, MC, V.*

$$ ⊞ **Zum Schwarzen Bären.** The "Black Bear" is a fine, traditional house near the center of the Old City, a block from the pedestrian zone, and incidentally was the birthplace of the renowned tenor Richard Tauber (1891–1948). The rooms are smallish but have recently been redone, and the baths (most with shower) are modern, if compact. ✉ *Herrenstr. 9–11, A–4020,* ☎ *0732/772477–0,* FAX *0732/772477–47. 35 rooms, 29 with bath. Restaurant, bar, weinstube. AE, DC, MC, V.*

Nightlife and the Arts

Linz is far livelier than even most Austrians realize. The local population is friendlier than in either Vienna or Salzburg, and much less cliquish than in those top resort towns. Nor has Linz lagged behind other Austrian cities in developing its own hot section, known as the Bermuda Triangle. Around the narrow streets of the Old City (Klosterstrasse, Altstadt, Hofgasse) are dozens of fascinating small bars and lounges; as you explore, you'll probably meet some Linzers who can direct you to the current "in" location.

THE ARTS

The **Linz opera company** is talented and often willing to mount venturesome works and productions. Most performances are in the Landestheater, some in the Brucknerhaus.

The tourist office's monthly booklet "Was ist los in Linz und Oberösterreich" ("What's on in Linz and Upper Austria") will give you details of theater and concerts. Two **ticket agencies** are Linzer Kartenbüro (✉ Herrenstr. 4, ☎ 0732/778800) and Ruefa (✉ Landstr. 67, ☎ 0732/662681–0, FAX 0732/662681–33).

Concerts and recitals are held in the **Brucknerhaus,** the modern hall on the banks of the Danube. From mid-September to early October, it's the center of the International Bruckner Festival. In mid-June, the hall hosts the biggest multimedia event in the area, the Ars Electronica, a musical and laser-show spectacle. ✉ *Untere Donaulände 7,* ☎ *0732/7612–0,* FAX *0732/783745.* ☉ *Box office weekdays 10–6.*

NIGHTLIFE

A good starting point, where both the young and the older will feel comfortable, is the bar **S'Linzerl** (✉ Hofberg 5), which is open Monday–Saturday 9 PM–3 AM.

The Linz **casino,** with roulette, blackjack, poker, and slot machines, is in the Hotel Schillerpark; the casino complex includes a bar and the Rouge et Noir restaurant. A passport is required for admission. ⊠ *Rainerstr. 2–4,* ☎ *0732/654487–0,* FAX *0732/654487–24.* ▨ *AS210 (includes 5 AS50 tokens).* ⊙ *Daily 3 PM–3 AM. Closed Nov. 1 and Dec. 24.*

For the young crowd there are several choices for popular late-night clubs. One of the most frequented is **Sassi** (⊠ Spittelwiese 6–12, ☎ 0732/787850), in the Arkade Shopping Mall on the pedestrian Landstrasse, which features behind the bar a pyramid of champagne bottles that can only be reached by stepladder. Open every day from 9 to the wee hours, the modern bar also offers soup, sandwiches, and light pasta dishes. **Jedermans** (⊠ Spittelwiese 6-8, entrance on Landstrasse, ☎ 0732/787868) is another hopping establishment, located next door to the Arkade Shopping Mall and open every day from 5 on, with live music on Sunday and Monday at 8.

Shopping
Linz is a good place to shop; prices are generally lower than those in resorts and the larger cities, and selections are varied. The major shops are found in the main square and the adjoining side streets, in the old quarter to the west of the main square, in the pedestrian zone of the Landstrasse and its side streets, and in the Hauptstrasse of Urfahr, over the Nibelungen Bridge across the Danube.

For local handmade items and good-quality souvenirs, try **O. Ö. Heimatwerk** (⊠ Landstr. 31, ☎ 0732/773376–0), where you'll find silver, pewter, ceramics, fabrics, and some clothing. Items from clothing to china are sold at the **Flea Market,** open March–mid-November, Saturday 7–2, on the Hauptplatz (main square). From mid-November through February the market moves across the river next to the new city hall and runs Saturday from 8 to 2. At the state-run **Dorotheum auction house** (⊠ Fabrikstrasse 26, ☎ 0732/773132–0), auctions take place every Wednesday at 1:30.

For antiques head for the Old City, on the side streets around the main square. Try **Otto Buchinger** (⊠ Bethlehemstr. 5, ☎ 0732/770117), **Richard Kirchmayr** (⊠ Bischofstr. 3a, ☎ 0732/797711), **Kunsthandlung Kirchmayr** (⊠ Herrenstr. 23, ☎ 0732/774667), or **Ute Pastl** (⊠ Wischerstr. 26, Urfahr, ☎ 0732/737306).

For jewelry, try **Pfaffenberger** (⊠ Landstr. 42, ☎ 0732/772495) or **Wild** (⊠ Landstr. 49, ☎ 0732/774105–0).

Outdoor Activities and Sports
Buy tickets for sports events at **Kartenbüro Ruefa** (⊠ Landstr. 67, ☎ 0732/662681–0, FAX 0732/662681–33). The office is open weekdays 8:30–noon and 2–6 and Saturday 8:30–noon.

BICYCLING
Cyclists appreciate the relatively level terrain around Linz, and within the city there are 89 km (55 mi) of marked cycle routes. Get the brochure *Cycling in Linz* from the tourist office. You can rent a bike through **Fahrradzentrum B7** (⊠ Oberfelderstr. 12, ☎ 0732/330550) or **LILO Bahnhof** (⊠ Coulinstr. 30, ☎ 0732/600703) or at the **Hauptbahnhof** (⊠ Main rail station, Bahnhofstr. 3, ☎ 0732/6909–0).

GOLF
Fairly close to Linz is the 9-hole, par-72 **Golfclub St. Oswald-Freistadt** (⊠ Promenade 22, St. Oswald, ☎ 07945/794528). The 18-hole, par-72 **Böhmerwald Golfpark** (⊠ Seitelschlag 50, Ulrichsberg, ☎ 07288/8200) is near Linz. East of Linz is the relatively new 18-hole, par-71

Linzer Golf Club Mühlviertel (✉ Am Luftenberg 1a, Luftenberg, ☎ 07237/3893), playable mid-March–November.

ICE-SKATING

Linz is an ice-skating city. From late October to late February, there's outdoor skating at the city rink, daily 2–5, and also Friday–Wednesday 6–9, weekends 9–noon; it's also available late September to April indoors at the adjoining indoor sports complex, the **Eishalle,** Wednesday 9–noon, Saturday 2–5, and Sunday 10–noon, 2–5, and 6–9. Hockey and skating competitions are also held in the Eishalle. ✉ *Untere Donaulände 11,* ☎ *0732/778513.*

SOCCER

Soccer matches are played in Linz in the **Stadion** (✉ Roseggerstr. 41, ☎ 0732/660670 or 0732/601115).

TENNIS

Tennis matches and other sports events are held at the **Stadthalle** (☎ 0732/657311–0).

WATER SPORTS

The Danube is not suitable for swimming, but alternatives exist. The closest swimming is at **Pleschinger Lake**; to get there, take Tram 1 to Urfahr/Reindlstrasse and Bus 32 to the lake. This is a pleasant spot for family swimming, although it tends to be crowded on sunny, warm weekends. The **Kral Waterskiing School** (✉ Talgasse 14, ☎ 0732/731494) offers waterskiing and other water sports.

EXCURSIONS FROM LINZ

Many travelers find Linz the most practical point of departure for visits to the Mühlviertel and the Gothic and Baroque sights found in the towns of St. Florian, Kremsmünster, and Steyr, although Steyr certainly merits an overnight itself. North of Linz toward Freistadt and the Czech border, the Mühlviertel (a "mill district" now in the agricultural, not industrial, sense) is made up of meadows and gentle wooded hills interspersed with towns whose appearance has changed little since the Middle Ages. To the west of Linz, south of the Danube, lies the Innviertel, named for the Inn River (which forms the border with Germany before it joins the Danube), a region of broad fields and meadows, and enormous woodland tracts, ideal for cycling, hiking, and riding. To the south, the hilly landscape introduces the foothills of the Austrian Alps.

Freistadt

★ ㉖ *41 km (26 mi) northeast of Linz.*

Freistadt developed as a border defense city on the salt route into Bohemia (now the Czech Republic), which accounts for the wall, towers, and gates, still wonderfully preserved today. To get to Freistadt, a preserved walled city in the eastern part of the Mühviertel, cross the Danube to Linz-Urfahr and turn right onto Freistädter Strasse (Route 125/E55).

A walk around the wall gives an impression of how a city in the Middle Ages was conceived and defended; it takes about a half hour. Look at the late-Gothic **Linzertor** (the Linz Gate), with its steep, wedge-shape roof, and the **Böhmertor,** on the opposite wall, leading to the Czech Republic. The city's **central square,** aglow with pastel facades, is virtually the same as it was 400 years ago; only the parked cars intrude into the picture of antiquity. Pause for a local beer; the town's first brewery dates from 1573. The 15th-century parish church of **St. Catherine's** was redone in Baroque style in the 17th century but retains its slender tower, whose unusual balconies have railings on all four sides.

The late-Gothic castle to the northeast of the square now houses the **Mühlviertel Heimathaus** (district museum); the display of painted glass in the chapel and the hand tools in the 163-ft tower are especially interesting. ☎ 07942/72274. ⌨ AS20. ⊙ *Tour May–Oct., Tues.–Sat. at 10 and 2, Sun. at 10; Nov.–Apr., Tues.–Fri. at 10, Tues. and Thurs. at 10 and 2.*

Centering on Freistadt is a historical road called the **Museumstrasse,** which takes you to points of interest from the glory days of the Mühlvietal, when this area was famous for its mills. Among places to stop and visit are historical mills, a former dyeing-works museum, and a leather-working museum. Contact the Mühlviertel Tourist Office (⌧ Blütenstr. 8, A–4040, ☎ 0732/735020, ℻ 0732/712400) in Linz for information.

Dining and Lodging

$$ ✕⌗ **Zum Goldenen Adler.** Here you'll be in another 600-year-old house;
★ it has been run by the same family since 1807, so tradition runs strong. The medium-size rooms are modern yet full of country charm; hotel service is exceptionally accommodating. The newly renovated garden, with a piece of the old city wall as background, is a delightful oasis. The restaurant can be variable but is known for regional specialties such as *Böhmisches Bierfleisch* (beef cooked in beer). The desserts are outstanding. ⌧ *Salzgasse 1, A–4240,* ☎ *07942/72112–0,* ℻ *07942/72112–44. 30 rooms. Restaurant, pool, sauna, exercise room. AE, DC, MC, V.*

Kefermarkt

㉗ *9 km (5½ mi) south of Freistadt.*

From Freistadt, you can get to Kefermarkt either via marked back roads or by turning east off of Route 125/E14. Both towns can be visited on a loop excursion from Linz. The late-Gothic **church of St. Wolfgang** boasts one of Austria's great art treasures, a 42-ft-high winged altar intricately carved from linden wood, commissioned by Christoph von Zelking, and completed in 1497. So masterly is the carving that it has been ascribed to famous 15th-century sculptors Veit Stoss and Michael Pacher, but most historians now attribute it to Jürg Huber and Martin Kriechbaum. Some figures, such as St. Christopher, are true masterpieces of northern Renaissance sculpture. The church also has some impressive 16th-century frescoes.

Eferding

㉘ *25 km (16 mi) west of Linz.*

Eferding, a centuries-old community with an attractive town square, lies west of Linz. You can easily drive the 25 km (16 mi) on Route 129, but the more adventurous route is via the **LILO** (Linzer Lokalbahn) interurban railway from Coulinstrasse 30 (☎ 0732/654376), near the main rail station.

In Eferding, the double door in the south wall of the 15th-century **church of St. Hippolyte** is a gem of late-Gothic stonecutting, with the Madonna and Child above flanked by Saints Hippolyte and Agyd. Inside, note the Gothic altar with its five reliefs and the statues of Saints Wolfgang and Martin. Visit the **Spitalskirche** (built in 1325) and note the Gothic frescoes in the Magdalen chapel, which date to about 1430.

Dining and Lodging

$$$$ ✕ **Dannerbauer.** Two kilometers (1 mile) north of Eferding, on the road
★ to Aschach and directly on the Danube, is one of the area's best restau-

rants. It serves many species of fish—some you probably never heard of—to your taste: poached, grilled, broiled, or fried. Many of the fish come from the river; some are raised in the house ponds, to ensure freshness. There are meat dishes, too, and game in season, and the soups (try the nettle soup) are excellent. The place has a pleasant outlook with lots of windows. ⊠ *Brandstatt bei Eferding,* ☎ *07272/2471. AE, DC. Closed Mon.–Tues. and mid-Jan.–mid-Feb.*

$ 🏨 **Zum Goldenen Kreuz.** The golden facade indicates a typical country-style hotel, simple and with the appealing charm of a family-run establishment. You'll sleep under fluffy feather-bed coverlets. The restaurant is known for its good regional cuisine, and there are occasional specialty weeks. ⊠ *Schmiedstr. 29, A–4070,* ☎ *07272/4247–0,* FAX *07272/4249. 21 rooms. Restaurant. AE, DC, MC. Closed Christmas wk.*

Hartkirchen

㉙ *12 km (7 mi) north of Eferding, 26 km (16¼ mi) northwest of Linz.*

The **parish church** at Hartkirchen is worth a visit to see fine Baroque wall and ceiling frescoes, dated 1750, that create the illusion of space and depth. To reach Hartkirchen, take Route 130 north from Eferding to Pupping and continue 3 km (2 mi).

Aschach

㉚ *2 km (1 mi) north of Hartkirchen, 21 km (13¼ mi) northwest of Linz.*

Aschach, a small village that was once a river toll station, is the birthplace of Leonard Paminger, one of the most noted 16th-century Austrian composers. It features several gabled-roof burghers' houses, a castle, and a late-Gothic church that are all well preserved. Less intact is the castle, now semi-ruined, that once belonged to the regal Counts of Harrach, located near the town.

Lodging

$$ 🏨 **Faust Schlössl.** Once a toll-collection station belonging to the
★ Schaunberg family (ruins of the family castle are nearby), this castle is on the river directly across from Aschach. Rumor has it that the place is haunted by the Devil, who is said to have built it in a single night for Dr. Faustus. Ignore the tale and enjoy simple but modern comfort in the towers and turrets of the converted castle. ⊠ *Oberlandshaag 2, A–4082 Feldkirchen,* ☎ *07233/7402–0,* FAX *07233/7402–40. 25 rooms. Restaurant, pool, fishing, bicycles. AE, MC, V.*

$$ 🏨 **Zur Sonne.** The welcome of the bright yellow facade carries over to the comfortable, traditional decor inside. You're right on the Danube here, and the best rooms have a river view. This popular restaurant offers regional specialties and, of course, fish, including fresh trout. ⊠ *Kurzwernhartpl. 5, A–4082 Aschach/Donau,* ☎ *07273/6308. 12 rooms. Restaurant. No credit cards.*

St. Florian

★ ㉛ *13 km (8 mi) southeast of Linz.*

St. Florian is best known for the great Augustinian abbey, considered among the finest Baroque buildings in Austria. Composer Anton Bruckner (1824–96) was organist for 10 years and is buried in the abbey. From Linz, you can drive south through Kleinmünchen and Ebelsberg to St. Florian, or for a more romantic approach, try the **Florianer Bahn,** a resurrected electric interurban tram line, which runs museum streetcars on Sundays from May through the end of September, 6 km

(4 mi) from Pichling to St. Florian (☎ 0732/387778); streetcars depart at 10:44, 2:14, and 3:44.

Guided tours of **Stift St. Florian** (Abbey of St. Florian) include a magnificent figural gate encompassing all three stories, a large and elegant staircase leading to the upper floors, the imperial suite, and one of the great masterworks of the Austrian Baroque, Jakob Prandtauer's **Eagle Fountain courtyard,** with its richly sculpted figures. In the splendid **abbey church,** where the ornate decor is somewhat in contrast to Bruckner's music, the Krismann organ (1770–74) is one of the largest and best of its period. Another highlight is the **Altdorfer Gallery,** which contains several masterworks by Albrecht Altdorfer, the leading master of the 16th-century Danube School and ranked with Dürer and Grunewald as one of the greatest northern painters. ⊠ *Stiftstr. 1,* ☎ *07224/8902–10.* ☜ *AS60.* ☉ *1½-hr tour Apr.–Oct., daily at 10, 11, 2, 3, and 4.*

Nightlife and the Arts

Summer concerts are held in June and July at the Kremsmünster (☞ *below*) and St. Florian abbeys; for tickets, contact Oberösterreichische Stiftskonzerte (⊠ Domgasse 12, ☎ 0732/776127). A **chamber music festival** (☎ 0732/775230) takes place in July at Schloss Tillysburg, 1½ km (1 mi) from St. Florian. In July and August, a series of **concerts** on the Bruckner organ are given on Sunday afternoons at 4:30 in the church (☎ 07224/8903).

Kremsmünster

�932 *36 km (22½ mi) south of Linz.*

The vast Benedictine **Stift Kremsmünster** was established in 777 and remains one of the most important cloisters in Austria. Most travelers arrive here by taking Route 139 (or the train) heading southwest from Linz. Inside the church is the Gothic memorial tomb of Gunther, killed by a wild boar, whose father, Tassilo, duke of Bavaria (and nemesis of Charlemagne), vowed to build the abbey on the site. Centuries later, a Baroque extravaganza replaced the initial structures. There are magnificent rooms: the Kaisersaal and the frescoed library with more than 100,000 volumes, many of them manuscripts. On one side of the Prälatenhof courtyard are Jakob Prandtauer's elegant fish basins, complete with sculpted saints, holding squirming denizens of the deep, and opposite is the Abteitrakt, whose art collection includes the Tassilo Chalice, from about 765. The eight-story observatory houses an early museum of science. ☎ *07583/275–216.* ☜ *Rooms and art gallery AS45, observatory and tour AS50.* ☉ *Rooms and art-gallery tour (minimum 5 people) Easter–Oct., daily at 10, 11, 2, 3, and 4; Nov.–Easter at 11 and 2. Observatory tour (minimum 5 people) May–June and Sept.–Oct., daily at 10 and 2; July–Aug., daily at 10, 2, and 4.*

☾ **Schloss Kremsegg,** has a collection of old-fashioned cars and motorcycles. ⊠ *Rte. 139,* ☎ *07583/52470,* ℻ *07583/5395.* ☜ *AS70.* ☉ *Sept.–June, Sat. 1–5, Sun. 10–noon and 1–5; July–Aug. Sat. and Sun. 10–noon, 1–5.*

Bad Hall

�933 *9 km (5½ mi) southeast of Kremsmünster, 36 km (22 mi) south of Linz.*

Bad Hall is a curious relic from earlier days when "taking the cure" was in vogue in Europe. It's still a spa and its saline-iodine waters are prescribed for internal and external application, but you can also enjoy the town for its turn-of-the-century setting. Since those on the cure need amusement between treatments, the town lays on numerous sports offerings—-during warm weather, there are especially excellent opportunities for golf and tennis—and an operetta festival in summer.

Lodging

$$$$ 🏨 **Schlosshotel Feyregg.** You'll be in an exclusive setting in this Baroque
★ castle just outside town, once the elegant summer residence of an abbot. The comfortable, spacious guest rooms on the ground floor are furnished in period style. The golf course is within an easy stroll. ⊠ *A–4540,* ☎ *07258/2591. 11 rooms. Bar. No credit cards.*

Steyr

★ ㉞ *18 km (11 mi) east of Bad Hall, 40 km (25 mi) south of Linz.*

If you travel to Steyr from Kremsmünster, follow Route 139 until it joins Route 122 and take the road another 17 km (10½ mi).

Steyr is one of Austria's best-kept secrets, a stunning Gothic market town that watches over the confluence of the Steyr and Enns rivers. Today the main square is lined with pastel facades, many with Baroque and rococo trim, all complemented by the castle that sits above. The Bummerlhaus at Number 32, in its present form dating to 1497, has a late-Gothic three-story effect. On the Enns side, steps and narrow passageways lead down to the river.

In Steyr you are close to the heart of Bruckner country. He composed his Sixth Symphony in the Parish House here, and there is a Bruckner room in the Meserhaus where he composed his "sonorous music to confound celestial spheres." Schubert also lived here for a time. So many of the houses are worthy of attention that you will need to take your time and explore. Given the quaintness of the town center, you'd hardly guess that in 1894 Steyr had Europe's first electric street lighting.

The **Steyrertalbahn** (☎ 07252/46569 or 0732/250345), a narrow-gauge vintage railroad, wanders 17 km (10½ mi) from Steyr through the countryside on weekends June–September.

The **Museum Industrielle Arbeitswelt** (industrial museum) set in former riverside factories is a reminder of the era when Steyr was a major center of ironmaking and armaments production; hunting arms are still produced here, but the major output is powerful motors for BMW cars, including those assembled in the United States. ⊠ *Wehrgrabengasse 7,* ☎ *07252/77351–0.* ⌨ *AS55.* ☉ *Tues.–Sun. 10–5.*

Dining and Lodging

$$ ✕ **Schloss Lamberg.** This large, wood-paneled restaurant located on the castle grounds serves traditional Austrian fare in a rustic atmosphere. Besides the ubiquitous schnitzels and boiled beef, there are a number of fresh fish dishes from which to choose. ⊠ *Bergg. 2,* ☎ *07252/48675. AE, DC, MC, V. Closed Mon.–Tues. Jan.–Mar.*

$ ✕ **Cafe Illecker.** This modern cafe is tucked away on a narrow cobblestone street leading up from the main square. The selection of pastries is tempting, and along with the wonderful aroma of freshly brewed coffee, it's no wonder this is a favorite gathering place for locals. ⊠ *Pfarrg. 6,* ☎ *07252/53926. No credit cards.*

$ ✕ **Treff Bar.** Just off the main square is a narrow passageway going down to the banks of the river, through which you must duck under an ancient archway to reach this old establishment. It's dark and cozy inside, with candlelit tables and odd scraps of artwork on the walls. There's a full cocktail menu, and light dishes are served as well. In summer tables are set outside on the stunning riverfront terrace, perfect for sipping a cold beer. ⊠ *Goldschmiedg. 3,* ☎ *07252/47237. No credit cards.*

$$$ ✕☷ **Minichmayr.** From this traditional hotel the view alone—out over the confluence of the Enns and Steyr rivers, up and across to Schloss Lamberg—will make your stay memorable. The rooms don't quite measure up to the charm of the building's exterior and public rooms; your best bet is to ask for one on the river side. The restaurant offers light cuisine, specializing in fresh fish. The grilled trout with almond butter is especially good. The hotel is one of the Romantik Hotel group. ✉ *Haratzmüllerstr. 1–3, A–4400,* ☎ *07252/53410–0,* ℻ *07252/48202–55. 51 rooms. Restaurant, bar, weinstube, no-smoking rooms, sauna, exercise room, bicycles. AE, DC, MC, V.*

$$ ✕☷ **Mader/Zu den Drei Rosen.** In this very old family-run hotel with small but pleasant modern rooms, you're right on the attractive town square. The restaurant offers solid local and traditional fare, with outdoor dining in a delightful garden area within the ancient courtyard. ✉ *Stadtpl. 36, A–4400,* ☎ *07252/53358–0,* ℻ *07252/53358–6. 53 rooms. Restaurant, weinstube. AE, DC, MC, V.*

THE WACHAU ALONG THE SOUTH BANK OF THE DANUBE

South of the Danube and east of Linz, the gentle countryside is crossed by rivers that rise in the Alps and eventually feed the Danube. Little evidence remains today, in this prosperous country of small-industry and agriculture, that the area was heavily fought over in the final days of World War II. From 1945 to 1995, the River Enns marked the border between the western (U.S., British, and French) and the eastern (Russian) occupying zones.

Enns

③⑤   *20 km (12 mi) southeast of Linz.*

A settlement has existed continuously at Enns since at least AD 50; the Romans set up a major encampment shortly after that date. Contemporary Enns is dominated by the 184-ft square city tower (1565–68) that stands in the town square. A number of Gothic buildings in the center have Renaissance or Baroque facades.

Visit the **Basilika St. Laurenz,** built on the foundations of a far earlier church, west of the town center, to view the glass-encased archaeological discoveries from earlier civilizations. And outside, look for the Baroque carved-wood Pontius Pilate disguised as a Turk, alongside a bound Christ, on the balcony of the old sanctuary.

Guided tours (☎ 07223/3261) of the town's highlights, starting at the tower, are available for a minimum of three persons daily at 9:15 and 10:30, May–mid-September.

Lodging

$$$ ☷ **Lauriacum.** You might overlook this plain contemporary building, set as it is among Baroque gems in the center of town, but it's the best place to stay. The bright rooms offer modern comfort, and the quiet garden is a welcoming spot. ✉ *Wiener Str. 5–7, A–4470,* ☎ *07223/82315,* ℻ *07223/82332–29. 30 rooms. Restaurant, bar, café, sauna. MC, V.*

Mauthausen

③⑥   *14 km (8½ mi) southeast of Linz, 6 km (4 mi) north of Enns.*

Adolf Hitler had the **Mauthausen Konzentrationslager,** the main concentration camp in Austria, built here along the banks of the Danube bearing the same name. From Linz, follow signs to Enns and Perg, and then to the EHEMALIGE KL DENKMAL, the concentration-camp memorial. The pretty town of Mauthausen was selected as the site for a concentration camp because of the granite quarries nearby, which would provide material needed for the grand buildings in Hitler's projected "Führer-Cities." The grim, gray fortress was opened in August 1938 for male prisoners (including children), and the conditions under which they labored were severe even by SS standards. More than 125,000 lost their lives here before the camp was liberated by the American army in May 1945. The site includes a small museum and memorials, as well as a bookstore. ✉ *Erinnerungsstr. 1, A–4310,* ☎ *07238/2269 or 07238/3696,* ℻ *07238/4889.* ▦ *AS25.* ☉ *Feb.–Mar. and Oct.–Dec. 15, 8–4 (last admission 3 PM); Apr.–Sept., 8–6 (last admission 5 PM).*

Waidhofen an der Ybbs

㊲ *30 km (18 mi) east of Steyr.*

Waidhofen an der Ybbs is well worth a slight detour from the more traveled routes. This picturesque river town developed early as an industrial center, turning Styrian iron ore into swords, knives, sickles, and scythes. These weapons proved successful in the defense against the invading Turks in 1532; marking the decisive moment of victory, the hands on the north side of the town tower clock remain at 12:45. In 1871, Baron Rothschild bought the collapsing castle and assigned Friedrich Schmidt, architect of the Vienna city hall, to rebuild it in neo-Gothic style. Stroll around the two squares in the Altstadt to see the Gothic and Baroque houses and to the Graben on the edge of the Old City for the delightful Biedermeier houses and the churches and chapels. From Enns, take the A1 autobahn or Route 1 east to just before Amstetten, where Route 121 cuts south paralleling the Ybbs River and the branch rail line for about 25 km (16 mi).

Ybbs an der Donau

㊳ *69 km (43 mi) east of Linz.*

Floods and fires have left their mark on Ybbs an der Donau, but many 16th century houses remain, their courtyards vine-covered and shaded. The parish church of **St. Laurence** has interesting old tombstones, a gorgeous gilded organ, and a Mount of Olives scene with clay figures dating to 1450. To get to Ybbs an der Donau from Waidhofen an der Ybbs, make your way back to the Danube via Routes 31 and 22 east, then Route 25 north through the beer-brewing town of Wieselburg.

Melk

★ **㊴** *22 km (13 mi) east of Ybbs an der Donau, 18 km (11 mi) west of St. Pölten, 33 km (20¾ mi) southwest of Krems.*

The ideal time to approach the magnificent abbey of Melk is mid- to late afternoon, when the sun sets the abbey's ornate Baroque yellow facade aglow. As one heads eastward paralleling the Danube, the abbey, shining on its promontory above the river, comes into view— unquestionably one of the most impressive sights in all Austria. The glories of the abbey tend to overshadow the town—located along Route 1—but the riverside village of Melk itself is worth exploring. A self-guided tour (in English, from the tourist office) will head you toward the highlights and the best spots from which to photograph the abbey.

★ By any standard **Stift Melk** (Melk Abbey) is a Baroque masterpiece. Here the story of Umberto Eco's historical novel and film *The Name of the*

Rose took place, and in fact, as in fiction, the monastery did burn in 1297, in 1683, and again in 1735. The Benedictine abbey was established in 1089; the building you see today dates to architect Jakob Prandtauer's reconstruction, completed in 1736, in which some earlier elements are incorporated. Part palace, part monastery, part opera set, Melk is a classic vision thanks greatly to the upward-reaching twin towers, capped with Baroque helmets and cradling a 208-ft-high dome, and a roof bristling with Baroque statuary. Symmetry here beyond the towers and dome would be misplaced, and much of the abbey's charm is due to the way the early architects were forced to fit the building to the rocky outcrop that forms its base. A tour of the building includes the main public rooms: a magnificent library, with more than 70,000 books, 2,000 manuscripts, and a superb ceiling fresco by the master Paul Troger; the marble hall, whose windows on three sides enhance the ceiling frescoes; the glorious spiral staircase; and the church of Saints Peter and Paul, an exquisite example of the Baroque style. There is one tour in English at 3 PM. The **Stiftsrestaurant,** which is closed November–April, offers standard fare, but the abbey's excellent wines elevate a simple meal to a lofty experience—particularly on a sunny day on the terrace. ⊠ *Abt Berthold Dietmayr-Str. 1,* ☎ *02752/2312–232.* 🍴 *AS55, AS70 with tour; combined ticket with Schloss Schallaburg (☞ below).* ☉ *Apr.–Oct., daily 9–5 (50-min tour hourly; last tour at 4); tour Nov.–Mar., daily at 11 and 2.*

Dining and Lodging

$$–$$$ ✕🛏 **Stadt Melk.** This traditional hotel in the heart of town offers plain but adequate accommodations in smallish rooms (look before you register), but the main feature here is the excellent and attractive restaurant. The cuisine ranges from regional traditional to creative light; try one of the cream soups, stuffed chicken breast, or rack of lamb in an olive crust to enjoy the contrasts. Dishes here are individually prepared. ⊠ *Hauptpl. 1, A–3390,* ☎ *02752/52475 or 02752/52547,* 🅵🆇 *02752/2475–19. 16 rooms. Restaurant. AE, DC, MC, V. Closed mid-Nov.–mid-Dec.*

$$ 🛏 **Goldener Ochs.** Here in the center of town you're in a typical village *Gasthof* with the traditional friendliness of family management. The rather small rooms were renovated in 1990, and the restaurant offers solid, standard fare. ⊠ *Linzer Str. 18, A–3390,* ☎ *02752/ 52367–0,* 🅵🆇 *02752/52367–6. 35 rooms, 25 with bath. Restaurant, sauna, exercise room, bicycles. AE, DC, MC, V.*

Schallaburg

㊵   *6 km (4 mi) south of Melk.*

From Melk, take a road south marked to Mank to arrive at the restored Protestant **Schloss Schallaburg** (dating from 1573), a castle featuring an imposing two-story arcaded courtyard that is held to be the area's finest example of Renaissance architecture. Its ornate, warm brown terra-cotta decoration is unusual. The yard once served as a jousting court. Many centuries have left their mark on the castle: inside, the Romanesque living quarters give way to an ornate Gothic chapel. The castle now houses changing special exhibits. ⊠ *3382 Schloss Schallaburg,* ☎ *02754/6317 or 02754/6889.* 🍴 *AS65; AS20 with tour; combined ticket with Stift Melk (Melk Abbey) (☞ above) AS105.* ☉ *May–Oct., weekdays 9–5, weekends 9–6 (last admission 1 hr before closing).*

En Route   To return to the Wachau from Schallaburg, head back toward Melk and take Route 33 along the south bank. This route, attractive any time of the year, is spectacular (and thus heavily traveled) in early spring, when apricot and apple trees burst into glorious blossom. Among the palette of photogenic pleasures is **Schönbühel an der Donau,** whose unbelievably picturesque castle, perched on a cliff overlooking the Danube, is unfortunately not open to visitors. Past the village of Aggsbach Dorf you'll spot, on a hill to your right, the romantic ruin of 13th-century Aggstein Castle, reportedly the lair of pirates who preyed on river traffic.

Mautern

㊶ *34 km (21 mi) north east of Melk, 1 km (½ mi) south of Stein.*

Mautern, opposite Krems, was a Roman encampment mentioned in the tales of the Nibelungs. The old houses and the castle are attractive, but contemporary Mautern is known for one of Austria's top restaurants (☞ Dining and Lodging, *below*), in an inn run by Lisl Bacher; another culinary landmark—also excellent— is run by her sister (☞ Schickh *in* Göttweig, *below*).

Dining and Lodging

$$$$ ✕🖫 **Landhaus Bacher.** Lisl Bacher's creative, light cuisine has elevated
★ this attractive restaurant to one of the top six in the country. Quality is consistently outstanding and the setting is delightful. The light-flooded rooms are elegant but not pretentious, and there's an attractive garden for alfresco dining. Offerings change regularly, reflecting the season and Bacher's remarkable inventiveness—simple perfection in the combination of ingredients and courses. Among main dishes, you might find local lamb with olives and artichoke hearts or guinea fowl with truffles. Ask for advice on wines; the choice is wide. There are a few small and cozy rooms in an adjoining guest house. ☒ *Südtirolerpl. 208,* ☎ *02732/82937–0 or 02732/85429,* FAX *02732/74337. Reservations essential. DC, V. Closed Mon.–Tues. Nov.–Apr., and mid-Jan.–mid-Feb. No lunch Mon.–Tues. May–Oct.*

Göttweig

㊷ *4 km (2½ mi) south of Mautern, 7 km (4½ mi) south of Krems.*

★ You're certain to spot **Stift Göttweig** (Göttweig Abbey) as you come along the riverside road: The vast Benedictine abbey high above the Danube Valley watches over the gateway to the Wachau. To reach it, go along Route 33, turn right onto the highway south (marked to Stift Göttweig and St. Pölten), and turn right again (marked to Stift Göttweig) at the crest of the hill. Göttweig's exterior was redone in the mid-1700s in the classical style, which you'll note from the columns, balcony, and relatively plain side towers. Inside, it is a monument to Baroque art, with marvelous ornate decoration against the gold, brown, and blue. The stained-glass windows behind the high altar date to the mid-1400s. The public rooms of the abbey are splendid, particularly the Kaiserzimmer (Emperor's Rooms), in which Napoléon stayed in 1809, reached via the elegant emperor's staircase. ☒ *Furth bei Göttweig,* ☎ *02732/85581–231.* 🎫 *AS50.* ☉ *Daily 10–5; tours (minimum 8 people) Easter–Oct., daily at 10, 11, 2, 3, and 4.*

Dining

$$$ ✕ **Schickh.** This restaurant, tucked away among lovely old trees below
★ the north side of the Göttweig Abbey, is worth looking for. Creative ideas out of the kitchen transform seasonal and regional specialties. You might be offered asparagus wrapped in smoked lamb or tender roast baby lamb. In summer you'll dine in the garden, probably rubbing elbows with the knowledgeable Viennese elite. There's a handful of guest rooms available for overnights. ☒ *Klein-Wein 2, Furth bei Göttweig,* ☎ *02736/7218–0,* FAX *02736/7218–7. Reservations essential. No credit cards. Closed Wed.–Thurs. and Mar.*

$-$$ ✕ **Stiftsrestaurant.** The terrace restaurant on the abbey grounds offers not only good standard Austrian cuisine but, on a fine day, a spectacular view. It's a great spot for lunch, coffee, or a drink. The grilled chicken can be recommended without reservation. You might try—and buy by the bottle—the excellent wines produced by the abbey. ⊠ *Stift Göttweig, A–3511 Furth bei Göttweig,* ☎ *02732/84663. AE, DC, MC, V. Closed Nov.–Mar.*

St. Pölten

㊸ *18 km (11 mi) south of Göttweig, 65 km (40¼ mi) west of Vienna.*

St. Pölten, Lower Austria's capital to the south of the Danube, is a city of comfortable contrasts and, for some, will be worth a detour 20 km (12½ mi) to the south of the main stretch of the Wachau. The old municipal center, now mainly a pedestrian zone, shows a distinctly Baroque face. The originally Romanesque cathedral on Domplatz has a rich Baroque interior; the rococo Franciscan church at the north end of the Rathausplatz has four altar paintings by Kremser Schmidt.

In a moated castle north of Pottenbrunn, 6½ km (4¼ mi) east of St. Pölten, there's a fascinating museum, the **Zinnfigurenmuseum** (Tin Figure Museum) devoted to authentically detailed tin soldiers. Imagine a bird's-eye view of entire armies in battle formation; you'll see thousands of soldiers at their posts in the battles of Leipzig (1813), Berg Isel (Innsbruck, 1809), Vienna (1683), and World War I. ⊠ *Pottenbrunner Hauptstr. 77,* ☎ *02785/42337.* 🎫 *AS50.* ☉ *Apr.–Oct., Tues.–Sun. 9–5.*

Dining and Lodging

$$$ ✕ **Galerie.** Mellow furnishings from long-gone dining rooms and hotels lend atmosphere to this stylish restaurant. In contrast to the antiques, the kitchen strives to do new things—generally successfully—with Austrian standards like pork fillet and turkey breast. ⊠ *Fuhrmanngasse 1,* ☎ *02742/351305. AE, DC, MC, V. Closed Sun.–Mon. and 2 wks around Easter.*

$$$ 🏨 **Metropol.** Slick modern styling marks this modern hotel on the edge of the pedestrian zone at the heart of the Old City. Rooms are comfortable, if rather uniform. ⊠ *Schillerpl. 1, A–3100,* ☎ *02742/ 70700–0,* 🗚 *02742/70700–133. 100 rooms. Restaurant, bar, sauna, parking. AE, DC, MC, V.*

OFF THE
BEATEN PATH
HERZOGENBURG – The great Augustinian monastery of Herzogenburg is 11 km (6½ mi) north of St. Pölten (take Wiener Strasse/Route 1 out of St. Pölten heading east for 12 km/8 mi to Kapelln; then turn left to Herzogenburg). The present buildings date mainly to the mid-1700s. Fischer von Erlach was among the architects who designed the abbey. The church, dedicated to Saints George and Stephen, is wonderfully Baroque, with exquisitely decorated ceilings. ☎ *02782/83112–0.* 🎫 *AS40.* ☉ *1-hr tour Apr.–Oct., daily at 9–11 and 2–5 on the hr.*

En Route Small rural villages abound on the south bank plain, some quaint, some typical. From St. Pölten, head north on Route S33 or the parallel road, marked to Traismauer, and pick up Route 43 east. If you're ready for back roads (too well marked for you to get lost), cut off to the left to Oberbierbaum (Upper Beer Tree) and then proceed on to Zwentendorf (there's a fascinating black madonna in the side chapel of the parish church here). If you follow Route 43, it will land you on Route 1 at Mitterndorf; drive east and after 4 km (2½ mi), turn left off Route 1 onto Route 19, marked for Tulln.

Tulln

㊹ *41 km (24½ mi) northeast of St. Pölten, 42 km (26¼ mi) west of Vienna.*

At Tulln, you'll spot a number of charming Baroque touches in the attractive main square. There's a new **Egon Schiele Museum** to honor the great modern artist, who was born here (1890–1918); the museum showing a selection of his works is in the onetime district prison, with a reconstruction of the cell in which Schiele—accused of producing "pornography"—was locked up in 1912. ✉ *Donaulände 28,* ☎ *02272/64570.* ▨ *AS30, more for special exhibits.* ۞ *Tues.–Sun. 9–noon and 2–6.*

A former **Minorite cloister** now houses a collection of museums. Among the more interesting are the **Limesmuseum,** which recalls the early Roman settlements in the area, and the **Landesfeuerwehrmuseum,** documenting rural firefighting. Also look inside the well-preserved, late-Baroque (1750) Minorite church next door. ✉ *Minoritenpl. 1,* ☎ *02272/61915.* ▨ *Each museum AS30.* ۞ *Weekdays 3–6, Sat. 2–6, Sun. 10–6.*

Dining and Lodging

$$$$ ✕ **Zum Roten Wolf.** In an unpretentious but attractive rustic restau-
★ rant (one of Austria's top 20) in Langelebarn, 4 km (2½ mi) east of Tulln, the stylishly elegant table settings complement the consistently outstanding food. Neither preparation nor presentation leaves anything to be desired. Start with artichoke cream soup, followed by duck breast in a ginger curry sauce with juniper berries and rosemary rösti, or lamb in an olive crust with okra and vegetable lasagne. The service is especially friendly; ask for advice on the wines. You can get here by local train from Vienna; the station is virtually at the door. ✉ *Bahnstr. 58,* ☎ *02272/62567. Reservations essential. AE, DC, MC, V. Closed Mon.–Tues.*

$$ ☷ **Zur Rossmühle.** From the abundant greenery of the reception area to the table settings in the dining room, you'll find pleasing little touches in this attractively renovated hotel on the town square. The rooms are done in grand old yet brand-new Baroque. Take lunch in the courtyard garden; here, as in the more formal dining room, you'll be offered Austrian standards. ✉ *Hauptpl. 12–13, A–3430,* ☎ *02272/62411,* ℻ *02272/62411–33. 55 rooms. Restaurant, bar, sauna, horseback riding. AE, DC, V.*

Greifenstein

㊺ *10 km (6½ mi) northeast of Tulln.*

Greifenstein is east of Tulln along Route 14; turn left at St. Andrä-Wördern and stay on the Danube shoreline. Atop the hill at Greifenstein, yet another **castle** with spectacular views looks up the Danube and across to Stockerau. Its earliest parts date to 1135, but most of it stems from a thorough but romantic renovation in 1818. The view is worth the climb, even when the castle and inexpensive restaurant are closed. ✉ *Kostersitzgasse 5,* ☎ *02242/32353.* ۞ *Mar.–Dec., Wed.–Sun.*

Klosterneuburg

㊻ *13 km (8 mi) northwest of Vienna.*

The great Augustinian **abbey** dominates the scene at Klosterneuburg. The structure has changed many times since the abbey was established in 1114, most recently in 1892, when Friedrich Schmidt, architect of Vienna's city hall, added neo-Gothic features to its two identifying towers. Klosterneuburg was unusual in that until 1568 it housed both men's and women's religious orders. In the abbey church, look for the carved-wood choir loft and oratory and the large 17th-century organ. Among Klosterneuburg's treasures are the beautifully enameled 1181 Verdun Altar in the Leopold Chapel, stained-glass windows from the 14th and 15th centuries, Romanesque candelabra from the 12th century, and gorgeous ceiling frescoes in the great marble hall. In an adjacent outbuilding there's a huge wine cask over which people slide. The exercise, called *Fasslrutsch'n*, is indulged in during the Leopoldiweinkost, the wine tasting around St. Leopold's Day, November 15. ⊠ *Stiftspl. 1*, ☎ *02243/411–0.* ⌨ *AS50.* ☉ *1-hr tour Mon.–Sat. 9–11 and 1:30–4:30 on the hr, Sun. at 11 and on the hr 1:30–4:30.*

Dining

$$ ✕ Stiftskeller. The main dining rooms are on the ground floor, but instead seek out the atmospheric underground rooms in a historic part of the abbey. This is an authentic cellar in every sense of the word, with some of the fine wines even carrying the Klosterneuburg label. You can sample them along with standard Austrian fare, from Wiener schnitzel to rump steak with onions. ⊠ *Albrechtsbergergasse 1*, ☎ *02243/32070. No credit cards.*

OFF THE   **KAHLENBERGERDORF** – Near Klosterneuburg and just off the road tucked
BEATEN PATH   under the Leopoldsberg promontory is the charming small vintners' village of Kahlenbergerdorf, an excellent spot to stop and sample the local wines. You're just outside the Vienna city limits here, which accounts for the crowds (of Viennese, not international tourists) on weekends.

DANUBE VALLEY A TO Z

Arriving and Departing

By Boat

Large riverboats with sleeping accommodations ply the route between Vienna and Linz and between Passau on the German border and Linz from late spring to early fall. Smaller day boats go between Vienna and the Wachau Valley, and there you can change to local boats that crisscross the river between the colorful towns.

For information on boat schedules, contact **DDSG/Blue Danube Schiffahrt** (⊠ Friedrichstr. 7, A–1010 Vienna, ☎ 01/588800, ℻ 01/58880–440; ⊠ Untere Donaulände 10, A–4010 Linz, ☎ 0732/783607) or **Fitzcaraldo Donauschiffahrt** (⊠ Ottensheimer Str. 37, A–4010 Linz, ☎ 0732/0664/140–4568). Danube boat services from Melk to Krems with stops between within the Wachau region are operated by **Brandner Schiffahrt** (⊠ Ufer 50, A–3313 Wallsee, ☎ 07433/2590–0).

By Car

A car is certainly the most comfortable way to see this region, as it conveniently enables you to pursue the byways. The main route along the north bank is Route 3; along the south bank, there's a choice of autobahn Route A1 or a collection of lesser but good roads.

By Plane

Linz is served mainly by Austrian Airlines, Lufthansa, Swissair, and Tyrolean. Regular flights connect with Vienna, Amsterdam, Berlin, Düsseldorf, Frankfurt, Paris, Stuttgart, and Zürich. The **Linz airport** (☎ 0732/07221/600–0) is in Hörsching, about 12 km (7½ mi) southwest of the city. Buses run between the airport and the main railroad station according to flight schedules.

By Train

Rail lines parallel the north and south banks of the Danube. Fast services from Vienna run as far as Stockerau; beyond that, service is less frequent. The main east–west line from Vienna to Linz closely follows the south bank for much of its route. Fast trains connect German cities via Passau with Linz.

Getting Around

By Boat

Bridges across the river are few along this stretch, so boats provide essential transportation; service is frequent enough that you can cross the river, visit a town, catch a bus or the next boat to the next town, and cross the river farther up- or downstream. You can take a day trip from Vienna and explore one of the stops, such as Krems, Dürnstein, or Melk. Boats run from May to late September.

By Bus

If you link them together, bus routes will get you to the main points in this region and even to the hilltop castles and monasteries, assuming you have the time. If you coordinate your schedule to arrive at a point by train or boat, you can usually make reasonable bus connections to outlying destinations. You can book bus tours in Vienna (☞ Guided Tours, *below*); in Linz, ask at the municipal bus station (⊠ Bahnhofpl. 12, ☏ 0732/1671).

By Car

A car is certainly the most hassle-free way to get around. Roads are good and well marked, and you can switch over to the A1 autobahn, which parallels the general east–west course of the route (☞ Driving *in* the Gold Guide).

By Train

Every larger town and city in the region can be reached by train, but the train misses the Wachau Valley along the Danube's south bank. The rail line on the north side of the river clings to the bank in places; service is infrequent. You can combine rail and boat transportation along this route, taking the train upstream and crisscrossing your way back on the river. From Linz, the delightful **LILO (Linzer Lokalbahn)** interurban line (☏ 0732/654376) makes the run up to Eferding. A charming narrow-gauge line meanders south to Waidhofen an der Ybbs.

Contacts and Resources

Bicycle Rentals

For details on the scenic Danube river route, ask for the folder "Danube Cycle Track" (in English, from Niederösterreich-Information; ⊠ Heidenschuss 2, A–1010 Vienna, ☏ 01/533–3114–0 or 01/53110–6200, FAX 01/535–0319). The brochure "Radfahren" is in German, but lists contact numbers for cycle rentals throughout Upper Austria. You can rent a bike in Linz (☞ Sports and Outdoor Activities *in* Linz, *above*) at the **Freistadt railroad station** (☏ 07942/2319), the **Steyr railroad station** (☏ 07252/595–385), or privately in Kremsmünster at **Tenniscenter Stadlhuber** (☏ 07583/7498–0).

Canoeing

The Danube is fast and tricky, so you're best off sticking to the calmer waters back of the power dams (at Pöchlarn, above Melk, and near Grein). You can rent a canoe at Pöchlarn. You can also canoe on an arm of the Danube near Ottensheim, about 8 km (5 mi) west of Linz. For information call Ruderverein Donau (☏ 0732/736250) or Ruderverein Ister-Sparkasse (☏ 0732/774888).

Car Rentals

Cars can be rented at the airports in Vienna (☞ Vienna A to Z *in* Chapter 2) or Linz. Linz contacts are as follows:

Avis (✉ Schillerstr 1, ☏ 0732/662881), **Buchbinder** (✉ Untere Donaulände 15, ☏ 0732/773051), **EuroDollar** (✉ Coulinstr. 13, ☏ 0732/658360), **Hertz** (✉ Bürgerstr. 19, ☏ 0732/784841–0).

Emergencies

Police, ☏ 133. **Fire,** ☏ 122. **Ambulance,** ☏ 144. If you need a doctor and speak no German, ask your hotel how best to obtain assistance.

Fishing

In the streams and lakes of the area around Linz, you can fly-cast for rainbow and brook trout and troll for pike and carp. Check with the town tourist offices about licenses and fishing rights for river trolling and fly-casting in Aggsbach-Markt, Dürnstein, Emmersdorf, Grein, Kleinpöchlarn, Krems, Mautern, Mauthausen, Persenbeug–Gottsdorf, Pöchlarn, Schönbühel/Aggsbach Dorf, Spitz, Waidhofen/Ybbs, and Ybbs.

Guided Tours

Tours out of Vienna take you to Melk and back by bus and boat in eight hours, with a stop at Dürnstein. Bus tours operate year-round except as noted, but the boat runs only April–October. Operators include the following: **Cityrama/Gray Line** (✉ Börsegasse 1, ☏ 01/534–13–0, ℻ 01/534–13–28), for AS790; **Citytouring Vienna** (✉ Penzinger Str. 46, ☏ 01/894–1417–0, ℻ 01/894–3239), for AS950, including a light snack; and **Vienna Sightseeing Tours** (✉ Stelzhammergasse 4/11, ☏ 01/712–4683–0, ℻ 01/714–1141), for AS790.

Day-boat trips with loudspeaker announcements in English run daily to and through the Wachau from Vienna May–September. Contact the **DDSG/Blue Danube Schiffahrt** (✉ Friedrichstr. 7, ☏ 01/588800, ℻ 01/58880–440). The cruise trips leave from Schwedenbrücke, by Schwedenplatz, in Vienna, daily at 10:30, 1, 2:30, and 4:30.

Hiking

Local tourist offices have maps and route details of the fabulous trails in the area, and in Linz you can get the booklet "Urban Hiking Paths in Linz." For information on the Mühlviertel from Freistadt to Grein, call ☏ 0732/735020.

Travel Agencies

In Linz, leading travel agencies include the following: **American Express** (✉ Bürgerstr. 14, ☏ 0732/669013, ℻ 0732/655334), **Carlson Wagonlit Travel** (✉ Bismarckstr. 8, ☏ 0732/771492–0, ℻ 0732/771492–9), **Kuoni** (✉ Hauptpl. 14, ☏ 0732/771301, ℻ 0732/775338), and **Oberösterreichisches Landesreisebüro** (✉ Hauptpl. 9, ☏ 0732/771061–0, ℻ 0732/771061–49).

Visitor Information

For general information on the area, check with the following district tourist offices:

Lower Austria (✉ Walfischg. 6, A–1010 Vienna, ☏ 01/513–8022, ℻ 01/513–8022–30). **Upper Austria** (✉ Schillerstr. 50, A–4010 Linz, ☏ 0732/602210, ℻ 0732/600220). **Linz** (✉ Hauptpl. 5, A–4020 Linz, ☏ 0732/7070–1777, ℻ 0732/772873), where you can pick up the latest *Linz City News* in English as well as German.

Most towns have local *Fremdenverkehrsamt* (tourist offices): **Bad Hall** (✉ Kurhaus, A–4540, ☏ 07258/200–0, ℻ 07258/200–20). **Dürnstein** (✉ Parkpl. Ost, A–3601, ☏ 02711/219, ℻ 02711/442). **Eferding** (✉ Stadtpl. 1, A–4070, ☏ 07272/5555–20, ℻ 07272/5555–33). **Freis-**

tadt (⊠ Hauptpl. 12, A−4240, ☎ 07942/72974, FAX 07942/73207). **Grein** (⊠ Hauptstr. 3, A−4360, ☎ 07268/6680 or 07268/7290, FAX 07268/ 7290). **Klosterneuburg** (⊠ Niedermarkt 4, A−3400, ☎ 02243/32038, FAX 02243/26773). **Krems/Stein** (⊠ Undstr. 6, A−3500, ☎ 02732/ 82676, FAX 02732/70011). **Melk** (⊠ Babenbergerstr. 1, A−3390, ☎ 02752/2307−32, FAX 02752/2307−37). **Pöchlarn** (⊠ Regensburger Str. 11, A−3380, ☎ 02757/2310−30, FAX 02757/2310−66). **St. Pölten** (⊠ Rathauspl. 1, A−3100, ☎ 02742/353354, FAX 02742/333−2819). **Steyr** (⊠ Stadtpl. 27, A−4400, ☎ 07252/53229 o. 07252/48154, FAX 07252/ 48154−15). **Tulln** (⊠ Minoritenpl. 2, A−3430, ☎ 02272/5836, FAX 02272/5838). **Wachau** (⊠ Undstr. 6, A−3500 Krems, ☎ 02732/82676, FAX 02732/70011). **Waidhofen an der Ybbs** (⊠ Obere Stadtpl. 32, A−3340, ☎ 07442/511−255, FAX 07442/511−259). **Weissenkirchen** (⊠ Gemeinde Weissenkirchen, A−3610, ☎ 02715/2600, FAX 02715/2600).

6 Salzburg

Mozart, Mozart, Mozart! Birthplace of the great 18th-century composer, Salzburg is a world-class music mecca that hosts the world's most elegant music festival every summer. But many come to tour this Golden City of High Baroque to the strains of music from the film that made Salzburg a household name. From Winkler Terrace to Nonnberg Convent, it's hard to go exploring without hearing someone hum "How Do You Solve a Problem Like Maria?"

Updated by
Bonnie Dodson

ALL SALZBURG IS A STAGE," Count Ferdinand Czernin once wrote. "Its beauty, its tradition, its history enshrined in the grey stone of which its buildings are made, its round of music, its crowd of fancy-dressed people, all combine to lift you out of everyday life, to make you forget that somewhere far off, life hides another, drearier, harder, and more unpleasant reality." Shortly after the count's book, *This Salzburg*, was published in 1937, reality arrived, but having survived the Nazis, Salzburg once again became one of the Austria's top drawing cards. Art lovers call it the Golden City of High Baroque; historians classify it the Florence of the North, or the German Rome; and, of course, being the birthplace of Mozart, music lovers know it as the Festival City— home of the world-famous Salzburger Festspiele (Salzburg Festival).

The natural setting is perfect. Salzburg lies on both banks of the Salzach River, at the point where it is pinched between two mountains, the Kapuzinerberg on one side, the Mönchsberg on the other. In broader view are many beautiful Alpine peaks. Man's contribution is a trove of buildings worthy of such surroundings. Salzburg's rulers pursued construction on a grand scale ever since Wolf Dietrich von Raitenau—the "Medici prince-archbishop who preached in stone"—began his regime in the latter part of the 16th century. Astonishingly, they all seem to have shared the same artistic bent, with the result that Salzburg's many fine buildings blend into a harmonious whole. Perhaps nowhere else in the world is there so unanimous a flowering of Baroque architecture.

While Salzburg is a visual pageant of Baroque motifs, music is the aural element that shapes the life of the city. It is heard everywhere: in the churches, castles, palaces, and, of course, the concert halls. Although the young Mozart was the wonder boy of Europe, Salzburg did him no particular honor in his lifetime. It is making up for it now. Since 1920, the Salzburg Festival has honored its native son, with performances by the world's greatest musicians. To see and hear them, crowds pack the city from mid-July until the end of August. Whether performed in the festival halls (Grosses und Kleines Festspielhaus) or outdoors with opulent Baroque volutes and scrolls of Salzburg's architecture as background, Mozart's music remains the heartbeat of the city.

Only the tourist who visits Salzburg outside of the festival season will have time to explore its other fascinating attractions. Many visitors love to make the town's acquaintance by visiting all the sights featured in *The Sound of Music*, filmed here in 1964. It's hard to take in the Mirabell Gardens, Winkler's Terrace, the Pferdeschwemme fountain, Nonnberg Convent, the Residenzplatz, and all the other filmed locations without imagining Maria and the von Trapp children trilling "Do-Re-Mi." (Like Mozart, the von Trapp family—who escaped the Third Reich by fleeing their beloved country—were little appreciated at home; Austria was the only place in the world where the film failed—it closed after a single week's showing in Vienna and Salzburg.) Whether it's the melodies of Rodgers and Hammerstein or of Joannes Chrysostomus Wolfgangus Amadeus Theophilus Mozart filling your head, the city of Salzburg is a symphony of both sounds and sights.

Pleasures and Pastimes

A Lot of Night Music

Music in Salzburg is not just *Eine Kleine Nächtmusik* (*A Little Night Music*), to mention one of Mozart's most famous compositions. The city's nightlife is livelier than its reputation. Folklore performances are given twice a week during the summer season at the Augustinerbräu. In winter "in" areas include the "Bermuda Triangle" (Steingasse, Imbergstrasse) and Rudolfskai; young people tend to populate the bars and discos around Gstättengasse. Of course, Salzburg is most renowned for its **Salzburger Festspiele** (summer festival) of music and theater (mid-July–August), and most visitors come during this season. Much of Salzburg's very special charm can, however, best be enjoyed and discovered off-season. For instance, real Mozart connoisseurs come to Salzburg in January for the **Mozart Week** (a 10-day festival held around Mozart's birthday, on January 27). And in general music lovers face an embarrassment of riches in this most musical of cities, ranging from concerts of chamber music held in the Marble Hall of the Mirabell Palace or the Golden Hall of the Fortress to the numerous concerts organized by the International Mozarteum Foundation from October to June in the Great Hall of the Mozarteum. Salzberg's concerts by the Camerata Academica under director Sándor Végh are now just as much in demand as the subscription series by the Vienna Philharmonic in the Musikverein in Vienna. The **Landestheater** season runs from September to June and presents opera, operetta, plays, and ballet. No music lover should miss the chance to be enchanted and amazed by the skill and artistry of the world-famous **Salzburg Marionette Theater** performing operas by Mozart, Rossini, Johann Strauss, and Offenbach.

Bicycling

As most Salzburgers know, one of the best and most pleasurable ways of getting around the city and the surrounding countryside is by bicycle. Bikes can be rented (☞ Salzburg A to Z, *below*), and the tourist office has maps of the extensive network of cycle paths. The most delightful ride in Salzburg? The **Hellbrunner Allee** from Freisaal takes you past Frohnburg Palace and a number of elegant mansions on either side of the tree-lined avenue out to Hellbrunn Palace. The more adventurous can go farther afield, taking the **Salzach cycle path** north to the village of Oberndorf or south to Golling and Hallein.

Dining

Salzburg has some of the best—and most expensive—restaurants in Austria; even better, the city is plentifully supplied with good eateries, offering not only solid, good Austrian food (not for persons on a diet) but peppery Hungarian dishes, spiced Slav specialties, and newer-than-now *Neue Küche* (nouvelle cuisine) delights. There are certain dining experiences that are quintessentially Salzburgian, including restaurants perched on the town's peaks that offer "food with a view"—in some cases, it's too bad the food isn't up to the view!—or rustic inns that offer "Alpine evenings" with entertainment. A favorite dish is the *Forelle blau getsotten*—trout, served with its price tag attached, as you pay according to the weight of the fish—and don't forget to have a *Schmankerltorte* for dessert. Finally, everyone knows the top place at cocktail time is the gemütlich bar of the Goldener Hirsch, where countesses and opera divas use up every square inch of space from five to seven—and where you can get that rarity in Europe, a genuine martini.

CATEGORY	COST*
$$$$	over AS550
$$$	AS400–AS550
$$	AS200–AS400
$	under AS200

*per person for a three-course meal, including house wine, 10% service, and VAT, but excluding extra tip

Lodging

The Old City has a wide variety of hotels and pensions, some with surprising locations and considerable atmosphere, but everything has its price and there are few bargains. In high season, and particularly during the festival (July and August), some prices soar and rooms are very difficult to find, so try to reserve at least two months in advance. Note that during the high season, rate differences may push a hotel into the next-higher price category. If you don't have a reservation, go to one of the tourist information offices or the accommodations service (*Zimmernachweis*) on the main platform of the railway station. If you're looking for something very cheap (less than AS500 for a double), clean, and comfortable, stay in a private home, though the good ones are all a little way from downtown. The tourist information offices don't list private rooms; try calling Eveline Truhlar of Bob's Special Tours (☎ 0662/872484), who runs a private-accommodations service.

CATEGORY	LOW SEASON*	HIGH SEASON*
$$$$	over AS2,200	over AS3,300
$$$	AS1,300–AS2,200	AS1,800–AS3,300
$$	AS900–AS1,300	AS1,200–AS1,800
$	under AS900	under AS1,200

All prices are for a standard double room for two, with bath, including breakfast (except where noted) and VAT.

Skiing

In the immediate vicinity of Salzburg, it is possible to ski down the **Gaisberg** or the **Untersberg.** These may not be ski resorts to please the expert; nevertheless, to take the cable car up the Untersberg and then ski down to the village of Fürstenbrunn can be a breathtaking experience—just right for a free morning or afternoon. Cross-country skiing is possible in **Hellbrunn Park** and around the **Gaisberg.** The tourist office on Mozartplatz will inform you about skiing facilities farther afield. In addition, Salzburg is a good base for excursions to the many ski resorts of Land Salzburg.

EXPLORING SALZBURG

The Altstadt, or Old City, where most of the major sights are concentrated, is a very compact area between the jutting outcrop of the Mönchsberg and the Salzach River. The cathedral and interconnecting squares surrounding it form what used to be the religious center, around which the major churches and the old archbishops' residence are arranged. The rest of the Old City belonged to the wealthy burghers: the Getreidegasse, the Alter Markt (old market), the town hall, and the tall, plain burghers' houses (like Mozart's Birthplace). The Mönchsberg cliffs emerge unexpectedly behind the Old City, crowned to the east by the Hohensalzburg Fortress. Across the river, in the small area between the cliffs of the Kapuzinerberg and the riverbank, is Steingasse, a narrow medieval street where the working people lived. Northwest of the Kapuzinerberg lie Mirabell Palace and its gardens, now an integral part of the city but formerly a country estate on the outskirts of Salzburg.

It's best to begin by exploring the architectural and cultural riches of the Old City, then go on to the fortress and after that cross the river to inspect the other bank. Ideally you need two days to do it all. An alternative, if you enjoy exploring churches and castles, is to stop after visiting the Rupertinum and go directly up to the fortress, either on foot or by returning through the cemetery to the funicular railway.

Numbers in the text correspond to numbers in the margin and on the Salzburg map.

Great Itineraries

IF YOU HAVE 1 DAY

It is the tourist who comes to Salzburg outside of the festival who will have most time to explore its many fascinating attractions. But even for busy festival visitors, making the acquaintance of the town is not too difficult, for most of its sights are compactly located in a comparatively small area. Of course, if you are doing this spectacular city in just one day, there is always a flip-book-fast way to take a course in Salzberg 101—take one of those escorted bus tours through the city. However, much of Salzburg's historic city center is for pedestrians only, and the bus doesn't get you close to some of the best sights—so it's best just to join the army of bipeds and explore by foot.

Start at the **Mozartplatz** ①—not just to sweeten your tour with a few *Mozart Kugeln,* the omnipresent candy balls of pistachio-flavored marzipan rolled in nougat cream and dipped in dark chocolate—but to make a pit stop at the main tourist information office. Flower-bedecked cafés beckon, but this is no time for a coffee—one of the glories of Europe is just a few steps away: the **Residenz** ③, which is the veritable center of Baroque Salzburg. Nearby are the **Dom** ④, Salzburg's grand cathedral, and two of Salzburg's most opulent churches, **St. Peter's Abbey** ⑥ and the **Franziskanerkirche** ⑦. You're now ready to take the funicular (it's just behind the cathedral) up to the **Fortress Hohensalzburg** ⑰—the majestic castle atop the Mönchsberg peak that overlooks the city. Enjoy a rest at the Grand Café Winkler, or opt for enjoying some picnic provisions or lunch at the Burgerwehr-Einkehr restaurant. Descend back down to the city via the Mönchsberg express elevators, which will deposit you at Gstättengasse 13. Head over to the **Pferdeschwemme** ⑫—the Baroque and royal horse trough that is a somewhat bewildering tribute to the chevaline race—then over to the **Getreidegasse,** the Old City's main shopping street, for some serious retail therapy and visit **Mozarts Geburtshaus** ⑯. Welcome twilight with a *Kaffee mit Schlag* (coffee with whipped cream) at the famous Café Tomaselli on the charming **Alter Markt** square. Choose one of the more than 40 pastries and congratulate yourself: You haven't seen everything in Salzburg, but you have missed few of its top sights.

IF YOU HAVE 3 DAYS

With three days, you can explore the **Old City** and the **Fortress and the New Town** as described in the two walking tours below. Try to catch an evening **concert**—hopefully of Mozart's music—at one of the many music halls in the city (before you arrive in Salzburg, do some advance telephone calls to determine the music schedule of the city for the time you will be there and, if need be, book reservations; if you'll be attending the summer Salzburg Festival, this is a must). For your third day, try one of three options: Book a *Sound of Music* tour (☞ Close-up box, *below*) then, in the afternoon, relax and take a ride up the **Untersberg** (☞ Short Side Trips from Salzburg, *below*) or try to arrange an excursion to the beautiful **Salzkammergut** (☞ Chapter 7) to the picture-book town of Mondsee or St. Wolfgang.

The Old City: In Mozart's Footsteps

To most people, Salzburg today means the city of Mozart. Ever since the film *Amadeus,* Wolfgang Amadeus Mozart has been the 18th-century equivalent of a rock star. Born in Salzburg on January 27, 1756, he crammed a prodigious number of compositions into the 35 short years of his life, many of which he spent in Salzburg (he moved to Vienna in 1781). Start by exploring the Altstadt (Old City), the heart of the Baroque Salzburg Mozart knew. Other Mozart-related sights are included in our second Salzburg tour (☞ The Fortress and the New Town, *below*). Don't forget to take Mozart tapes along for your Walkman.

A Good Walk

In Salzburg, as anywhere else, if you have the right departure point, you will have a good journey and ultimately arrive at the right place. For this city, there is no more appropriate center-of-it-all than **Mozartplatz** ①, the square named to honor the genius who set lovely Salzburg to music. Get in the proper mood by taking in, near the statue of Mozart, the street violinists who are usually playing a Mozart sonata or two. Walk past the Glockenspiel café into the next square, the Residenzplatz, centered by the 40-ft-high Court Fountain, often illuminated at night. Take in the famous **Glockenspiel** ② atop the Neubau Palace (chances are the tunes it plays will be by you-know-who); then enter the **Residenz** ③, the opulent Baroque palace of Salzburg's prince-archbishops and Mozart's patrons. From the Residenzplatz, walk through the arches into Domplatz, the majestic cathedral square of the city—in August, set out with seats for the annual presentation of Hofmannsthal's play *Jedermann*. The **Dom** ④ (Salzburg Cathedral) is among the finest Italian-style Baroque structures in Austria. Walk into the Kapitelplatz through the arches across the square and go through two wrought-iron gateways into **St. Peter's Cemetery** ⑤—one of the most historic and beautiful places in Salzburg. Enter the church of **St. Peter's Abbey** ⑥. Above the main entrance the Latin inscription reads: "I am the door—by me if any man enters here, he shall be saved." If it's nearing lunchtime, you may want to stop at the Stiftskeller St. Peter—so legendary a restaurant that the story has it Mephistopheles met Faust here.

As you leave the church of St. Peter's, look up to the right to see the thin Gothic spire of the **Franziskanerkirche** (Franciscan Church) ⑦. Leave the courtyard in this direction, cross the road, and enter the church by the side entrance, which will bring you directly into the Gothic apse crowned by the ornate red marble altar designed by Fischer von Erlach. Go down the aisle and leave the church by the front entrance, which opens on Sigmund-Haffner Gasse. Opposite is the back entrance to Salzburg's museum of 20th century art, the **Rupertinum** ⑧— its café is a handy spot for a lunch break. Turn left around the corner into **Toscaninihof** ⑨, the square cut into the dramatic Mönchsberg cliff. The wall bearing the harp-shape organ pipes is part of the famed **Festspielhaus** ⑩. The carved steps going up the Mönchsberg are named for Clemens Holzmeister, architect of the festival halls. If you climb them, you get an intimate view of the Salzburg churches at the level of their spires, and if you climb a little farther to the right, you can look down into the open-air festival hall, cut into the cliffs. From Hofstallagasse, you can either walk directly up to Herbert-von-Karajan-Platz or, preferably, walk around by Universitätsplatz to take a look at one of Fischer von Erlach's Baroque masterpieces, the **Universitätskirche** ⑪. In Herbert-von-Karajan-Platz is another point at which building and cliff meet: the **Pferdeschwemme** ⑫, a royal horse trough decorated with splendid paintings. To the left is the Neutor, the impressive road tunnel blasted through the Mönchsberg in 1764. Looking back toward Universitätsplatz, you'll see the famous hotel the Goldener Adler, its two buildings painted pink and blue. The arcaded Renaissance court on your left houses the **Spielzeugmuseum** ⑬, a delightful toy museum.

Pass by the tiny church of St. Blasius, built in 1350, and follow the road on through the Gstättentor to the **Mönchsberg elevator** ⑭ for a trip up the hill to the Winkler Terrace, Salzburg's most famous outlook. After you descend from the heights, turn left into the short street

leading to Museumsplatz to explore the **Carolino Augusteum Museum** ⑮.
Walk back toward the Blasius church, which stands at the beginning
of the Old City's major shopping street, Getreidegasse, aglitter with
numerous signs (featuring little wrought-iron cobblers and bakers—
few people could actually read centuries ago). Amid all the boutiques
and Salzburg's own McDonald's (featuring its own elegant sign) is
Mozarts Geburtshaus ⑯. Continue down the street, pass the Rathaus
(town hall), and enter the Alter Markt, the old marketplace adorned
with historic buildings, including the Café Tomaselli (1703) and the
Baroque Hofapotheke (court apothecary, 1591), still kept as it was back
then. Finish up with some "I Was Here" photographs of the marble
St. Florian's Fountain, and then head back to Mozartplatz.

TIMING

The Old City—the left bank of the Salzach River—contains many of
the city's top attractions. Other than exploring by horse-drawn cabs
(*Fiakers*), which can be rented at Residenzplatz, most of your exploring will be done on foot, since this historic section of town has banned
cars. The center city is compact and cozy, so you can easily see it in
one day. Note that many churches close at 6 PM, so unless you're
catching a concert at one of them, be sure to explore them during day-
light. In addition, several of the main attractions, such as the Residenz
palace, can only be seen by guided tour; refer to the hours we list and
try to plan your day with such tours in mind.

Sights to See

Alter Markt (Old Market). Right in the heart of the Old City is the Alter
Markt, the old marketplace and center of secular life in past centuries.
The square is lined with 17th-century middle-class houses, colorfully
hued in shades of pink, pale blue, and yellow ocher. Look in at the old
royal pharmacy, the **Hofapotheke,** with its incredibly ornate black-and-
gold rococo interior built in 1760. Inside, you'll notice a curious
apothecarial smell, thanks to the shelves lined with old pots and jars
(labeled in Latin). These are not just for show: This pharmacy is still
operating today. You can even have your blood pressure taken—but
preferably not after drinking a *Doppelter Einspänner* (black coffee with
whipped cream, served in a glass) in the famous **Café Tomaselli** just
opposite. In warm weather, the café's terrace provides a wonderful spot
for watching the world go by as you sip a *mélange* (another coffee specialty, served with frothy milk or cream), or, during the summer months,
rest your feet under the shade of the chestnut trees in the Tomaselli
garden at the top end of the square. Next to the coffeehouse, you'll
find the **smallest house in Salzburg,** now an optician's. Note the slant-
ing roof decorated with a dragon gargoyle. In the center of the square,
surrounded by flower stalls, the marble **St. Florian's Fountain** was dedicated in 1734 to the patron saint of firefighters.

⑮ **Carolino Augusteum Museum.** Here you can see remains of Salzburg's
old Roman ruins, the famous Celtic bronze flagon found earlier this
century on the Dürrnberg near Hallein (10 km/6 mi south of Salzburg),
and an outstanding collection of old musical instruments. Special exhibitions are mounted throughout the year. ⊠ *Museumspl. 1,* ☎ *0662/
843145, 0662/820–37221,* 𝕱𝖠𝖷 *0662/841134–10.* 🎫 *AS40; combined
ticket with Spielzeugmuseum (☞ below) AS60.* ☉ *Tues. 9–8, Wed.–
Sun. 9–5.*

★ ❹ **Dom** (Cathedral). When you walk through the arches from the Residenzplatz into the **Domplatz,** it is not difficult to see why Max Reinhardt chose it in August of 1920 as the setting for the annual summer
production of Hugo von Hofmannsthal's *Jedermann* (*Everyman*). The
plaza is a complete, aesthetic concept and one of Salzburg's most beau-

tiful urban set pieces. In the center rises the Virgin's Column, and at one side is the cathedral, considered to be the first early Baroque building north of the Alps and one of the finest. Its facade is of marble, its towers reach 250 ft into the air, and it holds 10,000 people. There has been a cathedral on this spot since the 8th century, but the present structure dates from the 17th century. Archbishop Wolf Dietrich took advantage of (some say he caused) the old Romanesque-Gothic cathedral's destruction by fire in 1598 to demolish the remains and make plans for a huge new building facing onto the Residenzplatz. His successor, Markus Sittikus, and the new court architect, Santino Solari, built the Renaissance-style cathedral, which was consecrated with great ceremony in 1628. The simple gray-and-white interior of the church, a peaceful counterpoint to the usual Baroque splendor, dates from a later renovation. Mozart was christened the day after he was born in the 13th-century font inside the cathedral, where he was organist from 1779 to 1781. Some of his compositions, such as the *Coronation Mass*, were written for the cathedral, and many were performed there for the first time. On Sunday, mass is sung here at 10 AM—the most glorious time to experience the cathedral in full splendor. Many of the church's treasures are in a special museum on the premises. ⊠ *Domplatz*, ☎ *0662/ 844189*, 𝔽𝔸𝕏 *0662/840442.* ▨ *AS40.* ☉ *Mid-May–mid-Oct., Mon.– Sat. 10–5, Sun. 11–5.*

❿ Festspielhaus (Festival Hall Complex). To attend the world famous Salzburg Festival, all music lovers head for the Hofstallgasse, the street where the three main festival theaters are located. The street owes its name to the fact that in the 17th century the court stables were located here. Now, in the place of prancing horses, festival visitors promenade along the Hofstallgasse during the intervals of summer performances, showing off their suntans and elegant attire. The festival complex consists of the **Kleines Festspielhaus** (Small Festival Hall, sometimes referred to as the Mozart Stage), built in 1937 and nowadays used mainly for productions of Mozart operas and chamber concerts, and the **Grosses Festspielhaus** (Great Festival Hall), built into the solid rock of the Mönchsberg and opened in 1960, with a maximum stage width of 104 ft and an auditorium seating more than 2,000. In recent seasons the Grosses Festspielhaus, nicknamed the Wagner Stage because of its width, has been the venue for spectacular productions such as *Boris Godunov* and *Der Rosenkavalier*. Stage directors are faced with the greatest challenge in the **Felsenreitschule,** the former Summer Riding School, which—hewn out of the rock of the Mönchsberg during the 17th century—offers a setting more dramatic than anything on stage. Max Reinhardt made the first attempt at using the Summer Riding School for Salzburg Festival performances in 1926. With its retractable roof it gives the impression of an open-air theater; the three tiers of arcades cut into the rock of the Mönchsberg linger in the mind of lovers of *The Sound of Music* film, for here the von Trapps were portrayed as singing "Edelweiss" in their last Austrian concert. The theaters are linked by tunnels (partially in marble and with carpeted floors) to a spacious underground garage in the Mönchsberg. If you want to see the inside of the halls, it's best to go to a performance, but guided tours are given and group tours can be booked on request. ⊠ *Hofstallg. 1,* ☎ *0662/ 8045.* ▨ *AS70.* ☉ *Group tour July 22–Aug., daily at 9, 2, and 4:30; individual tour July 22–Aug., daily at 10:30, 2, and 3:30.*

❼ Franziskanerkirche (Franciscan Church). The graceful, tall spire of the Franciscan Church stands out from all other towers in Salzburg and the church itself encompasses the greatest diversity of architectural styles. Even at the time of St. Virgil, in the 8th century, a church existed on this spot but it was destroyed by fire. The new one was consecrated with a Romanesque nave, still to be seen, as are other Romanesque features, such as a stone lion set into the steps of the pulpit. In the 15th century the choir was rebuilt in Gothic style, crowned by an ornate red marble and gilt altar designed by Austria's most famous Baroque architect, Fischer von Erlach. Mass—frequently one of Mozart's—is celebrated here on Sunday at 9 AM. ⊠ *Franziskanerg. 5,* ☎ *0662/843629.* 🎫 *Free.* ⊙ *Winter, daily 6:30–6; summer, daily 6:30 AM–8 PM.*

Getreidegasse. This is the main shopping street in the Old City center. According to historians the historic name means "trade street"—not "grain street," as many people believe. Today it is the address of famous and elegant fashion houses, international shoe chains, and McDonald's (note its wrought-iron sign—one of many on the street—and classy bronze lettering: Like all the other stores, it has conformed with Salzburg's strict Old City conservation laws). Other than coming to shop, visitors flock to this street because at Getreidegasse 9 they'll find **Mozarts Geburtshaus** (☞ *below).* Needless to say, in the summer the street is as closely packed with people as a corncob is with kernels. You can always escape for a while through one of the many arcades, mostly flower-bedecked and opening into delightful little courtyards, that link the Getreidegasse to the river and the Universitätsplatz.

❷ Glockenspiel (Carillon). The famous carillon tower is perched on top of the **Residenz Neubau** (New Residence), Prince-Archbishop Wolf-Dietrich's government palace and his first attempt at the Baroque style. The carillon is a later addition, brought from the Netherlands in 1688 and finally put in working order in 1702. The 35 bells play classical tunes (usually by Weber, Haydn, and you-know-who) at 7 AM, 11 AM, and 6 PM—with charm and ingenuity often making up for occasional musical inaccuracy. (You can get a deafening close-up of the action on a tour, at 10:45 AM and 5:45 PM in good weather, daily mid-March–October, weekdays November–mid-March). From Easter to October, the bells are immediately followed by a resounding retort from the 200-pipe "Bull" organ housed in the Hohensalzburg Fortress. Details of the music are listed on a notice board across the square on the corner of the Residenz building. ⊠ *Mozartpl. 1,* ☎ *0662/8042–2076,* 🎫 *AS20.* ⊙ *Daily 7 and 11 AM and 6 PM.*

⓮ Mönchsberg elevator. Just around the corner from the Pferdeschwemme (☞ *below),* at Neumayr Platz, you'll find the Mönchsberg elevator, which takes you up through solid rock to the **Winkler Terrace,** where you can walk along wooded paths while enjoying spectacular vistas of Salzburg. In summer this can be a marvelous and fast way to escape the tiny crowded streets of the Old City. At the top of the Mönchsberg, follow the signs and path south to **Burgerwehr-Einkehr,** a popular café-restaurant open May–mid-October with a magnificent view of the churches and the fortress from its outdoor garden. ⊠ *Gstätteng. 13.* 🎫 *Round-trip AS27, one-way AS16.* ⊙ *Tues.–Sun. 9 AM–11 PM, Mon. 9–7.*

⓰ Mozarts Geburtshaus (Mozart's Birthplace). Pilgrims to the city of Mozart's birth usually make this their first stop. Mozart was born on the third floor of this tall house on January 27, 1756, and the family lived here, when they were not on tour, until 1773 (the child prodigy composed many of his first compositions in these rooms). Mozart's piano and tiny violin are on display, as well as portraits of the family, autograph letters, and manuscripts, which are exhibited in cases illuminated by laser to make them easier to read. On the first floor, miniature stage models from various productions of Mozart operas are on display, and on the second floor a special annual exhibition is mounted, which opens the last week in January and runs until early October. ⊠ *Getreideg.*

9, ☎ 0662/844313. ☒ AS70. ☺ Sept.–June, daily 9–6; July–Aug., daily 9–7.

NEED A
BREAK?
On the ground floor of Mozart's Birthplace, stop in at **Trzesniewski's** (☒ Getreideg. 9) for a light snack of open sandwiches (18 different spreads on fresh whole-meal bread) and an excellent cup of coffee.

❶ **Mozartplatz** (Mozart Square). Right in the center of the square stands the statue of Wolfgang Amadeus Mozart, the work of sculptor Ludwig Schwanthaler and unveiled in 1842 in the presence of the composer's two surviving sons. It was the first sign of public recognition the great composer had received from his hometown since his death as a pauper in Vienna in 1791. As you will notice, the Mozart memorial industry has grown considerably since then. In fact, in 1991—the 200th anniversary of Mozart's death—a local sculptor caused an uproar, when, in protest against the overcommercialization of Mozart, he had the statue buried under a mountain of 200 supermarket shopping carts. The statue shows a 19th-century stylized view of Mozart, draped in a mantle, holding a page of music and a copybook. A more appropriate bust of the composer, modeled by Viennese sculptor Edmund Heller, is to be found on the Kapuzinerberg. It contains the inscription *Jung groß, spät erkannt, nie erreicht*—"Great while young, belatedly appreciated, never equaled."

⑫ **Pferdeschwemme** (Royal Horse Drinking Trough). At the western end of the Hofstallgasse is the Herbert-von-Karajan-Platz (named after Salzburg's second greatest son, maestro Herbert von Karajan, the legendary conductor and music director of the Salzberg Festival for many decades). On the Mönchsberg side of the square is the Pferdeschwemme—a royal trough where prize horses used to be washed and watered, constructed in 1695; as they underwent this ordeal they could delight in the frescoes of their pin-up fillies on the rear wall. Looking back toward Universitätsplatz, you'll see the famous hotel and restaurant the Goldener Hirsch, its two buildings painted pink and blue. ☒ *Herbert-von-Karajan-Platz.*

Rathaus (Town Hall). Where the Sigmund-Haffner-Gasse meets the Getreidegasse you will find the Rathaus, a remarkably insignificant building in the Salzburg skyline—apart from its clock, which chimes every quarter hour—no doubt reflecting the historical weakness of the burghers vis-à-vis the church. ☒ *Getreideg, and Sigmund-Haffner-Gasse.*

❸ **Residenz.** Situated at the very heart of Baroque Salzburg, the Residenz overlooks the spacious Residenzplatz and its famous horse fountain. The palace was built between 1600 and 1619 as the home of the prince-archbishops. The *Kaisersaal* (Emperor Room) and the *Rittersaal* (Knight's Hall), one of the city's most regal concert halls, can be seen with the rest of the state rooms on a guided tour. Today, the Residenz is often used for official functions, banquets, and exhibitions. In recent seasons, its courtyard has been the lovely setting for opera productions of the Salzburg Festival. The **Residenzgalerie,** an art museum specializing in 17th-century Dutch and Flemish art and 19th-century paintings of Salzburg, is situated on the second floor of the Residenz. ☒ *Residenzpl. 1, ☎ 0662/840451. ☒ AS50, Residenzgalerie AS50, combined ticket AS80. ☺ Apr.–Sept., daily 10–5; Oct.–Mar., Thurs.–Tues. 10–5. Tour July–Aug., daily 10–4:30 every ½ hr; Sept.–June, weekdays at 10, 11, noon, 2, and 3.*

❽ **Rupertinum.** If you are interested in 20th-century art, don't miss the chance to see the outstanding permanent collection of paintings and graphic art on display here in this gallery. Take a rest in the museum's excellent café. ⊠ *Wiener-Philharmoniker-Gasse 9,* ☎ *0662/8042–2336.* ☒ *AS40.* ⊘ *Tues. and Thurs.–Sun. 10–5, Wed. 10–9.*

❻ St. Peter's Abbey. The most sumptuous church in Salzburg, St. Peter's Abbey is where Mozart's Mass in C Minor premiered in 1783; his *Requiem* is performed every year on the anniversary of his death. The porch has beautiful Romanesque vaulted arches from the original structure built in the 12th century; the interior was decorated in the characteristically voluptuous late-Baroque style when additions were made in the 1770s. Note the side chapel by the entrance, with the unusual crèche portraying the flight into Egypt and murder of all first-born male infants. ⊠ *St. Peter Bezirk,* ☎ *0662/844576.* ☒ *Free.* ⊘ *Fall–spring, daily 8–12:30 and 2–6; summer, daily 8–12:30 and 2–8.*

❺ St. Peter's Cemetery. This eerie but intimate cemetery is the oldest Christian graveyard in Salzburg, dating back to 1627. Enclosed on three sides by wrought-iron grilles, Baroque vaults contain chapels belonging to old patrician families of Salzburg. The graveyard is far from mournful: The individual graves are tended with loving care, decorated with candles, fir branches, or flowers—especially pansies (because their name means "thoughts"). In Crypt XXXI is the grave of Santino Solari, architect of the cathedral; in XXXIX that of Sigmund Haffner, for whom Mozart composed a symphony and a serenade, naming them after his patron. The final communal crypt contains the body of Mozart's sister, Nannerl, and the torso of Joseph Haydn's brother, Michael (his head is inside an urn in St. Peter's church). ⊠ *St. Peter Bezirk,* ☎ *0662/844578–0.* ☒ *AS12.* ⊘ *Tour May–Sept., daily 10–5 on the hr; Oct.–Apr., daily 10:30–3:30 (check times on notice board).*

❀ ⓭ Spielzeugmuseum (Toy Museum). On a rainy day this is a delightful diversion for both young and old, with a collection of dolls, teddy bears, model railways, and wooden sailing ships. On some Wednesday and Friday afternoons at 3, special Punch and Judy puppet shows are performed Wednesday and Friday at 3. ⊠ *Bürgerspitalpl. 2,* ☎ *0662/847560.* ☒ *AS30.* ⊘ *Tues.–Sun. 9–5.*

❾ Toscaninihof (Arturo Toscanini House). The famous Italian maestro Arturo Toscanini conducted some of the most legendary performances at the Salzburg Festival during the 1930s. Throughout the summer months the courtyard here is a hive of activity, with sets for the stage of the Kleines Festspielhaus being brought in through the massive iron folding gates.

⓫ Universitätskirche (Kollegienkirche, or Collegiate Church). Consecrated in 1707, this is architect Fischer von Erlach's masterpiece of the genre in Salzburg as well as one of the finest examples of Austrian Baroque. The interior has a liberating feeling of space and light, which stage directors have used to great advantage in recent years for Salzburg Festival performances of contemporary music. ⊠ *Universitätsplatz,* ☎ *0662/841–327–72.* ☒ *Free.* ⊘ *Daily 9–6.*

Wiener Philharmonikergasse. Previously known as Marktgasse (Market Street), an open food market is held here every Saturday morning (note that a daily fruit and vegetable market is held on the Universitätsplatz every day). The street was renamed after the world famous Vienna Philharmonic Orchestra in recognition of the unique contribution they make annually to the Salzburg Festival by playing for most opera productions and for the majority of orchestral concerts.

The Fortress and the New Town

According to a popular saying in Salzburg, "If you can see the fortress, it's just about to rain; if you can't see it, then it's already raining." Fortunately there are plenty of days when spectacular views can be had of Salzburg and the surrounding countryside from the top of the fortress. Looking across the River Salzach, you can pick out the Mirabell Palace and Gardens, the Landestheater, the Mozart Residence and the Mozarteum, the Church of the Holy Trinity, and the Kapuzinerkloster perched on the Kapuzinerberg. Ranging from the "acropolis" of the city—the medieval Fortress Hohensalzburg—to the celebrated Salzburg Marionette Theater, this part of Salzburg captures the city in all its charm. If you want to see the most delightful Mozart landmark in this part of town, the Zauberflötenhäuschen—the mouthful used to describe the little summerhouse where he finished composing *The Magic Flute*—note that you have to make a special appointment at the Mozarteum.

A Good Walk

Start with Salzburg's number one sight—especially the case at night, when it is spectacularly spotlit—the famed **Fortress Hohensalzburg** ⑰, the 12th-century castle that dominates the town. Take the Mönchsberg elevator or the funicular railway on Festungsgasse, located behind the cathedral near St. Peter's Cemetery. If it's not running, you can walk up the zigzag path that begins a little farther up Festungsgasse; it's steep in parts but gives a better impression of the majesty of the fortress. Once you've explored the largest medieval fortress in Central Europe, head back to the footpath but turn right toward the **Nonnberg Convent** ⑱ rather than taking the steps back into town. Explore the church—Maria von Trapp almost found her calling here—then return along the path to the first set of steps, walk down them into Kaigasse, and continue on to Mozartplatz. From here you can cross the Salzach River over the footbridge, Mozartsteg. Cross the road and walk west a minute or two along Imbergstrasse until you see a bookstore on the corner. Here a little street runs into **Steingasse** ⑲—a picturesque medieval street. After exploring this "Time Machine," walk through the Steintor gate, past the chapel of St. Johann am Imberg to the Hettwer Bastion on the **Kapuzinerberg Hill** ⑳ for a great vista of the city.

Continue up the path to the simple Kapuziner-Kloster. From here, follow the winding road down past the stations of the cross. Turn right at the bottom of the road into Linzergasse, the New Town's answer to the Getreidegasse. Continue up this street until St. Sebastian's church on the left. An archway will lead you into the tranquil **St. Sebastian's Cemetery** ㉑—if it looks somewhat familiar that's because this setting inspired the scene at the end of *The Sound of Music* where the von Trapps are nearly captured. When you leave the cemetery, walk north through a passageway until you reach Paris-Lodron-Strasse. To the left as you walk west down this street is the Loreto Church. At Mirabellplatz, cross the road to the **Mirabell Gardens** ㉒—the Pegasus Fountain (remember "Do-Re-Mi"?) and the Dwarfs' Garden are highlights here.

Take in the adjacent **Mirabell Palace** ㉓ and its noted 18th-century Angel Staircase. Turn left out of the park on the busy Schwarzstrasse. Along this road you will find the **Mozarteum** ㉔. Next door is the **Marionettentheater** ㉕—home to those marionettes known round the world. Turn left at the corner, around the Landestheater, and continue onto Makartplatz, which is dominated at the far end by Fischer von Erlach's **Dreifaltigkeitskirche** ㉖. Across from the Hotel Bristol is the **Mozart Wohnhaus** ㉗, where you can complete your homage to the city's hometown deity.

SOUND OF MUSIC TOURS

FEW SALZBURGERS WOULD publicly admit it, but *The Sound of Music,* Hollywood's interpretation of the trials and joys of the local von Trapp family, has become their city's most eminent emissary when it comes to international promotion. The year after the movie's release, international tourism to Salzburg jumped 20%, and soon *The Sound of Music* was a Salzburg attraction. The soundtrack and other movie and von Trapp memorabilia are hot-selling items around town.

A May–September **dinner show** in the grand ballroom of the K+K Stieglkeller (✉ Festungsg. 10, ☎ 0662/832029) features Rodgers and Hammerstein songs, folk dancing, a three-course meal, and drinks. Included in the AS520 price tag, the *plat de résistance* is that preposterous but genuinely Andrews–von Trapp combination: schnitzel and noodles. A 10-minute video interview with Maria von Trapp, in which she tells of her courtship with Baron von Trapp.

Perhaps the most important *Sound* spin-off are the **tours** offered by several companies (☞ Guided Tours *in* Salzburg A to Z, *below*). Besides showing you some of the film's locations (usually very briefly), these four-hour rides have the advantage of giving a very concise tour of the city. The buses generally leave from Mirabellplatz; lumber by the "Do-Re-Mi" staircase at the edge of the beautifully manicured Mirabell Gardens; pass by the hardly visible Aigen train station, where the von Trapps caught the escape train; and then head south to Schloss Anif. This 16th-century water castle, which had a cameo appearance in the opening scenes of the film, is now in private hands and not open to the public.

First official stop for a leg-stretcher is at the gazebo in the manicured park of Schloss Hellbrunn, about 6 km (4 mi) south of Salzburg (☞ Short Side Trips from Salzburg, *below*). This is where Liesl von Trapp sings "I Am Sixteen Going on Seventeen" and where Maria and the Baron woo and coo "Something Good." The simple little structure, which was in fact rebuilt in Hollywood a size larger for choreographic reasons, is the most coveted prize of photographers.

After driving by another private castle with limited visiting rights, Schloss Leopoldskron (used for the scene where Maria and the Baron dance on the balcony during the ball), and the Nonnberg Convent at the foot of the daunting Hohensalzburg fortress (☞ *below*), the bus leaves the city limits for the luscious landscape of the Salzkammergut. These are the hills "alive with music," where Julie Andrews prances about in the opening scenes and forgets all about her fellow nuns. You get a chance for a meditative walk along the shores of the Wolfgangsee in St. Gilgen, before the bus heads for the pretty town of Mondsee (☞ Chapter 7). In real life, Maria and Georg von Trapp were married at the Collegiate Church here.

Tour guides are well trained and often have a good sense of humor, with which they gently debunk myths about the movie and its making. Did you know, for example, that all interior scenes were built in the Fox studios, even the superb replica of the convent's halls? And Switzerland was "moved" 160 km (100 mi) eastward so the family could hike over the mountains to freedom (while singing "Edelweiss")? Well, in Hollywood as in Salzburg and its magical environs, anything is possible.

– Marton Radkai

TIMING

Allow yourself half a day for the fortress, to explore it fully both inside and out. If you don't take an intermission at one of the restaurants on the Mönchsberg, you can stock up on provisions at Schwaighofer (Kranzlmarkt 3 in the Old City) for a picnic in the beautiful Mirabell Gardens. Call the Mozarteum to see if there will be evening recitals in their two concert halls; hearing the Linz Symphony or the *Davidde Penitente* cantata could be a wonderfully fitting conclusion to your day.

Sights to See

㉖ **Dreifaltigkeitskirche** (Church of the Holy Trinity). The Makartplatz is dominated at the top (east) end by Fischer von Erlach's first architectural work in Salzburg, built 1694–1707. It was modeled on a church by Borromini in Rome and prefigures von Ehrlach's Karlskirche in Vienna. Dominated by a lofty, oval-shape dome—which bears a painting by Michael Rottmayr—this church was the result of the archbishops' concern that Salzburg's new town was developing in a haphazard fashion. The Dreifaltigkeitskirche was intended to create order by introducing a spectacular monument of the Baroque—the signature style of the city—on the Makartplatz. The interior is small but perfectly proportioned, surmounted by its dome, whose trompe-l'oeil fresco seems to open the church to the sky above. ⊠ *Dreifaltigkeitasg. 14,* ☎ *0662/ 877495.* 🎟 *Free.* ☉ *Mon.–Sat. 6:30–6:30, Sun. 8–6:30.*

Festungsbahn (funicular railway). This is the easy way up to Fortress Hohensalzburg (☞ *below*); it's located behind St. Peter's Cemetery. ⊠ *Festungsg. 4,* ☎ *0662/842682.* 🎟 *Round-trip AS69, one-way AS37.* ☉ *Oct.–mid-Nov., mid- to late Dec., and Feb.–Apr., daily 9–5 every 10 min; May–Sept., daily 8 AM–9 PM every 10 min.*

⑰ **Fortress Hohensalzburg.** Founded in 1077, the Fortress Hohensalzburg is Salzburg's Acropolis and the largest preserved medieval fortress in Central Europe. Brooding over the city from atop the Festungsberg, it was originally built by Salzburg's Archbishop Gebhard, who had supported the pope in the political struggle against the Holy Roman Emperor. Over the centuries, the archbishops gradually enlarged the castle and used it first as a residence, then as a siege-proof haven against invaders and the rebellions of their own subjects. Outside, the fortress may look grim, but inside there are lavish state rooms, such as the glittering **Golden Room,** the **Burgmuseum**—a collection of medieval art— and the **Rainersmuseum,** with its brutish arms and armour. Politics and church are in full force here: There's a torture chamber not far from the exquisite late-Gothic **St. George's Chapel.** In 1502, the fortress acquired the 200-pipe organ, played daily after the carillon in the Neugebäude. It is best to listen to it from a respectful distance, as it is not called the Bull without reason. Everyone will want to climb up the 100 tiny steps to the **Reckturm,** a lookout post for its sweeping view of Salzburg and the mountains. Remember that queues can be long to the fortress, so try to come early.

You can either take the funicular railway, the ☞ **Festungsbahn,** up to the fortress (advisable with young children) or walk up the zigzag path that begins just beyond the Stieglkeller on the Festungsgasse. Note that descent on foot is possible only if you have a ticket for the fortress. ⊠ *Mönchsberg 34,* ☎ *0662/842430.* 🎟 *Fortress AS35, fortress and tour AS70.* ☉ *Oct.–May., daily 8–6; June–Sept., daily 8–7; 50-min tour Nov.–Mar., daily 10–4:30 every ½ hr; Apr.–June and Sept.–Oct., daily 9:30–5 every ½ hr; July–Aug., daily 9–5:30 every ½ hr.*

BONUS MILES MAKE GREAT SOUVENIRS.

MCI Calling Card

123 456 7891 2345
J. D. SMITH

WorldPhone

Earn Miles With Your MCI Card.

Take the MCI Card along on this trip and start earning miles for the next one. You'll earn frequent flyer miles on all your calls and save with the low rates you've come to expect from MCI. Before you know it, you'll be on your way to some other international destination.

Sign up for MCI by calling 1-800-FLY-FREE

Earn Frequent Flyer Miles.

AmericanAirlines'
A'Advantage®

Continental Airlines
OnePass

▲ Delta Air Lines
SkyMiles®

NORTHWEST AIRLINES
WORLDPERKS®

✈ **MILEAGE PLUS.**
United Airlines

US AIRWAYS
DIVIDEND MILES

Is this a great time, or what? :-)

MCI

Easy To Call Home.

1. To use your MCI Card, just dial the WorldPhone access number of the country you're calling from.
2. Dial or give the operator your MCI Card number.
3. Dial or give the number you're calling.

# Austria (CC) ♦	022-903-012
# Belarus (CC)	
From Brest, Vitebsk, Grodno, Minsk	8-800-103
From Gomel and Mogilev regions	8-10-800-103
# Belgium (CC) ♦	0800-10012
# Bulgaria	00800-0001
# Croatia (CC) ★	0800-22-0112
# Czech Republic (CC) ♦	00-42-000112
# Denmark (CC) ♦	8001-0022
# Finland (CC) ♦	08001-102-80
# France (CC) ♦	0-800-99-0019
# Germany (CC)	0800-888-8000
# Greece (CC) ♦	00-800-1211
# Hungary (CC) ♦	00▼800-01411
# Iceland (CC) ♦	800-9002
# Ireland (CC)	1-800-55-1001
# Italy (CC) ♦	172-1022
# Kazakhstan (CC)	8-800-131-4321
# Liechtenstein (CC) ♦	0800-89-0222
# Luxembourg	0800-0112
# Monaco (CC) ♦	800-90-019
# Netherlands (CC) ♦	0800-022-9122
# Norway (CC) ♦	800-19912
# Poland (CC) ÷	00-800-111-21-22
# Portugal (CC) ÷	05-017-1234
Romania (CC) ÷	01-800-1800
# Russia (CC) ÷ ♦	
To call using ROSTELCOM ■	747-3322
For a Russian-speaking operator	747-3320
To call using SOVINTEL ■	960-2222
# San Marino (CC) ♦	172-1022
# Slovak Republic (CC)	00-421-00112
# Slovenia	080-8808
# Spain (CC)	900-99-0014
# Sweden (CC) ♦	020-795-922
# Switzerland (CC) ♦	0800-89-0222
# Turkey (CC) ♦	00-8001-1177
# Ukraine (CC) ÷	8▼10-013
# United Kingdom (CC)	
To call using BT ■	0800-89-0222
To call using C&W ■	0500-89-0222
# Vatican City (CC)	172-1022

CHASE

Flying to France on Friday? Get Francs from Chase on Thursday. Call Currency To Go at 935-9935 for overnight delivery.

CHASE CURRENCY TO GO 935-9935

*O*r pounds for London. Or Deutschmarks for Düsseldorf. Or any of 75 foreign currencies. Call **Chase Currency To Go**℠ **at 935-9935** in area codes 212, 718, 914, 516 and Rochester, N.Y.; all other area codes call 1-800-935-9935. We'll deliver directly to your door.* Overnight. And there are no exchange fees. Let Chase make your trip an easier one.

CHASE. The right relationship is everything.℠

㉚ Kapuzinerberg Hill. Directly opposite the Mönchsberg on the other side of the river, Kapuzinerberg Hill is crowned by several interesting sights. By ascending a stone staircase near Steingasse 9 you can start your climb up the peak. At the top of the first flight of steps is a tiny chapel, **St. Johann am Imberg,** built in 1681. Farther on is a signpost and gate to the **Hettwer Bastion,** part of the old city walls and offering one of the most spectacular viewpoints in Salzburg. At the summit is the gold-beige **Kapuzinerkloster** (Capuchin Monastery), dating from the time of Prince-Archbishop Wolf-Dietrich. Pope John Paul II stayed here during his visit to Salzburg in 1988. The road downward is called Stefan Zweig Weg, after the great Austrian writer who had a house on the Kapuzinerberg until 1935 when he had to flee Austria and the Anschluss. Along the road are the stations of the cross.

㉕ Marionettentheater (Marionette Theater). This is both the world's greatest marionette theater and—surprise!—a sublime theatrical experience. Many critics have noted that viewers quickly forget the strings controlling the puppets, which assume lifelike dimensions and provide a very real dramatic experience. The Marionettentheater is identified above all with Mozart's operas, which seem particularly suited to the skilled puppetry; a delightful production of *Così fan Tutte* captures the humor of the work better than most stage versions. The company is famous for its world tours but is usually in Salzburg around Christmas, during the late-January Mozart Week, Easter, and from May to September (schedule subject to change). ⊠ *Schwarzstr. 24,* ☎ *0662/ 872406,* FAX *0662/825859.* ⊠ *AS250–AS500.* ☉ *Box office Mon.–Sat. 9–1 and 2 hrs before performance; Salzburg season May–Sept., Christmas, Mozart Week, Easter.*

㉒ Mirabell Gardens. While there are at least four entrances to the Mirabell Gardens—from the Makartplatz, the Schwarzstrasse, and the Rainerstrasse—you'll want to enter from the Rainerstrasse and head for the Rosenhügel (Rosebush Hill): You'll arrive at the top of the steps where Julie Andrews and her seven charges showed off their singing ability in *The Sound of Music.* This is also an ideal vantage point for admiring the formal gardens and offers one of the best views of Salzburg, as it shows how harmoniously architects of the Baroque period laid out the city. The center of the gardens—one of Europe's most beautiful parks, partly designed by Fischer von Erlach, and grand setting for the Mirabell Palace (☞ *below*)—is dominated by four large groups of statues representing the elements and designed by Ottavio Mosto, who came to live in Salzburg from Padua. A bronze version of the horse Pegasus stands in front of the southern facade of the Mirabell Palace in the center of a circular water basin. The most famous part of the Mirabell Gardens is the **Zwerglgarten** (Dwarfs' Garden), which can be found opposite the Pegasus fountain. Here you'll find 12 statues of dwarves sculpted in marble—the real-life models of which were presented to the bishop by the landgrave of Göttweig. Prince-Archbishop Franz Anton von Harrach had the stone figures made for a theater that was later closed. It's open daily 7 AM–8 PM. The **Baroque Museum** (⊠ Orangeriegarten, ☎ 0662/877432), beside the Orangery of the Mirabell Gardens, features a collection of late-17th- and 18th-century paintings, sketches, and models illustrating the development of the extravagant vision of life. Works by Giordano, Bernini, and Rottmayr are some of the highlights of the collection. The museum is open Tuesday–Saturday 9–noon and 2–5 and Sunday 9–noon; admission is AS 40.

㉓ Mirabell Palace. The "Taj Mahal of Salzburg," the Mirabell Palace was built by Prince-Archbishop Wolf-Dietrich for his mistress, Salomé Alt, and their 10 children: It was originally called *Altenau* in her honor.

Over the centuries the Mirabell Palace, now the City Hall, has undergone many extensive alterations. Due to the fire that ravaged Salzburg in 1818, nothing remains of the original palace except the Marble Hall upstairs, nowadays regarded as the most beautiful registry office in the world because it is used for civil wedding ceremonies (candlelit chamber concerts are also held here in the evenings). Recently restored, the hall now looks more splendid than ever, with its marble floor in strongly contrasting colors and the walls of stucco marble ornamented with elegant gilt scrollwork.

The only other part of the palace to survive the fire was the magnificent marble staircase, sculpted by Georg Rafael Donner. Staircases of important buildings afforded many Baroque artists ideal opportunities for ingenious and exuberant ornamentation, and Donner produced a particularly charming example of this highly specialized art in Mirabell. Romantically draped with white marble putti, the staircase is adorned with a multitude of these cherubs—their faces and gestures reflect a whole range of emotions, from questioning innocence to jeering mockery. Outdoor concerts are held at the palace and gardens, May though August, Sunday mornings, and Wednesday evenings. ⊠ *Off Makartpl.,* ☎ *0662/8485–86.* ▣ *Free.* ◷ *Weekdays 8–6.*

Mozart Audio and Video Museum. In the same building as the Mozart Wohnhaus (Residence) (☞ *below*) is the Mozart Audio and Video Museum, an archive of thousands of Mozart recordings as well as films and video productions, all of which can be listened to or watched on request. ⊠ *Makartpl. 8,* ☎ *0662/883454.* ▣ *Free.* ◷ *Mon.–Tues. and Fri. 9–1, Wed.–Thurs. 1–5.*

🐚 ㉗ **Mozart Wohnhaus** (Mozart Residence). The Mozart family moved out of their cramped surroundings in the Getreidegasse to this house on the Hannibal Platz, as it was known then, in 1773. Wolfgang Amadeus Mozart lived here until 1780, his sister Nannerl stayed here until she married in 1784 and father Leopold lived here until his death in 1787. The house is, therefore, now referred to as the Mozart Residence, signifying that it was not only Wolfgang who lived here. During the first Allied bomb attack on Salzburg in October 1944, the house was bombed and partially destroyed. Despite international protest at the time a six-story office block was built in its place. Now, in an exemplary building and sponsorship project, the office block has been demolished and the house reconstructed according to how it used to look. Mozart composed the "Salzburg Symphonies" here, as well as violin concertos, church music and sonatas, and parts of his early operatic masterpieces. Besides an interesting collection of musical instruments, among the exhibits on display are the books Leopold Mozart had in his library. Autograph manuscripts and letters can be viewed, by prior arrangement only, in the cellar vaults. One room is devoted to more personal details about Mozart—his height, color of his hair, his method of dress, and his numerous travels across Europe. ⊠ *Makartpl. 8,* ☎ *0662/883–4544–0,* ℻ *0662/872924.* ▣ *Mozart residence AS65, combined ticket for Mozart Residence and Birthplace AS110.* ◷ *Daily 10–6.*

㉔ **Mozarteum.** Two institutions share the address here—the International Mozarteum Foundation, set up in 1870, and the Academy of Music and Performing Arts, founded in 1880. Both are important centers of academic research; the Mozarteum also organizes the annual Mozart Week festival in January and is sponsor of concerts from October to June in its two recital halls, the Grosser Saal (Great Hall) and the Wiener Saal (Vienna Hall). ⊠ *Schwarzstr. 26,* ☎ *0662/88940–21.*

⑱ Nonnberg Convent. Situated just below the south side of the Fortress Hohensalzburg—and best visited in tandem with it—this convent was founded around AD 700 by St. Rupert, and his niece St. Erentrudis was the first abbess (in the archway a late-Gothic statue of Erentrudis welcomes the visitor). It's more famous these days as Maria's convent—both the one in *The Sound of Music* and that of the real Maria. She returned to marry her Captain von Trapp here in the Gothic church. Each evening in May at 6:45, the nuns sing a 15-minute service called *Maiandacht*. Their beautiful voices can be heard also at midnight mass on December 24. Parts of the private quarters for the nuns, which feature some lovely, intricate woodcarving, can even be seen by prior arrangement. ⊠ *Nonnbergg. 2,* ☎ *0662/841607.* ☉ *Fall–spring, daily 7–noon and 1:30–5; summer, daily 7–noon and 1:30–7:30.*

㉑ St. Sebastian's Cemetery. Located in the shadows of St. Sebastian's Church, the Friedhof St. Sebastian is one of the most peaceful spots in Salzburg. Prince-Archbishop Wolf Dietrich commissioned the cemetery at the end of the 16th century to replace the old cathedral graveyard, which he planned to demolish. It was built in the style of an Italian *campo santo,* with arcades on four sides, and in the center of the square he had an unusual, brightly tiled, mannerist mausoleum built for himself, where he was buried in 1617. Several famous people are buried in this cemetery, including the physician and philosopher Paracelsus, who settled in Salzburg during the early 16th century (the grave is by the church door); Mozart's wife, Constanze; and Mozart's father, Leopold (by the central path leading to the mausoleum). If the gate is closed, try going through the church, or enter through the back entrance on Paris-Lodron-Strasse. ⊠ *Linzerg.* ☉ *Daily 7 AM–7 PM.*

⑲ Steingasse. This narrow medieval street, walled in on one side by the bare cliffs of the Kapuzinerberg, ran along the riverfront before the Salzach was regulated. Nowadays it's a fascinating mixture of artists' workshops, antiques shops, and trendy nightclubs, but with its high houses the street still manages to convey an idea of how life used to be in the Middle Ages. **Steingasse 9** is the house where Josef Mohr, who wrote the words to the Christmas carol "Silent Night, Holy Night," was born in 1792. The **Steintor** marks the entrance to the oldest section of the street; here on summer afternoons the light can be particularly striking. House Number 23 on the right still has deep, slanted peep-windows for guarding the gate.

Short Side Trips from Salzburg

Gaisberg and Untersberg. Adventurous people might like to ascend two of Salzburg's "house mountains" (not on the same day!). You can take the bus to the summit of the Gaisberg, where you'll be rewarded with a spectacular panoramic view of the Alps and the Alpine foreland. In summer the bus leaves from Mirabellplatz at 9 AM and 11 AM, and the journey takes about half an hour. The Untersberg is the mountain Captain von Trapp and Maria climbed as they escaped the Nazis in *The Sound of Music.* In the film they were supposedly fleeing to Switzerland; in reality, the climb up the Untersberg would have brought them almost to the doorstep of Hitler's retreat at Eagle's Nest above Berchtesgaden. A cable car from St. Leonhard (about 13 km/8 mi south of Salzburg) takes you up 6,020 ft right to the top of the Untersberg, giving you a breathtaking view. In winter you can ski down (you arrive in the village of Fürstenbrunn and taxis or buses take you back to St. Leonhard); in summer there are a number of hiking routes from the summit. ⊠ *Untersbergbahn,* ☎ *06216/72177.* ▨ *Round trip*

AS215. ⊘ Mar.–June and Oct. 1–26, daily 9–5; July–Sept., daily 8:30–5:30; Dec. 20–Feb. 28, daily 10–4.

OFF THE BEATEN PATH	**NEUKIRCHEN/VÖCKLA** – In this tiny village about 50 km (30 mi) north of Salzburg is the Freilichtmuseum Stehrerhof, which houses a 400-year-old furnished farmhouse with related exhibits and even a still. From Salzburg go in the direction of Linz on the B1, turning north at Vöckla-markt. From here follow signs east to Langwies and then to Neukirchen. ⌂ *AS45. ⊘ Open Apr.–Oct., 10–noon and 1–5; July–Oct., 10–5.*

Oberndorf. This little village 21 km (13 mi) north of Salzburg has just one claim to fame; it was here, on Christmas Eve, 1818, that the organist and schoolteacher Franz Gruber composed the Christmas carol "Silent Night, Holy Night" to a lyric by the local priest, Josef Mohr. The church where the masterpiece was created was demolished and replaced in 1937 by a tiny commemorative chapel containing a copy of the original composition (the original is in the Carolino-Augusteum Museum in Salzburg); stained-glass windows representing Gruber and Mohr; and a nativity scene. About a 10-minute walk from the village center along the riverbank, the local **Heimatmuseum** (⊠ Stille-Nacht-Pl. 7, ☏ 06272/4422), opposite the chapel, documents the history of the carol. The museum is open March–January, daily 9–noon and 1–5; admission is AS40. You can get to Oberndorf by the local train (opposite the main train station), by car along the Oberndorferstrasse, or by bicycle along the River Salzach.

★ ☾ **Schloss Hellbrunn** (Hellbrunn Palace). Just 6½ km (4 mi) south of Salzburg, the Lustschloss Hellbrun was the pleasure palace of the prince-archbishops. It was built in the early 17th century by Santino Solari for Markus Sittikus, after he'd imprisoned his uncle, Wolf Dietrich, in the fortress. The castle has some fascinating rooms, including an octagonal music room and a banquet hall with a trompe l'oeil ceiling. From the magnificent gardens and tree-lined avenues to the silent ponds, Hellbrunn Park is often described as a jewel of landscape architecture. It became famous far and wide because of its **Wasserspiele,** or trick fountains: In the formal Baroque gardens, some of the exotic and humorous fountains spurt water from strange places at unexpected times—you will probably get wet. A visit to the gardens is highly recommended: Nowhere else can you experience so completely the fantasy that the grand Salzburg archbishops delighted in. The **Monatsschlösschen,** the old hunting lodge, contains an excellent folklore museum. The palace deer park now sports a **zoo** featuring freeflying vultures and Alpine animals that largely roam unhindered. You can get to Hellbrunn by Bus 55, by car on Route 159, or by bike or on foot along the beautiful Hellbrunner Allee past several 17th-century mansions. The restaurant in the castle courtyard serves good food. ⊠ *Fürstenweg 37, Hellbrunn,* ☏ *0662/820372. ⌂ Tour of castle, water gardens, and museum AS70; park free. ⊘ Apr. and Oct., daily 9–4:30; May–Sept., daily 9–5:30; evening tour July–Aug., daily at 6–10 on the hr.*

DINING

The prices in Salzburg's excellent restaurants are certainly higher than in much of the rest of Austria but, in general, justifiably so: You can experience some truly exquisite cuisine. Many restaurants favor the *Neue Küche*—a lighter version of the traditional, somewhat heavy specialties of Austrian cooking, but with more substance than nouvelle cuisine. The only truly indigenous Salzburg dish is *Salzburger Nockerln,* a snowy meringue of sweetened whisked egg whites with just a hint of lemon, but the Salzburgers have a wonderful way with fish—often a fresh catch from the nearby lakes of the Salzkammergut. In the more expensive restaurants, the set menus give you an opportunity to sample the chef's best; in the less expensive ones, they help to keep costs down. Note, however, that some restaurants limit the hours during which the set menu is available. Many restaurants are open all day; otherwise, lunch is served from approximately 11 to 2 and dinner from 6 to 10. In more expensive restaurants it's always best to make a reservation. At festival time, most restaurants are open seven days a week and have generally more flexible late dining hours.

$$$$ ✕ **Bei Bruno.** A short walk from Schloss Mirabell, this intimate restau-
★   rant in the Bristol Hotel offers some of the best food in the entire city. Chef Bruno Plotegher specializes in fresh fish, lightly prepared, and the menu changes frequently to showcase what's in season, such as the delicious *Steinpilze* (porcini mushrooms) and potato casserole. Look for sea bass in a champagne sauce with Chinese peas and spaghettini or monkfish in a saffron sauce with potato ravioli and asparagus. There are also chicken, beef, and vegetarian dishes. Bei Bruno is a perfect choice for after-theater dining. Service is friendly and attentive. ⊠ *Makartpl. 4,* ☎ *0662/8485–11–861. Reservations essential. AE, DC, MC, V.*

$$$$ ✕ **Paris Lodron.** The restaurant in the Schloss Mönchstein is a retreat into Old World elegance. Antique furniture, exquisite porcelain, and heavy plated cutlery provide a wonderful contrast to the Austrian nouvelle cuisine. The chef specializes in fresh seafood creations and lamb, and the food is among the best Salzburg has to offer, with a frequently changing menu. The sophisticated ambience makes dining here an especially memorable experience. Opt for the tiny terrace in summer. It's very popular, especially at festival time. ⊠ *Mönchsberg 26,* ☎ *0662/ 848555–0,* ℻ *0662/848559. Reservations essential. Jacket and tie. AE, DC, MC, V.*

$$$$ ✕ **Purzelbaum.** Tucked away under the Nonnberg in the Nonntal district, this restaurant (whose name means somersault) is a fine choice if you want to combine an outstanding gastronomic experience with enjoyable, relaxed surroundings and unobtrusive but attentive service. The light green and white decor has the flair of a Parisian bistro, with small square tables and subdued lighting in the rear room; in summer you can dine outside on the patio, discussing festival performances until well into the night. Specialties include fish caught in the lakes of the Salzkammergut served in delectable sauces. Ingenious combinations of vegetables are a delight for the eye as well as for the palate. But save enough room for a dessert—the variations on ice cream truffles or even traditional Austrian curd-cheese dumplings are unequaled. ⊠ *Zugallistr. 7,* ☎ *0662/848843,* ℻ *0662/844352. Reservations essential. AE, DC, V.*

$$$ ✕ **Stadtkrug.** You'll receive a warm welcome from the owners of this family-run hotel and restaurant—the owners, Hugo and Eva, often wear traditional Austrian costume, and together with their team of charming waiters they ensure that any meal here is both a gastronomic and social occasion. The combination of Austrian rustic elegance and cosmopolitan flair makes this a favorite spot for theatergoers and music critics. Try the superb cream of lettuce soup, locally caught rainbow trout or char, or fillet of lamb from the Lech valley in Vorarlberg. This is also one of the best places in town for *Salzburger Nockerl*—but who can resist the *Heisse Liebe* (extra creamy ice cream with hot raspberries). Allow plenty of time to eat here: Service can be slow, but the food is always well worth waiting for. ⊠ *Linzerg. 20,* ☎ *0662/873545 or 0662/878244,* ℻ *0662/879588. Reservations essential. AE, DC, MC, V. Closed Tues.*

224

Salzburg Dining and Lodging

Breitenfelderstrasse

Stauffenstrasse

Plainstrasse

Elisabethstrasse

Rainerstrasse

Last enstrasse

Merianstrasse

Bayerhamerstrasse

Haunspergstrasse

St. Julien-Strasse

Gabelsbergerstrasse

Lasserstrasse

Sterneckstrasse

KEY

AE American Express Office

i Tourist Information

N

Weiserstrasse

Haydnstrasse

Paracelsusstrasse

Auerspergstrasse

Faberstrasse

Markus-Sittikus-Strasse

Auerspergstrasse

Rainerstrasse

Franz-Josef-Strasse

Rupertgasse

23

Hubert-Sattler-Gasse

Mirabellpl.

Schrannengasse

Wolf-Dietrich-Strasse

Schallmooser Hauptstrasse

Mirabell Gardens

Schwarzstrasse

Paris-Lodron-Strasse

Kapuzinerberg

Dreifaltigkeitsgasse

Bergstrasse

Priesterh

Linzergasse

22

Franz-Josef-Ka

Elisabethkai

Makart-platz

Stef. Zweig Weg

21

20

9

10

Makart-steg

Hauptstrasse

Gstättengasse

Platzl

Staats-brucke

Salzach

Imbergstrasse

Steingasse

Giselakai

Museumplatz

A.-Neumayr-Pl.

Griesgasse

Rudolfskai

Mozart-steg

3

4

7

8

Getreidegasse

Judengasse

13

Herbert-von-Karajan-Pl.

5

6

Universitätsplatz

12

11

14

15

Goldgasse

i

AE

Nonntaler Brücke

Hofstallgasse

Sigmund-Haffner-Gasse

Brodgasse

Residenz-platz

Pfeifergasse

Kaigasse

Dr. Ludwig Prahauser-Weg

17

16

Buckl reuthstr.

18

Herrengasse

Kaigasse

19

Festungsgasse

$$$ ✕ **Zum Eulenspiegel.** Delicious food matches the unique setting in this
★ house, which is hundreds of years old. Tables are set with white linen
in wonderful nooks and crannies reached by odd staircases. It's right
in the middle of the Old City, and the staff speaks English. Try the potato
goulash with chunks of sausage and beef in a creamy paprika sauce,
or the house specialty, fish stew Provençale. These are served at lunch,
or all day in the bar downstairs. ✉ *Hagenauerpl. 2,* ☎ *0662/843180–
0,* FAX *0662/843180–6. Reservations essential. AE, DC, MC, V. Closed
Sun. except during festival, and Jan.–mid-Mar.*

$$ ✕ **K+K am Waagplatz.** This upstairs restaurant is particularly pleasant, with white linen tablecloths, candles and flowers, and windows
opening onto the street. Menu selections consist of locally caught fish,
delicious chicken breast medallions in a cheese crust with pasta and
basil-tomato sauce, and lentil salad with strips of goose breast, as well
as traditional Austrian dishes and game in season. Service is friendly.
✉ *Waagpl. 2,* ☎ *0662/842156,* FAX *0662/84211770. AE, DC, MC, V.*

$$ ✕ **Stiftskeller St. Peter.** In what is said to be Europe's oldest *Gasthaus,*
founded by Benedictine monks in the 9th century, choose between the
fairly elegant, dark wood-paneled *Prälatenzimmer* (Prelate Room) or
one of the several less formal rooms. Locals claim that Mephistophe-
les met Faust here. In summer the dramatic gray-stone courtyard is a
favorite. You'll find standards ranging from Wiener schnitzel to the del-
icate poached St. Peter's fish. Specialties include the *Klostertopf,* thick
soup served in a loaf of bread, fish caught in local rivers and lakes,
and, of course, *Salzburger Nockerl.* ✉ *St. Peter Bezirk 4,* ☎ *0662/
848481,* FAX *0662/841268–75. AE, DC.*

$$ ✕ **Zipfer Bierhaus.** The arched ceilings, brick floors, and wooden tables provide the right setting for good, standard local fare such as roast
pork with a dumpling, served with Zipfer beer, of course. This is one
of Salzburg's oldest *Gasthäuser;* look down the ancient cistern in the
passageway connecting the two main rooms. ✉ *Sigmund-Haffner-
Gasse 12/Universitätspl. 19,* ☎ *0662/840745,* FAX *0662/853234. No
credit cards. Closed Sun.*

$$ ✕ **Zum Mohren.** Good food, a central location by the river, a welcoming
atmosphere, attentive service, and reasonable prices have made Zum
Mohren very popular with both Salzburgers and tourists. The restau-
rant is in the basement of a 15th-century house; tables can be cramped.
Offerings are not overly adventuresome, but the menu always offers
at least one vegetarian item and several fish dishes among a selection
of Austrian specialties like sautéed veal liver and roast hare. ✉ *Judeng.
9/Rudolfskai 20,* ☎ *0662/842387. AE, MC, V. Closed Sun. and mid-
June–mid-July.*

$ ✕ **Augustinerbräu.** Salzburg's homegrown version of a Munich beer
house is at the north end of the Mönchsberg. You can bring your own
food; pick up a stone jug of strong, frothy (not fizzy) beer; and sit down
in the gardens or at a dark-wood table in one of the large halls. Shops
in the huge monastery complex sell salads that can look a little weary
later on in the day, sausage, and fried chicken, and a little stall has tasty
spirals of salted radish. If you don't feel up to cold beer, there's an old
copper beer warmer in the main hall. ✉ *Augustinerg. 4,* ☎ *0662/431246,*
FAX *0662/431246–20. No credit cards.*

$ ✕ **Bistro Bio Terra.** Located inside the Rupertinum Galerie, this casual
vegetarian restaurant serves tasty dishes entirely free of animal prod-
ucts or preservatives. The chef takes Italian recipes and creates his own
vegetarian versions. The blackboard menu changes daily, but look for
bruschetta with a variety of toppings or arugula and grilled oyster mush-
rooms with a Parmesan-paprika puree. You could make an entire meal
of the enticing antipasti bar. Several fresh fruit juices are also on offer.
✉ *Philharmonikerg. 9,* ☎ *06222/849414. No credit cards. Closed Mon.*

$ ✕ **Humboldtstube.** The main room, reminiscent of a hunting lodge, sets the atmosphere for good local food, such as roast veal and pork with sauerkraut. Salad aficionados choose from 18 varieties. You can find hot food here until 2 AM year-round and in summer dine outdoors at tables set on the street. ✉ *Gstätteng. 6*, ☎ *0662/843171. No credit cards.*

$ ✕ **Ristorante Pizzeria al Sole.** Located by the Mönchsberg elevator, this
★ Italian restaurant is owned by two friendly brothers who regularly travel over the border to Italy to bring back the freshest ingredients. The thin-crust pizzas are especially scrumptious, with a wide variety of toppings, including Gorgonzola and sage. Pasta dishes are numerous and delicious, such as tagliatelle with grilled shrimp or cheesy vegetarian lasagne. This is also the place to come for a light lunch of soup or salad with tuna and olives or chicken. Sit upstairs in a pretty room lined with Venetian prints or in the more casual downstairs area. In summer tables are set outside on the street. ✉ *Gstätteng. 15*, ☎ *0662/843284*, FAX *0662/843284. AE, DC, MC, V.*

$ ✕ **Sternbräu.** This place seems big enough to have fed half the Austro-Hungarian army. The restaurant is divided into a series of rooms with varying degrees of formality. There are two beer gardens where you can sit on warm evenings in the shade of chestnut trees and enjoy local beer or a refreshing *weiss g'spritztzt* (white wine with water) and special Salzburg dishes with products supplied from local farms. One part of the restaurant (La Stella) also serves Italian food. ✉ *Griesg. 23 and 34*, ☎ *0662/842140–0*, FAX *0662/842140–81. No credit cards.*

$ ✕ **Zum Fidelen Affen.** The name means "At the Faithful Ape," which
★ explains the ape motifs in this popular *Gasthaus*, dominated by a large circular bar and stone pillars under a vaulted ceiling. Besides the microbrewed beer on tap, the kitchen offers tasty, filling dishes, such as *Gemuse gröstl*, which is home-fried potatoes with vegetables and polenta, or spinach spaëtzle in a ham cream sauce and cheese gratiné. The garlic cream soup with black-bread croutons is outstanding. Service is especially warm and friendly. ✉ *Priesterhausg. 8*, ☎ *0662/877361. No credit cards. Closed Sun. No lunch.*

LODGING

It is difficult for a Salzburg hotel not to have a good location—you can find a room with a stunning view over the Kapuzinergberg or Gaisberg or one that simply overlooks a lovely Old City street. Many hostelries are charmingly decorated in *Bauernstil*—the rustic, peasant-luxe look of Old Austria. Note that many hotels in the Old City have to be accessed via footpower, as cars are not permitted on many streets. If you have a car, of course, you may opt to do what many do—find a hotel or converted castle on the outskirts of the city. Needless to say, if you're planning to come at festival time, you must book as early as possible. If you don't have a reservation, go to one of the tourist information offices or the accommodations service (*Zimmernachweis*) on the main platform of the railway station.

$$$$ 🏨 **Bristol.** No two rooms are alike in this luxurious turn-of the-century hotel, which has great views of the river and fortress. In the last couple of years all rooms have been completely renovated with great care in a unique and sumptuous style and feature marble bathrooms and all the little extras. The staff is especially friendly. Added bonuses are its close proximity to both the Old City and Schloss Mirabell, buffet breakfast, and the excellent restaurant, Bci Bruno (☞ Dining, *above*). ✉ *Makartpl. 4, A–5020*, ☎ *0662/873557*, FAX *0662/873557– 6. 60 rooms. Restaurant, bar. AE, DC, MC, V. Closed Jan.–Feb.*

$$$$ ☎ **Goldener Hirsch.** The "Golden Stag" has the best location of all
Salzburg's luxury hotels, right down the street from Mozart's Birthplace. Rooms in this nearly 600-year-old town house have a simple,
rustic charm with bright rag rugs; the stag motif is everywhere, including
the lamp shades, which were hand-painted by an Austrian countess.
Breakfast is not included in the room price. ⊠ *Getreideg. 37, A–
5020,* ☎ *0662/8084–0,* FAX *0662/848511–845. 70 rooms. 2 restaurants, bar, parking fee. AE, DC, MC, V.*

$$$$ ☎ **Österreichischer Hof.** Clientele at this beautiful hotel on the banks
★   of the Salzach River have ranged from the Beatles and the Rolling Stones
to, more recently, Hillary and Chelsea Clinton. It's owned by the
Gürtler family, who also own the famous Hotel Sacher in Vienna.
Each room is different, but all are exquisitely decorated, with care and
attention given to every possible whim or need, and the staff is warm
and friendly. The danger here is that the rooms are so lovely and comfortable you won't want to leave to explore the city. Room prices include a delicious buffet breakfast, including Sekt (Austrian sparkling
wine). In nice weather tables are set outside on the terrace where you
can enjoy a salad or hamburger (called a "Salzburger") for lunch while
gazing across at the fortress. ⊠ *Schwarzstr. 5–7, A–5020,* ☎ *0662/
88977,* FAX *0662/88977–14. 120 rooms. 3 restaurants, bar, exercise room,
meeting rooms. AE, DC, MC, V.*

$$$$ ☎ **Schloss Mönchstein.** This palatial mountain retreat is in its own mag-
★   ical world with gardens and hiking trails, yet just minutes from the city
center. Within these ancient, ivy-covered walls is a treasure trove of
lovely, luxurious rooms, some hung with tapestries and others with views
of the woods and Salzburg in the distance. Service is pleasant and dis-
creet, and the Paris Lodron restaurant is the epitome of Old World elegance (☞ Dining, *above*). The castle has its own wedding chapel, which
is particularly popular with American and Japanese couples. Getting
in and out of town calls for a car or taxi, unless you are willing to negotiate steps or take the nearby Mönchsberg elevator, which is about
an eight-minute walk away. ⊠ *Mönchsberg 26, A–5020,* ☎ *0662/
848555–0,* FAX *0662/848559. 17 rooms. Restaurant, bar, café, tennis
court, chapel, free parking. AE, DC, MC, V.*

$$$ ☎ **Elefant.** The prime location makes this one of Salzburg's most pop-
ular mid-level hotels. The public rooms are well decorated with Bieder-
meier furniture, though this doesn't carry over to the bedrooms, which
are standard. Under glass at the reception desk is a copy of a personal
check to the hotel from the real Maria von Trapp, written when she stayed
here in 1981. ⊠ *Sigmund-Haffner-Gasse 4, A–5020,* ☎ *0662/843397,*
FAX *0662/840109–28. 36 rooms. 2 restaurants. AE, DC, MC, V.*

$$$ ☎ **Stadtkrug.** This historic family-run hotel is cut into the stone of the
Kapuzinerberg, accounting for the various floor levels; the rock behind
the reception desk is real, not decoration. In many of the rooms, dark
wood contrasts with light walls and Oriental carpets. The suites are
elegantly spacious, with original wood-beamed ceilings, canopied bed,
and period furniture. Marble baths are equally expansive. Side rooms
have little or no view but are quieter, despite the pedestrian zone. The
garden terrace adjacent to the fourth floor offers a hilltop view out over
the city. ⊠ *Linzerg. 20, A–5020,* ☎ *0662/873545,* FAX *0662/879588.
34 rooms. Restaurant, café. AE, DC, MC, V.*

$$ ☎ **Blaue Gans.** At press time the "Blue Goose" was undergoing ex-
★   tensive renovations with plans to reopen soon as a more expensive hotel,
possibly pushing it into the $$$ category. Supposedly, bathrooms are
being added to the older rooms, along with an updated reception area.
Stepping straight out onto Getreidegasse with Mozart's Birthplace just
a few houses away makes this 500-year-old hotel a top choice, so

make reservations early. ⊠ *Getreideg. 43, A–5020,* ☎ *0662/841317,* FAX *0662/841317–9. 88 rooms. Restaurant. AE, DC, MC, V.*

$$ 🖫 **Weisse Taube.** A traditional family-run hotel, close to the Mozart-platz, the "White Dove" is a good choice and centrally located. The 14th-century house, with its uneven floors and ancient stone archways, is a historic property, though the rooms are furnished plainly with dark wood. Several no-smoking rooms are available, and the main section of the breakfast room is also no-smoking. The staff is friendly and helpful. ⊠ *Kaig. 9, A–5020,* ☎ *0662/842404,* FAX *0662/841783. 33 rooms. Bar, no-smoking rooms, meeting room. AE, DC, MC, V. Closed 2 wks in Jan.*

$$ 🖫 **Wolf.** The embodiment of Austrian gemütlichkeit, just off the Mozartplatz, the Wolf offers spotlessly clean and cozy rooms at reasonable prices. The rooms in this small family-run hotel are idiosyncratically arranged on several upper floors, connected by narrow, winding stairs, and are decorated with a pleasing Salzburg mix of rag rugs and rural furniture. The staff is friendly and helpful; borrow a bright umbrella from the stand by the door for use against the inevitable Salzburg showers. ⊠ *Kaig. 7, A–5020,* ☎ *0662/843453–0,* FAX *0662/ 842423–4. 12 rooms. AE. Closed mid-Feb.–mid-Mar.*

$ 🖫 **Bergland.** Just about a 10-minute walk from the train station, this cheerful, pleasant family-owned pension offers comfortable rooms with breakfast included in the price. The sitting room features an English library. ⊠ *Rupertg. 15, A–5020,* ☎ *0662/872318.* FAX *0662/ 872318–8. 17 rooms, 15 with bath. No credit cards. Closed late Oct.–Dec. 20.*

$ 🖫 **Schwarzes Rössl.** Once a favorite with Salzburg regulars, this traditional *Gasthof* now serves as student quarters for most of the year but is well worth booking when available. Rooms are fresh and immaculate, if not charming, and the location is excellent—close to the nighttime action. ⊠ *Priesterhausg. 6, A–5020,* ☎ *0662/874426,* FAX *01/ 401–76–20. 51 rooms with bath. AE, DC, MC, V. Closed Oct.–June.*

NIGHTLIFE AND THE ARTS

The Arts

Information and Tickets

Information and tickets for the main Salzburg Festival (late July–August), the Easter Festival (early April), and the Pentecost Concerts (late May) can be obtained from **Salzburger Festspiele** (⊠ Hofstallg. 1, A–5020 Salzburg, ☎ 0662/844501–0 or 0662/8045–361 for Easter Festival, FAX 0662/846682 or 0662/840124 for Easter Festival). You must reserve well in advance. Any office of the Salzburg Tourist Office (☞ Visitor Information *in* Salzburg A to Z, *below*) and most hotel concierge desks provide schedules for all arts performances, and you can find listings in the daily newspaper *Salzburger Nachrichten*. Tickets can be purchased directly at the box office, at your hotel, via the **Salzburg Ticket Service** (⊠ Mozartpl. 5, ☎ 0662/842296 or 0662/840310, FAX 0662/842476), or at a ticket agency like **Polzer** (⊠ Residenzpl. 3, ☎ 0662/846500, FAX 0662/840150) or **American Express** (⊠ Mozartpl. 5, ☎ 0662/8080–0, FAX 0662/8080–9).

Music

There is no shortage of concerts in this most musical of cities. The Salzburg Palace Concerts, the Fortress Concerts, and the Mozart Serenades take place year-round. In addition, there are the Easter Festival, the Pentecost Concerts, Mozart Week (January 24–February 2), and the Salzburg Cultural Days (October). The Mozart Week is always special; in recent seasons, Nicholas Harnoncourt, Carlo Maria Giulini, and John Eliot Gardiner have conducted the Vienna Philharmonic.

For jazz, check **Jazzclub Live Salzburg** (✉ Urbankeller, Schallmooser Hauptstr. 50, ☎ 0662/646424) for its Friday events. The **Riff Bar und Musikcafé im Rockhaus** (✉ Schallmooser Hauptstr. 46, ☎ 0662/ 878097) has live music on Monday nights in a 400-year-old cellar.

Opera
The great opera event of the year is, of course, the **Salzburg Festival.** The **Marionettentheater** is also devoted to opera, with a particularly acclaimed production of *Così fan Tutte* to its credit, and gives performances the first week of January, during Mozart Week, May–September, and after December 25.

The season at the **Landestheater** (✉ Schwarzstr. 22, ☎ 0662/871512–0) runs from September to June. New productions in 1999 will include Richard Strauss's *Daphne*, Chekhov's *Onkel Wanja,* and Offenbach's *Orpheus in der Underwelt.* You make place ticket orders by telephone Tuesday–Friday 10–1 and 5–5:30 and Saturday 10–1.

Theater
The Salzburg Festival performs Hugo von Hofmannsthal's morality play *Jedermann* (in German) annually in the forecourt of the cathedral. Customarily, the festival features the Vienna Philharmonic, but other orchestras can be expected to take leading roles as well.

Nightlife

Bars/Nightclubs
Bazillus (✉ Imbergstr. 2a, ☎ 0662/871631) is small, scruffy, and makeshift, but very cool; it's open daily 11 AM–1 AM. **Chez Roland** (✉ Giselakai 15, ☎ 0662/874335) is the haunt of "Loden-preppies," or the wealthy and stylish young, and is open Monday–Saturday 6 PM– 1 AM. **Seitensprung** (✉ Steing. 11, ☎ 0662/881377), which means "having someone on the side," is an elegant cocktail bar with food, open daily 8 PM–3 AM. **Shamrock Irish Pub** (✉ Rudolfskai 12, ☎ 0662/ 841610) attracts the young crowd and is always packed. Guinness is on tap. One of Salzburg's most popular bars is **Vis à Vis,** which resembles a '60s nightclub with its cavelike atmosphere (✉ Judeng. 13, ☎ 0662/841290); it's open daily 7 PM–3 AM.

Casino
Salzburg's **Casino** (☎ 0662/845656–0) has found its new home in Schloss Klessheim, a bit out of the center. A free shuttle bus will bring you from the Mönchsberg elevator or Mirabellplatz to Schloss Klessheim and back; your hotel can tell you the nearest departure point. Departures are hourly starting at 2:30 PM; check schedules if you also want to return by bus. Admission is free; you'll receive a free "welcome jeton," entitling you to purchase tokens worth AS250 for AS210. It's open daily from 3 PM except Good Friday, November 1, and December 24. Remember to take your passport.

Discos
Disco Seven (✉ Gstätteng. 7, ☎ 0662/844181) is large, has a youngish crowd, and goes for the American market; it's open daily 9 PM–4 AM and takes credit cards. **Half Moon** (✉ Anton-Neumayr-Pl. 5, ☎ 0662/ 841670) caters to yuppies and beautiful people and is open daily 10

PM–4 AM. The local disco scene has become more volatile, so check with the tourist office for the current best attractions.

OUTDOOR ACTIVITIES AND SPORTS

Bicycling

The Hellbrunner Allee out to Hellbrunn Palace and the Almkanal path out past Leopoldskron Palace are two of the nicest and least strenuous routes. The tourist office has maps of cycle paths, and rentals are available (☞ Getting Around *in* Salzburg A to Z, *below*).

Fishing

There is plenty of fishing around Salzburg, largely for trout, carp, and pike. The season runs from May to December. Day licenses are available for around AS250, depending on season and waters, from **Sport Rehm** (✉ Rudolf-Biebl-Str. 5a, ☎ 0662/435751), **Sporthaus Markus Maier** (✉ Rainerstr. 2, ☎ 0662/871441), or **Starfish** (✉ Auerspergstr. 10, ☎ 0662/877000).

Golf

The **Golf and Country Club Salzburg** (✉ Schloss Klessheim, Salzburg-Klessheim, ☎ 0662/850851), just west of the city, is a 9-hole course at Klessheim castle. Take the A1 freeway to the Klessheim exit.

Skiing

Within Salzburg, the Gaisberg and the Untersberg have good ski slopes. Cross-country skiing is possible on the Hellbrunner Allee and around the Gaisberg (Rauchenbühelhütte). The tourist office at Mozartplatz will inform you about skiing facilities farther afield; Salzburg is often used as a base for excursions to the many ski resorts of the Land Salzburg district.

Skis can be rented at **Sporthaus Markus Maier** (✉ Rainerstr. 2, ☎ 0662/871441). For **snow reports** in winter (in German) call ☎ 0662/1584.

Swimming

The **Paracelsus-Kurhaus** (✉ Auerspergstr. 2, ☎ 0662/883544–0) has a large swimming pool with a sauna and Turkish bath. There are several outdoor pools: Try **Freibad Alpenstrasse** (☎ 0662/620832), which you can reach on Bus 3; **Freibad Leopoldskron** (✉ Leopoldskronerstr. 50, ☎ 0662/829265–0); or **Freibad Volksgarten** (☎ 0662/623183–0), which you can reach via Bus 6 or 49.

Tennis

Salzburg has plenty of courts, although not in the center of town. The best tennis clubs are **Salzburger Tenniscourts-Süd** (✉ Berchtesgardner Str. 35, ☎ 0662/820326), which you can reach via Bus 5; **Tennishalle Liefering** (✉ Unter der Leiten/Lieferinger Spitz, ☎ 0662/432197), which you can reach on Bus 29; and **Tennisklub Salzburg** (✉ Ignaz-Rieder-Kai 3, ☎ 0662/622403–0), which you can reach on Bus 6 or 49.

SHOPPING

For a small city, Salzburg has a wide range of stores. The specialties are traditional clothing, like lederhosen and loden coats, jewelry, glassware, handicrafts, confectionery, dolls in native costume, Christmas decorations, sports equipment, and silk flowers. A *Gewürzsträussl* is a bundle of whole spices bunched and arranged to look like a bouquet of flowers (try the markets on the Universitätsplatz). At Christmas there is a special Advent market on the Domplatz. Stores are generally open weekdays 8–6 and Saturday 8–noon. Many stores stay open until 5 on the first Saturday of the month and on Saturday during the festival and before Christmas. Some supermarkets stay open until 8 on Thursday or Friday. Only shops in the railway station, the airport, and near the general hospital are open on Sunday.

Shopping Streets

The most fashionable specialty stores and gift shops are to be found along Getreidegasse, Judengasse, and around Residenzplatz. Linzergasse, across the river, is less crowded and good for more practical items. There are also interesting antiques shops and jewelry workshops in the medieval buildings along Steingasse and in the Goldgasse.

Specialty Stores

Antiques

Along Gstättengasse you'll find, among others, **Kirchmayer** (⊠ Gstätteng. 3, ☎ 0662/842219), **Marianne Reuter** (⊠ Gstätteng. 9, ☎ 0662/842136), **Peter Paul Burges** (⊠ Gstätteng. 23, ☎ 0662/848115), and **Schöppl** (⊠ Gstätteng. 5, ☎ 0662/842154). For an amazing assortment of secondhand curiosities, try **Trödlerstube** (⊠ Linzerg. 50, ☎ 0662/871453). An annual antiques fair takes place from Palm Sunday to Easter Monday in the state rooms of the Residenz.

Confectionery

If you're looking for the kind of *Mozartkugeln* (chocolate marzipan confections) you can't buy at home, try the two stores that claim to have discovered them: **Konditorei Fürst** (⊠ Brodg. 13, ☎ 0662/843759–0) and **Konditorei Schatz** (⊠ Getreideg. 3, Schatz passageway, ☎ 0662/842792).

Crafts

Fritz Kreis (⊠ Sigmund-Haffner-Gasse 14, ☎ 0662/841768) sells ceramics, wood carvings, handmade glass objects, and so on. **Salzburger Heimatwerk** (⊠ Residenzpl. 9, ☎ 0662/844119) has clothing, fabrics, ceramics, and local handicrafts at good prices.

Galleries

Salzburg is a good place to buy modern paintings, and there are several galleries on Sigmund-Haffner-Gasse. One of the best known, which also has an exhibition gallery plus a tiny coffee bar, is **Galerie Welz** (⊠ Sigmund-Haffner-Gasse 16, ☎ 0662/841771–0).

Jewelry

For exquisite costume jewelry and antique pieces, go to **Anton Koppenwallner** (⊠ Klampfererg. 2, ☎ 0662/841298), **Paul Koppenwallner** (⊠ Alter Markt 7, ☎ 0662/842617; ⊠ Universitätspl. 4, ☎ 0662/841449), or **Gerhard Lährm** (⊠ Getreideg. 27, ☎ 0662/843477–0), which is somewhat more expensive. **Franz Moltner** (⊠ Getreideg. 14, ☎ 0662/348116) offers costume jewelry, including lovely Fabergé eggs that can be attached to a necklace.Explore the **Schmuckpassage** (Jeweler's Passageway), which joins buildings between Universitätsplatz and Getreidegasse.

Men's Clothing

Men's outfitters are everywhere; the best are **Boss Herrenmoden** (⊠ Schwarzstr. 12, ☎ 0662/875026) and **Resmann M Exclusiv** (⊠ Getreideg. 25, ☎ 0662/843214–0).

Traditional Clothing

Dschulnigg (⊠ Griesg. 8, ☎ 0662/842376) is a favorite among Salzburgers for lederhosen, dirndls, and *Trachten,* the typical Austrian costume with white blouse, print skirt, and apron. For an enormous range of leather goods, some made to order, try **Jahn-Markl** (⊠ Residenzpl. 3,

☎ 0662/842610). **Lanz** (✉ Schwarzstr. 4, ☎ 0662/874272) sells a wide selection of long dirndls, silk costumes, and loden coats. **Madl am Grünmarkt** (✉ Universitätspl. 12, ☎ 0662/845457) has more flair and elegance in its traditional designs. A more specialized place, selling wool and silk shawls and chamois-leather skirts and waistcoats, is **Wacht** (✉ Griesg. 7, ☎ 0662/841622).

Women's Clothing

If dirndls are not your style, try **Lady** (✉ Schwarzstr. 4, ☎ 0662/ 878331; ✉ Sigmund-Haffner-Gasse 6, ☎ 0662/840156), **La Femme** (✉ Hildmannpl. 1a, ☎ 0662/845203), or **Resmann Couture** (✉ Rudolfskai 6/Getreideg. 15, ☎ 0662/841213–0).

SALZBURG A TO Z

Arriving and Departing

By Car

The fastest routes to Salzburg are the autobahns. From Vienna (320 km/198 mi), take A1; from Munich (150 km/93 mi, A8 (in Germany it's also E11); from Italy, A10. The only advantage to having a car in Salzburg is that you can get out of the city for short excursions or for cheaper accommodations. The Old City on both sides of the river is a pedestrian zone (except for taxis), and the rest of the city, with its narrow, one-way streets, is a driver's nightmare. A park-and-ride system covering the major freeway exits is being developed, and there are several underground garages throughout the city.

By Plane

Salzburg airport (✉ Innsbrucker Bundesstr. 96, ☎ 0662/8580 or 0662/ 8580–251 flight information), 4 km (2½ mi) west of the city center, is Austria's second-largest international airport. There are direct flights from London and other European cities, but not from the United States.

Americans can fly to Munich and take the 90-minute train ride to Salzburg. Alternatively, you can take a transfer bus from or to the Munich airport; in Salzburg the contact is **Salzburger Mietwagenservice** (✉ Ignaz-Harrer-Str. 79a, ☎ 0622/8161–0, ℻ 0622/436324).

Taxis are the easiest way to get downtown from the Salzburg airport; the ride costs around AS150 and takes about 20 minutes. City Bus 77, which goes by the airport every 15 minutes, takes you to the train station (about 20 minutes), where you change to Bus 1, 5, 6, 51, or 55 for the city center. Alternatively, you can take Bus 77 four stops to Aiglhof (look for a Mobil gas station on the corner), cross the road, and take Bus 29 (every 10–15 minutes) to the center of town.

By Train

You can get to Salzburg by rail from most European cities, arriving at **Salzburg Hauptbahnhof** (✉ Südtirolerpl., ☎ 0662/1717, ℻ 0662/8887– 31–69), a 20-minute walk from the center of town in the direction of Mirabellplatz. A taxi should take about 10 minutes and cost AS75. Train information is available by phone (☎ 0662/1717); don't be put off by the recorded message in German—eventually, you will be put through to a real person who should be able to speak English. You can buy tickets at any travel agency or at the station. The bus station and the suburban railroad station are across the street. Major building works are still in progress in front of the station and hamper access.

Getting Around

The Old City, composed of several interconnecting squares and narrow streets, is best seen on foot. An excellent bus service covers the rest of the city. A tourist map (available for AS10 from tourist offices in Mozartplatz and the train station) shows all bus routes and stops; there's also a color-coded graphic public-transport-network map that's free, so you should have no problem getting around. Virtually all buses and trolleybuses (O-Bus) run via Mirabellplatz and/or Hanuschplatz.

By Bicycle

Salzburg is fast developing a network of bike paths as part of its effort to get cars out of the city. A detailed bicycle map with suggested tours (about AS70–AS80) will help you get around.

Bikes can be rented year-round at the **Salzburg Hauptbahnhof** railway station (⊠ Südtirolerpl., Counter 3, ☎ 0662/8887–0), with savings for holders of that day's train tickets. You can rent a bike by the day or the week from **Albert Hager** (⊠ Fürstenallee 39, ☎ 0662/823723, FAX 0662/829623). Also check **Top-Bike Handels-OEG** (⊠ Aribonenstr. 18, ☎ 0662/862529, FAX 0662/434300–0), which is considerably more expensive but will deliver and pick up the bike. It's best to call and reserve in advance; you will need to leave your passport or a deposit.

By Bus or Trolleybus

Single tickets bought from the driver cost AS20. Special multiple-use tickets, available at tobacconists (*Tabak-Trafik*), ticket offices (main office, ⊠ Griesgasse 21, ☎ 0662/620551), and tourist offices, are much cheaper. You can buy five single tickets for AS15 each (not available at tourist offices), a single 24-hour ticket for AS40, or five transferrable 24-hour tickets at AS32 each.

By Horse-Drawn Carriage

One of the most delightful ways to tour Salzburg is by horse-drawn carriage. Most of Salzburg's **Fiakers** are stationed in the Residenzplatz. In the Christmas season, large, decorated horse-drawn carts take people around the Christmas markets. ☎ 0662/844772; ☜ *AS380 per Fiaker (up to 4 people) for 20–25 min, AS740 for 50 min.*

By Taxi

There are taxi stands all over the city; for a radio cab, call 0662/8111. Taxi fares start at AS30. Limousines can be hired for AS600 per hour (three-hour minimum) from **Salzburg Panorama Tours** (☎ 0662/883211–0 or 0662/874029, FAX 0662/871618).

Contacts and Resources

Changing Money

Banks are open weekdays 8–12:30 and 2–4:30. You can change money at the railway station in summer daily 7 AM–10 PM and in winter daily 7:30 AM–9 PM.

Consulates

The **U.S. consulate** (⊠ Alter Markt 1/2/2, ☎ 0662/848776, FAX 0662/849777) is open Monday, Wednesday, and Friday 9–noon. The U.K. consulate (⊠ Joseph Messner Str. 24/20, ☎ 0662/648528) is open weekdays 9–noon.

Doctors and Dentists

If you need a doctor or dentist, call the **Ärztekammer für Salzburg** (⊠ Schranneng. 2, ☎ 0662/871327–0); for emergency service on weekends and holidays, call the **Ärzte-Bereitschaftsdienst Salzburg-Stadt** (⊠ Paris Lodron Str. 8A, ☎ 0662/141).

The main **hospital** is the Landeskrankenhaus (⊠ Müllner Hauptstr. 48, ☎ 0662/44820), just past the Augustinian monastery heading out of town.

Emergencies

Police, ☎ 133. **Fire,** ☎ 122. For **ambulance** or medical emergency, ☎ 144.

English-Language Bookstores

American Discount (⊠ Alter Markt 1, ☎ 0662/845640), the only English-language bookstore in Salzburg, concentrates on popular paperbacks and magazines. You can, however, find some books in English in most good bookstores. **Hintermayer** (⊠ Imbergstr. 23, ☎ 0662/875754–1), across the footbridge from Mozartplatz, sells discount paperbacks in English.

Guided Tours

Because the Old City is largely a pedestrian zone, bus tours do little more than take you past the major sights. You would do better seeing the city on foot unless your time is really limited.

DAY TOURS FROM VIENNA

American Express (⊠ Kärntnerstr. 21–23, 1010 Vienna, ☎ 01/515–40–0, FAX 01/515–40–70) and **Vienna Sightseeing Tours** (⊠ Stelzhammerg. 4/11, 1030 Vienna, ☎ 01/712–4683-0, FAX 01/714–1141) run one-day bus trips Tuesday, Thursday, and Saturday to Salzburg from Vienna; the AS1,290 fare includes a tour of the city. On Sunday, Wednesday, and Friday, **Cityrama/Gray Line** (⊠ Börseg. 1, 1010 Vienna, ☎ 01/534–13–0, FAX 01/534–13–28) offers a similar tour. The Monday and Friday tours of **Citytouring Vienna** (⊠ Penzinger Str. 46, ☎ 01/894–1417–0, FAX 01/894–3239) include lunch and are slightly more expensive.

ORIENTATION

Bob's Special Tours (⊠ Dreifaltigkeitsg. 3, ☎ 0662/872484, FAX 0662/872–4844), **Salzburg Panorama Tours/Gray Line** (⊠ Mirabellpl. at St. Andrä Church, ☎ 0662/874029, FAX 0662/871618), and **Salzburg Sightseeing Tours** (⊠ Am Mirabellpl. 2, ☎ 0662/881616, FAX 0662/878776), conduct 1½- to 2-hour city tours. The desk clerks at most hotels will book for you and arrange hotel pickup. Depending on the number of people, the tour will be in either a bus or a minibus; if it's the former, a short walking tour is included, since large buses can't enter the Old City. Tours briefly cover the major sights in Salzburg, including Mozart's Birthplace, the festival halls, the major squares, the churches, and the palaces at Hellbrunn and Leopoldskron.

SOUND OF MUSIC TOURS

The *Sound of Music* tour (☞ Close-Up box, *above*) has been a staple of visits to Salzburg for the past 20 years and is still a special experience. All tour operators conduct one. The bus company actually featured in the film, Albus, offers a 3½-hour tour departing daily, which includes such sights as Anif Castle, Mondsee Church, and the little summerhouse in the gardens of Hellbrun. (⊠ Mirabellpl. 2, ☎ 0662/881616, FAX 0662/633790). Some travelers say the most personal approach is found with **Bob's Special Tours** (☞ *above*).

WALKING

The tourist office's folder "Salzburg—The Art of Taking It All In at a Glance" describes a self-guided one-day walking tour that's marked on a map.

Pharmacies

In general, pharmacies are open weekdays 8–12:30 and 2:30–6, Saturday 8–noon. When they're closed, the name and location of a pharmacy that's open are posted on the door.

Travel Agencies

American Express (☏ 0662/8080–0, FAX 0662/8080–9) is next to the tourist office at Mozartplatz 5–7. **Thomas Cook** can be found under the name Wagons-Lit Travel (✉ Münzg. 1, ☏ 0662/842755–0, FAX 0662/ 842755–5) in the Old City.

Visitor Information

The **Salzburg City Tourist Office** (✉ Auerspergstr. 7, A–5024 Salzburg, ☏ 0662/88987–0, FAX 0662/88987–32) handles written and telephone requests for information. You can get maps, brochures, and information in person from **Information Mozartplatz** in the center of the Old City (✉ Mozartpl. 5) and from the **Railway Station** (✉ Platform 2A, ☏ 0662/88987–330).

Don't forget to consider purchasing the Salzburg Card. **SalzburgKarten** are good for 24, 48, or 72 hours at AS200, AS270, and AS360, respectively, and allow no-charge entry to most museums and sights, use of public transport, and special discount offers. Children under 15 pay half.

All the major highways into town have their own well-marked information centers: **Salzburg-Mitte** (✉ Münchner Bundesstr. 1, ☏ 0662/ 432228), open April–October, daily 9–7, and November–March, Monday–Saturday 11–5; **Salzburg-Süd** (✉ Alpenstr. 67, ☏ 0662/ 620966), open November–March, Monday–Saturday 11–5, and April–October, daily 9–7; **Salzburg-West-Airport** (✉ Innsbrucker Bundesstr. 95, ☏ 0662/852451), open April–May and September–October, Monday–Saturday 9–6, and June–August, daily 9–7; **Salzburg-Nord** (✉ Autobahn, Kasern service facility, ☏ 0662/663220), open March–June and October, Monday–Saturday 9–7, and July–September, daily 9–7.

7 Salzkammergut

Remember the first five minutes of The Sound of Music? *Castles fronting on water, mountains hidden by whipped-cream clouds, and flower-strewn valleys crisped with cool blue lakes? It might seem too good to be true, but those scenes were filmed just a few miles from Salzburg in the melismatic hills of the Salzkammergut, and aside from the vastly improved amenities, little has changed here since the film was made. St. Wolfgang, Bad Ischl, St. Gilgen, and Fusch are picturesque towns with long and venerable histories. Even getting caught on a rainy summer day in a town such as Hallstatt is a delight.*

Updated by
Marton Radkai

THE TRIPS IN THIS CHAPTER touch heights both physical and spiritual. From the Schafberg, above St. Wolfgang, you can see just about every lake in the entire region, and in the pilgrimage church below, Michael Pacher's great late-15th-century winged altar, 10 years in the making, rises like a prayer. Ready your camera, dust off your supply of *wunderschöns*, and prepare for enchantment as you head into this compact quarter of Austria. The Lake District of Upper Austria, centered on the region called the Salzkammergut (literally, "salt estates"), presents the traveler with soaring mountains and needlelike peaks; a glittering necklace of turquoise lakes; forested valleys that are home to the *Rehe* (roe deer) immortalized by Felix Salten in *Bambi*—Austria at its most lush and verdant. Some of these lakes, like the Hallstätter See and Gosauer See, remain quite unspoiled, partly because the mountains act as a divider from busier, more accessible sections of the country. Another—historic—reason relates to the presence of the salt mines, which date back to the Celtic era; with salt so common and cheap nowadays, we forget it was once a luxury item mined under strict government monopoly. The Salzkammergut was therefore closed to casual visitors for centuries, opening up only after Emperor Franz Josef I made it his official summer residence in 1854 and turned it into the "drawing room" of the Lake District. Lured by idyllic landscapes and cosmopolitanism, a host of prominent people from crowned heads and their ministers to artists of all stamp soon flocked regularly to Bad Ischl.

To the west of Bad Ischl are the best known of all the Salzkammergut's 27 lakes—the Wolfgangsee, the Mondsee, and the Attersee (*See* is the German word for "lake"). Not far beyond these lakes the traveler will find one of Austria's loveliest spots, Gosau am Dachstein. Here, the three Gosau lakes are backdropped by a spectacular sight that acts as a landmark for many leagues: the Dachstein peak. Baron Friedrich von Humboldt, the 19th-century biologist and traveler, called Gosau am Dachstein one of the most beautiful spots in the world, and few persons at that time had seen more of the world than he. It is not surprising that Gosau inspired Wagner while he was writing *Parsifal*. Even today, Gosau remains a world's end, a place where people are content simply to drink in the view.

However, many activities beckon nearby. In summer, vacationers head for the lakes, streams, meadows, and woods for boating, fishing, swimming (the taller the lakeside peak, the colder the water), and stimulating pine-needle baths. A favorite passion for Austrians is *Das Wandern,* or hiking. The Lake District has many miles of marked trails, with lovely stretches around Bad Ischl—with more than 100 km (62 mi) of trails alone; the Attersee area, which has one great 35-km (22-mi) course that takes about 7½ hours to complete; the mountains in the Hallstatt and Altaussee/Bad Aussee areas; and Bad Aussee, with more than 150 km (93 mi) of trails. Cycling is also a quickly growing sport and a fine way to see lots of landscape at a human pace and take care of your fitness requirements. In winter, many come to the region to ski in the mountains of Salzburg Province and Styria. Amid this pastoral perfection, many enticing restaurants have sprung up; you can stay in age-old *Schloss* hotels or modern mansions. And shoppers come to buy the linens and ceramics, wood carvings, and painted glass of the region.

Pleasures and Pastimes

Dining

If you wander into a simple and pretty Gasthaus, be ready for meaty dishes, from the famous *Wiener schnitzel* (breaded veal) to various other cutlets and roasts (*Braten*). *Knödel* are a nice specialty, bread or potato dumplings usually filled with meat or jam. Desserts are doughy as well, though *Salzburger Nockerl* consists mainly of air, sugar, and beaten egg whites. The lakes and streams are home to several types of fish, notably trout, carp, and perch. They come in a variety of recipes, from plain breaded (*gebacken*) to smoked and served with horseradish, to fried in butter (*gebraten*). Sometimes at country fairs you will find someone charcoaling trout wrapped in aluminum foil with herbs and butter: it's worth every schilling. And finally, keep an eye out for seasonal specialties: In summer the restaurants often serve chanterelle mushrooms (*Eierschwammerl*) with dumplings, and in October it's time for delicious venison and game during the *Wildwochen* (game weeks).

There are culinary shrines around Mondsee, but in many of the towns of the Salzkammergut you'll find country inns that have dining rooms but few, if any, separate restaurants, other than the occasional, very simple *Gasthaus*. Prices for meals include taxes and a service charge but not the customary small additional tip.

CATEGORY	COST*
$$$$	over AS500
$$$	AS300–AS500
$$	AS200–AS300
$	under AS200

per person for a typical three-course meal, with a glass of house wine

Lodging

In the grand old days, the aristocratic families of the region would take paying guests at their charming castles. Today, most of those castles have been degentrified, if you will: They're now schools or are very fine hotels. You needn't stay in a castle to enjoy Salzkammergut—there is a wide range of accommodations, ranging from luxurious lakeside resorts to small country inns or even guest houses without private baths, and in most places, the *Herr Wirt*, his smiling wife, and his grown-up children will do everything to make you feel comfortable. While we cover the best in every category, note that every village, however small, has a Gasthaus or village inn. In peak summer season St. Wolfgang is packed, and you may find slightly less crowding and the same magnificent settings 3 km (2 mi) up the lake at Ried or back at Strobl.

Room rates include taxes and service and almost always breakfast, except in the most expensive hotels, but it is wise to ask. It is customary to leave a small additional tip (AS20) for the chambermaid. Happily, these hotels do not put their breathtakingly beautiful natural surroundings on the bill.

CATEGORY	COST*
$$$$	over AS1,500
$$$	AS1,000–AS1,500
$$	AS700–AS1,000
$	under AS700

All prices are for a standard double room for two, including local taxes (usually 10%) and service (15%).

Exploring the Salzkammergut

Whether you start out from Salzburg or set up a base in Bad Ischl—the heart of the Lake District—it's best to take in the beauties of the Salzkammergut in two separate courses: first around the Mondsee, the Wolfgansee, and Bad Ischl, and then south to the Hallstätter See, Gosau am Dachstein, then to Bad Aussee and the Altausseer See, returning via the Pötschen mountain pass.

Numbers in the text correspond to numbers in the margin and on the Salzkammergut/Lake District map.

Great Itineraries

IF YOU HAVE 2 DAYS

Setting out early from Salzburg, head to the core of the Lake District, **Bad Ischl** ⑤. It will be an easy transition from the imperial Austria of Salzburg. Franz Lehár—the composer of so many operettas that glorified the region—had a vacation villa here, where he could rub elbows with many other notables eager to holiday in Franz Josef's favorite getaway. After exploring the emperor's villa, a majestic manor in the warm "imperial" yellow so typical of Austria, created for his empress Elizabeth—the immortal "Sissi"—stop in at Zauner (just as Franz Joseph did) for some of the best pastries in Europe. Delicious, but beware: *Two* to a person will be plenty! After quickly taking in this history-rich spa—today, it is one of the best equipped in Austria—head south on Route 145 toward Hallstatt. After Bad Goisern bear right past Au and then turn right over the bridge to cross the River Traun into Steeg (don't worry about the factory smokestack—it's an isolated affair in these parts!). Traveling alongside the Hallstätter See, you will think you have made a magical detour into Norway: The lake, surrounded by towering peaks, almost looks like a fjord. Twenty-nine kilometers (18 mi) from Bad Ischl you'll come to a junction with Route 166. Here you should turn right into the ravine of the Gosaubach River. After heading through very scenic territory framed by steep wooded slopes for some 32 km (20 mi), you'll reach 🏕 **Gosau am Dachstein** ⑧, which spreads out in a comfortable north–south valley at the end of which lie the famous Gosau lakes. You have reached one of Austria's most beautiful spots. There are three lakes here, several miles apart from each other and all framed by the craggy heights of the Dachstein range. After drinking in the views, spend the night in the village and awaken to a dazzling dawn glistening over the snow-swept Bischofsmütze peak.

Head back to Route 145 and south to **Hallstatt** ⑦, not just the "world's prettiest lakeside village" but the oldest settlement in Austria. After spending quality time with your Nikon (do your photography in the morning when the village is nicely lit), check out one of either two natural wonders: the salt mines above Hallstatt (accessible by funicular or by a good one-hour walk) or, continuing around the southern end of the lake for 5 km (3 mi), the **Dachstein Ice Caves** ⑨ at Obertraun. Leaving Upper Austria, head for **Bad Aussee** ⑩ along the romantic old road that follows the Traun River. It is still in part covered with hand-hewn paving stones and has at one point an impressive gradient of 23° (closed in winter). Explore the town's picturesque 15th- and 16th-century architecture, and you should still have time for a stroll around neighboring **Altaussee** ⑪, whose romantic setting inspired so many artists and poets. Return to Bad Aussee, and then catch Route 145 north across the Pötschen pass, enjoying spectacular vistas along the way back to Bad Ischl.

IF YOU HAVE 4 DAYS

After your first taste of Salzkammergut superlatives, as outlined above, head west to explore more of the Lake District. A magical mix of in-

Salzkammergut/The Lake District

timacy (simple inns and rural hamlets) and publicity (tour buses, celebrities, and vacationing opera stars) will greet you at such destinations as St. Wolfgang and Mondsee. We once again start out at the unofficial "capital" of the region, 🎔 **Bad Ischl** ⑤ (where, if you are doing this four-day tour of the region, you will have booked an overnight stay for your second night, after seeing the sights outlined above on your second day). Heading west on Route 158, then bearing right at Strobl, you reach 🎔 **St. Wolfgang** ④—a town that all but clicks your camera shutter for you. For centuries it secretly harbored one of Austria's great art treasures, the great altarpiece by the late-Gothic woodcarver Michael Pacher in the parish church. However, it was the inn—now Hotel Weisses Rössl (White Horse)—which stands near the dock, that spread the fame (and made the fortune) of this little Alpine town: It became the subject of a very popular operetta composed for the most part by Ralph Benatzky and premiered in Berlin in 1930. After an enchanting steamer trip on the lake, enjoy the popular excursion by rack rail to the top of the nearby Schafberg mountain; then return to St. Wolfgang for a dinner of trout *blau* (steamed) and an overnight stay. The next morning, backtrack to Strobl, and then follow signs for Salzburg to join Route 158. The road bypasses the bulge of Abersee, which consists mainly of camping sites and very crowded beaches (one of which offers a beautiful view of St. Wolfgang), and reaches **St. Gilgen** ③ after another 7 km (4½ mi). St. Gilgen gets very crowded in summer, especially along the shore, which is lined with ice-cream parlors and souvenir shops. But the little house near the dock on Ischler Strasse where Mozart's mother and sister were born should be on your itinerary. For lunch (be sure to make reservations), head for **Fuschl** ② and the famous Hotel Schloss Fuschl, overlooking the western tip of the Fuschlsee, former address to the prince-archbishops of Salzburg; this is food with a view, as the dining room and terrace have grand vistas. Back on Route 158, **Mondsee** ① awaits after a bucolic journey north on a little road forking off toward Thalgau on Route 158, with its charming Marktplatz square full of lively cafés and restaurants, and impressive St. Michael Parish Church. From here, return west to Salzburg or east to Bad Ischl—vowing, undoubtedly, to return to the Lake District one day to buy a hillside chalet.

When to Tour the Salzkammergut

Year-round, vacationers flock to the Lake District; however, late fall is the worst time to visit the lake country, for it is rainy, cold, and many sights are closed or operating only part-time. By far the best months are July and September. August, of course, sees the countryside overrun with visitors from the nearby Salzburg Music Festival (even so, who can resist a visit on August 18 to Bad Ischl, when Emperor Franz Josef's birthday is still celebrated). Another seasonal highlight is the annual Narcissu Festival held at the beginning of June at Bad Aussee (the town is blanketed with flowers). Bad Aussee also has a special Carnival celebration, with men dressed as women and banging drums (the so-called *Trommelweiber*) on the Monday, and on Tuesday the *Flinserln* parading in costumes with silvery paillettes. Others like to visit Hallstatt for its annual Corpus Christi procession across the lake.

ON THE ROAD TO ST. WOLFGANG AND BAD ISCHL

The mountains that form Austria's backbone may be less majestic than other Alps at this point, but they are also a lot less stern; glittering blue lakes and villages nestle safely in valleys without being under the constant threatening eye of a riprap of huge peaks. Here you'll find what travelers come to the Lake District for: elegant restaurants, Baroque churches, meadows with getaway space and privacy, lakeside cabanas, and forests that could tell a story or two.

Mondsee

❶ *35½ km (22 mi) east of Salzburg, 100 km (62 mi) southwest of Linz.*

Mondsee is the gateway to the Salzkammergut for many tourists and Salzburgers alike. *Mondsee* means "Moon Lake," a name whose origins are the subject of some debate. Some say this body of water (11 km/7 mi long and 2 km/1 mi wide), which vaguely resembles a moon crescent, was named after prehistoric lunar deity, whereas others say it was named after a person. The Mondsee Monastery has its own story about a Bavarian duke being saved from falling in the water by a full moon that showed him the way, after which he vowed to found a monastery. The water is warmer than in any other of the high-placed lakes, which makes it a good place for swimming, and Mondsee has some of the best dining the Salzkammergut has to offer. Most travelers first head for the town square to visit the marvelous Baroque twin-towered **St. Michael Parish Church,** built in 1470. This is the largest parish church in Upper Austria, possibly because its original role was as church of the 8th-century Benedictine monastery. It holds a special place in the hearts of many travelers, as they remember it as the church in which Maria finally wed her Captain von Trapp in *The Sound of Music.*

Dining

$$$$ ✕ **Hotel/Restaurant Eschlböck.** Karl Eschlböck, who apprenticed at Troisgros in France, is ranked among Austria's top chefs. His 300-year-old Alpine chalet overlooking the lake south of Mondsee is still a fine restaurant, although quality roller-coasters from superb to mundane. Still, you're unlikely to be disappointed. What's offered in the individual dining rooms is what's fresh in the market that day; it could be anything from calf's tongue in mustard sauce to terrine of lake fish. The menu includes variations on classical Austrian dishes. ⊠ *St. Lorenz 41, Plomberg-Mondsee,* ☎ *06232/2912. Reservations essential. AF, DC, MC, V. Closed Tues.–Wed. Sept.–Mar.*

$$$$ ✕ **Seehof.** At this lakeside restaurant, the terrace setting is idyllic, the cuisine excellent, and the range of Italian, French, and Austrian wines comprehensive. Choices range more toward Austrian standards; specialties include venison on a bed of sauerkraut, spring lamb, and fresh fish from the lake. Located in the huge Park of the Seehof Hotel, this restaurant is a favorite of Mondseers in the know. ⊠ *Au 30, Loibichl-Mondsee,* ☎ *06232/5031,* 𝖥𝖠𝖷 *06232/5031–51. Reservations essential. AE, DC, MC, V. Closed mid-Sept.–mid-May.*

$$$ ✕ **La Farandole.** Just above Mondsee on Route 154, you'll find an in-
★ timate restaurant offering creative French-Swiss-Austrian cuisine with French emphasis, under the able hand of Wolfgang Buchschartner, who is manager, chef, and sommelier all in one. Specialties change with the season, fawn in aspic (*Kitzsülze*) or a fish soup, or a delicious suckling lamb in a garlic and thyme sauce. The apple-cake dessert is superb. ⊠ *Schlössl 150/Tiefgraben,* ☎ *06232/3475. Reservations essential. No credit cards. Closed Sun.–Mon. No lunch Sept.–June.*

Outdoor Activities and Sports

GOLF

The **Golfclub Sankt Lorenz** (⊠ Keuschen 166, ☎ 06232/5656, 𝖥𝖠𝖷 06232/5656–6) has 18 holes and a par-72. Greens fees weekdays are AS500, weekends AS600. The course is open March–November.

Fuschl

❷ *20 km (12 mi) south of Mondsee, 30½ km (19 mi) east of Salzburg.*

Fuschl is so close to Salzburg that many festival goers to the Salzburger Festspiele choose to stay in a hotel here, enjoying urban comforts while savoring rural pleasures at the same time. Located on Route 158, the town is on the Fuschlsee, a gem of a small lake with very clear, bluish-green, deep waters ideal for swimming, surrounded by a nature preserve. There's not much to do in Fuschl, the beaches being very limited in number—though those willing to hike can reach the extremely narrow strip on the northern shore, which is especially popular with nudists. The town of Fuschl, however, boasts many good places to eat and spend the night, including Schloss Fuschl, one of the finest establishments in the Salzkammergut.

Dining and Lodging

$$$$ ✕ **Brunnwirt.** You'll have to knock to be admitted, but once inside, you'll
★ find elegantly set tables in this atmospheric 15th-century house. Frau Brandstätter presides over a kitchen that turns out good-size portions of excellent Austrian and regional dishes. You might be offered game (in season) or roast lamb, but always with a light touch. Fish fresh from the lake is a regular specialty. ⊠ *Brunn 8,* ☎ *06226/8236. Reservations essential. Jacket and tie. AE, DC, MC, V. Closed Sun. and last 3 wks of Jan. No lunch except during Salzburg Festival wks.*

$$$$ ✕⌂ **Hotel Ebner's Waldhof.** This somewhat overly large Alpine chalet, with bright red geraniums on the balconies, seems perfect in its setting against the lake and mountains. The hotel is a member of the Silence Hotel group. You'll feel comfortable in the paneled public room, warmed by the open fireplace. The restaurant emphasizes local duck and game dishes, and gourmands enjoy the variations on lake-caught fish. ⊠ *Seepromenade, A–5330,* ☎ *06226/8264,* FAX *06226/8644. 64 rooms, 13 apartments. Restaurant, bar, indoor pool, lake, sauna, tennis court, archery, exercise room, windsurfing, boating, bicycles. No credit cards. Closed Mar. and late Oct.–mid-Dec.*

$$$$ ✕⌂ **Hotel Schloss Fuschl.** This grand hotel overlooking the western tip
★ of the lake just of Route 158 was built in the late 15th century and was first mentioned in a 1555 document. Once the hunting castle of the prince-archbishops of Salzburg, it was rebuilt in the 19th century and is now tastefully adapted and modernized. The sturdy principal building enjoys a setting about as perfect as you could imagine. Fireplaces and timbered ceilings abound amid the stonework. The hotel's elegant restaurant with a view of lake is one of Austria's best. You can expect innovative variations on such regional specialties as rack of venison and lake fish. Schloss Fuschl is a member of Leading Hotels of the World. ⊠ *A–5322 Hof bei Salzburg,* ☎ *06229/2253–0,* FAX *06229/ 2253–531. 62 rooms, 22 suites. Restaurant, bar, indoor and outdoor pools, beauty salon, sauna, 9-hole golf course, tennis court, bowling, exercise room, beach. AE, DC, MC, V.*

St. Gilgen

❸ *10 km (6 mi) south of Fuschl, 34 km (21 mi) east of Salzburg.*

Rather overbuilt around the edges and overwhelmed by an invasion of foreign visitors, the center of St. Gilgen is pleasant enough. All the local color left to St. Gilgen is its indirect musical ties: A Mozart fountain in the town square commemorates the fact that Mozart's mother and sister Nannerl were both born here, in a little house near the dock on Ischler Strasse. The town features a nice beach, the northernmost on the Wolfgansee.

Dining and Lodging

$$ ✕ **Grossgasthof Kendler.** St. Gilgen is a rather basic place when it comes to food, and the right place for a homey Salzkammergut experience is the big and friendly Kendler, right in the middle of town, which does its own butchering, so the meat is always fresh (lamb kebabs, venison in season, pork dishes), but the trend is also toward lighter foods, including good salads and spinach dumplings. The Kendler also has a guest house. ⊠ *Kirchenplatz 3, A–5340,* ☎ *06227/2223,* FAX *06227/720390. 40 rooms. Restaurant, sauna, steam room, exercise room. DC, MC. Early Nov.–mid-Dec.*

$$ ✕☱ **Hotel Gasthof zur Post.** This house, one of the most attractive in town, dates to 1415. The rooms are comfortable and complete with modern baths. The restaurant emphasizes regional fare; try the cream of garlic soup or the boiled beef. ⊠ *Mozartpl. 8, A–5340,* ☎ *06227/2239–0,* FAX *06227/2698. 15 rooms, some with bath. Restaurant, sauna. AE, MC. Closed early Nov.–early Dec.*

$$$–$$$$ ☱ **Parkhotel Billroth.** This elegant villa, decorated in turn-of-the-century style, is set in a huge park 10 minutes from the town center but close to the lake. The house is pleasantly worn at the edges yet spaciously arranged and luxuriously appointed, with a fine dining room. Sun terraces are particularly inviting. ⊠ *Billrothstr. 2, A–5340,* ☎ *06227/2217,* FAX *06227/2218–25. 44 rooms. Restaurant, bar, massage, sauna, tennis court, exercise room, beach, boating. AE, V. Closed Oct.–May.*

St. Wolfgang

★ ❹ *19 km (12 mi) east of St. Gilgen, 50 km (31 mi) east of Salzburg.*

A delightful way of entering the picture-book town of St. Wolfgang is to leave your car at Strobl, at the southern end of the Wolfgangsee, and take one of the steamers that play the waters of the lake. Strobl itself is a delightful setting, but not as fashionable as St. Wolfgang; if you want a quiet vacation base, that may be its attraction for you. Between St. Wolfgang and Strobl, the Wolfgangsee still retains its old name of "Abersee." One of the earliest paddleboats on the lake is still in service, a genuine 1873 steamer called the *Kaiser Franz Josef.* Service is regular from May to mid-October. The view of the town against the dramatic mountain backdrop is one you'll see again and again on posters and postcards. If you decide to drive all the way to town, be prepared for a crowd. Unless your hotel offers parking, you'll have to park on the fringes of town and walk a short distance, as the center is a pedestrian zone.

The town has everything: swimming and hiking in summer, skiing in winter, and natural feasts for the eyes at every turn. Here, you will find yourself in the Austria of operetta. Indeed, St. Wolfgang became known round the world thanks to the inn called **Weisses Rössl** (☞ Dining and Lodging, *below*), which was built right next to the landing stage in 1878. It featured prominently in a late-19th-century play, which only achieved fame as an operetta by Benatzky in 1930. Ironically, the two original playwrights, Gustav Kadelburg and Oskar Blumenthal, had another Weisses Rössl in mind.

You shouldn't miss seeing Michael Pacher's great altarpiece in the 16th-century **parish church,** one of the finest examples of Late-Gothic woodcarving to be found anywhere. This 36-ft masterpiece took 10 years (1471–81) to complete. The crowning of the Virgin Mary is depicted in detail so exact that you can see the stitches in her garments. Surrounding her are various saints, including the local patron, the hermit St. Wolfgang. Since the 15th century, his namesake town has been a place of pilgrimage. ⊙ *May–Sept., daily 9–5; Oct.–Apr., daily 10–4; altar closed to view during Lent.*

SCHAFBERG – From May to mid-October the rack railway trip from St. Wolfgang to the 5,800-ft peak of the Schafberg offers a great chance to survey the surrounding countryside from what is acclaimed as the "belvedere of the Salzkammergut lakes." On a clear day, you can see forever—or at least as far as the Lattengebirge mountain range west of Salzburg. Figure on crowds, so reserve in advance (☏ 06138/2232-0) or start out early. The train—itself a curiosity dating to 1893—departs hourly: mid-May to mid-June, daily from 8:30 AM to 4:30 PM; mid-June to mid-September, daily from 7 AM to 6:26 PM; and mid-September to mid-October, daily from 8:30 AM to 6 PM. Allow at least a good half day for the outing, which costs AS250.

Dining and Lodging

$$$–$$$$ ✕▥ **Hotel Weisses Rössl.** Despite a brutal modernization, the golden ★ yellow house, featured in films and theater over the years (thanks to the famous operetta set here), has kept its reputation for outstanding accommodations and service and is now part of the Romantik Hotel group. Rooms are comfortably country-rustic. The dining terraces, built on stilts over the water, are enchanting; fresh lake fish is served to the sound of zither music. Vegetarians and others alike can delight in hearty vegetable strudels and refreshing salads. Keep in mind that this hotel is world famous (busloads that come "to have a look"); book well in advance, especially for the summer. ⊠ *Markt 74, A–5360,* ☏ *06138/2306–66,* ℻ *06138/2306–41. 72 rooms. Restaurant, bar, indoor pool, lake, sauna, tennis court, exercise room, windsurfing, boating. AE, DC, MC, V. Closed Nov.–mid-Dec.*

$$$–$$$$ ✕▥ **Landhaus zu Appesbach.** Very secluded and quiet and offering excellent service, this old manor is the place to get away from it all while at the same time enjoying the activities of the region. It even has its own restaurant for guests only. ⊠ *A–5360 St. Wolfgang am See,* ☏ *06138/2209,* ℻ *06138/2209–14. 26 rooms, 9 suites. Restaurant, sauna, steam room, tennis court, beach, dock. AE, DC, MC, V.*

$ ✕▥ **Gasthof Zimmerbräu.** In this pricey town, it's a pleasant surprise to find a budget Gasthof. The house, which is four centuries old, was once a brewery; for the last hundred years, it's been run by the Scharf family. Centrally located, the Zimmerbräu is not near the lake but does feature its own bathing cabana by the water. The decor is traditional, most rooms have balconies, and the chef can even whip up some vegetarian specialties. ⊠ *Im Stöck 85, A–5360,* ☏ *06138/2204,* ℻ *06138/242745. 24 rooms with bath. Restaurant. No credit cards.*

Nightlife and the Arts

Concerts are held in St. Wolfgang every Monday from June to September; there are also band concerts every Wednesday and Saturday evening at 8:30 on the Marktplatz. Folk events are usually well publicized with posters. Not far from St. Wolfgang, the town of Strobl holds a Day of Popular Music and Tradition in early July—"popular" meaning brass band, and "tradition" being local costume. Check with the regional tourist office for details.

Bad Ischl

❺ *56 km (35 mi) east of Salzburg, 16 km (10 mi) southeast of St. Wolfgang.*

Many travelers used to think of Bad Ischl primarily as the town where Zauner's pastry shop is located, to which connoisseurs drove miles for the sake of a cup of coffee and a *Torte.* Pastry continues to be the best-known drawing card of a community that symbolizes, more than any other place except Vienna itself, the old Austria of uniforms and balls and waltzes and operettas. For Bad Ischl was the place where Emperor

Franz Josef chose to establish his summer court (there is a story, too, that his mother, Sophie, had stayed at the spa in 1829, when trying to conceive the future emperor). Today, you can enjoy the same sort of pastries *mit Schlag* that the emperor loved. Afterward, you can hasten off to the town's modern spa, one of the best known in Austria. The town initially grew up around the curative mineral springs that are still the raison d'être for the classic 19th-century *Kurhaus* (spa building) and the baths in the adjoining new buildings.

You'll want to stroll along the shaded **Esplanade,** where the pampered and privileged of the 19th century loved to take their constitutionals, usually after a quick stop at the spa pavilion of the **Trinkhalle,** still in the middle of town on Ferdinand-Auböck-Platz.

★ However, the quickest way to travel back in time to the 1880s in Bad Ischl is to head for the **Kaiservilla,** the imperial-yellow residence (the color of gold and power), rather like a miniature Schönbrunn. Markus von Habsburg, great-grandson of Franz Josef I, still lives here, but you can tour parts of the building to see the ornate reception rooms and the surprisingly modest residential quarters. ⊠ *Kaiserpark,* ☎ *06132/ 23241.* 🎫 *Grounds AS30; combined ticket, including tour of villa, AS90.* ☉ *Easter, Apr. weekends, and May–mid-Oct., daily 9–noon and 1–5.*

Don't overlook the small but elegant "marble palace" built nearby the Kaiservilla for Empress Elisabeth, who used it as a teahouse; it now is the home of a **photography museum.** (The marriage of Franz Josef and Elizabeth was not an especially happy one. A number of houses in Bad Ischl bearing women's names are said to have been quietly given by the emperor to his various lady friends around town (☞ Villa Schratt, *in* Dining and Lodging, *below*). You'll first need to purchase a ticket to enter the park grounds. ⊠ *Kaiserpark,* ☎ *06132/24422.* 🎫 *AS30.* ☉ *Apr.–Oct., daily 9:30–5.*

Composers followed the aristocracy and the court to Bad Ischl. Bruckner, Brahms, Johann Strauss the Younger, and Oscar Straus all spent summers here, but it was Franz Lehár, composer of *The Merry Widow,* who left the most lasting musical impression. The operetta festival in summer (☞ Music *in* Nightlife and the Arts, *below*) always includes one Lehár work. **Lehár's villa** is now a museum, open for guided tours. ⊠ *Pfarrgasse 11,* ☎ *06132/26992.* 🎫 *AS45.* ☉ *Easter and May–Sept., daily 9–noon and 2–5; last tours at 11:30 and 4:30.*

Bad Ischl is accessed easily via various routes. From St. Wolfgang, backtrack south to Strobl and head eastward on Route 158. To get to the town directly from Salzburg, take the A1 to Mondsee, then Routes 151 and 158 along the Wolfgangsee and the Mondsee. There are many buses that depart hourly from Salzburg's main railway station; you can also travel by train via the junction of Attnang-Puchheim or Stainach-Irdning (several transfers are required)—a longer journey than the bus ride, which is usually 90 minutes.

Dining and Lodging

$$$$ ✕ **Villa Schratt.** This is the villa where the brilliant Katharina "Kati" Schratt once lived, Emperor Franz Josef's most favored confidante (and a good friend of his wife as well). You'll be treated to some of the finest food in the area. Choose between modern decor and a rustic atmosphere replete with antlers; in either room, the setting is elegant and service attentive. Try any of the fish compositions, or beef tenderloins with mushrooms in a cream sauce. For dessert, order the traditional *Guglhupf* sponge cake. ⊠ *Steinbruch 43,* ☎ FAX *06231/27647. Reservations essential. AE, MC. Closed Tues., Wed., early–mid-Nov., and various wks during spring.*

$$-$$$ ✕ **Weinhaus Attwenger.** This restaurant is set in a turn-of-the-century
★ gingerbread villa under massive trees overlooking the river. In summer
the garden alone is worth a visit; the question is whether new management will uphold a reputation for good food as well as service. Ask
for seasonal recommendations; the fish and game dishes are always particularly good. In the cozy wood-paneled rooms inside, the environment is rustic. ✉ *Lehárkai 12,* ☎ ⅁⅂ *06132/23327. AE, DC. Closed
Tues. and mid-Jan.–mid-Mar.*

$$ ✕ **Café Zauner.** If you haven't been to Zauner, you haven't been to Bad
★ Ischl. The desserts—particularly the house creation, *Zaunerstollen,* a
chocolate-covered confection of sugar, hazelnuts, and nougat—have
made this one of Austria's best-known pastry shops. Other possibili-
ties include lunch or early dinner in the tree-shaded inner court or the
garden restaurant alongside the river in summer. ✉ *Pfarrgasse 7,* ☎
06132/23522, ⅁⅂ *06132/26716. MC. Closed Tues. Oct.–May 1.*

$$$ ✕⊞ **Kurhotel.** This fairly new and, for Bad Ischl, high-rise hotel, within
a two-minute walk of the railroad station, serves as a training insti-
tute for the regional hotel school, so you're sure to get attentive, enthusiastic service. The rooms are modern in dark browns and beige;
many have magnificent views of the mountains around the city. An underground passageway leads to the nearby mineral baths; use of the
pool and sauna is free. The hotel restaurant specializes in regional dishes
and game in season. ✉ *Voglhuberstr. 10, A–4820,* ☎ *06132/204,* ⅁⅂
*06132/27682. 115 rooms. Restaurant, bar, pool, sauna, tennis court.
AE, DC, MC, V.*

$$$ ✕⊞ **Zum Goldenen Schiff.** This traditional family-run house, overlooking
★ the river, offers typical country comfort. Rooms with a balcony on the
river side are preferred, but all are appealing, with lots of natural
wood in evidence. The restaurant specializes in fish. ✉ *Adalbert-
Stifter-Kai 3, A–4820,* ☎ *06132/24241–0,* ⅁⅂ *06132/24241–58. 56
rooms. Restaurant. AE, DC, MC, V.*

Nightlife and the Arts

The main musical events of the year in the Salzkammergut are the July
and August operetta festivals held here in Bad Ischl. In addition, per-
formances of at least two operettas (*The Merry Widow* is a standard
favorite) take place every season in the **Kurhaus** (☎ 06132/23766), where
tickets are sold. For early booking, contact the Operrettengemeind (✉
Wiesingerstr. 7, A–4820 Bad Ischl, ☎ 06132/23839, ⅁⅂ 06132/23384).

Outdoor Activities and Sports

GOLF

Bad Ischl Golfclub (☎ 06132/26340, ⅁⅂ 06132/26708), in Aschau, 6
km (4 mi) from the center of town, has 18 holes, par-71, and is open
April–November.

TENNIS

The Salzkammergut is great tennis territory, with courts in almost
every town. The best is probably the **Tennisclub Bad Ischl,** which has
indoor and outdoor courts, ball-throwing machines, and equipment
rentals (☎ 06132/24432 or 06132/23926).

Gmunden

❻ *76 km (47 mi) northeast of Salzburg, 40 km (25 mi) southwest of Linz,
32 km (20 mi) northeast of Bad Ischl.*

Gmunden, at the top of the Traunsee, is an attractive town to stroll about
in. The tree-lined promenade along the lake is reminiscent of past days
of the idle aristocracy and artistic greats—Schubert, Brahms, and the Duke
of Württemberg were just some who strolled under the chestnut trees.

In the town hall you'll find a famous carillon, with bells made from local clay. The gloriously ornate, arcaded yellow-and-white **town hall,** with its corner towers topped by onion domes, can't be overlooked. You can easily walk to the **Strandbad,** the swimming area, from the center of town. The beaches are good, and you can sail, water ski, or windsurf.

Take time to look at, or visit, two castles: The "lake" castle, **Schloss Orth,** on a peninsula known as Toskana, was originally built in the 15th century. Its last owner was Archduke Johann, who gave up his title after marrying an actress and thereafter called himself Orth. He disappeared with the casket supposedly holding the secret of the Mayerling tragedy after the death of Emperor Franz Josef's son Rudolf. The **Landschloss** on the shore is a simple 17th-century affair now operating as a government school of forestry; you can visit the courtyard, with its coats of arms and rococo fountain, daily 8 AM–dusk.

★ From Gmunden, take a lake trip on the *Gisela,* built in 1872, the oldest coal-fired steam side-wheeler running anywhere. It carried Emperor Franz Josef last century and is now restored. For departure times, check with Traunseeschiffahrt Eder (☎ 07612/5215 or 07612/66700, FAX 07612/66741). Boat lines crisscross the whole 12-km (7-mi) length of the lake.

From beyond the railroad station, take the 12-minute cable-car ride to the top of the **Grünberg.** From here you will have a superb view out over the Traunsee, with the Dachstein glacier forming the backdrop in the south. In the winter, there are good ski runs here. ⊠ *Freygasse 4,* ☎ *07612/4977–0.* 🎫 *Round-trip AS115, one-way AS85.* ☉ *May–June and Sept., daily 9–5; July–Aug., daily 9–6; Oct., daily 9–4:30.*

To get to Gmunden from Bad Ischl, take Route 145 along the western shore of the Traunsee—note the Traunstein, Hochkogel, and Erlakogel peaks on the eastern side, the latter nicknamed *Schlafende Griechin* (Slumbering Greek Girl)—and then along the Traun River. You can also take a train to the town via Attnang-Puchheim from Salzburg, or from the main station in Linz.

OFF THE
BEATEN PATH

TRAUNKIRCHEN – About 4½ km (3 mi) north of Ebensee on Route 145 you'll come to Traunkirchen; stop for a look at the "fishermen's pulpit" in the parish church. This 17th-century Baroque marvel, carved from wood burnished with silver and gold, portrays the astonished fishermen of the Sea of Galilee pulling in their suddenly full nets at Jesus' direction.

Dining and Lodging

$$ ★ ✕ **Lambi Mambi.** Ignore the apparently corny name—actually it's Finnish for "warm and friendly"—and try this chic but charming *Gasthaus* for some of the best food in the area. The choice is limited but imaginative; you might encounter an apple-celery soup with shrimp or fillet of lamb with a potato and leek crust. Finish with apple dumpling and cinnamon cream. ⊠ *Linzer Str. 37,* ☎ *07612/67488. No credit cards. Closed Sun.–Mon. No lunch.*

$$$ ★ 🏨 **Parkhotel am See.** This traditional-style house, separated from the lake by the promenade, is a five-minute walk from the town center. Although the building has recently been renovated, its antique furnishings continue to set the scene. There's a private pier for swimming. ⊠ *Schiffslände 17, A–4810,* ☎ *07612/4230–0,* FAX *07612/4230–66. 50 rooms. Bar, golf privileges, tennis court, bicycles. MC, V. Closed Oct.–mid-May.*

$$$ 🏨 **Grünberg am See.** This architecturally unimpressive hotel right on the lake has a good restaurant with lots of Upper Austrian Knödel specialties and a wide assortment of fresh fish dishes. Be thankful for the

superb sportive opportunities, from hiking to cycling to swimming. ⊠ *Traunsteinstr. 109, A–4810,* ☎ *07612/777–00,* FAX *07612/777–33. 30 rooms. Restaurant, bar, tennis court, hiking, beach, bicycles. MC. Closed 2 wks in Feb.*

Shopping

Among the many souvenirs and handicrafts you'll find in Salzkammergut shops, the most famous are the handcrafted ceramics of Gmunden. The green-trimmed, white country ceramics are decorated with blue, yellow, green, and white patterns, including the celebrated 16th-century *Grüngeflammte* design, solid horizontal green stripes on a white background. You'll find them at the **Gmundner Keramik** shop (⊠ Keramikstr. 24, ☎ 07612/5441–0).

HALLSTATT, GOSAU, AND BAD AUSSEE

It is hard to imagine anything prettier than this region of the Salzkammergut, which takes you into the very heart of the Lake District. The great highlight is Gosau am Dachstein—a beauty spot that even the least impressionable find hard to forget. But there are other notable sights, including Hallstatt, the Dachstein ice caves, and the spa of Altaussee. Lording over the region is the Dachstein range itself—the backbone of Upper Austria, Styria, Land Salzburg, and a true monarch of all it surveys.

Hallstatt

❼ *89 km (55 mi) southeast of Salzburg, 19 km (12 mi) south of Bad Ischl.*

As if rising from Swan Lake itself, the town of Hallstatt is the hero of thousands of travel posters. "The world's prettiest lakeside village" perches precariously on the lakeside, on what seems the smallest of toeholds to prevent it from tumbling into the dark waters of the Hallstättersee. Down from the steep mountainside above it crashes the Mühlbach waterfall, a sight that can keep you riveted for hours. Today, the town is a thriving tourist center and a bit too modernized, considering that Hallstatt is believed to be the oldest community in Austria. More than a thousand graves of prehistoric men have been found here, and it has been such an important source of relics of the Celtic period that this age is known as the Hallstatt epoch.

Most of the early relics of the Hallstatt era are in Vienna (including the greatest Iron Age totem of them all, the *Venus of Willendorf,* now a treasure of Vienna's Naturhistorisches Museum, ☞ Chapter 2) but some are here in the **Prähistorisches Museum** (Prehistoric Museum). ⊠ *Seestr. 56,* ☎ *06134/8398.* 🎫 *AS40.* ☉ *Apr. and Oct., daily 10–4; May–Sept., daily 10–6.*

Salt has been mined in the area for at least 4,500 years, and the **Hallstatt mines** are the oldest in the world. Take the cable car up and tour the mines above town; after a 10-minute walk, you enter the mines on a little miner's train (tall people, keep your heads down!) and go deep into the mountain, sliding down wooden chutes to an artificial subterranean lake, which is used to dissolve the salt. There is also an Iron Age cemetery and a restaurant up here. ⊠ *Salzberg (Salt Mountain),* ☎ *06134/8251–72.* 🎫 *Cable car round-trip AS97, one-way AS60; mine and tour AS135.* ☉ *Early Apr.–May and mid-Sept.–Oct. 26, daily 9:30–3; June–mid-Sept., daily 9:30–4:30.*

★ The Hallstatt market square, now a pedestrian area, is bordered by colorful 16th-century houses. Be sure to visit the **parish church of St. Michael,** which is picturesquely sited near the lake. Within the 16th-century Gothic church, you'll find a beautiful winged altar, which opens to reveal nine 15th-century paintings. The charnel house beside the church is a rather morbid but regularly visited spot. Because there was little space to bury the dead over the centuries in Hallstatt, the custom developed of digging up the bodies after 12 or 15 years, piling the bones in the sun, and painting the skulls. Ivy and oak-leaf wreaths were used for the men, Alpine flowers for the women, plus names, dates, and often the cause of death. The myriad bones and skulls are now on view in the charnel house. The lakeside vistas are spectacular, and people love to feed the fish by the shore.

In Gasthof Hallberg there is a curious **war museum** containing Nazi gold and propaganda materials that were to be air-dropped on Britain, discovered by the owner, Gerhard Zauner, on diving expeditions in nearby lakes. ⊠ *Seestr. 113,* ☎ *06134/8286.* ⌨ *Free.* ⊘ *Daily.*

To get to Hallstatt from Bad Ischl, head south on Route 145 to Bad Goisern—which also has curative mineral springs but never achieved the cachet of Bad Ischl. Just south of town, watch the signs for the turnoff to the Hallstättersee. Since the lake is squeezed between two sharply rising mountain ranges, the road parallels the shore, with spectacular views. The Hallstatt railroad station is on the opposite side of the lake; if you arrive by train, a boat (*Hemetsberger,* ⊠ Hallstättersee-Schiffahrt, ☎ 06134/8228) will take you across to the town. Embark via train for Hallstatt from Bad Ischl or via the Stainach-Irdning junction. From Bad Ischl, you can also take a half-hour bus ride to Hallstatt.

Dining and Lodging

$$$$ ✕⬚ **Grüner Baum.** Hallstatt is proud of not having succumbed to the
★ architectural horrors of some other tourist spots. Things here are "just like home." One of the best inns is this friendly, rambling house directly on the lake, in traditional yellow with white trim, dating from 1760. The house cats sit about the reception desk and worn armchairs—terrific atmosphere. Most of the comfortable rooms overlook the lake, yet you're right in the center of town. The restaurant is known for its fish specialties. ⊠ *Markpl. 104, A–4830,* ☎ *06134/8263,* ⅎΑX *06134/8420. 34 rooms. Restaurant, bar, lake. AE, DC, MC, V. Closed mid-Nov.–mid-Dec.*

$–$$ ✕⬚ **Gasthof Simony** A few steps from the Grüner Baum, this friendly,
★ family place is right on a lake. Sit in the large entrance hall and enjoy breakfast and the kids and grandkids running around the place. The restaurant has regional specialties and is inexpensive. ⊠ *Wolfenstrasse 105, A–4830,* ☎ ⅎΑX *06134/8231. 14 rooms, some without shower. Restaurant, lake. No credit cards. Closes very sporadically in winter.*

Outdoor Activities and Sports

BOATING

The lakes of the Salzkammergut are excellent for **canoeing** because most prohibit or limit powerboats. Try canoeing on the Hallstätter See (for information, contact Alois Zopf, ⊠ Hauptstr. 327, Bad Goisern, ☎ 06135/8254, ⅎΑX 06135/7409) or white-water **kayaking** on the Traun River (for information, call Fritz Schiefermeyer, ☎ 06134/8338).

HIKING

There are many great hiking paths around Hallstatt; contact the local tourist office for information about the path along the Echerntal to Waldbachstrub past pleasant waterfalls, or the climb to the Tiergartenhütte, continuing on to the Wiesberghaus and, two hours beyond, the Simony-Hütte, spectacularly sited at the foot of the Dachstein glacier. From here mountain climbers begin the ascent of the Hoher Dachstein, the tallest peak of the Dachstein massif.

Gosau am Dachstein

★ ⑧ *10 km (6 mi) west of the Hallstättersee.*

Lovers of scenic beauty should not leave the Hallstatt region without taking in Gosau am Dachstein, considered the most beautiful spot in Austria by 19th-century travelers but unaccountably often overlooked today. This lovely spot is 10 km (6 mi) west of the Hallstätter See, just before the Geschütt pass. You travel either by bus, rail, or motorboat as far as Gosaumühle—the village makes a good lunch stop (and, with its many *Gasthöfe* and pensions, could be a base for your excursion)— and from there you must walk, at the most an hour or two, depending on your speed, but you won't regret the hike. Of the three Gosauseen (Gosau lakes), the first—the Vorderer Gosausee—is the crown jewel, located some 8 km (5 mi) to the south of the town itself. Beyond a sparkling, almost fjordlike basin of water rises the amazing Dachstein massif, majestically reflected in the mirrorlike surface of the lake. Other than a restaurant and a gamekeeper's hut, the lake is undefiled by man-made structures. At the right hour—well before 2:30 PM, when, due to the steepness of the mountain slopes, the sun is already withdrawing—the view is *königlich* (regal). Following the path around the lake will clarify some of the greatest passages in Richard Wagner's *Parsifal,* which were composed with these vistas in mind. Then you may choose to endure the stiff walk to the other two lakes (not as spectacularly located), which will take another two hours; take a cable car up to the Gablonzer Hütte on the Zwieselalm (you might consider skiing on the Gosau glacier); or tackle the three-hour hike up to the summit of the Grosser Donnerkogel. At day's end, head back for Gosau am Dachstein, settle in at one of the many Gasthöfe (reserve ahead) overhung with wild gooseberry and rosebushes (or stay at one of Gosau's charming *Privatzimmer* accommodations). Cap the day off with a dinner of fried *Schwarzrenterl,* a delicious regional lake fish. To get to Gosau, travel north or south on Route 145, turning off at the junction at Route 166, and travel 36 km (20 mi) east through the ravine of the Gosaubach River.

Dining and Lodging

$$$ ✕🏨 **Hotel Koller.** One of the most charming hotels in Gosau, the
★   Koller was originally the home of famed industrialist Moriz Faber. With peaked gables and weather vanes the Koller has a fairy-tale aura when seen from its pretty park. Inside are an open fireplace and warm woodwork; guest rooms—many featuring breathtaking views—are newly renovated with blond-wood furniture. A special feature is the tavern's gala dinners, complete with folk music and regional barbecued specialties and health foods supplied fresh by the farmers of Gosau. Half board is required. ✉ *A–4824 Gosau am Dachstein,* ☎ *06136/88410,* 🖷 *06136/884150. 18 rooms with bath, 5 suites. 2 restaurants, bar, pool, sauna, steam room, playground. No credit cards. Closed late Oct.– mid-Dec.*

Dachstein Ice Caves

★ ⑨ *5 km (3 mi) east of Hallstatt.*

Many travelers to Hallstatt make an excursion to one of the most impressive sights of the eastern Alps, the **Dachstein Ice Caves.** From Hallstatt, take the scenic road around the bottom of the lake to Obertraun; then follow the signs to the cable car, the *Dachsteinseilbahn,* which will ferry you up the mountain (if you prefer, you can hike all the way up to the caves). From the cable-car landing, a 15-minute hike up takes you to the entrance (follow signs to DACHSTEINEISHÖHLE) of the vast ice caverns, many of which are hundreds of years old and aglitter with ice stalactites and stalagmites illuminated by an eerie light. The most famous sights are the **Rieseneishöhle** (Giant Ice Cave) and the **Mammuthöhle** (Mammoth Cave), but there are other caves and assorted frozen waterfalls. The cave entrance is at about 6,500 ft, still well below the 9,750-ft Dachstein peak farther south. Be sure to wear warm, weatherproof clothing; inside the caves it's cold, and outside, the slopes can be swept by chilly winds. ☎ *06131/362 or 06131/273–0.* ▨ *Cable car round-trip AS168, Giant Ice Cave AS90, Mammoth Cave AS90, combined ticket for both caves AS130.* ☉ *May–mid-Oct., daily 8:45–4:50 (5:50 for Mammoth Cave); last tours at 3:10 (Mammoth Cave) and 4:10 (Giant Ice Cave); cable cars for last tours depart at 2:10 (Mammoth Caves or combined) and 3:10 (Giant Ice Cave), 1 hr later July–Aug.*

Bad Aussee

⑩ *81 km (50 mi) southeast of Salzburg, 24 km (15 mi) west of Hallstatt.*

Following the bumpy old road westward (often closed in winter) from Hallstatt, you'll find yourself in company with the railroad and the Traun River (watch out for the precipitous 23° gradient at one point) and enter a region dotted with small lakes. The heart of this region is Bad Aussee, a great mecca in the summertime, for the town's towering mountains and glacier-fed lake keep the area cool. Even in midsummer, the waters of the lake are so cold that the presence of the municipal swimming pool is easy to account for. In the town, salt and mineral springs have been developed into a modern spa complex, yet the town retains much of its 15th- and 16th-century character in the narrow streets and older buildings, particularly in the upper reaches. The 1827 marriage of Archduke Johann to the daughter of the local postmaster brought attention and a burst of new construction, including some lovely 19th-century villas. Bad Aussee is a good base for hiking in the surrounding countryside in summer and for excellent skiing in winter. Many travelers come to Bad Aussee via the train from Salzburg, making a connection southward at the Attnang Puchheim junction.

Dining and Lodging

$$$$ ✕▥ **Erzherzog Johann.** A golden yellow facade identifies this tradi-
★ tional house, which, though in the center of town, is quiet. A direct passageway connects the hotel to a spa next door, with a swimming pool and cure facilities. The hotel rooms are modern and immaculate in their country decor. The first-floor restaurant serves the best creative cooking in the area in an ambience that is elegant but nevertheless intimate. Try the dishes with the famous Styrian pumpkinseed oil (*Kürbiskernöl*). ✉ *Kurhauspl. 62, A–8990,* ☎ *03622/52507,* ⅻ *03622/52394–680. 62 rooms. Restaurant, bar, indoor pool, sauna, spa, exercise room. MC. Closed late Nov.–mid-Dec.*

$$$ ▥ **Kristina.** Set in a lovely wooded park, this hotel is decorated with
★ antlers and trophies in the style of a hunting lodge; its rooms are appropriately outfitted with older furniture. ✉ *Altausser Str. 54, A–8990,* ☎ *03622/52017,* ⅻ *03622/52017–1. 11 rooms. Restaurant. AE, DC, MC, V. Closed mid- to late Jan. and Nov.–mid-Dec.*

$$ ▥ **Wasnerin.** This Styrian-style chalet above town offers magnificent views of the Dachstein peak. The rooms are simple but adequate, and the management is especially friendly. Half board is standard. ✉ *Sommersbergseestr. 19, A–8990,* ☎ *03622/52108. 33 rooms. Restaurant, bar, tennis court. No credit cards. Closed wk after Easter and of Oct.–mid Dec.*

Altaussee

⓫ *4 km (2½ mi) north of Bad Aussee.*

Taking a fairly steep road from Bad Aussee, you'll find Altaussee tucked away at the end of a lake cradled by gentle mountains. This is one of the most magical spots of the Salzkammergut. Over the years, it attracted dozens of fine artists who came for inspiration, for example Johannes Brahms, Arthur Schnitzler, and Hugo von Hofmannsthal—until one named Alex Storm drew the lake as an inkwell "into which we all dip our quills." The town is completely unspoiled, perfect for those who simply want an Alpine idyll: to do nothing, hike in the meadows, climb the slopes, or row on the lake. The end of May to the beginning of June is perhaps the best time to visit; the field flowers have burst forth and Bad Aussee holds its famous narcissus festival, which includes a procession to Altaussee.

During World War II, Nazi leaders stored stolen art in underground caverns near Altaussee. In their hurry to get the job done, they skipped a few details; one story has it that a famous painting from Vienna, possibly a Rubens or a Rembrandt, was overlooked and spent the remaining war years on the porch of a house near the entrance to the mines. At the end of the war, Allied forces were directed to the mines by the local populace, and, once unsealed, the caverns released a treasure unlikely ever again to be assembled in one place.

Salt is still dug in the nearby Sandling Mountain, and the **mines** are open to visitors. Check with the tourist office or phone for details of guided tours. ☎ *03622/713643.* ✂ *AS130.* ☉ *Apr.–Oct., daily 10–4; Nov.–Mar., tour daily at 2.*

If time allows and you feel fit enough, do the approximately 2½-hour walk up the Loser Mountain that begins at the end of Altaussee (follow the colored marks and occasional signs) to Loser-Bergrestaurant (⊠ Panorama Strasse, ☎ 03622/71315–16, FAX 03622/71315–13) up top for some very solid Styrian and Austrian cooking, and an extraordinary view. Shortly before is a small farm (*Alm*) where a young man makes fine soft cheeses. There is also a toll road leading up, but it's not nearly as fun as hiking.

Dining and Lodging

$$ ✕☷ **Zum Loser.** The rooms are simple but inviting in this attractive family-managed hostelry. The restaurant, specializing in fish, game, and pork, offers excellent local dishes. (You must order the delicious smoked trout a day in advance.) Local musicians entertain on Thursday evenings. ⊠ *Fischerndorf 80, A–8992,* ☎ *03622/71373,* FAX *03622/ 71373–15. 8 rooms. Restaurant. AE, DC, MC, V. Closed Nov.–mid-Dec. and mid-Apr.–May.*

$$$ ☷ **Hotel Seevilla.** This elegantly rustic hotel (part of the Silence chain)
★   is one of the loveliest in the Salzkammergut, thanks to its location amid towering trees and directly on the shores of Altaussee's picture-book lake. The balconied rooms upstairs, reached by a stone staircase, are spacious and furnished in a modern country style; baths are elegant and efficient. The hotel was completely renovated in 1994 and now features a gracious café. ⊠ *Fischerndorf 60, A–8992,* ☎ *03622/ 71302–0,* FAX *06322/71302–82. 46 rooms with bath, 7 apartments. Bar, café, indoor pool, sauna, exercise room, beach. AE, DC. Closed Nov.–mid-Dec.*

En Route   To get back to Bad Ischl, your best bet is to return to Bad Aussee and then take Route 145 north. It's only 28 km (18 mi), but a great deal of this consists of precipitous ups and downs, the highest point being at 3,200 ft before you head down through the Pötschen pass. Not surprisingly, the views are spectacular; don't miss the lookout point at a hairpin turn at Unter, far above the Hallstätter See.

SALZKAMMERGUT A TO Z

Arriving and Departing

By Car

Driving is by far the easiest and most convenient way to reach the Lake District. From **Salzburg,** you can take Route 158 east to Fuschl, St. Gilgen, and Bad Ischl or the A1 autobahn to Mondsee. Coming from **Vienna** or Linz, the A1 passes through the northern part of the Salzkammergut; get off at the Steyrermühl exit or the Regau exit and head south on Route 144/145 to Gmunden, Bad Ischl, Bad Goisern, and Bad Aussee. From the Seewalchen exit, take Route 152 down the east side of the Attersee, instead of the far less scenic Route 151 down the west side.

By Plane

The Lake District is closer to Salzburg than to Linz, but ground transportation is such that there is little preference for one departure point over the other. The **Salzburg** airport is about 53 km (33 mi) from Bad Ischl, heart of the Salzkammergut; the **Linz** airport (Hörsching) is about 75 km (47 mi). Both cities have good connections to European destinations but no flights to or from North America. A number of charter lines fly into Salzburg, including some from the United Kingdom.

By Train

The geography of the area means that rail lines run mainly north–south. Trains run from Vöcklabruck to Seewalchen at the top end of the Attersee and from Attnang-Puchheim to Gmunden, Bad Ischl, Hallstatt, Bad Aussee, and beyond. Both starting points are on the main east–west line between Salzburg and Linz.

Getting Around

By Bus and Train

Railroad service is fairly good, but you won't get off the beaten path. Where the trains don't go, the post office or railroad buses do, so if you allow enough time, you can cover virtually all the area by public transportation. Check at the railroad station in Salzburg or Bad Ischl on the availability of a "Salzkammergut Ticket," good for unlimited travel on all trains within the Salzkammergut region and for a 50% reduction on the lake steamers and Schafbergbahn mountain railway on any four days within a 10-day period from May to the end of October.

By Car

For sheer flexibility—plus being able to stop when you want to admire the view—travel by car is the most satisfactory way to see the Salzkammergut. Roads are good, and traffic is excessive only on weekends (although it can be slow on some narrow lakeside stretches). Just remember that gasoline is expensive in Austria, almost US$5 a gallon for unleaded.

Contacts and Resources

Bicycling

Much of the Salzkammergut is rather hilly if you are just a casual cyclist, but you'll find reasonably good cycling country around the lakes, including the Wolfgangsee (though Route 158 can become quite noisy and fumey). Sports shops throughout the area rent bikes; local tourist offices can point you to the right place. You can cycle the 14 km (9 mi) from St. Wolfgang to Bad Ischl on back roads. Bicycle rentals are available at the railroad station in **St. Wolfgang** (☎ 06138/2232–0).

Canoeing

Helpful firms for the entire Salzkammergut region are **Intersport Steinkogler** (✉ Salzburger Str. 3, Bad Ischl, ☎ 06132/23655) and **Pro-Travel Salzkammergut Aktiv** (✉ Markt 94, St. Wolfgang, ☎ 06138/2525–0, FAX 06138/3054).

Emergencies

The emergency numbers are ☎ 133 for the **police,** ☎ 144 for an **ambulance,** and ☎ 122 for the **fire department.** Call ☎ 120 for the **automobile club ÖAMTC.** If you need a doctor and speak no German, ask your hotel how best to obtain assistance.

Fishing Licenses

The Salzkammergut is superb fishing country for casting or trolling—the main season runs June–September—but you'll need a license. Many townships have their own licensing offices. **Attersee:** Matthäus Hollerweger (✉ Esso station, Nussdorf, ☎ 07666/8063–4). **Bad Ischl:** Ischler Waffen, Manfred Zeitler (✉ Schröpferpl. 4, ☎ 06132/23351). **Ebensee:** (✉ Langbathsee 1, Baier/Landgasthof in der Kreh, ☎ 06133/6235). **Gmunden:** Forstverwaltung Gmunden (✉ Klosterpl. 1, ☎ 07612/4529, FAX 07612/5664); Höller Kammerhof (✉ Kammerhofgasse 6, ☎ 07612/3308); Gasthof Steinmaurer (✉ Traunsteinstr. 23, ☎ 07612/4239–0). **Hallstatt:** Zentrasport Janu (✉ Seestr. 50, ☎ 06134/8298–0). **Mondsee:** Peter Schickl (✉ Pyrofex-Maximus-Str. 1, ☎ 06232/2881, FAX 06232/2040); Drogerie Maritsch (✉ Rainerstr. 1, ☎ 06232/3436). **St. Wolfgang:** Fischerhaus Höplinger (✉ Dr.-Rais-Promenade 79, ☎ 06138/2241).

A number of hotels in the **Altaussee–Bad Aussee** area have packages that combine a week's stay with the fishing license; for details and booking, contact Steirischer Tourismus (✉ St. Peter–Hauptstr. 243, A–8042 Graz, ☎ 0316/403033 or 0316/403013, FAX 0316/403013–10).

Guided Tours

Daylong tours of the Salzkammergut whisk you all too quickly from Salzburg to St. Gilgen, St. Wolfgang, and Mondsee: **Albus/Salzburg Sightseeing Tours** (✉ Mirabellpl. 2, A–5020 Salzburg, ☎ 0662/881616, FAX 0662/878776); **Salzburg Panorama Tours** (✉ Schrannengasse 2, A–5020 Salzburg, ☎ 0662/883211–0, FAX 0662/871618). Full-day tours to Salzburg from Vienna pass through Gmunden and the Traunsee, Bad Ischl, the Wolfgangsee, St. Gilgen, and Fuschlsee, but you can't see much from a bus window: **Cityrama/Gray Line** (✉ Börsengasse 1, A–1010 Vienna, ☎ 01/534–13–0, FAX 01/534–13–22); **Vienna Sightseeing Tours** (✉ Stelzhammergasse 4/11, A–1031 Vienna, ☎ 0222/712–4683–0, FAX 0222/712–4683–77).

Swimming and Water Sports

There's every kind of water sport in the Salzkammergut, from windsurfing to sailing. You can waterski at Strobl and St. Wolfgang on the Wolfgangsee and at most towns on the Attersee and Traunsee. At Ebensee, check with **Diving School Gigl** (✉ Strandbadstr. 12, ☎ 06133/6381), which also offers skin diving. In Gmunden, contact **Wasserskischule** (✉ Traunsteinstr., ☎ 07612/3602). A "round" will cost you about AS120.

You can explore the mysterious depths of the Hallstätter See by scuba diving with **Tauchschule und Bergefirma Zauner** (✉ Markt 113, ☎ 06134/8286).

Visitor Information

The main tourist offices for the provinces and regions covered in this chapter are as follows:

Land Salzburg (⊠ Wiener Bundesstr. 23, Pf. 1, A–5300 Hallwang bei Salzburg, ☎ 0662/6688–0, FAX 0662/6688–0; ⊠ Mozartpl. 5, A–5020 Salzburg, ☎ 0662/843264). **Salzkammergut** (⊠ Wirerstr. 10, A–4820 Bad Ischl, ☎ 06132/26909–0, FAX 06132/26909–14). **Styria** (⊠ St. Peter–Hauptstr. 243, A–8042 Graz, ☎ 0316/403033–0, FAX 0316/403033–10). **Tourismusverband Ausseer Land** (⊠ Kurhauspl. 55, A–8890 Bad Aussee, ☎ 03622/54040–0, FAX 03622/54040–7). **Upper Austria** (⊠ Schillerstr. 50, A–4010 Linz, ☎ 0732/600–221–0, FAX 0732/600220).

Most towns in the Salzkammergut have their own *Fremdenverkehrsamt* (tourist offices):

Altaussee (⊠ Fischerndorf 44, A–8992, ☎ 03622/71643, FAX 03622/71187). **Bad Aussee** (⊠ Chlumeckypl. 44, A–8990, ☎ 03622/52323, FAX 03622/52324). **Bad Ischl** (⊠ Bahnhofstr. 6, A–4820, ☎ 06132/27757, FAX 06132/27757–77). **Gmunden** (⊠ Am Graben 2, A–4810, ☎ 07612/4305, FAX 07612/71410). **Gosau am Dachstein** (⊠ Tourismusverband Gosau, A–4824, ☎ 06136/8295, FAX 06136/8255). **Hallstatt** (⊠ Seestr. 169, A–4830, ☎ 06134/8208, FAX 06134/8352). **Mondsee** (⊠ Dr.-Franz-Muller-Str. 3, A–5310, ☎ 06232/2270, FAX 06232/4470). **St. Gilgen** (⊠ Mozartpl. 1, A–5340, ☎ 06227/348 or 06227/7267–0, FAX 06227/7267–9). **St. Wolfgang** (⊠ Markt 28, A–5360, ☎ 06138/2239, FAX 06138/2239–81).

8 Carinthia

Carinthia could be labeled "Extract of Austria" since it contains a greater variety of Austria's charms than any other province. Routine-numb Viennese dream of its Austrian Riviera, where waterside gaiety emanates from such resorts as Maria Wörth and Velden; the scenic cities of Klagenfurt and Villach beckon; and art treasures await— Spittal's Porcia palace, Gurk's great Romanesque cathedral, and the model for the Gothic castle in Walt Disney's Snow White—Hochosterwitz Castle.

By George W. Hamilton

Updated by Marton Radkai

N 1877 THE GERMAN COMPOSER Johannes Brahms wrote of an unexpected holiday he spent in Carinthia: ". . . the first day was so lovely that I determined to stay for a second, and the second was so lovely that I have decided to stay here for the time being." Little has changed since.

If you approach Carinthia from Vienna not by the official A2 autobahn that passes through Graz but on Route 83 from the Murtal in the north that passes through Bad Einöd and Friesach, you will be taking one of the main gateways into Austria's sunniest province. The broad, open countryside you cross from there to the Wörther See—Austria's warmest lake and mecca of sun worshipers—is only one aspect of Carinthia. If you approach the province from any other direction, you will get a very different impression—that of an area walled in by towering mountains, surmountable only through a few, mostly high passes. Carinthia has Austria's highest peak (the famous Grossglockner, which rises to 12,470 ft), architectural treasures such as the Romanesque Gurk Cathedral, Renaissance gems like Schloss Porcia in Spittal, and Baroque beauties everywhere. Then there is also the waterside gaiety of such resorts as Maria Wörth and Velden, set within the pleasure-land that is the Austrian Riveria. Carinthia has the best summer weather in all of Austria (great for bicycling, fishing, hiking, and water sports), which means reservations usually need to be booked well in advance for such towns.

Klagenfurt is the official seat of the government, but over the course of time, Villach, an equally attractive small city, has emerged as the "secret" capital, especially when the spirit of carnival captivates Austria; the Villach Carnival takes over during the week before Lent. Its costume parades, floats, parodies, and cabarets are now televised annually for international consumption. Another event is the Carinthian Summer Festival, held here and in various other places in the region in July and August.

An interesting general note about Carinthia: It is a multiethnic area, whose three nationalities, the Austrian (German), Slovene, and Italian, are gradually becoming proud of their common identity. Since the post–World War I days, when parts of Carinthia were almost given away to the new Yugoslav state, the spirit in the land has changed. The more Europe grows together, it seems, the more the sense of solidarity and regional identity is growing.

Pleasures and Pastimes

Dining

Thanks to the region's many lakes and rivers, this is fish country: carp, pike, perch, eel, bream, crawfish (when in season, which is rather short), and, best of all, a large variety of trout. Austrian brook trout and rainbow trout are delicious. The most popular way of serving them is "blue," the whole fish boiled in a court bouillon and accompanied by drawn butter. Or try it *Müllerin*—sautéed in butter to a crisp brown— wonderful! In summer try cold smoked trout with lemon or horseradish for a delicate hors d'oeuvre. Carinthia's basically peasant tradition, however, is also reflected in its culinary specialties, such as *Sterz* (cornmeal served either sweet or salty) and *Hauswürste* (smoked or air-cured hams and sausages, available at the butcher). Through much of Carinthia you'll discover that, other than simple *Gasthäuser,* pizzerias, and the ubiquitous Chinese restaurants, most dining spots are not independent establishments but belong to country inns. When a hotel dining operation is especially noteworthy, we flag it by including it under the heading of "Dining and Lodging." Prices for meals include taxes and a service charge but not the customary small additional tip of 5%–7%.

CATEGORY	COST*
$$$$	over AS500
$$$	AS300–AS500
$$	AS200–AS300
$	under AS200

*per person for a typical three-course meal, with a glass of house wine

Lodging

Accommodations range from luxurious lakeside resorts to small country inns or even guest houses without private baths. Room rates include taxes and service and almost always breakfast, except in the most expensive hotels, but it is wise to ask. When comparing prices, note that many hotels in the resort towns require half board (one meal in addition to breakfast). The larger hotels offer a choice of menu. When staying two or three days or longer, it is customary to leave a small additional tip (AS20) for the chambermaid.

CATEGORY	COST*
$$$$	over AS1,500
$$$	AS1,000–AS1,500
$$	AS700–AS1,000
$	under AS700

*per person for a standard double room with bath, including service and tax

Exploring Carinthia

You can get a taste of Carinthia in a weekend, or savor it all during a weeklong stay. For our shortest itinerary, we tackle the Austrian Riviera; for a longer stay, Villach makes a good base.

Great Itineraries

Numbers in the text correspond to numbers in the margin and on the Carinthia map.

IF YOU HAVE 3 DAYS

If your time is limited, head to the Austrian Riviera, balm to travelers who wish simply to sun and soak. Start off with a visit to the provincial capital **Klagenfurt** ① before heading out to the most popular lake, the Wörther See. You can make stops along the way at resorts such as **Krumpendorf** ② and **Pörtschach** ③, before spending the night and next day in 🏨 **Maria Wörth** ④, with its postcard-perfect spired chapel overlooking the lake. For the next night, head to chic 🏨 **Velden** ⑤. On your final day, take in the towns of Maria Gail, **Egg am Faaker See** ⑥, and **Viktring** ⑦, with its Cistercian monastery dating back to 1142.

IF YOU HAVE 5 DAYS

The best place to start your trip is to take a day to explore 🏨 **Spittal an der Drau** ⑧, the principal town in Upper Carinthia. After an overnight stay, head for the medieval walled town of **Gmünd** ⑨ and continue on to the resorts on the Millstätter See, with your next night spent at 🏨 **Millstatt** ⑩. The Roman baths at 🏨 **Bad Kleinkirchheim** ⑪ are a treat for tired muscles on your third day; spend your third night at one of the spa's friendly chalet-style hotels. On your fourth day pass the quiet resort town of Feld am See on the Feldsee before pulling into 🏨 **Villach** ⑫—one of Carinthia's most historic cities—for your last night and day.

IF YOU HAVE 7 DAYS

Start your visit in 🏨 **Villach** ⑫, nestled on the banks of the Drau River, wandering the meandering lanes of the Altstadt (Old Town). Spend the

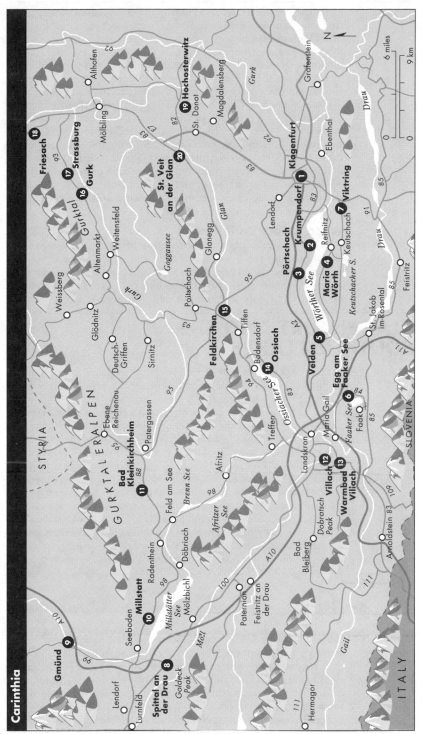

Carinthia

night in the city or head for the nearby spa of **Warmbad Villach** ⑬; the next day, relax with a massage or soak in the soothing hot springs, and then check out the imposing ruins of Landskron Castle. Spend your third day enjoying the resort town of ⌸ **Ossiach** ⑭ and its 11th-century monastery, where the soft sounds of music waft through summer nights during the annual music festival. Stay two nights there, for you'll want to get an early start on the day's full schedule of sightseeing attractions, including the medieval city of **Feldkirchen** ⑮; the massive Romanesque cathedral at **Gurk** ⑯; and a stop in **Strassburg** ⑰, formerly the seat of the bishopric. Pull into ⌸ **Friesach** ⑱, where it's easy to imagine lords and ladies descended from the Middle Ages living in this village, for your fifth evening. Spend your fifth night back in Friesach, a good base for touring. On the sixth day discover **St. Veit an der Glan** ⑳, Carinthia's capital until the 16th century; then move on to the amazing castle-fortress of **Hochosterwitz** ⑲. For your last evening and day, return to ⌸ **Klagenfurt** ①.

When to Tour Carinthia

If you wish to see the province in its best festive dress of blue and emerald lakes, framed by wooded hills and rocky peaks, and also do some swimming, you should come between mid-May and early October. Early spring, when the colors are purest and the crowds not yet in evidence, or fall, is perhaps the best time for quiet sightseeing.

KLAGENFURT AND THE SOUTHERN LAKES

Because of the resorts, the elegant people, the cultural events, and the emphasis on dawn-to-dawn indulgences, the region surrounding Carinthia's pleasure lakes has been nicknamed "Austria's Riviera." The most popular of the Funf Schwesterseen (Five Sister Lakes) is certainly the central lake, the Wörther See, sprinkled with such resorts as Krumpendorf, Velden, and Maria Wörth—once called the quietest village in all Austria and subsequently overrun by hordes of tourists. The Wörther See is 17 km (10½ mi) long and the warmest of Carinthia's large lakes; people swim here beginning in early May. A great way to see the lake is from one of the boats that run from end to end, making frequent stops along the way. Try to book passage on the S.S. *Thalia*, built in 1908 and now beautifully restored. You can follow the north shore to Velden by way of Pörtschach, bubbling with celebrities and excitement, or swing south and take the less traveled scenic route; in any case, you should visit picturesque Maria Wörth on the south shore.

Klagenfurt

❶ *329 km (192 mi) southwest of Vienna, 209 km (130 mi) southeast of Salzburg.*

Klagenfurt became the provincial capital in 1518, so most of what you see today dates from the 16th-century or later. And while Klagenfurt itself may not pulse with excitement, it's an excellent base for excursions to the rest of Carinthia. You can hardly overlook the *Lindwurm*, Klagenfurt's emblematic dragon with a curled tail, which adorns the fountain on Neuer Platz (New Square). The notion of Klagenfurt dragon became more intriguing when the fossilized cranium of a prehistoric rhinoceros was found nearby.Through the Kramergasse you reach the longish **Alter Platz,** the oldest square of the city and the center of a pleasant pedestrian area with tiny streets and alleys. South of the Neuer Platz (take Karfreitstrasse and turn left on Lidmansky-Gasse) is the **Domkirche** (cathedral) completed as a Protestant church in 1591, given over to the Jesuits and reconsecrated in 1604, and finally declared a cathedral in 1787. The 18th-century side-altar painting of St. Ignatius by Paul Troger, the great Viennese rococo painter and teacher, is a fine example of the transparence and light he introduced to painting.

One of the most notable sights of the city is the **Landhaus** (district government headquarters), with its towers and court with arcaded stairways. It was completed in 1591 and at the time formed a corner of the city wall. The only interior on view is a winner: The dramatic **Grosser Wappensaal** (Great Hall of Coats of Arms) contains 665 coats of arms of Carinthia's landed gentry and a stirring rendition of the Fürstenstein investiture ceremony portrayed by Fromiller, the most important Carinthian painter of the Baroque period. ⊠ *Alter Pl.,* ☎ *0463/ 577570.* ▣ *AS10.* ⊙ *Apr.–Sept., weekdays 9–noon and 12:30–5.*

From Klagenfurt, take the Villacher Strasse (Route 83) rather than the autobahn to the Wörther See, Austria's great summer-resort area. You'll pass by the **Minimundus** park, literally meaning "miniature world," with more than 175 models at a 1:25 scale of such structures as the White House, Independence Hall, the Eiffel Tower, and the Gur-Emir Mausoleum from Samarkand (Uzbekistan). ⊠ *Villacher Str. 241,* ☎ *0463/ 21194–0.* ▣ *Adults AS90.* ⊙ *Mid–late Apr. and early–mid–Oct., daily 9–5; May–June and Sept., daily 9–6; July–Aug., Sun.–Tues. and Thurs.–Fri. 8–7, Wed. and Sat. 8 AM–9 PM; folklore performance July– Aug., Wed. at 8; live big-band and jazz concerts Sat. at 8.*

OFF THE
BEATEN PATH **PYRAMIDENKOGEL** – On the banks of the Keutschacher lake, about 8 km (5 mi) west of Klagenfurt, lies the town of Keutschach, with the Romanesque church of St. George, a Baroque castle and an 800-year-old linden tree. A winding 5-km (3-mi) road ascends to the observation tower atop the 2,790-ft Pyramidenkogel; on a clear day you can see out over half of Carinthia.

Dining and Lodging

$$$$ ✗ **À la Carte.** This small and unpretentious restaurant in the center of ★ the city has catapulted almost overnight into Austria's top ranks. Co-owner and chef Harald Fritzer trained under several of Europe's best cooks. Ask for help in translating the handwritten menu, and don't overlook the superb fish. The six-course evening feast can be trimmed to your appetite. Wines come from Austria, France, and Italy. ⊠ *Khevenhüllerstr. 2,* ☎ *0463/516651. Jacket and tie. AE. Closed Sun.–Mon., holidays, Easter wk, and mid-July–mid-Aug.*

$$$$ ✗ **Präsent–Lido am See.** The gorgeous setting, with a view out over the Wörther See, is the backdrop for some of the area's best dining. Fish is the obvious choice, but don't overlook lamb chops, regional specialties, or such less predictable items as rabbit. Dishes are seasonal, depending on what's fresh in the market that day. The wine list features Austrian vintages but includes a good Bordeaux selection as well. ⊠ *Friedelstrand 1,* ☎ *0463/261723,* ℻ *0463/262453. AE, DC, MC, V. Closed Tues. Sept.–June.*

$$ ✗ **Peterwirt.** In Walddorf, about 6 km (4 mi) north of Klagenfurt on ★ Route 83, you'll find one of the better-kept restaurant secrets. This is country cooking at its best, with no pretensions. You won't need to ask for recommendations—there's no written menu; choose from such Austrian standards as roast chicken and beef roulade. ⊠ *Klagenfurt/Walddorf 1,* ☎ *0463/42646. No credit cards. Closed 2 wks in May and Nov.*

$$$ 🏨 **Musil.** This hotel is part of a chain, but modern amenities have been ★ tastefully incorporated into a 15th-century nobleman's palace in the center of town. The style is personal, intimate, and different in each room, ranging from Baroque to elegant Biedermeier and simple Austrian rural. Rooms open onto a series of interior balconies. The popular café serves cakes from the hotel's own bakery. The candlelit restaurant is good; try the game in season (September–October). You'll need to book a couple of months ahead. ⊠ *10-Oktober-Str. 14, A–9010,* ☎ *0463/511660,* FAX *0463/511660–4. 15 rooms. Restaurant, bar, café. AE, DC, MC, V.*

$$ ⊞ **Moser-Verdino.** Renovations have kept pace with the times at this
★ striking pink-and-white hostelry, the city's leading hotel for 100 years (owned by Bernhard Musil, who owns the Musil; ☞ *above*). The Art Deco design carries over into some of the rooms, no two of which are alike. The café is nearly always full and is a good spot for a snack. ⊠ *Domgasse 2, A–9010,* ☎ *0463/57878,* FAX *0463/516765. 74 rooms. Bar, café, sauna. AE, DC, MC, V.*

$$ ⊞ **Sandwirt.** This centrally located hotel, incorporated into a 17th-cen-
★ tury town house, has large rooms with high ceilings and traditional, comfortable furnishings. The family management is hospitable and friendly, and the food can be relied upon for being well prepared and tasty. The hotel is now part of the Best Western group. ⊠ *Pernhartgasse 9, A–9010,* ☎ *0463/56209,* FAX *0463/514322. 40 rooms. Restaurant. AE, DC, MC, V.*

$$ ⊞ **Schlosshotel Wörthersee.** At the end of the lake, on its own beach,
★ this glowing yellow mansion with fancy woodwork, towers, and balconies will remind you of the era of the grand hotels. The rooms are modern and comfortable; the preferred ones overlook the lake. The restaurant has been restyled along the lines of an informal *Heuriger* weinstube. ⊠ *Villacher Str. 338, A–9010,* ☎ *0463/21158–0,* FAX *0463/21158–8. 41 rooms. Restaurant, bar, café, sauna, beach, bicycles. AE, DC, MC, V.*

$ ✕ **Kirschnerhof.** This old restaurant, 11 km (7 mi) south of Klagen-
★ furt off Route 91, gives you the opportunity to plunge into genuine Carinthian culture and people and enjoy local specialties in a large and shady "guest garden." ⊠ *Kirschnerstr. 10, Maria Rain,* ☎ *04227/84922,* FAX *04227/84137. MC.*

Nightlife and the Arts

Opera and operetta are performed at the Stadttheater in Klagenfurt year-round, a pretty Art Nouveau building designed by the famous theater architects Helmer and Fellner of Vienna and completed in 1910. On the 1999 schedule are Mozart's *La Clemenza di Tito* and Imre Kálmán's *Csárdásfürstin.* For details and tickets, contact **Stadttheater Klagenfurt** (⊠ Theaterpl. 4, A–9020, ☎ 0463/55266). The box office is open September–June, Tuesday–Saturday 9–noon and 4–6, July and August, Tuesday–Saturday 9–noon and 5–7.

For a true after-hours scene in Klagenfurt, head for the Pfarrplatz-Herrengasse area, where you'll find a number of intimate bars and cafés. In the Old City, the Klagenfurt crowd gathers at any number of jaunty places, such as the **Tapferes Schneiderlein** on Herrengasse, but the **Scotch and Lemon** (⊠ Pfarrpl. 20, ☎ 0463/54097) remains the top dancing venue.

Outdoor Activities and Sports

BICYCLING

You can rent bicycles at the **Klagenfurt main station** (☎ 0463/5811359). Many visitors enjoy biking trips to the nearby Wörther See.

GOLF

Golfplatz Klagenfurt-Wörthersee at Schloss Seltenheim (☎ 0463/40223, FAX 0463/40223–20) recently expanded from 9 holes to a full 36-hole course. The greens fee is AS600, and the club is open March–October.

TENNIS
If you're in the mood to take to the courts, check out **Tenniscenter All-round** (⊠ Welzeneggerstr., ☎ 0463/31571) or **Tennisplätze M. Schoklitsch** (⊠ Feschnigstr. 209, ☎ 0463/41140).

Krumpendorf

❷ *10 km (6 mi) west of Klagenfurt.*

The first town on the north side of the Wörther See is less chic and far less pretentious than the other resorts, but pleasant all the same, particularly for those families seeking to escape the higher prices and singles invasions of other areas. The resort's water sports and down-home atmosphere appeal to families.

Lodging
$ ⊞ **Schloss Hallegg.** Just east of Krumpendorf, a small road heading
★ north leads to an early 13th-century castle, tucked away on the edge of a nature preserve above the lake. Now adapted as a hotel, it has rooms that are spacious and comfortable. You'll get breakfast only, but there is a choice of restaurants in town. There's a small lake for swimming and fishing, and ample grounds for hunting and riding. ⊠ *Hallegger Str. 131, A–9201, ☎ 0463/49311. 15 rooms. Lake, tennis court, horseback riding, fishing. No credit cards. Closed mid-Sept.–mid-May.*

Pörtschach

❸ *6 km (4 mi) west of Krumpendorf.*

Midway along the Wörther See is Pörtschach, one of the two top vacation spots on the lake. Here, the water is often warm enough for swimming as early as May, which is very early indeed for an Alpine region. You'll find dozens of places to stay and even more things to do under the stars: The nightlife here is as varied as the daytime activities. Elegant villas line the peninsula, which is often abloom with flowers and verdant foliage during the summer months. Chicly dressed visitors head for the lakeshore promenade to enjoy the view.

Dining and Lodging
$$$ ✕ **Rainer's.** Make your way through the bar to this "in" restaurant. The most favored tables are on the balcony overlooking the lake, although the two inside rooms have an intimacy of their own. Food choices are limited but good; try the grilled shrimp in herb sauce or the roast hare, or settle for a steak. ⊠ *Monte-Carlo-Pl. 1, ☎ 04272/2300,* FAX *0427/2300–17. AE, MC, V. Closed mid-Sept.–mid-May. No lunch.*
$$$ ✕⊞ **Schloss Leonstain.** This appealing 500-year-old castle, complete
★ with tower and antique furnishings, is unfortunately situated between the railroad and the highway (quiet is hard to find). The restaurant is among the best in town and is well worth a visit on its own. In summer, tables are set up in the courtyard as well as in the historic rooms. ⊠ *Hauptstr. 228, A–9210, ☎ 04272/2816–0,* FAX *04272/2823. 35 rooms. Restaurant, lake, sauna, golf course, tennis court, boating. AE, DC, MC, V. Closed early Oct.–early May.*
$$$–$$$$ ⊞ **Schloss Seefels.** About 3 km (2 mi) west of Pörtschach, this hotel attracts a prominent international clientele. The sprawling, interconnected buildings are set in a huge park on the lake, the staff is friendly, and the elegantly furnished rooms are in the grand-hotel mode. You can go by boat directly to Klagenfurt and to the Kärntner golf course across the lake. Half board is required. ⊠ *A–9210, Pörtschach/Töschling, ☎ 04272/2377,* FAX *04272/3704. 73 rooms. Restaurant, bar,*

indoor-outdoor pool, sauna, golf course, tennis court, exercise room, beach, boating, fishing. AE. Closed mid-Oct.–late Apr.

$$–$$$ ⊞ **Europa.** This modern hotel, uninspired on the outside, stands directly on the water. Ask for a room on the lake side and enjoy the sunniest corner of the lake. Half board is standard. The view is wonderful from the restaurant. ⊠ *Augustenstr. 24, A–9210,* ☎ *04272/2244–0,* FAX *04272/2298. 47 rooms. Restaurant, lake, golf course, tennis court, boating, bicycles. No credit cards. Closed Oct.–Apr.*

$$–$$$ ⊞ **Strandhotel Kärntnerhof.** This large, slightly rambling edifice is only a hotel, but the price is right, the rooms pleasant and light, and the beach right at your doorstep. It's an ideal place to set up a base to visit the rest of the region. ⊠ *Hauptstrasse 217, A–9210,* ☎ *04272/ 2347,* FAX *04272/2347–22. 25 rooms. Bar, beach. No credit cards. Closed early Oct.–Apr.*

Outdoor Activities and Sports

GOLF

You can improve your swing at the 18-hole, par-72 **Golfanlage Moosburg-Pörtschach** (☎ 04272/83486, FAX 04272/82055). The club is open April–early November. Greens fee is AS550 for adults.

HORSEBACK RIDING

Riding is a nice way to see some land. Contact the **Reitstall Knoll** in Wölfnitz (☎ 0463/49273); special offers including lodging.

WATER SPORTS

Pörtschach is a center of activity for windsurfing, parasurfing, and sailing. Check **Herbert Schweiger** (⊠ 10-Oktober-Str. 33, ☎ 04272/2655). Several hotels on the Wörther See offer sailing and surfing packages.

Maria Wörth

❹ *10 km (6 mi) west of Klagenfurt.*

The spire of Maria Wörth's parish church reflected in the waters of the Wörther See is one of Austria's most-photographed sights. This unpretentious little town is situated on a wooded peninsula jutting out toward the center of the lake, almost entirely surrounded by water. It actually has two notable churches, both dating from the 12th century. The smaller **Rosary church** in the town itself is basically Romanesque with later Gothic additions. The interior has a Romanesque choir with fragments of 12th-century frescoes of the apostles, a stained-glass Madonna window from 1420, and Gothic carved-wood figures. The larger **parish church,** despite its Romanesque portal, is mainly Gothic, with a Baroque interior, revealing all the "wrinkles" acquired since the days of its appearance in the 9th century. Skulls and bones can still be seen in the round Romanesque charnel house in the cemetery.

Lodging

$$$ ⊞ **Astoria.** This massive, comfortable villa on the lake is just 2 km (1 mi) from the 18-hole, par-71 Kärntner Golf Club course at Dellach; the hotel offers golf-holiday packages. The rooms are attractively furnished; those overlooking the lake are preferred. You'll have to take half board. ⊠ *A–9082,* ☎ *04273/2279,* FAX *04273/2279–80. 45 rooms. Restaurant, weinstübe, indoor pool, sauna, tennis court. No credit cards. Closed mid-Oct.–mid-May.*

$$$ ⊞ **Seewirt.** This large, sprawling hotel in Dellach right by the lake has all the amenities to make a stay on the southern shore of the Wörther See pleasant. The hotel's own farm produces some of the food you eat, and the fishing is also done "in-house." Golf players get a 30% discount on the greens fee at the golf course (☞ Outdoor Activities and Sports, *below*). ⊠ *Fischerweg 12, A–9082 Dellach,* ☎ *04273/2257,*

FAX *04273/28052. 19 rooms. Restaurant, sauna, 18-hole golf course, tennis court, exercise room, beach, boating, baby-sitting. No credit cards. Closed Oct.–May.*

Outdoor Activities and Sports

GOLF

Enjoy the scenic view while getting in your 18 holes at the **Kärntner Golf Club,** one of Austria's oldest golf clubs, at Dellach (☎ 04273/2515, FAX 04273/2606). The club is open April–October. Greens fees are AS600 on weekdays, AS700 on weekends.

Velden

❺ *8 km (5 mi) west of Maria Wörth.*

Velden, the most noted resort on the lake, is perched at the west end of the Wörther See. The atmosphere here strives to retain its international chic—classy and lively—and the summer carnival in August adds to the action. The fact that a casino has settled here says a lot about Velden, which has very little in the way of sights otherwise. The town's most famous beauty spot is the lakeside promenade, accented by turn-of-the-century lamps and mansions. However, if you're looking for a tranquil holiday, Velden may be too exuberant. The town gets pricey in the July–August main season.

Dining and Lodging

$$$$ ✕ **Casino-Restaurant.** If you're looking for fine cuisine plus a view, this place offers a wondrous vista over the lake. The cuisine ranges from international to regional and seasonal specialties. Keep an eye out for chanterelles in summer and venison at the end of September. The casino complex (☞ Nightlife, *below*) is limited to those 18 and over, and you'll need your passport for identification. ⊠ *Am Corso 17,* ☎ *04274/2948–57. Jacket and tie. AE, DC, MC, V.*

$$$–$$$$ ✕🏨 **Golf-Park-Hotel Velden.** This exclusive establishment, set in a park amid a stand of huge old trees, has been luxuriously renovated to offer every comfort, attracting tennis stars and Saudi royals. From the spacious lobby to the modern guest rooms, you'll find elegance and attentive service. The gourmet restaurant is particularly noted and, for this region, is distinctively cordon bleu in style and quality. ⊠ *Seecorso 68, A–9220,* ☎ *04274/2298–0,* FAX *04274/2298–9. 89 rooms. 2 restaurants, bar, indoor pool, beauty salon, sauna, spa, 3 tennis courts, exercise room. AE, DC, MC, V. Closed mid-Oct.–mid-Apr.*

$$–$$$ ✕🏨 **Hubertushof.** Two typical resort houses from the turn of the century comprise this family-run complex directly on the lake. A touch of the original Art Deco carries over into some of the rooms, most of which have balconies. The best rooms face the lake. The Hubertusstuberl is gaining a reputation for its way with regional specialties, such as lamb. ⊠ *Europapl. 1, A–9220,* ☎ *04274/2676–0,* FAX *04274/ 2657–60. 46 rooms. Restaurant, indoor pool, sauna, exercise room, boating. DC, MC, V. Closed mid-Oct.–mid-Apr.*

Nightlife

The **casino** in the center of Velden is a focal point of the evening, but you must be 18 or over. Along with the gambling tables and slot machines, the complex contains a disco, bars, and a restaurant (☞ Dining and Lodging, *above*), whose terrace overlooks the lake. You'll need your passport to enter the casino. ⊠ *Am Corso 17,* ☎ *04274/ 2064,* FAX *04274/2982. Jacket and tie.* ❂ *Daily 3 PM–3 or 4 AM.*

Outdoor Activities and Sports
WATER SPORTS
Velden is another good site for windsurfing, parasurfing, and sailing. Rentals are available at **Segel-und-Surfschule Wörthersee/Berger** (⊠ Seecorso 40, ☎ 04274/2691–0 or 04274/2956–0).

OFF THE BEATEN PATH	**MARIA GAIL** – The Romanesque parish church here has an unusually good 14th-century Gothic winged triptych altar. To get to Maria Gail, 15 km (9 mi) west of Velden, take the Villacher Strasse, Route 83, out of Velden. If you're heading on to Faaker See, you'll pass, several miles beyond Maria Gail, one of the most famous roadside shrines in Austria: framed by lake and mountain, this *Manterl* is a great photo op.

Egg am Faaker See

⑥ *4 km (2½ mi) east of Maria Gail.*

With turquoise-green waters that seem almost Mediterranean, the Faaker See presents an idyllic setting for swimming and boating. Boating aficionados take to the lake in droves with a rainbow array of sails skimming across the horizon (motorboats are not allowed); even so, the round lake—with its tiny island in the middle—remains less crowded than other resort areas here. Watching over all is the mighty pyramid of the Mittagskogel of the Karawanken range.

Dining and Lodging

$$$$ ✕▥ **Karnerhof.** A huge chalet with a long, low extension is set in a
★ quiet park right on the lake, with the mountain range serving as a scenic backdrop. This affiliate of the Silencehotel group offers attractive rustic rooms and the excellent Götzelstube restaurant. All dishes are freshly prepared, and the fish is particularly fine. ⊠ *Egger-Seeprome-nade 4/Karnerhofweg 10, A–9580,* ☎ *04254/2188,* ℻ *04254/3650. 105 rooms. Restaurant, café, indoor-outdoor pool, sauna, tennis court, exercise room, beach. AE, DC, V. Closed mid-Oct.–Mar.*

$$–$$$ ✕▥ **Sonnblick.** This family-run modern hotel is not especially attractive, but it has pleasant sun-drenched balconies, windows festooned with bright red geraniums, and a gemütlich atmosphere. Guests are greeted with a "welcome" cocktail and evening barbecues on the terrace overlooking the mountains. The hotel justifiably prides itself on its extensive wine cellar, featuring regional and European vintages. ⊠ *Dreimühlenweg 23, A–9580,* ☎ *04254/21670,* ℻ *04254/216715. 32 rooms. Restaurant. AE, DC, MC, V.*

Outdoor Activities and Sports
GOLF
Take in a game of golf at the 18-hole, par-72 **Golfanlagen Velden-Kösten-berg** (☎ 04274/7045, ℻ 04274/708715). The club is open April–early November.

Viktring

⑦ *17 km (10½ mi) east of Egg am Faaker See, 6½ km (4 mi) southwest of Klagenfurt.*

From the west and the Faaker See, you can get to Viktring by following the Rosental Valley on Route 85 until you come to the junction with Route 91 and then turn north toward Klagenfurt. Alternatively, take the narrow country road along the Pyramidenkogel (☞ Klagenfurt, *above*); it begins in Lind and goes by Keutschach and its pretty little lake. From Viktring it's 6½ km (4 mi) back to Klagenfurt.

You can still see parts of the moat remaining from the **Cistercian convent,** established here in 1142. Don't miss the convent's arcaded cloisters, and look for the 14th- to 16th-century stained glass in the choir of the church, behind the Baroque high altar. Every summer the old walls are the setting for music learning and performance, modern to jazz, at **Musikforum Viktring** (⊠ Stift-Viktring-Strasse 25, A–9073 Klagenfurt, ☎ 0463/28–22–41, FAX 0463/28–16–26).

THE DRAU VALLEY

The Drau Valley is a Carinthia for all reasons—there's a little here of the best of everything you can find in the province. One of the most impressive Renaissance castles in the country can be found in Spittal an der Drau, which comes alive with a series of theatrical events and concerts during the summer months. Take a ride on the wild side with a visit to the Porsche Museum, which documents the history of the innovative carmaker. Or you can soothe tired muscles at a Roman bath before relaxing away from the crowds at the quiet lakeside resort on the Feldsee. We begin, however, at the main town in Upper Carinthia, Spittal an der Drau.

Spittal an der Drau

❽ *31 km (20 mi) northwest of Villach.*

The name Spittal, meaning "hospital" or "station," goes back to the Middle Ages—this little town was an important stop on north–south route across the Alps. The ancient building was then used as a basis for the impressive Gothic church (on your left as you enter the town, autobahn exit Spittal-Ost), which was completed in 1311. But the name Spittal an der Drau is synonymous with the architecturally superb **Schloss Porcia,** built in the 16th century by the imperial treasurer Count Gabriel von Salamanca. This castle-palace, in the center of town next to a lovely park, is one of the most beautiful Renaissance buildings in Austria, especially in its gracefully arcaded Italianate courtyard stairways and open corridors, which provide a dreamlike setting for summer performances of classical plays, often Shakespeare. The upper floors house a museum highlighting regional culture of the past. Otherwise, besides the cozy inner town and its central square, Spittal is unremarkable. By the way, north–south traffic still goes by on the A10 autobahn. ☎ 04762/2890. ⊡ AS50. ☉ Mid-May–Oct., daily 9–6; Nov.–mid-May, weekdays 1–4.

☾ The **Goldeckbahn,** the aerial tramway that leaves from behind the tennis hall on Ortenburgerstrasse (☎ 04762/2864–0), will take you up to the 6,960-ft peak of the Goldeck mountain, from which you get splendid panoramic views to the north and east.

Dining and Lodging

$–$$ ✕⊡ **Langasthof Tell.** In the village of Paternion, halfway between Villach and Spittal, stands a nicely renovated 700-year-old country inn with a real familial feeling and excellent Carinthian cooking—homemade sausages, liverwurst, and all sorts of so-called *Pfandlgerichte* (dishes fried in a pan). The traditional interior courtyard is very pretty. ⊠ *Marktplatz 14, A–9711 Paternion,* ☎ 04245/2931, FAX 04245/3026. *16 rooms. Restaurant, fishing, bicycles. MC. Closed in late fall for 2 wks.*

$$ ⊡ **Alte Post.** This traditional, friendly house in the center of town has comfortable modern rooms, a good restaurant, and the bonus of fishing rights on a reserved stretch of the Drau River. ⊠ *Hauptpl. 13, A–9800,* ☎ 04762/2217–0, FAX 04762/5125–57. *42 rooms. Restaurant, bar. AE, DC, MC, V. Closed Jan.*

$ ☎ **Ertl.** This salmon-fronted, family-run hotel in a beautiful 19th-century building is just steps from the railroad station but away from heavy traffic. It even has a garden of sorts. If you're touring by train it's ideal; the rooms are large and attractively decorated. ⊠ *Bahnhofstr. 26, A– 9800,* ☎ *04762/2048–0,* ℻ *04762/2048–5. 40 rooms. Restaurant, pool, bicycles. AE, DC, MC, V. Closed Nov.*

Nightlife and the Arts

In Spittal an der Drau, from mid-July through August, the **Kmödien-spielen,** three or four plays focusing on human foibles and virtues, are presented with a minimum of pomp in the marvelous setting of Schloss Porcia. The experience is always great fun. Spittal is also the setting for an international **choir festival,** usually held in mid-July. Program information and ticket details for both events are from the same source (☎ 04762/3420 or 04762/3161 after July 1, ℻ 04762/3237).

Outdoor Activities and Sports

GOLF

An 18-hole course, a driving range, a pro shop, a nice restaurant, wonderful views of the lake and the mountains—one couldn't one ask for more at **Golfclub Millstätter See.** ⊠ *Millstatt,* ☎ *04762/82548,* ℻ *04762/82548–10.* ☜ *Greens fees are AS550 in the high season, AS450 in the off-season.*

HIKING

There's unusually good hiking starting from Spittal, and even better from Gmünd, Seeboden, Millstatt, Bad Kleinkirchheim, Feld am See, and Afritz. Local visitor information offices will have suggestions for routes and for combining a hike with a return by local bus.

Gmünd

❾ *19 km (12 mi) north of Spittal an der Drau via Rte. 99 (Gmündner Strasse).*

Not far from where the Malta mountain stream rushes into the Lieser is the colorful town of Gmünd. The warm pastels of the town's building facades on the oval-shape central square stand in contrast to the dark green of the surrounding forested hills. This little 16th-century town with medieval walls has been carefully restored. The "new" **castle** (1651) is watched over by the old castle, in ruin above the town. See the **parish church** and the ancient fresco on the outside wall, which shows the town as it was in the 17th century, little different from the way it looks today, except that the old castle is complete. The **town museum** can be found in the lower gate tower.

The automobile designer Ferry Porsche was born and worked in Gmünd; an informative and fascinating **Porsche Museum** shows a series of the cars and experimental models he designed and built. The museum is located directly northwest of the old walled town. ☎ 04732/2471. ☜ *AS65.* ☉ *Mid-May–mid-Oct., daily 9–6; mid-Oct.– mid-May, daily 10–4.*

Dining and Lodging

$$ ✕ **Alte Burg.** You might not expect to find a gemütlich setting within the ruins of a 13th-century castle, but you'll discover this attractive restaurant, set amid renovated dungeons and battlements, decorated with Carinthian wrought iron and antiques. On the menu, look for regional specialties such as roast lamb and Carinthian cheese noodles (a local form of ravioli with cream-cheese filling). This food comes with a view, as the castle picturesquely overlooks the town. ⊠ *Alte Burg,*

☎ 04732/3639. *AE, DC, MC, V. Closed Wed.–Thurs. Sept.–June, and mid-Jan.–wk before Easter.*

$ 🏨 **Kohlmayr.** Behind the pinkish facade of this family-run hotel on the town square you'll find a particularly friendly staff and modern, attractive rooms in rustic decor. Up the stone steps is a large reception room furnished with country antiques (including a spinning wheel). The rooms in front have a stunning view over the square. The whole town gathers in the *Bierstube* in the late afternoon and on Sunday morning. The restaurant offers good standard Austrian country fare. ⊠ *Hauptpl. 7, A–9853,* ☎ *04732/2149,* FAX *04732/2153. 22 rooms. Restaurant, weinstube. No credit cards. Closed Nov.*

Outdoor Activities and Sports
HIKING

In summer you can head up the scenic Malta Valley to see the massive hydroelectric dam and lake and hike at the top.

Millstatt

⑩ *5 km (3 mi) southeast of Gmünd.*

The largest resort on the Millstätter See is crowned by an impressive **Benedictine abbey** and adorned with imposing towers, antique courtyards, and centuries-old linden trees. The abbey was founded in the 11th century but secularized in the 18th. The twin-towered Romanesque church of the abbey complex was partially rebuilt in Gothic style and later given some Baroque ornamentation, but its 12th-century Romanesque portal remains its outstanding feature. Note also the *Kreuzgang*, the arcaded cloister between the church and the monastery, with its complicated pillar ornaments.

There is an old legend that St. Domitian cast 1,000 heathen statues in the lake around the turn of the 8th century. The statues along the waterfront promenade here are the beginning of an extensive artistic initiative called "1,000 statues," aimed at foiling old Domitian posthumously.

Dining and Lodging

$$$ ✕🏨 **Alpenrose.** This attractive house, with rustic-style rooms, advertises itself as Austria's first "bio-hotel." It is constructed entirely of natural materials (primarily wood and brick) and uses no plastic. The excellent restaurant continues the theme, featuring only natural ingredients (many of the vegetables are organically grown in the side garden). Half board is required. In winter there's free transport to nearby ski areas. ⊠ *Obermillstatt 84, A–9872,* ☎ *04766/2500–0,* FAX *04766/ 3425. 34 rooms. Restaurant, pool, sauna. No credit cards. Closed late Nov.–mid-Dec.*

$$–$$$ ✕🏨 **See-Villa.** This beautiful old villa in burnt yellow with a splendid garden was once a private mansion belonging to the Counts Tacoli. Count Anton Tacoli still is the master of the house; his guests are many and all are satisfied. The selection for vegetarians is picked from the villa's own vegetable garden, as are the herbs; fish are from the lake. ⊠ *Seestrasse 68, A–9872,* ☎ *04766/2102,* FAX *04766/2221. 18 rooms. Restaurant, beach, surfing. MC. Closed Oct. 16–Apr. 30.*

$$ ✕🏨 **Die Forelle.** This four-story balconied house sprawls along the lake, its tree-shaded terrace directly over the water. The public rooms are elegant but comfortable, the guest rooms bright and welcoming. The hotel has its own stretch of fishing water. Fish is featured at the ambitious and successful restaurant. ⊠ *Fischergasse 65, A–9872,* ☎ *04766/ 2050–0,* FAX *04766/2050–11. 68 rooms. Restaurant, pool, sauna, tennis court, boating, fishing. No credit cards. Closed Nov.–Apr.*

Nightlife and the Arts

In Millstatt there's something going on throughout much of the year: Musical Spring runs mid-May–June; International Music Weeks take over during July and August, followed by Musical Autumn in September. Most events take place in the Benedictine abbey. For program details and ticket reservations, contact the secretariat, Musikwochen Millstatt (⊠ Stiftgasse 1, A–9872, ☎ 04766/2165, FAX 04766/3479).

Outdoor Activities and Sports

BICYCLING

The Millstätter See is a naturally beautiful area to cycle, with well-tended and -marked paths going all around the lake and over to other places, such as up the Malta Valley from Gmünd (☞ *above*) or over to Seeboden. For information contact the tourist office in Millstatt (☞ Carinthia A to Z, *below*). Bicycles can be rented at the Spittal train station, among other places (☎ 04762/3976–390).

Bad Kleinkirchheim

⓫ *6 km (4 mi) north of Radenthein via Rte. 88.*

Barely known 30 years ago, the town of Bad Kleinkirchheim has become a booming and stylish resort thanks to its terrific combination of sports, activities, and the spa, which attracts people seeking a variety of cures. Although it's popular in summer, the town is unquestionably Carinthia's top ski resort, and Austrians flock to the slopes here in winter for great cross-country skiing, snowboarding, and skating. After a day on the slopes you can plunge into the (re-created) **Roman baths,** fed by thermal mineral springs. Nearby, the **Katharinenkapelle** (St. Catherine's Chapel) marks the location of one of the springs. It has an organ loft with carved-wood reliefs and a late-Gothic winged altar. Stop at **St. Oswald,** north of town, to look at the unusual iron hinges on the doors of the late-Gothic church, and step inside to admire and to see its frescoes of 1514 and the groined vaulting on the ceiling.

Lodging

$$$–$$$$ ⌕ **Pulverer.** This friendly hotel, in a group of interconnected chalet-style buildings, is not only in the center of town but is one of the centers of activity. You can take a cure with the medicinal thermal waters, then undo the good work at the enticing buffets: breakfast, salad, strudel, and hors d'oeuvres. The guest rooms are done in elegant country-rustic decor. ⊠ *Bach 1, A–9546,* ☎ *04240/744 or 04240/550,* FAX *04240/793. 40 rooms, 50 apartment-suites. Restaurant, indoor-outdoor pool, sauna, spa, golf privileges, exercise room. No credit cards. Closed mid- to late Apr. and Nov.–mid-Dec.*

$$$–$$$$ ⌕ **Ronacher.** You can easily spoil yourself at this family-managed combination sports-and-cure facility, with its in-house thermal baths and luxurious balconied rooms in modern-rustic decor. The large hotel is off the main road in the middle of town. It organizes many activities for those who dislike the chores of planning. Half board is required. ⊠ *Bach 18, A–9546,* ☎ *04240/282,* FAX *04240/282–606. 92 rooms. Restaurant, indoor-outdoor pools, sauna, spa, exercise room. AE, DC, V. Closed Apr. and late Oct.–mid-Dec.*

$$ ⌕ **Putz-Römerbad.** This family-run chalet-style hotel, tucked away behind fir trees, is a bit east of the center. A thermal-mineral spring bath is just down the hall, and sports facilities are a short walk away. Public rooms are spacious, balconied guest rooms slightly less so; the warmth of the rustic decor creates a comfortable atmosphere. Rooms on the south side have a view of the mountains. Half board is required. ⊠ *Zirkitzen 69, A–9546,* ☎ *04240/8234–0,* FAX *04240/8234–57. 32 rooms. Restaurant, sauna, spa, exercise room. AE, DC. Closed Nov.*

Outdoor Activities and Sports

GOLF

Golfclub Bad Kleinkirchheim (☎ 04275/594 or 04240/8282–16, FAX 04275/504 or 04240/8282–18) is challenging for beginners and advanced golfers alike, thanks to a fine 18-hole, par-72 course. The greens fee is AS400–AS600, depending on the season, and the club is open May–October.

SKIING

Made famous by local ski legend Franz Klammer, the ski resort at **Kleinkirchheim** has more than 100 km (60 mi) of prepared trails. Less famous and glamorous than the resorts in neighboring Tirol, the region caters to parents and their children. The combination spa is the clincher as far as pure rest and relaxation go. The Römerbad spa, for example, has an outdoor pool open in winter, which is a delightful feeling after a long day on the slopes. Local hotels and tourist offices can provide information on lesson and lift packages (in some cases use of the two spas, Römer and St. Kathrein, is included). For information, contact the tourist office (☞ Carinthia A to Z, *below*).

THE GURKTAL REGION

Storybook names, such as Tannhaüser, Snow White, and the Holy Hemma, are encountered throughout the Gurktal region of Carinthia. The region is populated with medieval strongholds, idyllic lakes, and towns that remain charming down to the last cobblestone.

Villach

⑫ *50 km (30 mi) west of Klagenfurt.*

Carinthia's "other" capital (Klagenfurt is the official one) sits astride the Drau River. The Romans may have been the first to bridge the river here for their settlement of Bilachium, from which the present name Villach is derived. The city is compact, with narrow, twisting lanes (restricted to pedestrians) winding through the Old City south of the river. Small, attractive shops are tucked into arcaded buildings, and each corner brings a fresh and surprising perspective. Renaissance houses surround the main square, which has a Baroque column in honor of the Trinity. The 16th-century alchemist and physician Theophrastus Bombastus Hohenheim, better known as Paracelsus, the inventor of homeopathic medicine, lived at Hauptplatz 14; his father was the town physician.

The late-Gothic 14th-century **parish church of St. Jacob** was Protestant during the mid-1500s, making it Austria's first Protestant church. Its marble pulpit dates to 1555; the ornate Baroque high altar contrasts grandly with the Gothic crucifix. If the stair entry is open and you don't mind the rather steep climb, the view from the 310-ft tower is marvelous. Near the river, at the intersection of Ossiacher Zeile and Peraustrasse, the pinkish **Heiligenkreuz parish church,** with two towers and cupola, is a splendid example of fully integrated Baroque. A good time to visit Villach is around August 1, when the townspeople and those from surrounding villages don their traditional clothes and celebrate *Kirtag* with music, folk dancing, and general merrymaking.

In the summer, a particularly lovely way to explore the Drau river from Villach is to take a cruise on the **MS Landskron;** watching the sun set over the mountains while you dine onboard makes for a memorable evening. For schedule and details, check with the tourist office or Drau-Schiffahrt (✉ Neubaugasse 32, ☎ 04242/58071, FAX 04242/58072).

OFF THE
BEATEN PATH

LANDSKRON – An interesting stopping point is this ruined castle, which has spectacular views over Villach, the Ossiach lake, and the Karawanken mountain range to the south. The original castle here dated from 1351 and was destroyed by fire in 1861; since then, sections have been rebuilt. It is also a keep for birds of prey, which are trained for shows. To get here, take Route 83 about 4 km (2½ mi) northeast of Villach.

Dining and Lodging

$$$–$$$$
★

✕ **Bleibergerhof.** North of Villach via Route 86 and then 13 km (8 mi) from Untere Fellach via a scenic road (there's also bus service), Bad Bleiberg is the site of one of Austria's dozen top restaurants. You'll dine in elegant but unpretentious splendor on superb international and Carinthian seasonal specialties. The service is impeccable; ask for advice on wines. The family-run Bleibergerhof also has excellent spa facilities. ⊠ *Drei Lärchen 150, Bad Bleiberger,* ☎ *04244/2205,* 🖷 *04244/2205–70. No credit cards. Closed Nov.–mid-Dec. No dinner Sun.–Tues., no lunch Mon.–Wed.*

$$

✕🎝 **Hotel Mosser.** You won't be able to miss the Hotel Mosser, with its orange and green candy-striped columns and peach exterior in the center of town. The welcome by the staff is equally cheery and exuberant. The furnishings are a bit nondescript, but the rooms are large and comfortable; ask for one facing the courtyard to avoid the noise from the street below. The hotel's restaurant serves classic Austrian fare, from schnitzel to wurst. ⊠ *Bahnhofstr. 9, A–9500,* ☎ *04242/24115,* 🖷 *04242/ 24115–222. 29 rooms. Restaurant, massage. AE, DC, MC, V.*

$$
★

✕🎝 **Post.** This beautifully adapted Renaissance palace, which dates from 1500, is in the pedestrian zone in the heart of the old city. Architects have cleverly created an elegant, modern hotel while preserving Old World features of the building such as the arcaded inner court. Service is personal and friendly. The restaurant serves light Austrian nouvelle cuisine and such traditional Carinthian specialties as cheese noodles. The Post is a member of the Romantik Hotel group. ⊠ *Hauptpl. 26, A–9500,* ☎ *04242/26101–0,* 🖷 *04242/26101–420. 77 rooms. Restaurant, bar, sauna, exercise room. AE, DC, MC, V.*

$

🎝 **Europa.** You'll be across the river from the Old City but just two minutes from the main rail station in this attractive yellow-and-white hostelry. The rooms are done with reproduction 19th-century furnishings; those on the inner side are quieter. The house is associated with the Best Western group. ⊠ *Bahnhofstr. 10, A–9500,* ☎ *04242/ 26766,* 🖷 *04242/26766–50. 44 rooms. Café, bar, sauna, exercise room, parking. AE, DC, MC, V.*

Outdoor Activities and Sports

HIKING

Southwest of Villach, the extremely scenic 16-km (10-mi) Villach Alpine highway climbs the mountain ridge to about 5,000 ft. From there, a lift gets you up to Hohenrain; then you can hike the marked trail— or take the train—up to the peak of the **Dobratsch mountain,** towering 7,040 ft into the clouds and providing a spectacular view. Close to parking lot 6, at 4,875 ft, is an Alpine botanical garden, which is open mid-June–August, daily 9–6. The 11 parking and outlook points along the highway offer great panoramas.

TENNIS

In the Villach area, try **Tennisplätze ASKÖ** (⊠ Landskron, Süduferstr., ☎ 04242/41879) or **Tenniscamp Warmbad** (⊠ Villach–Warmbad Villach, ☎ 04242/32564).

Warmbad Villach

⑬ *3 km (2 mi) southwest of Villach.*

On the southern outskirts of Villach lies Warmbad Villach, its name reflecting the hot springs of radioactive water, which is believed to combat aging, among other things. This remains one of the classic spas of Carinthia—one discovered by the Romans already!—and people also come to enjoy its thermal springs and swimming pools for various rheumatic ailments. Many hotels have been built around the *Kurpark,* the wooded grounds of the spa.

Dining and Lodging

$$$ ✕⊞ **Warmbaderhof.** With a tranquil park setting and a comfortable
★ meandering house seducing you into relaxation, the cure's the thing here. Ask for one of the modern, balconied rooms overlooking "Napoléon's meadow." The Bürgerstube restaurant offers regional and national specialties, including game in season. The Das Kleines Restaurant, with its wood and brass decor, changes its offerings with the seasons. ⊠ *Kadischenallee 22–24, A–9504,* ☎ *04242/3001–0,* ☏ *04242/3001–80. 123 rooms. 2 restaurants, bar, indoor-outdoor pool, sauna, exercise room, horseback riding. MC.*

$$–$$$ ⊞ **Josephinenhof.** Modern without being impersonal, this hotel is set in the comfortable isolation of the Kurpark. A unique program is devoted to age-control. The hotel will book only full-week packages in the main season. The restaurant is unexciting, but ample other possibilities are close by. ⊠ *Kadischenallee 8, A–9504,* ☎ *04242/3003–0,* ☏ *04242/3003–89. 61 rooms. Restaurant, indoor-outdoor pool, sauna, spa, tennis court. AE, DC, MC, V. Closed late Nov.–mid-Dec.*

$$–$$$ ⊞ **Karawankenhof.** The larger rooms in this hotel will appeal to those who want to take the cure or use this as a base for further excursions in Carinthia. Children are particularly welcome. An underground passageway leads to the spa, with its water slide and pools. The glassed-in terrace restaurant is a delight, but the kitchen, alas, does not quite live up to the decor. ⊠ *Kadischenallee 25–27, A–9504,* ☎ *04242/3002–0,* ☏ *04242/3002–61. 80 rooms, 9 apartments. Restaurant, bar, indoor-outdoor pool, sauna, exercise room. AE, DC, V.*

Ossiach

⑭ *19 km (12 mi) northeast of Warmbad Villach via Rte. 83.*

The resort town of Ossiach is now the center of the Carinthian Summer Festival (☞ Nightlife and the Arts, *below*) and is afflicted with wall-to-wall tourists during the high season. The festival, which since its launch in 1969 has expanded to include use of the Congress Center in Villach, covers all styles of music from Baroque to modern, from Gershwin to klezmer. There are other attractions, including what was originally an 11th-century **monastery,** a typical square building around an inner court, with a chapel at the side. The chapel, despite its stern, conservative exterior, is wonderfully Baroque. The monastery was razed by the Turks in 1484 and promptly rebuilt, though Baroque renovations have left it with its current look. Legend has it that in the 11th century the Polish king Boleslaw II lived incognito in the monastery for eight years, pretending to be mute, in penance for murdering the bishop of Kraków. A tombstone and a fresco on the church wall facing the cemetery commemorate the story.

Dining and Lodging

$ ✕ **Forellenstation Niederbichler.** This unpretentious, small, dark-stained wood cabin serves some of the freshest fish you're likely to find in Austria. Caught right in the nearby pond, the trout—*blau,* grilled or breaded and fried—makes a memorable meal at a bargain price. Linger outdoors under the brightly colored umbrellas sipping a *Gespritzter* (wine with soda water). ⊠ *Alt Ossiach 76,* ☎ *04243/8225. No credit cards.*

$$$ 🏨 **Stiftshotel Ossiach.** This first-class hotel was once a monastery (dating from the 1620s). Try for one of the high-ceilinged rooms in front overlooking the lake. The rooms (particularly the front corner suites) are spacious, with reproduction period furnishings. The hotel has its own private pier and beach, and the lake boat docks in front. ⊠ *A–9570,* ☎ *04243/8664–0,* 🖷 *0222/408–4976. 50 suites. Restaurant, beach, dock. AE, DC, MC, V. Sometimes closed Oct.–Apr.*

$ 🏨 **Seewirt Köllich.** This large rustic house in a quiet corner directly on the lake next to the monastery church offers simple but comfortable rooms with views over the lake (preferred) or of the lush green hills. The hotel has its own lakeside beach and paddle boats and is adjacent to the waterskiing school. The restaurant offers standard fare such as roast pork and goulash. ⊠ *A–9570,* ☎ *04243/2268. 15 rooms. Restaurant, beach, boating. No credit cards. Closed Nov.–mid-May.*

Nightlife and the Arts

Even though Ossiach is a small town (with a population of less than a thousand), it hosts an internationally renowned music event, the **Carinthian Summer Festival,** which has attracted many notable musicians, including Leonard Bernstein, the Collegium Musicum Pragense, and soloists from the London Symphony Orchestra. It is held in July and August and emphasizes 20th-century composition; along with Benjamin Britten's *Prodigal Son* opera, however, you might also hear some Mozart and Vivaldi, plus a little jazz and pop. Chamber concerts are all the more attractive for their setting in the Baroque chapel or the monastery in Ossiach. For a schedule or tickets, contact Carinthischer Sommer, through late May (⊠ Gumpendorfer Str. 76, A–1060 Vienna, ☎ 01/596–8198, 🖷 01/597–1236) or after early June (⊠ Stift Ossiach, A–9570 Ossiach, ☎ 04243/2510, 🖷 04243/2353).

In resort centers like Ossiach, you'll find regular evenings of folk music and dancing, some of them organized by the hotels. The local tourist offices will have details, and notices are often posted around the area.

Outdoor Activities and Sports

BICYCLING

The area around the Ossiacher See is excellent for cycling, and many of the main roads have parallel cycling paths. Rental bicycles are in great demand throughout this area, so reserve in advance. You can rent a bicycle at the **Ossiach-Bodensdorf railroad station** (☎ 04243/2218), where there's also a dock; you can put the bike on the boat, get off and cycle to the next boat landing, and return by boat when you run out of energy.

Feldkirchen

🄯 *6 km (4 mi) northeast of Ossiach.*

Feldkirchen is a modest little town that hides well the fact that it is one of Carinthia's oldest communities, having been officially mentioned in a document dating to 888. Some relics of the ancient medieval wall that once surrounded Feldkirchen remain in indistinct form; otherwise the town has a pleasant provincial Baroque look, with pastel facades and a shady central square with a fountain dribbling in the middle and a few cafés and Italian ice-cream parlors occupying space on the sidewalks. The relief of the Virgin Mary over the old pharmacy (*Apotheke*) is the only eye-catcher here. At the north end of town (Kirchgasse), look at the parish church in early Romanesque style, with a Gothic choir and Baroque decor. In addition, the town features some Biedermeier-style houses. Though small, Feldkirchen is an important crossroad: One road (Route 93) goes to Gurk, another (Route 94) heads to St. Veit an der Glan, and yet another (Route 95) traverses the remote Nock mountains up to the Turracher Höhe, a high pass between Carinthia and Styria with a dangerous 23° gradient, a mountain summer resort, and fine skiing center, on a pretty lake.

En Route Traveling north along Route 93 out of Feldkirchen are myriad small roads leading to colorful villages. **Goggau** has a small but charming lake; **Sirnitz** (☎ 04279/303, 04279/7145 atelier, FAX 04279/3034) has an interesting little castle called Schloss Albeck, with a fine restaurant, Sunday-morning concerts (at 11), and an atelier selling clothing made of hand-spun linen. At **Deutsch-Griffen,** with a picturesque defense church accessed by a long covered staircase, an easy hike up the Meisenberg takes you through Carinthia's first bird sanctuary, an initiative by Gottfried Topf, a retired German businessman who moved to the village permanently in 1990. In **Glödnitz** a road leads up to Flattnitz, a solitary but very beautiful spot with a little skiing and a few isolated houses. **Altenmarkt** has another defense church, this one having officially held off the Turks at one time (admittedly it was not the Pasha's main army but rather a marauding gang). **Weitensfeld** was the setting for one of Carinthia's most charming stories. In the 16th century, the plague decimated the population of this tiny town, southwest of Gurk. Only three young men and a noblewoman who lived in nearby Thurnhof castle survived. A race was proposed to determine which of them should win her in marriage, and although history failed to record the outcome, the tradition of the race continues every Pentecost weekend. The winner now kisses the noblewoman's statue plus any other attractive female within reach, and the celebration goes on. Thurnhof Castle is up on the left after you leave Weitensfeld.

Gurk

⑯ *34 km (21 mi) northeast of Feldkirchen.*

Gurk's claim to fame is its massive Romanesque **Dom** (cathedral) surmounted by two onion cupolas and considered the most famous religious landmark in Carinthia. It was founded in the 11th century by Hemma, Countess of Zeltschach, who, after losing her two sons and husband, decided to turn to religious works. She had two oxen tied before a cart and let them walk until they stopped. At that point she founded a cloister and gave all her belongings to the Church for building a cathedral. She did not live to see Gurk become a bishopric (in 1072). Construction on the cathedral itself began in 1140 and ended in 1200. Hemma wasn't canonized until 1938. Her tomb is in the crypt, whose ceiling and hence the cathedral itself, is supported by 100 marble pillars. The "Hemma-Stein," a small green-slate chair from which she personally supervised construction, is also there and alleged to bring fertility to barren women. In the church itself, the high altar is one of the most important examples of early Baroque in Austria. Note the *Pietà* by George Rafael Donner, who is sometimes called the Austrian Michelangelo. The 900-square-ft Lenten altar cloth of 1458 shows 99 scenes from the Old and New Testaments—a beautiful example of a *Biblia Pauperum,* a "poor man's Bible," to teach the Scriptures to those who could not read. It is displayed from Ash Wednesday to Good Friday. The bishop's chapel includes rare late-Romanesque frescoes, among the oldest in Europe. The guidebook in English is helpful. At the end of August a concert series is held in the cathedral. Despite the schedule, tours are restricted by church services or insufficient participation; tours at 1 and 3:45 are limited to 15 people and include the bishop's chapel. ☎ 04266/8520, ℻ 04266/8520–4. ☜ *Donation requested, tour AS35.* ☉ *Daily 9–6; tour Ash Wednesday–Oct., daily at 11 and 2:30; May–mid-Oct., Mon.–Sat. at 9:30, 1:30, and 4:15, Sun. at 9:30, 10:30, 1:30 and 4:15.*

Ⓒ The **Zwergenpark** is a vast natural setting filled with amusing garden statuary, the typically Austrian-German garden gnomes; children can traverse the park via a miniature railway. ☎ 04266/8077. ☜ *AS60, train AS40.* ☉ *May–June and Sept.–mid-Oct., daily 10–6; July–Aug., daily 9–6.*

Strassburg

⓱ *3 km (2 mi) northeast of Gurk.*

The seat of the Gurk bishopric until 1787, the episcopal palace, overlooking the Strassburg hamlet and now restored, houses small museums covering the history of the valley and of the diocese. The Gothic parish church, one of the most beautiful in Carinthia, has stained-glass windows dating from 1340. Also of note is the Heilig-Geist-Spital Church, constructed in the 13th century.

Outside Strassburg, at the intersection of Route 93 and Route 83/E7, you'll see the 18th-century **Pöckstein Castle,** belonging to the Carinthian bishops. In the distance off to the left you'll notice a castle on a hilltop, which you can see close-up by turning left at Mölbling on a road marked "Treibach/Althofen." The castle is actually in Ober Markt, an unusually picturesque town with 15th-century decorated houses.

Ⓒ Across the highway from the Pöckstein Castle is the northern terminal of a small narrow-gauge railway, the **Gurktaler Museumbahn.** The train meanders for 30 minutes under steam power down to Treibach on weekends and holidays, from mid-June to mid-September. For an additional contribution, you can ride in the locomotive alongside the engineer. ☎ 04262/4783, 04242/317530, or 04229/3528. ☜ *Round-trip AS60.* ☉ *Departures Sat. at 1, 2:30, and 4; Sun. at 10:30, 1, 2:30, and 4.*

En Route At Zwischenwässern and Hirt, Route 93 joins Route 83 coming from Klagenfurt. Heading north (toward Friesach), you'll come to **Brauerei Hirt** (☎ 04268/2524), a brewery since 1270. You might have a draft beer under the huge tree in the garden in the shade of a Renaissance arcade or in one of the paneled rooms. The food is good, standard Austrian and inexpensive.

Friesach

⓲ *16 km (9 mi) northeast of Strassburg via Rte. 83/E7.*

One of the oldest settlements of Carinthia, romantic Friesach is great for wandering. You'll immediately find the **Hauptplatz** (main square), with its old town hall and picturesque 19th-century facades, and as you stroll you'll discover parts of the medieval-era town: the double wall and the towers, gates, and water-filled moat. Among the medieval tournaments of gallantry that took place here, 600 knights participated in the famous one of May 1224; the Styrian minnesinger Ulrich von Liechtenstein, who appeared dressed and equipped all in green, alone broke 53 lances on his opposing adversaries. Look into the churches. The 12th-century **Romanesque parish church** on Wiener Strasse has some excellent stained glass in the choir. The 13th-century **Dominican church** north of the moat was the first of its order in Austria and contains a wonderful early Gothic choir. If you believe that Tannhäuser was a creation of Wagner's imagination, you will be surprised to learn that the descendants of his family were Salzburg administrators in Friesach; a **Tannhäuser Chapel** was erected in 1509 in this church, with a red marble tomb of Deputy Dean Balthasar Tannhäuser added after his death, in 1516. From a footpath at the upper end of the main square, take a steep 20-minute climb up to the impressive remains of **Schloss Petersberg** to see 12th- and 13th-century frescoes and a museum with beautiful late-Gothic art.

Lodging

$$ ✕🖿 **Metnitztalerhof.** This delightful hotel has overlooked Friesach's me-
★ dieval town square for more than 400 years. Rooms are furnished with country charm: rich, dark wood pieces to the floral fabrics covering chairs, curtains, and beds. Make sure to ask for a room overlooking the imposing castle ruins. The hotel also hosts gatherings for guests, from wine tastings to medieval feasts. ✉ *Hauptpl. 11, A–9360,* ☎ *04268/25100,* ℻ *0468/2510–54. 27 rooms. Restaurant. MC.*

$ ✕🖿 **Friesacherhof.** This comfortable hotel is incorporated into a cen-
★ turies-old building on the main square. The rooms in front look out over the square and the Renaissance fountain and can be somewhat noisy. ✉ *Hauptpl. 4, A–9360,* ☎ *04268/2123–0,* ℻ *04268/2123–15. 20 rooms. Restaurant, café. AE, DC, MC, V. Closed mid- to late Jan.*

Nightlife and the Arts

From late June to mid-August, there's open-air theater at the outdoor stage of the Dominican Monastery, performed in German, at Friesach. Check with the local tourist office (☞ Carinthia A to Z, *below*) for details and tickets.

Outdoor Activities and Sports

HIKING

Trails crisscross the hills and mountains near Friesach. Local visitor information offices will have suggestions for routes and for combining a hike with a return by local bus.

SKIING

Friesach is developing as a ski area, particularly for cross-country enthusiasts. The local tourist office (☞ Carinthia A to Z, *below*) can offer you information on trails, maps, and ski rentals.

Hochosterwitz

🄆 *31 km (19 mi) south of Friesach.*

The dramatic 13th-century **Hochosterwitz Castle,** looking out of a fairy tale, crowns the steep, isolated mountain on which it is built. You can hardly ignore the Disneyland effect, and in fact, this was the inspiration for Walt Disney's *Snow White* castle. Disney and his staff stayed here for many weeks studying it, and you will find Walt's fantasy to be fact. It was first mentioned in 860, and after a tumultuous few centuries, ended up in the possession of the Counts of Khevenhüller (1571), where it has remained ever since. It was in this castle that the besieged "Pocket-Mouthed Meg"—Margarethe Maultasch, the original of Feuchtwanger's *Ugly Duchess*—slaughtered the last ox of the starving garrison and dropped it onto the heads of the attacking Tyrolese. The stratagem succeeded and, dispirited by such apparent proof of abundant supplies, the Tyrolese raised the siege. The most recent fortifications were added in the late 1500s against the invading Turks; each of the 14 towered gates is a small fortress unto itself. Inside there's an impressive collection of armor and weaponry plus a café-restaurant in the inner courtyard. There's an elevator (which can accommodate wheelchairs), which costs AS40 from a point near the parking-lot ticket office. The hike up the rather steep path to the Hochosterwitz, of course, adds to the drama. It's easy to envision yourself as some sort of transplanted knight trying to vanquish the fortress. Your reward at the summit are spectacular vistas from every vantage point. Get to the castle on the back road from Treibach or via Route 83/E7. ✉ *Laundsdorf-Hochosterwitz,* ☎ *04213/2010 or 04213/2020,* ℻ *04213/202016.* ⌨ *AS40.* ⊙ *Easter–June and Sept.–Oct., daily 9– 5; July–Aug., daily 8–6.*

St. Veit an der Glan

⑳ *10 km (6 mi) west of Hochosterwitz via Rte. 82.*

Formerly the capital of Carinthia until 1518, this old ducal city remains largely unchanged, with the town hall's Baroque facade and ancient patrician houses forming the main square. Be sure to walk into the arcaded Renaissance courtyard of the **town hall,** overflowing with flowers in summer; the main state rooms can be seen on guided tours. The 12th-century Romanesque **parish church** was later given Gothic overtones; note the attractive entry. The **ducal palace** at the north end of town now houses a small medieval collection; the building itself has a marvelous arcaded stairway in the courtyard.

Dining and Lodging

$$$ ✕ **Pukelsheim.** Despite its enlargement, this restaurant remains
★ crowded—which testifies to its good reputation. You'll find regional specialties such as the ravioli-like *Nudeln* as well as variations on Austrian themes, such as veal tongue with vegetables or stuffed roast chicken. The chef's recommendations are invariably good. Pukelsheim is best known for its desserts: superb cakes and pies made with fruit in season. ✉ *Erlgasse 11,* ☎ *04212/2473. AE, MC, V. Closed Mon., 1 wk in Feb., and 1st wk in Sept. No dinner Sun.*

$$$ ☷ **Weisses Lamm.** Originally built in 1412, the Weisses Lamm retains the romantic atmosphere of the bygone era when St. Veit an der Glan was the home of the Carinthian aristocracy. Full modern amenities have been provided, while the ancient charm of the sturdy rooms, furnished with rustic antiques, has been preserved. The delightful arcaded courtyard is just the spot to while away a lazy afternoon. The small dining room serves regional favorites with a strong selection of Austrian vintages on the wine list. ✉ *Unterer Pl. 4-5, A–9300,* ☎ *04212/2362,* ℻ *04212/2362–62. 27 rooms. Restaurant, parking. AE, DC, MC, V.*

CARINTHIA A TO Z

Arriving and Departing

By Car

The most direct route from Vienna is via the Semmering mountain pass through Styria, entering Carinthia on Route 83 just above Friesach and going on to Klagenfurt. From Salzburg, the A10 autobahn tunnels beneath the Tauern range and the Katschberghöhe (the tunnels cost AS70 each!) to make a dramatic entry into Carinthia, although the parallel Route 99, which runs "over the top," is the scenic route. A pretty alternative here that leads you straight into the Nock mountains or Gurk Valley is to leave the A10 at St. Michael after the Tauern tunnel, head toward Tamsweg, and then take Route 97 through the Mur Valley: At Predlitz the pass road begins its climb over the steep Turracherhöhe into the Nock mountains. The fork-off to Flattnitz, the most scenic way into the Gurk Valley, is at Stadl. Several mountain roads cross over from Italy, but the most traveled is Route 83 from Tarvisio.

By Plane

Carinthia is served—mainly by Austrian Airlines and its subsidiary Tyrolean Airways—through the **Klagenfurt–Wörther See airport** (☎ 0463/41500–0), just northeast of Klagenfurt. Several flights daily connect the provincial capital and Vienna. In summer, service is also available from Zürich, Rome, and Frankfurt.

By Train

The main rail line south from Vienna parallels Route 83, entering Carinthia north of Friesach and continuing on to Klagenfurt and Villach. From Salzburg, a line runs south, tunneling under the Tauern mountains and then tracing the Möll and Drau River valleys to Villach. A line from Italy comes into the Drau Valley from Lienz in East Tirol. The main line north from Udine in Italy runs through Tarvisio and up to Villach; other rail lines tie Slovenia with Klagenfurt.

Getting Around

By Bus

As in all of Austria, the post office or railroad (*Bundesbahn*) buses go virtually everywhere, but you'll have to allow plenty of time and coordinate schedules carefully so as not to get stranded in some remote location.

By Car

Highways in Carinthia are good, although you can hit some stretches as steep as the 23-degree gradient on the Turracher pass road (Route 95), for example. Hauling trailers is not recommended (or is forbidden). The north–south passes are kept open in winter as far as possible, but the tunnels under the Tauern and Katschberg mountains ensure that Route A10 is now passable all year.

By Train

Much of Carinthia's attractive central basin is bypassed by the rail routes. Though you can get into and through Carinthia fairly easily by train, to see the inner province you'll need to rely on a car or the network of buses.

Contacts and Resources

Bicycling

Rental bicycles are in great demand throughout this area, so reserve in advance. The area around the Ossiacher See is excellent for cycling, as are the larger resort towns around the Wörther See along the Austrian Riviera: Rent bikes at **Faak am See** (☎ 04254/2149), **Klagenfurt main station** (☎ 0463/5811–399), or **Velden** (☎ 04274/2115–39). The area around the Millstätter See is about the only area good for cycling north of Villach. You can rent bicycles at the **Spittal-Millstätter See railroad station** (☎ 04762/3976–390). **Central bike reservations** for Carinthia is at ☎ 04242/3109.

Discounts

The **Kärnten Card** costs AS365, lasts for any three consecutive weeks between May 9 and October 4, and allows you free access to 80 museums and other sites of interest. Inquire at the tourist office or call the Carinthia Hotline (☎ 0463/3000).

Fishing

The Ossiacher See, Wörther See, and Faaker See all have excellent fishing. You'll need a license, issued by the tourist office. Some lakeside hotels offer fishing packages and allow you to fish in reserved waters. The booklet *Kärnten Fischen* from Kärntner Tourismus gives details (in German) about fishing waters, season, possible catch, bait, and local license-issuing authorities. Check also with your hotel or boat-rental shops (*Bootsverleih*); some can issue licenses.

Hiking

Local visitor information offices will have suggestions for routes and for combining a hike with a return by local bus. You may want to investigate *Hütten,* the refuges up in the mountains, where you can spend delightful nights, either in your own room or in a common room. Kärntner Tourismus has information on the huts.

Horseback Riding

Carinthia offers superb riding terrain, from mountains to woodlands, on more than 550 km (340 mi) of riding paths. In nearly 50 towns you'll find stables; an hour's outing will cost you about AS150; day rates are negotiable. A number of hotels offer riding package holidays. The brochure *Reiten* (in German), from Kärntner Tourismus, has details. Or contact **Reit Eldorado Kärnten** (⊠ Gerlitzenstr. 11 A−9551, Bodensdorf, ☎ 04243/2322, ℻ 04243/2322−20).

Tennis

Most of the large towns have public courts, but you'll have to wait if you don't book in advance. Many hotels around the southern lakes have their own courts, some of them indoors. In Feld am See, the **Hotel Alte Post** specializes in tennis packages.

Visitor Information

The official tourist office for the province is **Kärntner Tourismus** in Velden (⊠ Casinopl. 1, A−9220, ☎ 04274/52100−0, 0463/3000 24-hr hot line, ℻ 04274/52100−50).

The following are the leading regional *Fremdenverkehrsamt* (tourist offices): **Bad Kleinkirchheim** (⊠ A−9546, ☎ 04240/8212, ℻ 04240/8537). **Friesach** (⊠ Hauptplatz 1, A−9360, ☎ 04268/4300). **Gmünd** (⊠ Hauptpl. 20, A−9853, ☎ 040732/2222, ℻ 04732/3978). **Klagenfurt** (⊠ Rathaus, A−9010, ☎ 0463/537223, ℻ 0463/537295). **Maria Wörth/Reifnitz** (⊠ Verkehrsamt, A−9081, ☎ 04273/2240−0, ℻ 04273/3703). **Millstatt** (⊠ Kurverwaltung, Marktpl. 8, A−9872, ☎ 04766/3700, ℻ 04766/37008). **Ossiach Lake area** (⊠ A−9520 Sattendorf, ☎ 04248/2336−0, ℻ 04248/2336−5; ⊠ A−9570 Ossiach, ☎ 04243/497 or 04243/2246, ℻ 04243/363). **Pörtschach** (⊠ Hauptstr. 153, A−9210, ☎ 04272/2354, ℻ 04272/3770). **Spittal an der Drau** (⊠ Burgpl. 1, A−9800, ☎ 04762/3420, ℻ 04762/3237). **Velden** (⊠ Kurverwaltung, Seekorso 2, A−9220, ☎ 04274/2103, ℻ 04274/51078; ⊠ Villacher Str. 14, ☎ 04274/3919). **Villach** (⊠ Europapl. 2, A−9500, ☎ 04242/24444−0, ℻ 04242/24444−17).

9 Eastern Alps

It's easy to feel on top of the world if you take the Grossglockner High Alpine Highway—the most thrilling pass over the Alps. Nestled in a nearby valley is Heiligenblut, a town commemorated in a thousand postcards. Everywhere, breathtaking Alpine vistas and centuries-old castles polka-dot the landscape. For many travelers the Eastern Alps, concentrated around the Grossglockner peak, represent not only the most fascinating part of Austria's mountainous landscape but its most unspoiled as well.

By George W.
Hamilton

Updated by
Marton Radkai

EILIGENBLUT, AS THE MOST PHOTOGRAPHED village in the country, is the icon of the Eastern Alpine region. With the majestic Grossglockner—Austria's highest mountain—for a backdrop, it cradles the pilgrimage church of St. Vincent. Though every Austrian hamlet seems to have a church, nowhere else does a steeple seem to find such affirmation amid a setting of soaring peaks.

While this little town is a visual treat, the whole Eastern Alps region is dramatic countryside, with breathtaking scenery and great winter sports equal to those in Switzerland. Here, majestic peaks, many well over 9,750 ft, are home to slow-moving glaciers that give way to sweeping Alpine meadows, ablaze with wildflowers in spring and summer. Long, broad valleys (many names have the suffix -au, meaning "meadow") are basins of rivers that cross the region between mountain ranges, sometimes meandering, sometimes plunging. The land is full of ice caves and salt mines, deep gorges, and hot springs. Today, most tourism is concentrated in relatively few towns, but wherever you go, you'll find good lodging, solid local food, and friendly folk; it is countryside to drive and hike and ski through, where people live simply, close to the land.

Western Carinthia and East Tirol are dotted with quaint villages that boast charming churches, lovely mountain scenery, and access to plenty of outdoor action—from hiking and fishing in summer to skiing in winter. Across the southern tier, a series of scenic routes pass from Carinthia to that political anomaly, Osttirol (East Tirol). In 1918, after World War I, South Tirol was ceded to Italy, completely cutting East Tirol off from the rest of Tirol and the administrative capital in Innsbruck. The mountains along the Italian border and those of the Hohe Tauern, to the north, also isolate East Tirol, which has consequently been neglected by tourists.

Pleasures and Pastimes

Dining

While this region contains fine restaurants—in fact, two of the country's top dozen dining establishments are here—most of the dining you'll do in the small towns of the Eastern Alps will take place in a *Gasthöfe/Gasthaüser* (country hotels/inns), where the dining rooms are not necessarily separate restaurants. Note that, in many cases, such inns are open only in the peak season. In resort areas, you may be required to take half board (that is, breakfast and one other meal). Prices for meals include taxes and a service charge but not the customary small additional tip.

CATEGORY	COST*
$$$$	over AS500
$$$	AS300–AS500
$$	AS200–AS300
$	under AS200

*per person for a three-course meal, including a glass of house wine

Lodging

When you think of Alpine hotels, you probably think of chalet-style inns with flower-decked balconies and overhanging eaves. Not surprisingly, that's mainly what you find in the Eastern Alps, though the range runs from family-run country inns to professionally managed resorts. Interiors are generally done in a rustic, country decor that's very homey. This part of Austria is relatively inexpensive, except for the top resort towns of Saalbach, Badgastein, and Zell am See. Even there, however, cheaper accommodations are available outside the center of town or in pensions. Prices out of season may be as low as half those of the high season. Room rates include taxes and service and almost always breakfast, except in the most expensive hotels, but it is wise to ask. Half board is required in some lodgings. It is customary to leave a small additional tip (AS20) for the chambermaid.

CATEGORY	TOP RESORTS*	OTHER TOWNS*
$$$$	over AS2,200	over AS1,500
$$$	AS1,500–AS2,200	AS1,000–AS1,500
$$	AS900–AS1,500	AS700–AS1,000
$	under AS900	under AS700

for a standard double room with bath in high season

Exploring the Eastern Alps

Austria's Eastern Alps straddle four different provinces: Carinthia, East Tirol, Salzburg, and Styria. Imposing mountain ranges ripple through the region, isolating quaint Alpine villages whose picture-postcard perfection has remained unspoiled through the centuries. The mountainous terrain makes some backtracking necessary if you're interested in visiting the entire area, but driving through the spectacular scenery is part of the appeal of touring the region.

Great Itineraries

Numbers in the text correspond to numbers in the margin and on the Eastern Alps map.

IF YOU HAVE 3 DAYS

Start in the charming villages of **Hermagor** ① and **Kötschach** ②, stopping off at the Geo-Trail, which traces 50 million years of geological history. Then spend the afternoon exploring the East Tirolean capital of ⛰ **Lienz** ③. Castle ruins, picturesque churches, and more spectacular landscapes are in store on your second day as you visit **St. Jakob in Defereggen** ④ and **Matrei in Osttirol** ⑤ before returning to Lienz. On your final day, crown your trip with a visit to that Alpine jewel **Heiligenblut** ⑦, making stops at **Döllach** ⑥ and elsewhere along the imposing Grossglockner highway.

IF YOU HAVE 5 DAYS

Begin your trip in East Tirol's capital, **Lienz** ③, before heading to picture-perfect ⛰ **Heiligenblut** ⑦. As long as it's not wintertime, your second day can be spent taking the scenic Grossglockner High Alpine Highway through the Hohe Tauern National Park to the lake resort of ⛰ **Zell am See** ⑨. On day three, make a day trip to the mountain resorts of **Saalbach** ⑩ and **Saalfelden** ⑪, and descend into the depths with a tour of the **Lamprechtshöhle** (caves). On your fourth day, travel to ⛰ **Badgastein** ⑫ and take the cure. Then use your last day to visit the cathedral in **St. Johann im Pongau** ⑭ and the **Liechtensteinklamm** ⑬, the deepest, most dramatic gorge in the Eastern Alps.

IF YOU HAVE 7 DAYS

With a week at your disposal, you can see even more of the charming Alpine towns that dot the awesome landscape. Explore **Lienz** ③ and the lovely town of ⛰ **Heiligenblut** ⑦ on your first day. Then take on the twists and turns of the Grossglockner highway before lingering by the lake at the resort town of ⛰ **Zell am See** ⑨. On your third day, see the spectacular **Liechtensteinklamm** ⑬ gorge, and then overnight in ⛰ **St. Johann im Pongau** ⑭. Villages seemingly unchanged by the years are on the agenda for the fourth day, with visits to the charming town

of **Altenmarkt** ⑮, the medieval haven of **Radstadt** ⑯, and the former silver-mining town of ⬚ **Schladming** ⑰. A cable car will whisk you to the top of the Hunerkogel the next day during a stop at **Ramsau am Dachstein** ⑱, and then it's on to the resort town of ⬚ **Filzmoos** ⑲. On your sixth day, make an excursion to the dramatic underworld of the **Eisriesenwelt** ice caves near ⬚ **Werfen** ㉑, winding up your journey with a trip to the magnificent medieval castle, where birds of prey still swoop over the imposing fortress, and a final evening culinary blow-out at Obauer, one of the finest restaurants in Austria.

When to Tour the Eastern Alps

Depending on your interests, the Eastern Alps make a good destination at various times of year. Snowy conditions can make driving a white-knuckle experience, but winter also brings extensive, superb skiing throughout the region—often at a fraction of the cost of the more famous resorts in Tirol. In summer, the craggy mountain peaks provide a challenge to hikers, while cavers head into the bowels of the behemoths. Placid lakes and meandering mountain streams attract anglers for some of the best fishing to be found in the country.

TO LIENZ, UP THE DEFEREGGENTAL, AND BACK

Take Route 86 south out of Villach, through Warmbad Villach, and then Route 83 to Arnoldstein, about 10 km (6 mi) away. You're in the Gail River valley here, with the magnificent Karawanken mountains rising in Yugoslavia on your left. Just beyond Arnoldstein, turn right onto Route 111, marked for Hermagor. On the way up, the views now will be on the right, the dramatic Gailtal Alps in the background as you head west.

Hermagor

❶ *46 km (29 mi) west of Villach.*

This town is best known as a summer resort, offering hiking, climbing, and swimming in the nearby Pressegger Lake, but it also has skiing in winter. During the Middle Ages, villagers believed that the decorated keystones in Hermagor's late-Gothic **parish church** symbolized Jesus Christ's efforts to hold the framework of the church together. Dating from 1484, the church is also notable for its intricately carved and painted winged altar in the south Wolkenstein chapel.

Did the creation of the world take place in this area? Geologists from all over the world are fascinated by the possible answers that are believed to lie within the nearby Gartnerkofel mountain south of Hermagor off Route 90. Amateur sleuths can join in the experience by

★ following the **Geo-Trail,** along which you can gather fossils and trace 50 million years of geological history. Maps are available from the local tourist office. Botanists are equally intrigued by the blue *Wulfenia,* which blankets the Nassfeld mountain area farther along Route 90 on the Italian border each June. The flower, which is protected under Austrian law, can be found only here and in the Himalayas.

En Route From Hermagor, both Route 87, running northwest to Greifenburg, and Route 111 up to Kötschach offer gorgeous views, and the distances to Lienz on both are about 55 km (35 mi). If you choose Route 87, you can turn right shortly before Greifenburg for a detour to the blue-green **Weissensee,** a virtually undeveloped narrow lake 11 km (7 mi) long, tucked in between high mountain ridges, where there's excellent fishing and boating. Then, at Greifenburg, turn west onto Route 100 up the Drau River valley toward Lienz.

Kötschach

② *25 km (16 mi) west of Hermagor.*

Most visitors travel to this town and Mauthen, its twin across Route 111, to enjoy the natural beauty the area has to offer and to pay a call on the Kellerwand, one of Austria's top restaurants. The year-round resort is a good base for excursions via the Plöcken pass over the border into Italy or up the picturesque Lesach Valley through the Austrian (Lienzer) Dolomites. The early frescoes and unusual decorated arched ceiling that adorn Kötschach's **parish church,** which dates from 1527, make it worth a stop, too.

Dining and Lodging

$$$–$$$$ ✕🏠 **Kellerwand.** Elegant tables in a quiet, luxurious atmosphere high-
★ light the superb quality of the food, an uncommonly imaginative treatment of area specialties, including outstanding delicate pasta dishes and roast lamb or venison. (Frau Sonnleitner was named cook of the year in 1990.) The unpretentious residence includes a small hotel, where rooms and luxury suites are attractively decorated in a country style with tile floors. ⊠ *Mauthen 24, A–9640 Mauthen,* ☎ *04715/269–0 or 04715/378–0,* 🇫🇦🇽 *04715/378–16. 12 rooms, 8 suites. Restaurant, bar, sauna. AE, DC, MC, V. Closed 1 wk in mid-Apr., and mid-Nov.– mid-Dec.*

$$$ ✕🏠 **Naturabenteuer Hotel Post.** This interesting house of eccentric design, with odd balconies and a triangular garden, is in the center of town. Excursions, climbing, rafting, and fishing are offered, and rooms are attractively decorated. ⊠ *Hauptpl. 66 A–9640 Kötschach-Mauthen,* ☎ *04715/221,* 🇫🇦🇽 *04715/222–53. 24 rooms. Restaurant, bar, café, pool, sauna, exercise room, fishing. No credit cards. Closed end of Oct.–mid-Apr.*

En Route The scenic Route 110 north over the Gailberg will bring you, after about 14 km (9 mi) and some dramatic twists and turns, to Route 100 at Oberdrauburg. From here to Lienz (20 km/12 mi) the highway follows the Drau River valley, with splendid views up into the Kreuzeck mountain range on your right. The Romans recognized the strategic importance of the region and about AD 50 established **Aguntum** here to protect the important trade route against possible usurpers. About 4 km (2½ mi) before you reach Lienz, you'll come to the excavations to the right of the road. You can explore the site, where archaeologists have been unearthing remains of this ancient civilization, quite freely.

Lienz

③ *55 km (34 mi) northwest of Kötschach–Mauthen.*

Tucked in at the confluence of the Drau and Isel rivers, with the Dolomites a dramatic backdrop to the south, Lienz, a summer and winter resort, is now the capital of the region. The awe-inspiring peaks rising around the town might make your first impression one of human insignificance in the face of overwhelming power and glory. Such feelings of reverence may account for the number of notable churches in Lienz; at least five are worth a visit, particularly the parish church of **St. Andrä,** on Patriadorfer Strasse, which you can reach by walking up Muchar Gasse and Schweizergasse or by following the Rechter Iselweg along the river. A Romanesque lion decorates the doorway, giving witness to the church's early roots. The present-day Gothic edifice was completed in 1457, while the interior is Baroque, from the winged high altar to the vividly colored ceiling fresco (1761). Note the ornate marble tombstones of the noble Görz family.

Three blocks away from St. Andrä—cross the Pfarrbrücke into Beda Weber-Gasse and turn left into Patriadorferstrasse—you'll find the **war memorial chapel,** designed in 1926 by Clemens Holzmeister, the architect responsible for Salzburg's Festspielhaus and Felsenreitschule (the festival theaters). The wall paintings are by Albin Egger-Lienz (1868–1926), who is renowned for his ability to portray human strength and weakness and who is also buried here. Close to the center of town, the **Franciscan church** on the Muchargasse was originally a Carmelite cloister, founded in 1349 by the Countess Euphemia of Görz. The church was taken over by the Franciscans in 1785 and restored in 1947–48. A Gothic *pietà* from about 1400 adorns the left side altar at the back; its wall frescoes are from the 15th century.

A wooden statue dedicated to St. Wolfgang can be found on the Schweizergasse in the 1243 **Dominican church,** which was subsequently rebuilt in late-Gothic style. **St. Michael's** on Michaeler Platz on the north side of the Isel was completed in 1530, but the north tower, with its onion dome, dates only to 1713. Note the fancy ceiling ornamentation, the 1683 high altar, and the gravestones. The rococo **St. Joseph's,** by the Spitalsbrücke, was badly damaged in 1945 and rebuilt in 1957. **St. Antonius** on the Hauptplatz dates to the 16th century. The recently restored 16th-century **Lieburg palace** on the Hauptplatz, with two towers, now houses provincial government offices.

A massive tower looms over the **Schloss Bruck,** a battlemented residential castle that dates to 1280 and now serves as the city museum. The remarkably well preserved castle also has a Romanesque chapel with a late-15th-century ceiling and wall frescoes. Works by Egger-Lienz and Franz Defregger (1835–1921), another Tirolean painter, are displayed here, along with Celtic and Roman relics from nearby excavations. ⊠ *Iseltaler Str.,* ☎ *04852/62580.* ⊡ *AS45.* ☉ *Palm Sunday–mid-June and mid-Sept.–Oct., Tues.–Sun. 10–5; mid-June–mid-Sept., daily 10–6.*

Dining and Lodging

$$$$ ✕⊞ **Traube.** In summer, the striped awnings of this central hotel (part
★ of the Romantik Hotel group) shade the cafés on the street and balcony. The atmosphere is elegant, thanks to a mix of older furniture and antiques, and rooms are spacious and comfortable. The historic hotel has its own fishing waters and a rooftop swimming pool with wonderful views of the surrounding mountains. The restaurant's food is not quite up to the setting, but take the recommendations and you won't be unhappy; the cellar disco offers evening entertainment. ⊠ *Hauptpl. 14, A–9900,* ☎ *04852/64444,* ℻ *04852/64184. 51 rooms. 2 restaurants, bar, café, indoor pool, sauna, fishing, dance club. AE, DC, MC, V.*

$$$ ✕⊞ **Parkhotel Tristachersee.** A little more than 4 km (2½ mi) south-
★ east of Lienz (take the road via Amlach marked to Tristacher See) is a small lake hidden away up a hill. It's a magical setting for this diminutive, totally renovated country hotel, whose rooms sport dark paneled walls and lots of fabrics. A lakeside terrace provides opportunity for relaxation, and an excellent restaurant features regional cuisine, including fresh fish from the hotel's own ponds. ⊠ *Tristachersee 1, A–9900,* ☎ *04852/67666,* ℻ *04852/67699. 40 rooms, 8 suites. Restaurant, bar, indoor pool, lake, sauna. No credit cards. Closed Nov.–mid-Dec. and last 2 wks in Apr.*

$ ✕⊞ **Gasthof "Goldener Stern."** If you are watching your budget but would like to stay in historic surroundings, then this is the place to go: the "Golden Star" was built around 1400. The interiors are done in simple peasant style, nothing fancy, everything cozy. Some of the rooms in the new annex have balconies. There's no restaurant, but coffee and homemade cake in the afternoon will make you feel right at home. ⊠ *Schweizerg. 40, A–9900,* ☏ FAX *04852/62192. 20 rooms. No credit cards.*

Outdoor Activities and Sports

HIKING

Lienz and its surrounding area have miles of marked trails, and detailed maps are available from the tourist office that show mountain lodges where you can spend the night and other facilities. Trails in Tirol are designated as easy, moderate, or difficult. Just before Schloss Bruck (☞ *above*), you'll find a chairlift that rises nearly to the crest of the 6,685-ft **Hochstein** mountain, from which you get a splendid panoramic view over Lienz and to the east. You'll have to hike the last kilometer (½ mi) to reach the very top.

If you want to learn to climb, contact Leo Baumgartner at the **Alpinschule Lienz** (⊠ Gaimberg, A–9900, ☏ 04852/68770).

WHITE-WATER RAFTING

Stretches of the **Isel River** from Matrei down to Lienz are raftable from May to mid-October. The Drau, which always has enough water, is used for easy rides or beginners. If you are a hard-core rafter, you'll enjoy the Schwarzach in the Defereggental, known as "Ostirol's toughest river." For outfitters, check with a tourist office, or contact the **Osttiroler Kajak Club** in Lienz (☏ 04852/67777 or 048542/65811). Several companies offer tours at prices beginning around AS500 per person and a minimum of five people. Try Dieter Messner at the **Raftingzentrum Ainet** (⊠ House 41, A–9951 Ainet, ☏ 04853/5231) or Reinhard Fischl at the **Aqua Alpin Rafting** (⊠ House 108, A–9951 Ainet, ☏ 04853/5295, 0663/066490 cellular; FAX 04853/5595).

St. Jakob in Defereggen

④ *43 km (27 mi) northwest of Lienz.*

Few tourists venture into the Defereggen mountain range, although its craggy slopes are sprinkled with unspoiled villages. The small resort of St. Jakob in Defereggen is one of the most charming and picturesque in East Tirol. Sports enthusiasts flock to the area for hiking, climbing, rafting, and fishing in summer and skiing in winter. There are also sulfur baths at nearby St. Leonhard and a waterfall at Mariahilf. To reach St. Jakob from Lienz, head northwest on Route 108, following the Isel Valley, and turn left at the village of Huben, about 19 km (12 mi) out of Lienz, onto a scenic side roadway that takes you up the valley, the Defereggental. St. Jakob is 23 km (14 mi) from Huben. The right-hand side of the Defereggental constitutes the beginning of the **Hohe Tauern National Park,** an area of mountains that touches on three states (Salzburg, Carinthia, and Tirol) and includes the Grossglockner Group. The more hardy traveler may want to spend a few days hiking and lodging at any one of several refuges, where one is sometimes treated to very rustic, homemade victuals (cheeses and hams). The national park has several offices; the nearest to Lienz is in Matrei (Nationalparkverwaltung Tirol, ⊠ Rauterplatz 1, A–9971 Matrei in Osttirol, ☏ 04875/5161–0, FAX 04875/5161–20).

Dining and Lodging

$$$$ ✕🖭 **Alpenhof.** A large chalet, set against a velvet green hillside, is an ideal starting point for summer hiking and for skiing. From the outside it is completely out of style with the modest houses of the Defereggental, but the rooms are comfortable, with flower-decked balconies, and the hotel pays particular attention to families with children. The restaurant features regional dishes; ask for recommendations. ⊠ *Innerrotte 35, A–9963,* ☏ *04873/5351–0,* FAX *04873/5351–500. 85*

rooms. Restaurant, bar, indoor pool, sauna, nightclub, children's programs. AE, DC, MC, V. Closed May and mid-Oct.–mid-Dec.

$ ⊞ **Farmhouses.** If you fall in love with the Hohe Tauern mountains (which happens instantly for the most part) and decide you may want to stay for a while, ask at any tourist office about booking rooms at a farmhouse. Some even offer meals. It's a wonderful way of getting close to the land itself. Prices range from about AS150 per person per day to AS 230. The little brochure *Urlaub am Bergbauernhof* will whet your appetite, and you may consider moving to Osttirol at once, for good. For more information contact Hohe Tauern Süd-Werbung (⊠ Rauterplatz 1, A–9971 Matrei in Osttirol, ☎ 04875/5330, ⅏ 04875/5331).

Matrei in Osttirol

❺ *31 km (19 mi) northeast of St. Jakob in Defereggen.*

Because of its strategic location on one of the easier north–south routes over the Alps, Matrei in Osttirol has a long history to look back on, including Celtic and then Roman periods. Every year on the eve of St. Nicholas's Day (December 6), fantastically dressed characters with furs and bells storm through town in an old tradition called *Klaubaufgehen,* a way to frighten off bad spirits. The **parish church of St. Alban** in town is definitely worth entering for its rich interior. The real treasure, however, is the Romanesque **church of St. Nicholas,** which is on the other side of the Isel at the beginning of the Virgen Valley. It contains some simple carvings, such as the 15th-century statue of St. Nicholas, and its late-13th-century frescoes of various biblical scenes elevate it to a high work of art. Remarkably well preserved 14th-century frescoes decorate the outside walls. Just north of Matrei, standing on a daunting rock, is **Schloss Weissenstein,** a 12th-century castle that underwent substantial rebuilding in the 1800s and is now privately owned.

Dining and Lodging

$$$–$$$$ ✕⊞ **Rauter.** With an ultramodern facade, clean lines, and slick surfaces,
★ this fashionable house offers elegant comfort in stark contemporary contrast to the usual rustic Alpine style. Here, too, are many diversions and the best restaurant in East Tirol. The fish comes from the hotel's own waters, the lamb from the nearby mountains, and the house bakery supplies the café. A hotel bus brings you to and from hiking areas in summer, ski slopes in winter. Fishing is available for guests staying three days or longer, and there is riding nearby. ⊠ *Rauterpl. 3, A–9971,* ☎ *04875/6611,* ⅏ *04875/6613. 50 rooms. Restaurant, bar, café, indoor and outdoor pools, sauna, exercise room, fishing. No credit cards. Closed Nov.–mid-Dec.*

$ ⊞ **Alpengasthof Tauernhaus.** There's quiet comfort in this simple rus-
★ tic *Gasthof,* about 14 km (9 mi) up the Tauern Valley at the base of the Felbertauern pass. The hotel began as a rest house, founded in 1207 by the archbishops of Salzburg. It is a good starting point for hiking and skiing. ⊠ *A–9971,* ☎ *04875/8811,* ⅏ *04875/8812. 41 rooms, 21 with full bath, 12 with shower. Restaurant, sauna. No credit cards. Closed Nov.*

ACROSS THE GROSSGLOCKNER PASS

This is the excursion over the longest and most spectacular highway through the Alps, the Grossglockner High Alpine Highway, an engineering achievement of the first magnitude. There is one thrill every hundred yards along this scenic route, but your first will be sighting Heiligenblut, one of Austria's prettiest towns, at the foot of the Grossglockner.

To explore this region, winter travelers have no choice but to drive north out of Lienz on Route 108, arriving in Mittersill in Salzburg province via the 5-km (3-mi) Felbertauern toll tunnel (winter AS110, summer AS190) under the Tauern mountains, and taking Route 168 east to Zell am See. But if the road is open, go north over the Grossglockner mountain highway. (The trip can be done by car or bus.) Leave Lienz via Route 107, but stop on the way up the hill outside Iselsberg–Stronach for a great panoramic view over the city. As you go over the ridge, you'll be entering Carinthia again. At Winklern the road follows the Möll River valley, and after about 11 km (7 mi) you'll come to Döllach.

Döllach

❻ *28 km (17 mi) northeast of Lienz.*

Prospectors once searched for gold in Döllach (Grosskirchheim), in the Möll River valley. Today, the history of local gold mining is chronicled in a museum in the **Schloss Grosskirchheim.** ☎ *04825/226.* ✉ *AS35.* ☉ *May–Oct., Mon.–Sat. 10–noon and 1:30–5; tour Mon.–Sat. at 10, 11, 1:30, 3, and 4:30.*

Don't overlook the Gothic **St. Maria Cornach church,** with its ornate Baroque interior.

Dining and Lodging

$$$–$$$$ ✕🏠 **Schlosswirt.** Rooms range from somewhat spartan to elegant in this appealing chalet hotel at the base of the mountains on the fringe of the Grossglockner. In season you can climb, hike, ski, and ride horseback in the gorgeous "hidden valley" of the Graden brook. The hotel has its own fishing streams and lake, and it organizes dinners and wine tastings in the local 500-year-old castle. The restaurant has slipped since it started serving tour groups but is still worth a try; ask for recommendations. ✉ *A–9843,* ☎ *04825/211–0 or 04825/411–0,* ℻ *04825/211–165. 25 rooms. Restaurant, bar, pool, lake, sauna, tennis court, horseback riding, fishing. No credit cards. Closed 3 wks in Apr.*

Heiligenblut

★ ❼ *10 km (6 mi) north of Döllach.*

Some say the best time to experience this little slice of paradise is after a leisurely dinner at one of the many *Gasthöfe,* gazing out at the starry firmament over the Hohe Tauern range. Others relish standing around an early morning thaw-out fire, used by hikers setting out to conquer the mighty foothills of the Grossglockner peaks, the highest in Austria. This small town nestled in a valley is known for its picturesque church set against an equally picturesque mountain backdrop, but it's the famed mountain-climbing school and climbing and skiing facilities that draw flocks of all-out active types.

According to local legend, St. Briccius, after obtaining a vial of the blood of Jesus, was buried by an avalanche, but when his body was recovered, the tiny vial was miraculously found hidden within one of the saint's open wounds. The town gets its name, Heiligenblut (Holy Blood), from this miraculous event. Today the relic is housed in the Sakramenthäuschen, the chapel of the small but beautiful Gothic **parish church of St. Vincent.** Completed in 1490 after more than a century of construction under the toughest conditions, the church is marked by its soaring belfry tower. Sublimely, the sharply pointed spire finds an impressive echo in the conic peak of the Grossglockner. St. Vincent contains a beautifully carved late-Gothic double altar nearly 36 ft high, and the Coronation of Mary is depicted in the altar wings, richly carved by Wolfgang Hasslinger in 1520. The region's most important altarpiece, it imparts a feeling of quiet power in this spare, high church. The church also has a noble crypt and graveyard, the latter sheltering graves of those lost in climbing the surrounding mountains.

You can get to Heiligenblut by bus from Lienz or Zell am See (note that some buses stop in the tiny hamlet of Winkl directly below the town). During the winter, buses run from Heiligenblut to nearby ski runs. Heiligenblut loves tourists, and special deals are usually offered, ranging from bargain cards issued to visitors staying more than three days to cut-rate, one-day ski passes.

Dining and Lodging

$$$$ ✕🖬 **Glocknerhof.** This dark-wood chalet in the center of the village fits perfectly into the surroundings. You'll feel comfortable in its cozy, attractive rooms. Close to climbing in summer and skiing in winter, the hotel has its own fishing streams for guests. Tour groups stop here on the way over the Grossglockner road, and the restaurant is good. They serve their own trout and other mountain-stream fish; ask if there is *Gams* (local chamois) on the menu. ⊠ *Hof 3, A–9844,* ☎ *04824/ 2244,* 𝐅𝐀𝐗 *04824/2244–66. 52 rooms. Restaurant, bar, indoor pool, sauna, fishing, children's programs. MC. Closed mid-Apr.–mid-June and Oct.–early Dec.*

$$$–$$$$ 🖬 **Kärntnerhof.** Several chalet-style houses set close together have been combined to make up this intimate, family-run complex on the edge of thick woods about 2 km (1 mi) from the center of town. There's entertainment twice weekly. ⊠ *Winkl 3, A–9844,* ☎ *04824/ 2004,* 𝐅𝐀𝐗 *04824/2004–89. 43 rooms. Restaurant, bar, indoor and outdoor pools, sauna, exercise room. DC. Closed Easter–May and mid-Oct.–mid-Dec.*

$$$–$$$$ 🖬 **Panoramagasthof Lächenhof.** This charming *Gasthaus* lives up to its name, thanks to spectacular views of the surrounding Alpine scenery from balconied rooms festooned with flowers. The chalet-style building is perched on a mountain slope and surrounded by lush forest, so it's easy to feel you've left civilization behind. Rooms are comfortably appointed with pastel fabrics and sturdy wood furniture. ⊠ *Hof 70, A–9844,* ☎ *04824/2262,* 𝐅𝐀𝐗 *04824/2262–45. 23 rooms. Restaurant, bar, sauna. AE, DC, MC, V.*

$$$–$$$$ 🖬 **Senger.** Weathered wood and flowered balconies highlight this old farmhouse chalet, which has been cleverly enlarged while keeping its original rustic atmosphere. The rooms and romantic apartments, with lots of pillows and country prints, continue the attractive rural theme. It's a bit outside the center of town. ⊠ *Heiligenblut 23, A–9844,* ☎ *04824/2215,* 𝐅𝐀𝐗 *04824/2215–9. 9 rooms, 8 apartments. Restaurant, bar, sauna, exercise room. No credit cards. Closed 1 wk after Easter– June and mid-Oct.–mid-Dec.*

Outdoor Activities and Sports

DIGGING FOR GOLD

From mid-June through September, you can pan for gold in the streams around Heiligenblut. Buy a ticket for an excursion in the town at the "gold-digging office"—the tourist office or Raimund Granögger (☎ 04824/2109). The price (AS130) includes the necessary equipment and a permit to take home your finds.

HIKING AND MOUNTAIN CLIMBING

This is a hiker's El Dorado, with (in summer) more than 240 km (150 mi) of marked pathways and trails in all directions. There are relatively easy hikes to the Kalvarienberg (½ hour), Wirtsbauer-Alm (two hours), and the Leiterfall, a 400-ft-high waterfall (two hours). **Guided tours** are available and enjoyable. They cost anywhere from AS650 to

AS3,900 per person and can last two days. The National Park Programs Office (☎ 04825/616114) has all the information.

Grossglockner Highway

★ **8** *14 km (10 mi) north of Heiligenblut.*

From Heiligenblut the climb begins up the Carinthian side of the Grossglockner. You'll be tapped here for a AS350 toll (AS340 from season opening to June 16 and from September 16 to season closing) allowing you to use the Grossglockner High Alpine Highway as much as you like on the same day. There's also a ticket for AS480 good on any two days within a calendar year or for AS450 on any eight consecutive days. The peak itself—at 12,470 ft the highest point in Austria—is off to the west. You can get somewhat closer than the main road takes you by following the highly scenic but steep Gletscherstrasse westward up to the Gletscherbahn on the Franz-Josef-Plateau, where you'll be rewarded with absolutely breathtaking views of the Grossglockner peak and surrounding Alps, of the vast glacier in the valley below, and, on a clear day, even into Italy.

The Grossglockner road twists and turns as it struggles to the 8,370-ft Hochtor. At this point you've crossed into Salzburg province. Completed in 1935 after five years of labor by 3,200 workers, the highway provides the only passage over the high mountain ranges anywhere between the Brenner and the Radstadt Tauern passes, which are 160 km (100 mi) apart. You're now on Edelweiss-Strasse. A stop at the **Edelweissspitze** yields an unbelievable view out over East Tirol, Carinthia, and Salzburg, including 19 glaciers and 37 peaks over the 9,600-ft mark. The rare white edelweiss—the von Trapps sang its praises in *The Sound of Music*—grows here. Though the species is protected, don't worry about the plants you get as souvenirs; they are cultivated for this purpose. It is strictly forbidden to pick a wild edelweiss (and several other plant species), should you ever happen to come across one. Be sure to visit the visitor center and the Alpine museum. An excellent short film (in English) tells the story of the area, and computer-driven dioramas show how animals survive the extreme climatic changes atop the mountain range. ⌂ *Grossglockner Hwy., Km 26,* ☎ *0662/873673 road information.* 🎫 *Free.* ☉ *Early May–late Oct., daily 9–5.*

Zell am See

★ **9** *8 km (5 mi) northwest of the Grossglockner.*

After the toll station on the north side of the Grossglockner peak, the highway finally exhausts its hairpin turns (more than 30) and continues to Bruck an der Grossglocknerstrasse. From here it's only about 8 km (5 mi) west on Route S11 and then north on Route 311 to Zell am See. This lovely lakeside town got its name from the monks' cells of a monastery founded here in about AD 790.

In the quaint town center, visit the 17th-century Renaissance **Schloss Rosenberg,** now the town hall. The **Kastnerturm,** built around 1300, was originally a fortified tower for an abbey and then a granary. It now houses the city museum, with an eclectic collection of old furnishings and handicrafts, open June–September, Monday, Wednesday, and Friday 2–5. Unusually fine statues of St. George and St. Florian can be found on the west wall of the splendid Romanesque **parish church of St. Hippolyte.** Built in 1217 (the tower came about two centuries later), the church was beautifully renovated in 1975.

Several locations offer up stunning vistas of the town and its environs. On ground level, take a boat ride to the village of **Thumersbach,** on the opposite shore, for a wonderful reflected view of Zell am See. For a bird's-eye view, a cable car leads virtually from the center of Zell am See up to the **Schmittenhöhe** for a 180-degree panorama that takes in the peaks of the Glockner and Tauern granite ranges to the south and west and the very different limestone ranges to the north. This sweep will impress upon you the geology of Austria as no written description ever could. In addition, there are four other cable-car trips up this mountain, offering some of the most spectacular vistas of the Kitzbühel Alps.

The romantic narrow-gauge **Pinzgauer railroad** winds its way under steam power on a two-hour trip through the Pinzgau, following the Salzach River valley westward 54 km (34 mi) to Krimml. Nearby are the famous Krimmler waterfalls, with a 1,300-ft drop, which you can see from an observation platform or explore close at hand (if you can manage a hike of about 3½ to four hours). Be sure to take a raincoat and sneakers. ☎ 06542/17000. *Round-trip AS240. Trains depart July–Aug., Tues., Thurs., and weekends at 9:15; Sept., Sat. at 9:15.*

Dining and Lodging

$$$$ ✕▦ **Grand.** In the style of the great turn-of-the-century resort hotels, this totally renovated house right on the lake is, as its name implies, probably the grandest (and most charming) place to stay in Zell, even without all the amenities and health facilities other Zell hotels provide. It stands on its own peninsula, is decorated with mansard roofs and whipped-cream stuccowork, and serves up some fine dining. Most of the accommodations are small apartments, complete with kitchenette and fireplace; the best are those farthest out on the small peninsula. *Esplanade 4, A–5700,* ☎ *06542/2388,* FAX *06542/2388–305. 111 rooms. 2 restaurants, bar, kitchenettes, indoor pool, lake, sauna, golf, squash, boating, dance club. AE, DC, MC, V. Closed Nov.*

$$$$ ✕▦ **Salzburgerhof.** Sophisticated travelers often pick this impressive
★ family-managed chalet, not far from the lake and the ski lift, as the town's foremost hotel; comfort and personal service are the rule. Each of the attractive rooms and suites has a flower-bedecked balcony. The restaurant is truly excellent; try the *Tafelspitz* (boiled beef) or rack of lamb in an herbed pastry crust. The pleasant garden is used for barbecues and evenings of folkloric entertainment. Golfer guests get a 30% discount at the local club. Brand new is the little wellness pavilion with an outdoor pool in the park and a program of thalasso therapy, mud packs, Reiki, and yoga courses. *Auerspergstr. 11, A–5700,* ☎ *06542/ 765–0,* FAX *06542/76566. 36 rooms, 24 suites. Restaurant, bar, indoor pool, lake, sauna, spa, exercise room. AE, DC, MC, V. Closed Nov.*

$$$$ ✕▦ **Schloss Prielau.** Sporting turreted towers and striped shutters, this
★ castle looks as if it stepped out of a fairy tale. Elegantly furnished rooms with sumptuous fabrics and traditional carved wooden furniture can be a bit dim, however, because of the narrow, old-fashioned windows. But the service will make you feel as if you are the newest member of royalty to take up residence here. The restaurant serves classic Austrian dishes like schnitzel but with a lighter, more refined touch than you find in most other establishments. *Hofmannsthalstr., A–5700,* ☎ *06542/2609,* FAX *06542/2609–55. 12 rooms. Restaurant, bar, lake, sauna. AE, DC, MC, V.*

$$ ✕▦ **St. Hubertushof.** On the opposite side of the lake from town, this sprawling hotel complex offers a great view across the water. Paneling and antlers over the fireplace in the lounge add to its rural style. Golfers get a 30% reduction at the local course. The dance bar draws a regular crowd, and the restaurant offers a wide range of international and local dishes. *Seeuferstr. 7, A–5705 Thumersbach,* ☎ *06542/*

3116, FAX *06542/3116–71. 112 rooms. Restaurant, bar, café, sauna.
AE, DC, MC, V. Closed Nov.*

Nightlife and the Arts

The emphasis in Zell is more on drinking than on dancing, but the scene
does change periodically. At the moment, one of the "in" places is the
Crazy Daisy (☎ 06542/2516), a dance pub near the Kurhaus, where
town events often take place. Also near the Kurhaus and popular is
the pub **Zuckersake** (☎ 06542/4151). A mature crowd gathers at the
Wunderbar (☎ 06542/23870), in the Grand hotel (☞ Dining and
Lodging, *above*). Check out the action in the cellar of the **Sporthotel
Lebzelter** (☎ 06542/24110).

Outdoor Activities and Sports

BICYCLING

The area around Zell am See is a gorgeous spot for bicycling. If you
left your wheels at home, you can rent some at the **train station** (☎
06542/3214–380) for AS150 (AS90 if you have a valid rail ticket) for
a normal city bike, AS200 (or AS160) for a mountain bike. Renting
by the week is cheaper. From April to October, bike tours run from
south of Zell am See up to St. Johann and Salzburg via the Tauern cycle
route. Check with **Austria Radreisen** (✉ Joseph-Haydn-Str. 8, A–
4780 Schärding, ☎ 07712/5511–0, FAX 07712/4811).

FISHING

The lake's tranquil waters offer fine fishing. Many hotels in the area
have packages for avid anglers.

GOLF

Zell am See and Kaprun share two 18-hole courses (each par-72). ✉
Golfstr. 25, ☎ *06542/56161,* FAX *06542/56035.* ◷ *Apr.–Oct.*

WATER SPORTS

Boating—from paddleboating to sailings—and swimming are excellent
on the uncrowded Zeller See. Since powerboats are restricted on many
Austrian lakes, you won't find much waterskiing, but there is a waterskiing school, **Wasserskischule Thumersbach** (✉ Strandbad, Thumersbach, ☎ 06542/4362), on the lake.

Saalbach

🔟 *17 km (9 mi) northwest of Zell am See.*

Noted skiing meccas Saalbach and its neighbor Hinterglemm are part
of an area, comprising also Kaprun and Zell am See, that becomes a
ski circus in winter. A clever layout of lifts and trails enables you to
ski slopes without duplication and still get back to your starting point.
When the snow melts, the region offers sensational hiking; both towns
offer a wide variety of sports. Saalbach and Hinterglemm have each
banned cars from their village center. You can drive to your hotel to
unload baggage; watch carefully for signs or ask for specific directions—
the routes are convoluted and confusing. Take the **Kohlmais cable car**
north out of Saalbach to the top of the ridge for a superb 360-degree
view of the surrounding mountain ranges.

To get to Saalbach from Zell am See, continue north on Route 311 to
Maishofen, where the Glemm Valley opens to the west; then continue
about 9 km (5½ mi) to the west. For those traveling by train or bus,
head first to Zell am See for transfers up the valley.

Dining and Lodging

$ ✕ **Iglsbergerhof.** This utterly unpretentious family-run *Gasthof* serves
★   up some of the best authentic regional specialties in the area. Start with

beef bouillon with *Pinzgauer Käspressknödel* (cheese dumplings), then have *Speckknödel* (bread dumpling with bacon chunks) with sauerkraut, and finish with a *Pinzgauer Bauernkrapfen* (a delicious filled doughnut). ⊠ *Vorderglemm 340, Saalbach,* ☎ *06541/6491. No credit cards. Closed Wed. and Nov.–mid-Dec.*

$$$–$$$$ 🏨 **Glemmtalerhof.** This massive chalet is surprisingly intimate inside, with pleasant paneled rooms and 20 apartments in Alpine style, most with balconies. It is mainly a winter resort, but there's still plenty to do in summer. Golfers get a 30% reduction on greens fees at Zell am See courses. ⊠ *Glemmtaler Landstr. 150, A–5754 Hinterglemm,* ☎ *06541/7135–0,* FAX *06541/7135–63. 62 rooms. 2 restaurants, 2 bars, café, pool, sauna, exercise room, horseback riding, nightclub, children's programs. AE, DC, MC, V. Closed mid-Apr.–mid-May and mid-Oct.–mid-Dec.*

$$$–$$$$ 🏨 **Saalbacher Hof.** This family-run chalet complex in the center of town is identified by a rustic bell tower and overflowing pots of red geraniums against weathered dark wood. Warm paneling and a large fireplace welcome you; the rooms are spacious and comfortable. The hotel can make arrangements for golf and tennis. Every guest gets one free tennis hour daily on the hotel's own court. ⊠ *Dorfstr. 27, A–5753,* ☎ *06541/7111–0,* FAX *06541/7111–42. 90 rooms. 2 restaurants, bar, pool, sauna, golf privileges, tennis court, nightclub. AE, DC, MC, V. Closed mid-Apr.–May and Oct.–Nov.*

$$$–$$$$ 🏨 **Theresia.** The term "garden hotel" applies here. Intimate wood-paneled reception rooms spill over into a garden area topped with pools tucked into the hillside behind. On the quieter edge of Hinterglemm, the hotel is close to ski lifts and hiking trails. Spacious rooms feature light wood, and the restaurant is excellent. Zell am See courses offer a 30% greens-fee reduction. ⊠ *Glemmtaler Landestr. 208, A–5754,* ☎ *06541/7414–0,* FAX *06541/7414–121. 37 rooms. Restaurant, bar, pool, sauna, golf privileges, exercise room, bicycles. DC. Closed mid-Apr.–mid-May and Nov.–mid-Dec.*

Outdoor Activities and Sports

SKIING

In addition to offering tobogganing, sleigh riding, and curling, Saalbach and Hinterglemm have some of the finest skiing in Land Salzburg. There are more than 40 ski lifts, numerous cross-country ski trails, and, for ski potatoes, races and competitions are often run on the Saalbach–Hinterglemm Slalom. The most popular run is on the Schattberg mountain—a cable car takes you there from the center of Saalbach—where, on high, a restaurant offers fine dining. Ski schools are also here for beginners.

Nightlife

BARS

Saalbach has a number of places that crowd up quickly as the slopes are vacated. The tourist office has a list of bars and discos. For dancing and music, try the **Hinterhagalm** disco-bar (☎ 06541/7212) or the **Visage** disco in the Hotel Kristall (☎ 06541/6376–45). The **Alpenhotel** has its Arena Club, with live music (☎ 06541/6666–0), and **Neuhaus** (☎ 06541/7151–0) features small local bands. There's action at the **Almbar** in the Hotel Glemmtalerhof (☎ 06541/7135–0) and at the **Pinzgauer Stüberl** in Hotel Wolf in Hinterglemm (☎ 06541/6346–37). The Londoner and Knappenkeller in the **Hotel Knappenhof** (☎ 06541/6497) in Hinterglemm offer disco or live music in winter and are currently among the "in" spots. Among **bars,** Stamperl, Flockerl, Pfiff, and Kuhstall in Saalbach and Lumpie's, Bla-Bla, and Rudi's Kneipe in Hinterglemm are current favorites.

Saalfelden

⑪ *25 km (15 mi) northeast of Saalbach.*

Saalfelden nestles at the foot of the **Steinernes Meer** (Sea of Stone), the formidable ridge that divides Austria from Germany. The town, farther up Route 311 from Saalbach, is a climber's mecca, but only for those who are experienced and who can tackle such challenges as the 9,560-ft Hochkönig. At the edge of the Steinernes Meer, signs lead you to a late-Gothic **cave chapel,** containing a winged altarpiece near a stone pulpit and hermit's cell. Saalfelden is a main stop on the Innsbruck–Salzburg train route.

Sights in town include a 19th-century Romanesque parish church with a late-Gothic winged altar (1539); the nearby 14th-century Farmach Castle, which is now a retirement home; and the 13th-century Lichtenberg Castle, which is now privately owned. For many, the most interesting attraction is the **Ritzen Castle** museum, where the Christmas-manger collection of artisan Xandl Schläffer as well as exhibits on minerals, native handicrafts, and local history are on view. ▨ *AS38.* ☉ *Mid-June–mid-Sept., daily 10–noon and 2–5; mid-Sept.–mid-June, Wed. and weekends 2–4.*

Very enjoyable is the 1½-km (1-mi) **summer toboggan run.** With 63 curves and three tunnels, it is the longest such run in Europe. Take the chairlift up the Huggenberg southwest of Saalfelden on the road to Zell. Other well-marked attractions in the area include the **Vorderkaserklamm gorge.** The **Hirschbichl pass** was a strategic route where several battles were fought during the Napoléonic Wars.

OFF THE
BEATEN PATH

LAMPRECHTSHÖHLE – About 14 km (8 mi) northwest of Saalfelden on Route 311 heading toward Lofer, you come to Weissbach, whose claim to fame is a system of caves totaling about 35 km (19 mi). An old legend has it that a treasure is buried here, but no one has ever found it, not for lack of trying. ☎ *06582/8343.* ▨ *AS38.* ☉ *May 15–Oct. 15, daily 9–7; Oct. 16–May 14, daily 9–4.*

Dining and Lodging

$$–$$$ ✕ **Schatzbichl.** The reputation of this simple *Gasthaus* slightly east of
★ Saalfelden draws guests from near and far. The pine-paneled interior is bright and cheerful, as is the usually overworked staff. Regional dishes are simply prepared and presented; try the garlic soup, lamb chops, or any of the fish offered. ✉ *Ramseiden 82,* ☎ *06582/73281,* 🖷 *06582/73281–4. Reservations essential. No credit cards. Closed Tues. Mar.–May and Sept.–Oct., 2 wks in Apr., and Nov.*

$$$$ ✕🏨 **Hotel Gut Brandlhof.** This sprawling ranch, about 5 km (3 mi) outside town, is perfect for an active vacation. The vast complex provides all manner of sports facilities, including the 18-hole, par-72 Saalfelden golf course, which belongs to the hotel. The comfortable rooms are done in Alpine-country style. In the wood-panelled restaurant, a *Kachelofen* (tiled brick stove) radiates warmth; the cuisine is first class and Austrian, with an eye to healthy light meals, fresh salads, seasonal specialties, and some international fare. ✉ *Hohlwegen 4, A–5760,* ☎ *06582/7800–0,* 🖷 *06582/7800–598. 150 rooms. Restaurant, 2 bars, indoor and outdoor pools, sauna, 18-hole golf course, tennis court, bowling, exercise room, horseback riding, squash, fishing, children's programs. AE, DC.*

$$$ ✕🏨 **Gasthof Hindenburg.** This 500-year-old inn in the center of town has been newly renovated from top to bottom to provide modern comfort while retaining historic touches. Room colors are warm and inviting, complementing the wood flooring and the combination of antique and modern furnishings. Some suites have a duplex layout. In summer, the garden restaurant is particularly inviting. There are very pleasant spa facilities on its fourth floor. ✉ *Bahnhofstr. 6, A–5760,* ☎ *06582/793–0,* FAX *06582/793–78. 38 rooms, 6 apartments. 4 restaurants, bar, sauna, steam room. AE, DC, MC, V.*

$ 🏨 **Pension Klinglerhof.** This is just one of several modest bed-and-breakfasts in Saalfelden, where things are simple and comfortable and inexpensive, and the service is all by owners (the Hölzls in this case), who enjoy taking care of their guests. The Klinglerhof is quiet, right near the golf course and the cross-country ski trails and the lifts. ✉ *Schinking 1, A–5760,* ☎ *06584/7713. No credit cards.*

Outdoor Activities and Sports
BICYCLING

The valley leading to Saalfelden is a great place for seeing sights on two wheels. You can rent a bike at the **railroad station** (☎ 06582/2344–0).

HIKING

From Saalfelden, you can head off through the magnificent Saalach Valley on any of three five- or six-day self-guided expeditions called **"Hiking without Luggage."** Your bags are transported, your choice of accommodation is prebooked, and guidebooks are available in English. The exhilaration can't be described in words. Information is available from Saalfelden's Pinzgau regional tourist office (✉ *Lofererstr. 5, A–5760,* ☎ *06582/4017,* FAX *06582/4017–4).*

MOUNTAIN SPAS AND ALPINE RAMBLES

Glacier-covered Alps and hot springs, luxurious hotels, and tranquil lakes are the enticing combinations this Austrian region superlatively serves up. Gold and silver mined from the mountains was the source of many local fortunes; today, glittering gold jewelry finds many buyers in the shops of Badgastein's Empress Elizabeth Promenade. To set off on this trip, head south from Salzburg on the A10 and take the Bischofshofen exit toward St. Johann im Pongau, which gets you to Route 311 and, 17 km (11 mi) later, the Route 167 junction. From Zell am See, head east on Route 311 to pass Bruck again, continue through Taxenbach to Lend, and turn south at the intersection of Route 167.

Badgastein

🄬 *54 km (34 mi) southeast of Zell am See.*

Though it traces its roots all the way back to the 15th century, this resort, one of Europe's leading spas, gained renown in the last century, when VIPs from emperors on down to pecunious philosophers flocked to the area to "take the cure." Today, Badgastein retains much of its 19th-century ambience. The stunning setting—a mountain torrent, the Gasteiner Ache, rushes through the unusual town—adds to the attraction. Most attempts at rejuvenating this turn-of-the-century jewel have met with failure, and we can be thankful for it. The old buildings still dominate the townscape, giving it a wonderful feeling of solidity and charm. The baths themselves, however, are state of the art, as evidenced by the Felsenbad baths in the rocks and the **Kur-und-Kongresszentrum** (Treatment Complex). The most unusual spa is the "healing mine" in **Böckstein,** near the Empress Elizabeth Promenade; it's an abandoned gold mine with very special air. For complete information on the town's main spas, contact the Badgastein tourist office (☞ The Eastern Alps A to Z, *below*).

A very special tradition in Badgastein is the old heathen *Perchtenlaufen* processions on January 4: People wearing big masks and making lots of noise chase the winter away, bring good blessings for the new year.

Badgastein is serviced by many rail lines, with many expresses running from Salzberg and Klagenfurt. You can also reach the town by bus from Salzberg.

Dining and Lodging

$$$$ ✕▥ **Hotel Weismayr.** This grand old hotel in the middle of town is without a doubt the top address in Badgastein—a 66-room palace with a reputation for luxury and service going all the way back to 1832. Everything is done here to make sure your stay will be pleasant, even healthy: It's a typical spa hotel with all the applications local nature can offer. It also organizes such interesting excursions as hunting tours. The expansive dining rooms in Biedermeier style are the setting for luxurious meals including many seasonal dishes (asparagus in May and June, fish, game in autumn), but the menu also reflects the fact that you are at a spa and health club (fresh salads, vegetarian dishes). ✉ *Kaiser-Franz-Josef-Str. 6, A–5640,* ☎ *06434/2594–0,* ℻ *06434/2594–14. Restaurant, piano bar, mineral baths, spa, exercise room. AE, MC, V, DC.*

$$$$ ✕▥ **Villa Solitude.** In this central turn-of-the-century villa overlooking the gorge below, six elegant suites offer every comfort. Rooms are wood-paneled, with furnishings appropriate to the period. The management is the same as at the Grüner Baum (☞ *below*). In the excellent restaurant, the Brasserie, try fish or fillet of beef; if you're here in summer, you can enjoy meals on the terrace. ✉ *Kaiser-Franz-Josef-Str. 16, A–5640,* ☎ *06434/5101–0,* ℻ *06434/5101–3. 6 suites. Restaurant. AE, DC, MC, V. Closed Nov.*

$$$–$$$$ ✕▥ **Grüner Baum.** You're out of the center of town here, in a relaxing, friendly hotel village set amid meadows and woodlands. The guest list in this Relais et Châteaux group hotel has included Austrian Empress Elizabeth and Saudi king Saud. Five separate houses have comfortable rustic, wood-paneled rooms, giving the complex a feeling of intimacy and personality. Children are well looked after. The elegant restaurant has an excellent reputation. ✉ *Kötschachtal, A–564,* ☎ *06434/2516–0,* ℻ *06434/2516–25. 80 rooms. Restaurant, bar, indoor and outdoor pools, sauna, tennis court, exercise room, children's programs. AE, DC, MC, V. Closed Nov.*

$$$$ ▥ **Elisabethpark.** The dining and drawing rooms and music bars go on and on in this elegant hotel—modern but of the old school—in the center of town. The grand-hotel atmosphere is underscored by Oriental carpets, marble, and crystal chandeliers. Rooms, with period furnishings, are particularly comfortable, and service has a pleasantly personal touch. ✉ *A–5640,* ☎ *06434/2551–0,* ℻ *06434/2551–10. 109 rooms. Restaurant, bar, café, indoor pool, sauna, spa, exercise room. AE, DC, MC, V. Closed mid-Apr.–early June and Sept.–mid-Dec.*

$$ ▥ **Krone.** Most of the pleasant, bright rooms in this in-town hotel have balconies, and you're about three minutes from the cable car up the mountain. In addition, the thermal spa is next door. ✉ *Bahnhofspl. 8, A–5640,* ☎ *06434/2330–0,* ℻ *06434/2330–86. 60 rooms. Restaurant, bar, spa. MC, V. Closed mid-Apr.–mid-May and Oct.–Nov.*

Nightlife and the Arts

The **Grand Hotel de l'Europe casino** (✉ Kaiser-Franz-Josef-Str. 14, ☎ 06434/2465, ℻ 06434/246525) has baccarat, blackjack, roulette, and slot machines. A passport is required. The casino is open July–mid-September and December 26–March, daily 7 PM–2 AM. Keep an eye out also for concerts, especially at the **Kongresshaus** in the middle of town (New Year's concerts are held here, for example).

Outdoor Activities and Sports

As a good spa town, Badgastein keeps its guests entertained with all sorts of events from snowboarding competitions to dog-sleigh races. You will not be bored.

GOLF

The **Golfclub Gastein** has an attractive 9-hole, par-36 course. The greens fee is AS650 weekdays, AS750 weekends. Inquire at the nearest tourist office about special golfing packages and whether your hotel is a golf partner, which means you might get a 30% reduction. ☎ 06434/2775, FAX 06434/2775–4. ☉ Late Apr.–Oct.

HANG GLIDING

Flinging yourself off high places with a few sails is ideal in the Alps. You'll find a school and a rental company at the cable car in Dorfgastein 16 km (10 mi) north of Badgastein (☎ 06433/223–0, FAX 06433/344–10).

SKIING

Though other Austrian winter sports areas are more popular, don't let this discourage you from trying the excellent facilities and good slopes in Sportgastein, some 9 km (5½ mi) south of Badgastein. The main ski run near Badgastein is the Graukogel peak, which also offers a restaurant and great Alpine hikes.

Liechtensteinklamm

⑬ *38 km (24 mi) north of Badgastein.*

Traveling from Badgastein along Route 311, turn east toward Schwarzach in Pongau, where the road heads north, to find, between Schwarzach and St. Johann, the **Liechtensteinklamm,** the deepest (1,000 ft), narrowest (12½ ft), and most spectacular gorge in the Eastern Alps. At its far end is a 200-ft waterfall. A tour on a wooden walkway crisscrossing the gorge takes about 45 minutes. ☎ 06412/8572. ▧ AS32. ☉ Early May–Oct., daily 8–5.

St. Johann im Pongau

★ ⑭ *43 km (27 mi) north of Badgastein.*

St. Johann has developed into a full-fledged, year-round resort. The area is favored by cross-country and intermediate downhill skiers, as the gentle slopes provide an almost endless variety of runs. The huge, twin-spired parish church, built in 1861 in neo-Gothic style, is known locally as the **Pongau Cathedral**—a mammoth structure that rises quite majestically out of the townscape.

Every four years during the first week of January, the people of St. Johann, like the Badgasteiners, celebrate Pongauer Perchtenlauf, which can be poetically translated to mean "away with winter's ghost." Taking to the streets, they ring huge cowbells and wear weird masks and costumes to drive away evil spirits. The next celebration will be in the year 2000; check with the tourist office for the exact date. St. Johann is on the rail lines connecting Munich, Klagenfurt, and Salzburg.

Dining and Lodging

$$$–$$$$ ✕▨ **Sporthotel Alpenland.** The newest hotel in town has a somewhat more commercial approach to innkeeping than do the family-run chalets, but you get an attractive room, efficient service, and plenty of facilities. Three restaurants offer pizza, steaks, and such local specialties as lamb. ⊠ *Hans-Kappacher-Str. 7–9, A–5600,* ☎ *06412/7021–0,* FAX *06412/7021–51. 137 rooms. 3 restaurants, bar, indoor and outdoor pools, sauna, tennis court, exercise room. AE, DC, MC, V.*

Outdoor Activities and Sports

GOLF

An 18-hole, par-70 course near Schwarzach in Pongau is open May–October. ✉ *Off Rte. 311, Box 6, Goldegg,* ☎ *06415/8585,* FAX *06415/8585–4.*

SKIING

Linked by buses and 80 km (50 mi) of ski runs with other towns in the Pongau Valley, St. Johann remains the ski capital of the region called **Sportwelt Amadé,** which boasts a total of 135 lifts and more than 350 km (218 mi) of well-groomed slopes. St. Johann alone has more than 40 ski lifts plus several cable-car ascents. Along with other Pongau Valley runs, the town offers a Drei-Taler-Skischaukel (three-valley) pass. Inquire at the local tourist office what the best deal is, because they are constantly coming up with new commercial ideas.

Altenmarkt

⑮ *22 km (14 mi) east of St. Johann im Pongau.*

You cross over to Altenmarkt by leaving St. Johann im Pongau on Route 163 heading east across Wagrain and Reitdorf. Altenmarkt is small, but the **parish church of St. Mary's** contains the *Schöne Madonna,* an outstanding statue of the Virgin Mary that dates to before 1384. Outside of town, look for the **Schloss Tantalier,** built in 1450 for a noble family, reconstructed in 1569, and now serving as a youth hostel. The castle is unusual for its virtually square shape, with round towers on the south side and square ones on the north. Nearby streams make the town a prime fishing site in summer, and skiing takes the spotlight during the winter months.

Dining and Lodging

$$$$ ✕ ⌂ **Lebzelter.** Even though it's in the center of town, this comfortable,
★ family-run hotel has its own fishing stream. The excellent, window-filled country restaurant has a broad reputation. Dishes range from steaks to fish to vegetarian meals, but the emphasis is on traditional fare. ✉ *Marktpl. 79, A–5541,* ☎ *06452/6911,* FAX *06452/7823. 29 rooms. Restaurant, bar, sauna, exercise room, fishing, bicycles. AE, DC, MC, V.*

$$–$$$ ✕ ⌂ **Markterwirt.** This traditional house in the center of town dates back 900 years. The personal style of the family who runs it is reflected in the charming country decor of the comfortable rooms. The main dining room and the informal *Stube* are good, and half board is required. The hotel has its own lake for fishing. ✉ *Marktpl. 4, A–5541,* ☎ *06452/5420,* FAX *06452/5420–31. 28 rooms. Restaurant, café, sauna, fishing. MC, V. Closed Nov.*

Radstadt

⑯ *4 km (2½ mi) east of Altenmarkt.*

Despite wars and fires, the picturesque walled town of Radstadt still retains its 12th-century character. Standing guard over a key north–south route, Radstadt was once granted the right to warehouse goods and to trade in iron, wine, and salt, but the town's present prosperity is due to tourism: The area is growing in popularity as a skiing destination and has been a longtime mecca for hiking in the summer. Radstadt's north and west walls, dating to 1534, are well preserved, as are three of the towers that mark the corners of the old town. Most of the buildings around the square are also from the 16th century. The late-Romanesque **parish church,** north of the square, dominates the town, but reconstructions over the ages have destroyed much of its original character. The interior contains several Baroque altars. To get to Radstadt, motorists usually take the A10 from Salzburg. Trains and buses, too, connect Salzburg with Radstadt (occasionally with a change over at Bischofshofen).

Dining and Lodging

$$$ ✕⬚ **Sporthotel Gründler.** The emphasis here is on water, and the sport is fishing; the hotel has rights on 16 km (10 mi) of the Enns River. It also has ties to the Radstadt golf club. In summer, huge outdoor pools and a water slide offer great fun for children. The restaurant specializes in trout. ✉ *Schlossstr. 45, A–5550,* ☎ *06452/5590–0,* 🖷 *06452/ 5590–28. 10 rooms, 18 apartments. Restaurant, 3 indoor and outdoor pools, sauna, fishing. MC, V. Closed mid-Apr.–mid-May and mid-Oct.– mid-Dec.*

Outdoor Activities and Sports

GOLF

During the April–November season, hills and a 16th-hole island pose challenges on the town's 18-hole, par-72 course. ✉ *Römerstr. 18,* ☎ *06452/5111,* 🖷 *06452/7336.* ⊙ *Apr.–Nov.*

Schladming

⑰ *20 km (13 mi) east of Radstadt.*

In the 14th and 15th centuries, Schladming was a thriving silver-mining town; then in 1525 the town was burned in an uprising by miners and farmers. Most of what you see today dates to 1526, when reconstruction began, but traces of the earlier town wall and the old miners' houses stand as testament to the town's former glory. Dominating the skyline is the Romanesque tower of the **St. Achaz parish church.**

Schladming is popular as a year-round resort. This is an area where sport is taken seriously; not only does it attract the world's best skiers, but it also gives beginners ample scope. And in happy contrast to fashionable resorts in Tirol and Vorarlberg, Schladming and its surroundings are reasonably priced. To get to Schladming from Radstadt, take scenic Route 146 east along the Enns River valley for about 20 km (13 mi) over the provincial border into Styria at Mandling. The town is also accessible by rail via the Salzburg–Graz line.

Dining and Lodging

$$$–$$$$ ✕⬚ **Alte Post.** This traditional house in the center of town dates to
★   1618 and is notable for its particularly attractive *Stube* and the older rooms with vaulted ceilings. Guest rooms are cozy and comfortable. The restaurants offer good regional and Austrian cuisine in an appropriately genuine atmosphere. It's the place to sit outside in summer, watch people go by, and enjoy solid Austrian cooking, cholesterol and all. Golf arrangements can be made for the nearby Dachstein-Tauern club. ✉ *Hauptpl. 10, A–8970,* ☎ *03687/22571,* 🖷 *03687/22571– 8. 40 rooms. 2 restaurants, bar, golf privileges, tennis court. AE, DC, MC, V. Closed mid- to late Apr. and mid- to late Nov.*

Outdoor Activities and Sports

FISHING

From May to mid-September you can cast a fly for trout in the nearby Enns River. Contact **Walter Dichtl** (✉ Hauptpl. 28, ☎ 03687/23539).

GOLF

Schladming-Haus (Haus is a little village incorporated into Schladming) has an Alpine setting that's reason enough to play the 18-hole, par-71 course at the **Golf & Country Club Dachstein-Tauern.** ☎ *03686/2630– 0,* 🖷 *03686/2630–15.* ⊙ *May–Oct.*

The main ski runs here are on the Hochwurzen and Planai peaks, both offering cable cars, chairlifts, and expert downhill runs. The Dachstein-Südwand cable car ascends to a height of almost 9,000 ft, allowing skiing well into June. Another lure here is the bustling après-ski scene.

Ramsau am Dachstein

⑱ *6 km (4 mi) north of Schladming.*

Heading north out of Schladming, you take a narrow, winding road that offers increasingly spectacular views of the Enns Valley and ends in a broad, sun-bathed valley at the foot of the mighty Dachstein range. After passing through Kulm, take a left at the next intersection to reach the small resort town of Ramsau am Dachstein. About 4½ km (3 mi) west of Ramsau, a small toll road road (AS35 per adult) forks off to the north into the Dachstein itself, a majestic craggy outcrop of 9,826 ft. Take the impressive 20-minute **Hunerkogel cable car ride** to the top of the Alps; a round-trip without skis AS245. A phone call to ☎ 03687/81315 will tell you in German what the weather's like up there. To the north lie the lakes of the Salzkammergut; to the west, the Tennen mountain range. South and east lie the lower Tauern mountains. A snowmobile ride will take you very close to the Dachstein peak, or you can hike over if you're wearing proper hiking boots. In summer the south cliff at Hunerkogel is a favorite "jumping-off spot" for paragliders. To get to Ramsau without a car, you need to take a bus from Schladming.

Dining and Lodging

$$–$$$ ✕▣ **Pehab-Kirchenwirt.** *Kirchenwirt* means "next to the church," and that's exactly where this rustic hotel is. It's been family-run—for the past 200 years! Many of the comfortable rooms have balconies; those in the back have the best mountain view. You're close to hiking trails in summer and the hotel-operated ski lift and ski runs in winter. Hotel guests can use the nearby indoor pool, which has a sauna and solarium. The restaurant serves good Styrian specialties, among other things, for which it received an accolade. ⊠ *A–8972,* ☎ *0368//81/32,* ℻ *03687/81655. 40 rooms, 5 apartments. Restaurant, café, weinstube. AE, MC. Closed Nov. and 1 month after Easter.*

$$$ ▣ **Peter Rosegger.** This rustic chalet in a quiet area on the forest's edge
★ is decorated with homey mementos—framed letters and embroidered mottoes—of the Styrian writer after whom it is named. This is the place to stay when you've come for climbing, as Fritz Walcher heads the Alpine school. Rooms are country comfortable, and though the kitchen is the best in the area, the restaurant is only for hotel guests, who are treated to such local specialties as house-smoked trout, Styrian corned pork, and stuffed breast of veal. ⊠ *A–8972,* ☎ *03687/81223–0,* ℻ *03687/ 81223–8. 13 rooms. Restaurant, sauna, exercise room. No credit cards. Closed mid-Apr.–May and Nov.–mid-Dec.*

Outdoor Activities and Sports

HIKING

If you're interested in learning to climb in the difficult Dachstein area, contact the **Alpinschule Dachstein** (⊠ Ramsau am Dachstein 233, A–8972, ☎ 03687/81223–0) or **Bergsteigerschule Dachstein** (⊠ Ramsau am Dachstein 101, A–8972, ☎ 03687/81424).

SKIING

The famous **Dachstein glacier** can be skied year-round, although summer snow conditions require considerable expertise. The altitude, however, guarantees good snow conditions late into the winter season. As usual, you can purchase a whole variety of different cards depending on your needs and desires.

Shopping

In the nearby village of Rössing, you'll find Richard Steiner's **Lodenwalker** (☎ 03687/81930), which, since 1434, has been turning out that highly practical feltlike fabric called loden. Here you can find various colors and textures at reasonable prices. It's open weekdays.

Filzmoos

⑲ *14 km (9 mi) west of Ramsau am Dachstein.*

Filzmoos is still a well-kept secret. Though skiing in the nearby Dachstein mountains is excellent, the not terribly expensive winter resort has yet to be discovered by foreign tourists. During the summer months, meandering mountain streams and myriad lakes attract anglers eager for trout, while hikers come to challenge the craggy peaks. Filzmoos calls itself a balloon village, because it relies heavily on hot-air balloons to show its guests the region. Contact **Büro Dachstein-Tauern-Ballons** (☎ 06453/2781).

Dining and Lodging

$$$ ✕🏠 **Hubertus.** In this highly personal hotel in the center of town,
★ every last detail—from romantic furnishings to modern conveniences—is done to perfection. Fishing enthusiasts have 20 km (12 mi) of mountain streams and two small lakes at their disposal. The restaurant is the best in the area: Frau Maier's way with trout (which you might have caught yourself) is exquisite, but don't overlook the game, roast poultry, or veal sweetbreads. Finish with *Topfenknödel* (cream cheese dumpling), a house specialty. ⊠ *Am Dorfpl. 1, A–5532,* ☎ *06453/ 204,* 𝖥𝖠𝖷 *06453/2066. 17 rooms. Restaurant, bar, café, sauna, exercise room, fishing. No credit cards. Closed mid-Apr.–mid-May and mid-Oct.–mid-Dec.*

$$–$$$ 🏠 **Alpenkrone.** From the balconies of this chalet complex, you'll have a great view of the surrounding mountains. Rooms are simple and in no particular style, but the friendly management has succeeded in providing four-star comfort at three-star prices even when the customary half board is considered. ⊠ *Filzmoos 133, A–5532,* ☎ *06453/280–0,* 𝖥𝖠𝖷 *06453/280–48. 51 rooms. Restaurant, bar, indoor pool, sauna, exercise room. DC, MC, V. Closed Easter–mid-May and mid-Oct.–mid-Dec.*

En Route From Filzmoos, rejoin Route 99/E14 again at Eben im Pongau. Here you can take the A10 autobahn north to Salzburg, if you're in a hurry. But if you have time for more majestic scenery and an interesting detour, continue about 4 km (2½ mi) on Route 99/E14, and turn north on Route 166, the **Salzburger Dolomitenstrasse** (Salzburg Dolomites Highway), for a 43-km (27-mi) swing around the Tennen mountains. Be careful, though, to catch the left turn onto Route 162 at Lindenthal; it will be marked to Golling. Head for Abtenau.

Abtenau

⑳ *44 km (28 mi) northwest of Filzmoos.*

Abtenau is a charming little town with a pretty old village square flanked by colorful burgher's houses and the 14th-century **St. Blasius parish church,** which has late- Gothic frescoes and a Baroque high altar. A **museum** of local history, which documents primarily the life of the farmers, has been set up south of town in the Arlerhof, an ancient house, which was built in 1325. It's open June–mid-September, Tuesday, Thursday, and Sunday 2–5. Nearby, nature has arranged its own museum, the Trickl and Dachser **waterfalls,** with the nearby cave known as the "cold cellar" (*der kalte Keller*), where beer used to be stored (*gelagert* means "stored" in German, hence the name "lager" beer).

Dining and Lodging

$$$ ✕⌑ **Post.** This older, centrally located hotel, decorated in rustic style with natural wood, has comfortable rooms with up-to-date facilities. And transportation is at the door; the Windhofer family also runs the town's taxi and bus service. The restaurant is good; try the rump steak Tirol or any of the other beef dishes. ⊠ *Markt 39, A–5541,* ☎ *06243/ 2209–0,* FAX *06243/3353. 40 rooms. Restaurant, café, indoor pool, sauna. DC. Closed Apr. and Nov.–mid-Dec.*

$$$$ ⌑ **Moisl.** This group of typical Alpine chalet–style houses in the center of town, with flower-laden balconies and overhanging eaves, dates back to 1764, but its services and facilities are absolutely up-to-date. Rooms are done in country decor. Evening entertainment includes folk dancing and wine and grill parties. ⊠ *Markt 26, A–5441,* ☎ *06243/ 21630,* FAX *06243/2232–612. 75 rooms. Restaurant, bar, café, indoor pool, sauna, tennis court, bowling. No credit cards. Closed Apr. and mid-Oct.–mid-Dec.*

Outdoor Activities and Sports

BICYCLING

The hilly town of Abtenau has a program of mountain biking and plenty of rental bikes. To find out more about individual biking tours, contact **Austria Radreisen** (⊠ Holzingerstr. 546, A–4780 Schärding, ☎ 07712/5511, FAX 07712/4811).

WHITE-WATER RAFTING

From May to the middle of October, you can raft the Salzach and Lammer rivers. The Lammer, with its "Hell's Run," is particularly wild. Runs begin at AS500 per person. For details, call either of Abtenau's two active clubs, **Club Alpin Extra** (☎ 06243/2939–0, FAX 06243/2939–15) or **Club Zwilling** (☎ 06243/3069 or 06243/3339, FAX 06243/3069–17).

Werfen

㉑ *41 km (26 mi) from Abtenau.*

The small town of Werfen, adorned with 16th-century buildings and a lovely Baroque church, belies its importance for it actually is the base for exploring three extraordinary attractions: the largest and most fabulous ice caverns in the world; one of Austria's most spectacular castles; and a four-star culinary shrine, Obauer. The riches of Werfen, in other words, place it on a par with many larger, much-touted Austrian cities.

★ From miles away, you can see **Burg Hohenwerfen,** looming over the Werfen, one of the most formidable fortresses of Europe (it was never taken in battle), which dates to 1077. Though fires, reconstructions, and renovations, most recently in 1948, have altered the appearance of the formidable fortress, it still maintains its medieval grandeur. Hewn out of the rock on which it stands, the castle was called by Maximilian I a "plume of heraldry radiant against the sky." Inside, it has black-timber beamed state rooms and an enormous frescoed Knights' Hall. It even has a torture chamber. Eagles, falcons, and other birds of prey swoop dramatically above the castle grounds, adding considerably to the medieval feel. The castle harbors Austria's first museum of falconry, and the birds of prey are rigorously trained. Call to confirm the show schedule, which may change. ☎ *06468/7603ßßß,* FAX *06468/7603–4.* ⌑ *Admission, tour, and birds-of-prey performance AS120.* ☉ *Fortress Easter–Oct., daily (may be closed Mon. in Apr. and Oct.); tour Apr.*

and Oct., Tues.–Sun. 10–4; May and Sept., daily 10–3; July–Aug., daily 11–5. Birds-of-prey performance Apr.–early July and late Aug.–Oct., daily at 11 and 3; early July–late Aug., daily at 11, 2, and 4.

OFF THE BEATEN PATH

EISRIESENWELT – The "World of the Ice Giants," just southwest of Abtenau, houses the largest known complex of ice caves, domes, galleries, and halls in Europe. It extends for some 42 km (26 mi) and contains a fantastic collection of frozen waterfalls and natural statuesque formations. Drive to the rest house, about halfway up the hill, and be prepared for some seriously scenic vistas. Then walk 15 minutes to the cable car, which takes you to a point about 15 minutes by foot from the cave, where you can take a 1¼-hour guided tour. You can also take a bus to the cable car from the Werfen railroad station (☎ 06468/293), but be sure to leave at least an hour before the start of the next scheduled cave trip. The entire adventure takes about half a day. And remember, no matter how warm it is outside, it's below freezing inside, so bundle up, and wear appropriate shoes. ☎ *06468/291 or 06468/248–0. ⌧ AS180, including cable car. ☉ Tours May–early Oct., daily 9:30–3:30 hourly; July–Aug., daily 9:30–4:30 hourly.*

Dining and Lodging

$$$$ ✕ **Obauer.** Worth a detour on your way back to Salzburg, this
★ *Landgasthaus* (country inn) is one of Austria's top half dozen restaurants—some would argue the best. The gourmet temple draws people from around the nation, so reserve well in advance and allow plenty of time: This is superlative cuisine. The menu constantly changes to match the imagination of the Obauer brothers, who share responsibilities as chefs. Diners choose a fixed menu or order à la carte, but either way, you'll find perfection in every offering. Ask for advice on the appropriate wines. You can also stay overnight here; the house has seven rooms (reserve in advance). ⌧ *Hauptstr. 46,* ☎ *06468/212–0,* 𝖥𝖠𝖷 *06468/212–12. Reservations essential. AE. Closed 2 (varying) days per wk; annual holiday closing also varies.*

$$ ▥ **Gasthaus Erzherzog Eugen.** You can't miss this hot pink *Gasthaus* with window boxes trailing garlands of geraniums. It's smack in the middle of town. Though the decor is basic and a bit bland—traditional white lace curtains and nondescript furniture—the staff extends a warm and hospitable welcome to its guests. The lodging is under the same management as the nearby Obauer (☞ *above*). ⌧ *Marktstrasse 38 17, A–5453,* ☎ *06468/210–0,* 𝖥𝖠𝖷 *06468/210–3. 12 rooms. Bar. No credit cards.*

EASTERN ALPS A TO Z

Arriving and Departing

By Car

If you're coming from northern Italy, you can get to Villach on the E55/A13 in Italy, which becomes the A2 and then the A10; from Klagenfurt, farther east in Carinthia, taking the A2 autobahn is quickest. The fastest route from Salzburg is the A10 autobahn, but you will have to take two tunnels into account at a total cost of AS140 (Tauern- and Katschbergtunnel). In summer on certain weekends (when the German federal states have their official vacations), the A10 southbound can become one very long parking lot, with hour-long waits before the tunnels. Taking the normal road over the passes, although long, is very attractive, but you will not be the only person who thought of it. If coming from abroad, don't forget to buy the autobahn sticker for Austria (☞ Driving *in* The Gold Guide).

By Plane

The closest airport is at Klagenfurt, 50 km (31 mi) from Villach. It is served by Austrian Airlines, Tyrolean Airways, and Swissair. Salzburg, too, has its own airport (☞ Salzburg A to Z *in* Chapter 6). Both have frequent connections to other Austrian cities and other points in Europe, but neither has scheduled overseas connections.

By Train

Villach and Salzburg are both served by frequent rail service from Vienna. Villach is also connected to Italy and Salzburg, which in turn is well connected to Germany. For train information, try one of the following: **Salzburg** (☎ 0662/1717), **Villach** (☎ 04242/1717), **Klagenfurt** (☎ 0463/1717).

Getting Around

By Bus

As is typical throughout Austria, where trains don't go, the post office and railroad buses do, though some side routes are less frequently covered. You'll need to coordinate your schedule with that of the buses, which is not as difficult as it sounds. The Austrian travel offices are helpful in this regard, or **bus information** is available (☎ 0660/5188) in Villach (☎ 04242/44410 or 04242/2020–4041) and in Salzburg (☎ 0662/167 or 0622/872150). You can take a post office bus from the **Zell am See rail station** (☎ 06542/2295) up and over the mountains to the glacier at Kaiser-Franz-Josefs-Höhe, a 2½-hour trip, or from the **Lienz rail station** (☎ 04852/67067) via Heiligenblut to the glacier, about two hours on this route. Buses run from early June to mid-October.

By Car

A car is by far the preferred means of seeing this area; the roads are good, and you can stop to picnic or just to marvel at the scenery. Be aware that the Grossglockner High Alpine Highway is closed from mid-November or possibly earlier (the first heavy snow) to mid-May or early June. Though many of the other high mountain roads are kept open in winter, driving them is nevertheless tricky, and you'll probably need chains. Keep in mind the cost of driving these roads as well: Tunnels, passes, and panoramic roads often have tolls.

By Train

You can reach most of the towns in the Eastern Alps by train, but the Grossglockner and Dachstein mountains are reachable in a practical sense only by road. If you do travel by rail, you can go from Villach to Hermagor, to Lienz, and northward (north of Spittal an der Drau) via Mallnitz and Badgastein to the main line at Schwarzach. There you can cut back westward to Zell am See or continue onward to Bischofshofen, connecting there via Radstadt to Schladming or staying on the main line north to Salzburg.

Contacts and Resources

Guided Tours

Bus tours from Salzburg include the Grossglockner mountain highway (☞ Salzburg A to Z *in* Chapter 6).

Visitor Information

For information about Carinthia, contact **Kärntner Tourismus** (✉ Casinopl. 1, A–9220 Velden, ☎ 04274/52100, FAX 04274/52100–50). The central tourist board for East Tirol is **Tirol-Information** (✉ Wilhelm-Greil-Str. 17, A–6010 Innsbruck, ☎ 0512/5320–170, FAX 0512/5320–174). For information about Salzburg Province, contact **Salzburger Land Tourismus** (✉ Wiener Bundesstr. 23, Postfach 1, A–5300 Hallwang bei Salzburg, ☎ 0662/6688, FAX 0662/6688–0). The main tourist bureau for Styria is **Steiermark Information** (✉ St. Peter–Hauptstr. 243, A–8042 Graz, ☎ 0316/403033–0, FAX 0316/403033–10).

Many individual towns have their own *Fremdenverkehrsamt* (tourist offices). **Badgastein:** Kur and Touristikbüro (✉ Kaiser-Franz-Josef-Str. 27, A–5640, ☎ 06434/2531–0, FAX 06434/2531–37). **Grosskirchheim/Döllach:** Verkehrsamt (✉ A–9843, ☎ 04825/521–0, FAX 04825/ 522–30). **Heiligenblut:** Tourismusverband (✉ Hof 4, A–9844, ☎ 04824/2001–21, FAX 04824/2001–43). **Hermagor:** Verkehrsamt (✉ Wulfeniapl. 1, A–9620, ☎ 04282/2043–0, FAX 04282/2043–50). **Kötschach–Mauthen** (✉ Kötschach 390, A–9640, ☎ 04715/8516, FAX 04715/8513–30). **Lienz** (✉ Europapl. 1, A–9900, ☎ 04852/65265, FAX 04852/65265–2). **Matrei in Osttirol** (✉ Rauterpl. 1, A–9971, ☎ 04875/5330, FAX 04875/5331). **Radstadt** (✉ Stadtpl. 17, A–5550, ☎ 06452/7472, FAX 06452/6702). **Ramsau am Dachstein** (✉ Kulm 40, A– 8972, ☎ 03687/81925 or 03687/81833, FAX 03687/81085). **Saalbach-Hinterglemm** (✉ Saalbach 550, A–5753 Saalbach, ☎ 06541/680068, FAX 06541/680069). **Saalfelden** (✉ Bahnhofstr. 10, A–5760, ☎ 06582/ 72513, FAX 06582/75398). **St. Jakob in Defereggen** (✉ Unterrotte 75AH, A–9963, ☎ 04873/5483 or 04873/5484, FAX 04873/5265). **St. Johann im Pongau** (✉ Hauptstr. 16, A–5600, ☎ 06412/6036, FAX 06412/ 6036–74). **Schladming** (✉ Erzherzog-Johann-Str. 213, A–8970, ☎ 03687/22268, FAX 03687/24138). **Werfen** (✉ A–5450, ☎ 06468/388 FAX 06468/7562). **Zell am See:** Information (✉ A–5700, ☎ 06542/770– 0, FAX 06542/72032).

10 Innsbruck and Tirol

Tirol has a great deal, if not everything: the Holy Roman Empire splendors of Innsbruck, Hansel-and-Gretel villages, majestic mountain peaks, masked Carnival revelers, and more—much more. Shine up your best lederhosen and set out to shop for cuckoo clocks; then try out your vibrato on some Jodeln, Tirolian singing. Then head for the great ski resorts—St. Anton, Kitzbühel, and St. Johann—where sport und Spiel are always in high gear.

Updated by
Bonnie Dodson

TIROL IS SO DIFFERENT from the rest of Austria that you might think you've crossed a border. In a way, you have. The frontier between the provinces of Salzburg and Tirol is defined by mountains; four passes make traffic possible. The faster trains cut across Germany rather than agonizing through the Austrian Alps. To the west, Tirol is separated from neighboring Vorarlberg by the Arlberg Range.

Relatively small as the province of Tirol is, the idea of Tirol remains all-encompassing—it is virtually the shop window of Austria. Its very name conjures up visions of great chains of never-ending, snowcapped mountains; remote, winding Alpine valleys; rushing mountain torrents; and spectacular glaciers that rise out of the depths like brilliant, icy diamonds. In the winter you'll find masses of deep, sparkling powder snow; unrivaled skiing and tobogganing; and bizarre winter carnivals with grotesque masked mummers. In the summer, you'll find breathtaking picture-postcard Alpine scenery, cool mountain lakes, and rambles through forests; and throughout the year, there are yodeling and zither music, villagers in lederhosen and broad-brimmed feathered hats, and, of course, the sounds of those distinctive cowbells.

As if the sheer physical splendor of Tirol weren't enough, the region can look back on a history filled with romance. Up to the beginning of the 16th century, Tirol was a powerful state in its own right, under a long line of counts and dukes, including personages of such varying fortunes as Friedl the Penniless and his son Sigmund the Wealthy. (On the whole, Tirolean rulers were more often wealthy than penniless.) The province reached the zenith of its power under Emperor Maximilian I (1459–1519), when Innsbruck was the seat of the Holy Roman Empire. Maximilian's tomb in Innsbruck gives ample evidence of this onetime far-reaching glory. Over the centuries, the Tiroleans became fiercely nationalistic. In 1809–10 Andreas Hofer led bands of local patriots against Napoléon in an effort to break free from Bavaria and rejoin Austria. After three successful battles, including the Battle of Bergisel just outside Innsbruck, Hofer lost the fourth attempt against combined French and Bavarian forces, was executed in Mantua, and became a national hero.

Today, Tirol looks to Vienna for political support in its perpetual dispute with Italy over the South Tirol, a large and prosperous wine-growing region that was ceded to Italy after World War I. Many Austrian Tiroleans still own property in South Tirol and consider it very much a part of their homeland. Yet even Austria's Tirol is physically divided: East Tirol, a small enclave of remarkable natural magnificence wedged between the provinces of Salzburg and Carinthia, belongs to Tirol, but it can be reached only through Italy or the province of Salzburg.

And what about the Tiroleans themselves? Like most other mountain peoples, the Tiroleans are very proud and independent—so much so that for many centuries, the natives of one narrow valley fastness had little communication with their "foreign" neighbors in the next valley. (It's still possible to find short, dark, and slender residents in one valley and strapping blond, blue-eyed giants in the next.) But Tirol can also be very cosmopolitan, as any visitor to Innsbruck can attest. The city is Tirol's treasure house—historically, culturally, and commercially. It's also sited smack dab in the center of the Tirolian region and makes a convenient base from which to explore. Even if you are staying at an area resort, spend a day or two in Innsbruck first: It will give you a far better perspective on the rest of the region.

Pleasures and Pastimes

Dining

Tirolean restaurants range from grand-hotel dining salons—favored spots for chic Innsbruckers—to little Tirolean *Bauernstuben,* rustic restaurants where you can enjoy hearty carrot, *Knödel* (dumpling), and zucchini soups while sitting on highly polished wooden seats (rather hard ones!). Don't forget to enjoy some of the fine Innsbruck coffeehouses, famous for their scrumptious cakes—mainly of the whipped cream variety—and remember that some daytime eating places turn into wine taverns late in the evening. Outside of Innsbruck, you'll find country inns that have dining rooms, but there are few, if any, separate restaurants. Prices for meals include taxes and a service charge but not the customary small additional tip of 3%–5%.

CATEGORY	COST*
$$$$	over AS400
$$$	AS300–AS400
$$	AS200–AS300
$	under AS150–AS200

per person for a typical three-course meal, with a glass of house wine

Hiking

Tirol has a good share of the more than 50,000 km (35,000 mi) of well-maintained mountain paths that ribbon the country. Hiking is one of the best ways truly to experience the awesome Alpine scenery, whether you just want to take a leisurely stroll around one of the crystal blue lakes reflecting the mountains towering above them or trek to the top of one of the mighty peaks. Mountain-climbing is a highly organized sport in Tirol, a province that features some of the greatest challenges to lovers of this sport: the Kaisergebirge (base: Kufstein), the Zillertaler and Tuxer Alps (base: Mayrhofen), the Wettersteingebirge and Karwendel ranges (base: Seefeld), the Nordkette range (base: Innsbruck), and the Oetz (base: Obergurgl). The instructors at the Alpine School Innsbruck are the best people to contact if you want to make arrangements for a mountain-climbing holiday or if you wish to attend a mountain-climbing school; if you already know how, contact the Österreichischer Alpenverein (☞ Outdoor Activities and Sports *in* Innsbruck, *below*).

Lodging

For one reason or another, travelers do not stay very long in Innsbruck itself. The rival attractions of the magnificent countryside, the lure of the mountains, and the countless Alpine valleys prove perhaps too strong—in any case, Innsbruck hotels report the average stay is usually two to three days, so there is a fast turnover and always a room to be had. Even so, if you travel during the high season, July–August and in the winter, it's best to book in advance. If you're driving, you may want to seek out a hotel in Innsbruck that has parking, since otherwise cars must be left some distance from the city center. Hotel rates vary widely by season, with the off-peak periods being March–May and September–November. Some travelers opt to set up their base not in Innsbruck but *overlooking* it, on the Hungerburg Plateau, on the top of a hill 3,000 ft above sea level, or in one of the hotels and inns perched still higher up on the Nordkette chain, both reached by funicular. If you choose these lofty aeries, you will have invigorating mountain air and a wonderful view of the Alps with Innsbruck spread at your feet (commuting to the city, of course, will add to your expenses).

In the popular resort towns, many hotels operate on a half-board basis (breakfast and one other meal a day must be taken) during the ski season, and some take no credit cards. Summer prices are often as much as 50% lower than during the ski season. If you're out for savings, it's a good idea to find lodgings in small towns nearby, rather than in the resorts themselves; local tourist offices may be able to help you, possibly even with accommodations in private homes if you book well ahead. In our listings, Kitzbühel, St. Anton, and Seefeld are the higher-priced resorts. Prices include tax and service.

CATEGORY	RESORTS*	SMALL TOWNS*
$$$$	over AS2,200	over AS1,000
$$$	AS1,500–AS2,200	AS800–AS1,000
$$	AS900–AS1,500	AS550–AS800
$	under AS900	under AS550

*per person for a standard double room with bath, including breakfast (except in $$$$ hotels), generally half board in resorts in winter

Skiing

Downhill was practically invented in Tirol, which came to the forefront as a prime tourist destination because of the excellence of its skiing. Modern ski techniques were developed here, thanks to the legendary skiing master Hannes Schneider, who took the Norwegian art of cross-country skiing and adapted it to downhill running. No matter where your trip takes you, world-class—and often gut-numbing—skiing is available, from the glamour of Kitzbühel in the east to the imposing peaks of St. Anton am Arlberg in the west. Even on the sultriest summer day, it's possible to slip on your skis and glide down a glacier.

Close to the Arlberg Pass is **St. Anton,** which, at 4,300 ft, is home to one of the finest ski schools in the world. The specialty at St. Anton is piste skiing—enormously long runs studded with mogels (and few trees), some so steep and challenging that the sport is almost more like mountain climbing. In fact, this is the only place you can heli-ski in Austria. It was here in the 1920s that Hannes Schneider started the school that was to become the model for all others. A short bus ride to the top of the pass brings you to **St. Christoph,** at 5,800 ft. Many excellent tours, served by the Galzip cable railway, start here, but the *Skihaserl,* or ski bunny, would do well to stay down at St. Anton where there are better—and gentler—nursery slopes.

Farther along the Inn is the Ötz Valley. From the Otztal station, you can go by bus to **Soelden,** a resort at 4,500 ft that is not as expensive as others, nor as highly organized. The village of **Obergurgl,** at 6,321 ft, lies at the head of the Ötz Valley, where you can ski until early summer. Not far from Innsbruck is **Seefeld,** at 3,870 ft, long the town of one of Austria's best-known aces, Toni Seelos. At the farther end of Tirol lies **Kitzbühel,** chic and *charmant,* perhaps most famous for its "Ski Circus," a system of ski lifts and trails, floodlit at night, whereby skiers can ski for weeks without retracing their steps. The best time for skiing around **Innsbruck** is January–March.

Exploring Innsbruck and Tirol

Innsbruck makes a good introduction and starting point for exploring Tirol, but Tirol's gorgeous geography precludes the convenient loop tour from the capital city. You must go up into the valleys to discover the hundreds of charming villages and hotels, and a certain amount of backtracking is necessary. We've outlined four tours over familiar routes, touching on the best of the towns and suggesting side trips and pleasures off the beaten track. "Around the Lower Inn Valley" will take you east of Innsbruck through the lower Inn Valley, then south into the Ziller and Tuxer valleys, with detours to the Achensee and to Gerlos. "From Jenbach to Kitzbühel," also east of Innsbruck, continues up the Inn Valley to Kufstein on the German border and to the ski resorts of St. Johann and Kitzbühel. "West from Innsbruck to Imst and Ötz Valley" explores the Inn Valley west of Innsbruck to Imst, then goes south up the Ötz Valley. "Landeck, Upper Inn Valley, and St. Anton" heads west from Imst, takes in Landeck and the upper Inn Valley, ending with St. Anton and the Arlberg. Whether you mix or match these tours or do them all, they'll allow you to discover a cross section of Tirol's highlights: the old and the new, glossy resorts, medieval castles, and always that superlative scenery.

Great Itineraries

Numbers in the text correspond to numbers in the margin and on the Innsbruck, Eastern Tirol, and Western Tirol maps.

IF YOU HAVE 3 DAYS

Head straight to the heart of Tirol to the provincial capital of ☷ **Innsbruck** ①–⑩; the city is conveniently situated for the traveler to Tirol, for it lies almost exactly in the center of the province on the Inn River. Even if you have already settled on a resort for your holiday, you should spend at least a day in the capital first to check out the beautiful buildings built by the Emperor Maximilian I—from the **Goldenes Dachl** ① to the **Hofburg** ⑤—and by Austria's empress Maria Theresa, who gave her name to the principal street of the town, the Maria-Theresien-Strasse (any sightseeing in Innsbruck begins on this street, which runs through the heart of the city from north to south and is the main shopping center). Far from being exhausting to explore, Innsbruck is only a half-hour walk from one end of the old town to the other. The next day, let the funicular whisk you up the **Hungerburg** for the breathtaking views of Innsbruck below. You can take a leisurely hike along the mountain trail and see the flora and fauna at the Alpine zoo. After returning to the capital city, set out on your final day to visit **Schloss Ambras,** with its impressive collections of medieval curiosities—pack a picnic and stay for a concert if you're traveling during the summer season. More ambitious travelers should consider a quick day trip to the seriously scenic **Stubatial Valley,** one of the showpieces of the Tirol—via the narrow-gauge electric Stubaitalbahn.

IF YOU HAVE 5 DAYS

Begin your Tirolian sojourn with two days in attraction-studded ☷ **Innsbruck** ①–⑩—but don't forget to experience your first taste of the region's grand Alpine setting by fitting in some quick excursions to the outlying **Hungerburg** peak, the **Schloss Ambras,** or the **Stubaital Valley.** On day three, charming Alpine villages are on the agenda with a visit to the Ötz Valley: head for **Telfs** ㉖, **Ötz** ㉘, and **Sölden** ㉙, ending your journey at Austria's highest mountain town, ☷ **Obergurgl** ㉚. On the fourth day, spend time exploring castle ruins, Baroque churches, and yet more spectacular scenery in **Imst** ㉗, **Landeck** ㉛, and **Ried** ㉜, with an overnight in ☷ **Serfaus** ㉝. For the peak experience of your trip—literally—head to the slopes on your final day at **St. Anton am Arlberg** ㉞. Keep in mind that modern highways can get you to your destination quickly, but often the most beautiful scenic views lie on off-the-beaten-track roads: Ask your hotel concierge for advice on finding the best beauty spots.

IF YOU HAVE 7 DAYS

☷ **Innsbruck** ①–⑩ makes a good base for discovering the entire region but is well worth spending two days exploring on its own. After seeing the riches of the old town of the imperial city and its neighboring attractions, the **Hungerburg** peak and **Schloss Ambras,** set out on the morning of the third day to see how the Habsburgs amassed their vast

Eastern Tirol

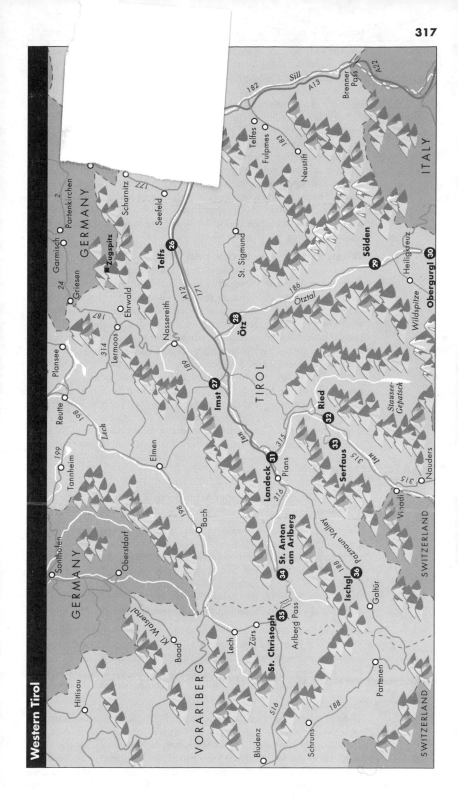

wealth: Visit the mint at **Hall in Tirol** ⑪ and the silver mines at **Schwaz** ⑫. Then spend the night overlooking the pristine ⚞ **Achensee** ⑬ or stay at ⚞ **Pertisau** ⑭. On your fourth day, head south following the Ziller river with stops along the way in **Zell am Ziller** ⑮ and **Mayrhofen** ⑯. From there you can head west to explore the beautiful **Tuxer Valley** ⑰ and the classic Alpine villages of Lanersbach and Hintertux or save your breath and head east to climb the impressive Kreuzjoch mountain in nearby ⚞ **Gerlos** ⑲. On the fifth day, challenge the slopes at either of the world-famous resorts of ⚞ **St. Johann** ㉔ or **Kitzbühel** ㉕—two towns that have become almost more fashionable as warm-weather destinations than skiing meccas. On day six, visit the smaller resorts of **Going, Ellmau,** and **Söll** before visiting Emperor Maximilian's pleasure palace in ⚞ **Kufstein** ㉓. On your final day, visit the medieval town of **Rattenberg** ㉒ and the castles of **Brixlegg** ⑳ on your way back to Innsbruck.

When to Tour Innsbruck and Tirol

Tirol is a province for all seasons, and the physical geography of the province makes it an especially ideal place in which to enjoy the outdoor life year-round. Ski-crazy travelers descend on the resorts during the winter months; in the summer, when the mountains are awash with wildflowers, camping tents spring up like mushrooms in the valleys as hikers, cavers, and mountain climbers take advantage of the palatial peaks. The annual Tirolean calendar is packed with special events: the famous Schemenlaufen, a procession of picturesque carved wooden masks, held in February in Imst; the Fasching balls, which reach their peak at the end of February in Seefeld; the Hahnenkamm ski race and curling competition held in winter in Kitzbühel; the glacier ski races in April at Obergurgl; the world-famous Gauderfest at Zell am Ziller during the first weekend in May; and the castle concerts at Kufstein and the folk festival in Mayrhofen during July and August.

INNSBRUCK

190 km (118 mi) southwest of Salzburg, 471 km (304 mi) southwest of Vienna.

The capital of Tirol is one of the most beautiful towns of its size anywhere in the world, owing much of its charm and fame to its unique setting. To the north, the steep, sheer sides of the Alps rise, literally from the edge of the city, like a shimmering blue-and-white wall—an impressive backdrop for the mellowed green domes and red roofs of the Baroque town tucked below. To the south, the peaks of the Tuxer and Stubai ranges undulate in the hazy purple distance.

Innsbruck has been an important crossroads for hundreds of years. When it was chartered in 1239, it was already a key point on the north–south highways between Germany and Italy and the east–west axis tying eastern Austria and the lands beyond to Switzerland. Today Innsbruck is the transit point for road and rail traffic between the bordering countries.

The charming Old World aspect of Innsbruck has remained virtually intact and includes ample evidence of its Baroque lineage. The skyline encircling the center suffers somewhat from high-rises, but the heart, the **Altstadt,** or Old City, remains much as it was 400 years ago. The protective vaulted arcades along main thoroughfares, the tiny passageways giving way to noble squares, and the ornate restored houses all contribute to an unforgettable picture.

Squeezed by the mountains and sharing the valley with the Inn River (Innsbruck means "bridge over the Inn"), the city is compact and very easy to explore on foot. Reminders of three historic figures abound: the local hero Andreas Hofer, whose band of patriots challenged Napoléon in 1809; Emperor Maximilian I (1459–1519); and Empress Maria Theresa (1717–80), the last two of whom were responsible for much of the city's architecture. Maximilian ruled the Holy Roman Empire from Innsbruck, and Maria Theresa, who was particularly fond of the city, spent a lot of time here.

Pick up a free Club Innsbruck card at your hotel for no-charge use of ski buses and reduced-charge ski-lift passes. For big savings, buy the **Innsbruck Card,** which gives you free admission to all the museums, mountain cable cars, the Alpenzoo and Schloss Ambras, plus free bus and tram transportation. Cards are good for 24, 48, and 72 hours at AS230, AS300, and AS370, respectively, and are available at the tourist office (☞ Visitor Information *in* Innsbruck and Tirol A to Z, *below*).

❶ Any walking tour of Innsbruck should start at the **Goldenes Dachl** (Golden Roof), which made famous the late-Gothic mansion whose balcony it covers. In fact, the roof is made of gilded copper tiles, and its recent refurbishment is said to have taken 14 kilograms (nearly 31 pounds) of gold. The house was built in 1420 for Duke Friedrich (otherwise known as Friedl the Penniless), and it is said that the indignant duke had the original roof covered with gold to counter the rumor that he was poor; the balcony was added in 1501 by Maximilian I as a sort of "royal box" for watching street performances in the square below. The structure was altered and expanded at the beginning of the 18th century, and now only the loggia and the alcove are identifiable as original. The magnificent coats of arms representing Austria, Hungary, Burgundy, Milan, the Holy Roman Empire, Styria, Tirol, and royal Germany are copies. You can see the originals (and up close, too) in the Ferdinandeum. The Golden Roof building now houses the **Maximilianeum,** which features memorabilia and paintings from the life of Emperor Maximilian I. ⊠ *Herzog Friedrich-Str. 15,* ☎ *0512/5360–575,* 🖅 *AS60,* ☼ *Mar.–Oct., daily 9:30–5:30; Nov.–Feb., Tues.–Sun. 9:30 5:30.*

❷ Down the street from the Goldenes Dachl is the **Stadtturm,** the 15th-century city tower, with a steep climb of 148 steps to the top. ⊠ *Herzog-Friedrich-Str. 21,* ☎ *0512/5759–62.* 🖅 *AS22.* ☼ *Mar.–June and Sept.–Oct., daily 10–5; July–Aug., daily 10–6.*

❸ Nearby is the dramatic blue-and-white **Helbling House,** originally a Gothic building (1560) to which the obvious, ornate rococo decoration was added in 1730. ⊠ *Herzog-Friedrich-Str. 10.*:The main attraction

❹ of the Baroque **Domkirche zu St. Jakob** is the high-altar painting of the Madonna by Lucas Cranach the Elder, dating from about 1520. The cathedral was built in 1722. The ornate Baroque interior also has dramatic painted ceilings. ⊠ *Dompl. 6,* ☎ *0512/5839–02.* 🖅 *Free.* ☼ *Sat.–Thurs. 6–noon and 2–5, Fri. 2–5.*

❺ One of the most historic attractions of Innsbruck is the **Hofburg** imperial palace, which Maximilian I commissioned in the 14th century. (The booklet in English at the ticket office will tell you more interesting tidbits about the palace than the tour guide will.) Center stage is the **Giant's Hall**—designated a marvel of the 18th-century as soon as it was topped off with its magnificent trompe-l'oeil ceiling, painted by Franz Anton Maulpertsch in 1775. The rococo decor and the portraits of Habsburg ancestors in the ornate white-and-gold great reception hall were added in the 18th century by Maria Theresa; look for the por-

Innsbruck

trait of "Primal" (primrose)—to use the childhood nickname of the empress's daughter, Marie-Antoinette. ✉ *Rennweg 1,* ☎ *0512/587186–13.* 🎫 *AS50.* ☉ *Tour mid-May–mid-Oct., daily 9–5 hourly; mid-Oct.–mid-May, Mon.–Sat. daily 9–5 hourly.*

❻ Close by the Hofburg is the **Hofkirche** (Court Church), built as a mausoleum for Maximilian I (although he is actually buried in Wiener Neustadt, south of Vienna). The emperor's ornate black marble tomb is surrounded by 24 marble reliefs portraying his accomplishments, as well as 28 larger-than-life statues of his ancestors, including the legendary King Arthur of England. Andreas Hofer is also buried here. Don't miss the 16th-century **Silver Chapel,** up the stairs opposite the entrance, with its elaborate altar and silver Madonna. The chapel was built in 1578 to be the tomb of Archduke Ferdinand II and his wife, Philippine Welser, the daughter of a rich and powerful merchant family. Visit the chapel in the morning to take pictures; the blinding afternoon sun comes in directly behind the altar. ✉ *Universitätsstr. 2,* ☎ *0512/584302.* 🎫 *AS20; combined ticket with Tiroler Volkskunstmuseum (☞ below) AS50.* ☉ *July–Aug., daily 9–5:30; Sept.–June, daily 9–5.*

❼ The **Tiroler Volkskunstmuseum** (Tirolean Folk-Art Museum), in the same complex as the Hofkirche, exhibits Christmas mangers, costumes, rustic furniture, and entire rooms from old farmhouses and inns, decorated in styles ranging from Gothic to rococo. Displays are somewhat static, and the information cards are in German. The small Christmas Manger Museum, on the other hand, is fascinating. ✉ *Universitätsstr. 2,* ☎ *0512/584302.* 🎫 *AS40; manger museum AS20.* ☉ *July–Aug., Mon.–Sat. 9–5:30, Sun. 9–noon; Sept.–June, Mon.–Sat. 9–5, Sun. 9–noon.*

↻ The **Schmetterlinghaus** (Butterfly House) in a corner of the Hofgarten is home to a fascinating collection of exotic live butterflies flitting about a sunny, flower-filled greenhouse. ✉ *Rennweg 2,* ☎ *0512/584803–27.* 🎫 *AS40.* ☉ *Mid-June–mid-Sept, daily 10–5.*

❽ The **Ferdinandeum** (Museum of Tyrol) houses Austria's largest collection of Gothic art, 19th- and 20th-century paintings, and medieval arms. Here you'll find the original coats of arms from the Goldenes Dachl balcony. ✉ *Museumstr. 15,* ☎ *0512/59489.* 🎫 *AS50.* ☉ *Oct.–Apr., Tues.–Sat. 10–noon and 2–5, Sun. 10–1; May–Sept., Fri.–Wed. 10–5, Thurs. 7–9.*

❾ The **Triumphpforte,** or Triumphal Arch (✉ Salurner-Str.) was built in 1765 to commemorate both the marriage of emperor-to-be Leopold II and the death of Emperor Franz I, husband of Empress Maria Theresa.

❿ The **Annasäule,** or St. Anna's Column (✉ Maria Theresien-Str.), commemorates the withdrawal of Bavarian forces in the war of the Spanish Succession in 1703 on St. Anna's Day. From here you'll have a classic view of Innsbruck, with the glorious mountains in the background.

↻ A visit to the 400-year-old **Grassmayr Bell Foundry** will give you an idea of how bells are cast and tuned. Take Bus J, K, or S south to Grassmayrstrasse. ✉ *Leopoldstr. 53,* ☎ *0512/59416–34.* 🎫 *AS20.* ☉ *Weekdays 9–6, Sat. 9–noon.*

Three Excursions

Hungerburg

↻ Just barely outside the city at the Hungerburg, a combination of funicular and cable car will take you soaring above Innsbruck's skyline. Take Streetcar 1 or Bus C to the base station (✉ Rennweg 41, ☎ 0512/586158). From here you take the funicular up to the Hungerburg (2,800 ft), then a two-stage cable car to Seegrube at 6,250 ft and

Hafelekar at the dizzying height of 7,500 ft. The round-trip to Hunger-burg costs AS48 with the Innsbruck Card; the round-trip to Hafelekar is AS230 with the Innsbruck Card. At all three stops you'll find hotels and restaurants commanding breathtaking views over the Tirolean Alps and Innsbruck.

If you're staying in Innsbruck for a few days, you may want to break up this excursion into stages. Starting with Hungerburg, visit a different al-titude and perspective each day, enjoying a leisurely lunch at each level.

The **Alpenzoo,** a short walk from the Hungerburg station, has an un-usual collection of Alpine birds and animals, including endangered species. The zoo alone is worth the trip up the Hungerburg; if you buy your ticket for the zoo at the base station, the trip up and back is free. ✉ *Weiherburggasse 37A,* ☎ *0512/292323.* ✍ *AS60.* ☉ *Spring–fall, daily 9–6; winter, daily 9–dusk.*

Schloss Ambras

When Archduke Ferdinand II wanted to marry for love to a commoner, Philippine Welser, the court grudgingly allowed it, but the couple was forced to live outside the city limits. Ferdinand revamped a 10th-cen-tury castle for his bride, which was completed in 1556 and every bit as deluxe as what he was accustomed to in town. Set in acres of gar-dens and woodland, it is a curiously inviting castle, with cheery red-and-white shutters on its many windows. The upper castle now houses rooms of noble portraits and the lower section has a collection of weaponry and armor. Be sure to inspect Philippine's sunken bath, a luxury for its time. Look around the grounds as well to see the fenc-ing field and a small cemetery with samples of earth from 18 battle-fields around the world. The castle is located 3 km (2 mi) southeast of the city. To reach it without a car, take Tram 3 to Ambras, or the shut-tle (AS30 roundtrip; leaves on the hour) from Maria–Therisien Strasse 45. ✉ *Schloss Str. 20,* ☎ *0512/348446.* ✍ *AS60; tour additional AS20.* ☉ *Tour Apr.–Oct., Wed.–Mon. 10–5; check with tourist of-fice for winter hrs.*

The Stubaital Valley

The delightful little Stubaital Valley, less than 40 km (25 mi) long, is one of the showpieces of the Tirol, with no fewer than 80 glistering glaciers and more than 40 towering peaks. If you just want to look, you can see the whole Stubaital in a full day's excursion from Inns-bruck. The narrow-gauge electric **Stubaitalbahn** (departure from the center of Innsbruck and in front of the main rail station, as well as from the station just below the Bergisel ski jump) goes as far as Fulpmes, partway up the valley. You can take the bus as far as Ranalt and back to Fulpmes, to see more of the valley, then return on the quaint rail line. Buses leave from Gate 1 of the Autobusbahnhof, just behind the rail station at Südtiroler Platz, about every hour (✉ Stubaitalbahn, ☎ 0512/5307–184).

Dining

$$$$ ✕ **Goldener Adler.** This is Innsbruck's most famous hotel (☞ Lodg-ing, *below*), and it also features a very good restaurant. A true rarity, the place is as popular with Austrians as it is with travelers. Two of the rooms are exceptionally beautiful; the others are by no means the poor man's hussar, offering luxe peasant decor. During the Christmas and Easter holidays you can listen to live zither music in the Goethe Stube (only open in the evening). The liveliest crowds favor the Batzen-häsl on the arcade ground-floor level. Start with an Adler-Royal, a glass of *Sekt* (Austrian sparkling wine) with a dash of blackberry liqueur while

Innsbruck Dining and Lodging

Dining
Café Valier, **22**
Central, **10**
Goldener Adler, **7**
Jörgele, **6**
Katzung, **12**
Ottoburg, **5**

Philippine, **23**
Schwarzer Adler, **8**
Sweet Basil, **13**
Theresian Brau, **20**
Tiroler Stuben, **16**
Weisses Rössl, **11**
Wienerwald, **9, 18**

Lodging
Alpotel, **16**
Binder, **25**
Goldener Adler, **7**
Innsbruck, **17**
Innsbrücke, **2**
Internationales
Studentenhaus, **15**

Kapeller, **24**
Maria Theresia, **19**
Rosen–Hotel
Höttinger Au, **3**
Rössl in der Au, **4**
Royal, **14**
Scandic Crown, **21**
Tautermann, **1**
Weisses Kreuz, **13**

you're perusing the menu, which features a modern slant on traditional dishes. Pork medallions are topped with ham and Gorgonzola, and the grilled chicken breast comes with a ginger cream sauce and spaëtzle. ✉ *Herzog Friedrich-Str. 6,* ☎ *0512/586334. Reservations essential. AE, DC, MC, V.*

$$$$ ✗ **Schwarzer Adler.** This intimate, romantic restaurant on the ground
★ floor of the Schwarzer Adler Hotel has lead-paned windows and rustic Tirolean decor, offering the perfect backdrop for a memorable meal. Specialties include lobster ragout with tagliatelle in a red wine sauce and grilled freshwater trout. It's a bit off the beaten track but worth the effort to go there. ✉ *Kaiserjägerstr. 2,* ☎ *0512/587109,* FAX *0512/561697. AE, DC, MC, V. Closed Sun.*

$$$ ✗ **Jörgele.** This flower-bedecked restaurant is in the heart of the old quarter near the Goldenes Dachl. Traditional Tirolean classics, such as game stew with mushroom as well as spinach dumplings and liver with bacon and tomatoes, are served in ample portions. The wine list is extensive, with vintages from around the globe, including Argentina, California, and France. ✉ *Herzog-Friedrich Str. 13,* ☎ *0512/571006. AE, DC, MC, V.*

$$$ ✗ **Sweet Basil.** Passersby often pause to look through the big window of this new, always crowded restaurant next to the Weisses Kreuz hotel, and it's easy to see why. Cozily arranged tables are topped with squat golden candles, made more dramatic because it's the only lighting used. Every month a different style of cuisine is featured, from Tex-Mex to Chinese to Italian, but traditional Austrian dishes are offered as well. Salads are also a big item here. ✉ *Herzog-Friedrich-Str. 31,* ☎ *0512/584996. AE, DC, MC, V.*

$$$ ✗ **Tiroler Stuben.** Highly regarded by locals, the Tiroler Stuben has a
★ broad seasonal menu including lots of vegetarian choices. Try the *Schlutzkrapferln,* Tirolean ravioli stuffed with cheese, potatoes, and spinach, topped with melted butter and Parmesan; the Tirolean braised beef in a bacon and onion cream sauce; or just a simple roast chicken and potato salad. End with profiteroles, vanilla ice cream–filled cream puffs covered with chocolate sauce. Despite the fact that the restaurant is always packed, service is attentive. Ask for help with the wine list, although the open wines, particularly the red St. Laurent, are excellent. ✉ *Innrain 13 (Ursulinenpassage),* ☎ *0512/577931. Reservations essential. AE, DC, MC, V.*

$$ ✗ **Ottoburg.** It's fun just to explore the rabbit warren of paneled rustic
★ rooms upstairs in this red-and-white shuttered house built in 1494. Several of the bay-window alcoves have great views toward the Goldenes Dachl square. The *Gaststube* downstairs is less intimate but offers a lower-cost selection. Try the trout, if it's on the menu, but the chicken and duck dishes are also excellent. ✉ *Herzog Friedrich-Str. 1,* ☎ *0512/574652. AE, DC, MC, V. Closed Tues. and 2 wks in mid-Nov.*

$$ ✗ **Philippine.** The food here is exclusively vegetarian, with so many tempting items to choose from it's hard to make a decision. You might start with polenta topped with Gorgonzola and ruby red tomatoes and then go on to cannelloni stuffed with potatoes and smoked tofu, or pumpkin risotto with pumpkin seeds, ginger, and Parmesan. All portions are substantial. The restaurant has a light, cheerful ambience, and tables are candlelit at night. ✉ *Müllerstr. and Templestr.,* ☎ *0512/ 589157. MC, V.*

$$ ✗ **Weisses Rössl.** In the authentically rustic rooms upstairs, an array of antlers and a private art gallery add to the decor. This is the right place for solid local standards, like *Tiroler G'röstl,* a tasty hash treatment, and veal cutlet, both of which taste even better on the outside terrace in summer. ✉ *Kiebachgasse 8,* ☎ *0512/583057. AE, MC, V. Closed Sun., early Nov., mid-Apr.*

$ ✕ Theresian Bräu. This new, multilevel brewhouse in the center of town is decorated to give the appearance of the inside of a ship, with what looks like a submarine control panel lining one wall and an assortment of other seafaring items scattered throughout, such as fishnets, steamer trunks, and even rowboats. But the focus here is on beer, brewed right on the premises. They also offer meals and snacks, including zucchini ragout with polenta gratiné, or *Tafelspitz*, a boiled beef dish. People of any age can be found here, but be prepared for loud music. ⊠ *Maria-Theresian-Str. 51–53,* ☎ *0512/587580,* FAX *0512/587580–5.*

$ ✕ Wienerwald. This chain started out with grilled chicken (and very good indeed) but now serves pastas as well as roast and grilled meats in a modern rustic environment. In summer, the gardens of both locations are particularly pleasant and are open till 11 PM. ⊠ *Maria Theresien-Str. 12,* ☎ *0512/584165;* ⊠ *Museumstr. 24,* ☎ *0512/588994. AE, DC, MC, V.*

Cafés

★ Cafe Valier. You'll have to walk a few minutes away from the city center to reach this café, but it's worth the effort and the calories you'll consume. Cafe Valier's pastries are so good that they have twice been invited to compete in the World Pastry Cup in Lyon, France. The coffee is also excellent, and service is friendly. ⊠ *Maximilianstr. 27,* ☎ *0512/586180. No credit cards. Closed Sun. and Aug.*

Central. Since 1878 this large, traditional café in the Viennese style has been *the* place to relax over a coffee. Recent renovations have also stripped away some atmosphere, but newspapers and magazines are still available, as is a variety of food and pastries. ⊠ *Gilmstr. 5, in the Central Hotel,* ☎ *0512/5920–0. AE, DC, MC, V. Closed Nov.*

Katzung. This café is just a few doors down from the Goldenes Dachl, and in summer you have a great view from the outdoor terrace. That's the main draw here, though the pastries are very good and they offer a variety of ice-cream sundaes. ⊠ *Herzog-Friedrich-Str. 16,* ☎ *0512/586183. No credit cards. Closed Sun.*

Lodging

$$$$ ⊡ Goldener Adler. Mozart, Goethe, and more recently John Glenn and the king and queen of Norway have stayed here. This traditional hotel, a 600-year-old house with stone walls, winding staircases, and a variety of nooks and crannies, has mostly spacious rooms, though a few readers have complained about closetlike rooms on the upper floors. The location is ideal, in the heart of the Old City and just down the street from the Goldenes Dachl. The hotel features one of Innsbruck's most popular restaurants (☞ Dining, *above*). ⊠ *Herzog Friedrich-Str. 6, A–6020,* ☎ *0512/586334,* FAX *0512/584409. 35 rooms. 2 restaurants. AE, DC, MC, V.*

$$$$ ⊡ Maria Theresia. Behind the elegant 1920s facade you'll find a freshly renovated hotel, now part of the Best Western chain. You couldn't be more central; choose between a room on the street overlooking the Anna Column and the active main thoroughfare or one on the inside, where it's considerably quieter. The rooms are stylishly furnished in neo-Baroque. ⊠ *Maria Theresien-Str. 31, A–6020,* ☎ *0512/5933,* FAX *0512/575619. 105 rooms. Restaurant, free parking. AE, DC, MC, V.*

$$$$ ⊡ Scandic Crown. This modern high-rise close to the railroad station looks out of place but offers contemporary comfort in friendly Scandinavian style. The rooms are simply furnished and efficiently modern. Look for Scandinavian specialties in the restaurants; the Sunday noon smorgasbord is justifiably popular. ⊠ *Salurner Str. 15, A–6020,*

☎ *0512/5935–0,* FAX *0512/5935–220. 172 rooms. 2 restaurants, bar, indoor pool, sauna, free parking. AE, DC, MC, V.*

$$$ 🏨 **Alpotel.** All rooms are quiet in this modern hotel tucked into a small square on the edge of the Old City. The building was designed for apartments, so many rooms are almost miniature suites; furnishings throughout are in warm colors and natural wood. Many rooms have balconies overlooking the quiet garden and mountains. The Tiroler Stuben restaurant (☞ Dining, *above*) is outstanding, and the breakfast buffet (included in the room price) features homemade whole-grain bread made from a secret recipe. ⊠ *Innrain 13 (Ursulinenpassage), A–6020,* ☎ *0512/577931,* FAX *0512/577931–15. 73 rooms. Restaurant, sauna, free parking. AE, DC, MC, V.*

$$$ 🏨 **Innsbruck.** Here, in one of the city's newest hotels, the mood is modern, from the lobby to the efficiently functional rooms with their accents of finished wood. From some of the rooms you'll get gorgeous views of the Old City and, from those on the river side, of the Nordkette mountains directly behind. ⊠ *Innrain 3, A–6020,* ☎ *0512/ 59868–0,* FAX *0512/572280. 91 rooms. Restaurant, indoor pool, sauna, free parking. AE, DC, MC, V.*

$$$ 🏨 **Kapeller.** Outside the center in Amras (take Streetcar 3), this friendly *Gasthof* offers cozy rooms as well as the advantage of a good in-house restaurant. ⊠ *Philippine-Welser-Str. 96, A–6020,* ☎ *0512/343106,* FAX *0512/343106–68. 36 rooms. Restaurant, free parking. AE, DC, MC, V.*

$$ 🏨 **Royal.** This modern hotel overlooks the river and is only steps from the Old City. Rooms are simple but spacious and comfortable. ⊠ *Innrain 16, A–6020,* ☎ *0512/586385,* FAX *0512/586385–10. 20 rooms. Breakfast room, free parking. AE, DC, MC, V.*

$$ 🏨 **Tautermann.** This red-shuttered house within walking distance of the city's center has been successfully turned into a friendly family-run hotel with rooms in natural woods and white. Some upper rooms on the west side have bay windows with gorgeous views of the imposing Hungerburg mountain. Bus A from the main station to Höttinger Kirchenplatz gets you close to the door. ⊠ *Stamser Feld 5/Höttingergasse, A–6020,* ☎ *0512/281572,* FAX *0512/281572–10. 28 rooms. Breakfast room, free parking. AE, DC, MC, V.*

$$ 🏨 **Weisses Kreuz.** At first encounter, you'll fall in love with this hotel, set over the stone arcades in the heart of the old city. It has seen massive renovations since the first *Gasthof* stood on this site in 1465, and the rooms are simple but comfortable, with mainly rustic furniture and lots of light wood. The service is friendly and accommodating. There are special rooms on the ground floor in which you can keep your skis; hotel reception and a restaurant are upstairs. ⊠ *Herzog Friedrich-Str. 31, A–6020,* ☎ *0512/59479,* FAX *0512/59479–90. 39 rooms. 2 restaurants. AE, MC, V.*

$ 🏨 **Binder.** A short streetcar trip (Number 3) from the center of town brings you to the less-costly comforts of this small, friendly family-run hotel. Rooms are modest but modern and attractive. Book well ahead, as Binder has many regular guests. ⊠ *Dr.-Glatz-Str. 20, A–6020,* ☎ *0512/33436–0,* FAX *0512/33436–99. 32 rooms. Bar, café, free parking. AE, MC, V.*

$ 🏨 **Innsbrücke.** Rooms at the front of this modest but comfortable hotel look across the river toward the Old City. You're five minutes from the center on foot or to the railroad station by Bus A or K. Rooms are in beige and light wood, and a few have baths. ⊠ *Innstr. 1, A–6020,* ☎ *0512/281934. 30 rooms, 8 with bath. Café. AE, DC, MC, V.*

Summer Hotels

Student accommodations in Innsbruck are turned into hotels from July to October and are extremely good value if you don't require the amenities of a full hotel; you may discover that Austrian university students don't live too badly. Check prices, as these can vary considerably from one hotel to another.

Internationales Studentenhaus. This is not only the best-located but also the cheapest option. ⊠ *Rechengasse 7, A–6020,* ☏ *0512/501912,* FAX *0512/50115. 275 rooms with bath. Free parking. AE, DC, MC, V.*

Rosen-Hotel Höttinger Au. Across the Inn River, this choice overlooks the city. ⊠ *Höttinger Au 84, A–6020,* ☏ *0512/2206–0 or 01/597–0689–0,* FAX *01/597–0689–89. 74 rooms without bath. Restaurant, free parking. AE, DC, MC, V.*

Rössl in der Au. Located across the Inn River, it affords a pleasant cityscape view. ⊠ *Höttinger Au 34, A–6020,* ☏ *0512/286846,* FAX *0512/ 293850. 125 rooms with bath. Free parking. AE, DC, MC, V.*

Nightlife and the Arts

The Arts

Each year at Pentecost the churches resound with organ music during the annual International Organ Week. In summer, concerts are held in various historic places around Innsbruck, including Schloss Ambras, and there are brass-band folk-music concerts in the public squares almost every day. It's said that Tirol has more bandleaders than mayors. Folk shows at the Hotel Europa Tyrol and other spots around the city feature authentic Tirolean folk dancing, yodeling, and zither music. The tourist office and hotels have details.

Concerts take place in the modern Saal Tirol of the **Kongresshaus** (⊠ Rennweg 3, ☏ 0512/5936–0). Innsbruck's principal theater is the **Tiroler Landestheater** (⊠ Rennweg 2, ☏ 0512/52074–4). Both opera and operetta are presented in the main hall, usually starting at 7:30; plays in the Kammerspiele start at 8. Get tickets at the box office or at the main tourist office.

Nightlife

The jazzy **casino** adjacent to the Scandic Crown hotel offers blackjack, baccarat, roulette, and plenty of slot machines, as well as a bar and good restaurant. You must present your passport to enter the casino. ⊠ *Salurner Str. 15,* ☏ *0512/587040–0.* 🎫 *AS210, exchangeable for AS250 worth of chips; admission free for those not playing.* ☉ *Daily 3 PM–3 AM.*

A popular spot is **Arcos** (⊠ Salurner Str., ☏ 0512/582423), next to the arch. The beautiful people gather at **Bellini** (⊠ Meranerstr. 5, ☏ 0512/560367). One of the more intriguing bars is the relaxed—or jammed, depending on the hour—**Café Brasil** (⊠ Leopoldstr. 7, ☏ 0512/ 583466), with its fireplace and comfortable, if stylishly shabby, furnishings. The atmosphere is cool modern at **Das Büro** (⊠ Badgasse 3, ☏ 0512/575633), by the cathedral.

Currently the basement **Blue Chip** disco (⊠ Wilhelm-Greil-Str. 17, ☏ 0512/565000) and the upstairs **Jimmy's** bar (⊠ Wilhelm-Greil-Str. 19, ☏ 0512/570473) are hot spots and packed nightly. Of the classic discos, the best and most enduring is **Kandinsky** (⊠ Anichstr. 7, ☏ 0512/582420).

Along the nightclub circuit, start first at **Filou** (⊠ Stiftgasse 12, ☏ 0512/ 580256), where in summer you can sit in an attractive garden until 10

PM, when things move indoors for the sake of neighborhood peace and quiet. **Lady O** (✉ Brunecker Str. 2, ☎ 0512/586432) is the traditional striptease nightclub; you can see a teaser program on the ground floor at 9 PM for an AS20 admission charge, but the first drink costs AS140.

Outdoor Activities and Sports

Golf

Golfclub Innsbruck/Igls in Lans, about 9 km (5½ mi) outside the city, has two 9-hole, par-66 courses (☎ 0512/377165). It is open April–November. **Golfclub Innsbruck/Igls** in Rinn, about 12 km (7½ mi) away, has 18 holes, with a par-71 (☎ 05223/78177). The course is open April–October. Both courses charge a AS460 greens fee on weekdays, AS580 on weekends, but you must be a member of a recognized club to use the courses. Several hotels—Europa-Tyrol in Innsbruck, Sporthotel Igls and Gesundheitszentrum Lanserhof at Lans, and the Geisler at Rinn—have special golfing arrangements.

Health and Fitness Clubs

In Innsbruck, try **City Fitness** (✉ Hunoldstr. 5, ☎ 0512/365696).

Hiking

Both easy paths and extreme slopes await hikers and climbers. From June to September, holders of the Club Innsbruck card (free from your hotel) can take free, daily guided mountain hikes. The tourist office has a special hiking brochure. If you want to learn to climb, look to the **Alpine School Innsbruck** (✉ Natters, In der Stille 1, ☎ 0512/546000–0). If you're already a pro, check in with the **Österreichischer Alpenverein** (✉ Wilhelm Greil-Str. 15, ☎ 0512/59547–34).

Horseback Riding

Horseback riding can be arranged through **Reitclub Innsbruck** (✉ Langer Weg, ☎ 0512/347174).

Skiing

In winter, check with the tourist office for information on snow conditions and transportation to the six ski areas. Your Club Innsbruck membership card will get you free transportation to the areas and reductions on a number of ski lifts. If you're a summer skier (and can take the altitudes), there's year-round skiing on the Stubai glacier, about 40 km (25 mi) from Innsbruck, via the "ST" bus from the train station. You can book with the **Schischule Innsbruck** (☎ 0512/582310) Ski schools and hotels have details on winter ski kindergartens.

Swimming

Around Innsbruck there are plenty of lakes, but in town you have little choice other than pools, indoor and out. Outdoors, try the **Freischwimmbad Tivoli** (✉ Purtschellerstr. 1, ☎ 0512/342344); indoors, try **Hallenbad Amraser Strasse** (✉ Amraser Str. 3, ☎ 0512/342585), **Hallenbad Höttinger Au** (✉ Fürstenweg 12, ☎ 0512/282339), or **Hallenbad Olympisches Dorf** (✉ Kugelfangweg 46, ☎ 0512/261342).

Tennis

Innsbruck has an abundance of courts, although they tend to be scattered and booked well ahead. Your hotel or the tourist office can help.

Try the **Olympia-Eissportzentrum** (✉ Olympiastr. 10, ☎ 0512/33838) or the **Tennisclub IEV** (✉ Reichenauer Str. 144, ☎ 0512/346229); your Club Innsbruck card will get you a reduction at both.

Shopping

The best shops are along the arcaded Herzog Friedrich-Strasse in the heart of the Old City; along its extension, Maria Theresien-Strasse; and the cross-street Maximilianstrasse in the newer part of town. Innsbruck is *the* place to buy native Tirolean clothing, particularly lederhosen. Look also for cut crystal and wood carvings; locally handmade, delicate silver-filigree pins make nice gifts. A lively flea market takes place each Saturday from 8 to 1 on Innrain, near St. John's Church (Johanneskirche).

Galerie Thomas Flora (⊠ Herzog Friedrich-Str. 5, ☎ 0512/577402) sells graphics by the droll Tirolean artist Paul Flora; you'll find much to smile at here, and maybe even to take home. **Rudolf Boschi** (⊠ Kiebachgasse 8, ☎ 0512/589224) turns out reproductions of old pewterware, using the original molds when possible. Among other items, he has locally produced, hand-decorated beer mugs with pewter lids. **Tiroler Heimatwerk** (⊠ Meraner Str. 2–4, ☎ 0512/582320) is the first place to look for local mementos and souvenirs of good quality. The extremely attractive shop carries textiles and finished clothing, ceramics, carved wooden chests, and some furniture. You can also have clothing made to order. **Trachten Wenger** (⊠ Herzog Friedrich-Str. 12, ☎ 0512/588336) is an outstanding source of dirndls, those attractive country costumes for women, with white blouse, dark skirt, and colorful apron. It also has children's clothing.

AROUND THE LOWER INN VALLEY

Northeast of Innsbruck the Inn River valley broadens out and courses right through Tirol toward Kufstein and the German border. Route 171 along the valley is a much more pleasant route than the autobahn running parallel.

Hall in Tirol

⓫ *9 km (5½ mi) east of Innsbruck.*

Hall in Tirol (Solbad Hall) is an old city founded by salt miners. The picturesque old part of the town is made up of narrow lanes running east–west, interrupted by a few short cross alleys. Stop and look around; from the main road, you cannot get a proper perspective of the fine old buildings. The **Rathaus,** built in the mid-15th century, has ornately carved councillors' rooms and beautifully worked mosaics covering the walls. The 17th-century **monastery church,** the oldest Renaissance ecclesiastical building in Tirol, and the **mint tower,** symbol of the town, are both interesting examples of local craftsmanship. The mint was moved to Hall from Meran, and the first coins were struck here in 1477. Legend has it that Duke Sigmund the Wealthy, son of Friedl the Penniless, got his nickname by tossing handfuls of Hall-minted coins to the populace wherever he went. The Inntal (Inn Valley) gave its name to the coin, known as the *Taler,* from which came the word "dollar."

Dining and Lodging

$$$ ✕🏨 **Hotel Restaurant Heiligreuz.** Perched on a hillside shrouded with trees, the Hotel Restaurant Heiligreuz is an intimate home away from home. Dark wood paneling and comfortable, overstuffed furniture decorate the hotel. Rooms are equally elegant and welcoming, as is the friendly staff. The restaurant offers traditional rib-sticking classics such as *G'röstl,* a concoction of eggs, bacon, and potatoes guaranteed to satisfy the heartiest of appetites. ⊠ *Reimmichlstr. 18, A–6060,* ☎ *05223/57114,* 🆚 *05223/571145. 38 rooms. Restaurant, bar. V.*

Shopping

Traveling east between Hall in Tirol and Schwaz, you'll pass the home of the Swarovski glass empire, in Wattens. Stop at the **Crystal Shop** (⊠ Innstr. 1, ☎ 05224/5886–0) to browse around and perhaps buy some of the famous crystal and glassware.

Schwaz

⑫ *16 km (10 mi) northeast of Hall in Tirol.*

The Hapsburg emperors in the 15th and 16th century owed much of their wealth to the silver and copper extracted from the mines here by the Fugger family, who emigrated from Augsburg. Founded in the 12th century, Schwaz, on the south bank of the Inn, evolved into a rich and important mining center. The mines of the **Silbergbergwerk Schwaz**—dug deep under the towering Tuxer Alps—indeed may have been the reason for setting up the mint in nearby Hall. ⊠ *Alte Land-str. 3a,* ☎ *05242/72372–0.* 🎫 *AS150.* ☉ *Jan.–mid-Nov., daily 8:30–5, mid-Nov.–Dec., daily 9:30–4 in winter.*

The 15th-and 16th-century houses built during those prosperous times still stand, and the marketplace has kept its atmosphere. Look at the vast **parish church,** the largest Gothic hall-church in Tirol. The church was expanded in 1490 and divided into two parts (once they were separated by a wooden wall): the southern chancel for the miners and the northern, or the "Prince's chancel," for the upper classes.

A fascinating new addition to Schwaz is the **Haus der Völker,** a museum dedicated to enthnography. Displays include ancient Asian sculptures as well as African art. ⊠ *Franz-Josef-Str. 26,* ☎ *05242/66090,* 𝖥𝖠𝖷 *05242/66091.* 🎫 *AS70.* ☉ *Daily 9:30–6.*

En Route **Jenbach,** 8 km (5 mi) north of Schwaz, across the river, is notable mainly as a rail and highway junction; from here Route 169 follows the Ziller River valley (Zillertal) south, past the Gerlos Valley (Route 165) and the Tuxer mountain range to Mayrhofen. The Achensee lies on the plateau to the north, fed by the Achen river rising high in the mountains beyond, on the German border. Both regions have become immensely popular.

Achensee

⑬ *25 km (17 mi) north of Schwaz, 17 km (12 mi) from Jesbach.*

From Jenbach, many travelers head to the Achensee. If you're driving, take Route 181; the initial stretch involves hairpin turns and a steep climb, but the views over the Inn Valley are exquisite.

You could take a bus, too, but the most adventuresome and romantic way to reach the Achensee is on the steam-powered train, the **Achensee-bahn** (☎ 05244/62243), built in 1889 as Tirol's first mountain cog railway. The line does its 1,300-ft climb in a nearly straight line more than 7 km (4½ mi) to the lower end of the Achensee (Seespitz), where you can get a lake steamer on to Buchau and Pertisau and to the north end.

The Achen Valley has fine skiing in winter, but the Achensee in summer, with water sports and excellent fishing, is the main attraction. It is the largest and most beautiful lake in Tirol—10 km (6 mi) long—with the great mountains of the Karwendel and Sonnwend ranges rising from its blue-green waters. The lake steamer connects the villages strung along its length.

Lodging

$$$$ ☎ **Posthotel.** This comfortable Alpine chalet is also a health center; you'll find every convenience for taking care of fitness, weight loss, and exercise. Horseback riders will find mounts ranging from Haflingers to Shetland ponies. Rooms are in typical Tirolean country style. ⊠ *Achenkirch, A–6215,* ☎ *05246/6522–0,* FAX *05246/6205–468. 97 rooms. Restaurant, indoor and outdoor pools, sauna, tennis court, exercise room, horseback riding, squash. No credit cards. Closed mid-Nov.–mid-Dec.*

Pertisau

⑭ *25 km (16 mi) north of Schwaz.*

This small, picturesque village set into the thick pine forest of a nature preserve is the only community on the western shore of the Achensee. It offers excellent swimming, sailing, tennis, fishing, and a golf course, all at budget prices. Although less popular, the eastern side of the lake enjoys at least two hours of sunshine more every day, and the water is consequently warmer. Because this area is so close to Innsbruck, the lake is crowded on summer weekends; try to visit on a weekday.

Dining and Lodging

$$–$$$ ✕☎ **Kristall.** This chalet lodge set against a wooded mountain offers friendly comfort in ample, elegant public rooms and cheerfully decorated bedrooms. You can take half board or not, and the restaurant is open to the public. ⊠ *A–6213,* ☎ *05243/5490,* FAX *05243/5374–19. 52 rooms. Restaurant, bar, indoor and outdoor pools, sauna, exercise room. No credit cards. Closed Nov.–mid-Dec.*

Outdoor Activities and Sports

GOLF

Golf-Club Achensee in Pertisau is an attractive 9-hole, par-70 Alpine course with 18 tees and many long, straight runs. ☎ *05243/5377.* ☉ *May–Oct.*

En Route   Scenic Route 181 leads along the eastern shore of the lake through Buchau to the northern end, passing through Achenseehof and Scholastika, among various small settlements belonging to the community of Achenkirch. Because this area is so close to Innsbruck, the lake is crowded on summer weekends; try to visit on a weekday.

The drive south from Jenbach on Route 169 follows the Ziller River, which rises high in the Alps to the south, in an area of perpetual glacier, then flows north. Route 169 parallels the narrow-gauge Ziller railway,
★ the **Zillertalbahn,** which makes daily runs between Jenbach and Mayrhofen, some under steam power. If your childhood dream was to drive a train, check in Jenbach (☎ 05244/63470, FAX 05244/63552) about renting this one; you can take a crash course in railroad operations and play engineer of the steam locomotive, all for a modest fee.

The first part of the Zillertal is broad and shallow, and the scenery is not very inspiring. But from Stumm onward, where you pass through some pretty Alpine villages, and particularly the stretch south of Zell am Ziller, the valley starts to live up to its reputation.

Zell am Ziller

⑮ *25 km (16 mi) southeast of Jenbach.*

The main town of the Zillertal—the biggest and most famous of the many beautiful Alpine valleys of the Tirol—is noted for its traditional 400-year-old **Gauderfest** (contact the local tourist board, ☎ 05282/2281), held on the first weekend in May, when thousands of tourists from far and wide pack the little market town of Zell am Ziller for the colorful skits, music, and singing—and great quantities of *Gauderbier,* a strong brew run up for the occasion. You can hear some of the country's best singing, by the valley residents, and listen to expert harp and zither playing, for which the valley is famous throughout Austria. Tradition runs strong here: Witness the Perchtenlaufen, processions of colorfully masked well-wishers going the neighborhood rounds on January 5, or the annual Almabtrieb during the last September and first October days, when the cows are hung with wreaths and bells and, amid celebrations, are herded back from the high Alpine pastures into the lower fields and barns. This is a typical Tirolean country town, with Alpine lodges and a round-domed pink village church (note the Baroque painting of the Holy Trinity); in winter it's a center for skiing and sports.

Dining and Lodging

$$–$$$ ✕⌂ **Bräu.** The core of this thick-walled, five-story, frescoed building
★ in the center of town dates to the 16th century; subsequent renovations and a new wing have brought it quite up to date. The rooms are decorated in warm Alpine style, in beiges, greens, and browns. The hotel can arrange fishing trips. The three-room restaurant complex serves fine food, with emphasis on fish and game. Reserve for the *Bräustübl,* and enjoy the house beer; the house brewery is also the source of the *Gauderbier.* ✉ *Dorfpl. 1, A–6280,* ☎ *05282/2313,* ℻ *05282/2313–17. 36 rooms. Restaurant, café, sauna. No credit cards. Closed Apr. and mid-Oct.–mid-Dec.*

$$–$$$ ✕⌂ **Zellerhof.** This variation on the traditional Alpine chalet is now a hotel school for most of the year, so you'll be looked after by a young and enthusiastic staff. The house is tastefully decorated in the local style, with ample natural wood, and the Tirolean ambience carries over to the comfortable rooms. The hotel can arrange fishing. The intimate restaurant upstairs is excellent. ✉ *Bahnhofstr. 3, A–6280,* ☎ *05282/2612–0. 40 rooms. Restaurant, bar, café, sauna. AE, DC, MC, V. Closed mid-Oct.–mid-June, except Christmas and Easter.*

Mayrhofen

⓰ *10 km (6 mi) south of Zell am Ziller.*

Down the road you'll come to Mayrhofen, end of the line for the narrow-gauge railway. This is the valley's main tourist base and the favorite summer resort of the British for many years. Mayrhofen is the starting point for summer hiking into the highly scenic valleys that branch off to the southeast, south, and southwest and for excursions into the Ziller glacier areas, at heights of 9,750 ft and more.

At Mayrhofen the valley splits into three *Gründe* (grounds): the Zillergrund, Stillupgrund, and Zemmgrund—prime examples of picture-postcard Alpine areas, swept at the top with glittering, pale-blue glaciers.

Dining and Lodging

$$$ ✕ **Wirtshaus zum Griena.** The restaurant tucked into this 400-year-old farmhouse is about a 10-minute drive north of Mayrhofen. The route is not simple, but everybody knows Griena's—ask at your hotel for directions. Once you get there, you'll find yourself in rustic surroundings of natural wood paneling. Such local favorites as beer soup, pasta dishes, and schnitzel are tempting. The beer is local and excellent, the wines somewhat disappointing. ✉ *Dorfhaus 768,* ☎ *05285/62778. No credit cards. Closed June–early July and Nov.–early Dec.*

$$$$ ✕⌂ **Elisabeth.** This newish house, in Tirolean style, radiates elegance
★ without being too formal. The same is true of the well-decorated, lux-

urious bedrooms, some with ceramic stoves and beautiful wood-carved walls and ceilings. Each room has a balcony overlooking the mountains, and a few have Jacuzzis set in a windowed alcove offering stunning views, plus fireplaces and canopied beds. The hotel has a loyal following, so book ahead. The excellent Gute Stube restaurant, decorated with pretty frescoes, offers international and local specialties such as roast veal or trout. Every Friday evening there is a huge Tirolean buffet and live music. ⊠ *Einfahrt Mitte 432, A–6290,* ☎ *05285/ 6767,* ℻ *05285/6767–67. 35 rooms. 2 restaurants, bar, café, indoor pool, sauna, exercise room. No credit cards.*

$$–$$$ ⌂ **Kramerwirt.** Here's the center of the action in Mayrhofen, where the crowd gathers. The welcoming warmth of natural wood in the lobby and *Stuben* (small, rustic dining room) is accented by the Asian carpets and Tirolean antiques. Still family-run, this hostelry has been around for centuries. You'll feel at home in the comfortable rooms. ⊠ *Am Marienbrunnen 346, A–6290,* ☎ *05285/6700,* ℻ *05285/6700– 502. 72 rooms. Restaurant, bar, sauna, exercise room, dance club, parking. No credit cards. Closed 2 wks in Dec.*

Outdoor Activities and Sports

CLIMBING

For the adventuresome, Peter Habeler at the **Alpinschule u. Schischule Mount Everest** (⊠ Hauptstr. 458, ☎ 05285/62829, ℻ 05285/64260) gives instruction in ice climbing.

Tuxer Valley

⑰ *15 km (9 mi) west of Mayrhofen.*

The fourth arm and highest in altitude of the Inn Valley is the Tuxer Valley, a summer ski region, which ends at the foot of the massive Olperer and Rifflerspitz glaciers, each nearly 11,000 ft high. Frequent buses leave Mayrhofen for **Lanersbach,** a small mountain village, and **Hintertux,** right at the doorway of the great glaciers. Hintertux is also a popular spa, with a small thermal swimming pool, and the center of an ancient wood-carving industry. Rubies (called Tirolean garnets) were once mined in this area, and you might run across local amethyst in the shops as well.

Dining and Lodging

$$$ ✕⌂ **Neu Hintertux.** In the shadow of the nearby mountains, this turreted hotel decorated with frescoes and carved wood exudes traditional Alpine charm. Rooms are delightfully decorated with canopied beds, brocaded fabrics, and tiled stoves. You can enjoy a drink after a day on the slopes around an open hearth in the bar, which is covered in dark, carved wood. Tirolean classics are served in the restaurant. ⊠ *A–6294 Hintertux,* ☎ *05287/8580–0,* ℻ *05287/8580–409. 54 rooms. Restaurant, bar, sauna, bowling, billiards. No credit cards. Closed Sept.*

$$$ ✕⌂ **Rindererhof.** This comfortable Alpine lodge at the end of the line is a good starting point for either climbing or skiing, since you're right at the base station for the cable cars up to the glacier. The outdoor Schirmbar (Umbrella Bar) is the "in" spot for après-ski in Hintertux. ⊠ *A– 6294 Hintertux,* ☎ *05287/8558–0,* ℻ *05287/87502. 30 rooms, 30 suites. Restaurant, bar, sauna. No credit cards. Closed mid- to late July and early–mid-Dec.*

$$$ ✕⌂ **Tuxerhof.** The welcoming open fireplace in the lounge sets the relaxed style for this attractive Alpine inn, whose rooms and restaurant are comfortably appointed. In winter, skiing starts literally at the door; in summer, hiking paths will lead you into the surrounding forests and mountains. ⊠ *Vorderlanersbach 185, A–6293 Lanersbach,* ☎ *05287/ 8511–0. 42 rooms, 4 suites. Restaurant, bar, pub, indoor pool, sauna, children's programs, parking. No credit cards. Closed May–June.*

$ ✕🏨 **Forelle.** This friendly mountain inn offers comfortable rooms in
★   typical Alpine decor and a good restaurant specializing in trout. The
hotel has its own fishing stream. ⊠ *Vorderlanersbach 216, A–6293
Lanersbach,* ☎ *05287/87214. 34 rooms. Restaurant, bar, indoor pool,
sauna, exercise room. No credit cards. Closed mid-Apr.–May and
Nov.–mid-Dec.*

Outdoor Activities and Sports
CLIMBING

Those particularly interested in ice climbing should contact Anton
Tomann at the **Hochgebirgs-und Wanderschule Tuxertal** (⊠ Juns 424,
A–6293 Lanersbach, ☎ 05287/87372).

Hainzenberg

⑱   *6 km (4 mi) south of Zell am Ziller.*

Hainzenberg was once a gold-mining town. Stop at the **Maria Rast pilgrimage church,** built in 1739 by the prospectors, to see its stuccos and
fine ceiling paintings. Don't look for the western transept wing of the
church; it slid down the precipice in 1910.

Gerlos

⑲   *18 km (10 mi) east of Zell am Ziller.*

The sensationally scenic Route 165 climbs east out of Zell am Ziller
up to Gerlos, a less glitzy but still splendid choice for a summer or winter holiday, with the 8,300-ft Kreuzjoch mountain looming in the
background. Scheduled buses make the run up from Zell am Ziller. The
Gerlos ski slopes are varied, and in summer the same slopes offer excellent hiking. Check in advance about hotel arrangements; many of
the better houses in Gerlos require a minimum of half board.

Lodging
$$$$ 🏨 **Gaspingerhof.** The three Alpine chalets that make up this family-
run, rustically furnished complex in the center of town are connected
by underground passages. Rooms are done in the bright local custom,
with natural woods and colorful fabrics. The nightlife is active. ⊠ *A–
6281,* ☎ *05284/5216. 73 rooms. Restaurant, indoor pool, sauna, tennis court. DC. Closed mid-Apr.–mid-May and mid-Oct.–early Dec.*

$$ 🏨 **Almhof.** In typical Tirolean style, this Alpine inn about 2 km (1 mi)
out of the center offers a friendly reception area and comfortable
rooms. ⊠ *Gerlos–Gmünd, A–6281,* ☎ *05284/5323–0,* 🆋 *05284/
5323–23. 45 rooms. Restaurant, indoor pool, sauna, tennis court, ex-
ercise room, parking. No credit cards. Closed May–early June and mid-
Oct.–mid-Dec.*

En Route   Beyond Gerlos, the highway climbs the 5,300-ft Gerlos Pass and
plunges into the province of Salzburg in a series of double-back hair-
pins close to the dramatic 1,300-ft **Krimmler Wasserfälle** (waterfalls).
You can complete the circuit back into Tirol by continuing east to Mit-
tersill and cutting north to Kitzbühel via the Thurn Pass.

FROM JENBACH TO KITZBÜHEL

Brixlegg

⑳   *16 km (10 mi) northeast of Jenbach.*

Starting again from Jenbach in the main Inn Valley, continue north-
east on Route 171 until you hit Brixlegg, a former copper-mining

town. It is the home of the Schloss Kropfsberg, built to defend the Ziller Valley from marauding invaders. Another castle from the 12th-century, the Schloss Matzen, is perched on a mountainside. For years, sufferers of rheumatism also have flocked to Brixlegg to soak in the radioactive sulfur waters of the Mehrn spa.

Dining and Lodging

$$$ ✕ **Herrnhaus.** The wood-paneled rooms lend a rustic, country atmosphere to this simple *Gasthaus* in the center of town, which is known for its good food. The menu offers regional dishes, including *Speckknödelsuppe* (bacon dumpling soup) and lamb medallions in a potato crust. Service is friendly but can be a little slow. ✉ *Herrnhauspl. 1, A–6230,* ☎ *05337/2223. No credit cards.*

$$$ ✕ **St. Leonard.** Located about a 10-minute drive from Brixlegg in Kundl, this excellent restaurant has *das gewisse Etwas,* or that certain something. Along with traditional Tirolean specialties, the roast Muscovy duck with a barley salad in a balsamic dressing is superb, as is the tantalizing dessert *Topfenknödel,* with fresh plum compote. ✉ *St. Leonard 2, A–6230,* ☎ *05338/7435,* ℻ *05338/8607. No credit cards.*

$$$$ ▦ **Schloss Matzen.** This lovely medieval castle, owned by a young Amer-
★ ican couple and run as a bed-and-breakfast, is the kind of place you'll want to settle into for several days. Guests are encouraged to feel at home in the remarkably preserved yet comfortable public rooms, some with original marble fireplaces, 14th-century frescoes, and carved wood walls and ceilings. The castle is full of cozy nooks and crannies that are perfect for reading or simply admiring the spectacular views of the countryside. Bedrooms are large and decorated with antiques, and all have great views. Baths are modern. In addition to breakfast, Austrian wine is served in the late afternoon. Guided tours of the castle are also offered. ✉ *A–6230,* ☎ *05337/62679,* ℻ *05337/66581. 10 rooms. MC, V.* ☯ *Open May–Oct. and possibly other months.*

Alpbach

㉑ *8 km (5 mi) southeast of Brixlegg.*

From Brixlegg a small side road runs down a valley to the unspoiled picture-book village of Alpbach. The town is nominally a winter-sports center, but it takes the international spotlight once a year in the spring when world leaders of government and industry gather to discuss global issues at the European Forum.

Dining and Lodging

$$$–$$$$ ✕▦ **Böglerhof.** Much of the original character has been preserved in
★ this beautifully restored old double chalet, with its heavily beamed ceilings and stonework. The rooms are attractively decorated in Tirolean style. The excellent restaurant, with its small *Stuben* (side rooms), is known for such Austrian specialties as cabbage soup and fillet points in light garlic sauce. The hotel is a member of the Romantik Hotel group. ✉ *A–6236,* ☎ *05336/5227. 50 rooms. Restaurant, bar, indoor and outdoor pools, sauna, tennis court, exercise room. MC, V. Closed mid-Apr.–May and mid-Oct.–mid-Dec.*

$$$ ▦ **Alpbacher Hof.** The massive fireplace sets the keynote in the public rooms of this typical chalet hotel, and the welcoming feeling carries over to the bedrooms. You may be asked to take minimum half board, but the policy is flexible. ✉ *A–6236,* ☎ *05336/5237,* ℻ *05336/5016. 55 rooms. Restaurant, café, indoor pool, sauna. No credit cards. Closed Apr.–mid-May and Oct.–mid-Dec.*

Rattenberg

㉒ *2 km (1 mi) northeast of Brixlegg.*

Just up the road from Brixlegg is this quaint medieval town once famous for its silver mines. When the mines were exhausted, Rattenberg lapsed into a deep sleep lasting, like Rip van Winkle's, for centuries. Were it not for the constant procession of cars and trucks (which the residents are trying to ban), you might think you were back in the Middle Ages. Narrow old streets full of relics of its past glory twine around the town, which has remained remarkably unchanged for centuries. Local legend purports that the ruins of Emperor Maximilian's massive castle, which looms above the town, are haunted by ghosts from a bygone era.

Dining

$ ⌂ **Hacker.** People come from miles around to sample the scrumptious
★ pastries and excellent coffee in this traditional café, which has been a coffeehouse since 1774. You can also choose from a variety of ice-cream sundaes. Service is especially friendly, and in summer tables are set outside. ✉ *Südtirolerstr. 46, A–6240,* ☏ *05337/62332. No credit cards.*

Shopping

If you're looking for something special and different, go to **Helga Danek** (✉ Inng. 60, 05337/63113), where you'll find beautiful painted glass. There is always a sale section available.

Across the river from Rattenberg lies Kramsach, a glass-production center since the 17th century. At the **glassworks school** (call ☏ 05337/62623 to arrange a visit) you can see etching, engraving, and painting on glassware.

En Route   Back on Route 171, the road leads to **Wörgl,** a rail junction where the main Austrian east–west line and the shortcut via the "German corner" come together. From Wörgl an extremely scenic road leads south to the small resort villages of Niederau, Oberau, and Auffach.

Kufstein

㉓ *28 km (17 mi) northeast of Brixlegg, 26 km (16 mi) from Rattenberg, 13 km (8 mi) north of Söll.*

Kufstein marks the border with Germany. The town was captured from Bavaria in 1504 by Emperor Maximilian I, who added it to the Habsburg domains.

You'll immediately notice that Kufstein is dominated by a magnificent fortress right out of a Dürer etching, the **Schloss Geroldseck,** originally built as a "castle for contemplation" in 1200. But Maximilian decided it was better suited for merrymaking and expanded and strengthened it in 1504, rechristening it *Lustschloss,* or "pleasure palace." The fortress, considerably renovated, contains a small **museum** and boasts the famed "Heroes' Organ" (said to burst into sound when a national hero dies). With sumptuous rooms and terraced gardens, Geroldseck ranks among the finest of the 1,001 Tirolian castles. The town of Kufstein itself has some beautiful medieval-period streets. ☏ *05372/62207, museum 05372/67038.* ▣ *Castle free, museum AS40.* ☉ *Castle May–Oct., daily 9–7; museum late Apr.–Oct., Tues.–Sun., tour Tues.–Sun. at 9:30, 11, 1:30, and 4:30.*

The center of town boasts a remarkable concentration of Art Nouveau buildings, both public and private. The **Burgher's Tower** houses the *Heldenorgel,* the world's largest outdoor organ, with 26 registers and

1,800 pipes. The instrument is played year-round daily at noon and in summer at noon and 6 PM.

Dining and Lodging

$$–$$$ ✕🖫 **Alpenrose.** This recently renovated house, on the edge of town in
★ green surroundings, welcomes you immediately with its friendly lobby, which seems to continue the outdoors; the feeling of relaxed comfort carries over into the attractive bedrooms as well. The elegant restaurant is the best in the area; the *Tafelspitz* (boiled beef) and fish, game, and goose in season are particularly recommended, as is the orange soufflé. ✉ *Weissachstr. 47, A–6330,* ☎ *05372/62122,* FAX *05372/62122–7. 19 rooms. Restaurant, bar. AE, MC. Closed wk before Easter.*

Shopping

Kufstein is home to the world-famous **Riedel glass works**; a visit to the factory (☎ 05372/64896–0) may be possible. Otherwise you can buy pieces at the factory outlet (✉ Weissach Str. 28–34, ☎ 05372/64896–0), which is open weekdays 9–noon and 1–5:30, Saturday 9–noon.

En Route At Wörgl most travelers begin to head east toward the great resorts of St. Johann and Kitzbühel, destinations described below. Route 312 takes you to St. Johann, the noted vacation center, about 30 km (19 mi) away. You can do the circuit of St. Johann and its more famous neighbor, Kitzbühel, by taking Route 161 for 10 km (6 mi) between the two resorts and returning to Wörgl via Route 170. Heading eastward, you first encounter the charming towns of Going, Ellmau, and Söll.

Going, Ellmau, and Söll

10 km (6 mi) to 40 km (25 mi) south of Kufstein.

The towns of Going, Ellmau, and Söll have developed into attractive, small winter and summer resorts. Their altitudes (and their snow) are about the same as those in Kitzbühel and St. Johann, and their prices are half as high but rising as popularity grows. Some of the region's finest restaurants and hotels are located around these towns.

Dining and Lodging

$$$$ ✕ **Rautnerwirt.** In its two small rooms with seven tables, this attractive restaurant in a country house offers imaginative local cuisine; depending on the season, you might find roast young goat or braised venison in a delicate mushroom sauce. You can watch the preparation through the picture window that divides kitchen and dining areas. ✉ *Going,* ☎ *05358/2784. AE, DC, MC, V. Closed June–early July. No lunch Mon.–Tues.*

$$ ✕ **Schindlhaus.** Original variations on Austrian dishes are served up in a modern setting at this restaurant. Try the lightly braised fillet of venison with red cabbage or one of the fish specialties, served with a delicate sauce. The gemütlich atmosphere and friendly staff provide the perfect finishing touches. ✉ *Dorf 134, Söll,* ☎ *05333/5161. AE, DC, MC, V. Closed Mon.*

$$$$ ✕🖫 **Der Bär.** Within walking distance of the village center, "The Bear," a member of the Relais & Châteaux group, is known throughout Austria as one of the foremost country inns. An elegant but friendly atmosphere pervades, with relaxed comfort in every respect, attractive bedrooms in Tirolean style included. The kitchen does best with local dishes; try roast lamb, game, or seafood. The wine list also has an extensive choice of Austrian, French, and Italian vintages. ✉ *Kirchbichl 9, A–6352 Ellmau,* ☎ *05358/2395,* FAX *05358/2395–56. 45 rooms. Restaurant, indoor and outdoor pools, sauna, exercise room. No credit cards. Closed mid-Apr.–May and early Nov.–mid-Dec.*

$$$$ 🏨 **Stanglwirt.** A 300-year-old coaching inn forms the core of this centrally located health-and-fitness complex, which is also a popular mealtime stop for tour buses. Rooms in the new section are spacious; some are studios with old-fashioned ceramic stoves, in keeping with the Tirolean decor. Guests can ride, swim, hunt, or ski in season or play tennis and squash. This hotel is a great favorite with Germans, who have ranked it among the top 12 resort hotels in Europe. ⊠ *Sonnseite 50, A–6353 Going,* ☎ *05358/2000,* 𝖥𝖠𝖷 *05358/2000–31. 62 rooms, 6 apartments. Restaurant, indoor and outdoor pools, sauna, tennis courts, exercise room, horseback riding, squash. AE, DC, MC, V.*

St. Johann

㉔   *32 km (24 mi) southeast of Kufstein, 14 km (9 mi) northeast of Kitzbühel.*

For years, St. Johann lived in the shadow of Kitzbühel, but today the town, with its colorfully painted houses, has developed a personality of its own and for better or worse is equally mobbed, winter and summer. The facilities are similar, but prices are still lower, although climbing. (The dark horse here could be Kirchdorf, 4 km/2½ mi north of St. Johann, where costs appear to be holding, or Fieberbrunn, 12 km/7 mi east on Route 164.) While in St. Johann, don't miss the magnificently decorated Baroque **parish church** or the Gothic **Spitalskirche**, with its fine late-medieval stained glass, just west of town in Weitau.

Dining and Lodging

$$$ ✕ **Das Braü.** A great place to stop on Highway 312 between Salzburg and Innsbruck is Das Braü, in the pretty village of Lofer. Josef Brüggler was head chef at the Hotel Arlberg in Lech (where he cooked for the late Princess Diana on three skiing visits) before returning to his roots and opening his own restaurant. There are two menus to choose from, one for casual dining and the other for a more elegant meal, and the excellent dishes include locally caught fish, fried chicken, and lamb. The setting is charmingly rustic, with red gingham tablecloths and cowbells, harnesses, and stirrups hanging from the wooden beams. If you don't feel like driving on, you can stay overnight in one of the 28 pleasant bedrooms upstairs. ⊠ *Hauptstr. 28,* ☎ *06588/82070,* 𝖥𝖠𝖷 *06588/820771. No credit cards. Closed Mon.*

$$$ ✕🏨 **Goldener Löwe.** This traditional chalet-style hotel is festooned with bright red geraniums in summer and white fairy lights in winter. The staff extends the gemütlich atmosphere through its friendly and outgoing service. Rooms are decorated in cool pastels and blond-wood furniture. Never mind that the decor seems a bit dated: The views from the room balconies of the surrounding mountain scenery are spectacular. The restaurant serves up hearty Tirolean specialties. ⊠ *A–6380,* ☎ *05352/62251,* 𝖥𝖠𝖷 *05352/62981. 64 rooms. Restaurant, café, bowling. AE, DC, MC, V.*

$$$ ✕🏨 **Post.** The painted stucco facade identifies this traditional hotel in the center of town. Natural woods and reds carry over from the public spaces and restaurant into the guest rooms. ⊠ *Speckbacherstr. 1, A–6380,* ☎ *05352/62230,* 𝖥𝖠𝖷 *05352/62230–3. 46 rooms. Restaurant, café. AE, DC, MC, V. Closed Apr. and Nov.*

$$$ 🏨 **Alpenapartment Europa.** This apartment hotel next to the recreation center (swimming, sauna, tennis) is attractively furnished in Baroque and regional decor. Many rooms have Tirolean four-posters and furnished kitchenettes. Exhausted skiers delight in knowing that breakfast is served until 11 AM. ⊠ *Achenallee 18, A–6380,* ☎ *05352/62285–0,* 𝖥𝖠𝖷 *05532/62285–5. 16 apartments. No credit cards.*

Kitzbühel

㉕ *20 km (12 mi) south of St. Johann, 71 km (44 mi) northeast of Gerlos.*

Long before Kitzbühel became one of the fashionable winter resorts, the town had gained a reputation for its summer season. Now, however, the accent is almost completely on skiing, with facilities among the finest in the world. The famous Ski Circus, a carefully planned, clever combination of lifts, cable railways, and runs that lets you ski for more than 80 km (50 mi) without having to exert yourself climbing a single foot, originally put this town on the map. Today, Kitzbühel is in perpetual motion and is always packed in December and again in February. But at anytime during the season there's plenty to do, from sleigh rides to fancy-dress balls.

Built in the 16th century with proceeds from copper and silver mining, the town itself is picturesque enough, but take time to also check out the churches: **St. Andrew's parish church** (1435–1506) has a lavishly rococo chapel, the Rosakapelle, and the marvelously ornate tomb (1520) of the Kupferschmid family; the **Church of St. Catherine,** built about 1350, houses a Gothic winged altar dating to 1515.

In summer, get a guest card stamped by your hotel for substantial reductions on various activities (some of which are then free), like tennis, riding, and golf. The best swimming is in the nearby Schwarzsee (Black Lake). To see Alpine flowers in their natural glory, take the cable car up the Kitzbühler Horn to the **Alpine Flower Garden Kitzbühel** at 6,500 ft; it leaves every half hour.

Dining and Lodging

$$$$ ✕ **Tennerhof.** Located in the Hotel Tennerhof, this elegant restaurant
★ is known as one of the best in Austria. Chef Hans Hauser, famous throughout Tirol for his innovative cooking, creates such specialties as *Spinattascherl* (spinach ravioli lightly touched with fried shallot butter), duck breast smoked in Jasmine tea with potato corn cakes, and lamb in a delicate mustard sauce with black-, white-, and green-bean ratatouille. Vegetables and herbs are straight from the hotel garden. In summer tables are set out on the terrace with the majestic mountains as a backdrop. ⊠ *Griesenauweg 26,* ☎ *05356/63181,* ℻ *05356/63181–70. Reservations essential. Jacket and tie. AE, DC, MC, V. Closed Apr.–mid-May and mid-Oct.–mid-Dec.*

$$$$ ✕ **Wirtshaus Unterberger Stuben.** In this former residence done up in typical Tirolean fashion, with beige and red decor, you may have to reserve weeks ahead to get a table in winter; the place is usually booked solid. The international cuisine is good if not always a match for the prices, offering such temptations as creamed pumpkin soup and stuffed oxtail. ⊠ *Wehrgasse 2,* ☎ *05356/66127,* ℻ *05356/66127–6. Reservations essential. No credit cards. Closed mid-May–June and Nov. No lunch Tues.–Wed. except during high season.*

$$ ✕ **Praxmair.** Après-ski can't begin early enough for the casually chic crowds who pile into this famous pastry shop–café, known for its Florentines. ⊠ *Vorderstadt 17,* ☎ *05356/62646. AE, DC, MC, V. Closed Apr. and Nov.*

$$$$ ✕🗖 **Romantik Hotel Tennerhof.** Hidden away slightly out of the cen-
★ ter, this is an elegant old country house set in a huge garden near the golf course, with towering mountains seemingly within reach. Over the years it has attracted celebrities from the Duke of Windsor to Kirk Douglas, but emphasis here is on family, including a special supervised children's room. The pretty bedrooms are done in Tirolean country furnishings, all different, some with ceramic stoves, and most with balconies. This is the kind of place you want to settle into for several days,

and the staff is exceptionally warm and accommodating. ✉ *Griese-nauweg 26, A–6370,* ☎ *05356/63181,* FAX *05356/63181–70. 40 rooms. Restaurant, indoor and outdoor pools, sauna, spa. AE, DC, MC, V. Closed Apr.–mid-May and mid-Oct.–mid-Dec.*

$$$ 🏨 **Schloss Lebenberg.** A onetime 16th-century castle on a hilltop outside town has been transformed into a wholly modern, owner-managed family hotel. The bedrooms are contemporary in flavor. You can literally start skiing at the front door, and if the youngsters are too small to go along, there's a nursery. ✉ *Lebenbergstr. 17, A–6370,* ☎ *05356/ 6901,* FAX *05356/64405. 109 rooms. Restaurant, indoor pool, sauna, tennis court, exercise room, nursery. AE, DC, MC, V.*

$$$ 🏨 **Schloss Münichau.** Four kilometers (2½ miles) outside town, just beyond the romantic Schwarzsee on the road to Reith, you'll find this quaint 15th-century hunting lodge from which you can still go hunting and fishing. The rooms are individual, with much Tirolean woodcarving in evidence. ✉ *A–6370 Reith bei Kitzbühel,* ☎ *05356/62962,* FAX *05356/62332–50. 58 rooms. Restaurant, sauna. AE, DC, MC, V. Closed mid-Apr.–May and Nov.*

$$ 🏨 **Goldener Greif.** The original building dates from 1271; renovations in the 1950s gave the house a more contemporary but still traditional Tirolean charm, emphasized by the magnificent vaulted lobby with open fireplaces and antiques. The rooms, too, are charming, some with four-posters, and a few apartments have fireplaces. The hotel is the locale of the Kitzbühel casino. ✉ *Hinterstadt 24, A–6370,* ☎ *05356/ 64311,* FAX *05356/65001. 47 rooms. Restaurant, bar, sauna, casino. AE, DC, MC, V. Closed Apr.–mid-June and Oct.–Nov.*

$$ 🏨 **Weisses Rössl.** This elegant but friendly hotel in the middle of town has open fireplaces ablaze in winter. The spacious rooms display much light pine and are particularly comfortable. ✉ *Bichlstr. 3–5, A–6370,* ☎ *05356/62541–0,* FAX *05356/63472. 38 rooms. Restaurant, 2 bars, tennis court, dance club. AE, DC, MC, V. Closed mid-Apr.–mid-May and mid-Oct.–early Dec.*

Nightlife and the Arts

Much activity centers on the **casino** in the Goldener Greif hotel, where you'll find baccarat, blackjack, roulette, and one-armed bandits galore. There's a restaurant and a bar, and no set closing time. You'll need your passport to enter the casino. ✉ *Hinterstadt 24,* ☎ *05356/62300.* 🎫 *Free.* ☉ *Dec. 25–Mar. and July–mid-Sept., daily 7 PM.*

The **Tenne** has for generations been *the* evening spot in Kitz. It's partly because there is a friendly atmosphere, the capacity, and the music (live), but most of all it's because you can meet people here. There's food, but emphasis is on drink and dance. ✉ *Hotel zur Tenne,* ☎ *05356/ 4444–0,* FAX *05356/4803–56. AE, DC, MC, V.* ☉ *Bar Dec. 25–mid-Mar. and Aug., daily 9 PM–3 AM.*

The disco crowd moves from place to place, but check out **Take Five** (✉ Hinterstadt 22, ☎ 05356/74131), the town's newest hot spot. Take Five's competition is **Roses** (✉ Bichlstr. 8, ☎ 05356/63425). Current among "in" spots are the **Stamperl** bar (✉ Franz-Reisch-Str. 7, ☎ 05356/62555); the **Londoner** (✉ Franz-Reisch-Str. 4, ☎ 05356/ 71428); and the **Fünferl** bar in the Kitzbüheler Hof (✉ Franz-Reisch-Str. 1, ☎ 05356/71300).

Outdoor Activities and Sports

GOLF

Golfclub Kitzbühel (05356/63007), 9 holes, par-36, is open April–October. **Golf-Club Kitzbühel-Schwarzsee** (☎ 05356/71645), 18 holes, par-72, is open April–October. Golf privileges can be arranged between the Kitzbühel courses and the Bichlhof, Erika, Rasmushof, Reisch, and Tennerhof hotels.

WEST FROM INNSBRUCK

Telfs

㉖ *32 km (20 mi) southeast of Reutte.*

The upper Inn Valley from Innsbruck to the Swiss border is beautiful countryside, particularly the narrow valleys that branch off to the south. Take Route 171 west from Innsbruck along the banks of the Inn, rather than the autobahn, which hugs the cliffs along the way. Mythical masked figures invade the streets of Telfs every five years when the town hosts its traditional Carnival celebration of **Schleicherlaufen.** Just before Lent in the year 2000 the whole population will celebrate in a festive masked procession. Some of the grotesque masks can be seen in the local museum.

Lodging

$$$$ 🏨 **Interalpen Tyrol.** This resort, outside town at 3,900 ft up the slopes, is simply huge, from the lobby with its vast expanse of carpet to the modern rooms. But the lobby's crackling fire is welcoming, and you'll find this a far quieter, more relaxing spot than you might guess from its original impression. ✉ *A–6410,* ☎ *05262/606,* ℻ *05262/606–190. 300 rooms. Restaurant, indoor pool, sauna, spa, tennis courts, exercise room. AE, DC, MC, V. Closed Apr.–early May and Nov.–mid-Dec.*

$ 🏨 **Tirolerhof.** You're within a couple of blocks of the center of town in this comfortable, balconied family-run hotel, convenient also to the indoor and outdoor pools and tennis and squash courts. The restaurant offers standard regional fare. ✉ *Bahnhofstr. 28, A–6410,* ☎ *05262/62237,* ℻ *05262/62237–9. 37 rooms. Restaurant. AE, DC, MC, V. Closed 3 wks before Easter.*

En Route From Telfs you have a choice of taking the very scenic Route 189/E6 to Nassereith and down to Imst or following the rail line along the river on Route 171. Like Telfs, both Nassereith and Imst are attractive for their richly decorated 15th- and 16th-century buildings and churches.

Imst

㉗ *35 km (22 mi) west of Telfs.*

Imst, a popular summer resort, lying a half-mile or so back from the Inn River and the railway line, makes an excellent base from which to explore the Paznaun Valley and the upper Inn Valley, leading into Switzerland and Italy.

Here the **Schemenlaufen,** a masked procession depicting the struggle between good and evil, takes place on Shrove Tuesday. Many of the magnificently carved masks worn by the mummers—especially those of the fearsome witches—are very old and works of art. The event is scheduled every four years and will next occur in the year 2000. The tradition is ancient, and as in Telfs, you can see some of the 100-year-old carved masks in the local **museum** (✉ Ballgasse 1); check with the tourist office for opening times. A great feature of these rustic carnivals is the ringing of cowbells of all shapes, sizes, and tones, and the resulting noise is quite deafening when the procession hits its stride. Don't overlook the 15th-century frescoed **parish church** in the upper part of Imst.

Dining and Lodging

$$ ✕⛺ **Post.** A 15th-century former castle, complete with onion-dome tow-
★ ers and set in the center of town next to a large park, is the heart of
this member of the Romantik Hotel group. The friendly interior is fur-
nished with antiques, and the modern bedrooms are cheerful. The
restaurant is recommended, particularly for game. ⊠ *E.-Wallnöfer-Pl.
3, A–6460,* ☎ *05412/66554,* FAX *05412/266519–55. 35 rooms. Restau-
rant, indoor pool. AE, DC, MC, V. Closed Nov.–Jan.*

$$ ⛺ **Linserhof.** This double-chalet hotel is outside town, set in a lush Alpine
meadow at the base of a wooded hillside. The attractive rooms are in
rustic Tirolean decor, with much natural wood; those on the south side
with balconies are preferable. ⊠ *A–6460 Imst/Teilwiesen,* ☎ *05412/
66415,* FAX *05412/66415–133. 42 rooms, 20 apartments. Restaurant,
bar, indoor pool, lake, sauna, tennis court, exercise room, bicycles. AE,
DC, MC, V.*

$ ⛺ **Zum Hirschen.** This comfortable *Gasthof-Pension,* attractively ren-
ovated and close to the center of town, pays particular attention to
families with children. ⊠ *Th.-Walsch-Str. 3, A–6460,* ☎ *05412/
6901–0. 53 rooms. Restaurant, bar, sauna. AE, DC, MC, V. Closed
early–mid-Dec.*

En Route The Ötz Valley climbs in a series of six great natural steps for nearly 42
km (26 mi) from the Inn River to the glaciers around Obergurgl, at 6,200
ft above sea level. The entire distance offers stunning scenery, with the
most dramatic part beginning around Sölden, where the final rise begins to the 8,100-ft pass over the Timmel Alps and across the Italian border into South Tirol. It was in this area that Ötzi, the Iceman mummy,
was discovered a few years ago. The body, which is more than 5,000
years old, was found by Austrians, who were unaware they had crossed
the Italian border. Ötzi is now in the possession of Italy, who at first wanted
nothing to do with him, thinking he was a recent murder victim. To reach
the valley, turn south off Route 171 onto Route 186.

Ötz

㉘ *21 km (12 mi) southeast of Imst, 23 km (14 mi) southwest of Telfs.*

Gothic houses with colorful fresco decorations grace this typically
Tirolean mountain village. The parish church of **St. George and St.
Nicholas,** its tower once a charnel house, sits on a rock promontory
above the village. The small St. Michael's chapel also has a splendid
altar dating to 1683.

Lodging

$ ⛺ **Alpenhotel.** This solid house fits the center of town well; here you'll
find traditional country warmth, friendliness, and comfortable rooms.
Minimum half board is required in winter. ⊠ *Bielefeldstr. 4, A–6433,*
☎ *05252/6232,* FAX *05252/6232–16. 45 rooms. Restaurant. No credit
cards. Closed mid-Apr.–May and Oct.–mid-Dec.*

$ ⛺ **Drei Mohren.** You can't miss the roof of this inn, with its wonder-
ful collection of odd towers and onion domes. Fortunately, the interior
is less exotic; the comfortable rooms are elegantly paneled, and most
have balconies. The restaurant, offering standard local fare, is intended
primarily for hotel guests and is tastefully decorated with old etchings.
⊠ *Hauptstr. 54, A–6433,* ☎ *05252/6301,* FAX *05252/2464. 22 rooms.
Restaurant, tennis court. AE, DC, MC, V. Closed Nov.–mid-Dec.*

Sölden

㉙ *28 km (18 mi) south of Ötz.*

The highest cable car in Austria squires skiers swiftly from Sölden over the glaciers to a permanent-snow area at almost 9,910 ft on Gaislacher Kogel, where you can ski all year. Sölden is the most famous village in the Ötz Valley, earning an international reputation for its natural skiing conditions. The towering Hochsölden (6,800 ft) ensures excellent snow for the whole season.

Dining and Lodging

$$$$ ✕☎ **Central.** Huge arches and heavy wooden timbers accent the antique furniture and set the atmosphere in this massive riverside hotel where the prominent are said to gather. The bedrooms are spacious and luxuriously furnished. Half board is standard. The intimate Ötztaler Stube restaurant is the best in town; sample the fillet of venison, and don't overlook the excellent desserts. ✉ *Hochsölden Hof 418, A–6450,* ☎ *05254/2260–0,* FAX *05254/2260–511. 92 rooms. Restaurant, indoor pool, sauna. No credit cards. Closed June–mid-July.*

$$$–$$$$ ☎ **Liebe Sonne.** You'll be right next to the chairlift to Hochsölden if you stay in this sprawling complex, recently rebuilt to include a new array of amenities. Its atmosphere is rustic, and the paneled rooms are cozy. Half board is required. ✉ *Rainstadl 85, A–6450,* ☎ *05254/2203–0,* FAX *05254/2423. 59 rooms. Restaurant, bar, indoor pool, sauna, spa, exercise room. No credit cards. Closed May and June.*

Outdoor Activities and Sports

CLIMBING

The nearby Venteral Valley burrows still farther into the Ötztal Alps, ending in the tiny village of Vent, a popular resort center. In summer, the village is transformed into a base for serious mountain climbers, experienced in ice and rock climbing, who want to attempt the formidable **Wildspitze** (12,450 ft) or other, even more difficult neighboring peaks. Hiring a professional local guide is strongly advised. To reach Vent from Sölden, turn off at the road marked to Heiligenkreutz.

Obergurgl

㉚ *11 km (7 mi) south of Sölden.*

Austria's highest village, tiny Obergurgl gained its reputation not only for superb winter sports but also as the place where the Swiss physicist Auguste Piccard landed his famous stratospheric balloon in the 1930s. In winter, a vast expanse of snow and ice shimmers all around you, and all year, the great peaks and glaciers of the Ötztal Alps appear deceptively close at hand. A high Alpine road takes you from Obergurgl to the hotel settlement at **Hochgurgl,** another excellent skiing spot, and farther up to the Timmelsjoch Pass through magnificent mountain scenery. From Hochgurgl, a three-stage chairlift brings you into an area of year round skiing. In summer, ask at the tourist office about river-rafting possibilities.

Lodging

$$–$$$$ ☎ **Bellevue.** This friendly Alpine chalet lives up to its name in every re-
★ spect: Is there another Bellevue among the probable millions in the world with a vista to equal the one here? You can ski right out the front door. Rooms are cozily comfortable, but you'll have to take half board. ✉ *A–6456,* ☎ *05256/6228. 26 rooms. Restaurant, indoor pool, sauna, exercise room. No credit cards. Closed May–June and Sept.–early Dec.*

$$–$$$$ ☎ **Edelweiss und Gurgl.** Traditionally, this is *the* place to stay. Reno-
★ vations have turned the massive house into an excellent family-run hotel

with a comfortable, relaxed ambience. The cheery rooms have attractive natural-wood touches. Minimum half board is required. ⊠ *A–6456,* ☏ *05256/6223. 100 rooms. Restaurant, bar, indoor pool, sauna. AE, DC, MC, V. Closed May–mid-June and Oct.–Nov.*

LANDECK, UPPER INN VALLEY, AND ST. ANTON

Landeck

③① *24 km (15 mi) southwest of Imst.*

On Route 171 west, Landeck is a popular place in summer and a good base from which to explore the Paznaun Valley and the upper Inn Valley, leading into Switzerland and Italy. Landeck is known for an ancient and awe-inspiring rite that takes place on **"Cheese Sunday,"** the first Sunday following Ash Wednesday. At dawn the young men set out to climb to the top of the great rocky crags that overshadow and hem in the old city on three sides. As dusk falls, they light huge bonfires that can be seen for miles around and then set fire to great disks of pinewood dipped in tar, which they roll ablaze down to the valley below. The sight of scores of these fiery wheels bounding down the steep slopes toward town is a fearsome spectacle worthy of Ezekiel.

The 13th-century **Burg Landeck castle** dominates from its position above the town. Climb up and catch the superb views from this vantage point. Also note the 16th-century winged altar in the 15th-century Gothic **parish church of the Assumption.** Downhill and, increasingly, cross-country skiing can be found in Landeck and throughout the Upper Inn Valley. Equipment is available for rent, though the selection and quality will vary from place to place.

Lodging

$ ☷ **Schrofenstein.** Directly in the middle of town, this older house still shows its original beamed ceilings and marble floors in the public areas. The rooms are comfortably modern, those overlooking the river preferred. ⊠ *Malser Str. 31, A–6500,* ☏ *05442/62395. 54 rooms. Restaurant. AE, DC, MC, V. Closed mid–late Apr. and Nov.–mid-Dec.*

$ ☷ **Schwarzer Adler.** Virtually in the shadow of the town castle, this traditional, family-run hotel offers solid comfort in typical Tirolean style, with red checks and light wood. ⊠ *Malser Str. 8, A–6500,* ☏ *05442/62316,* FAX *05442/62316–50. 32 rooms. Restaurant. No credit cards. Closed Nov.–mid-Dec.*

Outdoor Activities and Sports

HIKING
Would-be climbers can take lessons by contacting Hugo Walter at the **Bergsteigerschule Piz Buin-Silvretta** (⊠ *A–6563 Galtür,* ☏ 05443/260).

Ried

③② *19 km (12 mi) south of Landeck.*

At Landeck the Inn River turns southward along the edge of the Silvretta mountains. The valley, tucked between two dramatic ranges, climbs toward the Italian border. As you follow Route 315/S15 beside the river, you'll come across **Schloss Sigmundsried,** a small castle built by Duke Sigmund the Wealthy about 1470 around an earlier tower; the castle holds intriguing 16th-century coat-of-arms paintings. Today, you can canoe or raft the river along the edge of the Silvretta mountains.

Serfaus

㉝ *8 km (5 mi) southwest of Ried.*

At Ried, turn west off Route 315 for the scenic but steep climb up to Serfaus. This old village, perched on a plateau above the valley, has taken on new class in recent years as an important winter-sports center. There are several ski lifts, and the Komperdell cable car takes you in summer, too, up to points from which you can either hike or just enjoy the views.

Dining and Lodging

$$$–$$$$ ✕🏨 **Maximilian.** The transformation of a former Serfaus Gasthof into a modern hotel seems to have worked, successfully blending the old and the new, and the house is now a member of the Silence Hotel group. Rooms in the new section, some with open fireplaces, are more spacious, but all are comfortable. A separate, excellent restaurant in a cozy side room is open to the public in the evening, with two fixed menus available. ✉ *Herrenanger 4, A–6534,* ☎ *05476/6520,* FAX *05476/6520–52. 36 rooms. Restaurant, indoor pool, sauna, exercise room, children's programs. No credit cards. Closed May–June and Oct.–mid-Dec.*

$$$–$$$$ 🏨 **Cervosa.** This typical twin chalet is not only close to the center of town, it's the center of action in Serfaus. The family owners have preserved the hotel's informal ambience despite its rather elegant reconstruction. Rooms are welcoming and modern; there are apartments of various sizes as well. Half board is standard in winter. ✉ *Herrenanger 11, A–6534,* ☎ *05476/6211,* FAX *05476/6211–141. 70 rooms. Restaurant, indoor and outdoor pools, beauty salon, sauna, bowling, exercise room, squash. AE, DC, V. Closed mid-Apr.–mid-June and mid-Oct.–mid-Dec.*

St. Anton am Arlberg

㉞ *49 km (30 mi) northwest of Serfaus, 22 km (15 mi) west of Landeck.*

Tucked between the entrance to the Arlberg tunnel and the railway (if you're coming from Serfaus, backtrack to Landeck and take Route 316/S16 west toward Vorarlberg), St. Anton swarms with visitors at the height of the season. The wealthy, the prominent, and, occasionally, the royal appear regularly to see and be seen—some even to enjoy the winter sports. Their presence boosts prices into the very-expensive-to-outrageous category, but if you shop around, you can find accommodations outside the center of the action at a bearable price. St. Anton is a particularly lovely town in summer—which seems on the verge of becoming the more fashionable season.

Modern skiing techniques were created and nurtured in St. Anton. In 1921, Hannes Schneider (1890–1955), an unknown young ski instructor with innovative ideas, set up a ski school to teach his new technique, at the invitation of the just-founded Kandahar Ski Club. This "Arlberg School" method, developed by Schneider in the '20s and '30s, laid down the basic principles followed by all skiing courses the world over. St. Anton's remains one of the world's leading ski schools. Thanks to an amazing system of funicular trains, double chairlift, and interconnected T-bars, St. Anton can access skiers to the Arlberg's region's enormous 300-odd km (200-odd mi) of marked runs. If you decide to take to the slopes, remember that skiing remains serious business in St. Anton: Many slopes are so steep you'll be sharing them with mountain climbers.

Dining and Lodging

$$$$ ✕🏨 **Brunnenhof.** Set in the intimate, homey atmosphere of an old farmhouse in nearby St. Jakob is one of the best restaurants in the area.

From the excellent Tirolean and international menu you might choose a mushroom, garlic, or cheese soup and follow it with roast rack of lamb in an herb crust. The wine list is good. The 10-room hotel offers cozy comfort from December to April and from June to September at moderate prices. ⊠ *A–6580,* ☎ *05446/2293,* FAX *05446/2293–5. Restaurant. No credit cards. Closed May–June and Oct.–Nov.*

$–$$$ ⊞ **Schwarzer Adler.** The beautifully frescoed facade of this 420-year-
★ old inn in the center of town creates the right setting for the open fire-places, Tirolean antiques, and colorful Oriental carpets inside. Rooms are tastefully furnished in Alpine style and fully equipped. An annex across the street has somewhat less elegant (and cheaper) rooms. The lively Disco Klause is in the basement of the main house. ⊠ *A–6580,* ☎ *05446/2244–0,* FAX *05446/2244–62. 63 rooms. Restaurant, café, sauna, exercise room, dance club, baby-sitting. AE, DC, MC, V. Closed mid-Apr.–May and Oct.–Nov.*

$–$$ ✕⊞ **Karl Schranz.** Your first impression of this new and spacious Alpine lodge is made by the lobby's welcoming fireplace—a showcase for trophies won by the champion skier and owner-manager, Karl Schranz, from 1957 to 1972. A shuttle bus takes guests to and from the center of town. The rooms are large and modern, with elegant wood paneling. The Jägerstube restaurant features Austrian and Tirolean fare. ⊠ *A–6580,* ☎ *05446/2555–0,* FAX *05446/2555–5. 23 rooms. Restaurant, bar, sauna, exercise room, baby-sitting. No credit cards. Closed May– June and Oct.–Nov.*

Nightlife and the Arts

For some visitors to St. Anton, the show, not the snow, is the thing. Nobody complains about lack of action! Check out the popular après-ski spots:

Drop In (⊠ Sporthotel St. Anton, ☎ 05446/3131), the **Underground Piano Bar** (☎ 05446/2000), the **Postkeller** cellar disco (⊠ Hotel Neue Post, ☎ 05446/2213–274), the **terrace of the Hotel Alte Post** (☎ 05446/2553) in early springtime, and in St. Christoph, the **Siglu** at the Arlberghöhe (☎ 05446/2635–0). In Moos, Gunnar Munthe's **Krazy Kanguruh** bar with its cellar disco is a favorite gathering spot; it opens at 3:30 PM (☎ 05446/2633). Some of the best, original, local Alpine atmosphere for drinking and dining can be found at **Rodelalm** (☎ 0663/ 858855) and **Sennhütte** (☎ 05446/20048).

Outdoor Activities and Sports

SKIING

The *Skihaserl,* or ski bunny, as the beginner is called, usually joins a class on St. Anton's good "nursery" slopes, where he or she will have plenty of often very distinguished company. The school here is excellent and is considered by some to be the Harvard of ski schools. Once past the Skihaserl stage, skiers go higher in the Arlberg mountains to the superlative runs from the top of the Galzig and the 9,100-ft Valluga above it. Check with your hotel or ski-lift ticket offices about an **Arlberg Skipass,** which is good on cable cars and lifts in St. Anton and St. Christoph on the Tirol side and on those in Zürs, Lech, Oberlech, and Stuben in Vorarlberg—77 in all.

St. Christoph

③⑤ *2 km (1 mi) west of St. Anton am Arlberg.*

A hospice was founded, in what is now St. Christoph, as early as the 15th century to care for imperiled travelers stranded by the snows on the pass. Today, the snow is what attracts visitors to the area. Even the Austrian government has gotten in on the act, holding its exacting courses for aspiring ski instructors here. While St. Christoph hasn't the same social cachet as St. Anton, the skiing facilities are precisely the same (and even closer at hand). If you take your skiing seriously and are willing to forgo the high life as too distracting or too expensive, you may find winter sports per se more fun at St. Christoph.

Dining and Lodging

$$–$$$$ ✕⌨ **Arlberg Hospiz.** This huge pink building re-creates much of the
★ legendary ancient hospice that stood here until a fire in the 1950s. Carved wood paneling and rich Oriental carpets abound. The rooms are luxurious in the extreme; service is attentive but not obtrusive. The associated Hospizalm restaurant has earned a reputation for creative cooking: You might be offered cream of lobster or oyster soup, veal or venison, or fish dishes. The wine list is outstanding. ⌨ *A–6580 St. Christoph am Arlberg,* ☎ *05446/2611,* ⨎ *05446/3545. 102 rooms. Restaurant, bar, indoor pool, sauna, exercise room, dance club, babysitting. No credit cards. Closed May and Oct.–Nov.*

Ischgl

㊱ *67 km (42 mi) southeast of St. Christoph.*

Ischgl, the largest town in the Paznaun Valley, offers excellent skiing, particularly in the small Fimber Valley to the south, and in summer is a popular high-altitude health resort. You can get to the 7,500-ft Idalpe via the 4-km-long (2½-mi-long) Silvretta cable-car run. The enchanting Paznaun Valley follows the course of the Trisanna River for more than 40 km (25 mi). The valley runs into the heart of the Blue Silvretta mountains, named for the shimmering ice-blue effect created by the great peaks and glaciers. They are dominated by the Fluchthorn (10,462 ft) at the head of the valley near Galtür.

Slightly higher up the valley is **Galtür,** the best-known resort in the Paznaun, equally popular as a winter-sports area, as a summer resort, and as a base for mountain climbing. Although Galtür is a starting point for practiced mountaineers, many of the climbs up the Blue Silvretta are very easy and lead to the half dozen mountain huts belonging to the Alpenverein. Galtür and the Silvretta region inspired Ernest Hemingway's novella *Alpine Idyll*; the author spent the winter of 1925 here, and the town still remembers him.

Dining and Lodging

$$–$$$$ ✕⌨ **Madlein.** This modern chalet-style hotel not far from the center is the place to stay for sheer Alpine elegance and to see the town's action. The rooms are attractive, but you'll be tempted to spend your time in such places as the beamed Almbar with its large dance floor and friendly atmosphere. The main restaurant has a fine kitchen. ⌨ *A–6561,* ☎ *05444/ 5266,* ⨎ *05444/5636. 65 rooms. 2 restaurants, bar, indoor pool, sauna, nightclub. No credit cards. Closed May–June and Oct.–Nov.*

INNSBRUCK AND TIROL A TO Z

Arriving and Departing

By Bus

Innsbruck is connected by bus to other parts of Tirol, and the terminal (⌨ Südtiroler Platz, ☎ 0512/1717 or 0512/585155) is beside the main train station.

By Car

To get to Innsbruck, exit from the east–west autobahn (Route A12/ E60), or from the Brenner autobahn (Route A13/E45) running south to Italy. Since the Old City is a pedestrian zone and much of the rest of the downtown area is paid parking only, you'll be best off leaving the car in a central garage, unless your hotel has parking.

By Plane

The airport (0512/22525 flight information), 3 km (2 mi) west of Innsbruck, is served principally by **Austrian Airlines** and **Tyrolean. Buses** (Line F) to the city center (Maria-Theresien-Strasse) take about 20 minutes. Get your ticket from the bus driver; it costs AS18. **Taxis** should take no more than 10 minutes into town, and the fare is about AS100–AS150. Transfer services operated by **Four Seasons Travel** (⊠ Müllerstr. 14, ☎ 0512/584157, 🅵🅰🆇 0512/585767) run to and from the *Zentralbereich* at Munich airport, departing Munich at 7, 9, 11 AM and 4 PM. Service from Innsbruck to Munich is on demand; make arrangements in advance, allowing 2½ hours for travel. One-way fare is AS420, round-trip AS720; reservations are recommended.

By Train

Direct trains (☎ 0512/1717 information and reservations) serve Innsbruck from Munich, Vienna, Rome, and Zürich, and all arrive at the railroad station at Südtiroler Platz.

Getting Around

By Bus and Streetcar

In **Innsbruck,** most bus and streetcar routes begin or end at Maria-Theresien-Strasse, nearby Bozner Platz, or the main train station (Hauptbahnhof). You can get single tickets costing AS18 on the bus or streetcar. Multiple-ride tickets bought in advance at most tobacconists (*Tabak-Trafik*), the Verkehrsbetriebe (transportation services) office (⊠ Museumstr. 23), or the tourist office (☞ Visitor Information, *below*) are cheaper; a block of four tickets is AS44. A 24-hour ticket good for the city costs AS25; other 24-hour network tickets cover areas outside the immediate city. A weekly ticket costs AS105. For information, check with the tourist office. You can transfer to another line with the same ticket as long as you continue in more or less the same direction in a single journey. The bus is also the most convenient way to reach the six major ski areas outside the city. A Club Innsbruck pass (free from the tourist office or your hotel if you spend one night or more) gives you free transportation to the ski areas; many hotels provide shuttle service to the special ski bus stop. The public ski buses leave from the Landestheater on Rennweg, across from the Hofburg. Check with your hotel or the tourist offices for schedules.

In **Tirol,** as throughout Austria, where the train doesn't go, the post office or railroad bus does, and except in the most remote areas, buses are frequent enough so that you can get around. But bus travel requires time and planning. In summer, tour-bus operators run many sightseeing trips through Tirol that often include East and South Tirol. Check with your travel agent or the nearest tourist office.

By Car

Private cars are not allowed in **Innsbruck**'s Old City, and parking anywhere near the center in Innsbruck requires vouchers, which you buy from tobacconists, the tourist office (☞ Visitor Information, *below*), post offices, or blue coin-operated dispensers found around parking areas. Each half hour costs AS5. Maximum parking time is 1½ hours. Large blue *P* signs direct you to parking garages. The bus is about as convenient as a car for reaching the ski areas if you have to cope with chains and other complications of winter driving.

Driving is the best way to see the rest of **Tirol,** since it allows you to wander off the main routes at your pleasure or to stop and admire the view. Roads are good, but a detailed highway map is recommended. Watch your gas gauge, particularly on Sunday and holidays, when some stations may be closed.

The autobahns are fastest, but for scenery you'll be best off on the by-ways. One important exception is the 1¾-km (1-mi) Europa Bridge on the Brenner autobahn running south into Italy, although if you follow the parallel route from Patsch to Pfons, you'll have the views without the traffic. Roads with particularly attractive scenery are marked on highway maps with a parallel green line.

By Horse-Drawn Carriage

Horse-drawn cabs, still a feature of Innsbruck life, can be hired at the stand in front of the Landestheater. Set the price before you head off; a half-hour ride will cost around AS320.

By Taxi

In Innsbruck, taxis are not much faster than walking, particularly along the one-way streets and in the Old City. Basic fare is AS52 for the first 1½ km (1 mi). Call to order a radio cab (☎ 0512/5311, 0512/ 45500, or 0512/1718).

By Train

The railroad follows nearly all the main routes in Tirol, with highways and tracks sharing the same narrow valleys. Some of the most fascinating and memorable side trips can be made by rail: Two narrow-gauge lines steam out of Jenbach, for example, one up to the Achensee, the other down to Mayrhofen in the Zillertal. From Innsbruck, the narrow-gauge Stubaitalbahn runs south to Telfes and Fulpmes.

The main railway line of Tirol runs east–west, entering Tirol via the Griessen pass, then heading on to St. Johann and Kitzbühel before wandering over to Wörgl and onward to Jenbach, Hall in Tirol, and Innsbruck. From Innsbruck on, the line follows the Inn Valley to Landeck, then to St. Anton, where it plunges into an 11-km (7-mi) tunnel under the Arlberg range, emerging at Langen in Vorarlberg. From Innsbruck, a line runs north into Germany to Garmish-Partenkirchen and onward back into Austria, to Ehrwald and Reutte in Tirol and beyond, into Germany again. A line from Innsbruck to the south goes over the dramatic Brenner pass (4,465 ft) into Italy.

Contacts and Resources

Car Rentals

Avis (✉ Tourist Center, Salurner Str. 15, ☎ 0512/571754, FAX 0512/ 577149). **Budget** (✉ Michael-Gaismayr Str. 7, ☎ 0512/588468, FAX 0512/584580). **Europcar** (✉ Salurner Str. 8, ☎ 0512/582060, FAX 0512/ 582107).

Emergencies

Police (☎ 133). **Ambulance** (☎ 144).

Currency Exchange

In addition to banks (open weekdays 7:45–12:30 and 2:15–4) and post offices, you can **change money** in Innsbruck at the American Express office (✉ Brixnerstr. 3, ☎ 0512/582491), at the main train station (the office is open daily 7:30–12:30, 12:45–6, and 6:30–8:15) and the city tourist information office (☞ Visitor Information, *below*). But compare rates; you'll probably do best at a post office or bank.

Cash machines can be found in Innsbruck (⊠ Hofgasse 2 and Herzog-Friedrich-Strasse 7).

Guided Tours

In Innsbruck, bus tours with English-speaking guides cover the city highlights (two hours), leaving daily at noon, year-round, from the hotel information office at the Südtiroler Platz station. In summer, additional buses are scheduled at 10 AM and 2 PM; and a shorter, hour-long tour leaves the Volkskunstmuseum Monday–Saturday at 10:15, noon, 2, and 3:15. Guided 1½-hour walking tours on Saturday and Sunday highlight historic personalities and some offbeat features associated with the city. Your hotel or one of the tourist offices will have tickets and details.

Late-Night Pharmacies

Several pharmacies stay open late in Innsbruck on a rotational basis. The newspaper will give their names, addresses, and phone numbers. Ask your hotel for help.

Lodging

If you arrive in Innsbruck without a hotel room, check with the **Zimmernachweis** (room accommodation service) next to the railroad station (⊠ Südtiroler Pl., ☎ 0512/583766–0). The office is open summer, daily 8 AM–10 PM, and winter, daily 9–9. The same organization also has offices on the incoming west autobahn (☎ 0512/573543), the east autobahn (☎ 0512/346474), the Kranebitter Allee (north) autobahn exit (☎ 0512/284991), and the Brenner (south) autobahn (☎ 0512/577933). Call for information on **youth hostels** (☎ 0512/346179 or 0512/346180). The booklet "Children's Hotels" (in English, available from the Tirolean tourist office) lists Tirolean hotels that cater particularly to families with children.

Travel Agencies

American Express. ⊠ *Brixnerstr. 3,* ☎ *0512/582491–0,* ℻ *0512/573385.* ⊙ *Weekdays 9–5:30, Sat. 9–noon.*

Visitor Information

Innsbruck's main tourist office (⊠ Burggraben 3 A–6020, ☎ 0512/59850, ℻ 0512/59850–7) is open daily 8–7.

Österreichischer Alpenverein is the place to go for information on Alpine huts and mountaineering advice (⊠ Wilhelm-Greil-Str. 15, ☎ 0512/59547–34, ℻ 0512/575528). It's open weekdays 8:30–6, Saturday 9–noon.

Most small-town tourist offices have no specific street address and are accommodated in the village hall. Address letters to *Fremdenverkehrsamt* (tourist office) and include the postal code of the town.

Achenkirch (⊠ A–6215, ☎ 05246/6270, ℻ 05246/6780). **Brixlegg** (⊠ Marktstr. 6b, A–6230, ☎ 05337/62581, ℻ 05337/63882). **Gerlos** (⊠ A–6281, ☎ 05284/5244–0, ℻ 05284/5244–24). **Imst** (⊠ Johannespl. 4, A–6460, ☎ 05412/6910–0, ℻ 05412/6910–8). **Ischgl** (⊠ A–6561, ☎ 05444/5266, ℻ 05444/5636). **Jenbach** (⊠ Achenseestr. 37, A–6200, ☎ 05244/3901, ℻ 05244/3552). **Kitzbühel** (⊠ Hinterstadt 18, A–6370, ☎ 05356/2272, ℻ 05356/2307). **Kufstein** (⊠ Münchner Str. 2, A–6330, ☎ 05372/62207, ℻ 05372/61455). **Landeck** (⊠ Malserstr. 10, A–6500, ☎ 05442/62344, ℻ 05442/67830). **Mayrhofen** (⊠ Dursterstr. 225, A–6290, ☎ 05285/2305, ℻ 05285/4116–33). **Obergurgl/Hochgurgl** (⊠ A–6456, ☎ 05256/258, ℻ 05256/353). **Rattenberg** (⊠ Klostergasse 94, A–6240, ☎ 05337/63321, ℻ 05337/65417). **St. Anton am Arlberg** (⊠ A–6580, ☎ 05446/2269, ℻ 05446/2532). **St. Johann in Tirol** (⊠ Poststr. 2, A–6380,

☎ 05352/63335, FAX 05352/65200). **Schwaz** (⊠ Franz-Josef-Str. 26, A–6130, ☎ 05242/63240, FAX 05242/65630). **Serfaus** (⊠ Unteres Dorf 13, A–6534, ☎ 05476/6239, FAX 05476/6813). **Sölden/Hochsölden** (⊠ Rettenbach 288, A–6450, ☎ 05254/2212–0, FAX 05254/3131). **Tux/Lanersbach/Hintertux** (⊠ A–6293 Lanersbach, ☎ 05287/606–8506, FAX 05287/624–8508). **Zell am Ziller** (⊠ Dorfpl. 3a, A–6280, ☎ 05282/2281, FAX 05282/2281–80).

11 Vorarlberg

"What God has put asunder by a mountain, let no man join by a tunnel"—so said the Vorarlbergers of old. Once the Arlberg Tunnel linked Austria's westernmost province to the rest of the country, the secret was out. Vorarlberg—nicknamed the Ländle, the "Little Province"—was really Austria's Switzerland: cheaper in some ways, perhaps less efficient in others. The world at large discovered skiing slopes that rival those of Austria's neutral neighbor, gorgeous Lake Constance, and the lush forests of the Bregenzerwald. In colder months, a winter wonderland is the main lure— especially at Lech, now more in fashion than ever since the late Princess Diana vacationed there.

THEY SAY YOU CAN LEARN ALL ABOUT AUSTRIA just by going to the Vorarlberg. Like studying the ocean in a drop of water, this postage stamp–size province seems to be Austria in miniature—it features a sampling of the best of everything the country has to offer. Music devotees descend every summer on Hohenems for its elegant Schubertiade—held in a regal Renaissance castle—and on Bregenz for its famed lakeside music festival. Nature lovers head to the Bregenzerwald—a wide area of thick forests, charming valleys, and lush meadows dotted with thick clusters of red, white, and yellow Alpine flowers—a region that remains decidedly private, unostentatiously beautiful. Literature buffs arrive to see the sun set in the village of Schruns, where Hemingway spent several winters writing *The Sun Also Rises.* And merrymakers like to throng Lech and Zürs, two top ski resorts where the perfumes of hot chocolate and *Pfefferrminz Tee* mingle with the expensive perfumes worn by the jet set.

Updated by
Bonnie Dodson

Tiny Vorarlberg covers an area of less than 1,000 square mi and is the smallest (with the exception of Vienna) of Austria's federal states. As its name implies, the state lies "before the Arlberg"—that massive range of Alps, the watershed of Europe, mecca of winter sports—and forms the western tip of Austria. Until the tunnel was cut through, the Arlberg was passable only in summer; in winter, Vorarlberg was effectively cut off from the rest of the country. And while Austrians from the east may go skiing or take vacations in neighboring Tirol, and although they may be well traveled, many never make it to Vorarlberg in the course of their lives. The Viennese semi-affectionately refer to Vorarlberg as the *Ländle,* meaning the "Little Province."

Nowhere in Austria will you find such determined adherence to old customs as in the villages and towns of the Vorarlberg. You'll see folk costumes on people in the street, not in museums, and your chances are good of running into a local celebration at any time of year. The province has much in common with neighboring Switzerland. Not only are the dialects similar, but the landscape flows across the border with continuity. Both peoples descended from the same ancient Germanic tribes that flourished in the 3rd century BC. Both have the same characteristics of thrift, hard work, and a deep-rooted instinct for democracy and independence. In fact, after the collapse of the Habsburg monarchy following World War I, Vorarlberg came very close to becoming a part of Switzerland. In 1919, 80% of the populace voted in favor of negotiating with the Swiss to join the confederation, but the St. Germain peace conference put an end to such ideas, and Vorarlberg remained Austrian.

Pleasures and Pastimes

Dining

Vorarlberg's cuisine is lighter than in neighboring Tirol and the rest of Austria. Fresh ingredients from the region's farms, lakes, and forests are the norm, with an emphasis on dairy products from the cows that graze the mountains and meadows of the region. Be sure to try a slab of *Schweizer* cheese from one of the huge rounds produced at local farms. Cheese is also added to soups and noodle dishes and fried in fritters. Fresh river trout is caught in the waters of Lake Constance and in the surrounding lakes and streams. You'll see fish fried, broiled, and steamed on restaurant menus throughout Vorarlberg. In small towns throughout the region, restaurants are often the dining rooms of country inns.

CATEGORY	COST*
$$$$	over AS500
$$$	AS300–AS500
$$	AS150–AS300
$	under AS150

for a typical three-course meal with a glass of house wine, service, and tax, but excluding 3–5% tip

Lodging

Vorarlberg has loads of accommodation options from local farmhouses where you share chores to ski chalets perched on the slopes of the Western Alps to converted castle hotels high above the Bodensee. In ski resorts in Vorarlberg, hotel rates in season are often well above the range of our chart. At most of those hotels, the price includes a mandatory two meals a day, and often no credit cards are accepted. The tourist offices can usually help lead you to more moderate lodgings in private houses. In summer you can often find bargain rates at 50% of the winter tariff. In some towns, such as Bregenz, summer is the high season and may put the establishment into the next-higher price category.

CATEGORY	LECH/ZÜRS*	OTHER TOWNS*
$$$$	over AS2,200	over AS1,200
$$$	AS1,500–AS2,200	AS900–AS1,200
$$	AS900–AS1,500	AS600–AS900
$	under AS900	under AS600

per person per night for a standard double room in high season, including breakfast (in resorts, including one additional meal in winter), service charge of 10%, and tax

Skiing

One of the main attractions of a stay in Vorarlberg is the world-class skiing available in Austria's Western Alps. After all, modern ski techniques were developed in Vorarlberg by local Hannes Schneider, who founded the first ski school in Arlberg in the 1920s. From intimate, rustic resorts to the glamour of Lech and Zürs, the province has slopes to suit all tastes and levels, and fewer crowds than in the rest of the country.

The Sound—and Sights—of Music

Festival fever seizes the Vorarlberg every summer and summons the faithful to some of the finest concerts in Austria. Grand opera is offered lakeside at the **Bregenzer Festspiele** (Bregenz Summer Music Festival), while elegant recitals of the **Schubertiade** take place in the neighboring town of Feldkirch. The Bregenz festival is famed for its floating stage—in truth, a group of man-made islands mounted on pilings; now, when raindrops fall, there is a new indoor theater to accommodate the festivities. In Feldkirch—a spot some historians believe inspired the *Nibelungenlied*—Schubert *Lieder*-lovers come to hear fine musicians pay their homage to the great Biedermeier-era composer during a 10-day period in late June.

Exploring Vorarlberg

This chapter divides Vorarlberg into three sections. Our first exploring tour takes you through Bregenz, the region's historic capital. Then, we head out to the glorious countryside, taking in the legendary Bregenzerwald to Bludenz, following the Ill Valley to Feldkirch, and heading north again to Bregenz. Here, you can relax in a true backwoods atmosphere while enjoying the beautiful, if somewhat hair-raising, country roads as you pass through mountain hamlets, all with an Old

World charm of their own and few discovered by the guidebooks. The last excursion takes in the Arlberg ski resorts.

Great Itineraries

Numbers in the text correspond to numbers in the margin and on the Vorarlberg map.

IF YOU HAVE 2 DAYS

If you only have a weekend to visit Vorarlberg, head to the capital of ⊞ **Bregenz** ① on the banks of the Bodensee (Lake Constance). Spend a day wandering around the lakeshore and the lovely, romantic remains of the once fortified medieval town. The next day take a boat ride into neighboring Switzerland or Germany. Around the lake are extensive hiking and biking trails for those who'd rather see the sights on their own steam.

IF YOU HAVE 5 DAYS

Visit the resorts in the Arlberg and the Montafon Valley, which have attracted such notaries as Ernest Hemingway and the late Princess Diana. Start off your trip in ⊞ **Schruns** ⑪, visiting Hemingway's haunts. Now, you're ready for the Arlberg resorts. On your second day, head up north for **Stuben** ⑬, the hometown of skiing pioneer Hannes Schneider, moving on for your next overnight in ⊞ **Zürs** ⑭. After a little hobnobbing with film stars and royalty, spend your final two overnights in Vorarlberg's most famous ski resort, ⊞ **Lech** ⑮.

IF YOU HAVE 7 DAYS

If you have more time in Vorarlberg, begin by exploring the natural marvels of the **Bregenzerwald** and the history-rich sights of ⊞ **Bregenz** ①. After two overnights in Bregenz, you can venture off the beaten track on your third day by stopping for discount shopping in Egg on your way to the picturesque town of **Schwarzenberg** ②. Then head to ⊞ **Bezau** ③ to savor the beauty of the surrounding forests and mountains with a hike into the hills on your fourth day. That afternoon, visit breathtaking **Damüls** ④, where flowers blanket the hillsides during the summer and great skiing welcomes visitors in winter. Head for ⊞ **Bludenz** ⑤ to explore one of the five magical valleys surrounding the town. On the fifth day, follow the Ill Valley to the medieval town of ⊞ **Feldkirch** ⑦, and spend two days meandering through the narrow, winding streets admiring the burgher homes and castle from an earlier age when lords and ladies peopled the province. Make a stop in **Hohenems** ⑧ on your last day for a visit to the local Jewish Museum and **Dornbirn** ⑨, famous for its textiles, on your way back to the capital.

When to Tour Vorarlberg

Vorarlberg has something to offer visitors during every season. If you're in the province during warm weather, make sure to stop in Bregenz when the city comes to life with the Bregenzer Festspiele (Bregenz Summer Music Festival). Boat excursions to Switzerland and Germany are also a must. History buffs will enjoy the sights in Bregenz, Bludenz, and especially Feldkirch. And sports enthusiasts will love the wealth of hiking, biking, sailing, and fishing that is available around the region. Of course, if you travel to Vorarlberg during the winter months, then fasten on your bindings and head to the slopes.

BREGENZ

❶ *150 km (90 mi) west of Innsbruck, 660 km (409 mi) west of Vienna, 120 km (75 mi) east of Zurich, 193 km (120 mi) southwest of Munich.*

Lying along the southeastern shore of the Bodensee (Lake Constance) with the majestic Pfänder as its backdrop, Bregenz is where Vorarlbergers

Vorarlberg

Kressbronn

Lindau

GERMANY

Bodensee

Weiler-
Simmerberg

Oberstaufen

18

Altenrhein

Bregenz ①

Hard

202

Aach

Krumbach

SWITZERLAND

St. Margrethen

Lustenau

Alberschwende

200

Egg

Hittisau

Bregenzer Ache

Schwarzenberg ②

Dornbirn

Bezau ③

Reuthe

Hohenems ⑧

Mellau

Au

200

N13

A14

Götzis

BREGENZERWALD

Baad

Rankweil

Damüls ④

Hochkrumbach

Faschina

Sonntag

Fontanella

Schröcken

Warth

Feldkirch ⑦

Blons

193

Lutz

198

Lech ⑮

ILL

Frastanz

190

A14

Grosswalsertal

Zürs ⑭

Nenzing ⑥

Stuben ⑬

LIECHTENSTEIN

Bürserberg

Bludenz ⑤

Langen

316

516

St.
Anton

S16

Dalaas

Arlberg
Strassentunnel

Brand ⑩

Tschagguns ⑪

⑫ **Schruns**

188

Lunersee

Montafon

St.
Gallenkirch

TIROL

SWITZERLAND

Valley

Gaschurn

Galtür

N

Bielerhöhe

*Silvretta
Stausee*

0 ——————— 10 miles

0 ——————— 15 km

come to make merry, especially in summer. Along the lakeside beach and public pool cabanas and candy floss lure starched collars to let loose, while nearby, an enormous floating stage is the site for magnificent performances of Wagner and Strauss under the stars. Bregenz is the capital of Vorarlberg and has been the seat of the provincial government since 1819. The upper town has maintained a charming Old World character, but the lower part of the city fronting the lake's edge is largely unimpressive. Unfortunately, the waterfront is cut off by railroad tracks, though there is a strip of pedestrian walkway that hugs the shoreline.

★ Bregenz is pleasant at any time of year, but the best time to visit is during the **Bregenzer Festspiele** (Bregenz Summer Music Festival; ☞ Nightlife and the Arts, *below*). Acclaimed artists from around the world perform operas, operettas, and musical comedies on the festival's floating stage, part of the Festspiel-und Kongresshaus (Festival Hall and Congress Center) complex. In front of the stage, the orchestra pit is built on a jetty, while the audience of 6,000 is safely accommodated on the 30-tier amphitheater, built on dry land—a unique and memorable setting you are sure to enjoy. Reserve your tickets in advance, as performances sell out early.

The lake itself is a prime attraction, with boat trips available to nearby Switzerland and Germany. Don't forget to bring along your passport. The **Bodensee White Fleet** ferries offer several trip options. You can travel to the "flower isle" of Mainau or make a crossing to Konstanz, Germany, with stops at Lindau, Friedrichshafen, and Meersburg. The longest round-trip excursion is the Drei-Länder Rundfahrt, which includes stops in Germany and Switzerland. The ferries have different operating schedules, but most run only in the summer months. The Mainau excursion is the exception, running from May to mid-September. ✉ *Bodenseeschiffahrt Ticket Office, Seestr. 4,* ☎ *05574/42868,* FAX *05574/6755–520.*

Most of the important sights of Bregenz can be seen in the course of a walk of about two hours. The town's neoclassical main **Post Office** (✉ 5 Seestr.) was built in 1893 by Viennese architect Friedrich Setz. Because of the marshy conditions of the land, the post office is built on wood pilings to prevent it from sinking. Behind the post office, the **Nepomuk-Kapelle** (✉ Kaspar Moosbrugger Pl.) was built in 1757 to serve the city's fishermen and sailors. Today, the town's Hungarian community celebrates mass here. To the right of the Nepomuk-kapelle along Kornmarktstrasse is the **Gasthof Kornmesser,** built in 1720 and a gorgeous example of a Baroque town house. Just after the alley simply marked THEATER along Kornmarktstrasse you'll reach the **Theater am Kornmarkt,** originally constructed in 1838 as a grain storehouse when Bregenz was still an important commercial port; in 1954, the granary was converted into a 700-seat theater.

Next door to the Theater am Kornmarkt is the **Landesmuseum** (Provincial Museum), where relics from Brigantium, the Roman administrative city that once stood where Bregenz is today, are housed. Gothic and Romanesque ecclesiastical works are also on display in this turn-of-the-century building. ✉ *Kornmarktpl. 1,* ☎ *05574/46050.* ▣ *AS20.* ☉ *Sept.–June, Tues.–Sun. 9–noon and 2–5; July–Aug., daily 9–noon and 2–5.*

Originally used as a grain warehouse when it was built in 1685, the **Rathaus,** on the Rathausgasse, was turned over to the city in 1720. The ornate facade and tower were only added to the city hall in 1898. Next door to the Rathaus is the **Seekapelle** (Lake Chapel), topped with an onion dome. The chapel was put up over the graves of a defeated band of Swiss, who in 1408 attempted to incorporate Bregenz into Switzerland. Behind the Seekapelle is the traditional **Gösser Braugaststätte** (⌾ Anton-Schneider-Gasse 1). This might be just the moment for a cool beer, a cup of coffee, or the daily vegetarian special. Try to get a table in the Zirebenstuble, with its beautifully carved wood-paneled walls and ceiling.

From Deuringstrasse (which borders on Anton-Schneider-Gasse), take a left on Belrupstrasse, and you'll find the **Pfänderbahn** cable car, which takes you up to the 3,460-ft peak overlooking the city. You can see four countries—and almost 240 Alpine peaks—from here, and the restaurant is open June–mid-September. Children will enjoy a 30-minute circular hike to a small outdoor zoo, with deer, Alpine goats, mouflon, and wild boar. Admission is free. An added attraction is the **Adlerwarte** (☎ 0663/053040), where eagles and other birds of prey demonstrate their prowess in free flight May–September at 11 and 2:30; admission is AS40. ☎ 05574/42160. ⌾ *Round-trip AS98, Oct. 1– Mar. 20; AS125, Mar. 21–Sept. 30.* ⊙ *Dec.–Mar., daily 9–6; Apr.– Nov. 15, daily 9–7; service on hr and ½ hr. Closed last 2 wks of Nov.*

Off of Belruptstrasse, the **Herz-Jesu Kirche** (Sacred Heart Church) was built in 1908 in brick Gothic style. The stained-glass windows by Martin Hausle are especially bright and colorful. Go left from Belrupstrasse on to Maurachgasse. Walking up Maurachgasse, you'll reach the **Stadtsteig** (stone gate) guarding the entrance to the old city, which bears the emblem of a Celtic-Roman equine goddess (the original is now housed in the Landesmuseum; ☞ *above*). Inside the gate are the coats of arms of the dukes of Bregenz and of the dukes of Montfort, the latter crest now the Vorarlberg provincial emblem.

Next to the Stadtsteig, explore the interior of the tiny chapel called **Martinskirche** (⌾ Martinsplatz) for its fine 14th-century frescoes. The **Martinsturm** (⌾ Martinsg. 3b,) boasts the largest onion dome in Central Europe. The tower (1599–1602) has become a symbol of Bregenz and was the first Baroque construction on Lake Constance; it is closed Monday October–April. The remains of the ancient **city wall** are to the right of the tower on Martinsgasse. The coats of arms of several noble Bregenz families still remain on the house next to the wall's remains.

Angle on along Martinsgasse to Graf Wilhelm Strasse and the brightly shuttered **Altes Rathaus** (Old City Hall). The ornate half-timber construction was completed in 1622. Behind the Altes Rathaus on Eponastrasse stands the former **Gesellenspital** (Journeymen's Hospital); remnants of a fresco still visible on its wall depict St. Christopher, St. Peter, and a kneeling abbot. At the bottom of Eponastrasse is **Ehreguta Square,** named for the legendary woman who saved Bregenz during the Appenzell War of 1407–£09. Ehreguta was a maid who overheard the enemy planning an invasion of Bregenz. Discovered listening at the door, she was warned that she would be killed if she breathed a word to anybody. Torn between protecting the city and saving her own life, she decided to tell all to the fire in the kitchen one night but speaking loud enough for others to overhear and take action to save Bregenz. The **Montfortbrunnen fountain** in the center of the Ehreguta Square is the scene of a ritual washing of wallets and change purses, when the carnival jesters clean out their empty pockets and spin tales about the events of the previous year. The fountain honors the minnesinger Hugo von Montfort, who was born in the city in 1357. The small parallel streets running uphill from the Ehreguta Square roughly outline the boundaries of the town in the Middle Ages. Hidden around the corner of the building at the beginning of Georgen-Schilde-Strasse are the-

Meissnerstiege (Meissner steps), named after a local poet, that lead from the old city to the **parish church of St. Gallus.** At the bottom of the steps follow Schlossbergstrasse up the hill to the church, which combines Romanesque, Gothic, and rococo elements. The interior is decorated simply with pretty pastel colors instead of the usual excessive gilt. Empress Maria Theresa donated the money for the high altarpiece. You'll notice the monarch's features on one of the shepherdesses depicted there. From the hill outside the church there is a wonderful view of the southwestern wall of the old city, including the **Beckenturm,** the 16th-century tower once used as a prison and named after bakers imprisoned there who had baked rolls that were too small. The **Künstlerhaus Thurn und Taxis** (✉ Gallusstrasse 8) was owned by the regal Thurn und Taxis family until 1915. The building, erected in 1848, now contains a modern gallery. The **Thurn und Taxispark** contains rare trees and plants from around the world.

☺ Children and parents alike will enjoy a ride on the **Hohentwiel,** a restored old-time paddle-wheel lake steamship that cruises Lake Constance out of Hard, 8 km (5 mi) southwest of Bregenz. Sailings are scheduled irregularly; call for information (☎ 05574/48983, FAX 05574/42467–86).

Dining and Lodging

$$$ ✗ **Ilge-Weinstube.** This cozy, intimate *Keller* is old Bregenz at its best. Rustic decor in the basement of a 300-year-old house close to the oldest section of town draws the youngish "in" crowd. The atmosphere alone makes the Ilge-Weinstube worth a visit. ✉ *Maurachstr. 6,* ☎ *05574/43609. MC, V. Closed Mon. and 2 wks during Oct. or Nov.*

$$ ✗ **Maurachbund.** The elegant furnishings and soft lighting make dining at this restaurant an enjoyable, intimate experience. In summer diners can choose to eat outside on the back terrace. The menu features a wide variety of fish to choose from as well as traditional Austrian dishes. ✉ *Maurachg. 11,* ☎ *05574/44020. MC, V.*

$$ ✗ **Wirtshaus am See.** This half-timbered house with a gabled roof is right on the banks of Lake Constance, next to the floating stage used for the Bregenz Festival. The menu has the usual Austrian favorites from schnitzel to *Zwiebelrostbraten* (a skirt steak topped with crispy fried onions). The main attraction here is the spectacular lake view. You can watch the world go by from the restaurant's extensive outdoor terrace. ✉ *Seeanlagen,* ☎ *05574/42210,* FAX *05574/42210–4. No credit cards. Closed Jan.–Feb.*

$ ✗ **Café Götze.** Locals frequent this small, unpretentious café because it's known to have the best pastries in town. The location halfway between the waterfront and the old city is convenient. ✉ *Kaiserstr. 9,* ☎ *05574/44523. Closed Sun.*

$ ✗ **Goldener Hirschen.** Allegedly the oldest tavern in Bregenz and close
★ to the old city, this rustic restaurant offers delicious traditional fare and drink in a lively atmosphere. The ambitious chef occasionally highlights certain foods, as during the oft-repeated Noodle Week, when diners can choose from a special menu offering a mouthwatering selection of pasta dishes. Particularly good is the spicy spaghetti in a tomato, onion, bacon, and red pepper sauce, or spinach tagliatelle with grilled turkey in a tomato cream sauce with Gorgonzola gratiné. ✉ *Kirchstr. 8,* ☎ *05574/42815. AE, DC, MC, V. Closed Tues. and 2 wks in Sept.*

$$$$ ✗🛏 **Deuring-Schlössle.** This 400-year-old castle with its Baroque tower
★ has been the inspiration for paintings by Turner and Schiele. Rooms are tastefully furnished and have polished wood floors and lovely wainscoting. The owner is also the chef of the hotel's restaurant (closed Monday lunch), which is considered to be among the best in Austria.

Specialties include beautifully presented pike-perch on a bed of pumpkin puree with baby asparagus. If you want a blow-out meal in a lovely, romantic setting, this is the place to go. But be prepared for inflated prices, small portions, and inattentive service. ⊠ *Ehregutapl. 4, A–6900,* ☎ *05574/47800,* FAX *05574/47800–80. 13 rooms. Restaurant. AE, DC, MC, V.*

$$$ 🖫 **Kaiser Hotel.** This hotel behind a purple facade is rather hard to locate, but it's well worth the hunt. There is no sign for it on the front side of the building, but the hotel is on the second floor above Cafe Heitinger and Segafredo. All rooms have been thoroughly refurbished recently, successfully combining antiques with funky, modern decor. Guests will feel pampered with whirlpool baths, VCRs, and compact disc players. If there is no one on duty at the reception desk, ask for assistance in the cafe. ⊠ *Kaiserstr. 2, A–6900,* ☎ *05574/52980,* FAX *05574/52982. 8 rooms. Restaurant, 2 cafés, hot tubs. AE, DC, MC, V.*

$$–$$$ 🖫 **Mercure.** Adjacent to the Festival Hall and housing the casino, the house is typical of the chain: functionally modern, all rooms with balconies. Rooms looking out over the lake are best. ⊠ *Pl. der Wiener Symphoniker, A–6900,* ☎ *05574/46100–0,* FAX *05574/47412. 94 rooms. 2 restaurants, bar. AE, DC, MC, V.*

$–$$ 🖫 **Weisses Kreuz.** This traditional, family-run, turn-of-the-century house has been renovated with care and charm and is now a Best Western hotel. The location on the edge of the pedestrian zone is central, and the staff is particularly friendly. The rooms are comfortable and modern; those overlooking the private park out back are quieter. ⊠ *Römerstr. 5, A–6900,* ☎ *05574/4988–0,* FAX *05574/4988–67. 44 rooms. Restaurant, bar. AE, DC, MC, V. Closed Dec. 25–mid-Jan.*

Nightlife and the Arts

The cultural year starts with the **Bregenzer Frühling,** the spring music and dance festival that runs from mid-April to mid-May. Information and tickets are available through the tourist office (⊠ Bahnhofstr. 14, A–6900, ☎ 05574/4959). The big cultural event in Bregenz is the **Bregenzer Festspiele** (Bregenz Summer Music Festival), held mid-July to mid-August. For information and tickets, contact the festival office (⊠ Box 311, A–6901, ☎ 05574/4076, FAX 05574/407400). Tickets are also available at the Bregenz tourist office. In case of rain, the massive Festival Hall and Congress Center next door to the floating stage can accommodate at least half of the 4,200 seats for performances on the floating lake stage.

For the first time in nearly 100 years a new modern art museum, the **Kunsthaus,** has opened in Austria. Designed by Swiss architect Peter Zumthor, the scaled glass-and-concrete building creates a feeling of space and light with an innovative feature of 8-ft openings between each story, which allows sunlight to enter the translucent glass through the ceiling. This marvel of design bathes each gallery in natural light in spite of concrete walls. ⊠ *Karl Tizian Pl., A–6900,* ☎ *05574/485940,* FAX *05574/485948.* ⊙ *Open Tues.–Sun. 10–6; Thurs. 10–9.*

The **casino** is the site of much activity (⊠ Pl. der Wiener Symphoniker, A–6900, ☎ 05574/45127–0). The house opens at 3 PM. Bring your passport.

Outdoor concerts are held during the summer months in the horseshoe-shape **Music Pavilion** at the end of the promenade on the lake.

Outdoor Activities and Sports

Bicycling

The area around the lake offers superb cycling, and trails have been laid out to offer varying distances and degrees of difficulty. Maps and rental bikes are available; ask the tourist office for details.

Skiing

Skiers head for **Pfänder** mountain, in the backyard of Bregenz, which has a cable tramway and two drag lifts. The views are stunning from atop the peak, stretching as far as the Black Forest and the Swiss Alps.

Water Sports

With the vast lake at its doorstep, Bregenz offers a variety of water sports. You can even learn to sail, although a minimum of two weeks is required for a full course at **Segelschule Lochau.** ✉ *Box 7, Alte Fähre*, ☎ *05574/52247.*

THROUGH THE BREGENZERWALD TO BLUDENZ AND FELDKIRCH

Directly behind Bregenz lies the **Bregenzerwald** (Bregenz Forest), a beautiful area studded with densely wooded highlands, sweeping valleys, and lush meadows radiant in summer with wildflowers, all set against a fabulous backdrop of majestic, towering Alps. As you go along, you come across one town after another with *au*—meaning "meadow"— in its name: As the area developed, names were given to the meadows in which settlements were established. Here you will see the Vorarlbergers as they really are. In the little villages, you can spot women still wearing the handsome, stiffly starched folk dress of their ancestors. On festive occasions the girls wear a golden headdress shaped like a small crown, and the married women a black or white pointed cap. Men's costume is worn by musicians in the local bands (which seems to include nearly everyone), with the shape of the cap and the color of various parts of the clothing differing from town to town. Secure in their mountains and, until quite recently, feeling no call to mix with the outside world, Vorarlbergers have remained true to the traits of their forebears.

To reach the Bregenzerwald, travelers can take one of the daily bus services that leave Bregenz or Dornbirn on the main line from Feldkirch to Lindau in Germany—there are few train routes servicing the area. By car, leave Bregenz headed south on Route 190; then make a sharp left after crossing the river on a road marked to Wolfurt and Schwarzach. About 21 km (13 mi) farther, at Alberschwende, you'll come to Route 200; follow the signs for **Egg,** where you should note the old country houses before heading on to Schwarzenberg. If you haven't bought your Alpine hat before you get to Egg, go to the **Capo** hat and cap factory outlet here (✉ Mühle 534, ☎ 05512/2381–0). It's open weekdays 1– 4:30 and sells fashionable headgear as well as Alpine styles.

Schwarzenberg

❷ *31 km (19 mi) southeast of Bregenz.*

One of the region's most colorful villages is Schwarzenberg. The artist Angelika Kauffmann (1741–1807), who spent most of her life in England and Italy, still considered this her home. Even though she became one of the most renowned female artists of the 18th century, few people in Austria east of the Arlberg mountains knew of her until her picture appeared on a new issue of Austrian currency a few years ago.

You can see several of her larger works in the Baroque village church, including a painting of the 12 apostles she did at 16, and an altar painting of the Annunciation of Mary from about 1800 (the Landesmuseum in Bregenz has her portrait of the Duke of Wellington). The Schwarzenberg **town hall** (⊠ Hof 765, ☎ 05512/3166) has a room dedicated to Angelika Kauffmann. It's open Tuesday, Thursday, and weekends 2–4, or by appointment; admission is AS35.

Bezau

❸ *4 km (2½ mi) south of Schwarzenberg, 35 km (23 mi) east of Bregenz.*

According to local legend, Bezau's district hall was built on tall columns and was accessible only by ladder. Once the councillors were gathered inside, the ladder was removed until they came to a decision. The **Heimatmuseum,** slightly south of the center, contains exhibits on the town's interesting past, including local folk costumes. ⊠ *Ellenbogen 181,* ☎ *05514/2559.* ⬛ *AS30.* ☉ *June, Tues. and Thurs. 2–4; July–Sept., Tues., Thurs., and Sat. 3:30–5:30, Wed. 10–noon; Oct.–May, Tues. 2–3.*

☙ At the **Bregenzerwald Museumsbahn,** visitors can see all that is left of the onetime narrow-gauge railroad that ran from Bregenz to Bezau and was abandoned in 1980. The museum has managed to preserve more than 6 km (almost 4 mi) of track to Bersbuch, beyond Schwarzenau, and runs diesel and steam excursions. ⊠ *Bahnhof 147,* ☎ *05513/6192,* 𝔽𝔸𝕏 *05513/6192–4.* ⬛ *Round-trip by steam AS75, by diesel AS55.* ☉ *June–mid-Oct., weekends at 11, 2, and 3:30; also Thurs. at 11 and 2 July–Aug. Closed mid-Oct.–May.*

Dining and Lodging

$$ ✕ **Gasthof Engel.** The Gathof Engel has some of the best Italian food
★ you'll find in Austria. Fresh regional ingredients are served with elegant simplicity here. A whole page of fresh pasta dishes is featured on the menu as well as traditional meat and fish dishes. The wine list has a fine selection of Austrian and Italian vintages. The service is also exceptional; you'll feel like a long-lost member of the family. ⊠ *Pl. 29,* ☎ *05514/2203. No credit cards. Closed Wed. and Nov.*

$$ 🏠 **Gasthof Gams.** Dating from the 17th century, this friendly house
★ in the center of town offers every comfort and is a great base for exploring. The rooms are in attractive country-rustic decor, and the hotel welcomes families. ⊠ *Pl. 44, A–6870,* ☎ *05514/2220,* 𝔽𝔸𝕏 *05514/2220–24. 22 rooms, 5 suites. Restaurant, bar, pool, sauna, tennis court, exercise room. No credit cards. Closed Nov.–mid-Dec.*

Outdoor Activities and Sports

SKIING

Bezau has four regular trails for cross-country skiers and one lift that takes downhill skiers up to the 5,300-ft Baumgartenhöhe.

Damüls

❹ *14 km (9 mi) south of Bezau, 59 km (37 mi) southeast of Bregenz.*

If you turn right onto Route 193 at Au, you'll be on the way leading to Damüls—the road is narrow, with a 14 degree gradient at one point, but when you reach the town, you'll agree the climb was worth it. You're at 4,640 ft, the top of the Bregenzerwald. This is great skiing country in winter. There are enough slopes and lifts, and the crowds are generally elsewhere. In summer the area is knee-deep in wildflowers, but don't pick them; it's against the law. Check the frescoes in the parish church, which date to 1490, just after the church was built, but were rediscovered under later plaster only about 40 years ago.

Lodging

$–$$$ ⊞ **Damülser-Hof.** This group of chalets, spread over a meadow, forms an elegant but friendly hotel complex. It's warmly decorated and cozy, with brick, exposed wood, carpets, and open fireplaces. The rooms—also in country-rustic decor—in the older section have been renovated; the ones in the new section are well designed and executed. ✉ *NR 147, A–6884,* ☎ *05510/210–0,* 📠 *05510/543. 37 rooms. Restaurant, bar, café, indoor pool, sauna, tennis court, bowling. MC, V. Closed Nov.*

En Route   The **Grosswalsertal** (Great Walliser Valley) is extremely scenic. As you start the descent from Damüls heading toward Bludenz along Route 193, look across at the St. Gerold monastery to your right, but after reaching Blons, keep your eyes on the road: It's full of hairpin turns.

Bludenz

⑤   *22 km (13 mi) southwest of Damüls, 60 km (37 mi) south of Bregenz.*

Bludenz rests in the middle of five mountain valleys, sheltered in part by the Muttersberg peak, nicknamed "the Sun Balcony." In the old city the narrow streets are lined with tightly packed 17th-century houses and relics of the ancient town defenses, while the mountains are endowed with ski lifts, good slopes, and hiking trails. People here are pleased when you ask for a hot chocolate instead of coffee. Bludenz is a major chocolate-producing center, as you may detect if the wind is coming from the direction of the factories. The town, adorned with houses and pergolas that seem more Italian than Austrian, is a major transportation crossroads, serviced by frequent bus and train routes.

Dining and Lodging

$–$$ ⊞ **Schlosshotel.** Perched on a hill above the castle and overlooking the town, this modern hotel with balconies offers splendid views of the Rätikon mountain range to the south, on the Swiss border; ask for a room in front above the café terrace. The pseudo-rustic decor of the house continues into the guest rooms, whose clean lines and modern furnishings are, in fact, attractive. ✉ *Schlosspl. 5, A–6700,* ☎ *05552/63016–0,* 📠 *05552/63016–8. 42 rooms. Restaurant, café, miniature golf. AE, DC, MC, V.*

Nenzing

⑥   *12 km (7 mi) northwest of Bludenz.*

Nenzing is the jumping-off spot for the wildly romantic Gamperdonatal, the valley of the Meng river, which rises toward peaks that are 6,500 ft or higher. The valley is hikable, but it's barely passable for cars. The top of the valley is called *Nenzinger Himmel,* or Nenzing Heaven.

Feldkirch

⑦   *15 km (9 mi) northwest of Nenzing, 33 km (22 mi) southwest of Bregenz.*

Feldkirch is Vorarlberg's oldest town, with parts dating from the Middle Ages that contribute greatly to the town's romantic character. Picturesque arcades line the narrow main street, and wrought-iron oriels festoon some of the quainter town houses. Marvelous towers and onion domes top some of the buildings, watched over by an assembly of imposing stone blockhouses, which compose the Schattenburg castle complex just above the town.

A number of luminary figures have spent time in Feldkirch. James Joyce stopped for several months en route from Italy to Switzerland, saying later that he formed the basis for *Ulysses* here and that he gathered material for *Finnegan's Wake*. There is a plaque honoring him at the train station, where he spent hours every day observing people and trains for his writing. Promising student Sir Arthur Conan Doyle attended the Jesuit boarding school, Stella Matutina, which is now the Provincial Conservatory of Music. He wrote two short stories for the local newspaper, which are stored in the archives. And Thomas Mann used the same boarding school as a setting in *Magic Mountain*.

Although the composer Schubert had no ties to the town, Feldkirch is now home to the annual **Schubertiade** (☞ Nightlife and the Arts, *below*), a small but elegant music festival that has won world renown for the quality of performers—including Jessye Norman and Cecelia Bartoli—with events offered in May, June, and September.

An easy walk around the center of Feldkirch will take you to most of the town's highlights. Start at the **St. Nicholas cathedral** on Domplatz. A mystical light in this church, built in 1478, comes through the stained-glass windows. Walk toward the river, past the district government offices (once a Jesuit monastery) and the bishop's palace, a block back of Herrengasse, to the **Katzenturm** (literally, "cats' tower"; figuratively, "the clergy"), reconstructed by Emperor Maximilian I. This is the most prominent remnant of the town's fortifications and now holds the 7½-ton town bell. Down the Hirschgraben, you'll come to the Chur gate and beside it the **Frauenkirche** (Women's Church), dedicated to St. Sebastian in 1473. Now, for the **towers**: Head down Montfortgasse to where the Wasserturm (water tower) and the Diebsturm (thieves' tower) stand guard over the Schillerstrasse bridge. Wander down Vorstadt to the Pulverturm (powder tower) and across to the Mühlenturm (mill tower), whose contrast to the modern Leonhardsplatz is considerable. Turning left, you'll find the St. Johann Church (1218); behind it, the **market square** (market days Tuesday and Saturday), with its arcades; and at the far end, a five-story, half-timbered house. The square is the site of the annual wine festival during the second week of July. Across the pedestrian zone you'll come to Liechtenstein Palace, once the administrative center. On your right is the **Rathaus** of 1493, with its frescoes and paneled rooms.

Overlooking Feldkirch, in the Neustadt, is the 12th-century **Schattenburg,** a massive castle that now houses a museum devoted to the decorative arts and armor. Arcades climb up the hill to frame the castle in an intriguing vista. ⊠ *Burggasse 1,* ☎ *05522/71982 or 05522/73467.* ▨ *AS25.* ☉ *Mar.–Oct., Tues.–Sun. 9–noon and 1–5; Nov.–Feb. by appointment.*

Dining and Lodging

$$$ ✕ **Schäfle.** Tucked away in the heart of the old city, this *Gasthaus* offers atmosphere and food more typical of that in the countryside. The tables are elegantly set, and you can expect such regional fare as tongue, beef fillet, or perch from Lake Constance, all with delicate sauces and a fine touch. ⊠ *Naflastr. 3,* ☎ *05522/72203–0,* FAX *05522/72203–17. AE, DC, MC, V. Closed Sun. and mid-Dec.–mid-Jan. No lunch Mon.*

$$$ ✕▥ **Central Lowen.** The rooms are large and comfortable but lacking a bit in the charm department. However, the hotel staff is friendly and outgoing. A steam room and sauna are on the premises to help you relax. The hotel's restaurant has a huge selection of Austrian and international favorites. The schnitzel is especially good. ⊠ *Schlossgraben 13, A–6800,* ☎ *05522/72070–0,* FAX *05522/72070–5. 68 rooms. Restaurant, sauna, steam room. D, MC, V.*

\$\$ ☷ **Alpenrose.** This charming old burgher house in the center of the old
★ city has been renovated outside and in and offers unusually personal
service. Rooms are tastefully done in period furnishings. The house is
part of the Best Western group. ⊠ *Rosengasse 6, A–6800,* ☎ *05522/
72175,* FAX *05522/72175–5. 24 rooms. AE, DC, MC, V.*

Nightlife and the Arts

The **Schubertiade** presents an impressive series of concerts devoted to
Franz Schubert and his circle, offered in churches, castles, and audi-
toriums in Feldkirch during May, June, and September. Everyone from
Vladimir Ashkenazy to Dietrich Fischer-Dieskau has performed here,
starring along with the Vienna Philharmonic and Vienna Symphony.
⊠ *Schubertiade GmbH, Schubertpl. 1, A–6803,* ☎ *05522/38001–0,*
FAX *05522/38005.*

Hohenems

❽ *9 km (5½ mi) northeast of Feldkirch, 24 km (15 mi) southwest of
Bregenz.*

"The antiquity of Hohenems is so apparent, so forceful, it looms like
a presence, a mysterious knight, armored cap-a-pie, visor lowered,"
observed James Reynolds in his 1956 book *Panorama of Austria.* Hohenems is a town dominated by castles, both ruined (the 12th-century
Alt-Ems citadel atop the Schlossberg) and ravishing, especially the
Schloss Glopper and the castle of Prince-Archbishop Marcus Sittcus
von Hohenems, with its elegantly ornate Rittersaal. Empress Elizabeth
of Austria used to stay in this castle toward the end of her tragically
shortened life and, in fact, used the title of Countess Hohenems when
she traveled "anonymously" around the world. The **parish church,** dedicated to St. Carlo Borromeo and rebuilt in 1797, has a noted painted
altarpiece of the Coronation of the Virgin.

In 1617 a decree was signed that welcomed Jews to Hohenems and allowed them to live and work in peace. For the next 300 years a large
Jewish community thrived here, but by 1938 fewer than 20 Jews remained. The **Jüdisches Museum** (Jewish Museum), housed in the Villa
Heimann-Rosenthal, has a large library, as well as photographs and
historical documents on display. ⊠ *Schweizerstr. 5,* ☎ *05576/3989.*
▤ *AS30.* ⊙ *Wed.–Sun. 10–5.*

Dornbirn

❾ *4 km (2½ mi) northeast of Hohenems, 13 km (8 mi) southwest of
Bregenz.*

Dornbirn, the industrial center of Vorarlberg, is known as the "city of
textiles." The annual Dornbirn Fair, held in early September to tie in
with the Bregenz Music Festival, shows a range of goods and tech-
nologies, but textiles are especially featured.

Dining

\$\$\$ ✕ **Rotes Haus.** The "red" in the name of this 1639 gabled wood house
★ in the center of town refers to bull's blood, originally used as pigment
for the facade, which is still basically red, with decorative panels. Traditional cuisine is served here in a series of charming small rooms. You'll
find lamb, game, and fish on the menu. ⊠ *Marktpl. 13,* ☎ *05572/31555,*
FAX *05572/31625. AE, DC, MC, V. Closed Sun.*

THE ARLBERG AND MONTAFON RESORTS

The Western Alps are a haven for those who love the great outdoors. It's also a region that provides getaway space and privacy—Ernest Hemingway came to Schruns to write *The Sun Also Rises* and, more recently, the late Princess Diana came to Lech with William and Harry to escape from the media. In the spring, summer, and fall, travelers delight in riding, tennis, swimming and, of course, hiking the Montafon valley, which is dominated by the "Matternhorn of Austria," the Zimba peak, and probably the most attractive of Vorarlberg's many tourist-frequented valleys. When the first snowflakes begin to fall, skiers head to the hills to take advantage of the Arlberg mountain range, the highest in the Lechtal Alps. If you want to avoid the crowds that can clog Austria's other resorts, keep in mind that Lech and Zürs are resorts where the seeing is almost as important as the skiing. If you're traveling by train, Langen is the stop closest to the ski resorts; Route S16/316 takes you by car from Bludenz to Langen and beyond to Route 198 heading north.

Brand

⑩ *70 km (43 mi) south of Bregenz.*

Since it was first settled by Swiss exiles centuries ago, the lush and beautiful Brand Valley has attracted many travelers interested in visiting the enormous glaciers and one of the largest lakes in the Alps, located near the town. Today, Brand is known as a winter-sports center and as a health resort. Its hotels lie at the foot of the Scesaplana mountain group (which marks the Swiss border and is the highest range in the Rätikon). There are no rail lines to Brand, so the best way to reach the resort is to take the train to Bludenz and then the bus from there to Brand.

If you are fond of hiking, you can climb by easy stages along the forest paths without much exertion to the famous glacier lake, the **Lünersee.** In winter, the skiing is excellent, and there is a short, modern gondola-type cable railway up the Niggenkopf (5,500 ft) to take you up to the finest ski slopes in just a few minutes. Anyone interested in geology should pay a visit to the tiny village chapel, known as the **"trowel stone" chapel,** built of local rock that can be cut into shape quite easily with an ordinary saw. When exposed to the air, the masonry then shrinks slightly and hardens and becomes rather brittle.

Dining and Lodging

$$ ✕▥ **Sporthotel Beck.** The Beck family runs this sports hotel in the shadow of the nearby mountains. Rooms are comfortably furnished and light-filled and have flower-bedecked balconies that look out over spectacular view. The hotel's restaurant features classic Austrian fare like schnitzel but also lighter dishes for those watching their waistlines. Sports enthusiasts will like the wide range of activities available in the hotel as well as the great mountain-climbing nearby. ✉ *A-6708,* ☎ *05559/306–0,* FAX *05559/306–70. Restaurant, pool, massage, driving range, exercise room, horseback riding. AE, DC, MC, V.*

Outdoor Activities and Sports

GOLF

Golf Club Brand, set in a stunning Alpine valley and Vorarlberg's first course, has 9 holes, par-68. ☎ *05559/450,* FAX *05559/450–20.* ☉ *May–Oct.*

HIKING

From a leisurely stroll to serious mountain trekking, Brand has hiking galore. The most noted trail runs from Brand via Innertal (with a chairlift up to Melkboden) and the Schattenlagant-Alpe to the lower end of the Lünersee. Inquire at the local tourist office for maps.

SKIING

The Brandnertal has ski passes good for 3, 6, or 13 days, with rates for adults, children, and senior citizens varying according to season. The regional tourist office has details. Rental equipment is available.

Schruns-Tschagguns

10 km (6 mi) northeast of Brand, 60 km (39 mi) south of Bregenz.

Author Ernest Hemingway spent many winters at the Schruns–Tschagguns skiing area in the Montafon Valley. Today, neither of the towns—sited across the Ill River from each other—is as fashionable as the resorts on the Arlberg, but the views over the Ferwall Alps to the east and the mighty Rätikon on the western side of the valley are unsurpassed anywhere in Austria. In winter, the powdery snow provides wonderful skiing. Thanks to an integrated system of ski passes and lifts, the Montafon Valley is considered a "ski stadium" by skiers-in-the-know. They love
⑪ to head for the Hochjoch-Zamang—the main peak at **Schruns**—to have lunch on the spectacularly sited sun terrace of the Kapell restaurant.
⑫ Then it's on to Grabs-Golm over the river in **Tschagguns.** Others prefer the Silvretta-Nova run at Gaschurn and St. Gallenkirch. In summer, the heights are given over to climbers and hikers, the mountain streams to trout fishermen, and the lowlands to tennis players.

Dining and Lodging

$$$–$$$$ ✕🏨 **Löwen.** This central hotel looks huge, but inside, the country style works well, and the rustic dark-wood exterior is carried over elegantly into the modern rooms with balconies. The hotel is set in the center of a grassy garden platform, which forms a greenbelt around the main building and serves as a roof for the ground-floor pool and restaurants. The excellent Edelweiss restaurant, with its graceful table settings (candlelit at night), serves regional specialties done with a flair. ✉ *Silvrettastr. 8, A–6780,* ☎ *05556/7141,* ℻ *05556/73553. 85 rooms. 4 restaurants, bar, indoor pool, sauna, exercise room, dance club. AE, DC, MC, V. Closed mid-Apr.–mid-May and mid-Oct.–mid-Dec.*

$$–$$$ ✕🏨 **Montafoner Hof.** This cozy hotel in Tschagguns is perfect for families. The management is warm and friendly and makes guests feel at home. The hotel restaurant is also known for its popular restaurant, which features delicious, traditional Austrian cooking. ✉ *Kreuzg. 9, A–6774 Tschagguns,* ☎ *05556/7100-0,* ℻ *05556/7100-6. 48 rooms. Restaurant, 1 indoor and 1 outdoor pool, sauna. No credit cards.*

$$–$$$ 🏨 **Alpenhof Messmer.** Set on a lush green hillside slightly out of the
★ center of town, this oversize double chalet welcomes you with fireplaces and comfortable rustic furnishings. Most of the imaginatively decorated rooms have balconies with a view over the town. It is a member of the Silencehotel group. The family management is particularly friendly and helpful, and the same goes for the restaurant staff. ✉ *Grappaweg 6, A–6780,* ☎ *05556/72664-0,* ℻ *05556/76156. 35 rooms. Restaurant, bar, indoor pool, sauna, exercise room. No credit cards. Closed mid-Apr.–mid-May and mid-Nov.–mid-Dec.*

Outdoor Activities and Sports

FISHING

The local mountain streams and rivers are full of fish. Licenses are available; ask the regional tourist office in Bregenz for detailed information on seasons and locations.

SKIING

Ski passes are available for 3, 6, or 13 days, with rates for adults, children, and senior citizens varying according to season. The regional tourist office in Bregenz has details. Rental equipment is available.

Stuben

⑬   *38 km (23 mi) northeast of Schruns, 29 km (23 mi) east of Bludenz.*

Traveling through the Montafon via Route 316, you'll come to Stuben, hometown of that pioneer of Alpine ski techniques, Hannes Schneider. From December to the end of April the magnificent skiing, at 4,600 ft, makes Stuben popular among serious skiers who are willing to forgo the stylish resorts, such as Lech, just up the road. Stuben has skiing links with St. Anton, Lech, and Zürs. The town is poised right above the Arlberg Tunnel, so travelers can't—appearance to the contrary on maps—arrive there via rail from Innsbruck or Bregenz. They must detrain at Langen am Arlberg and then take a bus on to Stuben.

Dining and Lodging

$$$ ✕🏨 **Hotel Mondschein.** A welcoming exterior, accented with pink geraniums in flower boxes and dark green shutters, greets visitors as they come down the street from the town church. Inside this traditional Alpine country house, dating back to 1739, the greeting is almost as warm as the fires blazing in the hotel's hearths, while the pricey restaurant prides itself on its fish selections. Unlike other Stuben hostelries, this one is right in the center of town. Depending on the season, rates include half board. ✉ *A–6762,* ☎ *05582–511 or 05582/721,* FAX *05582–736. 25 rooms with bath. Restaurant, indoor pool, health club, baby-sitting. No credit cards. May and mid-Sept.–mid-Dec.*

En Route   Just past Stuben, the Flexen Road (Route 198) over the Arlberg pass begins its descent to the Züs Valley. It is protected from avalanches by concrete or timbered roofing; a triumph of engineering, it looks like a giant caterpillar crawling along the face of the cliffs. In summer, the treeless slopes are covered with Alpine flora.

Zürs

⑭   *13 km (8 mi) north of Stuben, 90 km (56 mi) southeast of Bregenz.*

The chosen resort of the rich and fashionable on this side of the Arlberg, Zürs is little more than a collection of large hotels. Perched at 5,600 ft, it is strictly a winter-sports community; when the season is over, the hotels close. But Zürs is more exclusive than Lech and certainly more so than Gstaad or St. Moritz in Switzerland—this is the place wealthy emirs bring their private ski instructors. Zürs is also the place where the first ski lift in Austria was constructed in 1937. In most hotels, you'll be asked to take full board, so there are relatively few "public" restaurants in town and little chance to dine around. But the hotel dining rooms are elegant; in many, jacket and tie are de rigueur in the evening.

Dining and Lodging

$$$–$$$$ ✕🏨 **Central-Sporthotel Edelweiss.** This 19th-century house has received an agreeable face-lift, giving it a colorful, contemporary interior, including the guest rooms. The Zürserl disco is *the* place in the evening. The restaurant, Chesa Verde, is the best in town, offering fresh fish, game, and other regional standards, but be sure to reserve. Prices include half board. ✉ *A–6763,* ☎ *05583/2662,* FAX *05583/3533. 66 rooms, 5 apartments. Restaurant, sauna, exercise room, dance club. No credit cards. Closed mid-Apr.–Nov.*

$$$$ 🏠 **Alpenhof.** The timber-frame windows here face a great panorama, but who has time to admire the scenery? If you're not on the slopes (the ski school is next door), the house offers dozens of other diversions. The Oriental carpets alone are worthy of a palace. The rooms are elegant yet comfortable. Prices include full board; half board is available by arrangement. ⊠ *A−6763,* ☎ *05583/2191 or 05572/21777 (off-season),* FAX *05583/3330. 41 rooms. Restaurant, piano bar, indoor pool, sauna, exercise room. No credit cards. Closed mid-Apr.−Nov.*

$$$$ 🏠 **Lorünser.** The hospitable elegance of this hotel draws royalty, including Prince Albert of Monaco and Queen Beatrix of the Netherlands. In the reception area, carved ceiling beams, open fireplaces, and attractive accessories create a welcoming ambience. Rustic wood is used to good effect in the stylish guest rooms. Prices include full board, half board by arrangement. ⊠ *A−6763,* ☎ *05583/2254−0,* FAX *05583/2254−44. 74 rooms. Restaurant, bar, sauna, exercise room. No credit cards. Closed mid-Apr.−early Dec.*

$$$$ 🏠 **Zürserhof.** This world-famous hostelry at the north end of town comprises five chalets—five of the most luxurious and expensive chalets in the world (prices can near $900 a day with board). Many of the accommodations are elegant, spacious apartments or suites with fireplaces; newer ones have Roman baths. The family-run house has nevertheless managed to preserve an intimate atmosphere. Prices include half board. When celebrities want to be private and exclusive, they come here. ⊠ *A−6763,* ☎ *05583/2513−0,* FAX *05583/3165. 97 rooms. Restaurant, bar, indoor pool, beauty salon, sauna, driving range, tennis court, exercise room, dance club. No credit cards. Closed mid-Apr.−Nov.*

Outdoor Activities and Sports

SKIING

There are two main chairlifts: East of Zürs, a lift takes you to Hexenboden (7,600 ft) and Trittkopf (7,800 ft), with a restaurant and sun terrace; to the west, a lift takes you to Seekopf (7,000 ft), where there is another restaurant. This is avalanche country, so skiers need to be particularly alert.

Lech

🔟 *9 km (5½ mi) north of Zürs, 90 km (56 mi) southeast of Bregenz.*

Just up the road from the Zürs resort, Lech is a full-fledged community—which some argue detracts from its fashionableness. But there are more hotels in Lech, better tourist facilities, bigger ski schools, more shops, more nightlife, and prices nearly as high as those in neighboring Zürs. Zürs has the advantage of altitude, but Lech is a less artificial and very pretty Alpine village. And Lech is a favorite winter vacation spot for Princess Caroline of Monaco and also the Belgian royal family. Be sure to check with the hotel of your choice about meal arrangements; some hotels recommend that you take half board, which is usually a good deal. You can't get to Lech via rail; take the train to Langen am Arlberg station stop, and then transfer to a bus.

Dining and Lodging

$$$$ ✕ **Brunnenhof.** This cozy dinner restaurant in the hotel of the same name, slightly north of the town center, has gotten increasingly better in recent years, justifying the tag "Gourmet-Hotel." The menu has offered such innovative dishes as fillet of perch over a bed of squash and fillet of beef with artichoke sauce. The wine list includes selections from Austria, France, Italy, Spain, Australia, and California. Be sure to reserve well in advance, for this is one of the best restaurants in town, and it's regularly full. ⊠ *House 116,* ☎ *05583/2349 or 05583/2902,*

FAX *05583/2349–59. Reservations essential. AE, DC, MC, V. Closed Sun. and mid-Apr.–mid-Dec.*

$$$–$$$$ ✕⌘ **Gasthof Post.** A *gemütlich* atmosphere dominates in this green-
★ shuttered chalet hotel, with murals, flower boxes, and a paneled wood interior. The à la carte restaurant is the best in town; try the medallions of lamb or grilled salmon, but save space for one of the outstanding desserts. ✉ *Dorf-11, A–6764,* ☎ *05583/2206–0,* FAX *05583/2206– 23. 40 rooms. Restaurant, bar, indoor pool, sauna. No credit cards. Closed mid-Apr.–June and mid-Sept.–Nov.*

$$$–$$$$ ✕⌘ **Montana.** In Oberlech, in the pedestrian zone just above the town,
★ you'll find this easygoing hotel, run by an outgoing expatriate Alsatian. He has installed a *Vinothek* (wine shop), where tastings are held and wine is sold by the glass or bottle. The bright interior colors contrast well with the weathered wood; the rooms are friendly and snug. The ski slopes are just outside the door. The restaurant, Zur Kanne, has French overtones and is remarkable for its attention to detail, both in the kitchen and in the table settings. Ingredients are fresh daily, and dishes range from lobster hash to beef fillet gratiné. Prices for the hotel include half board. ✉ *House 279, A–6764,* ☎ *05583/2460,* FAX *05583/2460–38. 42 rooms. Restaurant, bar, indoor pool, sauna, tennis court, exercise room. No credit cards. Closed May–Nov.*

$$–$$$$ ✕⌘ **Krone.** Directly across the street from two of the main lifts, this family-managed hotel grew out of a 250-year-old house and now belongs to the Romantik Hotel group. The adaptations and modernization have not affected the general ambience of comfort and well-being that's reflected in the beamed ceilings, tile stoves, and Oriental carpets. The restaurant, one of the town's three best, is noted for its game and regional specialties; try the fillet of whitefish on cucumber or the rack of lamb. ✉ *House 13, A–6764,* ☎ *05583/2551,* FAX *05583/2551–81. 56 rooms. Restaurant, sauna, exercise room, fishing, dance club. No credit cards. Closed mid-Apr.–mid-June and Oct.–Nov.*

$$ ⌘ **Solaria.** This hillside chalet, fairly close to the center of town, is not far from the lower station of two of the lifts, one of which runs in summer as well. The hotel is family-run and friendly; the rooms are cheerful and cozy. Half board is mandatory in winter. ✉ *NR 130, A–6764,* ☎ *05583/2214,* FAX *05583/3456. 18 rooms, 4 apartments. Restaurant, bar, children's program. No credit cards. Closed Apr.–Nov.*

Nightlife and the Arts

Lech is known almost as much for après-ski and nightlife as for the snow and the slopes. Ask at the tourist office about the "in" spots, as the crowd tends to move around. Prices vary from place to place, but in general, you'll pay AS65–AS80 for a mixed drink.

You can join the crowd as early as 11 AM at the outdoor and famed **Red Umbrella** bar for snacks and drinks at the Petersboden Sport Hotel at Oberlech (☎ 05583/3232). Activity continues at the late-afternoon **tea dance** at the Tannbergerhof (☎ 05583/2202).

Hot **après-ski** spots include the bars in the Goldener Berg (☎ 05583/ 2205), and Burg (☎ 05583/2291) hotels in Oberlech, and Monzabon (☎ 05583/2104) in Lech. Among the popular places for a **mid-evening drink** (starting at 9:30) are Pfefferkörndl in the Pfefferkörn Hotel (☎ 05583/2525–429) and Mohnenfluh in Oberlech (☎ 05583/3311). Also check on Walch's Italiener (☎ 05583/3734) and the Klausur bar (☎ 05583/3500–0) in the Almhof-Schneider hotel in Tannberg. The Kronen Bar in the Krone hotel (☞ Dining and Lodging, *above*) opens at 9 PM and goes on until 2 or 3 AM.

Outdoor Activities and Sports
SKIING

Lech is linked with Oberlech and Zürs with more than 30 ski lifts, all accessed by the regional ski pass, which allows skiers to take in the entire region. You can ski right from Zürs to Lech. In addition, there is a vast network of cross-country trails.

VORARLBERG A TO Z

Arriving and Departing

By Car

From Germany, the autobahn (Route A14/E17) takes you into Bregenz; roads from Switzerland lead to Lustenau and Hohenems; from Liechtenstein, Route 16 (Route 191 in Austria) goes to Feldkirch; and Routes A12/E60 from eastern Austria and 315 from Italy meet at Landeck become Route 316/E60, then head westward through the Arlberg auto tunnel (toll AS150). Alternatively, your car (and you) can get to Vorarlberg on the car train that runs to Feldkirch from Vienna, Graz, or Villach.

By Ferry

From May to October, passenger ships of the Austrian railroad's **Bodensee White Fleet** (☎ 05574/42868, ℻ 05574/44341–128) connect Bregenz with Lindau, Friedrichshafen, Meersburg, and Konstanz on the German side of the lake. The Eurailpass and Austrian rail passes are valid on these ships. You'll need your passport.

By Plane

The closest major airport is in Zürich, 120 km (75 mi) away. Munich is 190 km (119 mi) away, and Innsbruck is 200 km (125 mi) away. Several trains a day serve Bregenz from the **Zürich Kloten airport.** In winter a bus leaves the airport Friday, Saturday, and Sunday at 12:30 PM for resorts in the Arlberg and Montafon regions. You can book through Swissair. On the Austrian side, call Arlberg Express (✉ A–6754 Klösterle, ☎ 05583/2000, ℻ 05582/3155) for information and bookings.

Rheintalflug (☎ 01/7007–6911 in Vienna, 05574/48800 in Vorarlberg, 071/435120, ℻ 01/7007–6915 in Vienna, 05574/48800–8 in Vorarlberg) flies between Vienna and Altenrhein on **Lake Constance** in Switzerland. A direct bus service takes passengers free of charge to and from the airport and Bregenz, Dornbirn, and Lustenau.

By Train

The main rail line connecting with Vienna and Innsbruck enters Vorarlberg at Langen after coming through the Arlberg tunnel. Both the *Arlberg* and *Orient Express* trains follow this route, which then swings through Bludenz to Feldkirch. There the line splits, with the *Arlberg* going south into Liechtenstein and Switzerland, the other branch heading through Dornbirn to Bregenz and on to Lindau in Germany.

Getting Around

By Bus

Post office, railroad, and private bus services connect all the towns and villages not served by the railroad, using tracked vehicles when necessary in winter. Even so, some of the highest roads become impassable for a few hours.

By Car

A car is the most flexible way of getting about in Vorarlberg, but the roads can be treacherous in winter. You are not allowed on some mountain roads in the Arlberg without chains, which you can rent from a number of service stations.

By Taxi

Taxis start at AS41, so taking one even a short distance can be expensive. Call to order a radio cab (☎ 05574/65400 or 05574/42222).

By Train

The railroads connect the main centers of Vorarlberg remarkably well; besides the lines described above, the Montafoner electric (with occasional steam) rail line runs parallel to the highway from Bludenz southeast to Schruns.

Contacts and Resources

Car Rentals

Avis (✉ Rheinstr. 86, A–6900 Bregenz, ☎ 05572/78100). **Hertz** (✉ Auto Schneeweiss, Am Brand 2, A–6900 Bregenz, ☎ 05574/44995).

Discounts

A *Bodensee-Pass* includes the Swiss and German as well as the Austrian lake steamers, all at half price, plus area trains, buses, and cablecar lifts. The pass comes in one-, three-, and seven-day variations; the Vorarlberg information offices in Bregenz and Vienna have details.

Emergencies

In case of an emergency, call ☎ 133 for the **police,** ☎ 144 for an **ambulance,** and ☎ 122 for the **fire department.**

Visitor Information

The headquarters for **tourist information** about Vorarlberg is based in Bregenz (✉ Bahnhofstr. 14, A–6900 Bregenz, ☎ 05574/42525–0, ℻ 05574/42525–5); there is a branch office in Vienna (✉ Tuchlaubenstr. 18, A–1010 Vienna, ☎ 01/535–7890, ℻ 01/513–9116–76).

Other regional tourist offices (*Verkehrsamt, Verkehrsverein,* or *Fremdenverkehrsamt*) are located throughout the province at the following addresses:

Bezau (✉ Pl. 39, A–6870, ☎ 05514/2295, ℻ 05514/3129). **Bludenz** (✉ Werdenberger Str. 42, A–6700, ☎ 05552/62170, ℻ 05552/67597). **Bregenz** (✉ Bahnhofstr. 14, A–6900, ☎ 05574/4959). **Feldkirch** (✉ Herrengasse 12, A–6800, ☎ 05522/73467, ℻ 05522/79867). **Lech** (✉ A–6764, ☎ 05583/2161–0, ℻ 05583/3155). **Montafon Valley** (✉ Silbertalerstr. 1, A–6780 Schruns, ☎ 05556/72253, ℻ 05556/74856). **Zürs** (✉ A–6763, ☎ 05583/2245, ℻ 05583/2982).

12 Portraits of Austria

Powder-Perfect Skiing

Books and Videos

German Vocabulary

Menu Guide

POWDER-PERFECT SKIING

Austrian skiing is a fairy tale. Strip away the ski history and the tourist-brochure hype, and it's still a fairy tale. Austria has the same high, treeless bowls and slopes that make skiing all over the Alps so different from skiing in North America, plus something extra—the loveliest mountain villages in Europe. Classic Austrian ski villages look, and feel, like an art director's fantasy of Alpine charm.

It's hard for American skiers who haven't skied in the Alps to imagine the sheer size and scale of Alpine ski resorts, where many individual ski areas are linked together with a common ski pass and a spiderweb network of lifts, spanning and connecting different valleys and multiple mountains. These large, interconnected ski domains add a new dimension to skiing—that of exploration. To take full advantage of the promise of so much snowy terrain, American skiers should consider hiring a ski-instructor/guide for a day or two. Private instructors are much less expensive in Austria than in the United States, and the upper levels of Austrian ski-school classes are more about guiding than actual teaching.

Another surprise for the American skier in Austria will be the degree to which the entire country seems to embrace skiing (and winter sports in general, including cross-country skiing and, more recently, snowboarding). Skiing is deeply woven into the daily patterns of winter life in the Austrian countryside. A far greater percentage of the Austrian than the U.S. population skis. In Austria skiing isn't just another sport, it's the national sport. Ski racers are national heroes; the sports pages of Austrian newspapers award ski competitions banner headlines. Winter, Austria, and skiing are virtually synonymous.

hotel, and ski information, for the main Austrian ski regions. Contacting the tourist bureaus at individual resorts for this kind of information is a much slower process. But all of Austria's Alpine resorts do have tourist bureau–central reservation services that can make hotel reservations for you (☞ addresses and phone numbers for individual resorts, *below*).

Skiing is neither more nor less expensive in the Alps—and in Austria—than in the States. Some costs, like those for lift tickets, are lower; others, like those for fine meals, are higher. Some resorts, like Kitzbühel, are very posh indeed, but there are almost always budget alternatives nearby (neighboring ski villages with more modest prices that are nonetheless connected by lifts to the same large ski domain). Some airlines, notably Swissair, offer all-inclusive air-lodging-skiing packages to many Austrian resorts. (One of the easiest ways to reach the great resorts of the Vorarlberg and the Tirol is to fly to Zurich, then take a short and convenient train ride east into the Austrian Alps.)

The Austrian ski season typically runs from late November to April, depending on local snow conditions. Areas with glacier skiing are a better bet in dry snow years. A number of these very high glacier locations offer summer and autumn skiing. But summer ski zones are rather small; the real magic of Austrian skiing involves snow-frosted villages and endless slopes.

Austrians take their snow reports very seriously. In winter, one television channel is devoted exclusively to broadcasting images of snow conditions, captured by remote-control cameras, at ski areas across the country. Americans can check snow conditions by calling the **Austrian National Tourist Office** in New York and listening to its very accurate "snow-phone" survey of all major Austrian resorts (☎ 212/944–6880, ext. 993).

Packages, Discounts, and Information

Your best source for information about Austrian ski vacations and resorts is the Austrian National Tourist Office (✉ 500 5th Ave., Suite 2009, New York, NY 10110, ☎ 212/944–6880, FAX 212/730–4568). It has a wealth of brochures, with resort,

Favorite Destinations

There are so many choices when it comes to Austrian skiing that you're not going to see it all, and ski it all, in one lifetime. Ski areas dot the map of Austria like spots

Ski Areas

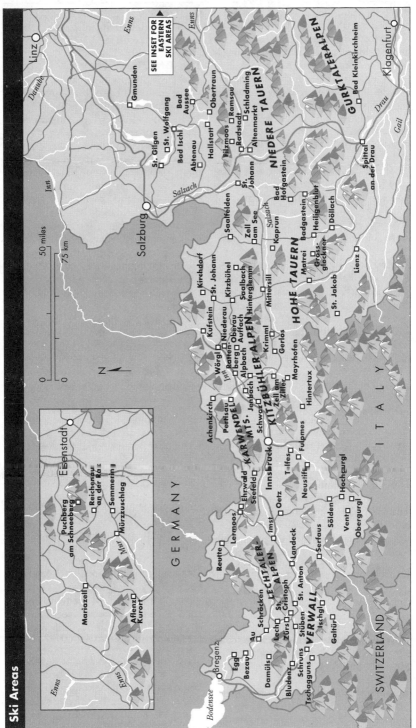

SEE INSET FOR
EASTERN
SKI AREAS

N

50 miles

75 km

GERMANY

SWITZERLAND

ITALY

Linz

Gmunden

Danube

Enns

Inn

Salzburg

Salzach

St. Wolfgang
St. Gilgen
Bad Ischl
Abtenau

Bad
Aussee
Obertraun
Hallstatt

Pillmoos
Ramsau
Radstadt
Schladming
Altenmarkt
Aftenmarkt

NIEDERE TAUERN

St.
Johann

Bad
Hofgastein

Heiligenblut
Döllach

Bad Kleinkirchheim

GURKTALERALPEN

Spittal
an der Drau

Klagenfurt

Drau

Gail

Saalfelden
Zell
am See
Kaprun

Badgastein

Grossglockner

Lienz

Matrei

St. Jakob

HOHE TAUERN

Kirchdorf
St. Johann
Kitzbühel
Saalbach
Hinterglemm

Mittersill
Krimml
Gerlos

Mayrhofen

Hintertux

Kufstein
Wörgl
Rattenberg
Niederau
Oberau
Auffach
Alpbach
Brixen

KITZBÜHLER ALPEN

Zell am
Ziller
Jenbach

Schwaz

Achenkirch
Pertisau

KARWENDEL MTS.

Innsbruck
Igls
Fulpmes
Talfes
Neustift

VERWALL

Ehrwald
Seefeld
Lermoos
Imst
Oetz
Landeck

Sölden
Vent
Obergurgl
Hochgurgl

Serfaus

Reutte

Schröcken
Lech
Zürs
St.
Christoph
St. Anton

LECHTALER-ALPEN

Ischgl
Galtür

Au
Egg
Bezau
Damüls
Bludenz
Schruns
Tschagguns

Bregenz

Bodensee

Enns

Eisenstadt

Puchberg
am Schneeberg

Reichenau
an der Rax
Semmering
Mürzzuschlag

Mariazell

Aflenz
Kurort

Mur

Enns

on a Dalmatian. Foreign ski enthusiasts and newcomers to Austrian slopes would do well to focus first on the biggest ski regions of the Arlberg and the Tirol. These mega-ski regions—places that Austrians sometimes call a *Skigrossraum* (big ski space)—showcase what makes Alpine skiing so special: an astonishing variety of slopes and lifts that allows the visitor to ski, day after day, often from one village to the next, without ever repeating a lift or a piste. True, there are many tiny and delightful ski villages in Austria, real discoveries for adventurous skiers, but it makes more sense to sample the feast of a major *Skigebiet* (interconnected ski region) first. Here, to get you started, are some of the finest.

The Arlberg

This is a capital of Austrian skiing: a double constellation of ski-resort towns—Zürs, Lech, and Oberlech, in the Vorarlberg; and, just across the Arlberg Pass to the east and thus technically in the Tirol, St. Anton, St. Christoph, and Stuben. These classic Arlberg resorts are interconnected by ski lifts and trails and share more than 200 km (120 mi) of groomed slopes (and limitless off-piste possibilities), nearly 80 ski lifts, and a common ski pass.

A skier in **St. Anton,** where Hannes Schneider started the first real ski school, can feel like a character out of a 1930s Luis Trenker ski film: from enjoying Jaeger tea after skiing to dinner at the Post Hotel. Neighboring **St. Christoph** is a spartan resort for skiing purists, a handful of handsome hotels lost in a sea of white, high above timberline, and the permanent home of the Austrian National Ski School training and certification courses. Several valleys farther west, the plaster walls of many of Lech's hotels are painted with folk art and poetry.

The pièce de résistance of Arlberg skiing is the all-day round-trip, on skis, from Zürs to Lech, Oberlech, and back. This ski epic starts with a 5-km (3-mi) off-piste run from the Madloch down to Zug and ends, late in the afternoon, many lifts and many thousands of vertical feet later, high on the opposite side of Zürs, swinging down the slopes of the Trittkopf.

VISITOR INFORMATION
Lech (Verkehrsbüro [tourist office], ⊠ A–6764 Lech am Arlberg, ☎ 05583/2161–

0, FAX 05583/3155); **St. Anton** (Verkehrs-büro, ⊠ A–6580 St. Anton am Arlberg, ☎ 05446/22690, FAX 05446/253215).

The Tirol/Innsbruck

The Tirol is really the heart of Austrian skiing—about a third of all Austrian ski resorts are found in this province. After St. Anton and the Arlberg, **Kitzbühel,** in the heart of the Tirol, is Austria's best-known ski destination and certainly its most elegant. "Kitz" is picture-perfect and posh—all medieval cobbled streets, wrought-iron signs, and candles flickering in the windows of charming restaurants. But *Achtung!* Kitzbühel's ski slopes are rather low in altitude, and the snow there is often not as good as at higher resorts. Check the snow depth before a trip here. Fortunately, the area served by the Kitzbühel super-ski pass includes nearby Mittersill, a much higher ski area that should have adequate snow even in dry years. A common pass lets you access 63 lifts serving 157 km (97 mi) of groomed slopes—the most celebrated of which is the Hahnenkahm, the course for Europe's toughest downhill race. Deep-snow enthusiasts will gravitate to the ungroomed slopes of the Schwarzkogel.

If you want to enjoy the chic atmosphere of Kitz, ski all the celebrated pistes of the Kitzbüheler Superskigebiet, but avoid high-end prices, consider staying just down the Brixen Valley in neighboring **Kirchberg,** cozy but happily not chic.

For an altogether different sort of ski vacation, especially for mixed groups of skiers and nonskiers, consider staying in downtown **Innsbruck** and making day trips to the various ski areas of the Innsbruck Skigrossraum. Innsbruck has twice hosted the winter Olympics and boasts a stunning collection of medium-size ski areas with grand views: Seegrube, Igls, Fulpmes, Mutters, and especially Axamer-Lizum.

My own favorite Austrian Skigebiet has to be the **Zillertal,** just south and east of Innsbruck. Almost unknown to American skiers, there are 10 different ski areas, strung like pearls up the long Ziller Valley, culminating in the Tuxer glacier at the very top (a popular summer-skiing site, too). Mayerhofen, a pretty town full of painted buildings halfway up the Zillertal, is a perfect base for skiing the whole valley. The Ahorn, right above Mayerhofen, is one of the smallest ski areas in this large valley, but it has the finest children's ski school I've ever seen. The Zillertal ski pass includes efficient bus and train transportation up and down the valley from one ski area to the next. Especially recommended are the slopes of the Königsleiten on a powder morning; the Penken above Mayerhofen for its wide-open slopes; the Eggalm, an intimate, uncrowded balcony of a ski area higher up the valley; and the Tuxer glacier for its on-top-of-the-world feeling. The common Ziller Valley ski pass lets you ski 400 km (240 mi) of groomed slopes and use 140 lifts.

VISITOR INFORMATION

Innsbruck (Tourismusverband, ⊠ Burggraben 3, A–6021 Innsbruck, ☎ 0512/59850, ℻ 0512/59850–7); **Kitzbühel** (Tourismusverband, ⊠ Hinterstadt 18, A–6370 Kitzbühel, ☎ 05356/2155, ℻ 05356/2307); **Zillertal** (Verkehrsbüro, ⊠ Dursterstr. 225, A–6290 Mayerhofen, ☎ 05285/2305, ℻ 05285/2305–33).

Salzburg

Farther east, in the province of Salzburg, there are also a number of stunning integrated ski regions. Despite its grandiose name, the **Europa-Sportregion** is only a grouping together of two—splendid—ski resorts, Kaprun and Zell am See. The skier population here, comes from all across Europe, and the large number of British and Scandinavian skiers guarantees that Americans without a word of German will feel at home here. Zell am See, a lakeside village, sits beneath the Schmittenhöhe, a wide mountain served by 25 ski lifts, known for its long runs. A few miles away, the village of Kaprun lies under the 10,509-ft Kitzsteinhorn peak, and its glacier skiing makes a winter vacation here very "snow safe." (This is also a major summer-skiing location.) Kaprun only has 16 ski lifts, but they climb quite high.

The **Gasteiner Tal** (Gastein Valley) is the place to combine skiing and spa vacationing. Badgastein and neighboring Bad Hofgastein are better known to Americans for their luxurious thermal and mineral baths. But their ski slopes, linked with those of Grossarl in the next valley over, comprise a beautiful and rather large ski region. Accommodations range from luxury hotels—Badgastein has a distinctly chichi reputation—to traditional Alpine farmhouses. The Gasteiner Tal and nearby Grossarl together offer 53 ski lifts serving 250 km (155 mi) of groomed slopes.

The slopes of **Saalbach-Hinterglemm,** linked with nearby Leogang, are not particularly steep or difficult, but this is a beautifully integrated ski offering with 200 km (120 mi) of groomed pistes and more than 70 lifts, one of which, the Schattbergbahn, is said to be the largest cable car in Austria. It's good choice for long, aesthetic intermediate ski runs.

The **Salzburger Sportwelt Amadé** Skigebiet drapes over three large valleys and a number of smaller ones. Resorts like Wagrain, Filzmoos, St. Johann im Pongau, Kleinarl, and Radstadt have never been written up in American ski magazines, which invariably stick with the big names like St. Anton and Kitz, but this ski region nonetheless links more than 320 km (200 mi) of groomed slopes with 120 lifts. Lower altitudes make this a recommended destination only in good snow years.

VISITOR INFORMATION

Europa-Sportregion (Kurverwaltung, ⊠ Brucker Bundstrasstr. 1, A–5700 Zell am See, ☎ 06547/2600, ℻ 06547/2032); **Gastein Valley** (Kur- und Fremdenverkehrsverband, ⊠ Kaiser-Franz-Josef-Str. 27, A–5640 Badgastein, ☎ 06434/2531-0, ℻ 06434/2531–37); **Saalbach-Hinterglemm** (Fremdenverkehrsverband, ⊠ Saalbach 550, A–5753 Saalbach, ☎ 06541/7272, ℻ 06541/7900).

Styria

The mountains tend to become lower and the snow conditions less certain as one travels east in the Austrian Alps, so it makes sense for American skiers to concentrate on the more westerly ski destinations. One possible exception is in Styria, the **Dachstein-Tauren Region.** Here the Dachstein glacier offers a bonus of high-altitude snow. Nine separate villages share a common pass that gives access to 78 lifts, serving 140 km (87 mi) of groomed slopes above the wide Enns river valley. But Dachstein slopes are not as interconnected as those in many other Austrian ski regions and you tend to wind up spending each skiing day above just one of the region's villages: Schladming, Rohrmoos-Unter-tal, Pichl, Haus im Ennstal, Aich-Assach, Pruggern, Gröbming, Mitterberg, and Ramsau am Dachstein. Cross-country skiing is as popular as downhill skiing in this valley with an amazing 240 km (152 mi) of prepared cross-country trails.

VISITOR INFORMATION

Dachstein-Tauren Region (Verkehrsbüro, ⊠ Erzherzog-Johann-Strasse 213, A–8970 Schladming, ☎ 03687/22268, FAX 03687/22268–21).

— Lito Tejada-Flores

BOOKS AND VIDEOS

Books

Gordon Brook-Shepherd's *The Austrians: A Thousand-Year Odyssey* traces the history of Austria through the postwar years. The 2,000-year history of Vienna is detailed in *The Viennese: Splendor, Twilight and Exile,* by Paul Hofmann. Alan Palmer's *Twilight of the Hapsburgs* covers the years of Emperor Franz Josef's life (1830–1916). For an intriguing portrait of Vienna in the months before and after the murder-suicide of Crown Prince Rudolf and his teenage mistress, read Frederic Morton's *A Nervous Splendor: Vienna 1888/1889.* *The World of Yesterday,* Stefan Zweig's haunting memoir, begins in what Zweig calls the "Golden Age of Security," the period that was shattered by the First World War. Zweig witnesses the rise of anti-Semitism, which causes him to flee Austria in the 1930s.

Austria has produced many great composers. Recommended as background reading are Maynard Solomon's *Mozart: A Life* and Richard Rickett's *Music and Musicians in Vienna.*

Wittgenstein's Vienna, by Allan Janik and Stephen Toulmin, tells the story of the brilliant young philosopher and his city in the waning days of the Austro-Hungarian Empire. In *Sigmund Freud,* Richard Wollheim provides a concise analysis of the man and his theories.

Robert Musil's most famous work, the sprawling, unfinished, three-volume modernist novel, *The Man Without Qualities,* is set in Vienna on the eve of World War I. John Irving's first novel, *Setting Free the Bears,* follows two university students as they conspire to liberate the animals at the Vienna Zoo.

Videos

Vienna and Austria have served as settings for a number of fine films. In *'38: Vienna Before the Fall* (1986), nominated for an Oscar for Best Foreign Language Film, a Gentile and a Jew fall in love just before the Nazi takeover. Postwar Vienna is the backdrop for Graham Greene's suspense classic *The Third Man* (1949), with direction by Carol Reed and zither music by Anton Karas (☞ Box in Chapter 2). Four soldiers—an American, a Russian, a Frenchman, and an Englishman—patrol occupied Vienna in *Four in a Jeep* (1951), arguing politics while helping an Austrian woman whose husband has escaped from a POW camp. Ethan Hawke and Julie Delpy are strangers in Richard Linklater's *Before Sunrise* (1995); they meet on a train and impulsively decide to spend Hawke's last hours in Europe together by wandering through Vienna. *Brother of Sleep* (1995), about a musical genius who is unhappy in love, was filmed in Vorarlberg and was nominated for a Golden Globe for Best Foreign Language Film. The young Dr. Freud (Montgomery Clift) battles with the Viennese medical establishment for acceptance of his beliefs in John Huston's *Freud* (1962). In *The Seven Percent Solution* (1976), a cocaine-addicted Sherlock Holmes (Nicol Williamson) and his sidekick, Dr. Watson (Robert Duvall), team up with Sigmund Freud (Alan Arkin) to rescue a beautiful woman in peril (Vanessa Redgrave). Omar Sharif, Ava Gardner, James Mason and Catherine Deneuve star in *Mayerling* (1968), an account of the murder-suicide of Crown Prince Rudolf and his mistress Marie Vetsera. Rodgers and Hammerstein's *The Sound of Music* (1965) was filmed in Salzburg and the Lake District; it won Oscars for Best Director (Robert Wise) and best picture and has become an integral part of tourist promotion for Salzburg (☞ Box in Chapter 6).

A number of films have been set in Austria, although they weren't actually filmed here: F. Murray Abraham won a Best Actor Oscar for his portrayal in *Amadeus* (1984) of Antonio Salieri, a second-rate composer whose jealousy for the first-rate Mozart leads him (the film would have us believe) to attempt to destroy his rival. The film also won Oscars for Best Director (Milos Forman) and Best Picture. Erich von Stroheim directed and stars in the silent classic *The Wedding March* (1928) about an impoverished Austrian nobleman who must choose between marrying for love or for money.

— Keith Besonen

GERMAN VOCABULARY

Austrian German is not entirely the same as the German spoken in Germany. Several food names are different, as well as a few basic phrases.

Umlauts have no similar sound in English. An ä is pronounced as "eh." An äu or eu is pronounced as "oy". An ö is pronounced by making your lips like an "O" while trying to say "E" and a ü is pronounced by making your lips like a "U" and trying to say "E".

Consonants are pronounced as follows:

CH is like a hard H, almost like a soft clearing of the throat.

J is pronounced as Y.

Rs are rolled.

ß, which is written "ss" in this book, is pronouced as double S.

S is pronounced as Z.

V is pronounced as F.

W is pronounced as V.

Z is pronounced as TS.

An asterisk (*) denotes common usage in Austria.

English	German	Pronunciation

Basics

English	German	Pronunciation
Yes/no	Ja/nein	yah/nine
Please	Bitte	**bit**-uh
May I?	Darf ich?	darf isch?
Thank you (very much)	Danke (vielen Dank)	**dahn**-kuh (**fee**-len dahnk)
You're welcome	Bitte, gern geschehen	**bit**-uh, gairn ge**shay**-un
Excuse me	Entschuldigen Sie	ent-**shool**-di-gen zee
What? (What did you say?)	Wie, bitte?	vee, **bit**-uh?
Can you tell me?	Können Sie mir sagen?	kunnen zee meer **sah**-gen?
Do you know _____?	Wissen Sie _____?	**viss**-en zee
I'm sorry	Es tut mir leid.	es toot meer lite
Good day	Guten Tag	**goo**-ten tahk
Goodbye	Auf Wiedersehen	owf **vee**-der-zane
Good morning	Guten Morgen	**goo**-ten **mor**-gen
Good evening	Guten Abend	**goo**-ten **ah**-bend
Good night	Gute Nacht	**goo**-tuh nahkt
Mr./Mrs.	Herr/Frau	hair/frow
Miss	Fräulein	**froy**-line
Pleased to meet you	Sehr erfreut.	zair air-**froyt**
How are you?	Wie geht es Ihnen?	vee **gate** es **ee**-nen?
Very well, thanks.	Sehr gut, danke.	sair goot, **dahn**-kuh

| And you? | Und Ihnen? | oont **ee**-nen? |
| Hi! | *Servus! | **sair**-voos |

Days of the Week

Sunday	Sonntag	**zohn**-tahk
Monday	Montag	**moan**-tahk
Tuesday	Dienstag	**deens**-tahk
Wednesday	Mittwoch	**mitt**-voak
Thursday	Donnerstag	**doe**-ners-tahk
Friday	Freitag	**fry**-tahk
Saturday	Samstag	**zahm**-stahk

Useful Phrases

Do you speak English?	Sprechen Sie Englisch?	**shprek**-hun zee **eng**-glisch?
I don't speak German.	Ich spreche kein Deutsch.	isch **shprek**-uh kine doych
Please speak slowly.	Bitte sprechen Sie langsam.	**bit**-uh **shprek**-en zee **lahng**-zahm
I don't understand	Ich verstehe nicht	isch fair-**shtay**-uh nicht
I understand	Ich verstehe	isch fair-**shtay**-uh
I don't know	Ich weiss nicht	isch vice nicht
Excuse me/sorry	Entschuldigen Sie	ent-**shool**-di-gen zee
I am American/ British	Ich bin Ameri-kaner(in)/Eng-länder(in)	isch bin a-mer-i-**kahn**-er(in)/**eng**-len-der(in)
What is your name?	Wie heissen Sie?	vee **high**-sen zee
My name is . . .	ich heiße . . .	isch **high**-suh
What time is it?	Wieviel Uhr ist es? *Wie spät ist es?	**vee**-feel oor ist es **vee** shpäte ist es
It is one, two, three . . . o'clock.	Es ist ein, zwei, drei . . . Uhr.	es ist ine, tsvy, dry . . . oor
Yes, please/	Ja, bitte/	yah **bi**-tuh/
No, thank you	Nein, danke	**nine** dahng-kuh
How?	Wie?	vee
When?	Wann? (as conjunction, als)	vahn (ahls)
This/next week	Diese/nächste Woche	**dee**-zuh/**nehks**-tuh **vo**-kuh
This/next year	Dieses/nächstes Jahr	**dee**-zuz/**nehks**-tuhs yahr
Yesterday/today/ tomorrow	Gestern/heute/ morgen	**geh**-stern/**hoy**-tuh/**mor**-gen
This morning/ afternoon	Heute morgen/ nachmittag	**hoy**-tuh **mor**-gen/**nahk**-mit-tahk
Tonight	Heute Nacht	**hoy**-tuh nahkt
What is it?	Was ist es?	**vahss** ist es
Why?	Warum?	vah-**rum**
Who/whom?	Wer/wen?	vair/vehn

Who is it?	Wer ist da?	vair ist dah
I'd like to have . . .	Ich hätte gerne . . .	isch **het**-uh gairn
a room	ein Zimmer	ine **tsim**-er
the key	den Schlüssel	den **shluh**-sul
a newspaper	eine Zeitung	i-nuh **tsy**-toong
a stamp	eine Briefmarke	i-nuh **breef**-mark-uh
a map	eine Karte	i-nuh **cart**-uh
I'd like to buy . . .	ich möchte . . . kaufen	isch **merhk**-tuh **cow**-fen
cigarettes	Zigaretten	tzig-ah-**ret**-ten
I'd like to exchange . . .	Ich möchte . . . wechseln	isch **merhk**-tuh . . . **vex**-eln/
dollars to schillings	Dollars in Schillinge	dohl-lars in **shil**-ling-uh
pounds to schillings	Pfunde in Schillinge	pfoonde in **shil**-ling-uh
How much is it?	Wieviel kostet das?	**vee**-feel **cost**-et dahss?
It's expensive/ cheap	Es ist teuer/billig	es ist **toy**-uh/**bill**-ig
A little/a lot	ein wenig/sehr	ine **vay**-nig/zair
More/less	mehr/weniger	mair/**vay**-nig-er
Enough/too much/ too little	genug/zuviel/ zu wenig	geh-**noog**/tsoo-**feel**/ tsoo **vay**-nig
I am ill/sick	Ich bin krank	isch bin krahnk
I need . . .	Ich brauche . . .	isch **brow**-khuh
a doctor	einen Arzt	I-nen artst
the police	die Polizei	dee po-lee-**tsai**
help	Hilfe	**hilf**-uh
Fire!	Feuer!	**foy**-er
Caution/Look out!	Achtung!/Vorsicht!	**ahk**-tung/**for**-zicht
Is this bus/train/ subway going to . . . ?	Fährt dieser Bus/ dieser Zug/ diese U-Bahn nach . . . ?	fayrt **deez**er buhs/ **deez**-er tsook/ **deez**-uh **oo**-bahn nahk . . .
Where is . . .	Wo ist . . .	**vo** ist
the train station?	der Bahnhof?	dare **bahn**-hof
the subway station?	die U-Bahn-Station?	dee **oo**-bahn-**staht**-sion
the bus stop?	die Bushaltestelle?	dee **booss**-hahlt-uh-**shtel**-uh
the airport?	der Flugplatz? *der Flughafen?	dare **floog**-plats dare **floog**-hafen
the hospital?	das Krankenhaus?	dahs **krahnk**-en-house
the elevator?	der Aufzug?	dare **owf**-tsoog
the telephone?	das Telefon?	dahs te-le-**fone**
the rest room?	die Toilette?	dee twah-**let**-uh
open/closed	offen/geschlossen	**off**-en/ge-**schloss**-en
left/right	links/rechts	links/recktz
straight ahead	geradeaus	geh-**rah**-day-owws
is it near/far?	ist es in der Nähe/ist es weit?	ist es in dare **nay**-uh? ist es vite?

MENU GUIDE

English	German
Entrées	Hauptspeisen
Homemade	Hausgemacht
Lunch	Mittagsessen
Dinner	Abendessen
Dessert	Nachspeisen
At your choice	Önach Wahl
Soup of the day	Tagessuppe
Appetizers	Vorspeisen

Breakfast

Bread	Brot
Butter	Butter
Eggs	Eier
Hot	Heiss
Cold	Kalt
Caffeine-free coffee	Café Hag
Jam	Marmelade
Milk	Milch
Juice	Saft
Bacon	Speck
Lemon	Zitrone
Sugar	Zucker

Soups

Stew	Eintopf
Goulash soup	Gulaschsuppe
Chicken soup	Hühnersuppe
Potato soup	Kartoffelsuppe
Liver dumpling soup	Leberknödelsuppe
Onion soup	Zwiebelsuppe

Fish and Seafood

Trout	Forelle
Prawns	Garnele
Halibut	Heilbutt
Lobster	Hummer
Crab	Krabbe
Salmon	Lachs
Squid	Tintenfisch
Tuna	Thunfisch
Turbot	Steinbutt

Meats

Veal	Kalb
Lamb	Lamm
Beef	Rindfleisch
Pork	Schwein

Game and Poultry

Duck	Ente
Pheasant	Fasan
Goose	Gans
Chicken	Hühner
Rabbit	Kaninchen
Venison	Reh
Turkey	Truthahn
Quail	Wachtel

Vegetables and Side Dishes

Red cabbage	Rotkraut
Cauliflower	Karfiol
Beans	Bohnen
Button mushrooms	Champignons
Peas	Erbsen
Cucumber	Gurke
Cabbage	Kohl
Lettuce	Blattsalat
Potatoes	Kartoffeln
Dumplings	Knödel
French fries	Pommes frites

Fruits

Apple	Apfel
Orange	Orangen
Apricot	Marillen
Blueberry	Heidelbeere
Strawberry	Erdbeere
Raspberry	Himbeere
Cherry	Kirsche
Cranberry	Preiselbeere
Grapes	Trauben
Pear	Birne
Peach	Pfirsich

Desserts

Cheese	Käse
Crepes	Palatschinken
Soufflé	Auflauf
Ice cream	Eis
Cake	Torte

Drinks

Tap water	Leitungswasser
With/without water	Mit/ohne wasser
Straight	Pur
Non-alcoholic	Alkoholfrei

A large/small dark beer	Ein Krügel/Seidel Dunkles
A large/small light beer	Ein Krügel/Seidel Helles
Draft beer	Vom Fass
Sparkling wine	Sekt
White wine	Weisswein
Red wine	Rotwein
Wine with mineral water	Gespritz

INDEX

Katharinekapelle (Bad Kleinkirchheim), 272

Katzenturm (Feldkirch), 364

Kefermarkt, 175, 190

Kinsky Palace (Vienna), 33, 35

Kirche Am Hof (Vienna), 33, 35

Kitzbühel, 314, 318, 334–341, 350

Klagenfurt, 6, 260, 262–265, 282

Kleinwetzdorf, 112

Klosterneuburg, 172, 175, 199–200, 203

Klosterwappen peak, 163

Kohlmais cable car (Saalbach), 297

Kohlmarkt (Vienna), 38–39

Koloman-Wallisch-Platz (Bruck an der Mur), 156

Korneuburg, 172, 175–176

Kornmesserhaus (Bruck an der Mur), 156

Kötschach, 285, 289, 310

Kötschach-Mauthen, 310

Krems, 172, 176–177, 203

Kremsmünster, 175, 192

Kremsmünstererhaus (Linz), 181, 184

Kriminal Museum (Vienna), 25, 28

Krimmler Wasserfälle (waterfalls), 334

Krumpendorf, 260, 265

Kufstein, 318, 336–337, 350

Kunstforum (Vienna), 33, 35

Kunsthaus (Bregenz), 360

Kunsthaus Wien (Vienna), 28

Kunsthistorisches Museum (Museum of Fine Art; Vienna), 22, 33, 48–49, 50

Künstlerhaus (Vienna), 58

Künstlerhaus Thurn und Taxis (Bregenz), 359

Kur-und-Kongresszentrum (Treatment Complex; Badgastein), 300

Kurpark (Baden), 109

L

Laa an der Thaya, 105, 106, 120, 126

Lake District. ☞ Salzkammergut

Lake Neusiedl, 5, 130, 132–133

Lamprechtshöhle caves, 285, 299

Landeck, 315, 344, 350

Landesfeuerwehrmuseum (Tulln), 199

Landesmuseum (Bregenz), 357

Landesmuseum (Eisenstadt), 138

Landesmuseum Joanneum (Graz), 144, 147

Landschloss (Gmunden), 249

Landestheater (Salzburg), 206, 230

Landeszeughaus (Graz), 144, 147–148

Landhaus (Graz), 144, 148

Landhaus (Klagenfurt), 263

Landhaus (Linz), 181, 184

Landskron, 274

Lanersbach, 333, 351

Langelebarn, 13

Lech, 7, 355, 369–371, 372

Lehár's villa (museum; Bad Ischl), 247

Leoben, 132, 156–157

Leopold Wing (Hofburg Palace; Vienna), 42, 45

Leopoldsteiner See, 159

Libraries

in Stift Admont, 159

Hofbibliothek Prunksaal (Vienna), 22, 42, 45

Lieburg palace (Lienz), 290

Liechtensteinklamm, 285, 302

Lienz, 6, 285, 288–292, 310

Limesmuseum (Tulln), 199

Linz, 5, 13, 15, 175, 181, 183–189, 202

excursions from, 189–194

Linz Castle, 181, 184–185

Linzertor (Freistadt), 189

Lipizzaner Museum, 42, 45–46

Lipizzaner stallions, 11, 42, 45–46, 152–153

Lipizzaner Stud Farm (Piber), 152–153

Lockenhaus, 140

Looshaus (Vienna), 38, 40

Luegg House (Graz), 147

Lünersee, 7, 366

Lurgrotte (cave; Peggau), 153

M

Magdalenenkirche (Judenburg), 158

Marchegg, 122

Märchengrotte Railroad (Fairy-tale Grotto; Linz), 184, 185–186

Maria am Gestade (church; Vienna), 24, 28

Maria-am-Wasser Kirche (Leoben), 157

Maria Gail, 268

Maria Himmelfahrt (church; Weissenkirchen), 179

Maria Rast pilgrimage church (Hainzenberg), 334

Maria Taferl, 180

Maria Taferl Basilica, 180

Maria Wörth, 6, 260, 266–267, 282

Mariazell, 130, 160–161, 168

Mariazeller Basilica, 160

Marionettentheater (Salzburg), 206, 216, 219, 230

Martinskirche (Bregenz), 358

Martinskirche (Linz), 181

Martinsturm (Bregenz), 358

Matrei in Osttirol, 285, 292, 310

Mautern, 175, 197

Mauthausen, 194–195

Mauthausen Konzentrationslager (concentration camp), 194–195

Mauttern (Customs Tower; Leoben), 157

Mayerling, 5, 105, 107, 110–111

Mayrhofen, 318, 332–333, 350

Mechanical Nativity figurines (Mariazell), 160

Melk, 5, 13, 172, 175, 195–196, 203

Michaelerkirche, 40

Michaelerplatz (Vienna), 38, 40

Millstatt, 260, 271–272, 282

Minimundus park, 263

Minorite cloister (Tulln), 199

Minoritenkirche (Linz), 181, 184, 185

Minoritenkirche (Stein), 177

Minoritenkirche (Vienna), 33, 35

Mint tower (Hall in Tirol), 329

Mirbachov palać (Bratislava), 124

Mirabell Gardens (Salzburg), 13, 216, 219

Mirabell Palace (Salzburg), 216, 219–220

Mixnitz, 156

Mödling, 105, 107–108, 126

Monastery (Ossiach), 275

Monastery church (Hall in Tirol), 329

Monatsschlösschen, 222

Mönchsberg elevator (Salzburg), 209, 213

Mondsee, 242, 243, 257

Montafon, 366–371, 372

Montfortbrunnen fountain (Bregenz), 358–359

Mörbisch, 137

Mozart Audio and Video Museum (Salzburg), 220

Mozart Week, 206

Mozartplatz (Salzburg), 208, 209, 214

WHEREVER YOU TRAVEL, *H*ELP IS NEVER FAR AWAY.

From planning your trip to providing travel assistance along the way, American Express® Travel Service Offices are always there to help you do more.

Austria

American Express Travel Service
3 Brixnerstrasse
Innsbruck
(43) (512) 582491 or 587386

American Express Travel Service
Mozartplatz 5-7
Salzburg
(43) (662) 8080

American Express Travel Service
Kaerntnerstrasse 21-23
Vienna
(43) (1) 51540-770

do more **AMERICAN EXPRESS**
Travel

www.americanexpress.com/travel

American Express Travel Service Offices are located throughout Austria.